Gerald Weales
Sept. 24, 1948
Columbia Univ.

Samuel Johnson

Other Books by Joseph Wood Krutch

THE AMERICAN DRAMA SINCE 1918

WAS EUROPE A SUCCESS?

EXPERIENCE AND ART

FIVE MASTERS

THE MODERN TEMPER

EDGAR ALLAN POE—A STUDY IN GENIUS

COMEDY AND CONSCIENCE AFTER THE RESTORATION

SAMUEL JOHNSON
From the painting by Sir Joshua Reynolds (1769)

Samuel Johnson

BY

JOSEPH WOOD KRUTCH

Brander Matthews Professor of Dramatic Literature,
Columbia University

NEW YORK: HENRY HOLT AND COMPANY

Published, November, 1944
Second printing, February, 1945
Third printing, April, 1945

A WARTIME BOOK
THIS COMPLETE EDITION IS PRODUCED IN FULL COMPLIANCE WITH THE GOVERNMENT'S REGULATIONS FOR CONSERVING PAPER AND OTHER ESSENTIAL MATERIALS

PRINTED IN THE UNITED STATES OF AMERICA

To Marcelle

Foreword

THE LITERATURE surrounding Samuel Johnson is enormous. His contemporaries recognized him as an all but incomparable subject and his death released a spate of anecdote, reminiscence, and biography of which Boswell's *Life* is only the best and the best-known specimen. Since that time his cult has never ceased to function and today there is probably no other English man of letters except Shakespeare whom so many people acknowledge as the chief interest of their lives. They not only write books and read papers, they also form clubs, give dinners, stage celebrations, and collect curios. In America a *Johnson News Letter* appears several times a year.

The "Johnsonians" include men of many types ranging all the way from the simple hobbyist to the most learned, meticulous, and indefatigable scholar whose passion for detail and accuracy has built up a vast literature dealing with the smallest as well as the largest facts ascertainable concerning either Johnson himself or Johnson's friends. But the very intensity of this specialization (as well, of course, as the tremendous reputation of Boswell's *Life*) has tended to discourage any attempt in recent times to produce a large inclusive book which would serve to give the general reader a running account of Johnson's life, character, and work as they appear in the light of contemporary knowledge and contemporary judgment. The specialist, after the way of specialists, knows too much to be willing to undertake anything of the sort, and that fact is the excuse here pleaded for attempting to supply something which the author hopes certain readers will welcome.

Certain readers, I say, for, though I have freely used the work of many professional Johnson scholars, this book is not addressed to them. They will no doubt find in it many deficiencies and, possibly, errors. But the risk must be run if the layman is to be given, as I have attempted to give him, a certain kind of book about Johnson which did not, I think, exist before. To read with delight over a considerable span of years both Johnson and the Johnsonians is almost inevitably to be tempted to write something about him. Probably many have resisted the temptation to write the kind of thing I have written. As the following pages demonstrate I succumbed to it.

Two readers whose knowledge and judgment command the greatest respect have accused me of "being hard on Boswell." This charge distresses me greatly, since Boswell was undoubtedly a very likable fellow whom I find attractive despite his foibles, and I can find only one explanation for the fact that I have evidently dissembled my love by kicking him downstairs. That explanation is as follows: The contrast between the Great Moralist and his sprightly companion is so piquant that one is insensibly led to stress that contrast by citing facts which illustrate it and which assume a disproportionately important place in the account. There is little or nothing that I have said and would like to take back, but I am sorry that I failed to give equal stress to those sides of his character which have made him so widely liked.

Certain sayings of Johnson's and certain anecdotes concerning him are referred to more than once in the text of my book. This repetition is not inadvertent. Where the remark or anecdote in question seemed relevant in a new connection I chose to repeat it instead of sending the reader back to a previous chapter.

Where I have taken a specific fact or opinion directly from some scholarly work I have usually acknowledged the fact by citing the work in question in its proper place among the references gathered together at the end of this volume, but my general debt to many not mentioned as well as to some who are cited only in connection with some single point is very great and is hereby acknowledged. For a reading of the manuscript and extremely valuable advice I am deeply grateful to Professor

Foreword

James L. Clifford, one of the most distinguished of the younger generation of Johnsonians, to Professor Frederick A. Pottle, whose work on Boswell has made him the leading authority, and to my colleague and friend of many years, Professor Mark Van Doren.

Perhaps I should say here that I have frequently quoted the text of Mrs. Thrale's *Anecdotes* even in cases where an earlier (and sometimes probably more accurate) version of the same story is available in the recently edited *Thraliana*. Of the fresh material in the latter I have made extensive use but in the case of well-known bits from the *Anecdotes* it seemed preferable to give them in the more finished as well as more familiar form. On one or two occasions where a disparity between the two versions seemed genuinely important I have called attention to the fact by giving a reference to the corresponding passage in *Thraliana*. Any reader curious to know how Mrs. Thrale polished (and sometimes improved upon) her original record in any given instance may easily satisfy that curiosity by using the table of references supplied in an appendix to Miss Katherine Balderston's edition of *Thraliana*.

I wish also to thank the Misses Mary and Ruth Stout for the patient typing of a messy manuscript and Mrs. Elizabeth C. Moore for the preparation of the indexes.

JOSEPH WOOD KRUTCH

Redding, Connecticut
May, 1944

Contents

List of Illustrations

List of Illustrations

Samuel Johnson

CHAPTER I

The Lichfield Prodigy

SAMUEL JOHNSON was a pessimist with an enormous zest for living. It has been said that no one was ever more typically English and it has also been said that he is one of the world's great eccentrics. But no other single trait of his character is quite so striking as the strange combination of deeply pessimistic convictions with an enormous—almost Gargantuan—appetite for learning, for literature, for good company, and for food.

Of his many categorical judgments none is better known than that which he puts into the mouth of Imlac, the philosopher in *Rasselas:* "Human life is everywhere a state, in which much is to be endured, and little to be enjoyed." Yet even Imlac is not made to say that life has no pleasures; only that its pains outnumber them. And Johnson had a wholehearted relish for such of the former as came within his reach.

"I hate," he said once, "a *cui bono* Man," and that remark suffices to indicate how well his pessimism taught him to value those goods he had, how it saved him from the cant of such philosophers as profess to find everything dust and ashes. But pessimism had another advantage, for it gave him courage. In a letter to his friend, Mrs. Thrale, he once wrote: "He that sees before him to his third dinner, has a long prospect."

Two things he was afraid of—madness and death—but there is no evidence that in the course of a long and often desperate life he ever feared anything else. The thought of madness came often to his mind and for good cause; death he dreaded chiefly for Hamlet's reason. Too much a believer not to fear divine punishment and too invincibly a skeptic to count his faith sufficient to save him, he clung desperately to known ills lest he be hurried to others he knew not of.

Madness was spared him. Death, with a full consciousness of its approach, came to him as it has come to other immortals. Shortly before the event he precipitately burned great masses of material including, says Boswell, "two quarto volumes, containing a full, fair, and most particular account of his own life, from his earliest recollection." Part of what may have been still another volume somehow escaped the conflagration and, though Boswell never saw it, it was to be published in 1805. A few bare facts as well as some familiar anecdotes of Johnson's early childhood are there preserved, but the manuscript reveals little of Johnson's inward life, some secrets of which probably perished forever in the conflagration. Boswell, whose sense of delicacy was intermittent to say the least, professes to have been unable to bring himself to ask certain questions, and for these as for other reasons there are things we shall never know. Johnson despised "complainers," especially those who sought sympathy for mental and emotional sufferings. His mind he exposed as fully and persistently as any man ever did; his heart was not worn upon his sleeve.[1]

So far, however, as the external facts of genealogy and chronology are concerned, we now know a good deal—much more than Boswell was able to gather and in some instances more than Johnson himself knew. Except for Shakespeare, no English author has been the center of a more eager band of scholarly devotees, and even within the past two decades the antiquarian skill plus the almost incredible industry of scholars has established dates which remained vague to all previous biographers and discovered facts about persons more or less remotely connected with Johnson which would have been news to the Doctor himself. What he spent for food while at Oxford, when he stopped being charged for food there, and when, by inference, he departed from the university without his degree can now be easily ascertained by anyone who cares to know. So too, for instance, can the name of the first wife of the husband of his wet nurse, Mrs. John Marklew, née Joan Winckley.

The picture which emerges from the facts and anecdotes concerning his childhood is the picture of a moody, sensitive and strong-willed boy, growing up under the care of respectable and respected parents who were oppressed by mediocre financial difficulties and, though willing enough to do the right thing for each other and their children, were yet not very happy either in their domestic affairs or in their individual lives. As a man Johnson spoke of his parents with affection and gratitude but he never idealized them. Indeed it is remarkable that, despite his strong Tory insistence upon the importance of the family as a legal and social institution, upon the rights of inheritance and the dignity of birth, he had an unexpectedly low opinion of parental authority, speaking with open contempt of mature persons who paraded their deference to the wishes of a father.

It is true that on one of his last visits to the town of his birth he disappeared from company at breakfast, did not return until the supper hour, and then, after an uneasy silence, explained his absence: "Fifty years ago, Madam, on this day, I committed a breach of filial piety, which has ever since lain heavy on my mind, and has not till this day been expiated. My father, you recollect, was a bookseller, and had long been in the habit of attending Uttoxeter market, and opening a stall for the sale of his books during that day. Confined to his bed by indisposition, he requested me, this time fifty years ago, to visit the market, and attend the stall in his place. But, Madam, my pride prevented me from doing my duty, and I gave my father a refusal. To do away the sin of this disobedience, I this day went in a postchaise to Uttoxeter, and going into the market at the time of high business, uncovered my head, and stood with it bare an hour before the stall which my father had formerly used, exposed to the sneers of the standers-by and the inclemency of the weather; a penance by which I trust I have propitiated heaven for this only instance, I believe, of contumacy toward my father."

But this incident doubtless occurred during one of those fits of scrupulosity to which he was subject and at least it ought to be read in connection with other remarks. "Poor people's children," he once said, "never respect them: I did not respect my own mother, though I loved her: and one day, when in anger she called me a puppy, I asked her if she knew what they called a puppy's mother." Of the marital state itself he found nothing better to say than: "Marriage has many pains, but celibacy has no pleasures"; and this is not, as we shall see, by any means the only one of his convictions which he had occasion to form in childhood.

Michael Johnson, the father, seems always to have been regarded by his wife as less wellborn than she, and it was probably of the paternal side that Samuel was thinking when he attempted to demonstrate the disinterestedness of his belief in the importance of a noble lineage by remarking that he could scarcely tell who his grandfather was. Very recent genealogical research has demonstrated, however, that Michael had respectable connections and might, had he cared to boast, have demonstrated that his family was as good as his wife's. He had been born at the village of Cubley in Derbyshire and baptized there on April 2, 1657, but the family had moved afterward to Lichfield from whence Michael went to serve an apprenticeship in the Stationers Company (probably in London). He was established as bookseller in Lichfield when, in 1706, he married Sarah Ford, some twelve years his junior and the daughter of a man well enough established to be denominated "gentleman."

She was, as has been indicated, somewhat proud of her various respectable connections, but among them none is so well-known today as her brother's son, the decidedly unrespectable "Parson Ford," at one time one of Lord Chesterfield's chaplains and said, on somewhat dubious authority, to be the clergyman sitting next the punch bowl in Hogarth's *Modern Midnight Conversation.*

In population Lichfield was no more than what we should call a village. As late as 1781 its inhabitants numbered less than four thousand, or about half those of Oxford, and it was not usual for towns of that size to have a bookseller. But Lichfield was primarily a cathedral town rather than a market or industrial one, and this meant that it was something of an intellectual center. Johnson's biographers sometimes speak of his father as a learned man and base their conviction on a letter written in 1716 by the Rev. George Plaxton in Trentham near Lichfield. In it the writer observes that "Johnson, the Lichfield Librarian, is now here; he propagates learning all over this diocese, and advanceth knowledge to its just height; all the Clergy here are his pupils, and suck all they have from him; Allen cannot make a warrant without his precident, nor quondam John Evans draw a recogizance *sine directione Michaelis.*" But it has recently been pointed out that the author of this tribute was an inveterate jester. And when that fact is taken together with the high-flown style of the remarks, it is not difficult to interpret the words as a comic description of the isolation of the country clergy and to see the praise of Johnson's learning as given much in the spirit of Goldsmith's tribute to the village schoolmaster. Michael Johnson had probably attended the Lichfield grammar school and knew some Latin; but he was a tradesman, not a scholar.[2]

With bookselling he combined the business of manufacturing parchment; he habitually visited neighboring towns to open a stall on market days; and he was what we should call the "publisher" of (i.e., had printed to be sold by himself) some not very important books which seemed likely to attract local customers. He was also well enough regarded by his fellow townsmen to be made sheriff of Lichfield and later to be elected magistrate of the city.

Financially his condition seems to have got worse as time went on. He appears to have been industrious but he was not methodical, and Johnson's childhood was a straitened one. If there is a paradox here, it is perhaps sufficiently explained by Johnson himself: "My mother concluded that we were poor, because we lost by some of our trades; but the truth was, that my father, having in the early part of his life contracted debts, never had trade sufficient to enable him to pay them, and maintain his family; he got something but not enough. It was not till about 1768, that I thought to . . . estimate his probable profits. This, I believe, my parents never did." A great many years later when the Doctor was reassuring Mrs. Thrale concerning her responsibility for the brewery which her husband had left her, he proclaimed in his most magisterial manner: "Trade could not be managed by those who manage it if it had much difficulty." Michael Johnson was not, apparently, one of those who could do even that.

Johnson remembered that in very early childhood he had read in school the legend of a great man who punished those whom he hated by making them rich, and he remembered also his delight in the fact that when he told his mother the tale he discovered that the paradox was beyond her comprehension. But her failure to understand how riches might be a curse was perhaps the result rather of too much experience than of too little mental acuteness, and Johnson himself, when he had acquired more of the former, included the philosopher's professed contempt for this world's goods as part of the sentimental cant to be rejected by a true but tough-minded moralist like himself.

Samuel, the Great Moralist, as Boswell liked to call him, was born in Lichfield on what was then known as September 7, 1709, though by our calendar the date would be September 18th. Michael Johnson was past fifty-two and Sarah past forty, but they had been married for only a little over three years and this was the first of their two sons. Johnson remembered the story that his father, who was then sheriff and due that day to make the annual official circuit of the county, was asked by his mother whom he would invite to the traditional banquet. "All the town now," he replied, and later feasted the citizens with uncommon magnificence.

But the infant whose arrival was thus celebrated was a far from promising one. He was born almost dead, he could not cry for some time, and when the man-midwife who had tended his mother in a long, difficult labor finally held the infant in his arms, he said: "Here is a brave boy." One of his godfathers was Dr. Samuel Swinfen, a young physician of some standing who then lodged with the Johnsons, and Dr. Swinfen later told him that he "never knew any child reared with so much difficulty." Johnson remembered, also, that an aunt remarked to him while he was still a child that "she would not have picked such a poor creature up in the street."

For some ten weeks he was left at the house of a wet nurse,

Mrs. John Marklew, but was taken away when it was discovered that his eyes were affected. Dr. Swinfen thought he had there contracted the scrofulous infection which was to impair his senses, distort his body, and lay the physical foundation for what he might have called, had Pope not first appropriated the phrase, "this long disease, my life." But Sarah Johnson, apparently concerned only for the social and not the physical soundness of her family, believed that he had inherited scrofula through her and this may well have been true. A few weeks after birth some sort of lesion appeared on his body; while he was still at nurse an "issue" was cut in his left arm and left open, Johnson thought, till he was about six years old. Sometime in 1710 or 1711 he was taken to a neighboring town to be examined by an oculist and finally, in 1712, to London, on the advice of Sir John Floyer, a distinguished physician, in order that he might be "touched for evil" at one of the public ceremonies held for the purpose by Queen Anne.[3]

Though Anne had the blood of the Stuarts in her veins, it is not recorded that the young Samuel received any benefits from either the royal touch itself or the amulet of gold which was presented as a token and which Johnson wore about his neck on a ribbon till it passed, on his death, to his old schoolfellow, Dr. Taylor of Ashbourne. He did, however, retain memories of the great event, of the queen herself, "a sort of solemn recollection of a lady in diamonds, and a long black hood," "of a cat with a white collar and a dog, called Chops, that leaped over a stick" in the house of the bookseller with whom they stayed in London; also of a small silver cup and spoon marked "Sam. I" which his mother bought for him there. This cup, he records, was one of the last pieces which he and his wife sold during one of those periods of distress concerning which he had later so little to say and concerning which so little is known. "One has," he said to Mrs. Thrale, while parrying an inquiry concerning his family, "*so* little pleasure in reciting the anecdotes of beggary."

Fortunately Johnson's physical inheritance was not all bad. His diseased body was a powerful one and his physical strength great. Almost to the end of his life he delighted to astonish friends by sudden undignified displays of agility or strength,

the cruelty accepted as a matter of course in schools; but Johnson, never very sympathetic toward the advanced ideas concerning education which were beginning to be current during his maturity, always took the position that rudiments must be learned, that they could not be other than dull, and that the soundest system was the simplest—punish those who failed to perform the necessary tasks. Fanny Burney tells how once when Dr. Rose was praising the mild treatment at school in more recent years, Johnson replied that "what they gain on one end, they lose at the other" but this was not, in intention at least, brutality. "I would rather," he said on another occasion, "have the rod to be the general terrour of all, to make them learn, than tell a child, if you do thus, or thus, you will be more esteemed than your brothers or sisters. The rod produces an effect which terminates in itself. A child is afraid of being whipped, and gets his task, and there's an end on't; whereas, by exciting emulation and comparisons of superiority, you lay the foundation of lasting mischief; you make brothers and sisters hate each other."

This theory had been well-tested on Johnson himself, for Hunter, headmaster of the Lichfield school, was notorious for his severity, though, in Johnson's own words, "Abating his brutality, he was a very good master." Once when Bennet Langton asked Johnson how he had acquired his remarkably accurate knowledge of Latin, he replied: "My master whipt me very well. Without that, Sir, I should have done nothing." But that was doubtless in part talking for effect, as Johnson was by no means unwilling to do, and on another occasion he described Hunter as "very severe, and wrong-headedly severe." "He used," he said, "to beat us unmercifully; and he did not distinguish between ignorance and negligence; for he would beat a boy equally for not knowing a thing, as for neglecting to know it. He would ask a boy a question; and if he did not answer it, he would beat him, without considering whether he had an opportunity of knowing how to answer it. . . . Now, Sir, if a boy could answer every question, there would be no need of a master to teach him."

Nevertheless, Johnson could maintain on another occasion

that "a boy at school was the happiest of human beings"—an opinion as surprising in view of his general contempt for similar sentimental platitudes as it is in view of his experience. What he says in defense of the opinion is curiously in accord with the view that corporal punishment is less painful than the distress occasioned by the spirit of emulation, and it suggests that Johnson, though physically tough, was abnormally sensitive where intellectual self-respect was involved. To Boswell's objection that the schoolboy was in terror of the rod, he replied: "Ah, Sir, a boy's being flogged is not so severe as a man's having the hiss of the world against him. Men have a solicitude about fame; and the greater share they have of it, the more afraid they are of losing it." Boswell silently asked himself: "Is it possible that the great SAMUEL JOHNSON really entertains any such apprehension?" The great JAMES BOSWELL, we know, certainly did.[5]

If Johnson retained to the end of his life a greater respect for learning of the most formal and traditional kind than was usual even in the eighteenth century among people of his breadth of experience, it was certainly not because the pill had been sugar-coated for him, and one wishes that we knew more than he ever revealed concerning the spontaneous mental activities of his childhood. We are told, to be sure, that his intellectual superiority was recognized at school, that his companions sometimes paid tribute to it by carrying their awkward school fellow on their shoulders. We are also told how, while still a child, he sat reading *Hamlet* in the family kitchen until he came to the ghost scene, which so captured his imagination that "he suddenly hurried up stairs to the street door that he might see people about him." But there is little evidence that as a boy he was very much more than merely unusually quick at routine school tasks or that during his brief academic career he particularly distinguished himself as a scholar.

Johnson's own testimony as well as the little furnished by others is contradictory and self-contradictory enough. His father's stock of books had of course always been available and his friend Dr. Shaw (who is said to have got his information from the daughter of Dr. Swinfen) declared in the first published sketch of Johnson's life that "he is said, when a mere schoolboy, to have read indefatigably." To Boswell Johnson once remarked: "I knew almost as much at eighteen as I do now." Yet, he called himself "idle" during the years immediately following his school days; said that he followed no plan of study beyond that of confining himself to standard literature; that he read only "as chance threw books in his way, and inclination directed him through them"; and that although he very early "loved to read poetry" he "hardly ever read any poem to the end."

Such, we know, were the habits of his mature life, for however much he may have believed in the virtue of discipline in connection with some activities he always insisted that one was not likely to profit much from any reading except that done for pleasure. Lady Mary Montagu's *Letters* was, so he told Mrs. Thrale, the only book "which he did not consider obligatory" that he had ever read through in his life. And to the same lady on another occasion: "A man is seldom in the humour to unlock his book-case, set his desk in order, and betake himself to serious study; but a retentive memory will do something, and a fellow shall have a strange credit given him, if he can but recollect striking passages from different books, keep the authors separate in his head, and bring his knowledge artfully into play." The *Anatomy of Melancholy* was the "only book that ever took him out of bed two hours sooner than he wished to rise" and he was scornful of those who read books *"through."* Yet Johnson also talked of the folly of those who supposed that conversation could make up for lack of reading and, apparently careless of inconsistency: "I used—*to read like a Turk."*

It has been suggested that his apparently extraordinary knowledge of literature may have been acquired in preparation for the dictionary for which he certainly read extensively, and yet when Boswell asked him how he had attained the astonishing familiarity with our language exhibited in that work, he replied that "it was not the effect of particular study; but that it had grown up in his mind insensibly." Perhaps the nearest we can hope to come to resolving the paradox is to say that Johnson was certainly a desultory reader and certainly got more out of the books he dipped into than others got by reading them *through.* But it is also to be remembered that his standards were high, and that what seemed like idleness to him would not have seemed like that to others.[6]

Johnson was above all a talker, a man who found in conversation a stimulus he did not find in study. It seems reasonable, therefore, to assume that he was first aroused to a sense of his own powers by social contacts, and if this is true, then it is easy to date the beginning of his career. His cousin Cornelius, or "Parson," Ford came to Lichfield in September, 1725, and doubtless because he then perceived some promise in his physically unprepossessing kinsman, invited him for a stay at his home at Pedmore. Cornelius was a man of the world, apparently not yet notorious for his vices, and at his house Johnson probably for the first time met people with some pretensions to social elegance and to an interest in "elegant learning."

Evidently the visit was a success, for it was extended to some months and indeed was the occasion for the refusal of the Lichfield school to take Johnson back after so long an absence. At the suggestion of Cousin Cornelius, he was accordingly sent to Stourbridge, where he would appear not as the son of a struggling bookseller, but as a kinsman of the Fords who were well-known there. Bishop Percy (he of the *Reliques* and a native of a neighboring village) could remember that at Stourbridge Johnson's "genius was so distinguished that, although little better than a school-boy, he was admitted into the best company of the place, and had no common attention paid to his conversation; of which remarkable instances were long remembered there."

At Stourbridge nevertheless he remained only for about a year, apparently returning to Lichfield in the autumn of 1726 when he was just completing his seventeenth year. The financial affairs of Michael Johnson were at an extremely low ebb and the assumption seems to have been that Samuel, whose education was now over, would devote himself to the family business. We know that he actually learned to bind books, for in later life he once recognized a specimen of his own handiwork; but, though he seems to have had no other definitely formulated ambition, he certainly entered with no enthusiasm into the career that seemed to lie before him. His father scolded him for his want of steady application and he had, he told Boswell, "no settled plan of life, nor looked forward at all, but merely lived from day to day." Probably it was during this period—it lasted two years—that he committed the sin later to be atoned for at Uttoxeter market.

But though Johnson spoke of his idleness, the period was probably far from wasted. It seems to have been then that he did a great deal of his solidest reading—not, he told Boswell, "voyages and travels, but all literature, Sir, all ancient writers, all manly." And it was during this time also that, frequenting some of the best provincial society, he acquired that ease in good company which always seemed somewhat paradoxical in a man who had, during so much of his early manhood, been shut out from it and whose downrightness of speech seemed at first sight more mere uncouthness than it actually was. Among others, Gilbert Walmesley, son of the M.P. for Lichfield and chancellor of the diocese, took him up. He was a man of sophistication and culture to whom Johnson was later to pay high tribute, and to whose intervention at a somewhat later crisis Johnson perhaps owed the direction of his career. With the young David Garrick, who had been a childhood visitor at the Walmesley residence in the bishop's palace, Johnson, so he himself says, "enjoyed many cheerful and instructive hours."

Anna Seward, the Swan of Lichfield, was the granddaughter of the schoolmaster Hunter and at one time lived with her parents in the house which had formerly been Gilbert Walmesley's home. "The Swan" was not one of Johnson's warmest admirers and was still unborn when Johnson was a youth. Moreover, she unscrupulously rewrote portions of her letters before she published them. But she did know the Lichfield tradition and what she says in one of her letters is worth quoting provided one bears in mind that her penchant for the dramatic would incline her to play up any situation for all it was worth. First she stresses the humbleness of the Johnsons' position by remarking that though Garrick's parents—his father was a half-pay lieutenant—were acquaintances of the Walmesleys, those of the young Samuel were not, since they did not move in Walmesley's "sphere." Then she writes:

"Within the walls which my father's family inhabits, in this very dining-room, the munificent Mr. Walmesley, with the taste, the learning and the liberality of Maecenas, administered to rising genius the kind nutriment of attention and praise. Often to his hospitable board were the school-boys, David Garrick and Samuel Johnson, summoned. The parents of the former were of Mr. Walmesley's acquaintance; but those of the latter did not move in his sphere.

"It was rumoured that my mother's father, Mr. Hunter, had a boy of marked ability upon his forms. The huge, over-grown, mis-shapen, and probably dirty stripling was brought before the most able scholar and the finest gentleman in Lichfield or its environs, who, perceiving far more ability than even rumour had promised, placed him at his table, not merely to gratify a transient curiosity, but to assure him of a constant welcome.

"Two or three evenings every week Mr. Walmesley called the stupendous stripling and his livelier companion, David Garrick, who was a few years younger, to his own plentiful board. There, in the hours of convivial gaiety, did he delight to wave every restraint of superiority formed by rank, affluence, polished manners and the dignity of advanced life; and there, 'as man to man, as friend to friend', he drew forth the different powers of each expanding spirit, by the vivid interchange of sentiment and opinion, and by the cheering influence of generous applause.

"Another circumstance combined to heighten the merit of this patronage. Mr. Walmesley was a zealous Whig. My grandfather, then master of the free school, perceiving Johnson's abilities, had, to his own honour, taken as much pains with him as with the young gentlemen whose parents paid an high price for their pupilage; but my grandfather was a Jacobite, and Sam. Johnson had imbibed his master's absurd zeal for the forfeit rights of the house of Stuart; and this, though his father had very loyal principles; but the anxiety attendant on penurious circumstances, probably left old Johnson little leisure or inclination to talk on political subjects.

"His son, I am told, even at that early period of life, maintained his opinions, on every subject, with the same sturdy, dogmatic and arrogant fierceness with which he now overbears all opposition to them in company.

"At present we can well conceive the probability of his dogmatism being patiently supported by attending admirers, awed by the literary eminence on which he stands. But how great must have been Mr. Walmesley's love of genius; how great his generous respect for its dependent situation, that could so far restrain a naturally impetuous temper, as to induce him to suffer insolent sallies from the son of an indigent bookseller, and on a subject which, so handled by people of his own rank, he would have dashed back in their faces with no small degree of asperity! . . ." [7]

The period of so-called idleness was brought suddenly to a close when in October of 1728, less than two months after he had entered his twentieth year, Johnson became a member of Oxford University. He was to remain for only a little more than a year and the move, especially the financing of it, has always been something of a mystery. Boswell felt the matter too delicate to permit his questioning Johnson himself, but he got from one of Johnson's old friends a story about a gentleman of Shropshire who undertook to support him as a companion to the gentleman's son, then in Oxford. There are, however, some difficulties involved in accepting the story just as told and there may be more significance in a fact recently discovered by Aleyn Reade, namely, that earlier in the year a rich cousin of Johnson's mother had died and left her a legacy of forty pounds. Though Johnson was poor (and proud) at the university, he went as a commoner, not as a servitor, and it has been calculated that forty pounds would be just about sufficient to pay his expenses during the little more than a year he was there. College bills indicate that his expenditures were about average.

Oxford, it is generally agreed, reached its lowest ebb in the eighteenth century. Johnson was not there long and there is no tangible evidence that his stay profited him much; but unlike some of his contemporaries—Gibbon, for one—who had also attended the university, he always spoke of it with glowing enthusiasm. Few things in his life gave him deeper satisfaction than the honorary degree conferred upon him and few pleasures delighted him more than those he enjoyed on visits to the university when he could chat learnedly with professional scholars. He had for colleges that almost romantic admiration which is, even today, less common among graduates than among those who had desired but could not get a formal education, and his respect for ancient institutions made him a strong champion of the idea of a university. "Emulation," which he thought so evil a thing in schools, he cites as one of the advantages of university study. The "excellent rules of discipline" were another. But he let the cat out of the bag when he added: "The members of an University may, for a season, be unmindful of their duty. I am arguing for the excellency of the institution." Oxford and Cambridge were the visible embodiments of England's regard for learning, just as the Church was the visible embodiment of its regard for religion; and Johnson, for all his hatred of cant, was almost tender-minded in this one respect. It hurt, angered and, one is almost tempted to say, frightened him when anyone treated with disrespect the visible embodiment of things he deeply cherished. Learning and religion, he seemed to feel, received so little recognition in the world that even the imperfect institutions testifying to that little respect ought to be almost exempt from criticism. Attacks on education or the church evidently seemed to him less likely to improve either than to encourage the worldly to neglect them altogether. Visiting Oxford after he had received his degree of M.A. he wore his gown with a punctilious regard for ceremony which was described as "almost ostentatious."

So far as his own behavior as a student is concerned there is nothing in the little we know to distinguish it from that of the average careless undergraduate—except possibly a more than usual casualness. The first day he came to college he visited his tutor but then, he told Boswell, he stayed away four to go sliding on the ice, and according to Hawkins he said to a tutor who had assessed him a small fine for an absence: "Sir, you have sconced me two-pence for non-attendance at a lecture not worth a penny."

Thus, though Johnson startled his tutor at a first interview by quoting Macrobius, his outward conduct was in general that of the usual casual undergraduate. Dr. William Adams, one of the Fellows of Pembroke at the time of Johnson's arrival, told Boswell that Johnson "was caressed and loved by all about him, was a gay and frolicksome fellow, and passed there the happiest part of his life." The Bishop of Dromore had heard from some of Johnson's contemporaries "that he was generally seen lounging at the College gate, with a circle of young students round him, whom he was entertaining with wit, and keeping from their studies, if not spiriting them up to rebellion against the College discipline, which in his maturer years he so much extolled." But Johnson's own comment is: "Ah, Sir, I was mad and violent. It was bitterness which they mistook for frolick. I was miserably poor, and I thought to fight my way by my literature and my wit; so I disregarded all power and all authority." Later he was to write of Lyttelton's *Persian Letters* that they "have something of that indistinct and headstrong ardour for liberty which a man of genius always catches when he enters the world, and always suffers to cool as he passes forward." Perhaps another explanation is simply that Johnson, like many other admirers of authority, formed his opinion while imagining himself exercising rather than submitting to it.

Though the college expense accounts may show that he was not starving himself, he was certainly suffering some of the deprivations of poverty. We are told that he used to call on a fellow student in a different college to get at second hand the lectures of a tutor whom he admired, but that he gave up the habit when the deplorable state of his shoes was observed; and we know also that he indignantly rejected an offer to supply him with a better pair. It is equally evident that his mental state was not that which his liveliness suggested. It was now that a reading of Law's *Serious Call* "was the first occasion" of his "thinking in earnest of religion," which he had become indifferent to in his ninth year and which, according to his own confession, he had *talked* against if not indeed *thought* against.[8]

More ominous is the fact that in 1729 his melancholy reached a serious crisis, which was probably responsible for his leaving the university and which certainly drove him to consult Dr.

Swinfen who was then not "physician of Lychfield," as Boswell calls him, but a physician in Birmingham some sixteen miles away. Johnson was evidently dating from this period when he wrote a friend in 1778: "My health has been, from my twentieth year, such as has seldom afforded me a single day of ease." He drew up an account of his case so acute and so eloquent that Dr. Swinfen showed it to several people (much to Johnson's displeasure), but the account has not survived and we have only vague information concerning the symptoms. According to Boswell, Johnson "felt himself overwhelmed with a horrible hypochondria, with perpetual irritation, fretfulness, and impatience; and with a dejection, gloom, and despair which made existence a misery." Describing his efforts to deal with the disorder, his remark to Boswell was "I did not then know how to manage it"; but if this is taken to imply that he later learned, the fact nevertheless remains that not only melancholy but a fear that he might be losing his reason frequently shadowed the rest of his life. He said that he inherited "a vile melancholy" from his father, which made him "mad all his life, at least not sober."

Boswell thought that this mental crisis occurred "in the college vacation of 1729" and that Johnson returned to remain at the university until 1731. The question how long he was actually in residence has been lengthily disputed for more than a century, but Reade has recently given what appears to be conclusive proof that he left for good in December, 1729, after a stay of thirteen months, and that the confusion is due to the fact that his name was kept on the college books, certain fixed charges continuing to be entered, long after he had left to return as a student no more. That Johnson planned to return is suggested by the fact that he left a rather large collection of books in the care of a friend, but there may have been financial reasons as well as those supplied by his mental state why he never did so. When he left he was already in arrears (later balanced by the forfeiture of his deposit or "caution money") and when he got to Lichfield he found his father in financial straits.[9]

Boswell evidently knew little concerning either the chronology or the details of the desperate years following his hero's short college career, but other contemporary sources, as well as, especially, more recent research, have fixed certain facts, though it is still not known how he employed himself between December, 1729, and sometime in 1731 when he made an unsuccessful application for the post of usher at the Stourbridge school. At some time (probably March) during the next year he did secure the post of undermaster at the school at Market Bosworth, where he endured, until July of the same year, days made miserable not only by the dull routine of the school but by the fact that he had also to serve as private chaplain to the school's patron, one Sir Wolstan Dixey, whom, so records show, he had good reason for calling "an abandoned brutal rascal." Shortly before he took this position, his father died (December, 1731) leaving an unprosperous business to be managed by Johnson's mother and his younger brother Nathaniel, then nineteen. According to Boswell, one of Johnson's little diaries records, under the date of July 15, 1732, the fact that he had just received twenty pounds "being all that I have reason to hope for out of my father's effects, previous to the death of my mother." Small as the sum was, it probably gave him the courage to free himself from the bondage of Market Bosworth and the humiliation involved in living with "an abandoned brutal rascal."

Before the end of the same month he wrote an unsuccessful letter of application for a position in the school at Ashbourne and some months later he accepted the invitation to visit an old school friend, Edmund Hector of Birmingham. There he was made acquainted with Thomas Warren, a prosperous bookseller and printer of the city, for whom he is said to have done some work. We also know from a surviving letter that in June, 1735, Johnson was living in the house of Thomas Whitby at Great Haywood near Lichfield where, though Boswell makes no mention of the fact, he was acting as tutor for Whitby's son.

More than five years had now passed since he had quitted Oxford for good and, on the basis of such of the scanty facts available as have so far been alluded to, it might seem that those five years had been spent with little profit. But the time was near when he was to launch himself definitely upon the world. At

Birmingham the essays, now lost, which he is supposed to have contributed to the local newspaper were probably his first published prose compositions and his translation from the French of the *Voyage to Abyssinia* by the Spanish Jesuit, Jeronimo Lobo, published in 1735, his first considerable literary chore. It was at Birmingham also that he first met Mrs. Henry Porter, whom he was soon to marry. Some eight months before that event, and before the *Voyage* was actually published, he had by letter applied unsuccessfully to Edward Cave, editor of *The Gentleman's Magazine,* for employment as a writer of literary articles and he had also, shortly before, issued abortive proposals to print by subscription the Latin poems of Politian. Since the application to Cave (and possibly also the missing proposals for Politian) is subsequent to the death, in August or September of 1734, of the first husband of his future wife, it is barely possible that these attempts to settle himself in literary occupations may have been inspired by thought of marriage.

In any event, responsibility for a widow who already had children of her own soon added urgency to the problem of finding a place for himself in the world. To what extent he had been, up to that time, merely drifting, it is impossible to say, but he seems always to have had confidence in his powers, if not in his ability to use them. Many years later, when he was to some degree famous as the author of *The Rambler* and the compiler of the *Dictionary,* he wrote to Bennet Langton: "When I was as you are now, towering in confidence of twenty-one, little did I suspect that I should be at forty-nine what I am now." Since Johnson was not one automatically to repeat cant about youth or about anything else, it is safe to assume from this passage that even in the desperate days after leaving college he was already expecting great things of himself.

Before giving him the responsibility of a wife and sending him forth to make a place in the world for himself and for her, we may take brief stock of him as he had doubtless done of himself. In 1735, then, Johnson was already twenty-six years old and had just made the first start toward a literary career at an age which has seen many a man of letters with important work behind him. Yet his temperament and physical constitution, as well as the outline of his opinions, were already fixed. Not only melancholy but also indolence had definitely claimed him as their own, for he dictated the translation of Lobo from bed; as for his physical appearance, we have evidence given Boswell by Mrs. Porter's daughter Lucy that it was not any more prepossessing then than in the days of his greatness. "Miss Porter told me, that when he was first introduced to her mother, his appearance was very forbidding: he was then lean and lank, so that his immense structure of bones was hideously striking to the eye, and the scars of the scrophula were deeply visible. He also wore his hair, which was straight and stiff, separated behind; and he often had, seemingly, convulsive starts and odd gesticulations, which tended to excite at once surprise and ridicule." That he could also already exhibit powers and charms sufficient to make himself acceptable despite the grotesqueness of his appearance is evident both from Miss Porter's further testimony and from the list of local persons who received and befriended him. As a child he is said to have been carried on the backs of admiring schoolfellows; at Oxford we have heard him described as lounging before the college gate and entertaining students with his wit. Even before that, his worldly cousin, Parson Ford, had found him an acceptable house guest, and more recently he had been invited to make a stay at Birmingham. Evidently, then, it was already not too difficult to forget what Johnson looked like.

There are tales of his frequenting the best houses around Lichfield and even more impressive is the behavior of Gilbert Walmesley. As we have already seen, he took the poor boy into his own social circle. "At this man's table," Johnson himself later wrote, "I enjoyed many cheerful and instructive hours, with companions, such as are not often found"; and a year or two after his marriage we hear of him as intimate not only with this gentleman, but also with ladies of some pretension to elegance and refinement.

Some considerable part of the vast store of literary knowledge which enabled him to talk and write so learnedly without research or other preparation had also probably already been acquired, though if one were to take literally his own testimony concerning his lifelong idleness and neglect of study one would be driven to the conclusion that literature had been communicated to him by some transcendental process and that he could analyze, with minute correctness, writers whom he had never read. Adam Smith, who is not likely to have been easily impressed, once declared that "Johnson knew more books than any man alive." The recently discovered list of the approximately one hundred books which he owned at college certainly indicates that he was then interesting himself not only in the classics and the Renaissance scholars, but also in Spenser, Dryden and Milton, as well as in other less important English writers.

Perhaps the strongest indication that Johnson's intellectual temperament had already declared and clarified itself, the best proof that not only his principles but also his attitude toward life had been fixed, is a few sentences from the Preface to his translation of Lobo. More than forty years later, when Boswell came across a copy of it, Johnson apparently did not like to be reminded of this early work, but it is characteristic enough to be worth noticing. Introducing his author, he said:

"The Portuguese traveller, contrary to the general vein of his countrymen, has amused his reader with no romantick absurdity, or incredible fictions; whatever he relates, whether true or not, is at least probable; and he who tells nothing exceeding the bounds of probability has a right to demand that they should believe him who cannot contradict him.

"He appears by his modest and unaffected narration, to have described things as he saw them, to have copied nature from the life, and to have consulted his senses, not his imagination. He meets with no basilisks that destroy with their eyes, his crocodiles devour their prey without tears, and his cataracts fall from the rocks without deafening the neighbouring inhabitants.

"The reader will here find no regions cursed with irremediable barrenness, or blest with spontaneous fecundity; no perpetual gloom, or unceasing sunshine; nor are the nations here described, either devoid of all sense of humanity, or consummate in all private or social virtues. Here are no Hottentots without religious polity or articulate language; no Chinese perfectly polite, and completely skilled in all sciences; he will discover, what will always be discovered by a diligent and impartial enquirer, that wherever human nature is to be found, there is a mixture of vice and virtue, a contest of passion and reason; and that the Creator doth not appear partial in his distributions, but has balanced, in most countries, their particular inconveniences by particular favours."

Since Boswell's time it has been repeatedly remarked that the sentence structure, the rhythm, and the rhetorical method of these sentences are manifestly those of Johnson's mature style. It has also been observed that the translation of this book probably suggested the choice of Abyssinia as the scene of *Rasselas.* But it seems to have been less often observed that the passage also suggests an important aspect of the theme of that tale and thus, indeed, already announces one of Johnson's fundamental convictions concerning human life as a whole.

Like many prefaces, this one was no doubt written chiefly because a preface would be expected, and the author may seem to be saying what he says chiefly because he must find something to say. At first sight, in other words, it may appear to be a mere formal exercise. But it is surely significant that the traveler should be praised chiefly for the absence of wonders in his tale; for his failure to encourage the belief that life in one part of the globe is so very different from life in another; for the confirmation which he might be thought to supply in behalf of one of Johnson's fundamental convictions—the conviction, namely, that the structure of the universe and the essential nature of man are so overwhelmingly the most important factors in determining the good and evil of the human lot as to render climate, government or social institutions secondary at best and insufficient in themselves to do more than make it somewhat better or somewhat worse.

Johnson accepted the miracles of the Bible because he could not refuse to do so without plunging himself into an abyss of intolerable doubt from the brink of which he always shuddered back; but even in works of pure imagination the supernatural was likely to trouble him, and what he said of the vein of "stubborn rationality" that kept him from the Roman Catholic Church may give warrant for the guess that he would have been more comfortable if even Anglicanism had put less strain upon it. That deficiency in the sense of wonder (if deficiency it be) which made him assume, worshiper of the classics though he was, that the mythology in Homer and other classical poets was merely a puerility to be put up with for the sake of the rational picture of men and manners found in the same works, was something more than the antiromantic tendency of which he was one of the last great representatives. It was not merely that he distrusted (outside official religion) the wonders of the supernatural, but almost equally that he distrusted the less extravagant wonders purveyed by those who drew in high relief the contrasts between men and men, nations and nations, the fortunate and the unfortunate. And he distrusted them because he was so sure that there were few exceptions to the generalization: "Human life is everywhere a state, in which much is to be endured, and little to be enjoyed."

Among rationalists, the sense of wonder is likely to manifest itself in the form of a love of the dramatic. The contrast and variety of life so exhilarates them that they love to emphasize it, and one way of extending the process is to imagine utopias in which the most violent possible contrast is drawn between things as they are and things as they might be. Johnson's own temperament was completely undramatic in this sense. It was the *mediocrity* of human life that struck him most forcibly and the uniformity of human existence that he was most prone to illustrate. Hence he found himself ready to respect and believe an author who, though traveling in remote lands, could find even there "no perpetual gloom, or unceasing sunshine . . . no Hottentots without religious polity or articulate language; no Chinese perfectly polite, and completely skilled in all sciences," but showed, on the contrary, "that wherever human nature is to be found, there is a mixture of vice and virtue, a contest of passion and reason; and that the Creator doth not appear partial in his distributions, but has balanced, in most countries, their particular inconveniences by particular favours."

This temperamental predisposition and this conviction (one is here hardly to be separated from the other) harmonized of course with his conservative leanings in politics and morality and, being antecedent to the latter, should probably be taken as to some extent determining them. Indeed, the passages quoted from the Preface may give as good a key as any to the greatest paradox in Johnson—the fact that a man so tenderhearted, so generous and capable of so many individual acts of benevolence, should have so often professed political and moral convictions which seemed almost inhumanly harsh to many of his contemporaries, as well as to much of posterity.

No doubt one must, in discussing his fear of social or political change, remember that the climate of opinion in which he lived was more influenced than he realized or would have cared to admit by ideas which came down through intermediaries from Hobbes. To him as to Hobbes, change risked anarchy and any government is better than no government. But there is more to the attitude than that. Johnson assumes that the risks involved by change are risks taken without real chance of betterment and his often extravagant insistence that the individual's happiness was not affected by the form of government under which he lived was, in part at least, dictated by his conviction of the universal and unalterable mediocrity of the human lot.

If, then, this analysis of the earliest extant example of Johnson's prose composition be accepted, it would seem to suggest that before he went up to London, even before he had contracted the marriage which spurred him on to begin his career, he had exhibited the most central feature of his philosophy of life. The conviction that man must in all respects forever remain in what Pope had called "a middle state" was more important than the political Toryism in which he was also already fixed, even perhaps more important than the great acceptance (and great refusal) which he had made when he accepted once and for all that Anglican version of Christianity which he never afterward permitted himself or others to debate, but which he kept carefully in a separate compartment of his mind.[10]

CHAPTER II

London; or, The Full Tide of Human Existence

IT IS not easy to think of the young Johnson as a bridegroom. We may with some difficulty imagine him as wanting a wife but why, may we ask, should a wife want him? The fact remains that on July 9, 1735, he married Elizabeth Jervis Porter, a widow whose husband had died some ten months before. The new Mrs. Johnson was forty-six years old and thus only a little less than twice her husband's age. She was already provided with three children of whom the eldest was a daughter nearly twenty

Johnson probably first met the Porters in Birmingham in 1733. Both Henry Porter and his wife were descended from a long line of small country squires, but Henry had not been successful in his business and from his estate his widow received little or nothing. But she possessed something like seven or eight hundred pounds inherited from other relatives and when Johnson began to court her soon after her husband's death, he was probably not unaware that her small fortune would mitigate the imprudence of a marriage. Nevertheless, everything we know of Johnson's character as well as of the subsequent history of the pair seems to justify the conclusion that this was, within any reasonably inclusive definition of the term, a love match on his side and probably on hers also. Johnson "archly" told his gay young friend, Topham Beauclerk, that it was; and though doubtless few young men of twenty-five would have had what Boswell makes Johnson call his "amorous propensities" deeply stirred by a widow of forty-six, Johnson's almost certainly were.[1]

It must be remembered that he had both strong sex impulses and rigid scruples—either one of which characteristics is likely to be troublesome alone, but to be much more so in combination with the other. It has been suggested that he may, on occasion, have yielded to impulse, but Boswell, himself a furious rake and ready enough to make allowance for masculine weakness, does not dare risk more than a guarded suspicion and, on another occasion, states flatly: "His juvenile attachments to the fair sex were, however, very transient; and it is certain, that he formed no criminal connection whatsoever." Yet Johnson repeatedly revealed his realization of the power of the sexual impulses in himself as well as in mankind in general. Tough-minded here as he was always unless inescapable Christian doctrine happened to be involved, Johnson refused to summon cant to the solution of a problem which had to be faced. In itself the sex impulse was no more an evil than money. There were merely lawful as well as unlawful ways of using it; and since marriage provided for most men a proper solution of the difficulty, he assumed that it would for him also. In that respect his opinion at twenty-five was no doubt identical with his opinion at sixty. Perhaps he was thinking of his own case when he remarked some quarter of a century later: "It is not from reason and prudence that people marry, but from inclination. A man is poor; he thinks, 'I cannot be worse, and so I'll e'en take Peggy.' "

Possibly he would have preferred a woman nearer his own age. Certainly in his later years he was strongly attracted to youth as many instances, including his fondness for Fanny Burney and, to take a slighter one, his sitting in Scotland with a Highland girl upon his knee, sufficiently prove. Indeed, Anna Seward (whose testimony is, however, not to be taken too seriously) liked to spread the story that Johnson had turned to Mrs. Porter only after he had decided that her nineteen-year-old daughter Lucy was not for him. Still, though Johnson no doubt knew that he did not have the whole world to choose from, there is no reason for supposing that he regarded Elizabeth Porter as a desperate *faute de mieux* or that he found her deficient in physical charms.

The relations between the Great Moralist and his beloved Tetty form an important part of the Johnson legend. His nearsighted admiration of her faded charms is too picturesque a detail to be overlooked by any commentator, but to what extent the grotesqueness of the pair was exaggerated with malicious humor it is not possible to say. Tetty shared Johnson's deepest obscurity but died just as he was beginning to emerge from it. Boswell never saw her, neither did Mrs. Thrale. The stories come chiefly either from Garrick, who knew well enough how much fun Johnson had made of him, or from Anna Seward, who was distinctly not one of the Doctor's idolaters. A surviving picture evidently made when Tetty was young indicates that she had not been without good looks, and there is no reason to suppose that they had completely vanished at forty-six. But she can hardly have remained for many years after their marriage the "pretty thing" he is reported to have continued to call her; and even after all due allowance has been made for humorous exaggeration, it seems safe enough to assume that Johnson's uxoriousness had its comic as well as its pathetic side.

It must, moreover, be remembered that all of Johnson's physical appetites were strong and hearty rather than delicate. In eating he was not undiscriminating but he was by no means finicky and he was not always repelled by foods which others thought heavy to the point of coarseness. Add the fact that, in later years at least, his vision was so bad that he could see nothing more than a few inches from his eyes, and even Garrick's picture of him peering with admiration at a face which heavy wrinkles and heavy painting made preposterous to others is not wholly incredible. Jonathan Swift, who in *Gulliver* took such pleasure in imagining how repulsive the most delicate of human skins would be if it could be seen suitably magnified, would no doubt have been delighted at the converse demonstration afforded by the spectacle of a nearsighted Brobdingnagian peering uxoriously at a countenance whose coarseness the ordinary man needed no lens to observe.

In judging Johnson it is fairer to look through no eyes but his own. Physically as well as otherwise Tetty inspired love, and to love her was lawful. Garrick might describe her to Boswell "as very fat, with a bosom of more than ordinary protuberance, with swelled cheeks, of a florid red, produced by thick painting, and increased by the liberal use of cordials; flaring and fantastick in her dress, and affected both in her speech and her general behavior." But even if that description was strictly true from Garrick's own point of view, it is certain that Johnson himself saw her in no such terms. Near the very end of his life he placed over her grave a stone with an inscription in which she is described as "formosa, culta, ingeniosa, pia," and there is no reason to suppose that in doing so he was claiming the privileges implied when he said on another occasion: "In lapidary inscriptions a man is not upon oath." [2]

Neither, for that matter, is there reason to suppose that Tetty's attractions were all physical. Johnson professed to despise learned ladies, especially when they competed with men, but he also more than once specified sprightliness and brains as necessary attributes of an attractive woman, and the few anecdotes which have survived concerning Tetty indicate that she was not only a woman of some judgment in intellectual matters but also that she possessed wit of a kind not unlike his own. Some stories which Johnson himself told are not incompatible with Garrick's account of her tendency to indulge on occasion in a kind of willful coquettishness hardly appropriate to her age or appearance, but there is every reason to believe that this was the result rather of a foible than of any fundamental folly. Lucy told Boswell that her mother was shocked by Johnson's appearance when he first came courting but she added that her mother, after hearing him talk, had said: "This is the most sensible man that I ever saw in my life." Johnson himself told Boswell that she remarked when he was writing *The Rambler:* "I thought very well of you before; but I did not imagine you could have written any thing equal to this."

Both Boswell and Mrs. Thrale tell as from Johnson himself

the farcical story of the first (as well as possibly the last) clash between Tetty's capriciousness and what Boswell calls Johnson's "manly firmness." It is said to have occurred on the way from Birmingham to the church at Derby where the ceremony took place; according to Boswell, Johnson's account was in the following words: " 'Sir, she had read the old romances, and had got into her head the fantastical notion that a woman of spirit should use her lover like a dog. So, Sir, at first she told me that I rode too fast, and she could not keep up with me: and, when I rode a little slower, she passed me, and complained that I lagged behind. I was not to be made the slave of caprice; and I resolved to begin as I meant to end. I therefore pushed on briskly, till I was fairly out of her sight. The road lay between two hedges, so I was sure she could not miss it; and I contrived that she should soon come up with me. When she did, I observed her to be in tears.' " Mrs. Thrale softens the whole by making the last sentence read: "But I believe there was a tear or two—pretty dear creature." [3]

Those who remember Johnson's outburst in Scotland when he thought he was being deserted by his companion may suspect that being on horseback put him in a sensitive mood, and the indefatigable Reade points out that the incident could hardly have occurred "on the wedding morn" since Johnson would have had to be in Derby the day before. Nevertheless, something of the sort must have occurred if Johnson told the story to at least two different persons and it was, as Boswell remarks, "a singular beginning of connubial felicity." [4]

But if this incident is to be read into the evidence concerning Tetty's brains and temperament, it should at least be balanced against a somewhat less often repeated story, told by Anna Seward. Johnson, it seems, had asked his mother's permission to marry and when she protested the rashness of the proposed step, he replied: "Mother, I have not deceived Mrs. Porter; I have told her the worst of me; that I am of mean extraction; that I have no money; and that I have had an uncle hanged. She replied, that she valued no one more or less for his descent; that she had no more money than myself; and that, though she had not had a relation hanged, she had fifty who deserved hanging." If Tetty really said this she was not only no fool but something of a wit in her husband's own manner, and the same conclusion might be drawn from another remark attributed to her, according to Boswell, by Johnson himself. Discussing Johnson's domestic arrangements and his love of good eating, Boswell once asked him if he and his wife never quarreled. Johnson replied that they often did and remembered the time when she had interrupted his grace before meat with the Johnsonian protestation: "Nay, hold, Mr. Johnson, and do not make a farce of thanking God for a dinner which in a few minutes you will protest not eatable." [5]

Lucy Porter accepted her mother's odd marriage with good grace and for many years lived in Lichfield with Johnson's mother, whom Johnson himself never saw again. Joseph Porter, the younger son, was in later years at least on good terms with Johnson, but Jervis Henry Porter, who had private means inherited from an uncle and seems to have been a worthy officer in the navy, apparently never forgave either his mother or her husband for a marriage which he evidently regarded as a disgrace to the family. "While they resided in Gough Court [i.e., Gough Square], her son, the officer, knocked at the door, and asked the maid if her mistress was at home? She answered, 'Yes, Sir, but she is sick in bed.' 'O!' says he, 'if it is so, tell her that her son Jervas called to know how she did;' and was going away. The maid begged she might run up to tell her mistress, and, without attending his answer, left him. Mrs. Johnson, enraptured to hear her son was below, desired the maid to tell him she longed to embrace him. When the maid descended, the gentleman was gone, and poor Mrs. Johnson was much agitated by the adventure; it was the only time he ever made an effort to see her." Johnson did what he could to comfort his wife and told Mrs. Williams: "Her son is uniformly undutiful; so I conclude, like many other sober men, he might once in his life be drunk, and in that fit nature got the better of his pride." [6]

Though at the time of his marriage Johnson had already made his first tentative efforts to establish himself in a literary career with the translation of Lobo and the unsuccessful offer of his services to the editor of *The Gentleman's Magazine,* he evidently saw no immediate hope of supporting himself in such a career and turned again to the schoolmastering which he hated and for which he had no great qualifications. We know that in August, 1735, shortly after his marriage, the ever-helpful Gilbert Walmesley attempted to get him a position at a school in Solihull but met with a discouraging objection. Inquiry, he was told, had revealed that the candidate was an excellent scholar and therefore deserving of something a good deal better than the position applied for, but also that "he has the character of being a very haughty, ill-natured gent., and yet he has such a way of distorting his face (Wh though he can't help) ye gent. think it may affect some young lads."

Even before this time, however, plans for setting up a school of his own seem to have been vaguely formed. The exact date on which the new venture was begun has never been established, but shortly after his marriage Johnson (probably with his wife's money and certainly with Walmesley's encouragement) rented a house at Edial, some two miles west of Lichfield, and inserted an advertisement in *The Gentleman's Magazine* announcing that there "young gentlemen are boarded and taught the Latin and Greek Languages, by SAMUEL JOHNSON." By way of a nest egg, Mr. Walmesley supplied one pupil in the person of another Lichfield protégé, a youngster whose grandfather had been a Huguenot refugee and whose father, a struggling lieutenant in the army, had married a Lichfield girl. The family name had been de la Garrique but the young man in question was now known as David Garrick.

Just how many pupils besides Garrick the Edial school ever had an opportunity to instruct is not known and neither is the date when the venture was abandoned as a failure, but the pupils were never more than a very few and the school must have been closed before March, 1737, or some twenty months after Johnson's marriage. Boswell speaks of its having lasted "a year and a half," which cannot be far wrong. Probably the lads of the Lichfield region were themselves disconcerted by the grimaces whose effect had been feared by the authorities at Solihull, and Garrick later professed to remember how (in Boswell's words) "The young rogues used to listen at the door of his bed-chamber, and peep through the key-hole, that they might turn into ridicule his tumultuous and awkward fondness for Mrs. Johnson, whom he used to name by the familiar appellation of *Tetty* or *Tetsey,* which, like *Betty* or *Betsey,* is provincially used as a contraction for *Elizabeth,* her christian name, but which to us seems ludicrous, when applied to a woman of her age and appearance." However brief the Edial experiment and however dismal its failure, it served to dispose for the time being of the idea that Johnson might support himself as a schoolmaster, and it led to a step as crucial in his career as it has been in that of so many other man—a move on the metropolis itself.[7]

Either in anticipation of failure or, more probably, in hope of escape, Johnson occupied his spare moments at Edial with the composition of an Oriental tragedy in blank verse, taking his subject from a history of the Turks borrowed for the purpose from Garrick's eldest brother, Peter. Johnson's genius was, of course, not dramatic and the play was not produced until many years later when Garrick did a kindness for his old friend. But it is perhaps worth remembering that in an age when bad historical tragedies often earned respectable returns there was nothing grotesque in the effort of a young schoolmaster to launch himself on the world in such a manner.*

One story has it that Garrick, applying his eye to a keyhole in what appears to have been according to the accepted Edial custom, saw Johnson at work on the manuscript and, since Garrick also was interested in the stage, promptly formed an alliance with him. Garrick was, to be sure, only eight years his master's junior, but if he had theatrical ambitions at that time they were certainly not yet confessed, and he could hardly have declared himself without admitting to the peeping which, even at Edial and even granting that he had in this instance applied himself to a study rather than a bedroom door, hardly seems

* Johnson's first draft has recently been published in the edition of Johnson's poetical works edited by Smith and McAdam (Oxford, 1941). Elsewhere but still more recently it has been ingeniously argued that one character in the play (Aspasia) is an idealized portrait of Tetty. (Bronson, Bertrand H., *Johnson and Boswell.* University of California Publications in English, Vol. 3, No. 9.)

probable. In any event, Walmesley is said to have been impressed by the incompleted play and to have prophesied for its author a career as a dramatist.

Shortly thereafter, on February 5, 1737, Walmesley wrote to an old friend at Rochester, a mathematician of some distinction, asking him to receive David Garrick as a pupil and to prepare this "sensible young fellow" for the study of the law. Johnson's tragedy was not yet completed, but apparently it was decided that the opportunity for the two to travel up to London together was not to be missed; therefore, on March 2nd they set out together to make the journey of one hundred and twenty miles, probably on horseback. It can seldom have happened that two young men, both destined to enduring fame, set out thus in each other's company to conquer the world, but the auspices were not particularly favorable. Johnson had, he once said, but twopence halfpenny in his pocket, and when Garrick objected to the alleged exaggeration, he replied: "I came with two-pence half-penny in *my* pocket, and thou, Davy, with three half-pence in thine."

Three days after the setting out, Johnson's only brother, Nathaniel, aged twenty-four, was buried in Lichfield, having possibly died from his own hand after some sort of difficulties, apparently not entirely honorable, which are vaguely referred to in a letter to his mother.

Since for Johnson the visit to London was to be merely exploratory, Tetty was left behind. According to one story, when he and Garrick arrived in the city and found themselves without money they applied to Wilcox, the bookseller, for a loan of five pounds and got it on no security except that afforded by their honest manner, thereby, perhaps, laying the foundations for Johnson's lifelong tenderness toward those in Wilcox's trade. According to another account, when the bookseller was informed that Johnson intended to live by authorship, he eyed his robust frame attentively "and with a significant look, said, 'You had better buy a porter's knot.' "[8]

Apparently Johnson soon parted from Garrick and the latter's financial difficulties were temporarily solved by a legacy. Johnson himself had no such luck, but when he came back to

Lichfield some months later he had evidently acquired sufficient confidence in himself to plan a permanent remove to London with his wife. She probably arrived there near the end of 1737, and though Johnson seems to have made, a little later, another effort to be appointed to a post in a country school, it is hard to imagine him leaving the metropolis once he had tasted its delights. He loved the city, he identified himself with it, and he learned to know it not only from one end to the other but also from the bottom up. It was for him at once the perfect setting and the perfect subject. It was his spiritual home because there only he felt himself "at home" and if he never after spoke without scornful irony of those who talked about the charms of a simple life in pastoral solitude it was in part because such talk seemed to him to imply some failure to appreciate properly the wonder of the metropolis. There is no record to indicate that he ever visited Lichfield again until after his mother's death. Neither is it recorded that he ever spoke of the great cathedral there with the slightest interest. But Fleet Street stirred him to eloquence and at Charing Cross he contemplated with a kind of awe "the full tide of human existence."

Johnson, of course, took pretty much for granted the squalor, the brutality and the suffering upon which was spread the thin film of Hanoverian elegance. This needs to be remembered, as does also the fact that the London to which he first came was a different and much less clean or orderly place than even the London in which he spent the last great years during which he made himself a legend. In 1737 Continental travelers who came provided with the certainly not high standards supplied by Paris were shocked at the dirt and disorder of London. The reform wave which was, during Johnson's own lifetime, to pave and light the streets, to substitute numbers for the picturesque menace of a thousand swinging signs, to provide elevated side footpaths for the pedestrians and what we call gutters beside them to drain the street from the center, was still years away. In 1737 Fleet ditch had just been arched over. In the streets the unfortunate foot traveler still picked his way through the muck of the highway, protected from the splattering carts of the street only by a row of stone posts, while householders emptied their garbage and slops from the windows above him and the open channel in the middle of the road ran sluggishly with every imaginable sort of filth, including the dead cats, etc., described with such relish by Swift.

The stench was terrific and neither the most elegant nor the most privileged could completely protect themselves from that or even from more tangible contacts. Only four years later Johnson himself was to write: "The most disgusting part of the character given by travellers, of the most savage nations, is their neglect of cleanliness, of which, perhaps, no part of the world affords more proofs than the streets of the British capital; a city famous for wealth, and commerce, and plenty, and for every other kind of civility and politeness, but which abounds with such heaps of filth, as a savage would look on with amazement. . . . That the present neglect of cleansing and paving the streets is such as ought not to be borne, that the passenger is everywhere either surprized and endangered by unexpected chasms, or offended or obstructed by mountains of filth, is well known to every one that has passed a single day in this great city; and that this grievance is without remedy is a sufficient proof that no magistrate has, at present, power to remove it." Yet twenty-one years were to pass before the city itself undertook to keep the streets clean instead of holding every man nominally responsible for the section in front of his own door.

To venture a mile beyond the outskirts of the city was to run imminent risk of meeting a highwayman; to be abroad after dark, even in the most populous centers and even in a chair or accompanied by a linkboy, was by no means to be immune from violence. To step from the conveyance which had brought a passenger from one little island of relative cleanliness and elegance to another was to run the risk of being at least splattered by the omnipresent filth. No one seems to have considered the possibility of making the city itself clean or orderly or safe. People aimed at no more than measures of individual self-protection and must have lived there almost as an explorer lives in a jungle, surrounded by savages and intent only on taking every possible precaution against too intimate contact with the barbarity and infection which reigned almost undisputed.[9]

All this Johnson saw but largely disregarded. Though his heart was as compassionate as his nose was insensitive, he also accepted as inevitable the more overwhelming morass of human suffering which he attempted to alleviate here and there by those individual acts of charity beyond which almost all Englishmen of the time seem to have assumed it impossible to go. Today we are often reminded that all great cities include their underworld, but it is difficult to remember how much the largest and most conspicuous part of the world of London was an underworld at its worst. The streets swarmed with beggars, thieves, prostitutes and outcasts of every description. Homeless children slept on ash heaps; whole areas were given over to destitution and disease utterly neglected. "Prison fever" and other maladies carried away hundreds of felons and poor debtors alike, while malefactors and unfortunates were so numerous that government could think of nothing to do except periodically to send certain batches to the colonies and other batches on processions to the gallows.

It is frequently recalled that pleasure seekers took tea on a Sunday afternoon while inspecting the madmen chained in Bedlam. Johnson himself made at least two visits there—and though it is not necessary to assume that he found the spectacle amusing, his companions did. "I had," says Boswell, his companion on the second occasion, "heard Foote give a very entertaining account of Johnson's happening to have his attention arrested by a man who was very furious, and who, while beating his straw, supposed it to be William, Duke of Cumberland, whom he was punishing for his cruelties in Scotland, in 1746." Boswell adds: "There was nothing peculiarly remarkable this day." But public cognizance had at least been taken of the inmates of the madhouse, while thousands of other unfortunates died unnoticed. Families engaged in domestic manufacture often lived and worked in one room. Thanks to the window tax, many persons lived in total darkness. In certain East End parishes infant mortality rose to one hundred per cent, and not many years after Johnson's first coming to the metropolis, Henry Fielding could write out of experience as a magistrate: "Gin . . . is the principal sustenance (if it may be so called) of more than a hundred thousand people in this metropolis. Many of these wretches there are, who swallow pints of this poison within twenty-four hours; the dreadful effects of which I have the misfortune every day to see, and to smell, too."

Nor could the authorities conceive of any method of dealing with the tide of crime other than the attempt to increase the rigor of the law until almost every felony except petty larceny was a capital offense. Johnson himself later devoted a number of *The Rambler* to protest against the insane harshness of the law and spoke with horror of the appointed days "when the prisons of this city are emptied into the grave"; but this is one of the relatively rather rare occasions when even he deals with what we should call a sociological rather than a moral subject. Much later (though this is an example of his contentiousness in argument rather than typical of his usually humane attitude) he could deplore the abolition of public hangings: "No, Sir, . . . it is *not* an improvement: they object that the old method drew together a number of spectators. Sir, executions are intended to draw spectators. If they do not draw spectators, they don't answer their purpose. The old method was most satisfactory to all parties; the public was gratified by a procession; the criminal was supported by it." And in so far as he was serious Johnson was here not so much relapsing, as he is sometimes accused of doing, into a special brutality of his own, but merely failing to rise above a kind of insensibility to certain accustomed things without which it was almost impossible to live at all in that age. Besides, he was always irritated by those who proposed, in the name of prudence or decorum, to deprive the poor of their few pleasures and he was obviously prepared to recognize public executions as one of them. The heads of traitors were still exposed at Temple Bar, ingenious entrepreneurs rented spyglasses at a halfpenny a look to passers-by who wanted a closer view, and Goldsmith could find a joke at Johnson's expense when they came to pass under the Bar.[10]

Nevertheless, and despite it all, London was to Johnson first and foremost not London's filth or suffering or degradation. For him London was above all the center of learning and poetry, the market to which any man might bring such wares as he had to sell. Cities were the characteristic product of man's effort to lift himself above the animal level, to create a world of thoughts and aims and institutions human rather than natural, and since London was the greatest of cities, it must be the greatest of man's achievements. It was, more successfully than any other human community, what all human communities aspired to be.

If something like this was the determining factor in Johnson's final judgment, it must nevertheless be remembered that few respectable men of the time were as intimately acquainted as he with the seamy side. Hereditary gentlemen had merely caught such glimpses as no one who stirred abroad could fail to catch; parvenu prigs like Richardson might have spent their lives picking their way carefully enough to avoid contact with all but a few of their fellows; but Johnson's knowledge of London became like Defoe's or like, in a later age, the knowledge of Sam Weller. It is probable that the journalistic connections which he soon established preserved him from himself falling, except on a few occasions, into the lowest depths of poverty. Nevertheless, he did on at least one occasion walk the streets all night with Richard Savage because neither of them had money to pay for the meanest lodging. There was certainly also another occasion when Tetty sold as their last piece of salable goods the little silver cup which his mother had bought when he was taken to be "touched" by Queen Anne; and twice, at least, he was in danger of the debtor's prison. For some years, in other words, he was never far from the abyss, and for a long time he was far closer to the world of wretches than he was to the world of fashion and security. Moreover, his sympathy for the unfortunate made him habitually look below him even when he was not far from the bottom himself, and he sought out the destitute to help them from his own small store.

In the days of his prosperity Johnson shared his lodgings with a small but motley group of men and women who had no other place to live; and from the beginning he had an extensive acquaintance among the unfortunate and the disreputable. What is more, he valued this acquaintance highly for he was as far from squeamishness as he was from any decadent or perverse enjoyment of the spectacle of misery, and he was also enough of a bohemian to value his knowledge of the underworld almost as

"JOHNSON'S WILLOW" NEAR LICHFIELD
From an old print (Courtesy Columbia University Library)

ST. JOHN'S GATE
Office of *The Gentleman's Magazine*
From an old print
(Courtesy Columbia University Library)

SHOP OF TOM DAVIES
where Johnson and Boswell
first met
From an old print (Courtesy
Columbia University Library)

much as his knowledge of the upper. To the end of his life he objected vehemently to that habit of referring to the members of the wealthy class as *the world,* and when Sir Joshua Reynolds happened to remark in his presence that "nobody" wore laced coats any more though "everybody" had once worn them, Johnson jeered in reply: "See now . . . how absurd that is; as if the bulk of mankind consisted of fine gentlemen that came to him to sit for their pictures. If every man who wears a laced coat (that he can pay for) was extirpated, who would miss them?" What Johnson had learned from the poor he never forgot. He was well past seventy when Boswell remarked that "the poor go about and gather bones, which I understand are manufactured," and Johnson answered out of a fund of information which he must have collected many years before: "Yes, Sir; they boil them, and extract a grease from them for greasing wheels and other purposes. Of the best pieces they make a mock ivory, which is used for hafts to knives, and various other things; the coarser pieces they burn and pound, and sell the ashes—for making a furnace for the chymists for melting iron." [11]

Eighteenth-century London had nothing that corresponds to a modern hotel—unless indeed one is willing to take account of the coaching inns where visitors rarely stayed more than a day or two. Even on his first exploratory visit Johnson had, accordingly, to take lodgings: first with a staymaker in Exeter Street; later, in Greenwich, where he might have quiet to proceed with the composition of his tragedy. When he returned from Lichfield with his wife, they lodged for a time in Woodstock Street near Hanover Square and afterward in Castle Street, now known as Castle Street East. *Irene,* the tragedy, was promptly rejected by Charles Fleetwood, the patentee of Drury Lane, but Johnson was soon engaged in work, humble but sufficiently remunerative to keep him alive.

A sound instinct had led him to Edward Cave, proprietor of *The Gentleman's Magazine,* one of the men who were making journalism a bearable (if just bearable) profession. In the preceding age it had become possible for a poet as extraordinary as Pope to earn large sums and possible for a miscellaneous writer as incredibly profuse as Defoe to earn a decent living; but miscellaneous writing was hardly yet a respectable trade and was, by common consent, the desperate refuge of wretches. *The Gentleman's Magazine* was the first magazine in the modern sense of the term to achieve any lasting success, the first to establish itself as a recognized institution in the literary world, and despite its low rate of pay, the first important literary enterprise to provide a regular outlet for the miscellaneous writer. Johnson, it will be remembered, had previously made an unsuccessful application to its editor by letter, and his persistent, finally successful effort to win a connection was probably at least partly the result of his sense that Cave's periodical stood for a future in which the writer would be, as Johnson himself wished to be, first of all a laborer worthy of his hire.

The famous letter to Chesterfield, still a good many years away, may not have been, as it has sometimes been picturesquely called, a death blow to the patron. But it did signalize Johnson's own confidence that authorship had by then been established as a profession dependent upon the public through the bookseller. There is no doubt of the fact that, Whiggish though the attitude may seem to us, Johnson did feel that a piece of writing is fundamentally an article of commerce and properly subject to the law of supply and demand. He was, moreover, consistent enough always to defend booksellers who, he believed, had freed the writer from the caprices of the patron and to assume that the public, being the purchaser of literary wares, was the final arbiter of their worth.

Cave himself was a tradesman in a new trade who had created an institution by virtue of shrewd and dogged persistence. He had been born in 1692, the son of a cobbler at Rugby, and he had managed to get an abbreviated education at Rugby school, which was already beginning to draw gentlemen's sons from afar but was required by its regulations to admit local boys. In his teens Cave had been apprenticed to a printer who sent him to establish a provincial newspaper and he had later been engaged in supplying news from London to other papers. Somehow he had conceived the idea (not in itself strictly original) of publishing a sort of digest of the innumerable newspapers and newsletters of the metropolis. He set up a print shop in St. John's Gate and then, in 1731, started *The Gentleman's Magazine,* which at first bore also the subtitle *Or Traders Monthly Intelligencer* and was supposed to be edited by one Sylvanus Urban, Gent.—a pseudonym apparently intended to suggest that the magazine would appeal equally to men of town and country.

There had been magazines before—notably *The Gentleman's Journal,* which began a short career as far back as 1692—and there were at the moment other digests of newspapers. But *The Gentleman's Journal* had been anemic and dilettante and *The Gentleman's Magazine,* perhaps because Cave understood and appealed to a much larger public including the newly important middle class, succeeded as no even remotely similar enterprise had succeeded. It gradually added essays, special articles, and reviews until it became the unmistakable prototype of the modern magazine; and though Cave himself died in 1754, it continued to be published under the same name until 1922. What is more important, it held in the eighteenth century a unique position as *the* magazine.[12]

Johnson's first proposal, made from Lichfield in 1734, had been that he should supply poems, inscriptions, etc., never published before, as well as short dissertations, critical remarks on authors ancient and modern, etc. This proposal was original, since the magazine at that time was almost exclusively political and newsy; it also suggested a direction which the magazine was presently to take. But though Cave is known to have answered the letter, nothing appears to have come of it except that Johnson, a few months after his first arrival in London and while he was still without his wife, again approached him by a letter dated July 12, 1737, in which he proposed to make a translation from the Italian of *The History of the Council of Trent,* a French translation of which with elaborate notes had recently been made. For the time being nothing came of this either, and Johnson apparently first made the contact some months later when he was shrewd enough to seize the opportunity afforded by some severe attacks on Cave by competitors and critics, to send him a complimentary poem, "Ad Urbanum," which was printed in the issue for March, 1738. It begins:

> Urbane, nullis fesse laboribus,
> Urbane, nullis victe calumniis,
> Cui ſrontc sertum in eruditâ
> Perpetuò viret et vircbit . . .

and was elegantly translated by an unknown correspondent in the May number thus:

> Hail, URBAN! indefatigable man,
> Unwearied yet by all thy useful toil!
> Whom num'rous slanderers assault in vain;
> Whom no base calumny can put to foil.
> But still the laurel on thy learned brow
> Flourishes fair, and shall forever grow.

This effusion seems to have seriously attracted Cave's attention at last. Johnson was soon employed, not only as a regular contributor but also in some supervisory capacity.

Of his employer Johnson always spoke with admiration and something like affection. He told Boswell that when he first saw St. John's Gate, where the magazine was published, he "beheld it with reverence" and Boswell, no doubt correctly, explains this apparently immoderate emotion by recalling how *he* himself felt toward the periodical which first bestowed upon him the blessings of publication. Possibly also Johnson knew that various regular contributors were accustomed to gather there and promised himself a share in the delights of literary society.

This group was not at the moment too dazzlingly distinguished, for among its chief luminaries were the poet Moses Browne and the busy scholar-hack, the Rev. Thomas Birch, of whom Boswell reports that Johnson is said to have said: "Tom Birch is as brisk as a bee in conversation; but no sooner does he take a pen in his hand, than it becomes a torpedo to him, and benumbs all his faculties." But it was also through Cave that Johnson met Mrs. Elizabeth Carter, whose friendship he valued through many years and concerning whom he wrote a Greek epigram, which he sent to Cave in the early days of their association, adding the remark that he thought Mrs. Carter "ought to be celebrated in as many different languages as Lewis le Grand." Some forty years later, Fanny Burney described her as "really a noble-looking woman" and declared: "I never saw age so graceful in the female sex yet; her whole face seems to beam with goodness, piety, and philanthropy." Johnson, who professed to believe that learning was not the first characteristic to be looked for in a woman, was willing to forgive her extraordinary knowledge of Greek because she could "make a pudding, as well as translate Epictetus." Probably he found it easier than we would to forgive her English poetry, of which the following three lines are a specimen taken from an *Ode to Melancholy,* called by her biographer her best work in verse:

> Here, cold to pleasure's airy forms,
> Consociate with my sister worms,
> And mingle with the dead.

As for "Poor dear Cave," as Johnson calls him, he was a born organizer and noted more for a devotion to his business amounting almost to obsession and for a slow shrewdness than for either polite learning or social polish. He "used to sell ten thousand of 'The Gentleman's Magazine'; yet such was then his minute attention and anxiety that the sale should not suffer the smallest decrease, that he would name a particular person who he heard had talked of leaving off the Magazine, and would say 'Let us have something good next month'." He was naïve enough to promise his new contributor, by way of reward, a glimpse of some hack writers in a tavern and not above increasing his business by advertising indecent books for sale at St. John's Gate. Moreover, it is hardly probable that he was any more generous at the beginning than he was in 1749, when it is said that one of his hacks, Samuel Boyse (his clothes being at the pawnbroker's), sat naked in bed writing verses with a pen stuck through a hole in his blanket. Indeed Johnson on his deathbed, speaking affectionately of Cave, had to admit that the publisher was "a penurious pay-master" who would "contract for lines by the hundred and expect the long hundred." "But he was a good man," Johnson added, "and always delighted to have his friends at his table." Probably the last-mentioned quality counted almost as much with Johnson as the fact that Cave was doing his part toward the establishment of journalism as a trade even though it was not yet quite a profession.[13]

Apparently Johnson never described to Boswell precisely the nature, the duration, or the shifting circumstances which surrounded the various functions he performed for Cave; but for a period of at least six or eight years, beginning soon after the appearance of his laudatory poem, he not only made frequent contributions including poems, brief "lives," and other miscellaneous items but also selected material for reprint, acted as judge of a prize contest, prepared copy for publication, and in general performed services which might not make it improper to think of him as editor, or at least an editor, of the magazine. Boswell itemizes the contributions in so far as he could ascertain them and certainly for some time Johnson owed his livelihood to his work for *The Gentleman's Magazine*. Boswell calls the latter "for many years . . . his principal resource for employment and support."

In a small way Cave was also a publisher of books, and after Johnson had begun work for the magazine he went ahead with the translation of *The History of the Council of Trent* which he had previously proposed. But though he received pay for his work, publication was abandoned when a rival translator (who also later fell by the wayside) appeared. When or how Johnson acquired his working knowledge of both French and Italian is not known. Sir John Hawkins had "some reason to think" that he frequented Slaughter's coffeehouse in the hope of learning to speak French but that he never succeeded in gaining great fluency.

By far the most often remembered of Johnson's contributions to the magazine are, of course, the parliamentary reports, thinly disguised as "Debates in the Senate of Magna Lilliputia," which he first edited and then himself composed. It had long been assumed that the proceedings of the House of Commons were privileged at least as long as Parliament was in session. Nevertheless, accounts were commonly published after recess had been taken and during the sessions surreptitious reports were circulated in the coffeehouses. Moreover, as early as 1728 Cave himself had got into some trouble when Robert Raikes, the proprietor of a provincial newspaper who had been summoned before the bar of the House to answer for his temerity in reporting parliamentary debates, testified that he had got his information from Cave. The latter was let off, however, after he had begged pardon on his knees; he had apparently learned a lesson, since next year, when Raikes was again summoned, the latter cited another person as the source of his news.

In 1732, nevertheless, the year after *The Gentleman's Magazine* was founded, Cave began to publish abbreviated reports of the debates; when a rival, *The London Magazine,* published an annual supplement with much fuller reports, Cave followed suit. Later he began to print what purported to be individual speeches in fuller form, and finally, on April 13, 1738, it was unanimously resolved in the lower House "That it is an high indignity to, and a notorious breach of the privilege of this House . . . to give any account of the Debates—as well during the Recess as the Sitting of Parliament."

The resolution dispelled any ambiguity, but it was a hard blow to the magazines, which had found their reports a popular feature. *The London Magazine* first invented a popular subterfuge by beginning to publish "Debates in the Political Club" in its issue for May, 1738, and *The Gentleman's Magazine* followed in June, 1738, with its "Debates in the Senate of Magna Lilliputia." They are introduced by an elaborate bit of foolery in which it is said that Gulliver's grandson, who has just returned from Lilliputia, reports that the latter country and its neighboring kingdoms constitute a perfect epitome of Europe and that he will report the debates which have taken place in the Lilliputian parliament. A brief sketch of the contemporary European and American situation is then given, with Spain represented as Iberia, America as Columbia, etc., while Walpole becomes Walelop, Halifax Haxilaf, etc. In succeeding numbers, individual speeches were reported and their makers indicated by easily identifiable anagrams. In passing, it may be remarked that immunity could be obtained through so transparent a device only because public opinion was unfavorable to parliamentary attempts to limit the freedom of the press and juries would not convict whenever they could be given the slightest pretext for refusing to do so. Such was, at least, the reason assigned a good many years later by Horace Walpole when he was commenting on the libelous freedom of newspapers in 1770.[14]

Johnson may have revised the debates from the very beginning, when they were compiled from information supplied by the Scottish "author by profession," William Guthrie, who attended sessions of the House and brought back what he could in his retentive memory and also, perhaps, from penciled notes made by Cave himself. Later, however, Johnson took more complete charge of the department and, out of sheer laziness no doubt, began composing the speeches entirely out of his own head. He told Boswell that "sometimes—he had nothing more communicated to him than the names of the several speakers, and the part which they had taken in the debate" though sometimes he had "scanty notes furnished by persons employed to attend in both houses of Parliament." To John Nichols he confessed that some of the speeches were "the mere coinage of his own imagination."

According to Boswell, Johnson said that he was the "sole composer" only during the years 1741-1743 inclusive, and the feature ceased to appear in the magazine after 1746; but it is not possible to say precisely to what extent Johnson is responsible for many of the others and the secret of his authorship was so well kept that it does not seem to have been generally known until after his death. For years after their original publication the speeches were commonly taken as genuine—notably by Smollett, who quoted them as such in his *History of England.* Yet for the most part they read like abstract dissertations, not like debates or even speeches, and they were written at top speed—faster, Johnson said, than anything else he ever wrote, and sometimes at the rate of three columns of the magazine per hour.

In 1792, and writing probably only from memory, Arthur Murphy told a story demonstrably inaccurate in certain details but probably authentic in the main and certainly too picturesque to be forgotten. Dining with Johnson and Murphy at the house of Samuel Foote, Dr. Philip Francis, the translator of Horace, happened to remark that a certain speech by Pitt was the best he had ever read and that, though he had spent eight years in the study of Demosthenes, he had met nothing in the latter's work equal to it. "That speech," announced Johnson, "I wrote in a garret in Exeter-street . . . I never had been in the gallery of the House of Commons but once. Cave—and the persons employed under him, gained admittance: they brought away the subject of discussion, the names of the speakers, the side they took, and the order in which they rose, together with notes of the arguments advanced in the course of the debate. The whole was afterwards communicated to me, and I composed the speeches in the form which they now have in the parliamentary debates." When one of the company praised Johnson for his impartiality and observed that he dealt out reason and eloquence with an equal hand to both parties, he made the celebrated explanation: "I saved appearances tolerably well; but I took care that the WHIG DOGS should not have the best of it."

Probably this last remark, which so perfectly exemplifies the sly humor with which Johnson exploited his prejudices, is more than any other single thing responsible for the fact that the "Debates" are so often remembered, but it is not actually more characteristic of him than the fact that he refused deliberately to deceive and told Boswell that he determined to write no more of the speeches when he found them taken for genuine. "He would not be accessory to the propagation of falsehood." To John Nichols he confessed that they were "the only part of his writings which then gave him any compunction."[15]

Just how well Johnson was paid for his multifarious activities is not known. The record of certain sums received from Cave has been preserved, but his total income can only be guessed at and different biographers have represented him as everything from destitute to comparatively well off during these early years in London. Even Boswell is hardly consistent, for having observed that from Cave Johnson "probably obtained a tolerable livelihood," he permits himself not many pages further along to draw a picture of the most desperate poverty. To him Johnson later talked gaily of the art of living on little as he had practiced it when he first came up to London, and he told of an Irish painter whom he had known in Birmingham and who had reassured him about the cost of living in London. "Thirty pounds a year," so the latter said, "was enough to enable a man to live there without being contemptible. He allowed ten pounds for clothes and linen. He said a man might live in a garret at eighteen-pence a week; few people would enquire where he lodged; and if they did, it was easy to say, 'Sir, I am to be found at such a place.' By spending three-pence in a coffee-house, he might be for some hours every day in very good company; he might dine for six-pence, breakfast on bread and milk for a penny, and do without supper. On *clean-shirt-day* he went abroad, and paid visits." Apparently Johnson made the painter his model, for he told Boswell: "I dined very well for eight-pence, with very good company, at the Pine Apple in New-street, just by. Several of them had travelled. They expected to meet every day; but did not know one another's names. It used to cost the rest a shilling, for they drank wine; but I had a cut of meat for six-pence, and bread for a penny, and gave the waiter a penny; so that I was quite well served, nay, better than the rest, for they gave the waiter nothing." [16]

The sums mentioned are not large but neither are they, when the purchasing power of money at the time is duly considered, fantastically small. Johnson "had a little money when he came to town"—perhaps from Walmesley, perhaps from his wife—and the shifts he was put to are merely those which have been practiced by thousands of young men from before Johnson's time down to the present moment. Even in the days of his relative prosperity he spent only a part of his income on himself, preferring to give the rest away to the needy, and living in the midst of a bohemian disorder that startled his friends.

The establishments which he provided for himself and his wife were no doubt much of the time highly satisfactory to him if not to her, for Tetty was something of a stickler for outward decency. We have it on the somewhat dubious authority of Sir John Hawkins that she refrained from attempting to keep her husband tidy and permitted him to go about in a state which made it unnecessary for him to proclaim, as he did, that for clean linen he had "no passion"; but when Mrs. Thrale asked him if he ever disputed with his wife: "Perpetually (said he):

my wife had a particular reverence for cleanliness, and desired the praise of neatness in her dress and furniture, as many ladies do till they become troublesome to their best friends, slaves to their own besoms, and only sigh for the hour of sweeping their husbands out of the house as dirt and useless lumber: a clean floor is *so* comfortable, she would say sometimes, by way of twitting; till at last I told her, that I thought we had had talk enough about the *floor,* we would now have a touch at the *ceiling.*"

It is comforting to know, on the other hand, that Tetty, though a distressingly good housekeeper, "read comedy better than any body he ever heard (he said); in tragedy she mouthed too much." And, seriously, it is not to be supposed that his domestic life was conspicuously stormy, partly no doubt because Johnson himself, for all his verbal cantankerousness, was too sociable as well as too fundamentally kindly to maintain bitterness toward any of his companions; and once when Mrs. Thrale mentioned a remark of Shenstone's to the effect that some little quarrel between lovers or relations was useful, "Why," he cried, "what a pernicious maxim is this now, *all* quarrels ought to be avoided studiously, particularly conjugal ones, as no one can possibly tell where they may end; besides that lasting dislike is often the consequence of occasional disgust, and that the cup of life is surely bitter enough, without squeezing in the hateful rind of resentment." [17]

Three bits of evidence are chiefly responsible for the contention that he suffered actual want during this period of his life. In the first place, there is the reference previously cited to the "small silver cup and spoon Sam. I" which "dear Tetty sold in our distress." This is certainly definite enough and must be taken to indicate that for some period, however short, he and Tetty were nearly destitute. But the incident may have occurred even before he was employed by Cave and the other two pieces of evidence prove less. In the second place, there is the story apparently told to more than one acquaintance about walking the streets with Richard Savage when neither of them could afford even the most miserable of lodgings. In the third place, there is a letter to Cave, published by Boswell and datable on internal evidence as not later than November, 1738, which concludes: "Yours, impransus, Sam. Johnson." This Boswell calls "a fair confession that he had not a dinner." But, in connection with the anecdote about Savage, Johnson says nothing of his wife and we can only assume either that he had provided a separate lodging for her or that this occurred during that brief interval when, according to Hawkins, the pair were separated by some incompatibility. As for the "impransus" letter, it contains nothing else to suggest that he considered himself ill-used and the subscripture may mean no more than simply: "in haste, since I have not yet had time to dine."

Two other small bits of evidence must, however, be added. Mentioning Johnson in his memoirs, Richard Cumberland, the dramatist, says he had "heard that illustrious scholar assert (and he never varied from the truth of fact) that he subsisted himself for a considerable space of time upon the scanty pittance of fourpence halfpenny per day." Furthermore, a letter written in Johnson's behalf by the future Lord Gower and belonging to August, 1739, speaks of Johnson's willingness to undertake a difficult journey to Dublin if necessary in order to get the M.A. which might make it possible for him to get a job as schoolmaster. He chooses, continues the letter, "rather to die upon the road, *than be starved to death in translating for booksellers;* which has been his only subsistence for some time past." But neither the epoch nor the duration of the "considerable space of time" referred to by Cumberland is specified and the phrase in Gower's letter suggests some degree of playful exaggeration. Johnson himself once told Boswell that he had never been hungry but once.

The fact that Boswell himself is ambiguous and makes no attempt either to balance the evidence or even to collect in one place what evidence he had suggests that he himself remained in doubt, and against the theory that Johnson passed years in something near to destitution must be placed not only Boswell's early statement about the "tolerable livelihood" but also the fact that Johnson was steadily doing a considerable amount of work for *The Gentleman's Magazine*. It is true that he called Cave "a penurious pay-master" but he also prided himself on demanding a fair sum for his writing and he would hardly have retained in his later days an affection for Cave's memory if he had felt that he had been outrageously treated. What is more, Boswell had in his possession an account which demonstrates that in connection with the ill-fated translation of *The History of the Council of Trent,* Cave paid Johnson various sums between August 2, 1738, and April 21, 1739, which total forty-nine pounds and seven shillings. When it is considered not only that these payments were for something quite aside from Johnson's work for the magazine, but also that Johnson himself had apparently accepted thirty pounds a year as sufficient for a man to live in London "without being contemptible," it becomes difficult to accept the picture of his chronically starving there. It is possible, of course, that he was then (as we know he was somewhat later) sending money to Lichfield for his mother and Lucy Porter and it is certain that as an almost unknown writer most of whose work was anonymous his income cannot have been very large. "Slow rises worth, by poverty depress'd." But if he went without dinner and without lodgings, the occasions on which he did so were probably extraordinary rather than usual.[18]

There is a vague story, for which Sir John Hawkins is responsible, that during the early years of their marriage Johnson and his wife for a time lived separately, possibly because, as Hawkins, always harsh in his judgments, suggests, Tetty could not endure Johnson's bohemian ways; possibly because Johnson could not provide adequate lodgings for both. It may, as has already been suggested, have been during this separation that he walked the streets with Richard Savage, and whether living at home or not, Johnson had certainly already begun to cultivate that large and miscellaneous collection of acquaintances and that all-inclusive knowledge of London which is one of the most astonishing things about him. It was apparently even before he had brought Tetty up from Lichfield that he made the acquaintance of "Harry Hervey," fourth son of the Earl of Bristol, whose house he frequented familiarly as he had frequented "good" houses in Lichfield and Birmingham. But it is not certain that he did not value more highly his obscure and even disreputable companions, some of whom he was already beginning to know.

"The most literary conversation that I ever enjoyed," he told Boswell, "was at the table of Jack Ellis, a money-scrivner behind the Royal Exchange, with whom I at one period used to dine generally once a week."

Johnson's knowledge and esteem of what we call low or coarse life was, says Mrs. Thrale, "prodigious" and to Fanny Burney he boasted: "I have known all the wits from Mrs. Montagu down to Bet Flint"—the latter lady being a woman of the town and on another occasion more fully described to Boswell thus: "I used to say of her that she was generally slut and drunkard;—occasionally, whore and thief. She had, however, genteel lodgings, a spinnet on which she played, and a boy that walked before her chair. Poor Bet was taken up on a charge of stealing a counterpane, and tried at the Old Bailey. Chief Justice ——, who loved a wench, summed up favorably, and she was acquitted. After which Bet said, with a gay and satisfied air, 'Now that the counterpane is *my own,* I shall make a petticoat of it'."

Johnson is most often referred to as a scholar and a moralist and he was, of course, both; but either term without further qualification is likely to suggest a temperament and a way of life very different from what was his. Of literature he said that he liked the biographical part best and that is one key to the nature of his literary interests, for even poetry and fiction, to say nothing of what he would have called the solider parts of learning, were fascinating to him chiefly not for the imagination or fancy to be found in them, not for the intoxication, the ecstasy or the escape into the ideal which in other times they have been supposed to afford, but largely because they conveyed to him some of that knowledge of men and manners which was his principal interest as well as principal solace, and which, moreover, he preferred when possible to get at first hand.

Writing was his trade but it was not his avocation. His famous contention that no one but a fool ever wrote for anything but money was not a casual paradox, for it is paralleled by other remarks such as, for instance, his reply when Hawkins congratulated him upon finding in the *Shakespeare* a congenial employment: "I look upon this as I did upon the Dictionary; it is all work, and my inducement to it is not love or desire of fame, but the want of money, which is the only motive to writing that I know of." What this means is not that he had a contempt for literature (which he certainly revered) or for fame (which he certainly did not scorn), but simply that he found in society a pleasure which only necessity could make him change for the labor of writing.[19]

Doubtless he was anxious enough, when establishing his connection with Cave, to get such employment in his trade as Cave would give him, but even then it was already a trade, and in the great days when he had retired because he thought that he had done enough for his contemporaries he could reply grandly to Arthur Murphy's twittings about his activity in supplying gratis a prologue to a theatrical performance for the benefit of Hugh Kelley's widow and an "Address" for Dr. Dodd, the convicted reverend-forger: "Why, Sir, when they come to me with a dead stay-maker [Kelley had served his apprenticeship in that trade] and a dying parson, what can a man do?" But he went on to say "that he hated to give away literary performances, or even to sell them too cheaply: the next generation shall not accuse me (added he) of beating down the price of literature: one hates, besides, ever to give that which one has been accustomed to sell; would not you, Sir (turning to Mr. Thrale,) rather give away money than porter?"—Mr. Thrale being, of course, the proprietor of a great brewery.

Bookish he was in the sense that he had read and understood many books but he was not bookish at all in the sense of preferring books to life. He reminded Boswell that when *The Rambler* was begun he had been "running about the world" more than most; he made it clear on other occasions that it was above all as a man of the world that he fancied himself most; and, as Fanny Burney remarked with surprise, he seemed always to prefer another "man of the world" to a scholar. It was a tavern chair, not an academic chair, which he called "the throne of human felicity"; not a library, but again a tavern of which he said that there was nothing else "contrived by man, by which so much happiness is produced."

Just as Johnson the scholar was saved by his sociability from pedantry, so too Johnson the moralist was saved by the same thing from any suggestion of priggishness. Samuel Richardson, whose work and whose principles Johnson later professed so much to admire, boasted that, so far as he knew, he had never been in the company of an immoral woman. Johnson, of course, freely admitted that he had not only been in the company of many but that he had found that company sometimes enjoyable, and nothing suggests more clearly the profound difference between the two men who had so much in common so far as the abstract principles they professed are concerned. The one was pharisaical and tender-minded, the other robust and sympathetic. In theory Johnson never relaxed the severity of his moral demands and he held himself strictly to their observance. But he forgave or, rather, overlooked the self-indulgence and sensuality of others, making usually the fantastic excuse that their "principles" were sound however reprehensible their conduct might be, and shutting his eyes to what it would have been too painful to contemplate in his friends. It was not merely the Bet Flints whom he loved—an astonishing number of his chosen intimates were men of conspicuously loose lives. He took up, then made himself the defender of, the outrageous Richard Savage; of Hervey, who was one of the first of his London acquaintances, he said: "Harry Hervey . . . was a vicious man, but very kind to me. If you call a dog HERVEY, I shall love him." And though he may never have suspected the extent of Boswell's insane wallowings, he was well aware that Topham Beauclerk, later one of his most valued acquaintances, was a rake.

These seem odd companions for a man of Johnson's mental character and grotesque physical disabilities. But it must be remembered that all companions were odd ones for a man whom nature had made something of a monster. In one sense he was at home with all sorts of people, from the Bet Flints through the Topham Beauclerks to the Joshua Reynoldses and even to the dons of Oxford. But in another sense he was not at home with anybody; he was something of an outsider in any society. He associated with "gay dogs," as he liked to call them, but he was not a gay dog; he moved during his later life among the famous and the fashionable, but whether tolerated or sought out he was in some sense an outsider here also. Even when he dominated a company, as he almost invariably did, he was not really one of it. He entered various orbits, but he did not and could not revolve through the whole course of any one of them.[20]

This he knew well enough, as he also knew it was not primarily his genius but his deficiencies that cut him off—his physical grotesqueness no less than his melancholy and his obsessions. He might go for a "frisk" with Beauclerk and the rest, but he knew well enough that the occasion was a special one for them as well as for him, that he could never participate fully in their life or in the lives of any other class of people. He was almost desperately sociable because he could never be part of any society. At every feast of wit or food he was a spectator and no matter how eagerly he tried to identify himself with the city and its multifarious life, of that too he was compelled to remain a spectator.

In one of the *Ramblers* he was to draw a ludicrous picture of a complacent lady vegetating in the country. She had been married at eighteen and as a bride she had spent one winter in London "where, having no idea of any conversation beyond the formalities of a visit, she found nothing to engage her passions; and when she had been one night at court, and two at an opera, and seen the monument, the tombs, and the tower, she concluded that London had nothing more to show, and wondered that when women had once seen the world, they could not be content to stay at home." But for him London was not a collection of sights. It was, first of all, simply the place where the largest number and greatest variety of men were to be found and hence the place where one was least likely to feel alone. "Sir," he said to Boswell, "if you wish to have a just notion of the magnitude of this city, you must not be satisfied with seeing its great streets and squares, but must survey the innumerable little lanes and courts. It is not in the showy evolution of buildings, but in the multiplicity of human habitations which are crowded together, that the wonderful immensity of London consists"; and again: "When a man is tired of London, he is tired of life; for there is in London all that life can afford." Yet to Johnson himself it afforded inns and lodgings, but no home; companions and admirers, but no fellows—no one to whom he was not a strange apparition rather than a man.

Just how early in youth he had realized that he was not and never could be like other men it is impossible to say, but it seems reasonable to guess from the completeness of his adjustment that he had resigned himself to the situation before he knew what he was doing. Nothing in his behavior is more striking than his tact. That may seem a strange word to apply to a man whose conversation was notoriously blunt, even at times hectoring and rude. But plain speaking was within his accepted character, the consequence of a license which he had demanded and got. He never failed, on the other hand, to remember what his character was. If he frisked, it was with a full realization that he was making a spectacle of himself, and he assumed that people would accept it as such. He never presumed (at least until the last sad days when he was on the point of death and may possibly have supposed that Mrs. Thrale might think of him as a normal human being) to that full intimacy which human beings of the same age and condition give to one another. He never, like Aesop's ass, climbed on to anyone's knees under the delusion that he was a lap dog. In argument he deferred to no one, but until his quasi-adoption by the Thrales he met others only for talk at appointed places: in the tavern, where every man was free to come and go; in the drawing room, to which one is invited with the understanding that one will go away again at the end of an appointed period, fully realizing that the degree of intimacy implied by an invitation is strictly limited by the more or less formal traditions of the drawing room itself. Many of the ten thousand commandments of politeness he broke; but there were ten thousand others which his physical and mental infirmities made applicable only to him, and these he kept.[21]

CHAPTER III

Running About the World

On November 3, 1746, Gilbert Walmesley, Johnson's old Lichfield patron, wrote a letter to Garrick, who was by that time well-established as the greatest actor of his age. In the course of it, he said: "When you see Mr. Johnson pray [give] my compliments, and tell him I esteem him as a great genius—quite lost both to himself and the world." [1]

Just how seriously this was meant as a reproach it is difficult to say but, at least by comparison with Garrick, Johnson had got nowhere. Of the two, Walmesley had probably expected more from Johnson, but the tragedy, *Irene,* which had so impressed him, was still unproduced, and though more than nine years had passed since Johnson first set out for London, he had by no means made himself famous. Most of what he had published in the *Magazine* was not only anonymous but ephemeral, and though he had also made three other and more ambitious attempts to display his powers—namely, by the publication of his poem *London,* in 1738; of his *An Account of the Life of Mr. Richard Savage,* in 1744; and his pamphlet *Miscellaneous Observations on the Tragedy of* Macbeth, in 1745—none of these had originally borne his name on the title page. The first had attracted a good deal of attention but had not been followed up. Probably Johnson was becoming well known to the booksellers and publishers, but his old patron in Lichfield was certainly justified in feeling that he had made no great stir in the world.

Samuel Johnson

London, a Poem, in Imitation of the Third Satire of Juvenal had been written not long after Johnson's first acquaintance with Cave and probably composed in the first flush of hope generated by the actual commencement of a literary career. With most un-Johnsonian modesty and dissimulation, it was submitted to Cave in a humble letter as the work of one of Johnson's needy acquaintances. At Johnson's suggestion, Cave apparently enlisted the interest of the much better-known publisher, Robert Dodsley, and the poem appeared with the latter's imprint in May, 1738—on the same day, according to Boswell, as Pope's satire *One Thousand Seven Hundred and Thirty Eight.* Apparently there was, about the success which it achieved, a kind of brilliance not to be enjoyed again by Johnson for a long time to come, if, indeed, it was ever quite equaled—since his subsequent successes were solid rather than spectacular. It had a second edition within the week, readers were convinced that a new poet, "greater even than Pope," had made his appearance; and Pope himself is said to have predicted that the unknown author would soon be "déterré." Boswell reports that Johnson got ten guineas for the copyright, which is not too contemptible a sum for a poem of only 263 lines long and by an unknown. He is also said to have refused to accept any less for the very characteristic reason that Paul Whitehead, the rakehell poet, had recently sold some verses for that amount.[2]

To Boswell, *London* is one of Johnson's major claims to literary fame and by title at least it is still one of his best-known works. A modern reader can, moreover, hardly fail to perceive that in it remarkable powers are exhibited. Yet it is probably not often reread except by students, and the reason is not simply that neoclassical poetry never completely regained the popularity it lost during the romantic revival. There are in *London* defects, or at least peculiar qualities, which render it to most modern readers less attractive than the best of Dryden or Pope. What these qualities are becomes plain enough if certain aspects of the poem be closely examined.

The genre to which it belongs—the adaptation and modernization of a classical satire—was, of course, then a familiar one to which Pope had given great currency. In his *Life of Pope,* Johnson describes it as "a kind of middle composition between translation and original design, which pleases when the thoughts are unexpectedly applicable and the parallels lucky" and "it seems," he adds, "to have been Pope's favorite amusement." One can only reply that it is not ours. To spend ingenuity in achieving and to experience delight in recognizing often strained parallels between what Juvenal could say of Rome and what Pope or Johnson can say of London is to be guilty of a kind of puerility possible to intelligent men only in an age when reverence for the classics had been carried to a point where it went beyond legitimate admiration for the virtues of the ancients and included an exaggerated interest in the ancient for its own sake. To recognize the importance of what is permanently true of human nature or human institutions is one thing, but it is another to marvel that, if there were too many Greeks in Rome to suit Juvenal's taste, Johnson can, without too much stretching a point, maintain that in London there are too many Frenchmen to suit his—or that, as Fluellen puts it in establishing the remarkable parallel between Alexander and Henry: "There is a river in Macedon, and there is also moreover a river at Monmouth; . . . and there is salmons in both." [3]

We must then, and without too much regret, recognize that we will be usually unaffected by what Johnson himself seems to assume the chief source of pleasure in this species of composition, namely, delight in noting "when the thoughts are unexpectedly applicable and the parallels lucky." To us the poem would probably be more impressive if it were *not* an imitation, if the observations had been made at first hand instead of being merely recognized as still usable. To us such a passage as

> But thou, should tempting villany present
> All Marlb'rough hoarded, or all Villiers spent,
> Turn from the glitt'ring bribe thy scornful eye,
> Nor sell for gold, what gold could never buy,
> The peaceful slumber, self-approving day,
> Unsullied fame, and conscience ever gay . . .

is at least none the better because Juvenal had said something of the same sort. And that much is true whether we happen to be or not to be among those who can find a certain relish in such a characteristically eighteenth-century antithesis as "sell for gold, what gold could never buy" or such an equally characteristic (and valid) distinction as that made so economically in contrasting "all Marlb'rough hoarded" with "all Villiers spent." That Marlborough's avariciousness was a commonplace and that Pope, in a brilliant passage, had previously made Villiers's squanderings equally well known would hardly, in the estimation of Boswell and his contemporaries, have detracted from the excellence of Johnson's lines. But to perceive how far Johnson was from being "an unknown poet, greater even than Pope," it is necessary only to compare any passage in *London* with, for example, the paragraph just referred to on Villiers, which is, of course, one of the purple patches in Pope's *Moral Essays.*

Mr. T. S. Eliot has recently written an introduction to a new edition of *London* and has stated in the strongest possible terms his contention that Johnson's best poetry has every right to the admiration of all those who value Augustan verse. But, as has already been suggested, *London* actually fails to achieve certain of the excellences which its close imitation of many of the formal aspects of such poetry might suggest, and may leave rather cold even those who have a deep love for Dryden and Pope.

Such persons would not expect to find in *London* any of the qualities of the lyric poet who infuses everything with a personal emotion. They take for granted, as readily as they take for granted the formal diction, the fact that Johnson assumed it to be the business of the poet to deal with the most general as well as fundamental aspect of human life and that at so late a date no fundamental aspect of human nature was like to remain unnoticed. Johnson's melancholy nature supplied him with sick fancies which, it is not unreasonable to suppose, might have appeared, in print, as novel as those of Rousseau or even Baudelaire. But like most of his contemporaries, it would never have occurred to him to regard them as suitable subjects for poetry. Of some he relieved himself through the prayers and meditations which it became his habit to write, but he would no more have published verses about them than he would have exhibited his physical peculiarities on a platform at Smithfield Fair.

However, even if we assume of *London,* as we assume of much of the poetry of Pope or Dryden, that the proper *subject* for such a poem is some objectively verifiable imitation of men and manners rather than some unusual personal emotion, we may still find some coldness, some effect of merely rhetorical ingenuity, which is decidedly not characteristic of all neoclassical poetry. Such deficiencies are, of course, more often characteristic of poetry as late as *London* than they are of the earlier Augustan epoch, and doubtless this is, in part at least, simply a result of the fact that the themes, the poetic devices, and the diction had hardened into a convention.

But that *London* is more of an exercise than a poem is further demonstrated by the fact that its opinions and attitudes are usually not really Johnson's. They are, on the contrary, those supplied in part by Juvenal and in part by the satiric clichés current in Johnson's own time. Thus it has often been observed that, despite the line

> Here falling houses thunder on your head

eighteenth-century buildings were not in the habit of collapsing. It has been less often remarked that the other half of the couplet

> And here a female atheist talks you dead

is one of the relatively few lines in the poem in which Johnson adds a touch revealing something of himself. Many of the sentiments are, on the other hand, quite contrary to his. He did not really believe that luxury was destroying the nation, for he often ridiculed those who thought that it was; he did not really believe that Britons were languishing in slavery; and, despite the conventional denunciation of Walpole, he, later, according to Boswell, "honestly acknowledged" Walpole's merit and called him a "fixt star" to be contrasted with "the meteor" (Pitt). Still more striking and significant is the conventional contrast between the country and the city, which is little short of fantastic coming as it does from a man who was as completely and contentedly urban as any who ever lived.

> Though grief and fondness in my breast rebel,
> When injur'd Thales bids the town farewell,
> Yet still my calmer thoughts his choice commend,
> I praise the hermit, but regret the friend;
> Resolv'd at length, from vice and London far,
> To breathe, in distant fields, a purer air.

On no other occasion did Johnson ever permit himself to "praise the hermit," and the self-delusion of those who thought that flowery meads and pastoral amusements would compensate them for the loss of what London had to offer was one of the favorite subjects of his ridicule. Indeed, it is hardly too much to say that most of the themes of the poem, from the sad fate of those condemned to suffer under a corrupt and tyrannical government to the felicities of rural retirement, come under the head of the cant which he so impatiently urged Boswell to "clear his mind of."[4]

It is hardly worth while to argue that Johnson may have later changed his opinions, for the present contention is not that *London* is consciously insincere, but simply that there is little of Johnson's real temper revealed in it and that, accordingly, it seldom rises above the level of a skillfully executed exercise and has little or none of the flavor characteristic, not only of Johnson's later talk, but also of his maturer writing. The point is worth laboring both because of its relevance to the history of his development as a man of letters and even more for the light it throws on the decline of neoclassical poetry. To search for the enduring truths and the best words in which to phrase them, to trust and to respect one's own convictions the more when one discovers that they are consonant with those of the wise ancients and the general consensus, is one thing; to repeat what has been said only because it has been said, even merely to choose for emphasis and development those themes which are usual rather than those which seem to oneself the most important or the most in need of such emphasis and development, is quite another. And when the cultivation of neoclassical poetry had come to mean what it has come to mean in *London,* then neoclassical poetry had entered into a decadent stage, which has quite unjustly influenced our judgment of the creators and great masters of the style.

Despite its very favorable reception, Johnson could not hope to receive a large sum for such a poem and neither could he hope to write such poems often. It was, as a matter of fact, ten years before a companion piece first appeared; but since the two are always quite properly considered together, something should be said of it here.

From Johnson's own time to the present the tendency has been pretty consistently to regard *The Vanity of Human Wishes* as superior to its predecessor and, indeed, it has generally been highly praised by all critics not committed to an exclusive admiration for romantic poetry. Byron called it "a grand poem—and so *true!*"; Walter Scott, in an essay on Johnson, said that it had "often extracted tears from those whose eyes wander dry over pages professedly sentimental"; and T. S. Eliot, in the Introduction previously referred to, makes a proper appreciation of a famous passage almost a test of the reader's ability to recognize genuine poetry.

One superiority over *London* it certainly has: it is no mere rhetorical exercise. In itself the theme proclaimed by Ecclesiastes is no less familiar than that elaborated by Juvenal, but Johnson, who can only in a moment of aberration have convinced himself that he hated London, believed in the deepest recesses of his being that "All is vanity." Hence the one poem is fundamentally sincere, the other fundamentally artificial. But when this has been said and when, in addition, the weighty opinions of others have been cited, one may venture the opinion that *The Vanity of Human Wishes* does, nevertheless, remain a poem in which the author fails to achieve either of the two effects which Johnson himself declares are inevitably produced by the "most engaging powers of an author." Here are certainly no new things to be made familiar; and, to one reader at least, the "familiar things are not made new."

The passage which was later revised to read:

> There mark what ills the scholar's life assail,
> Toil, envy, want, the patron and the gaol.

See nations, slowly wise and meanly just,
To buried merit raise the tardy bust.
If dreams yet flatter, once again attend,
Hear Lydiat's life, and Galileo's end . . .

is remembered because it has genuine vigor as well as because of the biographical reference. There are perhaps a dozen other lines equally vigorous—including those which compose the passage on senility from which the following couplets are taken:

The still returning tale, the ling'ring jest,
Perplex the fawning niece and pamper'd guest,
While growing hopes scarce awe the gath'ring sneer,
And scarce a legacy can bribe to hear;

. . . .

From Marlb'rough's eyes the streams of dotage flow,
And Swift expires a driv'ller and a show.

Even more numerous are the lines which it would not be too easy to distinguish from forgotten hundreds of eighteenth century pentameters.

But, as has already been noted, *The Vanity of Human Wishes* belongs to a period considerably later than that with which we are at present concerned. Perhaps because Johnson realized that *London* did not open up any vein which could be exploited in such a way as to make him a living, the next even moderately considerable of his efforts outside the magazine were two anonymous pamphlets: *Marmor Norfolciense,* a satire on the House of Hanover published in April, 1739, and *A Complete Vindication of the Licenser of the Stage, from the Malicious and Scandalous Aspersions of Mr. Brooke, Author of Gustavus Vasa,* an ironical piece published in May of the same year. Since Johnson himself was probably not greatly concerned over the question of the rightness or wrongness of the lord chamberlain in the exercise of his new duties as licenser of the stage and since, as he was later to confess, he really cared little whether the House of Hanover or the House of Stuart ruled England, both pamphlets were probably pure hack work.

There is, moreover, no evidence that either achieved any considerable success, and quite possibly it was about this time that

Johnson reached the lowest level of his discouragement as well as his worst financial straits. Certainly it was just at this time that he made what appears to have been his last effort to escape from hack work into schoolmastering. The letter from Gower (previously quoted) indicates that Johnson was candidate for a position at some school which has been, with considerable probability, identified as that at Appleby and that he needed an M.A., which Gower was trying to persuade "a friend of Dean Swift" to ask the Dean to ask Dublin for.

The degree was not granted and Johnson did not get the job, but he was evidently ready to try anything rather than the trade in which he was engaged, for it was, according to Boswell, "about this time" that he, through an intermediary, inquired of "Dr. Smalbroke of the [Doctors'] Commons, whether a person might be permitted to practice as an advocate there, without a doctor's degree in Civil Law." Quite characteristically he added that he was "a total stranger to these studies" but that "whatever is a profession, and maintains numbers, must be within the reach of common abilities, and some degree of industry"—thus exhibiting the courage and self-confidence which were so conspicuously his and also a certain equally characteristic tendency to pooh-pooh the supposed mysteries of occupations other than his own. The man who proposed to practice law without knowing anything about it, at least to begin with, is the same man who, more than forty years later, could write grandly to Mrs. Thrale, who had just inherited her husband's brewery: "Do not be frighted; trade could not be managed by those who manage it, if it had much difficulty." [5]

No doubt this willingness to assume that he could do what anyone else could was, in part, the consequence of one of his pet opinions: that talent was general, not specific, and that a man of ability could excel in whatever activity he chose to devote himself to. In part it was also a certain impatience when the abilities of others were too eagerly admired. In one of Shadwell's plays there is a gentleman who responds so automatically to the mention of any science or skill with a claim to great proficiency along the same lines that once, when pimping is referred to, he finds, before catching himself, that he has professed to be a great adept in that art also; and in view of the fact that Johnson exhibited a somewhat similar tendency, it is perhaps just as well that we have no record of any conversation in which the disreputable professions were discussed in his presence. Colley Cibber was merely "a fellow who claps a hump on his back, and a lump on his leg, and cries *'I am Richard the Third.'*" *Ossian* was merely such stuff as a man might write forever "if he would *abandon* his mind to it"; as for the composition of fables, there was nothing to it once the idea of making animals talk had been conceived.

"I might," he declared on another occasion, "as well have played on the violoncello . . . but I should have done nothing else. . . . A man would never undertake great things, could he be amused with small," and though he thought it "very strange, and very melancholy, that the paucity of human pleasures should persuade us ever to call hunting one of them," Mrs. Thrale believed that "no praise ever went so close to his heart" as that called out by a gentleman on an occasion when Johnson, yielding to one of the impulses toward violent physical activity which now and then seized him, had gone out with the Thrales upon Brighthelmstone (Brighton) Downs: "Why Johnson rides as well, for aught I see, as the most illiterate fellow in England." He was, in other words, not merely proud to demonstrate an unexpected accomplishment but also glad to prove that learning did not disqualify a man for anything.

"The true genius," he once wrote in serious development of his theme, "is a mind of large general powers, accidentally determined to some particular direction" and he could support this dubious contention with analogy less than dubious, as he did when he explained that "the man who has vigor may walk to the east just as well as to the west, if he happens to turn his head that way." Indeed, few things were more likely to bring out in full force his tendency to argue jeeringly for victory alone than his enthusiasm for this theory that talent is general, and his impatience at hearing special skills praised, and it is worth remembering that two of the very few occasions when he was completely silenced arose in connection with just this subject. One was that upon which Goldsmith retorted, to Johnson's contempt for those who thought it hard to make the animals in a fable talk: "This is not so easy as you seem to think; for if you were to make little fishes talk, they would talk like WHALES." The other was when, at Reynolds's house, the conversation happened to turn upon music and Johnson roundly proclaimed "that no man of talent, or whose mind was capable of better things, ever would devote his time and attention to so idle and frivolous a pursuit." Reynolds's niece whispered to her next neighbor: "I wonder what Johnson thinks of King David." Johnson, who overheard the remark but would not have yielded so easily to anyone except a young lady, had the grace to respond: "Madam, I thank you; I stand rebuked before you, and promise that, on one subject at least, you shall never hear me talk nonsense again." [6] How often others might hear him he did not say.

Apropos of Johnson's new failure to get himself appointed schoolmaster, Boswell finds it impossible to resist the inevitable comment: "It was, perhaps, no small disappointment to Johnson that this respectable application had not the desired effect; yet how much reason has there been, both for himself and his country, to rejoice that it did not succeed, as he might probably have wasted in obscurity those hours in which he afterwards produced his incomparable works." For reasons different as well as for reasons similar we may rejoice that he was also not encouraged to become an advocate. He might have won a good many cases but there is some reason to believe that a larger number than the law of averages requires would have been something less than triumphs for justice. Johnson is nearly always at his worst when extended and formal argument gives him an opportunity to display his ability to outrage common sense with an elaborate show of logic. Most Englishmen read *Taxation No Tyranny* with as little pleasure as do most Americans, and the arguments he prepared on more than one occasion for Boswell to use in behalf of the latter's clients do not make us regret that Johnson had no more numerous opportunities to act as advocate —though it must be admitted that Boswell had a knack for getting on the wrong side of cases, as he did, for instance, in that of the schoolmaster who beat his pupils. Johnson certainly did not, like Swift, hate mankind while loving John, Tom and Henry. But it is noticeable that he was nearly always humane in dealing with individuals whom he knew though often brutal in insisting upon harsh general principles.

After this failure to become either a schoolmaster or an advocate, Johnson seems never again to have sought escape from the career as writer for which nature had so obviously destined him, but there is evidence that these last efforts either caused, or were accompanied by, a considerable if temporary upheaval in his way of life. For one thing, he published nothing, so far as we know, in either *The Gentleman's Magazine* or elsewhere between May, 1739, and June, 1740. Apparently during this period he separated for a short time from his wife and in January, 1740, speaks of "the Rambles upon which I have been forced." Hawkins, though he alone, attributes this separation not to Johnson's efforts to establish himself in a new career, but to domestic discord arising out of Tetty's irritation with her husband's openhandedness. "She disliked the profusion, with which he constantly gave away all the money about him; and he found with astonishment and concern, that whatever he provided or laid up for family exigence, was always gone before he expected." This is certainly an accurate description of Johnson's habits, whether or not it is also an accurate description of Tetty's reaction to them; but the quarrel, if quarrel there was, cannot have lasted long since we now have a letter from Johnson to Tetty, unknown to Boswell and dated "January 31, 1739-40," which is couched in the most affectionate, though possibly also conciliatory, terms.

Dearest Tetty,

After hearing that you are in so much danger, as I apprehend from a hurt on a tendon, I shall be very uneasy till I know that you are recovered, and beg that you will omit nothing that can contribute to it, nor deny yourself anything that may make confinement less melancholy. You have already suffered more than I can bear to reflect upon, and I hope more than either of us shall suffer again. One part at least I have often flattered myself we shall avoid for the future, our troubles will surely never separate us more. If M does not easily succeed in his endeavours, let him not [tear] to call in another Surgeon to consult with him, Y [tear] have two or three visits from Ranby or Shipton, who is [tear] to be the best, for a guinea, which you need not fear to part with on so pressing an occasion, for I can send you twenty pounds more on Monday, which I have received this night; I beg therefore that you will more regard my happiness, than to expose yourself to any hazards. I still promise myself many happy years from your tenderness and affection, which I sometimes hope our misfortuncs have not yet deprived me of. David wrote to me this day on the affair of Irene, who is at last become a kind of Favourite among the Players, Mr. Fletewood promises to give a promise in writing that it shall be the first next season, if it cannot be introduced now, and Chetwood the Prompter is desirous of bargaining for the copy, and offers fifty Guineas for the right of printing after it shall be played. I hope it will at length reward me for my perplexities.

Of the time which I have spent from thee, and of my dear Lucy and other affairs, my heart will be at ease on Monday to give Thee a particular account, especially if a Letter should inform me that thy leg is better, for I hope you do not think so unkindly of me as to imagine that I can be at rest while I believe my dear Tetty in pain.

Be assured, my dear Girl, that I have seen nobody in these rambles upon which I have been forced, that has not contribute [*sic*] to confirm my esteem and affection for thee, though that esteem and affection only contributed to encrease my unhappiness when I reflected that the most amiable woman in the world was exposed by my means to miseries which I could not relieve.

I am

My charming Love

Yours

SAM. JOHNSON.

Jan. 31st, 1739-40.

Lucy always sends her Duty and my Mother her Service.

To Mrs. Johnson at Mrs. Crow's in Castle
Street near Cavendish Square, London.

Among other things, this letter certainly seems to indicate that Johnson's affection for his wife was not merely something he imagined after her death, and is almost sufficient by itself to dispose of Hawkins's characteristically cynical confession that he has "often been inclined to think, that if this fondness of Johnson for his wife was not dissembled, it was a lesson that he had learned by rote, and that, when he practiced it, he knew not where to stop till he became ridiculous." The twenty pounds which Johnson offers to send Tetty has been explained by the fact that on the very day on which the letter was written he had succeeded in mortgaging the Lichfield house and had received exactly twenty pounds as his share.[7]

Before the beginning of the summer of 1740, Johnson was probably back in London, for in the issue of *The Gentleman's Magazine* for June of that year he resumed his contributions with the first part of a life of Admiral Blake and was soon to become "sole composer" of the "Debates." No further publication of his outside the magazine is known until 1743, when his brief *Proposals for Printing Bibliotheca Harleiana* was published in the catalogue of the great collection which the bookseller, Thomas Osborne, had bought for thirteen thousand pounds with the intention of reselling it. The next year Johnson published an *Introduction* to the Harleian Miscellany, later reprinted as *An Essay on the Origin and Importance of Small Tracts and Fugitive Pieces*. Both compositions were, of course, merely commissions from a bookseller and neither is long, but they reveal Johnson's powerful mind at work and demonstrate his strong historical sense as well as his power of stating with great perspicuity large general principles. He had, literally, the instincts of a scholar though he was never able to summon the scholar's industry. The *Essay* also demonstrates how fully the main features of his most solemn and magisterial style had been formed. A brief quotation will illustrate that fact as well as indicate his restrained and not always consistently maintained enthusiasm for the liberty of the press, which indeed was the result of a somewhat wavering compromise between his abstract Tory principles and his temperamental impatience with most actual attempts to interfere with reasonable liberty for the individual: [8]

"The multiplicity of religious sects tolerated among us, of which every one has found opponents and vindicators, is another source of unexhaustible publication, almost peculiar to ourselves; for controversies cannot be long continued, nor frequently revived, where an inquisitor has a right to shut up the

SAMUEL JOHNSON

From an engraving of an unfinished sketch by James Barry, date unknown

disputants in dungeons; or where silence can be imposed on either party, by the refusal of a license.

"Not, that it should be inferred from hence, that political or religious controversies are the only products of the liberty of the British press; the mind once let loose to inquiry, and suffered to operate without restraint, necessarily deviates into peculiar opinions, and wanders in new tracks, where she is, indeed, sometimes lost in a labyrinth, from which though she cannot return, and scarce knows how to proceed; yet, sometimes, makes useful discoveries, or finds out nearer paths to knowledge."

Years later he could express a very characteristic doubt that the liberty of the press was really important to general happiness. "Now, Sir, there is the liberty of the press, which you know is a constant topick. Suppose you and I and two hundred more were restrained from printing our thoughts: what then? What proportion would that restraint upon us bear to the private happiness of the nation?" But he was himself well aware "of that partiality which almost every man indulges with regard to himself." "The liberty of the press is a blessing when we are inclined to write against others, and a calamity when we find ourselves overborne by the multitude of our assailants; as the power of the crown is always thought too great by those who suffer by its influence, and too little by those in whose favour it is exerted; and a standing army is generally accounted necessary by those who command, and dangerous and oppressive by those who support it." [9]

In the same year (1744) Johnson made a second attempt to establish himself as something more than a mere journalist when he published, anonymously, as in the case of *London,* his *Life of Richard Savage,* the biography of a minor poet and man about town with whom he had for a time lived on terms of great intimacy. This work, a book of some 180 pages, is one of the most vivid and lively of Johnson's works; delightful reading for its own sake and an obvious forerunner of *The Lives of the Poets,* where the method of the strictly biographical portions is precisely the same. He had, of course, some practice through writing the various short sketches which had been an important part of his work for *The Gentleman's Magazine,* but these were no more than compilations in which rather general formal observations held together the facts acquired at secondhand.[10] The *Savage,* on the other hand, was an intimate portrait of a sort that had for Johnson an especial fascination.

"The proper study of mankind is man." That injunction, which the eighteenth century so enthusiastically accepted as the perfect formulation of one of its most fundamental convictions, can, like its predecessor "Know thyself," be taken to mean rather different things. It may mean—and doubtless was sometimes taken to mean—that the most important subject of man's study is his own fundamental nature and his place in the universal scheme. So interpreted, it might be an invitation to metaphysics, and Pope himself, with his speculations concerning the Great Chain of Being, accepted the invitation. But the eighteenth century was certainly not a metaphysical age, and Johnson, despite his own rather surprising confession that metaphysics could have been his favorite subject, had an additional reason for interpreting the phrase in a narrower sense—namely, that the accepted truths of the Christian religion made unnecessary any further speculation concerning the nature, place and duty of man. Hence to him, and perhaps to most of his contemporaries, to say that the Proper Study of Mankind is Man was simply to express an almost inexhaustible curiosity concerning the variety of character and custom to be found within the limits of his own society. It was almost to proclaim that the Comedy of Manners is the one inexhaustible subject.

Such curiosity is, of course, also characteristic of the Elizabethan age, of the nineteenth century, of our own day, and indeed of all highly developed civilizations. But it has seldom had less competition from other curiosities than it had among the literary men of Johnson's time. The Elizabethans were even more interested in the exotic and the marvelous than they were in the familiar; the nineteenth century was at least as interested in the physical sciences; the twentieth is so convinced of the importance of formal psychological, political and economic theories as to suspect that any concern with the minutiae of manners is merely frivolous. But the eighteenth century, despite the fact that even Johnson shared the contemporary interest in chemistry, despite Gibbon's *Roman Empire,* despite Adam Smith's *Wealth of Nations,* despite Boswell's running after a Corsican hero, and despite society's concern with Omai, the noble savage—despite, in other words, a thousand things, was, nevertheless, primarily interested in contemporary social life and interpreted "social life" quite narrowly. This was one of the many ways in which it cultivated its garden and tended to what it regarded as its own business. Hence, of course, the endless chatty letters and hence also the fact that the age is the golden age of conversation and of the anecdote. If its journalism invented the gossip column and gave it a larger place in newspapers and magazines than it has ever held since (unless perhaps it be in our own time), Johnson and others invented also the picturesque biography of private and literary persons.

Biography was Johnson's own favorite reading. In it he obviously found a sort of substitute for, or extension of, the social intercourse of which he could never get enough, and scattered here and there he left abundant materials for a sketch of his idea both of the best methods of biographical writing and of the kind of profit to be got from it. To him history was meaningful only if it was social history or the biography of historical persons and he had little use for any other kind. "Sooner than hear of the Punic War," writes Arthur Murphy, "he would be rude to the person that introduced the subject"; and as we know from other recorded remarks, he used "the Punic War" as a catch phrase to indicate all those historic parallels or ancient instances of which many of his contemporaries were fond, but which he dismissed impatiently as *"that* stuff." "[Fox] talked to me at club one day . . . concerning Cataline's conspiracy—so I withdrew my attention, and thought about Tom Thum." Indeed, he could not endure what Boswell calls "the cant transmitted from age to age, in praise of the ancient Romans," and in exasperation he once wrote: "I know not why any one but a school-boy in his declamation should whine over the Common-wealth of Rome, which grew great only by the misery of the rest of mankind. The Romans, like others, as soon as they grew rich, grew corrupt; and in the corruption sold the lives and freedoms of themselves, and of one another." But veracious and realistic lives of people like ourselves were something quite different from pompous political history, or rhetoric about Virtue and Corruption. They give us "what comes near to ourselves, what we can turn to use." [11]

It may seem at first odd that Johnson, whose name the popular mind commonly associates with sonorous generalities, should insist so strongly upon the exclusive importance of the specific character and the individual trait. Yet he was, as *The Rambler* will demonstrate, an early champion of realistic prose fiction as well as of picturesque biography, and his own best writing is by no means the tissue of large generalities it is sometimes assumed to be. His vocabulary, to be sure, does tend to be abstract and for that reason his manner seldom seems familiar, but the observation or the comment which he so persistently "Johnsonizes" is often realistic, shrewd and detailed. Savage's habitual way of life is, for example, thus described:

"But no sooner had he received his pension, than he withdrew to his darling privacy, from which he returned, in a short time, to his former distress, and, for some part of the year, generally lived by chance, eating only when he was invited to the tables of his acquaintances, from which the meanness of his dress often excluded him, when the politeness and variety of his conversation would have been thought a sufficient recompense for his entertainment.

"He lodged as much by accident as he dined, and passed the night sometimes in mean houses, which are set open at night to any casual wanderers, sometimes in cellars, among the riot and filth of the meanest and most profligate of the rabble; and sometimes, when he had not money to support even the expenses of these receptacles, walked about the streets till he was weary, and lay down in the summer upon a bulk, or in the winter, with his associates in poverty, among the ashes of a glass-house.

"In this manner were passed those days and those nights which nature had enabled him to have employed in elevated speculations, useful studies, or pleasing conversation. On a bulk, in a cellar, or in a glass-house, among thieves and beggars, was to be found the author of the Wanderer; the man of exalted sentiments, extensive views, and curious observations; the man whose remarks on life might have assisted the statesman, whose ideas of virtue might have enlightened the moralist, whose eloquence might have influenced senates, and whose delicacy might have polished courts."

For all the formality of the manner, the information conveyed is detailed as well as picturesque. Johnson thought the best biography autobiographic and the second best that written by an intimate friend, who could and would tell the whole truth, not forgetting the little peculiarities which define character. "Nobody," he said, "can write the life of a man, but those who have eat and drunk and lived in social intercourse with him." [12]

That Johnson, as biographer of such a man as Richard Savage, should have fulfilled so adequately these conditions has always been the occasion of some astonishment to those who have written about him, for Savage was an odd companion for a moralist—an odder one, indeed, than James Boswell. He was a wastrel, a parasite, a debauchee and a weakling. He was egotistical, arrogant, vain and demanding, though utterly without that dignity or pride of which Johnson had so much and for which he had such great respect. He was also a poet of talents either so small or so little employed that even of his best-known poem, *The Bastard,* only one line is ever remembered—that in which the talented bastard, got, as Dryden says, "with some diviner lust," is called: "No tenth transmitter of a foolish face." And that line has been quoted so often that one is tempted to reply with the remark of Rivarol, when he had grown weary of hearing the praises of a certain famous couplet: "C'est fort bien, mais il y a des longueurs." [13]

If any explanation of Johnson's intimacy with Savage is necessary, other than that supplied by his interest in character and his social tolerance as opposed to his theoretical intolerance, then that explanation is probably adequately supplied by one phrase used in the biography of his friend: "In no time of Mr. Savage's life," he says, was it "any part of his character to be the first of the company that desired to separate." After Savage had left the scene, Johnson appears to have tried during all the rest of his own life to find another willing to outsit and outtalk him.

It has, indeed, been pointed out in addition that the number of general parallels which can be drawn between the temperament of Johnson, the moralist, and Savage, the wastrel, is surprising in view of the equally fundamental differences between them. When Johnson writes of Savage that he "always preserved a steady confidence in his own capacity" or that he "excelled in the arts of conversation and therefore willingly practiced them," Johnson might of course have been speaking of himself. When he describes how Savage, though destitute, refused to cnter a house until some clothes left for him "with some neglect of ceremonies" had been taken away, it is impossible not to remember Johnson and the shoes which he refused to receive at Oxford. Of either it might certainly be said that he "would prolong his conversation till midnight, without considering that business might require his friend's application in the morning" because "when he left the company, he was . . . abandoned to gloomy reflections." And Johnson might equally well have been writing of himself when he observed of Savage: "He had the peculiar felicity, that his attention never deserted him; he was present to every object, and regardful of the most trifling occurrences. . . . To this quality is to be imputed the extent of his knowledge, compared with the small time which he spent in visible endeavours to acquire it. He mingled in cursory conversation with the same steadiness of attention as others apply to a lecture . . . His judgment was eminently exact, both with regard to writings and to men." One is, even, tempted to go beyond the mere observation that Johnson describes Savage as in many respects much like himself and to wonder whether or not the resemblance was not consciously or unconsciously exaggerated; whether, in other words, Johnson was not, after the manner of many novelists, writing most vividly when he was drawing upon himself in order to give life to personages in the main outlines of their character very different.

According to Savage's own account—which Johnson accepts without question—he was the illegitimate son of the Countess of Macclesfield, who certainly did have an illegitimate son (presumably by Earl Rivers) on account of whom her husband divorced her. But in a lifetime spent in asserting his claim and denouncing the inhumanity of his mother, Savage never seems to have produced any documentary evidence to support his contention—not even the letters, first revealing even to him the secret of his birth, which he pretended to have discovered in the home of his nurse, and which, therefore, it is incredible that he should have lost or destroyed.

Like most sensational pretenders, Savage has, even today, his partisans. They point out that certain fashionable people championed him in his own time, that certain members of the family to which he claimed a relationship tried to keep him quiet by small gifts or allowances, and that no libel suit was ever brought against him. But none of these arguments is very strong. Society is notoriously inclined to take up, for a time at least, those who can make romantic claims for themselves; members of the family would not unnaturally have been glad to quiet a sensational scandal if it could be quieted at small expense; and no one who knows anything about eighteenth-century libel suits, about their malodorousness or the difficulty in getting a conviction, can wonder that the Countess of Macclesfield, whose adultery was established, had no great desire to have the whole scandalous mess publicly explored again. The cases of few such claimants as Savage have ever been studied more exhaustively than his and the consensus is overwhelmingly that he was either self-deluded or an out-and-out impostor.

If Johnson had not been blinded by his own partiality he would certainly have seen that the emphasis he places upon the pointless malignity attributed to the supposed mother, who is alleged not only to have denied her son without motive but also to have taken underhanded means to prevent others from aiding him, actually weakens the credibility of his case. To believe in the justice of Savage's claims one must believe that he had for a mother a monster of disinterested iniquity, whom Johnson himself all but declares incredible. But one may escape the necessity of believing in her if one is only willing to believe something not in itself improbable—that Savage was an impostor. Savage gave no evidence at all to support a contention that involves the highest degree of improbability so far as the behavior of his alleged mother is concerned. On the other hand, there is no reason why we should find it hard to believe that a few lies were told by a thoroughly unprincipled man who spent most of his life trying to persuade the world that it owed him a living.

Just when Johnson first met Savage and just how long their intimacy lasted is not known, but since Savage contributed verses to *The Gentleman's Magazine,* it may be assumed that the first meeting took place at St. John's Gate. Savage's one virtue seems to have been that he was an entertaining companion and that he had seen enough of "the world" to pass on to Johnson a good deal of the kind of information which the latter was always eager to acquire even at second hand. Possibly, as Boswell darkly hints, Johnson was occasionally seduced by his companion from the path of strict virtue but it can hardly have been far or for long. At the time of the acquaintance Savage was nearing the end of his rope and sinners in misery always found Johnson ready to pardon.

Even before Boswell's time it was suggested that the "injur'd Thales" of *London* was Savage, and certain parallels are striking. But there are chronological difficulties, which can hardly be explained away; Boswell rejected the identification; and to date the longest arguments have had to conclude with a "not proved." In any event, the association between Johnson and Savage must have come to an end when the latter left London for good in July, 1739, and went to Wales, where he died on August 1, 1743. Johnson's motives for writing the *Life* seem to have included a desire to serve the memory of his friend and he must have set to work soon after Savage's death. An undated letter to Cave reveals him making inquiry concerning certain of the materials which he needed and he had been heard to say: "I wrote forty-eight of the printed octavo pages of the Life of Savage at a sitting; but then I sat up all night." The volume came out from the shop of one Roberts in February, 1744, and appears to have been well-received. It reached a second edition in 1748, a third and fourth in 1767 and 1769, though the last two, of course, belong to the period when the author had become a very famous man. Johnson had sold the copyright to Cave for fifteen guineas shortly before publication.[14]

It has already been sufficiently indicated that the merits of the performance have nothing to do with the examination of the evidence to support Savage's claims to noble birth. To a degree almost fatuous Johnson takes them purely on Savage's own terms and blandly assumes that the latter's "wrongs" palliate, if they do not completely excuse, the outrageousness of his conduct. The great merit does, on the other hand, consist in the interest of the narrative and, more especially, in the full and vivid portrait of a complicated and picturesque personality equally interesting whether one assumes him to have been a victim or an impostor. Sir Joshua Reynolds told Boswell that he picked up the volume in Devonshire and, knowing nothing of the author, began to read it while he was standing with his arm leaning against a chimneypiece. "It seized his attention so strongly, that, not being able to lay down the book till he had finished it, when he attempted to move, he found his arm totally benumbed." A modern reader might easily have the same experience. Certain of the *Lives of the Poets,* which reveal an extraordinarily active and robust mind busily concerned with larger subjects, no doubt exhibit powers of a higher order. But probably none of Johnson's other writings equals the *Savage* as sheer entertainment or in the power to lead one from paragraph to paragraph in an eagerness to learn more about a picturesque human being.

In method Johnson is no Boswell. There is little or no direct discourse, no setting of the scenes with that elaborate choice of accidental detail which gives a kind of literal realism to Boswell's pages. If Johnson had had occasion to mention the models for the sort of biographical writing which he admired he might well have cited Plutarch and Tacitus, with possibly even an allusion to Suetonius or Diogenes Laertius. And though the first two, at least, might have been startled to find so much attention given to a man so little excellent and so little important to his country, the method is nevertheless more like theirs than it is like the method of Boswell. Doubtless it also owes something, as so much eighteenth-century portraiture in fiction as well as biography does, to the classical "characters" which come down from Earle and the rest through the *Spectator* and Johnson's own *Rambler*.

Anecdotes, though not told in Boswell's manner, do constitute an important part of the narrative. Much, however, is in the form of highly generalized discourse and where Boswell, nearly fifty years later, would have cited specific instances or told several stories, Johnson, for example, writes in such general terms as these: "[Savage] spent his time in mean expedients and tormenting suspense, living, for the greatest part, in fear of prosecutions from his creditors, and, consequently, skulking in obscure parts of the town, of which he was no stranger to the remotest corners. But, wherever he came, his address secured him friends, whom his necessities soon alienated; so that he had, perhaps, a more numerous acquaintance than any man ever before attained, there being scarcely any person eminent on any account to whom he was not known, or whose character he was not, in some degree, able to delineate." But Johnson's method, no less than Boswell's, has its virtues, and the method has seldom been more successfully used.

Savage lived (and died) on the bounty of others. He was chronically ungrateful and as incapable of thanks as he was ready to abuse those who gave too little or too seldom. The record of the multifarious gifts, allowances and other assorted gratuities which he received from various persons certainly suggests that the benevolence of the eighteenth-century gentleman was phenomenal even though it seems to us to have been exercised upon oddly chosen subjects, and Johnson's preposterous partiality leads him to extenuate the malignant parasitism of Savage as he extenuated the other faults of a man who seems to have exhibited nearly all the defects (except dullness) of which human nature is capable. Indeed, these extenuations, together with all that is baldly admitted, make certain passages in the *Life* read almost like *Jonathan Wild* or *Barry Lyndon*. But they do not, any more than Johnson's readiness to accept Savage's own story of his origin, prevent us from seeing or understanding the character of the man who is being so vividly portrayed. Johnson's forbearance does not persuade him to conceal anything, and his various summings-up are damning even when he himself hesitates to pronounce the sentence.

So too is the final conclusion, which runs: "Such were the life and death of Richard Savage, a man equally distinguished by his virtues and his vices; and at once remarkable for his weaknesses and abilities . . .

"He appeared to think himself born to be supported by others, and dispensed from all necessity of providing for himself . . . His temper was, in consequence of the dominion of his passions, uncertain and capricious; he was easily engaged, and easily disgusted; but he is accused of retaining his hatred more tenaciously than his benevolence.

"He was compassionate both by nature and by principle, and always ready to perform offices of humanity; but when he was provoked (and very small offences were sufficient to provoke him) he would prosecute his revenge with the utmost acrimony till his passion had subsided.

"His friendship was, therefore, of little value; for though he was zealous in the support or vindication of those whom he loved, yet it was always dangerous to trust him, because he considered himself as discharged, by the first quarrel, from all ties of honour or gratitude; and would betray those secrets which, in the warmth of confidence, had been imparted to him. . . .

"This relation will not be wholly without its use—if those who, in confidence of superior capacities or attainments, disregard common maxims of life, shall be reminded, that nothing will supply the want of prudence, and that neglect and irregularity, long continued, will make knowledge useless, wit ridiculous, and genius contemptible."

Like many other writers of the eighteenth century, Johnson was much more ready than we to give credit for good intentions even when they got nowhere near performance. To consider professed "respect for virtue," even in the absence of any practice of it, surprisingly important was one of his conspicuous foibles and could lead him to such absurdities as his praise of a man for always taking off his hat when he passed a church even though he never entered one. Hence he can say of Savage: "His actions, which were generally precipitate, were often blameable; but his writings, being productions of study, uniformly tended to the exaltation of the mind, and the propagation of morality and piety." In all seriousness he can even regret that Savage never carried into effect an intention to compose a poem called the *Progress of a Freethinker.* "That he did not execute this design is a real loss to mankind; for he was too well acquainted with all the scenes of debauchery to have failed in his representations of them, and too zealous for virtue not to have represented them in such a manner as should expose them either to ridicule or detestation."

Such passages of unintentional satire are, however, more than compensated for by passages which for the first time exhibit in Johnson's writing the irony—especially the ironic confrontation of cant and common sense—which is so large a component in the flavor of his best talk as well as of his best written prose. Savage, "having no profession, became, by necessity, an author." When his poem in honor of a member of the royal family was not only graciously received but outrageously overpaid, he "assumed the title of volunteer laureate, not without some reprehensions from Cibber [actually the laureate], who informed him, that the title of laureate was a mark of honour conferred by the king, from whom all honour derived, and which, therefore, no man has a right to bestow upon himself; and added, that he might with equal propriety style himself a volunteer lord or volunteer baronet." "It cannot," Johnson goes on, "be denied that the remark was just; but Savage did not think any title, which was conferred upon Mr. Cibber, so honourable as that the usurpation of it could be imputed to him as an instance of very exorbitant vanity, and, therefore, continued to write under the same title, and received every year the same reward." And when the time comes to recount how Savage, toward the end of his life, not only agreed to retire to Wales at the request of friends but even promised himself happiness amid the rural delights of which he certainly knew nothing except what he had read in pastoral poems, Johnson cannot resist the temptation to enlarge upon one of his favorite themes even at the expense of the man he was defending: "He imagined that he should be transported to scenes of flowery felicity, like those which one poet has reflected to another; and had projected a perpetual round of innocent pleasures, of which he suspected no interruption from pride, or ignorance, or brutality.

"With these expectations he was so enchanted, that when he

was once gently reproached by a friend for submitting to live upon a subscription, and advised rather by a resolute exertion of his abilities to support himself, he could not bear to debar himself from the happiness which was to be found in the calm of a cottage, or lose the opportunity of listening, without intermission, to the melody of the nightingale, which he believed was to be heard from every bramble, and which he did not fail to mention as a very important part of the happiness of a country life."

In April, 1745, or a little more than a year after the appearance of *The Life of Savage,* Johnson published a pamphlet entitled *Miscellaneous Observations on the Tragedy of* Macbeth, *with Remarks on Sir T.H's [Sir Thomas Hanmer's] Edition of Shakespeare.* Accompanying it were "Proposals" for a new edition of Shakespeare's plays.

The *Miscellaneous Observations* provides the first demonstration of Johnson's extraordinary ability as a critic, especially in the field of what we should call "criticism on historical principles." Since, however, many years and much other work were to intervene before the preface and notes to his edition of Shakespeare revealed the full extent of this ability, it will be best to consider the *Miscellaneous Observations* later in connection with the accomplishment toward which it pointed.[15]

CHAPTER IV

The Harmless Drudge

IF GARRICK relayed to Johnson the message sent in 1746 by Gilbert Walmesley and quoted at the beginning of the preceding chapter, it is not likely that Johnson was much troubled by it. He knew that he had not actually been as idle or accomplished as little as his old patron supposed, though he knew also that Walmesley had no way of knowing either how much work he had done or the extent to which he had built up a purely professional reputation "in the trade" as a man of solid parts who could be trusted to perform satisfactorily a literary job. That such a reputation had been achieved was soon to be demonstrated when a group of booksellers advanced him a considerable sum of money to prosecute a long, arduous and important enterprise which few other men in England would have undertaken and none, perhaps, have been able to carry to so satisfactory a conclusion. Just how the booksellers defined in their own minds the kind of reputation Johnson had earned, we can only guess, but a guess based on the evidence will help clarify the position he later held.

Before the end of his career Johnson was something more than merely the author of certain works. To call him a literary dictator would be to misstate as well as to overstate the case, but he was what might be termed the best-known professional in the world of letters; and it is obvious that in the forties he was already beginning to be recognized as at least potentially something of that sort even before he was much known outside publishing circles. He was more than a journalist, and yet so miscellaneous and so casual was his learning that one hardly thinks of him as a scholar. If he had been less able or if he had done his work less well, we would merely call him a hack and perhaps a superlatively good hack is just what he was.

Here, booksellers came to realize, was a man who could be commissioned to do some literary job (and all his major works were thus commissioned) in the full confidence that, though he would approach the job as a job, he would also do it better than anyone else working for love or fame at his chosen avocation would have done it. Here, in other words, was a great reservoir of information and ability which could be drawn upon for any sort of literary task, whether that task was to compile a great dictionary or merely to write a dedication or an epitaph. Not everyone found exactly to his taste what Johnson did. But even those whose taste he did not suit, and who certainly never dreamed of accepting his pronouncements as law, inevitably accepted him as a major figure nevertheless. Such a man was a godsend to those who printed and sold books: even if he did not make any of them rich, he conferred upon their trade a sort of solidity. Since Johnson's time there have been many who have established themselves less conspicuously and less successfully in a similar position but we still have no name for their profession.

The year 1746, which was that of Walmesley's mild reproach, happened also to be one in which Johnson's literary labors, whatever they may have been, left no decipherable record. No contribution by him to *The Gentleman's Magazine* has been traced during either 1745 or 1746, and it may be that there was some coolness between him and Cave which was later dispelled; but it may also be simply that the amount of space devoted in the magazine to the excitement caused by the threatened uprising in behalf of the Young Pretender crowded out the material which Johnson normally supplied. The suggestion that he might have been in hiding because of some active connection with treasonable plots is absurd, since Johnson's Jacobitism was merely something to talk about and he told Boswell not only that "he had never in his life been in a nonjuring meeting-house," but also "that if holding up his right hand would have secured victory at Culloden to Prince Charles's army, he was not sure he would have held it up." [1]

Possibly both 1745 and 1746 were spent chiefly in work on the proposed edition of Shakespeare which was, for external reasons, abandoned. Possibly, and more probably, some or most of his energy was devoted to forming the scheme for the *Dictionary of the English Language* which is already well-advanced when we first hear of it. In any event, Johnson was soon to be deep in the two works which first definitely established his reputation with a large public as distinguished from that which he enjoyed among journalists and booksellers. Oddly enough, however, neither of these works is much alive today. One of them, the *Dictionary*, ceased, like most works of scholarship, to be of any general interest when, partly upon the foundation which it laid, more elaborate edifices of the same sort were erected. The other, that series of periodical essays called *The Rambler*, is, despite striking sentences and even a few whole papers which deserve to be remembered, not likely ever to be much read again as a whole. Yet the *Dictionary*, successive revisions of which continued to bear his name, maintained a position as *the* dictionary of the English language not even disputed until the appearance of Webster and not definitely displaced until the appearance of the Oxford. *The Rambler* was so well known that many years later Boswell could frequently refer to its author by that assumed name. Had Johnson established no other claim to fame except that founded on the *Dictionary*, his name would have been as well known for a century as that of Noah Webster is known in America; if he had written nothing except *The Rambler*, his contemporaries would have regarded him as a very important literary figure.

Boswell is exasperatingly vague (and obviously not informed) concerning either the exact time when the work of compiling the *Dictionary* was begun or the precise circumstances under which the project was formed. Sir John Hawkins, who is not generally to be trusted too implicitly but who says that he saw the original contract, states that it was dated June 18, 1746. Boswell tells us that the booksellers who contracted with Johnson "single and unaided" were Dodsley, Charles Hitch, Andrew Millar, the two Messrs. Longman and the two Messrs. Knapton. He also tells us that the price stipulated was fifteen hundred and seventy-five pounds, out of which Johnson himself had to pay for his clerical assistance. From a passage in Johnson's own *Prayers and Meditations* we know that he began the second of the two folio volumes ("room being left in the first for Preface, Grammar, and History, none of them yet begun") on April 3, 1753. And he adds: "O God, who hast hitherto supported me, enable me to proceed in this labor, and in the whole task of my present state; that when I shall render up, at the last day, an account of the talent committed to me, I may receive pardon, for the sake of Jesus Christ. Amen."

Before the labor was finished he had received and spent the entire sum contracted for and indeed, at least according to Arthur Murphy, when the receipts were produced to him at a tavern dinner given by the booksellers, it appeared that something more than one hundred pounds above what was due him had been paid. That sum, in addition to what he earned from other work done during the same period, certainly kept him from serious financial worry and he expressed himself later as satisfied with his treatment. Boswell remarked: "I am sorry, Sir, you did not get more for your Dictionary," and Johnson's reply was: "I am sorry too. But it was very well. The booksellers are generous, liberal-minded men." [2]

According to his own statement, it was by Dodsley's "recommendation" that he was employed in the work; but that is not to be taken to mean that Johnson had not previously considered the possibility of doing something of the kind. That he *had,* as a matter of fact, previously thought about the need for a dictionary we know both from a statement made more than thirty years later when he said: "Dodsley first mentioned to me the scheme of an English Dictionary; but I had long thought of it," and from the anecdote told by James Dodsley, brother of the publisher, who remembered that several years before the plan of the *Dictionary* was published, he had heard his brother remark in Johnson's presence that a dictionary would be well received by the public and that "Johnson seemed at first to catch at the proposition, but, after a pause, said, in his abrupt, decisive manner, 'I believe I shall not undertake it.' "

In any event, the task was one for which English culture was now ready and also one for which Johnson had both technical equipment and something else equally necessary—the requisite understanding of the true function of a standard dictionary in stabilizing further a language already formed and entered upon its classic phase. It is true that on no other occasion did he undertake anything that demanded so much methodical labor. It is also true that at the time when he was engaged upon it he often spoke jocosely in depreciation of the profession he had assumed. In the *Dictionary* itself, when he comes to the word "lexicographer" he permits himself one of those rare but famous lapses into pleasantry by defining it as "a writer of dictionaries, a harmless drudge"; and in an essay published while he was still at work he speaks of men who "employed their minds in such operations as required neither celerity nor strength, in the low drudgery of collating copies, comparing authorities, digesting dictionaries," etc. Moreover, he himself says in the first paragraph of the *Plan* that when he first undertook the task "I knew that the work in which I engaged is generally considered as drudgery for the blind, as the proper toil of artless industry; a task that requires neither the light of learning, nor the activity of genius, but may be successfully performed without any higher quality than that of bearing burdens with dull patience, and beating the track of the alphabet with sluggish resolution." G. Birkbeck Hill quotes this passage in such a way as to make it appear that Johnson was describing his own conception of the lexicographer's task rather than the way in which it was "generally considered"; and the main body of the *Plan* makes it clear enough that Johnson's intention was to do something different from anything that had been done before and to make his work serve a purpose which no previous dictionary of the English language had served. Mere drudgery could not accomplish what he proposed.[3]

The first dictionaries were merely lists of hard words explained. Medieval scholars, when they found in a Latin text a word not familiar to them, were accustomed to "gloss" it by writing above in a smaller hand either an easier Latin word or an equivalent in their own language. A list compiled from such interlinear notations was called a Glossarium or Glossary, and the earliest extant probably go back to originals as remote as the seventh century. They were the ancestors of the Latin-English vocabularies used by schoolboys as early as the thirteenth century and these vocabularies served in their turn as models for the various French-, Spanish- or Italian-English vocabularies printed during the sixteenth century. But all such vocabularies were either bi- or polylingual and the first exclusively English word list, *The Table Alphabetical of Hard Words,* published in 1604 by a schoolmaster named Robert Cawdrey, reveals through its title the fact that such word lists were thought of, not as in any sense philosophical or as tending to fix or even influence the language, but merely as aids to the unlearned.

It was not until more than a hundred years later that the idea of a dictionary containing *all* the English words seems to have occurred to anyone willing to undertake the task of compiling it, and no attempt was made to furnish such a work until Nathaniel Bailey published, in 1721, his *Universal Etymological English Dictionary.*

Bailey went through many editions; Johnson took it as a working basis, and it was by no means completely displaced in popular use by his own work. But it must be noted that Bailey's purpose in including *all* English words, even the most familiar, was merely to give etymologies on the indisputable assumption that his readers would be ignorant of the origin of many words whose meaning would present no difficulty. None of his imitators or rivals, before Johnson, went beyond this, and it was Johnson who made the final step. To him a dictionary was not merely a list of hard words which might need explanation. Neither was it even merely a list of *all* words with their derivations. It was also a history of good usage, illustrated by quotation, and an authority by reference to which questions concerning correctness and propriety might be answered. It records usage, but also to some extent fixes it. The conception of such a work could not have been formed until the contributory conceptions of elegance and propriety in language as distinguished from the merely crude *meaning* of words had come to seem extremely important, and Johnson's *Dictionary* was thus a contribution to a much more inclusive task which the eighteenth century had set itself—the task, namely, of discovering and establishing in all human affairs (including language) the most reasonable, most durable, most efficient and most elegant procedure. It was his purpose to stabilize in the English language the order and consistency which writers of the golden age (i.e., seventeenth and eighteenth centuries) had conferred upon it.[4]

In 1747, the year following the signing of the contract, Johnson published in a pamphlet of thirty-four pages *The Plan of an English Dictionary* and dedicated it to Philip Dormer, Earl of Chesterfield, "one of His Majesty's principal Secretaries of State." This *Plan* is evidently the product of much careful thought, and not only outlines the general scope of the proposed work but also explains what decision has been taken concerning various problems of detail. The intention is to list all the words in general use, to indicate their pronunciation, to give their etymologies, to define them, and to illustrate their uses by examples taken chiefly from standard authors. Obsolete words will be included when they occur in works still commonly read, technical and scientific terms only if they have passed into the general language and are no longer used only in connection with the trade or science which originally invented them. The *Dictionary* is to be designed "not merely for critics but for popular use" and "the chief intent of it is to preserve the purity, and ascertain the meaning of our English idiom."

That Johnson realized even this early what kind of difficulties would inevitably arise in the effort to follow the principles laid down may be illustrated by his remarks in connection with the rules to govern the inclusion of technical words:

"The academicians of France, indeed, rejected terms of science in their first essay, but found afterwards a necessity of relaxing the rigour of their determination; and, though they would not naturalize them at once by a single act, permitted them by degrees to settle themselves among the natives, with little opposition; and it would surely be no proof of judgment to imitate them in an errour which they have now retracted, and deprive the book of its chief use, by scrupulous distinctions.

"Of such words, however, all are not equally to be considered as parts of our language; for some of them are naturalized and incorporated; but others still continue aliens, and are rather auxiliaries than subjects. This naturalization is produced either by an admission into common speech, in some metaphorical signification, which is the acquisition of a kind of property among us; as we say, the *zenith* of advancement, the *meridian* of life, the *cynosure* of neighbouring eyes; or it is the consequence of long intermixture and frequqent use, by which the ear is accustomed to the sound of words, till their original is forgotten, as in *equator, satellites;* or of the change of a foreign to an English termination, and a conformity to the laws of the speech into which they are adopted; as in *category, cachexy, peripneumony.*

"Of those which still continue in the state of aliens, and have made no approaches towards assimilation, some seem necessary to be retained, because the purchasers of the *Dictionary* will expect to find them. Such are many words in the common law, as *capias, habeas corpus, præmunire, nisi prius:* such are some terms of controversial divinity, as *hypostasis;* and of physick, as the names of diseases; and, in general, all terms which can be found in books not written professedly upon particular arts, or can be supposed necessary to those who do not regularly study them. Thus, when a reader not skilled in physick happens in Milton upon this line,

> ——— pining atrophy,
> Marasmus, and wide-wasting pestilence,

he will, with equal expectation, look into his dictionary for the word *marasmus,* as for *atrophy,* or *pestilence;* and will have reason to complain if he does not find it."

The phrase "to preserve the purity . . . of our English idiom" is indication enough that Johnson assumed the existence of some sort of standard and that he intended his *Dictionary* to help fix practice in accordance with that standard. It is not, however, to be assumed that his intention was naïvely authoritarian. No doubt he knew less than modern scholars know of the way in which languages grow and function; no doubt he was somewhat less inclined than they to acquiesce gladly in the tendency of usage gradually to legitimatize novelties and barbarisms. But "I am," he can say, "not yet so lost in lexicography, as to forget that *words are the daughters of earth, and that things are the sons of heaven.*" He can also quote with approval Quintilian's observation that "speech was not formed by an analogy sent from heaven," and go on to add: "It did not descend to us in a state of uniformity and perfection, but was produced by necessity, and enlarged by accident, and is, therefore, composed of dissimilar parts, thrown together by negligence, by affectation, by learning or by ignorance." [5]

But, though he is not naïvely authoritarian, he is equally far from assuming that no choice can be made between various usages or that language ought to be left entirely and forever to the chance which produced it. He recognizes that language is not in its origins logical or consistent, that it was at first not the shadow of an idea but a rude practical contrivance, that in the beginning was not the word but the thing. Nevertheless, he goes on to assume that the order and consistency and stability, which language does not have of itself, should to some extent be artificially imposed upon it once it has arrived at a certain state of perfection. Where religion was not concerned, Johnson was, like most of his educated contemporaries, a skeptic and a rationalist. But again like most of his contemporaries, and without taking any more pains than most of them did to assure metaphysical consistency with other notions, he also tended to assume, after the fashion of Pope's *Essay on Criticism* and *Essay on Man,* that there is a certain kind of order and consistency—some one order and consistency rather than merely *some* order and *some* consistency—which is natural to man and therefore enduring, however little it may be manifest in the spontaneous growth of language. Though he never quite says so, he would probably have maintained that the "best usage" is best, not simply because it has the authority of the best writers but because the best writers have found out what the best really is—because, as Pope argued, "the rules" of literary composition are discovered rather than promulgated and are therefore merely "nature methodized."

Johnson knew of the French Academy and its lexicographical labors to which he made jocose reference. But he did not really need such an example: his general principle was one which not only suited his age but was made inevitable by it. A century and a quarter earlier, Bacon could take it for granted that the English language was too unstable to be entrusted with anything that readers a hundred years hence might want to know. Within Johnson's own lifetime Pope had written, though perhaps with less real conviction, "For such as Chaucer is will Dryden be." But Johnson and certain of his immediate predecessors, as well as his contemporaries, now felt both that the language could be fixed and that it had reached a point of development where such fixing was desirable. To stabilize it might mean that further development or improvement would be impeded at least; but it also meant protection against that decline from gold to silver, and finally to lead, which the history of Roman literature seemed to suggest was the likely course of a language that had reached the stage they thought had been reached in the best writing of their own time and, more especially, of the century and a half immediately preceding it. From an allusion of Lady Mary Wortley Montagu's, it appears that Addison had once considered an enterprise something like Johnson's; quite recently it has been discovered that Ambrose Philips published undated proposals for a dictionary; and Johnson himself implies in the *Plan* that Pope had originated some dictionary project or had at least given Johnson a list of writers who might be regarded as authorities. But Johnson was the first actually to undertake to accomplish a work the desirability of which had been increasingly recognized.[6]

Anything like an arbitrary remaking of the language was far from his intention. He was ready to assume that good usage is generally the final test of correctness and he proposed to use his own authority only where literary usage could not be cited to settle a question. But it is significant that he assumed *literary* usage to be the only sort which carries much weight, and that he did undertake to make his own taste or judgment the deciding factor where literary usage seemed inconsistent. In a passage that ends with a flowery compliment to Chesterfield, amusing enough in view of what was later to happen, he writes:

"With regard to questions of purity or propriety, I was once in doubt whether I should not attribute too much to myself, in attempting to decide them, and whether my province was to extend beyond the proposition of the question, and the display of the suffrages on each side; but I have been since determined, by your Lordship's opinion, to interpose my own judgment, and shall, therefore, endeavour to support what appears to me most consonant to grammar and reason. Ausonius thought that modesty forbad him to plead inability for a task to which Cæsar had judged him equal:

Cur me posse negem posse quod ille putat?

And I may hope, my Lord, that since you, whose authority in our language is so generally acknowledged, have commissioned me to declare my own opinion, I shall be considered as exercising a kind of vicarious jurisdiction, and that the power which might have been denied to my own claim, will be readily allowed me as the delegate of your Lordship."

He had already promised that "the present usage of spelling, where present usage can be distinguished, will . . . be generally followed," though he adds that such spellings are often "tolerated rather than chosen." So, too, he will endeavor to prevent those changes in the accentuation of polysyllables which tend to make older poets seem unmetrical and he will accomplish this purpose by attempting to standardize the accents employed by the best writers—giving as an example "dolorous" and "sonorous" for the difference between which he sees no reason, but which were so accented by Milton. As to syntax: "The soldier died *of* his wounds, and the sailor perished *with* hunger; and every man acquainted with our language would be offended with a change of these particles, which seem originally assigned by chance, there being no reason to be drawn from grammar why a man may not, with equal propriety, be said to die *with* a wound or perish *of* hunger. . . . Our syntax, therefore, is not to be taught by general rules, but by special precedents."

The extent to which Johnson's *Dictionary* actually did fix the language would be difficult to measure. That it did not absolutely fix even the use of the preposition is evident enough when we consider that it is now "to die with hunger" rather than "to die of hunger" which offends every ear. And in so far as he did tend to establish certain ideas of propriety he did so less because of the authority he undertook to exercise on definitely specified occasions than because of the fact that he assumed not only the existence of "good usage" as something usually distinguishable from mere "usage" but also that, no doubt following the general tendency of his age, he fixed in accordance with his own lights the chronological limits of the period within which usage had authority. Good usage, he explains in his Preface to the *Dictionary* as it was finally published, means, first of all, the usage of those good writers who flourished between Sir Philip Sidney, the earliest writer to be extensively used, and the beginning of that deterioration of the language which Johnson believed began to manifest itself toward the end of the seventeenth century. "So far have I been from any care to grace my pages with modern decorations, that I have studiously endeavoured to collect examples and authorities from the writers before the Restoration, whose works I regard as *the wells of English undefiled,* as the pure sources of genuine diction." The usage of even the best writers of a given period is, in other words, to be followed only if it is not too old or too new. "Our language, for almost a century, has, by the concurrence of many causes, been gradually departing from its original Teutonic character, and deviating towards a Gallic structure and phraseology, from which it ought to be our endeavour to recall it, by making our ancient volumes the ground-work of style, admitting among the additions of later times only such as may supply real deficiencies, such as are readily adopted by the genius of our tongue, and incorporated easily with our native idioms."

Writers before the Restoration broke precedents to establish new ones but it is, he implies, our business only to follow where they led. And if Johnson had been asked why he proposed to serve the language by fixing it, while at the same time admitting that this same language had been at its best in its most licentious period; or if it had been suggested that he could not consistently object to Frenchification in the eighteenth century without objecting to Frenchification in the twelfth or thirteenth, and should, therefore, propose a return to Anglo-Saxon if he wanted to preserve its "original Teutonic character," he would doubtless have replied in terms of the passage which immediately follows that just quoted:

". . . as every language has a time of rudeness antecedent to perfection, as well as of false refinement and declension, I have been cautious lest my zeal for antiquity might drive me into times too remote, and crowd my book with words now no longer understood. I have fixed Sidney's work for the boundary, beyond which I make few excursions. From the authors which rose in the time of Elizabeth, a speech might be formed adequate to all the purposes of use and elegance. If the language of theology were extracted from Hooker and the translation of the Bible; the terms of natural knowledge from Bacon; the phrases of policy, war, and navigation from Raleigh; the dialect of poetry and fiction from Spenser and Sidney; and the diction of common life from Shakespeare, few ideas would be lost to mankind, for want of English words, in which they might be expressed." [7]

Johnson originally allowed himself three years for "beating the track of the alphabet with sluggish resolution," and when a friend protested that the forty members of the French Academy took forty years to accomplish a similar task he could only reply: "Sir, thus it is. This is the proportion. Let me see; forty times forty is sixteen hundred. As three is to sixteen hundred, so is the proportion of an Englishman to a Frenchman." "With so much ease and pleasantry," adds Boswell, "could he talk of that prodigious labor." But nine years were actually to pass between the signing of the contract and the date of publication and so, in terms of man-years, one Englishman turned out to be worth only one-third as much as Johnson calculated but the proportion was still one which might permit him to agree with the judgment of "old Meynell," whom he had met at Ashbourne some ten years before and who had observed after what must have been due reflection: "For anything I see, foreigners are fools."

After several removes Johnson finally settled himself in Gough

Square, Fleet Street, the first of his London residences concerning which much is known. There "he had an upper room fitted up like a counting house" where his amanuenses could labor. All in all there were six of these, and five, as the often easily pleased Boswell points out with pride, were "natives of North-Britain, to whom he is supposed to have been so hostile." Indeed, Boswell seems to have been more interested in the nationality of the copyists than he was in the method by which the *Dictionary* was compiled, for of the latter his account is not only brief but obviously muddled. It would surely not have been practical to proceed, as he implies that Johnson did, by making first a list of words and then searching for quotations to illustrate them. Boswell may, as he says, have seen several of the books which Johnson used "marked—with a black-lead pencil, the traces of which could be easily effaced," but the following account left by Bishop Percy is certainly more nearly correct:

"He began his task by devoting his first care to a diligent perusal of all such English writers as were most correct in their language, and under every sentence which he meant to quote, he drew a line, and noted in the margin the first letter of the word under which it was to occur. He then delivered these books to his clerks, who transcribed each sentence on a separate slip of paper, and arranged the same under the word referred to. By these means he collected the several words and their different significations; and when the whole arrangement was alphabetically formed, he gave the definitions of their meanings, and collected their etymologies from Skinner, Junius, and other writers on the subject. In completing his alphabetical arrangement, he, no doubt, would recur to former dictionaries, to see if any words had escaped him; but this, which Mr. Boswell makes the first step in the business, was in reality the last."

Sir John Hawkins not only supplies scarcely needed confirmation to what Bishop Percy has to say about the use of some previous compilation, but also suggests that, as one would suppose, such use was both more important and more closely integrated with the rest of the procedure than the phrase "last step" would suggest. "An interleaved copy of Bailey's dictionary in folio," says Hawkins, "he made the repository of the several articles."

Hawkins also adds that the books Johnson used for choosing quotations "were what he had in his own collection, a copious but a miserably ragged one, and all such as he could borrow; which latter, if ever they came back to those that lent them, were so defaced as to be scarce worth owning, and yet, some of his friends were glad to receive and entertain them as curiosities." The ill nature of this last sentence is quite characteristic of Hawkins but what he says is true enough, for Johnson was notoriously not one of those scholars who had great respect for books as physical objects. Once indeed he drove Garrick almost to distraction by flinging about the fine bindings of which Garrick was, perhaps, too proud.[8]

For all that Johnson said about humble drudges and sluggish resolution, he did not apparently find his task especially disagreeable. It is true that he was later to remark that "it was easier to him to write poetry than to compose his *Dictionary*" because "his mind was less on the stretch in doing the one than the other," but when the volumes were about to appear he wrote to one of his friends: "I wish, come of wishes what will, that my work may please you, as much as it now and then pleased me, for I did not find dictionary making so very unpleasant as it may be thought." He did not underestimate the task but he had the incalculable advantage of those who, through whatever difficulties they pass and no matter what misfortunes, neglects and injustices they may suffer, never doubt their own strength. Even after due allowance has been made for the fact that even Johnson probably spoke somewhat more jauntily of his labors after they were finished than he did when the goal was still far ahead, there is much to be learned from one incomparable bit of dialogue recorded long after the *Dictionary* was finished: BOSWELL. "You did not know what you were undertaking." JOHNSON. "Yes, Sir, I knew very well what I was undertaking,—and very well how to do it,—and have done it very well."

When he looked back upon the nine years during which this work was his chief concern, he must have realized, as any biographer inevitably does, that they were among the most important of his whole life, not only because he did much other work in addition to what went into the *Dictionary* and laid the secure foundations of his fame but because both his character and his career then took final shape. When he signed the contract with Dodsley *et al.* he was unknown to any considerable public and still in the position of a man whose lifework had not with any certainty been laid out. When it was finished he was already well known as an author, especially as the author of the series of periodical essays called *The Rambler* and of the somber satiric poem *The Vanity of Human Wishes* (1749). The *Dictionary* could then appear as possibly the *magnum opus* of a personage well established in the literary world. His character, his tastes and his private way of life also are during these years pretty well fixed.[9]

It is true that neither Boswell nor Mrs. Thrale was to make his acquaintance for some time yet and that, accordingly, we cannot know him with the intimacy which their record of incidents and conversations makes possible, but we begin to catch glimpses of his daily life, to see him more clearly, not merely as a name but as a person. Even though Boswell and Mrs. Thrale have not yet entered upon the scene, other persons only a little less important a part of the Johnsonian legend begin to appear —Levett, the humble medical practitioner; Miss Williams, who was to be later the blind hostess at his tea table; Francis Barber, the black valet whose ministrations did not seem to accomplish much; and Bennet Langton, the elegantly learned, who brought with him that gay dog, Topham Beauclerk. It was also during the early part of this dictionary epoch that he formed "a little club," the vaguely known precursor of a much more famous one, that "used to meet weekly" for dinner at a famous beefsteak house known as the King's Head, in Ivy Lane near St. Paul's. It included, among others, Dr. Hawkesworth, to whose later periodical essay Johnson contributed; Sir John Hawkins, later one of Johnson's biographers ("Sir John, Sir, is a very *unclub-able* man"); and possibly "Dear Bathurst," the "good hater," of whom Johnson was to say after the latter's death that he loved him better than he "loved any human creature."

Even from the days of his first coming up to London, Johnson, it will be remembered, managed to find talk and to think it good even when he found it in such unexpected places as "the table of Jack Ellis, a money-scrivener behind the Royal Exchange." But it was probably at Ivy Lane that he began to taste to the full the delight of spreading himself, and in Hawkins's crabbed account one can see the main outlines of Johnson's later manner. "Our conversations," he says, "seldom began till after a supper, so very solid and substantial, as led us to think, that with him it was a dinner. By the help of this refection, and no other incentive to hilarity than lemonade, Johnson was, in a short time after our assembling, transformed into a new creature; his habitual melancholy and lassitude of spirit gave way; his countenance brightened." Already Johnson talked for victory and disputed for the sake of victory; "At one time, *good,* at another *evil* was predominant in the moral constitution of the world. Upon one occasion, he would deplore the non-observance of Good-Friday, and on another deny, that among us of the present age there is any decline of public worship, at this versatility of temper, none, however, took offence; as Alexander and Cæsar were born for conquest, so was Johnson for the office of a symposiarch, to preside in all conversations; and I never yet saw the man who would venture to contest his right." But even Sir John Hawkins has the grace to stress equally that gaiety of Johnson which Boswell seems unwilling to emphasize. "Not only in Johnson's melancholy there were lucid intervals, but he was a great contributor to the mirth of conversation. . . . In the talent of humour there hardly ever was his equal . . . he was enabled to give to any relation that required it, the graces and aids of expression, and to discriminate with the nicest exactness the characters of those whom it concerned. In aping this faculty I have seen Warburton disconcerted, and when he would fain have been thought a man of pleasantry, not a little out of countenance."

Nor was Johnson, even while a practicing lexicographer, any more anxious to go to bed than in after years when he was a pensioner with nothing but a conscience to get him up again the next day. Hawkins remembered that once (in December, 1750), when a first novel by Mrs. Charlotte Lennox was about to appear, he insisted upon celebrating the event and, despite Hawkins's protest that he had never sat up a whole night in his life, herded a company, including the lady and her husband, into the Devil Tavern for a dinner at eight. "The night passed, as must be imagined, in pleasant conversation, and harmless mirth, intermingled at different periods with the refreshments of coffee and tea. About five, Johnson's face shone with meridian splendour, though his drink had been only lemonade; but the far greater part of us had deserted the colours of Bacchus, and were with difficulty rallied to partake of a second refreshment of coffee, which was scarcely ended when the day began to dawn. This phenomenon began to put us in mind of our reckoning; but the waiters were all so overcome with sleep, that it was two hours before we could get a bill, and it was not till near eight that the creaking of the street-door gave the signal for our departure."

On this great occasion Mrs. Johnson does not appear to have been present, though at least one lady—she who served as excuse for the festivities—is definitely mentioned. Mrs. Johnson was at the time past sixty and no doubt her age is sufficient to explain this particular absence. Moreover, the increasingly important disparity of age between Johnson and his wife must inevitably have tended to make his social life something more and more apart from hers. But this is not all. Though once she had been near enough his own age to marry him, there does not survive a single reference to her in any social gathering outside her own home, and the fact is odd even though it is true that references of any kind are not numerous. Speaking of her reputed character, Hawkins makes the casual remark: "As, during her lifetime, [Johnson] invited but few friends to his house, I never saw her," which certainly seems to take it for granted that she would not be seen anywhere else and thus raises a delicate question. Was Tetty, whom Garrick represents as overfond of the bottle, socially unpresentable for this or other reasons? Or did she, perhaps, simply not care for society? Did Johnson, who was so long a widower and whose tastes and habits became so eminently bachelorlike that it is always difficult to think of him as having ever been married, tend in certain respects himself to forget that he was—even during Tetty's lifetime? And does this have something to do with the self-reproach which colors certain of his meditations on Tetty's death? [10]

Of course, due allowance must be made for the fact that the eighteenth century was still predominantly a man's century, even though it was becoming less so both legally and socially; even though the battle cry "Rights of Women" was to be heard before the century was over and Samuel Foote could make the aging rake in one of his plays regret that he had been born too soon. "What vast improvements are daily made in our morals! What an unfortunate dog am I, to come into the world at least half a century too soon! What would I give to be born twenty years hence! There will be damned fine doings then! hey, Tom." In Johnson's time it was no more taken for granted than it is in Latin countries today that a man's home is necessarily open to all of even his intimate acquaintances. Women could, as a passage in Boswell's *Life* makes clear, come to the public rooms in a tavern but they were certainly not usually taken there, and it is difficult to escape the suspicion that one of the reasons why men gathered at taverns, coffeehouses, and the clubs which made taverns their headquarters was their desire to be secure from female intrusion. At least from the age of the Restoration on down through the Regency even the rakes seem to have spent more time in such masculine amusements as gambling and drinking than in what was the professed business of their lives, and this remained true whether their specialty was simply wenching, or the—as one would suppose—more time-consuming practice of seduction. Thus Vanbrugh can make his Lord Foppington, who has been describing how his days are spent, reply airily to the objection that he seems to have left inadequate time for a certain important activity: "Those who intrigue with Women of Quality, have rarely occasion far above half an Hour at a time: People of that Rank being under those Decorums they can seldom give you a langer View, than will just serve to shoot 'em flying. So that the Course of my other Pleasures is not much interrupted by my Amours." Even when a gentleman entertained guests at dinner in his own home, the ladies retired as soon as the wine appeared, in accordance with a tradition which foreign visitors found somewhat barbarous, though the Englishmen, as

CHARING CROSS
("The full tide of human existence")
From a painting by Samuel Scott

THE MALL
From a painting by Samuel Scott
(The Marshall Field Collection, Courtesy of M. Knoedler & Co.)

one of them remarked, showed as great a delight in being thus liberated as ever schoolboys did in the departure of a schoolmaster.

Yet despite everything tending to keep the sexes apart, it is abundantly evident from innumerable diaries and letters (ranging socially as well as chronologically all the way from Pepys's priceless record to that of Thomas Turner, a small shopkeeper, flourishing just about the time with which we are now concerned) that men and women did manage to see a good deal of one another in one way or another, including, for example, informal evenings at home as well as expeditions to the amusement parks scattered about the outskirts of the city. "The Pantheon," famous for its assemblies, did not open until 1772, and the first club for both men and women was founded in 1770 with Horace Walpole among the original members. But even in the forties and fifties mixed society was by no means unobtainable.

Johnson did not dance and he did not play cards—though he justified a well-known adage concerning the latter by regretting late in life that he had never learned any of the games. Thus he was cut off from two of the chief amusements which brought men and women together in the eighteenth century. Yet Johnson himself, in the course of a long life, knew many attractive women with whom he loved to banter, and by whom he allowed himself to be petted in one way or another. Granted, then, that Tetty was neither enough an intellectual nor enough a woman of fashion to claim the freedoms that the bluestocking or the great lady might enjoy; granted also that Johnson's domestic establishment was not one where formal dinner parties could be imagined—the verdict must still be that Tetty was less in evidence so far as his social life is concerned than she, or at least some other woman, might have been. Perhaps it is not too remarkable that she was not. Neither is it to be taken as too much merely what one would expect.

There is, however, no possible doubt that Johnson loved her or that, in one way, she meant much to him. When she died on March 17 (Old Style), 1752, her husband was in the midst of his compilation of the *Dictionary* and had recently concluded

The Rambler, but because he was then only beginning to be famous, she was so little known to anyone else that she is now hardly more than a comic legend remembered most vividly as she was burlesqued by a great actor. What her illness was, how long it lasted, and for how long a time before her death Johnson suspected that he must lose her, we do not know. We do know that more than thirty years later, when he was approaching his own last day and considering the advisability of "sleeping out of town" for his health, he told Fanny Burney a melancholy anecdote: "My wife, when she was near her end, poor woman, was also advised to sleep out of town; and when she was carried to the lodgings that had been prepared for her, she complained that the staircase was in very bad condition, for the plaster was beaten off the walls in many places. 'Oh,' said the man of the house, 'that's nothing but the knocks against it of the coffins of the poor souls that have died in lodgings!'" Boswell implies, nevertheless, that her end came in London.

When she died, Johnson dispatched, after midnight, a letter to his friend, the Rev. Dr. Taylor, who came to comfort him. She was buried at Bromley in Kent "to which he was probably led by the residence of his friend Hawkesworth at that place," and Johnson composed for her a funeral sermon which was never, however, delivered. From the surviving fragments of his *Prayers and Meditations,* we discover that he long made it a habit to remember the day of her death. Indeed, his prayers for her throw a curious light on the vexed question arising out of the conflict between his "stubborn rationality" and his tendency to accept as literal fact even some of those pious beliefs which many Christians of his own day were content to regard as mere mythology. As various passages show, he steadily maintained that neither the significance of dreams nor the reality of ghosts had been disproved and something more than a month after his wife's death he could pray: "O Lord! . . . if thou hast ordained the Souls of the Dead to minister to the Living, and appointed my departed Wife to have care of me, grant that I may enjoy the good effects of her attention and ministration, whether exercised by appearance, impulses, dreams or in any other manner agreeable to thy Government." [11]

More than two years later he wrote to Thomas Warton: "You know poor Mr. Dodsley has lost his wife; . . . I hope he will not suffer so much as I yet suffer for the loss of mine. . . . I have ever since seemed to myself broken off from mankind; a kind of solitary wanderer in the wild of life, without any direction, or fixed point of view: a gloomy gazer on a world to which I have little relation." More than twenty-five years after Tetty's death, when an old fellow collegian whom he had not seen for half a century remarked to him: "I have been twice married, Doctor. You, I suppose, have never known what it was to have a wife." "Sir," replied Johnson, "I have known what it was to have a wife, and (in a solemn, tender faltering tone) I have known what it was to *lose a wife.*—It had almost broke my heart." While he was still living in Gough Square he would study only in the garret room (probably that in which the assistants had worked on the *Dictionary*) and when asked the reason he explained: "Because in that room only I never saw Mrs. Johnson."

But the most impressive testimony to the depth of his grief is that furnished by his rare but solemn references to it long after the time when new activities and new friends might be supposed to have made it almost forgotten. Writing, at the age of seventy-one, a letter of condolence, he says: "He that outlives a wife whom he has long loved, sees himself disjoined from the only mind that has the same hopes, and fears, and interest; from the only companion with whom he has shared much good or evil; and with whom he could set his mind at liberty to retrace the past, or anticipate the future. The continuity of being is lacerated; the settled course of sentiment and action is stopped; and life stands suspended and motionless, till it is driven by external causes into a new channel. But the time of suspense is dreadful."

Johnson's own life was "driven by external causes into a new channel." He undoubtedly mentioned his wife far less often than he thought of her, partly because she had not been known to many of those who became his most intimate companions, partly because he was much disinclined to give anyone a glimpse into that abyss of melancholy, of near-madness, from which he tried to distract as far as possible his own glancc. Since college days at least he had known that the abyss was just beside whatever path he trod, whether it was something he had inherited from a melancholy father or, possibly, something generated by some forgotten experiences never examined in the light of day. At its bottom lay nameless apprehensions and fears, an obscure sense of guilt—all, indeed, of the grisly forms which recent psychopathologists have tried to distinguish and catalogue. Perhaps it is hardly necessary to suggest that his wife's death, quite aside from the extent to which it added to his depression, served also as a rational incident to which floating and otherwise inexplicable distresses attached themselves. He was self-reproachful and apprehensive while she still lived, but regrets and reproaches found in her memory a new justification. All this he concealed so well that Mrs. Thrale could say: "Time, and resignation to the will of God, cured every breach in his heart before I made acquaintance with him [i.e., early in 1765], though he always persisted in saying he never rightly recovered the loss of his wife." Yet Mrs. Thrale was so far from knowing the truth that five or six years after the time referred to, Johnson himself was noting in his private papers: "This is the day on which in —52, I was deprived of poor dear Tetty. . . . When I recollect the time in which we lived together, my grief for her departure is not abated, and I have less pleasure in any good that befalls me, because she does not partake it. . . . When I saw the sea at Brighthelmston, I wished for her to have seen it with me." Five years after that, he noted in a perfunctory diary of a visit to Paris his reaction to the Palais Bourbon: "As I entered, my wife was in my mind; she would have been pleased. Having now nobody to please, I am little pleased." [12]

Johnson, it will be remembered, did not begin on the second volume of the *Dictionary* until slightly more than a year after his wife had died, but only a few days before the blow fell (and doubtless in anticipation of it) he had discontinued the semiweekly essays signed *The Rambler,* which had appeared regularly up to and including this 208th number. Of *The Rambler* two oddly contrasting things may be said: Probably none of his other literary compositions did so much to establish his reputation in his own day; certainly, on the other hand, none is equally responsible for the extent to which many now assume that he is, as a prose writer, quite unreadable. According to Samuel Rogers, Johnson himself was so far from anticipating the judgment of posterity as to say to one of Rogers's acquaintances: "My other works are wine and water; but my *Rambler* is pure wine." On the other hand, it is also recorded that on a still later occasion, when he read over one of the essays, he shook his head and said: "Too wordy."

He had begun the papers on March 20, 1750, partly in the hope of adding to his income and partly as a relief from the mechanical labor involved in compiling the *Dictionary*. Except for a few contributions from outsiders, including Samuel Richardson, the whole series was not only written by Johnson but as usual often written rapidly. Despite a certain number of satiric or humorous papers, *The Rambler* was predominantly devoted to moralizing discourses of a rather somber sort and could be said to be an imitation of the *Tatler* and *Spectator* only in the very general sense that all the essay periodicals of the time might be said to be such. Each number was printed on three half-sheets and was priced at 2d. As the essays appeared one by one they certainly did not sell well—Arthur Murphy says fewer than five hundred each, and hence not enough to make the undertaking a financial success at that time, since the publisher (Cave) was paying the author four guineas a week. They were, however, soon collected, and according to Boswell: "Its author lived to see ten numerous editions of it in London, besides those of Ireland and Scotland." Boswell also ventures the opinion that "its sale has far exceeded that of any other periodical papers since the reign of Queen Anne." For the collected edition Johnson made revisions, which do not seem to have been extensive.[13]

Throughout the rest of his career, Johnson's admirers and detractors alike were more likely to rest their respective cases upon *The Rambler* than upon any one of his other works. As has already been pointed out, certain qualities of his manner as well as of his thoughts were manifest in his first piece of published prose; a modern reader is almost certain to prefer strongly the style of either the notes to Shakespeare or the *Lives of the Poets,* and it is by these works that he will be judged in this book. But to Boswell, on the one hand, or to the satirist, Archibald Campbell, on the other, *The Rambler* was the undefiled well of Johnsonianism. Nowhere else is he so completely what Boswell liked to call him: "the great moralist"; nowhere else does his manner of writing exhibit so constantly or in so extreme a form those rhetorical devices and those peculiarities of diction for which he was famous. And it is worth noting as a testimony to the extent of his fame that even the severest of his contemporary critics take it for granted that he is a phenomenon too impressive and too influential not to be reckoned with seriously.

Today quotations from *The Rambler* are relatively infrequent even in the writings of professed Johnsonians who, for obvious reasons, prefer to cite from either Boswell's record of Johnson's conversation or from one or the other later works. Yet a surprising number of his favorite themes, interests, opinions and prejudices appear in these essays for the first time. Here, for example, and choosing almost at random, one may find his love of London and his strong sense of the difference between personal liberty, which he loved, and political liberty, which he distrusted; his contempt for parental authority and his admiration for realistic writing of the sort that was just giving birth to the novel; his distrust of "the rules" in literature and his assumption that public favor is the final test of literary excellence. His later criticism of Milton is foreshadowed in a paper on *Samson Agonistes* and his criticism of the "metaphysical poets" already implicit in a paper on wit. Indeed, if nothing of him survived except *The Rambler* it would still be possible to form a pretty accurate idea of his opinions on moral, intellectual and artistic questions. Yet we do not commonly so form our idea partly because of the relatively unattractive style in which the opinions are presented, even more because Johnson seems not yet to have learned the art of distilling his own essence. The characteristic opinions are lost among the more numerous commonplaces. One does not feel, as one so constantly does in later writing, the flavor of a personality which gives special significance to even the eccentricities and the perversities. This means, among other things, that if Johnson were known only by *The Rambler* we should never think of him as a "character." But it means more than that. We should also not think of him as a man whose opinions, even when conventional or even reactionary, were defended with an arresting originality and force.

Johnson's own recorded pronouncements concerning prose style and its characteristic excellences are few and singularly unilluminating so far as the theory behind his own practice is concerned. He held to a rather extreme degree the characteristic neoclassical opinion that literature deals with the general rather than the particular, and that opinion, no doubt, tends to justify the abstractness of so much of *The Rambler*. But he has little to say concerning rhetoric or diction and, indeed, in a passage written later in *The Idler* he heaps scorn upon a kind of writing which some would describe as exactly his own and which is, at least, too frequently suggested by *The Rambler*. In *The Idler* he speaks of "the ponderous dictator of sentences," of "the stately son of demonstration, who proves with mathematical formality what no man has yet pretended to doubt," and of "a mode of style—by which the most evident truths are so obscured that they can no longer be perceived." If, as appears, he saw nothing of himself in all this, one is evidently justified in concluding that the manner in which he wrote was in some sense either natural to him or had become so habitual as to be at the very least a second nature. He did not, in other words, deliberately translate thoughts into a special language; he wrote rapidly, if elaborately, because he thought in the terms of his writing. To that extent the style was if not the whole man, then one of the man's aspects, and if sometimes the effect is less displeasing than we feel it ought to be, the explanation no doubt lies there. Johnson did not merely write abstractly; he thought abstractly. He did not deliberately elaborate parallels and antitheses; it was through them that his thought evolved.

Parodies of Johnson's style, either by his contemporaries or later, have seldom been successful because those of its individual features which are readily distinguishable are integrated in some fashion which all but defies imitation. It is easy to see that his diction is abstract, that it contains a large proportion of words of Latin origin, and that it admits numerous strange words, only a few of which he seems to have invented but many of which are rarely used. Almost equally obvious is the fact that he habitually employs parallel phrases embodying thoughts sometimes parallel and sometimes antithetical. But the same thing may be said of other writers who produce an effect quite different from his, and deliberately to employ them all does not necessarily produce an even recognizable parody. His contemporaries noted that his fondness for balance led him to use frequently not only what they called the triplet but even what one of them called "quaternions." Yet even the most envenomed of his satirists never succeed in demonstrating what they wished to demonstrate —namely, that "a man might write such stuff for ever, if he would *abandon* his mind to it."

Among the scores of outlandish words which modern scholars have collected from his works may be mentioned, by way of example: adscidulous, abscinded, indiscerptible, fugacity, alexipharnick, oraculous, internerate and oppugner. Moreover, phrases, sentences and even whole paragraphs which one readily calls typical may be found in almost any number of *The Rambler*. The very first essay opens thus: "The difficulty of the first address on any new occasion, is felt by every man in his transactions with the world, and confessed by the settled and regular forms of salutation which necessity has introduced into all languages. Judgment was wearied with the perplexity of being forced upon choice, where there was no motive to preference; and it was found convenient that some easy method of introduction should be established, which, if it wanted the allurement of novelty, might enjoy the security of prescription." The last sentence of the last number is: "I shall never envy the honours which wit and learning obtain in any other cause, if I can be numbered among the writers who have given ardour to virtue, and confidence to truth." In between there is hardly a paragraph which one would not at first sight guess to be his, and there are hundreds of which the following is a by no means extreme example:

"Equally dangerous and equally detestable are the cruelties

often exercised in private families, under the venerable sanction of parental authority; the power which we are taught to honour from the first moments of reason; which is guarded from insult and violation by all that can impress awe upon the mind of man; and which, therefore, may wanton in cruelty without control, and trample the bounds of right with innumerable transgressions, before duty and piety will dare to seek redress, or think themselves at liberty to recur to any other means of deliverance than supplications, by which insolence is elated, and tears, by which cruelty is gratified."

But the thing one recognizes is by no means as easily described by a formula as would at first sight seem to be the case, and the structure appears, upon close examination, to present far greater diversity than one would imagine. We may call any of these passages "typical" but we should be careful not to assume too readily that we know all that makes them so, and a recent careful study has shown just how elaborate and how penetrating an analysis can be made while still leaving the conviction that the whole secret has not been plumbed.

It is somewhat odd that Johnson, who was not only interested in the contemporary comedy of manners but also had the example of Addison before him and had recently, in the *Life of Savage,* demonstrated his own ability to deal interestingly with the contemporary scene, should, in *The Rambler,* have devoted so relatively little attention to the local and the concrete. The occasional papers in which he does just that are, sometimes, delightful and reveal that sense of the ridiculous which, as his conversation demonstrated, was one of his outstanding characteristics. Indeed, in such a passage as the following, which describes the life of Lady Bustle, a country gentlewoman, there is a richness and robustness hardly equaled anywhere in the thinly elegant writings of Addison and Steele:

"It is, indeed, the great business of her life, to watch the skillet on the fire, to see it simmer with the due degree of heat, and to snatch it off at the moment of projection; and the employments to which she has bred her daughters, are to turn roseleaves in the shade, to pick out the seeds of currants with a quill, to gather fruit without bruising it, and to extract bean-flower water for the skin.

"Lady Bustle has, indeed, by this incessant application to fruits and flowers, contracted her cares into a narrow space, and set herself free from many perplexities with which other minds are disturbed. She has no curiosity after the events of a war, or the fate of heroes in distress; she can hear, without the least emotion, the ravage of a fire, or devastations of a storm; her neighbours grow rich or poor, come into the world or go out of it, without regard, while she is pressing the jelly-bag, or airing the store-room; but I cannot perceive that she is more free from disquiets than those whose understandings take a wider range. Her marigolds, when they are almost cured, are often scattered by the wind, and the rain sometimes falls upon fruit, when it ought to be gathered dry. While her artificial wines are fermenting, her whole life is restlessness and anxiety. Her sweetmeats are not always bright, and the maid sometimes forgets the just proportions of salt and pepper, when venison is to be baked. Her conserves mould, her wines sour, and pickles mother; and, like all the rest of mankind, she is every day mortified with the defeat of her schemes, and the disappointment of her hopes.

"With regard to vice and virtue she seems a kind of neutral being. She has no crime but luxury, nor any virtue but chastity; she has no desire to be praised but for her cookery; nor wishes any ill to the rest of mankind, but that whenever they aspire to a feast, their custards may be wheyish, and their pie-crusts tough."

But Johnson's more usual themes are suggested by such titles as "Life sufficient for all purposes if well employed"; "The narrowness of fame"; "Idleness an anxious and miserable state." Typical beginnings are: "That wonder is the effect of ignorance has been often observed"; "It is common, says Bacon, to desire the end without enduring the means"; "No complaint has been more frequently repeated in all ages than that of the neglect of merit associated with poverty, and the difficulty with which valuable or pleasing qualities force themselves into view, when they are obscured by indigence."

Boswell has, to be sure, brought himself to praise certain of the lighter pieces, but it is to the more stately ones that he gives preference as Johnson himself evidently did. The latter deal more often with sins than with follies and are more concerned with the abstract analysis of virtue and vice than with specific illustrations of either. In none of Johnson's other major prose works, except *Rasselas,* does he permit so constantly to prevail that somberness of mood into which he was likely to fall whenever he was not distracted by either society or literature. "The natural flights of the human mind are not from pleasure to pleasure, but from hope to hope," he observes in the second number, and in the thirty-second he writes one of the few sentences in the whole series now often quoted: "The cure for the greatest part of human miseries is not radical, but palliative." Even in the comic passage cited above, one of his favorite themes —the fact that no human being can hope to find a way of life freed from anxiety—gives the passage a certain gloomy undertone, and perhaps the finest piece of writing in the whole series is an expanse of somber rhetoric, which Boswell quotes:

"Thus every period of life is obliged to borrow its happiness from the time to come. In youth we have nothing past to entertain us, and in age, we derive little from retrospect but hopeless sorrow. Yet the future likewise has its limits, which the imagination dreads to approach, but which we see to be not far distant. The loss of our friends and companions impresses hourly upon us the necessity of our own departure; we know that the schemes of man are quickly at an end, that we must soon lie down in the grave with the forgotten multitudes of former ages, and yield our place to others, who, like us, shall be driven a while by hope or fear about the surface of the earth, and then like us be lost in the shades of death. . . .

"It is not therefore from this world, that any ray of comfort can proceed, to cheer the gloom of the last hour. But futurity has still its prospects; there is yet happiness in reserve, which, if we transfer our attention to it, will support us in the pains of disease, and the languor of decay. This happiness we may expect with confidence, because it is out of the power of chance, and may be attained by all that sincerely desire and earnestly pursue it. On this therefore every mind ought finally to rest. Hope is the chief blessing of man, and that hope only is rational, of which we are certain that it cannot deceive us."

In this passage the style, though unmistakably Johnson's, can hardly be charged with any of the major faults all too frequently exhibited in *The Rambler,* and the thoughts, though certainly not unfamiliar ones, seem to come home to the author as the familiar thoughts in other papers often do not—perhaps because the essay, one of the last, was probably written when the imminent death of Tetty was staring him in the face. One of the probable sources of Johnson's manner also is suggested. The passage is, if one likes, pure Johnson. But one also catches in it an echo of Sir Thomas Browne as well as an echo of all the great seventeenth-century preachers from Donne onwards.[14]

Between the conclusion of *The Rambler* and the publication of the *Dictionary,* Johnson appears to have devoted himself chiefly to his work as lexicographer. He did, however, supply his friend, Mrs. Lennox, with a dedication to her *Shakespeare Illustrated* and published in *The Gentleman's Magazine* a brief biographical sketch of its founder, Edward Cave, who had just died, leaving an estate valued at more than eight thousand pounds. He also made one of a small group which contributed more or less regularly to an essay periodical called *The Adventurer,* with which his dear friend Dr. Bathurst also was associated. The individual papers were signed only with initials or pseudonyms and Boswell evidently had some difficulty in making up his mind which were Johnson's. His final decision has been called in question and good reason given for believing that some, which Boswell rejected, are actually by Johnson.[15]

About four months before the *Dictionary* was actually published, Johnson sent to Lord Chesterfield the famous letter of which too much has no doubt been made, but which is, nevertheless, the climax of a story picturesque enough to be always remembered. It reads:

To the Right Honourable the Earl of Chesterfield.

My Lord,

I have been lately informed, by the proprietor of the World, that two papers, in which my Dictionary is recommended to the publick, were written by your Lordship. To be so distinguished, is an honour, which, being very little accustomed to favours from the great, I know not well how to receive, or in what terms to acknowledge.

When, upon some slight encouragement, I first visited your Lordship, I was overpowered, like the rest of mankind, by the enchantment of your address, and could not forbear to wish that I might boast myself *Le vainqueur du vainqueur de la terre;*—that I might obtain that regard for which I saw the world contending; but I found my attendance so little encouraged, that neither pride nor modesty would suffer me to continue it. When I had once addressed your Lordship in publick, I had exhausted all the art of pleasing which a retired and uncourtly scholar can possess. I had done all that I could; and no man is well pleased to have his all neglected, be it ever so little.

Seven years, my Lord, have now past, since I waited in your outward rooms, or was repulsed from your door; during which time I have been pushing on my work through difficulties, of which it is useless to complain, and have brought it, at last, to the verge of publication, without one act of assistance, one word of encouragement, or one smile of favour. Such treatment I did not expect, for I never had a Patron before.

The shepherd in Virgil grew at last acquainted with Love, and found him a native of the rocks.

Is not a Patron, my Lord, one who looks with unconcern on a man struggling for life in the water, and, when he has reached ground, encumbers him with help? The notice which you have been pleased to take of my labours, had it been early, had been kind; but it has been delayed till I am indifferent, and cannot enjoy it; till I am solitary, and cannot impart it; till I am known, and do not want it. I hope it is no very cynical asperity, not to confess obligations where no benefit has been received, or to be unwilling that the Publick should consider me as owing that to a Patron, which Providence has enabled me to do for myself.

Having carried on my work thus far with so little obligation to any favourer of learning, I shall not be disappointed though I should conclude it, if less be possible, with less; for I have been long wakened from that dream of hope, in which I once boasted myself with so much exultation,

My Lord,

Your Lordship's most humble

Most obedient servant,

SAM JOHNSON.

One of the glories of the eighteenth century is certainly that its wars were relatively bloodless and that its great men, though they may have acquiesced in a harsh social and economic system, seldom exhibited the ferocity characteristic of many ages—including those most inclined to boast of their civilization. Seventy-five years before, a great nobleman who had been first defied and then given a moral lecture by a low-born hack would probably have hired a gang of thugs to give the upstart a beating, as the Earl of Rochester did when he thought Dryden had insulted him in print. But Chesterfield, taking no revenge, admired the skill of his opponent; Johnson, far from overpublicizing his victory, was so chary of exploiting it that the text of the letter was all but lost, and when Lord Hardwicke once asked to hear it repeated, Johnson replied with a smile in which, it now seems, arrogance and magnanimity must have been mixed in proportions not easy to determine: "No, Sir; I have hurt the dog too much already." He was certainly not a humble man and when he defied "one of His Majesty's principal Secretaries of State" he was not demonstrating his courage so much as a proud confidence in his own powers. Nor was the battle a David and Goliath affair. It was a battle for prestige between two different sorts of giant—even though one of them was mostly stilts—and the whole story is too good not to be told from the beginning, especially since Boswell is a trifle disingenuous.

Johnson had, it will be remembered, dedicated the *Plan* to Chesterfield. More than thirty years later he said to Boswell: "Sir, the way in which the Plan of my Dictionary came to be inscribed to Lord Chesterfield was this: I had neglected to write it by the time appointed. Dodsley suggested a desire to have it addressed to Lord Chesterfield. I laid hold of this as a pretext for delay, that it might be better done, and let Dodsley have his desire. I said to my friend, Dr. Bathurst, 'Now if any good comes of my addressing to Lord Chesterfield, it will be ascribed to deep policy, when, in fact, it was only a casual excuse for laziness.' "

Johnson was a man who did not deliberately misrepresent facts, no matter how freely he sometimes defended opinions he did not really hold. Moreover, the reference to his delay in getting a necessary task completed is a detail that contributes verisimilitude. But the explanation can hardly be the whole truth. In the first place, it appears that the *Plan* had been discussed with and approved by Chesterfield before the dedication was offered. In the second place, Johnson himself had spoken of his prospective patron in terms very different from those he was later to use. No doubt he felt that the writer of a dedication, like the writer of an epitaph, is not "on oath." Even so, the high compliments which he pays Chesterfield would be hardly excusable if he had an active contempt for the man to whom they are addressed, and there is other evidence that he did not. Though Boswell does not allude to the fact when telling the story, he records, several hundred pages later, that Johnson, apparently speaking of the first interview, remarked: "His manner was exquisitely elegant, and he had more knowledge than I expected." Moreover, he did, by his own confession, accept ten pounds from Chesterfield and he makes it clear in the famous letter itself that he waited in vain in the nobleman's anteroom —though how often or how long is left rather conspicuously vague.

Despising patrons, he nevertheless cultivated one just enough to prove to himself that he had been outrageously neglected. Doubtless not as unreasonable as his friend Savage had been, he was certainly not a man upon whom favors could be conferred with impunity, nor is any desire to exculpate Chesterfield necessary in order to inspire the observation that Johnson, who respected booksellers but despised pretentious elegance, would probably have quarreled with any mere figurehead who thought his position entitled him to dole out benefits to genius. Moreover, Chesterfield was a peculiarly unfortunate choice. It was not merely—perhaps, indeed, not even importantly—that Chesterfield was a chronic dedicatee and hence a symbol of the old dependence of the writer upon a personage rather than upon a public. Neither was it merely that he was a cynical unbeliever and, in Johnson's later view, an apologist for elegant vice—for Johnson numbered among his own friends men whose private lives would certainly have scandalized Chesterfield himself. In addition, the formal opinions of the two men coincided almost as often as they clashed. The important thing is that their temperaments were more antithetical than their philosophies of life. The one was a strict moralist who, nevertheless, despised forms and lived his life with enormous gusto. The other was a professed worldling who, nevertheless, seemed to impose upon himself a discipline as strict in its own way as that of a religious order and led, for all the carefully calculated indulgences which he seems to have regarded as permissible, what must have been a joyless life. Gusto he completely lacked, his worldly wisdom was expressed in a singularly pedantic manner, and if he had a certain amount of wit he obviously had no humor whatsoever. The man in the bushy uncombed wig and the soiled shirt, who came happy from a tavern conversation, must have hated at sight the formal epicurean who could later write to his son that a wise man would be careful to dress as well as possible while, of course, despising clothes.

No doubt Chesterfield culpably neglected the struggling scholar from whom he had accepted a dedication, and the ten pounds which he tossed out was, as Johnson called it, "an inconsiderable sum"—though it happens to be almost precisely what Johnson had received for *London,* the only considerable literary work for which he was at the time well known. One need not take too seriously Chesterfield's alleged protest to Dodsley that "he would have turned off the best servant he ever had, if he had known that he denied him to a man who would have been always more than welcome." Johnson was certainly not at the time an important personage and would not have been, in accordance with the principles implied in that "great scheme of subordination" which Chesterfield cherished hardly more than Johnson, entitled to more than occasional condescension. Between a great (and busy) noble patron and a young man on the lookout for a cause of offense some such cause was certain to be found.

We do not know just how great Johnson's provocation was, but it is not difficult to date approximately the time when he decided that the pleasures of independence were worth more than the meager benefits of a noble protector. When *The Vanity of Human Wishes* was published in 1749, it did not, like the editions after 1755, list "the patron" among the hardships which the man of letters was compelled to endure. On the other hand, the ninety-first number of *The Rambler,* which was published on January 29, 1751, or almost exactly two years after the first edition of the poem, is an allegorical account of the progress of literature and concludes with this sentence: "The sciences, after a thousand indignities, retired from the palace of patronage, and having long wandered over the world in grief and distress, were led at last to the cottage of independence, the daughter of fortitude; where they were taught by prudence and parsimony to support themselves in dignity and quiet." He returned to disparage the patron again in a later number, and of course it is in the *Dictionary* itself that a patron is defined as "commonly a wretch who supports with insolence, and is paid with flattery." One may therefore at least amuse oneself with the inference that it was sometime between January, 1749, and January, 1751, that Johnson not only decided to get along without Chesterfield but found the disgust produced by his own personal experience crystallized into the general conviction that the age of patronage had passed.

The oft-repeated assertion that Johnson's letter gave literary patronage its deathblow belongs, of course, with the similar assertion about Cervantes and chivalry. The most that can truthfully be said is that it gave evidence of the fact that the system *was* dead, or dying, for the letter could never have been written if the literate public had not been by now prepared to support those whom it chose to admire. But the proud scholar who had defied the great lord was the talk of the town, and the letter itself is undoubtedly a magnificent piece of rhetoric—though on the whole somewhat less impressive when we know all the circumstances than it would be if they had been more nearly what the imagination almost insists upon assuming that they were. Johnson was not, as has already been remarked, quite a David sallying forth to slay a giant with his slingshot, though it is certainly in just that character that the letter is written, and he seems indeed to have been, at this moment, more in a mood to dramatize himself than he ever was either before or afterward. Thus he concluded the Preface to the *Dictionary* itself with two sentences more famous and more rhetorically effective than seem justified by the circumstances: "I may surely be contented without the praise of perfection, which, if I could obtain, in this gloom of solitude, what would it avail me? I have protracted my work till most of those, whom I wished to please, have sunk into the grave, and success and miscarriage are empty sounds: I, therefore, dismiss it with frigid tranquillity, having little to fear or hope from censure or from praise." It was doubtless the melancholy inspired by the loss of his wife which gave the tone to the passage, but it is not known what other companions, if any, had sunk into the grave. He certainly had already a numerous acquaintance and "success or miscarriage" certainly did not long remain "empty sounds." He had (though, of course, he could not know this) nearly thirty years more to live and a great deal "to fear or hope from censure or from praise." It was in very considerable measure because of the praise he got that the years remaining were probably the happiest of his life.

Chesterfield himself may well have felt that he also was to some extent an injured party. The two essays in *The World,* which Johnson so scornfully dismisses, appear to have been well meant and their author could have argued with some show of justification that, however inadequate Johnson might consider them as amends for any past neglect, it was hardly reasonable to assume that they were intended as anything else or that Chesterfield, an aging man already in possession of all the worldly honors he could well want, was meanly intriguing to get some reflected glory from the publication of a dictionary. In the first of the two essays, Chesterfield demonstrated that he understood the idea behind the work when he wrote: "The time for discrimination seems to be now come. Toleration, adoption, and naturalization have run their lengths. Good order and authority are now necessary. But where shall we find them, and, at the same time, the obedience due to them? We must have recourse to the old Roman expedient in times of confusion, and choose a dictator. Upon this principle, I give my vote for Mr. Johnson to fill that great and arduous post." The second essay, lighter in tone, was less fortunate and its rather dreary pleasantry about a young woman who misses an assignation because of her imperfect understanding of her native tongue was doubtless offensive to Johnson, who had certainly not spent arduous years in the hope of facilitating illicit amours. But Chesterfield was probably merely lapsing into something less than Chesterfieldian tact rather than practicing what Boswell (and apparently Johnson) insisted upon regarding as an artifice intended to gain himself credit which he did not deserve.

As for "the town," it appears to have taken Johnson's side, as "the town" usually does take the underdog's side—as soon as it becomes evident that he is coming out on top. Chesterfield seems to have made the best he could of a rather awkward situation. Instead of trying to hide what an attempt to suppress would certainly have caused to circulate more widely, he is said to have left the letter lying on his table where everyone might see it, and if he really did (as Dodsley told Dr. Adams) go so far as to call the severest passages to Dodsley's attention with the remark "this man has great powers," then he was practicing a shrewdness of policy worthy of his own reputation. Perhaps Johnson himself best summed the whole thing up in his contribution to the dialogue which took place when Dr. Adams, suggested that Chesterfield's excuses should be accepted since he was generally affable and easy of access, especially to men of letters. "Sir, (said Johnson) that is not Lord Chesterfield; he is the proudest man this day existing. No, (said Dr. Adams) there is one person, at least, as proud; I think, by your own account, you are the prouder man of the two. But mine, (replied Johnson, instantly) was *defensive* pride." Perhaps, on the other hand, it is not either Johnson or Chesterfield who comes best out of the incident; perhaps it is rather the century of which each has been taken as representative, a century which could see the importance of a battle of wits involving two of the strongest forces in the world—pride of place versus pride of ability—and could appreciate the fact that the battle was fought to a finish with no weapons other than those which intellect alone could furnish. Our own more brutal century may well admire and no less well feel some envy.[16]

The first edition of the *Dictionary* appeared in April, 1755, in two large folio volumes. It contained something more than forty-one thousand words; the printing account came to £1,239 11s. 6d.; and the work sold for the considerable price of £4 10s. Few equally laborious works have ever been completed by one man with so little help of any kind except of a purely clerical sort. Johnson's own boast in the Preface—that "the English Dictionary was written with little assistance of the learned, and without any patronage of the great; not in the soft obscurities of retirement, or under the shelter of academic bowers, but amidst inconvenience and distraction, in sickness and sorrow"—is as accurate in the first particular as in all the rest. To Boswell he remarked that "the only aid which he received was a paper containing twenty etymologies, sent to him by a person then unknown, who he was afterwards informed was Dr. Pearce, Bishop of Rochester."

Some three weeks after publication Johnson wrote to Bennet Langton that his Book, as he called it, "has, you see, no patrons and, I think, has yet no opponents, except the critics of the coffee-house, whose outcries are soon dispersed into the air, and are thought on no more." Some critics it was to have, but it sold well and there seems never to have been any doubt as to its success. Two thousand copies of the first edition were printed and attention has quite recently been called to the fact that, though these were not immediately sold out, the publishers almost at once put out proposals for a reprinting to be issued in 165 weekly numbers at sixpence per number. Apparently this extraordinary method of dictionary publishing (which would mean that subscribers would be accumulating their copy of the work over a period of more than three years) was adopted in order to meet the competition of the proprietors of *Bailey* who had recently adopted it for an edition of their cheaper work. In 1756 Johnson produced a one-volume abridgment of his own *Dictionary* and still later he revised the whole for the fourth (1773) edition of the unabridged version.

From what has just been said it is evident that his humbler rival Bailey was by no means superseded, but Johnson's name attached to the various latter editions and revisions of his original work identified the *Dictionary* as *the* dictionary until well into the nineteenth century. It was, for example, the inevitable gift to Becky Sharp when she went forth to her career. Years later Johnson was, despite his other achievements, still sometimes known as "Dictionary Johnson" to his admirers, just as "Lexiphanes" had by then become his accepted designation among the satirists. The French Academy acknowledged his labors by presenting him with a copy of its own work and, more important perhaps than anything else, the University of Oxford (having been properly prodded) conferred upon him, shortly before the *Dictionary* appeared, that degree of Master of Arts which Dublin had refused him not many years before. To posterity he has always seemed *Dr.* Johnson from the cradle, but Doctor he did not become (even of Dublin) until 1765, and of Oxford not until 1775. Now, however, he had received at least some recognition from an institution which he admired just a little less than he admired the Church itself, and for the first time he could appear as some sort of personage.[17]

Before a year had passed, the *Dictionary* was reviewed by Adam Smith in the first (and short-lived) *Edinburgh Review*. Smith credited the work with great merit but criticized its lack of philosophical understanding, so far as grammar was concerned. In general, however, the criticisms most commonly made were those still repeated today and these are in turn, for the most part, those to which Boswell gave currency. The *Dictionary's* greatest merit lies, of course, simply in the fact that nothing intended to serve the same purpose in English existed before. Its strongest individual parts are the illustrative quotations and, next, the definitions. Its greatest weakness, as Boswell admits, was the etymologies, though neither Boswell nor any but a very few men of the time could even begin to imagine just how bad, by modern standards, they are. Most of them Johnson professedly took from "authorities" who relied heavily on guesswork, and when he guessed himself the results are sometimes even more fantastic: "May not spider be spydor—the insect that watches the dor (or bumblebee)?" Johnson's own contemporaries did, however, grumble at the inclusion of such Johnsonian words as "versible," "advesperate," "adjugate," "agriculation" and "abstrude," which a modern scholar has pointed out in the *Dictionary*, and it is Boswell himself who is responsible for the fact that the standard example of Johnson's occasional tendency to make his definition harder than the word defined is the definition of network as "anything reticulated or decussated, at equal distances, with interstices between the intersections." It is Boswell also who has made the occasional whimsical definitions so well known that many seem to think of the *Dictionary* as essentially a comic work, and it is from him that so many have taken the familiar illustrations: "Pension. An allowance made to anyone without an equivalent. In England it is generally understood to mean pay given to a state hireling for treason to his country"; "Oats. A grain, which in England is generally given to horses, but in Scotland supports the people."

Most of the defects are such as would be inevitable in such a work undertaken by one man and in an age when aids were few; the rest arise out of Johnson's own nature, for he was a man with too much personality to be able to keep even lexicography completely impersonal. That he knew the nature of his own sportive divagations is evident enough from his remark when he was telling Boswell how, in defining "renegado," he had added: "Sometimes we say a Gower." "Thus," he added, "it went to the press; but the printer had more wit than I, and struck it out." In such a mood Johnson would probably have appreciated the reply, attributed to Lord Elibank, when the definition of "oats" was first pointed out to him: "Very true, and where will you find such *men* and such *horses?*" The whimsical definitions—even those of "pension" and "pensioner"—were allowed to stand in the fourth edition. They are after all few but since they have for long been so famous it is perhaps worth while to remind the reader both that a man might use the *Dictionary* for a lifetime without ever happening to come across one of them and that, in general, Johnson's definitions are extremely fine.

Many good stories center about the *Dictionary* and have long survived it to demonstrate that though works of erudition are supplanted by others which build upon them, wit, like other expressions of the creative impulses, cannot be superseded. Had Johnson not been for a period of years a harmless drudge, we should not have that perfect example of disarming candor he furnished when a lady asked him why he defined "pastern" as "the knee of a horse." "Ignorance, Madam, pure ignorance." We should also lack the equally perfect example of the retort courteous-discourteous made to the two other ladies who expressed their satisfaction that naughty words had been omitted: "What, my dears! then you have been looking for them." Nor, had he not been a lexicographer, would he have demonstrated the art (supposedly feminine) of drawing blood with what looks like a kind word as he did when a gentleman once told him that a friend of his had looked in vain for the word "ocean." "Sir, I doubt the veracity of your information!" He instantly stalked into his library; and, opening the work in question with the utmost impatience, at last triumphantly put his finger upon the subject of research, adding, "There, Sir; there is *ocean.*" And when the gentleman was preparing to apologize for the mistake, added (in a manner which Croker, source of the anecdote, rather oddly calls "good-natured"): "Never mind it, Sir; perhaps your friend spells *ocean* with an *s.*"

But perhaps nothing will serve better to close the subject than the little interchange between Johnson and the messenger who carried the last sheets of the great work to Andrew Millar, one of the proprietors and the man whom Johnson, thinking no doubt of the "death of patronage," once called "the Maecenas of the age." " 'Well, what did he say?'—'Sir,' (answered the messenger) he said, 'thank God I have done with him.' 'I am glad (replied Johnson, with a smile,) that he thanks God for any thing.' " [18]

CHAPTER V

The Bread and Tea of Life

During his early years in London, Johnson never had any fixed habitation for long, and he once consented to give Boswell a list of eleven addresses which he had used before the end of 1749. When, however, his contract for the *Dictionary* had given him some sense of security, he moved, as has already been mentioned, to the house in Gough Square, Fleet Street, where he was to remain for ten years. Here the *Dictionary* itself and *The Rambler* were composed; here his wife died; and here was found the garret to which he preferred to retire because it was the only room in which he had never seen Tetty. It was here also that he began to collect his strange household about him, and that we first see him receiving visitors.

Of his manner of life during this period Miss Reynolds, Sir Joshua's sister, gives a sufficiently lurid if syntactically imperfect account. "Before he had the Pension," she writes, "he literally dressed like a Beggar; and from what I have been told, literally lived as such; at least respecting common conveniences in his apartments, wanting even a chair to sit on, particularly in his study, where a gentleman who frequently visited him whilst writing his *Idlers* always found him at his Desk, sitting on one with three legs; and on rising from it, he remark'd that Mr. Johnson never forgot its defect, but would either hold it in his hand or place it with great composure against some support, taking no notice of its imperfection to his visitor. How he sat, whether on the window-seat, on a chair, or a pile of Folios, or how he sat, I do not remember to have heard. It was remarkable in Dr. Johnson that no external circumstances ever prompted him to make any apology, or to seem even sensible of their existence. Whether this was the effect of Philosophic pride, or of some partial notion respecting high breeding is doubtful."

Boswell himself is evidence for the fact that even in more prosperous days Johnson lived shabbily enough. Nevertheless, Miss Reynolds's description probably applies in full only to Johnson's own garret rather than to the house as a whole, and the elementary deficiencies of the furnishing were the result of his careless habits rather than of any desperate poverty. The house itself, which Carlyle was later to seek out and which has more recently served the Johnson Club for its quarterly suppers, was a typical example of the modest residence of the time. There is a basement kitchen with two open fireplaces, a parlor and dining room on the first floor, bedrooms on the second, and, finally, the garret which Johnson used as a study. He had certainly never been lodged so well before, and when he quitted Gough Square, it was to seek a cheaper place to live.[1]

To the Gough Square period belongs the first known portrait of Johnson—that painted by Reynolds in 1756, or when Johnson was forty-seven years old and had, just one year before, published the *Dictionary*. It is now in the National Portrait Gallery and shows him seated at a table with a pen in one hand. The face and figure are heavy—almost fat; the clothes are in some slight disarray and the expression, though more youthful than in any of the other pictures, is at once indolent and combative. There is little suggestion of the beggarly appearance to which Miss Reynolds refers; still less does the whole suggest the slovenly monster described by those who refer to his appearance a decade or more later. But probably the picture is, if not exactly idealized, at least kindly—even though Reynolds could probably at the time only guess something that he was later to learn, namely, that Johnson, who might not be disturbed by a missing chair leg, certainly did not like to have his personal defects too uncompromisingly set down for posterity. It was, at any rate, probably a few years before the picture was painted that the eager young man named Bennet Langton came to seek him out, and of his surprise Boswell gives the following account:

"Mr. Langton was exceedingly surprised when the sage first appeared. He had not received the smallest intimation of his figure, dress, or manner. From perusing his writings, he fancied he should see a decent, well-drest, in short, a remarkably decorous philosopher. Instead of which, down from his bed-chamber, about noon, came, as newly risen, a huge, uncouth figure, with a little dark wig which scarcely covered his head, and his clothes hanging loose about him. But his conversation was so rich, so animated, and so forcible, and his religious and political notions so congenial with those in which Langton had been educated, that he conceived for him that veneration and attachment which he ever preserved."

Whatever his appearance at this or any other period, it did not prevent the list of his friends from growing so long as to discourage even Boswell from any attempt to describe them all. At first sight strangers might take him for an idiot, as Hogarth quite literally did when, about 1753, he observed Johnson in the house of Samuel Richardson, "standing at a window in the room, shaking his head, and rolling himself about in a strange ridiculous manner." But once Johnson had begun to talk, most people quickly revised their opinion as Hogarth did his, for he was so struck with amazement that he "looked at him with astonishment, and actually imagined that this ideot had been at the moment inspired." [2]

Even before his wife's death, it will be remembered, Johnson had formed the Ivy Lane Club in order to assure for himself at stated intervals one dependable source of the sociability he could not get along without. Yet even at that time the list of his friends was evidently not only long but curiously varied, since the catalogue (supplied to Boswell by the servant, Francis Barber) of those who visited him just after Tetty's death does not end with his "dear Bathurst" and such expected names as those of Cave and Dodsley. It includes also the two bluestockings, Mrs. Carter and Mrs. Macaulay; the Earl of Orrery and Lord Southwell; and it also includes, at the opposite end of the social scale, "Mr. Ryland, merchant on Tower-Hill" and "Mrs. Gardiner, wife of a tallow-chandler on Snow-hill, not in the learned way, but a worthy, good woman." Just about this time, moreover, the first firm establishment of his fame began to make Johnson a man sought out as well as a man seeking companionship. At almost the same moment, the death of his wife freed him from any domestic responsibilities and made distraction even more necessary. Much as he had "run about the world" before, he now entered upon his career as companion and talker, and began to be more and more known in a great world whose fringes only he had previously touched.

Garrick, now reaching the heights, he had of course always known, though there had been a period when they had seen little of one another; Sir Joshua Reynolds he seems to have met some time after the latter's return from Italy in 1752, and they soon became intimate. About the same time the young and wellborn "Bennet Langton, Esq. of Langton, in Lincolnshire," then still in his 'teens, sought him out after reading *The Rambler* and later introduced his friend, Topham Beauclerk, whose dissipations, despite a love for literature, not only made him a strange companion for the rather serious Langton but *a fortiori* for Johnson who was, nevertheless, presently to add in the person of Boswell another young rake to his list of acquaintances. "In a short time, the moral, pious Johnson and the gay, dissipated Beauclerk, were companions." Garrick, when he first heard of the friendship, exclaimed: "What a coalition! I shall have my old friend to bail out of the Round house." But both Beauclerk and Langton long remained intimate friends; they play an important part in Boswell's *Life* and both, some ten years after Johnson's first meeting with the latter, became charter members of The Club.

It was to Beauclerk that Johnson said: "Thy body is all vice, and thy mind all virtue"; but his interest was so little exclusively in the mind that it was with Langton and Beauclerk that he went on the famous "frisk" in the early dawn after the two gay dogs, rousing him at three A.M., brought him to the door "in his shirt, with his little black wig on the top of his head, instead of a nightcap, and a poker in his hand." Beauclerk's satiric tongue once led Johnson to say to him: "You never open your mouth but with intention to give pain; and you have often given me pain, not from the power of what you said, but from seeing your intention." Yet Johnson permitted him a freedom that he was quick to resent in others.

There is abundant testimony to Beauclerk's attractive qualities, though not everyone showed Johnson's enthusiasm. Of him Lord Charlemont said: "Devoted at one time to pleasure, at another to literature, sometimes absorbed in play, sometimes in books, he was, altogether, one of the most accomplished, and, when in good humour, and surrounded by those who suited his fancy, one of the most agreeable men that could possibly exist." Even the perverse and grudging Hawkins permitted himself to say in a burst of wholly unaccustomed generosity that over all Beauclerk's behavior "there beamed such a sunshine of cheerfulness and good humour, as communicated itself to all around him." Mrs. Thrale allows herself to grant that "Topham Beauclerk (wicked and profligate as he wished to be accounted) was yet a man of very strict veracity." And then she adds, without pause or explanation: "Oh Lord! how I did hate that horrid Beauclerc!"

"Beauclerk," says Boswell, "was too polite, and valued learning and wit too much, to offend Johnson by sallies of infidelity or licentiousness," adding as a mealy-mouthed explanation of the strange friendship that "Johnson delighted in the good qualities of Beauclerk, and hoped to correct the evil." But Boswell is probably nearer one small part of the truth when he remarks that Johnson was not unaffected by the legitimate claims of Langton and Beauclerk alike to ancient lineage and that, in the case of the latter, his wholly romantic Jacobitism was certainly titillated by the fact that Beauclerk, as fifth son of the only son of the first Duke of St. Albans, was therefore a great-grandson of Charles II and Nell Gwyn.

But the most inclusive explanation is simply that Johnson liked youth and gaiety even more than most men do—partly because he himself had never been young and seldom been gay without arrière-pensée. He liked to experience vicariously what he could never experience directly, and by winning the love of gay young people he liked to assure himself that he was not quite so much of a monster—a learned, wise and virtuous monster, but a monster, nevertheless—as many of his other friends liked to assume. Cumbersome, melancholy and moral though he might be, he liked to think that there was something of the gay dog in him also. He was obviously complacent when his "frisk" was talked of in company, and when he recalled that Garrick had said to him: "I heard of your frolic t'other night. You'll be in the Chronicle," he remarked exultantly: *"He* durst not do such a thing. His *wife* wouldn't *let* him!" [3]

Johnson certainly did not want to be a rake; almost as certainly he would have resisted any temptation to break the continence which he regarded as one of the elementary obligations of a Christian. But, like most men virtuous in this respect, he did not like to assume that his abstinence was other than voluntary. Though Boswell never remarks on this fact, it is evident that he sensed it, for on more than one occasion he made some remark or engineered some situation which would emphasize the Great Moralist's unfitness for an amorous role and then, with that scientific cruelty characteristic of him, noted his victim's reaction to the unwelcome implications. He was, for example, once too pointedly amused at the Doctor's unguarded reference to certain arrangements he would insist upon if he kept a harem, and was punished by a sally which he edited out of his manuscript of the *Journal of a Tour to the Hebrides* and which remained unknown until the original was recently published—a sally in which Johnson indicated what office he would assign to Boswell in this same harem after the latter had been "properly prepared." Later, in the same tour, Boswell, having learned that something interesting might be expected when a banderilla was skillfully placed in the tender spot he had discovered, persuaded a Highland girl to sit on Johnson's lap and to give him a kiss. Boswell prepared to enjoy the spectacle but this time his victim found a better way out. He returned the kiss with the happy exclamation: "Do it again and let us see who will tire first."

Johnson's rigid principles prevented him from ever defending the more obvious vices of his gayer friends. It was of Beauclerk's wife, the famous Lady Diana, that he made the brutal remark: "The woman's a whore, and there's an end on't," when Boswell had attempted to defend her unfaithfulness to a former husband by alleging that husband's bad behavior. But the coarseness of the expression and the cruelty of the judgment were both probably more because of than despite the fact that Johnson was well aware who was being discussed and knew that Boswell might relay the remark to Beauclerk himself. And though he never defended vices as such, even when they happened to be those of his dearest friends, he certainly did forgive or overlook them, possibly because not to do so would have deprived him of friends and thus of one of the greatest consolations of his life; also, perhaps, out of respect for the Christian injunction to judge not, which he seldom remembered when mere strangers (whom he could consider merely as illustrations of theoretical principles) were concerned, but which he was very likely to obey when faced not with an abstraction, but with a person—especially, of course, if that person happened to be one whom he loved.

In this respect he behaved very much as he did when the question was one not of misconduct but of hardship. Johnson's theoretical Toryism made him sometimes advance the harshest opinions concerning the rights of property, but a suffering individual seldom left him untouched; and it is probable that he would have been willing to love even an American if he had ever come face to face with a colonist in distress. His tenderness toward sinners, if not toward sin, was manifest from his earliest days and his practical tolerance tended to grow (even while his abstract principles remained what they had always been) until he could say, much later: "As I know more of mankind I expect less of them, and am ready now to call a man a *good man,* upon easier terms than I was formerly."

In theory Johnson would probably have refused to accept the pronouncement of a more recent moralist, who has declared that in a given individual "no vice or virtue implies the existence of any other vice or virtue" but he tended to act as though he did accept it and was as ready to admit the foibles of the virtuous as he was to recognize what redeemed the vicious. Beauclerk was a rake whom he loved; Samuel Richardson was a good man whose goodness did not exempt him from stinging censure.

Johnson had early met this simpleton-genius—who was, by

the way, a perfect example of the danger of too much moral earnestness uncorrected by any "running about the world"—and was apparently on intimate terms with him during the fifties. Indeed, it was Johnson who had sought him out, as he once admitted, when he made Richardson an exception to his boast: "I never sought much after any body." He was a frequent visitor in Richardson's house and they exchanged compliments on one another's work. Richardson wrote to Cave of *The Rambler* papers: "There is but one man, I think, that could write them"; and in *The Rambler* Johnson called Richardson "an author who has enlarged the knowledge of human nature, and taught the passions to move at the command of virtue." But he neither failed to perceive nor failed to comment abundantly on the silly pomposity and folly of this great man. Comparing Richardson's novels with those of Fielding, he could say: "Sir, there is more knowledge of the heart in one letter of Richardson's than in all 'Tom Jones.'" But that did not prevent him from showing disgust with Richardson's eternal preoccupation with his own merits. To Langton Johnson boasted that he could make Richardson "rear," and what he meant by that is plain enough from an anecdote which Boswell relegated to a footnote.

"One day at his country-house at Northend, where a large company was assembled at dinner, a gentleman who was just returned from Paris, willing to please Mr. Richardson, mentioned to him a very flattering circumstance,—that he had seen his Clarissa lying on the King's brother's table. Richardson observing that part of the company were engaged in talking to each other, affected then not to attend to it. But by and by, when there was a general silence, and he thought that the flattery might be fully heard, he addressed himself to the gentleman, 'I think, Sir, you were saying something about,—' pausing in a high flutter of expectation. The gentleman, provoked at his inordinate vanity, resolved not to indulge it, and with an exquisitely sly air of indifference answered: 'A mere trifle, Sir, not worth repeating.' The mortification of Richardson was visible, and he did not speak ten words more the whole day. Dr. Johnson was present, and appeared to enjoy it much." [4]

"You think I love flattery," he once said to Mrs. Thrale, "and so I do; but a little too much always disgusts me: that fellow Richardson, on the contrary, could not be contented to sail quietly down the stream of reputation, without longing to taste the froth from every stroke of the oar." And after Richardson had passed on from this life to those rewards which, whatever they may be, he certainly still regards as inadequate, Johnson remarked: "That fellow died merely for want of change among his flatterers; he perished for want of more, like a man obliged to breathe the same air till it is exhausted."

But the fact that Johnson enjoyed the society of Langton and Beauclerk is, after all, more readily understandable than a corollary fact less often commented upon—the fact, that is to say, that Langton and Beauclerk enjoyed his. While he took pride as well as pleasure in being accepted as a companion by two gay young men, they, to be sure, no doubt took some pride as well as got some pleasure in the fact that they were publicly favored by a learned, wise and famous man. But it requires no great knowledge of the world to know that youth is usually less surprised and less touched by the tributes of age than age is by the tolerance of youth, and that the young and gay do not usually waste any large proportion of their time with even those of the older and graver whom they profess to admire, being generally content to pay hasty respects and then to go about their more entertaining business. Yet Langton and Beauclerk, like more distinguished but also fashionable elders such as Garrick and Reynolds, did pass in Johnson's company many hours that might have been passed in more glittering ways. And they did so despite the fact that Johnson, who demanded much, was not an easy companion; also despite the perhaps even more important fact that in appearance as well as, sometimes, in behavior he shocked their sense of propriety and embarrassed them before their friends.

Miss Reynolds writes, though in reference to a later period of Johnson's life:

"It is very certain that he piqued himself much upon his knowledge of the rules of true politeness, and particularly on his most punctilious observances of them towards the ladies. A remarkable instance of this was his never suffering any lady

JAMES BOSWELL

From a drawing by George Dance

to walk from his house to her carriage, through Bolt Court, unattended by himself to hand her into it (at least I have reason to suppose it to be his general custom, from his constant performance of it to those with whom he was the most intimately acquainted); and if any obstacle prevented it from driving off, there he would stand by the door of it, and gather a mob around him. Indeed they would begin to gather the moment he appear'd handing the lady down the steps into Fleet Street. But to describe his appearance, his important air (that indeed cannot be described) but his morning Habiliments, from head to foot, would excite the utmost astonishment in my reader, how a man in his senses could think of stepping outside his door in them, or even to be seen at home in them. Sometimes he exhibited himself at the distance of eight or ten doors distant from Bolt Court, to get at the carriage, to the no small diversion of the populace.

"And I am certain to all who love laughing a description of his dress from head to foot would be highly acceptable, and in general, I believe, be thought the most curious part of my Book. But I forbear, merely out of respect to his memory, to give the slightest intimation of it. For having written a minute description of his Figure, from his wig to his slippers, a thought occurred that it might probably excite some person to delineate it, and I might have the mortification of seeing it hung up at a Printshop as the greatest curiosity ever exhibited.

"His best dress was, at that time, so very mean, that one afternoon as he was following some ladies up stairs, on a visit to a lady of fashion, the Housemaid, not knowing him, suddenly seized him by the shoulder, and exclaimed, 'Where are you going?' striving at the same time to drag him back; but a gentleman who was a few steps behind prevented her from doing or saying more, and Mr. Johnson growled all the way up stairs, as well he might. He seemed much chagrined and apparently disposed to revenge the insult of the maid upon the mistress. Unluckily, whilst in this humour, a lady of high rank happening to call on Miss Cotterel, he was much offended with her for not introducing him to her Ladyship, at least not in the manner he liked, and still more for her seeming to shew more attention to this Lady than to him. After sitting sometime silent, meditating how to *down* Miss C., he address'd himself to Mr. Reynolds, who sat next him, and, after a few introductory words, with a loud voice said, 'I wonder which of us two could get most money by his trade in one week, were we to work hard at it from morning till night.' I don't remember the answer; but I know that the lady, rising soon after, went away without knowing what trade they were of . . . This incident Dr. Johnson used to mention with great glee—how he had *downed* Miss C., though at the same time he professed a great friendship and esteem for that lady."

No other argument disposes more completely of the absurd contention that Johnson is James Boswell's invention than the abundant evidence that many witty, learned and elegant people loved and cultivated him before Boswell came upon the scene. The fact is, of course, that Boswell, far from inventing or even discovering the fascination of Johnson's personality, deliberately sought him out because that personality was already famous; because he had, even in Edinburgh, heard Thomas Sheridan the elocutionist "frequently expatiate upon Johnson's extraordinary knowledge, talents, and virtues, repeat his pointed sayings, describe his peculiarities, and boast of his being his guest sometimes till two or three in the morning."

Both Johnson's intimate group and those who circulated around its periphery differed considerably from one another in the precise attitude they took toward him. Reynolds, for example, not only loved and admired Johnson but definitely made himself Johnson's intellectual disciple. He was, when he first came under Johnson's influence, just about to launch himself upon his great career. Johnson, he confessed, "may be said to have formed my mind, and to have brushed from it a great deal of rubbish." It is certainly also of Johnson that he is speaking in the seventh of the *Discourses,* where he pays tribute to all that a painter may learn from conversation with learned and ingenious men. Indeed, it seems probable that many of Reynolds's aesthetic ideas came in the first instance from Johnson—which is odd enough when one considers in what slight respect, in what contempt almost, Johnson held the art of painting: partly because he could not consider any of the arts except in literary terms, partly because the physical limitations of his vision were so great that he could scarcely have any direct experience with pictures capable of correcting his narrow conception of what a picture could do or be.

Other members of his circle certainly held their own, sometimes quite antithetical, opinions and prejudices, even though they also, in his presence, usually kept these opinions to themselves. Neither Garrick nor, later, Goldsmith, would have consented to be called a disciple. Boswell and Mrs. Thrale, though they professed and no doubt generally felt a respect for him amounting almost to reverence, also regarded him as something of an eccentric, an original, even as something of a curiosity. And when one has admitted that much one has touched on an aspect of Johnson's character and his position in his world that is hard to define. In many who knew him best, awe and amusement managed somehow to exist simultaneously and harmoniously together, just as they do in the minds of his subsequent admirers. But we do not have the delicate problem his contemporaries had, for they must manage somehow to maintain friendship with a man well aware of his own peculiarities yet ferociously determined that no one else should show awareness in any way that implied the slightest disrespect; with a man who violated many of the rules he demanded that others observe, and who would have resented nothing more than the knowledge that there was anything remotely condescending in the attitude of anyone toward him.

Perhaps it has never been sufficiently remarked that one reason for his domineering manner, for his insistence upon winning almost every argument by fair means or foul, is to be sought in his realization that he must dominate any group of which he did not expect to become quickly the butt. In many respects he was made to be laughed at. Awkward, unkempt, not too clean, and the victim of half a dozen ridiculous physical tics, he was also formal in diction, somewhat old-fashioned in appearance, and almost worst of all, a rigid moralist in an age little inclined to believe, for instance, that anyone seriously recommended chastity for men. If his companions had not feared as well as respected him, the freedoms they would have begun to take would soon have grown until he had become a butt whose grotesqueries were tolerated in society only because they furnished an opportunity for jest. Johnson had the power to halt familiarity as well as the shrewdness to see that anyone as open as he was to ridicule could escape it only by inspiring awe.

Sometimes he seems to have deliberately and humorously tested that power, as he did once after he had been unlucky enough to say of a certain woman of humble birth that she "had a bottom of good sense." The Bishop of Killaloe, so Boswell is careful to tell us, kept a straight face; but most of the company tittered and even Hannah More, whom one would have expected to equal at least a bishop in propriety, hid her face behind another lady's back. But Johnson, "resolved to assume and exercise despotick power, glanced sternly around, and called out in a strong tone, 'Where's the merriment?' Then collecting himself, and looking awful, to make us feel how he could impose restraint, and as it were searching his mind for a still more ludicrous word, he slowly pronounced, 'I say the *woman* was *fundamentally* sensible;' as if he had said, hear this now, and laugh if you dare. We all sat composed as at a funeral." On other occasions he resented what he regarded as dangerous rudeness (including, incidentally, even a remote approach to his own habitual manner) with all the solemn formality of the eighteenth-century code.[5]

To the amazement of his companions he evidently regarded himself as something of an authority on good breeding and good manners, which he certainly was not, but the readiness with which he both made apologies and, once he was convinced that no offense was intended, accepted them from others is proof enough that he did realize how impossible conversation of the sort he loved would become if the forms of civility were not preserved. The sometimes introductory and sometimes parenthetical "sir" Boswell no doubt consciously established as the Johnsonian trademark by seeing to it that it occurred somewhere in most of the reported remarks, especially those of the knock-down-and-drag-out variety. But the vocable is not a mere meaningless syllable. It served Johnson only somewhat more conspicuously than it served eighteenth-century conversation in general by enabling him to speak freely without degenerating into insult.

"Sir" used as an introduction to a vigorous attack means: "I acknowledge that this is a civilized gathering and that we are all ladies and gentlemen. In general you have a claim to be treated with respect and the claim I hereby acknowledge. But you will grant me the privilege, which one gentleman grants another, of speaking frankly." To have lost, as we have, the use of such formulae is to make conversation that is at once full-blooded and civilized more difficult. It makes it harder to escape from merely vapid amiability without falling into what looks like mere rudeness.

The formula did not, to be sure, always prove sufficient. Johnson not infrequently gave offense and not infrequently took it. Then if a permanent rupture of friendship was to be avoided—and usually it was—an elaborate ritual had to be gone through in the course of which the two parties alternately offered explanations or made partial apologies until at last, through a series of short steps, no one of which was too much to expect of either, the two parties were close enough together again to clasp hands.

Just how complicated was the ritual when apologies were to be exchanged is repeatedly illustrated in Boswell, as for instance in his account of the elaborate interchange between Johnson and Bishop Percy, when Johnson thought the latter had made an offensive reference to Johnson's defective vision. Or consider the occasion—which happens also to be one of the best examples of Boswell's power to bring the comedy of manners alive—when even the privileged Beauclerk went too far:

"In talking of Hackman, Johnson argued, as Judge Blackstone had done, that his being furnished with two pistols was a proof that he meant to shoot two persons. Mr. Beauclerk said, 'No; for that every wise man who intended to shoot himself, took two pistols, that he might be sure of doing it at once. Lord ——'s cook shot himself with one pistol, and lived ten days in great agony. Mr. ——, who loved buttered muffins, but durst not eat them because they disagreed with his stomach, resolved to shoot himself; and then he eat three buttered muffins for breakfast, before shooting himself, knowing that he should not be troubled with indigestion; *he* had two charged pistols; one was found lying charged upon the table by him, after he had shot himself with the other.'—'Well, (said Johnson, with an air of triumph,) you see here one pistol was sufficient.' Beauclerk replied smartly, 'Because it happened to kill him.' And either then or a very little afterwards, being piqued at Johnson's triumphant remark, added, 'This is what you don't know, and I do.' There was then a cessation of the dispute; and some minutes intervened, during which, dinner and the glass went on cheerfully; when Johnson suddenly and abruptly exclaimed, 'Mr. Beauclerk, how came you to talk so petulantly to me, as "This is what you don't know, but what I know?" One thing *I* know, which *you* don't seem to know, that you are very uncivil.' BEAUCLERK. 'Because *you* began by being uncivil, (which you always are.)' The words in parentheses were, I believe, not heard by Dr. Johnson. Here again there was a cessation of arms. Johnson told me, that the reason why he waited at first some time without taking any notice of what Mr. Beauclerk said, was because he was thinking whether be should resent it. But when he considered that there were present a young Lord and an eminent traveller, two men of the world with whom he had never dined before, he was apprehensive that they might think they had a right to take such liberties with him as Beauclerk did, and therefore resolved he would not let it pass; adding, 'that he would not appear a coward.' A little while after this, the conversation turned on the violence of Hackman's temper. Johnson then said, 'It was his business to *command* his temper, as my friend Mr. Beauclerk, should have done some time ago.' BEAUCLERK. 'I should learn of *you,* Sir.' JOHNSON. 'Sir, you have given *me* opportunities enough of learning, when I have been in *your* company. No man loves to be treated with contempt.' BEAUCLERK. (with a polite inclination towards Johnson) 'Sir, you have known me twenty years, and however I may have treated others, you may be sure I could never treat you with contempt.' JOHNSON. 'Sir, you have said more than was necessary.' Thus it ended; and Beauclerk's coach not having come for him till very late, Dr. Johnson and another gentleman sat with him a long time after the rest of the company were gone; and he and I dined at Beauclerk's on the Saturday se'nnight following." [6]

"If," wrote Mrs. Thrale in her diary, "he had unawares spoken harshly to a modest man, he would strive to make him amends as in the following Case. A young Fellow of great Fortune as he was sitting with a Book in his hand at our House one Day called to him rather abruptly & he fancied disrespectfully—Mr. Johnson says the Man—would you advise me to marry? I would advise *no Man* to marry answered he, bouncing from his Chair & leaving the Room in a fret—that is not likely to propagate Understanding. The young Fellow looked confounded & and had barely begun to recover his Spirits when the Doctor returned with a smiling Countenance and joining in the General Prattle of the Party, turned it insensibly to the Subject of Marriage; where he laid himself out in a Conversation so entertaining instructive & gay that nobody remembered the Offence except to rejoyce in its Consequences."

Of course not everyone, even after exposure to Johnson's conversation, thought it worth while to put up with either his grotesqueries or his not too infrequent rudeness. There was an anti-Johnsonian party in society as well as in literature. But an astonishing number of people, themselves worth seeking out, sought out Johnson. And even though he could give them no return except his conversation, even though he could not repay socially their entertainment, continued for many years to cultivate him, as Beauclerk himself had at the time of the little quarrel. Obviously they got, not only from his conversation but from the mere presence of his powerful personality, something of which they could not tire. If, on the other hand, one asks what he got from them the answer is "almost everything." He got an opportunity to exercise the greatest of his talents, he got assurance that he had powers sufficient to more than make up for his physical and mental disabilities, and perhaps most important of all, he won hours of freedom from his own sick mind—from that sense of the ultimate emptiness of life which he had rationalized into something like a philosophic system.

As the years went by, the circle of his friends grew larger and he came to have more and more opportunity to spend his time with the rich or the great. Yet he never lost touch with humbler people and now, in the period immediately following Tetty's death when he was just entering upon what may be called his social career, he was also, as has been mentioned, establishing that queer household of dependents to which he would return after his forays into another world. Nothing that has been said about him so far would suggest that Johnson was a man who had, in any sense of the term, domestic tastes. Even during the years of his married life he was certainly "running about the world" and spending much of his time in taverns or the back parlors of booksellers' shops. But a temporary lodging presided over by a woman twenty years his senior, and past sixty when he began to achieve his first success, is hardly a home in the usual sense of the term. There is, moreover, a comment scribbled by Mrs. Thrale (who certainly knew Johnson as well as anyone) in the margin of her copy of Boswell's *Life* which suggests that some of Johnson's habits may be looked at in a light somewhat different from any Boswell ever seems to have caught. In a letter written shortly before his death Johnson refers to Edmund Hector, whom he had known in the days of his poverty, as one of the only two friends of his youth still living, and Mrs. Thrale, exhibiting a touch of something like jealousy, makes a note: "to whom he perpetually turned . . . not to his Flatterers & Admirers. Ever sighing for the Tea & Bread & Butter of Life, when satiated with the Turtle & Burgundy of it."

From the Thrales, especially, he had had in his last years a good deal of the turtle and Burgundy and if he longed for tea and bread it was no doubt partly because he did not feel compelled to owe the latter to the amiable bounty of others. One catches the hint that Johnson, so habitually in either taverns or the homes of his friends, was more aware than he cared to admit of his own half-vagabond status and that he gathered the homeless about him not only because he had, as he certainly did, a heart easily touched by actual want, but also because they helped provide him with a sort of substitute for a family, with dependents to whom he could afford food, shelter and company instead of receiving them as he came more and more constantly to do from persons better off than himself. If he said "that a tavern chair was the throne of human felicity" and on another occasion "there is nothing which has yet been contrived by man, by which so much happiness is produced as by a good tavern or inn," the implication may be in part that Johnson was aware of his homelessness. The wonder and delight with which he contemplated the Burney household—apparently the first example of happy family life he had ever seen—must mean something. So too must the mock-serious dialogue recorded by Fanny Burney, though it took place some years later, when Johnson was no longer lodged in Gough Square:

"Mr. T[hrale].—'And pray who is clerk of your kitchen, sir?' Dr. J.—'Why, sir, I am afraid there is none; a general anarchy prevails in my kitchen, as I am told by Mr. Levat, who says it is not now what it used to be!' Mr. T.—'But how do you get your dinners drest?' Dr. J.—'Why, De Mullin [Desmoulins] has the chief management of the kitchen; but our roasting is not magnificent, for we have no jack.' Mr. T.—'No jack? Why, how do they manage without?' Dr. J.—'Small joints, I believe, they manage with a string, and larger are done at the tavern. I have some thoughts (with a profound gravity) of buying a jack, because I think a jack is some credit to a house.' Mr. T.—'Well, but you'll have a spit, too?' Dr. J.—'No, sir, no; that would be superfluous; for we shall never use it; if a jack is seen, a spit will be presumed!' " [7]

Johnson's household no doubt shifted, and it certainly grew. Writing of the period when she knew him, Mrs. Thrale, loosening the reins on her love for the picturesque, writes: "He nursed whole nests of people in his house, where the lame, the blind, the sick, and the sorrowful found a sure retreat from all the evils whence his little income could secure them: and commonly spending the middle of the week at our house, he kept his numerous family in Fleet-street upon a settled allowance; but returned to them every Saturday, to give them three good dinners, and his company, before he came back to us on the Monday night—treating them with the same, or perhaps more ceremonious civility, than he would have done by as many people of fashion—making the holy scriptures thus the rule of his conduct, and only expecting salvation as he was able to obey its precepts."

So far as the account of Johnson's attitude toward his pensioners is concerned, this account is doubtless accurate. It may also well be that various unfortunates were given temporary shelter; but Mrs. Thrale, who got her notions in part from Johnson's own humorously exaggerated accounts of the state of his household, is probably considerably too picturesque when she suggests that Johnson lived in quite so populous a Home for the Destitute. At least one may say that only five pensioners lived with him long enough to find significant places in any of the accounts left by his contemporaries, and that of these, two did not join him until after he had left Gough Square. There the permanent members of his household included only the black servant, Francis Barber, the unlicensed physician, Robert Levett, and the blind lady, Miss Anna Williams.

The last-named was the mistress of the establishment and, though there was a period when she lodged separately, remained so much his official hostess (if the phrase is not too formal to be used in connection with one of Johnson's disorderly life) that when Boswell was taken to have tea with her less than three months after he had first met Johnson he considered that he "had now made good my title to be a privileged man" and was much elated. Despite the suspicion that Miss Williams gauged the fullness of a teacup by holding one finger over the inner edge, he "willingly drank cup after cup, as if it had been the Heliconian spring," until the novelty wore off and he grew more fastidious. Later the Thrales' Italian tutor and friend, Joseph Baretti, noted that he dined at Johnson's house as seldom as possible because he "hated to see the victuals paw'd by poor Mrs. Williams, that would often carve, though stone blind"; and this is perhaps as good a time as any to observe that the question whether she was or was not guilty of putting her finger in the tea must still remain *sub judice*. On the one hand, Boswell himself, after describing his disgust, is conscientious enough to add in a footnote: "I have since had reason to think that I was mistaken; for I have been informed by a lady, who was long intimate with her, and likely to be a more accurate observer of such matters, that she had acquired such a niceness of touch, as to know, by the feeling on the outside of the cup, how near it was to being full." On the other hand, Mrs. Thrale, glossing this same footnote, observes: "Not She, poor Soul; the 1st Story is the truest." And yet those who remember Johnson's unexpected niceness in the matter of the sugar, and how, touring Scotland, he was infuriated by the waiter who took a lump in his fingers, will have to balance still another pair of questions: Would he have tolerated anyone's digit in his favorite beverage; is it possible that long intimacy with Miss Williams had persuaded him to tolerate in her what he would not have permitted a stranger?

The lady was the daughter of Dr. Zachariah Williams, a Welsh physician, who had spent many years in an attempt to win the reward offered for the discovery of a method of determining longitude at sea and for whom, during Dr. Williams's old age (1755), Johnson had written an account of the alleged method in an unsuccessful effort to enable him to collect at least part of the reward. It was apparently Mrs. Johnson who first made the acquaintance with Dr. Williams and while she was still alive the daughter was a frequent visitor at the Johnson establishment. She had come up to London in the vain hope of being cured of cataracts in both eyes and, after Tetty's death, she came under Johnson's roof; there she was to remain, except when he had no sufficiently commodious home, until her death which occurred not long before his own.

There is abundant testimony to Miss Williams's intellectual and other qualities as well as to the satisfaction Johnson took in her company. It is true that Boswell calls her "peevish" and that she quarreled with other and less attractive members of the household, but the favorable references are much more numerous. Mrs. Chapone, writing to a friend in 1753, or not long after Miss Williams had first made her home with Johnson, says: "I was charmed with Mr. Johnson's behavior to Mrs. Williams, which was like that of a fond father to his daughter. She . . . shewed very good sense, with a great deal of modesty and humility; and so much patience and cheerfulness under her misfortune, that it doubled my concern for her." She knew French and Italian, she wrote feeble verses, and more remarkably, she shared Johnson's dilettante interest in chemistry. Hannah More speaks of her "engaging" manners and of her "lively and entertaining" conversation, but no doubt her disposition did not improve with age and it is only fair to call attention to the subjunctive of unreal condition in Johnson's reference to her after her death. "Had she had," he wrote, "good humour and prompt elocution, her universal curiosity and comprehensive knowledge would have made her the delight of all that knew her." This, however, again refers to the last years of her life when Johnson was confessing: "Age and sickness, and pride, have made her so peevish, that I was forced to bribe the maid to stay with her, by a secret stipulation of half a crown a week over her wages."

In general his other references put beyond dispute the fact that his regard for her was deep. After her death he could write to Bennet Langton: "I have lost a companion, to whom I have had recourse for domestic amusement for thirty years, and whose variety of knowledge never was exhausted"; to Mrs. Montagu: "Thirty years and more she had been my companion, and her death has left me very desolate." Apparently Miss Williams was not wholly destitute when she came to live with Johnson; he obviously regarded her as socially as well as intellectually above any other members of his household, and he and his friends alike evidently sought as far as possible to soften her sense of dependence. In 1750, before she came to live with Johnson, proposals for printing by subscription her *Essays in Verse and Prose* were printed in *The Gentleman's Magazine;* nine years later Johnson was still signing receipts for subscribers to the same book, which was not published until 1766—thus establishing an example of procrastination which rivals Johnson's own delays in giving *Shakespeare* to his subscribers. In 1756 Johnson persuaded Garrick to give her a benefit at Drury Lane from which she got two hundred pounds. Much later, both her relative, Lady Philips, and Mrs. Montagu made her an allowance, and her income is said at one time to have amounted to thirty-five or forty pounds a year.[8]

Next below Miss Williams—and, though greatly her social and intellectual inferior, quite as much a fixture as she was—came his physician in ordinary, the destitute Robert Levett. We have Johnson's own statement in his *Prayers and Meditations* that he had known this strange man, "an old and faithful friend," "from about 46" and one may assume that he met him first in his professional capacity; but since it does not seem possible to determine when he joined Johnson's household, we must rest content with Boswell's statement that Levett had an apartment in Johnson's house "ever since I was acquainted with Dr. Johnson [1763], and many years before, as I have been assured by those who knew him earlier." Levett was an uncouth fellow with no such claims as Miss Williams had to being an entertaining companion. Only his rough goodness and his forlorn state recommended him. According to an account published in *The Gentleman's Magazine* at the time of his death: "His person was middle-sized and thin; his visage swarthy, adust and corrugated. His conversation, except on professional subjects, barren. When in dishabille, he might have been mistaken for an alchemist, whose complexion had been hurt by the fumes of the crucible, and whose clothes had suffered from the sparks of the furnace." According to Hawkins: "He had no learning . . . and though it may be said, that having lived for some years abroad, he must have seen and remarked many things that would have afforded entertainment in the relation, this advantage was counterbalanced by an utter inability for continued conversation, taciturnity being one of the most obvious features in his character." And Hawkins adds: "The consideration of all which particulars almost impels me to say, that Levett admired Johnson because others admired him, and that Johnson in pity loved Levett, because few others could find anything in him to love."

Levett, Johnson told Fanny Burney, "is a brutal fellow, but I have a good regard for him; for his brutality is in his manners, not in his mind." He lived with Johnson until his death in 1782 and Hawkins writes: "Whoever called in on Johnson at about mid-day, found him and Levett at breakfast, Johnson in dishabille, as just risen from bed, and Levett filling out tea for himself and his patron alternately, no conversation passing between them." Johnson, nevertheless, did not wish him to be regarded as an inferior and did not treat him as a dependent. Levett, he said, "was indebted to him for nothing more than house-room, his share in a penny loaf at breakfast, and now and then a dinner on a Sunday." [9]

The available accounts of Levett's life are fragmentary and

leave the chronology confused. It is, indeed, so far from clear just when he came to live with Johnson that if it were not for Boswell's statement (quoted above) one would be inclined to put the date later. He was apparently identical with the Robert Levett who was baptized at East Yorks near Hull in 1705 and, since his parents were poor, he is said to have been apprenticed to a woolen draper in Hull and to have learned something of medicine from a neighbor. He came up to London and worked, possibly as a servant, until he had saved enough money to visit France for the purpose of improving his medical knowledge. In Paris he is said to have worked as waiter in a coffeehouse frequented by surgeons, and through the latter to have obtained free admission to the lectures on pharmacy and anatomy delivered by the most renowned teachers of the time. After five years he returned to London and ultimately set up a practice among the poorest classes of the city. Even during the period of his residence with Johnson, he attended such medical lectures as were open to him without pay. "All his medical knowledge," said Johnson, "and it is not inconsiderable, was obtained through the ear. Though he buys books, he seldom looks into them, or discovers any power by which he can be supposed to judge of an author's merit."

The biography in *The Gentleman's Magazine* includes the summary of a somewhat ribald tragicomedy of which Johnson himself, in letters belonging to the years 1762 and 1763, makes brief mention without giving any of the details. The relevant sentences from *The Gentleman's Magazine* are as follows:

"He married . . . a woman of the town, who had persuaded him (notwithstanding their place of congress was a small coal-shed in Fetter-lane), that she was nearly related to a man of fortune, but was injuriously kept by him out of large possessions. . . . She regarded him as a physician already in considerable practice. . . . He had not been married four months, before a writ was taken out against him, for debts incurred by his wife. He was secreted; and his friend then procured him a protection from a foreign minister. In a short time afterward, she ran away from him, and was tried (providentially in his opinion) for picking pockets at the Old Bailey. Her husband was with difficulty prevented from attending the court, in the hope she would be hanged. She pleaded her own cause, and was acquitted; a separation between this ill-starred couple took place." [10]

To understand just how Levett fitted into the contemporary scheme of medical practice it is necessary to understand the peculiar outlines of that scheme. So far as the science of medicine and surgery was concerned, great progress was being made, as it was in most of the other sciences. Moreover, as the century proceeded, more and more effective means were evolved for putting science to the service of the individual patient, with the result that great triumphs—notably the control of smallpox and the lessening of jail fever—were accomplished. Nevertheless, the disappearance of the physician as scholarly gentleman and the appearance of the clinical practitioner were slow, and during most of Johnson's lifetime the absurd aloofness of the most dignified physicians often left the actual care of sick persons in hands as ignorant as Levett's.

In many respects the eighteenth century was the golden age of privilege. The universities were run for the benefit of the professors, the fellows and the tutors; the Church, for the benefit of its ministers—or at least for that relatively small number who had influence enough to accumulate for themselves the various benefices while leaving the incumbent duties to be performed by their less fortunate fellows to whom these duties were farmed out. In similar fashion, medicine existed for the benefit of its practitioners. Just as some of the learning of the college professor (assuming that he had any, for it should be remembered that Chesterfield only half jokingly suggests to his young son that the latter already knew enough Greek to be professor of the language at one of the universities, should he care for that way of life) might ultimately seep through to a student; and just as some of the piety of the successful priest (that is, in the even less likely case that *he* had any) might seep through to members of his flock—so, too, the successful physician, who stood at the head of the hierarchy of medicine, might assume that some benefits of his knowledge would ultimately reach a sufferer. But ordinarily he was not expected to trouble himself to the extent of personally observing a patient. The latter was commonly visited by an apothecary (a Freeman of the Society of Apothecaries) who then proceeded to the coffeehouse where he found the physician he was accustomed to consult, described the symptoms, and received a "bill," written in Latin, which described the medicines to be given and the other treatments to be followed. The apothecary then returned to his shop, compounded the prescription, and returned to treat the patient, administering such clysters, purges and emetics as might have been ordered, but summoning a barber-surgeon if bleeding were necessary and a cupper if cupping had been ordered. Only when the case was very serious did the physician himself consent to make a visit, and in that case his fee was a guinea or two-thirds of a guinea for every mile he was compelled to travel.

Thus, though wealthy and important persons might be visited in ordinary illness by their physician, the vast majority of middling people were lucky if they received his ministrations from a distance. And of course vast numbers could not afford the considerable expense involved and were dependent upon unlicensed physicians like Levett, who belonged to no Company, passed no examinations, were completely unregulated, and took as fees whatever the patient could give. Levett himself was said to be extremely conscientious and, within the limits of his education and mind, able. What the usual level of such men was can only be guessed.

One result of all this was that many men dosed themselves in accordance with vague theories of their own and that the eighteenth century was one of the heydays of the secret proprietary medicine. Like Horace Walpole, Johnson himself was a great believer in one of the most famous: "Dr. James's Powder for Fevers and Other Inflammatory Distempers" (a dangerous combination of antimony and phosphate of lime), invented by an old Lichfield friend. One Joanna Stevens achieved such fame through her secret remedy for stone that Parliament, acting purely in the public interest, paid her five thousand pounds to make the formula public. It consisted of a powder of calcined eggshells and snails, soap and honey, but Horace Walpole had so much faith in it that he took a course of treatment in which it has been calculated he consumed 180 pounds of soap and 1,200 gallons of lime water. In Walpole's letters his various theories concerning gout and its proper treatment figure prominently, but Johnson fancied himself even more as an amateur physician. He loved the company of members of the profession and boasted of "my knowledge of physick" which "I learned from Dr. James, whom I helped in writing the proposals for his medical Dictionary and also a little in the Dictionary itself." Sometimes in his letters we find him prescribing to his friends, as he did to Miss Boothby in 1755; and to his mother in her last illness he wrote: "I have just read a physical book, which inclines me to think that a strong infusion of the bark would do you good. Do, dear mother, try it."

In very serious cases Johnson sometimes consulted his old friend, Dr. Thomas Lawrence, at one time president of the College of Physicians, but ordinarily Levett served him, and he had been heard to say that "he should not be satisfied, though attended by all the College of Physicians, unless he had Mr. Levet with him." Yet most of the latter's patients were so poor that his only fee was frequently the food or drink which they had to offer him, and from this fact sprang his only vice. "Johnson would observe, he was, perhaps, the only man who ever became intoxicated through motives of prudence. He reflected, that if he refused the gin or brandy offered him by some of his patients, he could have been no gainer by their cure, as they might have had nothing else to bestow on him. This habit of taking a fee, in whatever shape it was exhibited, could not be put off by advice or admonition of any kind. He would swallow what he did not like, nay, what he knew would injure him, rather than go home with an idea, that his skill had been exerted without recompense. 'Had (said Johnson) all his patients maliciously combined to reward him with meat and strong liquors instead of money, he would either have burst, like the dragon in the Apocrypha, through repletion, or been scorched up, like Portia, by swallowing fire.' But let not from hence an imputation of rapaciousness be fixed upon him. Though he took all that was offered him, he demanded nothing from the poor, nor was known in any instance to have enforced the payment of even what was strictly his due."

When Levett died Johnson wrote in his memory a singularly touching poem. The rhythm and the diction are perhaps influenced by Gray's *Elegy*. Readers who have little taste for formal satire in couplets may well find it the best of Johnson's verse, and it is at least fine enough to deserve quotation in full.

Condemn'd to hope's delusive mine,
As on we toil, from day to day,
By sudden blasts, or slow decline,
Our social comforts drop away.

Well try'd, through many a varying year,
See Levet to the grave descend,
Officious, innocent, sincere,
Of ev'ry friendless name the friend.

Yet still he fills affection's eye,
Obscurely wise, and coarsely kind;
Nor, letter'd arrogance, deny
Thy praise to merit unrefined.

When fainting nature call'd for aid,
And hov'ring death prepar'd the blow,
His vig'rous remedy display'd
The pow'r of art, without the show.

In mis'ry's darkest cavern known,
His useful care was ever nigh,
Where hopeless anguish pour'd his groan,
And lonely want retir'd to die.

No summons, mock'd by chill delay,
No petty gain, disdain'd by pride;
The modest wants of ev'ry day
The toil of ev'ry day supply'd.

His virtues walk'd their narrow round,
Nor made a pause, nor left a void;
And sure the eternal master found
The single talent well-employ'd.

The busy day—the peaceful night,
Unfelt, uncounted, glided by;
His frame was firm—his pow'rs were bright,
Though now his eightieth year was nigh.

Then, with no fiery throbbing pain,
No cold gradations of decay,
Death broke, at once, the vital chain,
And freed his soul the nearest way.[11]

Mrs. Carmichael, the most troublesome of Johnson's dependents, did not come to live with him till later. While he was in Gough Square the household was completed by a Negro servant, Francis Barber, whom Dr. Bathurst's father had brought from Jamaica, and then, by his will, set free. Frank, as he was called, entered Johnson's service in 1752 and remained with him except for two intervals until the master's death. According to Mrs. Thrale, Johnson always appeared to think of Negroes as of "a race naturally inferior" but it is certain that, unlike some of his supposedly more liberal friends, he detested the institution of slavery with a vehemence not surpassed in intensity by any of his other feelings; and though he was not an egalitarian—he neither believed men to be equal in fact nor saw any objection to the recognition of formal distinctions between them—his kindness and consideration tended to be more conspicuous in proportion to the social or financial inferiority of the person with whom he was concerned. Frank was, accordingly, a great favorite. Johnson went himself to get oysters for the ailing cat, Hodge, lest Frank should be humiliated by being sent upon such an errand, and it was noted that when the various dependents quarreled among themselves, Johnson always sided with Frank—partly no doubt in order to avoid the suspicion that he could be unfair to a member of "a race naturally inferior." One may read in his own *Prayers and Meditations* how he instructed his servant in religion, and at one time he sent Frank to school—with what results is not recorded. Moreover, he shocked Mrs. Thrale by bequeathing him what she regarded as an absurdly large sum.[12]

Such, then, were Johnson's domestic companions for many

years; such, the household to which he would return both at the time when he was first making his sorties into the society of fine ladies and gentlemen and also long after, when he had grown accustomed to the luxuries of the Thrale establishment. Bohemianism is no unusual thing among men of letters, and the bohemian who, dressed in the semiformal evening attire which makes all who can afford that much equals, sallies forth from his hall bedroom to associate familiarly with those who hardly bother to guess how he lives in his own home is a familiar enough figure today. But Johnson's case is not parallel. His establishment was not bohemian in the ordinary sense of the term, for that suggests rootlessness and the deliberate avoidance of such ties as Johnson cultivated. He was not camping-out amidst casual disorder. His establishment was half eleemosynary but it was also half genuinely domestic. Perhaps it is worth while to separate the two elements.

Johnson had always been charitable up to the limit of his resources, even when he had been himself near the edge of destitution, and accustomed to slip pennies into the fists of sleeping urchins. Later, when his pension gave him a modest competence he is known to have systematically given away an astonishingly large part of it. Now, during the Gough Square period, when he was neither as poor as he once had been nor as comfortably off as he was to become, he automatically relieved the distress of those who came under his notice even though, as surviving letters reveal, he was himself financially insecure enough to be compelled to ask now and again for small loans from his friends and, in 1756, was actually under arrest for a debt of £5 18s.—which sum, happily, was advanced him by Samuel Richardson.

Theoretically he was opposed to giving to beggars. "It is an unhappy circumstance," he once said, "that one might give away five hundred pounds in a year to those that importune in the streets, and not do any good"; and again: "You are much surer that you are doing good when you *pay* money to those who work, as the recompense of their labour, than when you *give* money merely in charity." Yet he "frequently gave all the silver in his pocket to the poor, who watched him, between his house and the tavern where he dined." And, perhaps, just because he had no sociological theories, because his charitable impulse sprang directly out of his tenderness toward suffering and was not complicated by any scheme for redeeming mankind, it was uncontaminated by concern over the possible unworthiness of the recipient or any conviction that the poor should be made to feel the shame of their poverty. In his opinion, this sort of severity toward the poor was, according to Mrs. Thrale, a consequence of Whiggism, and he himself, "not contented with giving them relief—wished to add also indulgence." "'What signifies,' says one, 'giving halfpence to common beggars? they only lay it out in gin or tobacco.' 'And why should they be denied such sweeteners of their existence (says Johnson)? it is surely very savage to refuse them every possible avenue to pleasure, reckoned too coarse for our own acceptance. Life is a pill which none of us can bear to swallow without gilding; yet for the poor we delight in stripping it still barer, and are not ashamed to shew even visible displeasure, if ever the bitter taste is taken from their mouths.'" [13]

So much Johnson's more fortunate friends could at least comprehend, but they did not always even profess to understand why he found it necessary or even agreeable to live on intimate terms with those who were not only not his intellectual equals but were also quite far below him morally and spiritually. Many persons of that time freely admitted to a conviction which it has since become customary to conceal—the conviction, that is to say, that, certain extravagances of Christian theory notwithstanding, the "best people" socially and intellectually are also the "best people" spiritually. Thus the Duchess of Buckingham—genuinely shocked by the Wesleyan insistence that all mankind (even including the nobility) had corrupt hearts—could write in righteous protest to the pious Countess of Huntingdon: "It is monstrous to be told that you have a heart as sinful as the common wretches that crawl on the earth. This is highly offensive and insulting, and I cannot but wonder that your ladyship should relish any sentiment so much at variance with high rank and good breeding." More mildly, but in a similar spirit, Mrs. Thrale, who was certainly not, as people go, conspicuously illiberal or hardhearted, could write concerning Johnson's intimacy with Levett that the former, "always thinking neglect the worst misfortune that could befall a man, looked on a character of this description with less aversion than I do."

Asked by an intimate friend how he could bear to be surrounded by "such necessitous and undeserving people," his answer was: "If I did not assist them no one else would, and they must be lost for want." But that is only half the story, for Johnson was not forcing himself to do an unpleasant duty. It is evident that he liked such people and that in some way he identified himself with them, or at least with something in their state. "It was never against people of coarse life," says Mrs. Thrale, "that his contempt was expressed, while poverty of sentiment in men who considered themselves to be company for *the parlour,* as he called it, was what he could not bear." And again: "Dr. Johnson knew how to be merry with mean people too, as well as to be sad with them; he loved the lower ranks of humanity with a real affection: and though his talents and learning kept him always in the sphere of upper life, yet he never lost sight of the time when he and they shared pain and pleasure in common."

No doubt the last phrase is the most important of all. Johnson's abstract Tory principles, which certainly included an extremely high estimate of the rights of property, had been formed in the days when they were absurdly inconsonant with what present-day writers would call his "class interest" and he carried them unchanged through a life that brought him into closer and closer relation with people in whom such principles are less surprising. But emotionally he felt so much closer to those among whom his birth had first cast him that even in the days of turtle and Burgundy he was proud of his own understanding of low life and resentful of those who held it in ignorant scorn.

This contrast between his intellectual insistence upon the rights of property and his emotional identification with the dispossessed is, indeed, one of the many paradoxes of his personality and it remains such, even though we remember that the eighteenth century laid more stress than is now usual upon the Tory claim that the latter's sense of responsibility to the lower orders made him actually more concerned with their welfare than were the liberals with their doctrine of equal opportunity—and its corollary: let the devil take the hindmost. Discussing the poor merely as one of the abstractions in political economy, Johnson could sound very brutal. He could even, in the course of an argument, talk like some aristocratic duelist and maintain that "a poor man has no honour"—an opinion which led even Mrs. Thrale, certainly no leveler, to scribble "Shocking" in the margin of her copy of Boswell. But it is highly improbable that he would have allowed anyone else to say the same, and it was to the poor that he turned for "the bread and tea of life" which he so much needed.

Perhaps, indeed, the fact that they did not have to concern themselves with honor—a fantastic and insubstantial thing—was one of the reasons. Perhaps, at bottom, he despised that sort of honor, just as he openly despised what he called "the distresses of sentiment." Once when Mrs. Thrale lamented the loss of a first cousin killed in America, he replied in a vein which he frequently struck: "Pray, my dear, (said he) have done with canting; how would the world be worse for it, I may ask, if all your relations were at once spitted like larks, and roasted for Presto's [the dog] supper?" And if that anecdote was disputed by Boswell, there is another equally characteristic remark on another occasion: "These are the distresses of sentiment—which a man who is really to be pitied has no leisure to feel. The sight of people who want food and raiment is so common in great cities, that a surly fellow like me has no compassion to spare for wounds given only to vanity or softness."

Johnson's household was, then, something more than an eleemosynary institution and its inmates not merely wretches with whom he acknowledged a disagreeable Christian duty to associate. They were friends with whom he had something in common that he did not have with most of his more intellectual companions—a knowledge of the stern elementals of human existence. The house was not merely a house—it was a kind of home inhabited by the members of a kind of family, and therefore an important element in that adjustment which Johnson, something of a monster, succeeded in making to a life in which many of the normal things had to be done without, while substitutes took their place. He was an outsider with Boswell and Langton and Beauclerk, and, to some lesser extent, an outsider even with the Thrales and the Reynoldses and the Garricks and the Burneys. Luxury, elegance and fashion seemed less real to him than to many because he was never wholly part of the world in which they were taken for granted.

Many men, oppressed with a sense that most of life is fantastical and trivial, have sought in various ways to make contact with "reality." To some, that has meant hardship in remote places; to some, as to Thoreau, solitude and simplicity; to still others, it has meant the search for God in mystical experience. To Johnson it meant reminding himself of the struggle for existence on the most elementary level, refreshing association with people who knew, as he did, what it was to be close to illness and to want. To know how much one could do without and still desire to live, how much poverty and suffering one could endure, made him feel safe. And, by contrast, profusion frightened him. "All these things, David," he once said to Garrick when the latter was displaying his fine house and fine grounds, "make death very terrible." [14]

CHAPTER VI

Rasselas

IT WAS, as has already been remarked, from the garret work-room of the Gough Square house that the final pages of the *Dictionary* had gone forth. Johnson was to remain at the same address until 1759, and it was there that he was to enter upon his next important literary projects: an edition of Shakespeare (previously proposed but temporarily abandoned), a new series of periodical essays called *The Idler,* and *Rasselas,* that Oriental fable which was perhaps admired beyond its merits by Johnson's contemporaries but is today quite unjustly condescended to by those who have either forgotten what it is like or never taken the trouble to find out.

Though *The Rambler* and the *Dictionary* had made him at last really famous, fame did not relieve him from the necessity of earning his living almost from day to day. We have already seen that the advance payments for the *Dictionary* had been spent as received, and to March, 1756, belongs a letter to Samuel Richardson which vividly illustrates how easily the sure prospect of his third dinner ahead might seem to Johnson a large measure of security. The letter reads:

SIR,

I am obliged to entreat your assistance. I am now under arrest for five pounds eighteen shillings. Mr. Strahan, from whom I should have received the necessary help in this case, is not at home; and I am afraid of not finding Mr. Miller. If you will be so good as to send me this sum, I will gratefully repay you, and add it to all former obligations.

I am, Sir,

Your most obedient and most humble servant,

SAM JOHNSON.

Gough Square, March 16

Some light on the "former obligations" is thrown by a previous letter to the same person, which is dated February 19, 1756, and returns thanks for "the favour which you were pleased to do me two nights ago." Happily the letter just quoted in full is said to have borne on the margin this endorsement: "March 16, 1756. Sent six guineas. Witness, Wm. Richardson."

No doubt Johnson's need for immediate cash has something to do with the fact that the proposal to edit Shakespeare was not to bear fruit for a long time to come. It almost certainly has much to do with the further fact that a great deal of hack work—reviews, prefaces, dedications, and the like—belongs to the period immediately following the publication of the *Dictionary*. In May of 1756 appeared the first number of a new periodical called *The Literary Magazine, or Universal Review,* to which Johnson not only contributed over a period of some fifteen months but which he also, according to Boswell, "engaged to superintend." "What," Boswell continues, "were his emoluments from this undertaking, and what other writers he employed in it, I have not discovered"; but the dramatist, Arthur Murphy (who, unlike Boswell, was already acquainted with Johnson at this period), gives an account of the latter at work as editor that is picturesque enough though perhaps not to be trusted too implicitly:

"This employment engrossed but little of Johnson's time. He resigned himself to indolence, took no exercise, rose about two, and then received the visits of his friends. Authors, long since forgotten, waited on him as their oracle, and he gave responses in the chair of criticism. He listened to the complaints, the schemes, and the hopes and fears of a crowd of inferior writers, 'who,' he said, in the words of Roger Ascham, 'lived, *men knew not how, and died obscure, men marked not when.*' He believed, that he could give a better history of Grub-street than any man living. His house was filled with a succession of visitors till four or five in the evening. During the whole time he presided at his tea-table." [1]

Most of the hack work Johnson did at this time for the magazines was hack work and no more, but one review stands out both as a piece of extraordinarily vigorous writing and as a clear revelation of the fact that Johnson was thinking hard on one of the problems which greatly concerned his contemporaries. Such books as Thomas Birch's *History of the Royal Society of London* and Hampton's translation of Polybius he reviewed with perfunctory brevity, but when Soame Jenyns's *Free Enquiry into the Origin and Nature of Evil* came into his hands he rose to the occasion, and the ten thousand words in which he demolished that author were certainly not carelessly written.

Jenyns was a witty trifler—or at least a trifler who hoped to be witty. With the possible exception of James Boswell, who disposed of the arguments against Negro slavery in a jeu d'esprit, no one illustrates better the fatuousness into which feeble men could be led by the tendency of the eighteenth century to assume that a reasonable familiarity with what was called "polite learning" constituted a sufficient equipment for the solution of all problems political, moral or metaphysical. It is the glory of that century to have demonstrated more successfully than any other before or since how much common sense can accomplish and how charming a garden can be cultivated by those who are content not to look beyond the garden wall; but not even its greatest men—not even Johnson himself always—escaped fatuity when they adventured too far afield with too light an equipment.

Jenyns had formerly been a fellow contributor with Chesterfield to *The World* and he was later to aspire to a *View of the Internal Evidence of the Christian Religion.* At present he was merely endeavoring to justify the ways of God to man and performing the task with jaunty assurance. His book, as Johnson points out, is merely an expansion in prose of Pope's *Essay on Man,* to which little is added. But while it is as difficult to criticize Pope as it would be to criticize a display of fireworks, Jenyns's attempt at a methodical exposition of a coherent system lays all the unproved assumptions, all the sophisticated arguments, and all the glaring non sequiturs open to an attack which Johnson pushes home with remorseless vigor. It is, moreover, worthy of remark that, after declaring Jenyns's book far from the impious licentiousness of Bolingbroke, Johnson attacks it, not with weapons drawn from the armory of Christian orthodoxy but with logic of the sort Jenyns himself wished to use. In one respect Johnson is a better Popian than Jenyns—in this one respect, indeed, a better Popian than Pope—for he accepts without reservation the injunction "Presume not God to scan" and what he objects to most violently is the fact that Pope before, and Jenyns after him, proceed not only to scan God but to report confidently what no man can see.

Johnson was no mystic and he did not love mysteries. He found Christianity hard enough to accept and he took no pleasure, as Sir Thomas Browne professed to do, in believing what was difficult to believe. He was too much of a rationalist not to welcome anything that would help make Christianity seem rational, anything that would actually justify to human reason the ways of God. But he was also too honest to accept specious arguments merely because they were on his side. He could advise such a man as Jenyns "to distrust his own faculties, however large and comprehensive," and he could advise it not because Jenyns was attempting to damage trust in God and not because Johnson delighted in skepticism, but solely because he would not consent to have the grave difficulties which the spectacle of human misery puts in the way of faith in God, difficulties which he himself had painfully faced, explained away with feeble argument. On one page he exposes the conception of the Great Chain of Being for the insubstantial fancy that it is; on another he demonstrates that to accept as a premise the existence of a Supreme Being infinitely powerful, wise and benevolent is to render unnecessary all the succeeding argument intended to prove that the Supreme Being does have those attributes. The story of how Johnson "refuted" Bishop Berkeley's idealism by kicking a stone is all too well known. If this review in which he met logical argument with logical argument were equally familiar to readers, Johnson's reputation as a dialectician would be considerably higher than it is.

Even in this piece, however, the strongest—or at least the most flavorsome—passages are those in which it is not so much abstract logic that is brought to bear as it is common sense supported by that familiarity with human suffering which so regularly saves Johnson from the kind of complacency more privileged members of his century too often indulged in. For many of them it was easy, as it was for Jenyns, to explain away as part of God's plan those injustices for which society was responsible and to harden their hearts with the reflection that this is, after all, the best of all possible worlds. But Johnson, for all his lack of faith in sociological reform, seldom allowed to pass unchallenged the comfortable assumption that the sufferings of the underprivileged were not only part of God's mysterious plan but probably not really sufferings at all. He clearly rebuked one of the besetting sins of his age when he wrote in this review: "I am always afraid of determining on the side of envy and cruelty," and he then proceeded to illustrate what he meant by examining Jenyns's delighted demonstration: "Poverty, or the want of riches, is generally compensated for by having more hopes, and fewer fears, by a greater share of health, and a more exquisite relish of the smallest enjoyments, than those who possess them are usually blessed with." Commented Johnson:

"Poverty is very gently paraphrased by want of riches. In that sense, almost every man may, in his own opinion, be poor. But there is another poverty, which is want of competence of all that can soften the miseries of life, of all that can diversify attention or delight imagination. There is yet another poverty, which is want of necessaries, a species of poverty which no care of the publick, no charity of particulars, can preserve many from feeling openly, and many secretly. . . .

". . . The milder degrees of poverty are, sometimes, supported by hope; but the more severe often sink down in motionless despondence. Life must be seen, before it can be known. This author and Pope, perhaps, never saw the miseries which they imagine thus easy to be borne. The poor, indeed, are insensible of many little vexations, which sometimes imbitter the possessions, and pollute the enjoyments, of the rich. They are not pained by casual incivility, or mortified by the mutilation of a compliment; but this happiness is like that of a malefactor, who ceases to feel the cords that bind him, when the pincers are tearing his flesh. . . .

"[Jenyns] imagines, that as we have not only animals for food, but choose some for our diversion, the same privilege may be allowed to some beings above us, *who may deceive, torment, or destroy us, for the ends, only, of their own pleasure or utility.* This he again finds impossible to be conceived, *but that impossibility lessens not the probability of the conjecture, which, by analogy, is so strongly confirmed.*

"I cannot resist the temptation of contemplating this analogy, which, I think, he might have carried further, very much to the advantage of his argument. He might have shown, that these 'hunters, whose game is man,' have many sports analogous to our own. As we drown whelps and kittens, they amuse themselves, now and then, with sinking a ship, and stand round the fields of Blenheim, or the walls of Prague, as we encircle a cockpit. As we shoot a bird flying, they take a man in the midst of his business or pleasure, and knock him down with an apoplexy. Some of them, perhaps, are virtuosi, and delight in the operations of an asthma, as a human philosopher in the effects of the air-pump. To swell a man with a tympany is as good sport as to blow a frog. Many a merry bout have these frolick beings at the vicissitudes of an ague, and good sport it is to see a man tumble with an epilepsy, and revive and tumble again, and all this he knows not why. As they are wiser and more powerful than we, they have more exquisite diversions; for we have no way of procuring any sport so brisk and so lasting, as the paroxysms of the gout and stone, which, undoubtedly, must make high mirth, especially if the play be a little diversified with the blunders and puzzles of the blind and deaf. We know not how far their sphere of observation may extend. Perhaps, now and then, a merry being may place himself in such a situation, as to enjoy, at once, all the varieties of an epidemical disease, or amuse his leisure with the tossings and contortions of every possible pain, exhibited together." [2]

Rasselas

Why Johnson's supervision of *The Literary Magazine* came to an end we do not know, but it was perhaps to supply the loss of income from that source that he began in April, 1758, the series of weekly essays called *The Idler.* These, instead of being separate publications like *The Rambler,* appeared as part of a weekly newspaper called *The Universal Chronicle* and continued until April, 1760. Of the one hundred and three essays, all but twelve were written by Johnson himself and, again as in the case of *The Rambler,* they were later issued in book form. In its own day *The Idler* never achieved quite the degree of reputation which the earlier essays enjoyed and it is (if it be possible to compare accurately two degrees of popularity both of which are so nearly nil) even less read today, despite the fact that *The Idler,* being lighter, might be thought nearer the taste of our own time. Some of the essays, to be sure, might easily pass as *Ramblers,* but in general the proportion of pieces in a light tone is larger. The account of Dick Minim, the critic, is as near being well known as anything in either series, and one might easily choose various passages to illustrate Johnson's gift for good-humored satire.

Nevertheless, the only paragraph from *The Idler* still quoted from time to time is from the concluding number, and it is not difficult to understand why it has stood the test of time. Johnson's strain of melancholy exaggerated to a degree that made him conscious of it a certain psychological phenomenon which most readers recognize as having occurred in their own mental life only after Johnson has indicated it.

"There are few things not purely evil, of which we can say, without some emotion of uneasiness, *this is the last.* Those who never could agree together, shed tears when mutual discontent has determined them to final separation; of a place which has been frequently visited, though without pleasure, the last look is taken with heaviness of heart; and the Idler, with all his chilness of tranquillity, is not wholly unaffected by the thought that his last essay is now before him.

"The secret horrour of the last is inseparable from a thinking being, whose life is limited, and to whom death is dreadful. We always make a secret comparison between a part and the whole;

the termination of any period of life reminds us that life itself has likewise its termination; when we have done any thing for the last time, we involuntarily reflect that a part of the days allotted us is past, and that as more is past there is less remaining.

"It is very happily and kindly provided, that in every life there are certain pauses and interruptions, which force consideration upon the careless, and seriousness upon the light; points of time where one course of action ends, and another begins; and by vicissitudes of fortune or alteration of employment, by change of place or loss of friendship, we are forced to say of something, *this is the last.*" [3]

Johnson's style has no doubt been called "laborious" more often than it has been called anything else, but the implications of the adjective are not to be taken to include slowness of composition, for Johnson was likely to dash off at top speed even those compositions which seem heavy and involved. "When," he once observed, "a man writes from his own mind, he writes very rapidly. The greatest part of a writer's time is spent in reading, in order to write: a man will turn over half a library to make one book." And it is Boswell who tells Bennet Langton's story about the time when Johnson, on a visit to Oxford in 1759, asked him one evening when the post went out and, on being told that it would leave in about half an hour, said merely: "Then we shall do very well." He instantly sat down, composed an *Idler* (about a thousand words), and when Langton asked to read it, replied: "Sir, you shall not do more than I have done myself." He then folded the paper and dispatched it to London, where it was due at the printer's next day.

It was not until many years later that Johnson made his often-quoted remark: "No man but a blockhead ever wrote, except for money," but it is against the background of the profession of letters as he saw it at this time that the statement must be interpreted, and it is not cynical in the way that it is often assumed to be. Johnson did not love money, which he never accumulated and which he gave freely away. He put upon it the value commonly put upon it by the poor, and this is a very different thing from the value put upon it by the rich. To write for money meant, in Johnson's case, merely to write from necessity, and his statement means no more than that he could not conceive how anything except necessity could drive a man to do what he found so painful to his constitutional indolence, so much less entertaining than reading or conversation. Like many, perhaps like most, good writers, he found the process of composition disagreeable in itself even though he composed rapidly, and he spoke for many when he said: "I allow that you may have pleasure from writing, after it is over, if you have written well; but you don't go willingly to it again."

The desire to excel and to win admiration Johnson certainly had, but that desire alone was not enough to overcome his inertia, and it is noticeable that all his major works were accomplished either because he wrote under the pressure of immediate necessity or because he had previously committed himself to something from which he could not honorably escape. Thus *Rasselas* (1759), his most important work between the publication of the *Dictionary* and the appearance of his edition of Shakespeare, was composed, quite literally, to "defray the expense of his mother's funeral, and pay some little debts which she had left." The story is worth telling in full.[4]

It will be remembered that when Johnson first established himself permanently in London some twenty-two years before, he left his mother and his wife's daughter, Lucy, with the bookshop which had lost its founder when his father died in 1731. Mrs. Johnson continued to operate it until her death, when the remaining stock was added to that of the old maidservant, Catherine Chambers, who had apparently been conducting a trade in quasi independence of the original business which Mrs. Johnson had, no doubt, allowed to dwindle as she grew into extreme old age. During all these years she and Lucy had been living in the house on Market Street where Johnson was born, and indeed Lucy continued there until about 1766 when some money left by her brother, Captain Porter, enabled her to build a house of her own.

Boswell has little to say concerning Johnson's relations with the Lichfield establishment, doubtless because of Johnson's confessed reluctance to discuss the humiliating details of his poverty, but from various sources it is possible to piece together a picture of his struggles to keep his two dependents as well as himself afloat. A surviving document dated January 31, 1740, shows that he was compelled (jointly with his mother) to mortgage the Market Street house to one Theophilus Levett of Lichfield for the sum of eighty pounds, and it is obvious from his share of this sum that he promises, in a letter to Tetty dated the same day as the mortgage, to send her twenty pounds "which I have received this night" in order that she might be able to consult a good physician concerning a serious "hurt on a tendon" from which she was suffering.

This debt of eighty pounds was to plague Johnson over a long period. More than three years later (December 1, 1743) he wrote to John Levett, the son of the original mortgager, thanking him for his "forebearance" in the matter of interest and promising to pay twelve pounds "in two months." Yet the debt evidently grew, for some eight years after that (March 7, 1752) he wrote Levett thanking him again for "the long credit and kind forebearance I have received from you" and informing him that in consequence of having sold a piece of property he can now give him "a Draught of one hundred pounds upon a Bookseller of credit payable on the first of May and realizable in the meantime." Presumably the property referred to was the rights to a portion of the collected edition of *The Rambler* of which the last number was to be printed a week later. But it was not until June 27, 1757, or more than seventeen years after the obligation had originally been contracted and only eighteen months before his mother's death, that an endorsement on the mortgage preserved in the town records of Lichfield reveals that the debt was finally liquidated—presumably out of what Johnson had recently received for subscriptions to his proposed edition of Shakespeare, though that edition was not to be published until more than eight years after he had thus spent a portion of the proceeds! [5]

During all these years when he was struggling to keep a roof over his mother's head he does not appear ever to have seen her or indeed to have been in Lichfield at all between 1737 and her death. Writing to Bennet Langton in 1755, just after the publication of the *Dictionary* and referring to a possible journey, he said: "I have a mother more than eighty years old, who has counted the days to the publication of my book, in hopes of seeing me; and to her, if I can disengage myself here, I resolve to go." But he did not disengage himself. Nor were there lacking reasons other than his constitutional tendency to procrastination to excuse his neglect. Even the meticulous research done on his life since Boswell's time has failed to uncover any evidence that he was out of London more than two or possibly three times between 1737 and his mother's death: once when he went to Appleby in Leicestershire in 1740 to seek a schoolmaster's job; once when he visited Oxford in 1754; and, possibly, once when he appears to have been in the same place again the following year. Johnson was poor, he was often ill, and the journey to Lichfield was not to be undertaken lightly by an even more energetic man. More than a decade later he set out from London on Thursday at nine, and arrived at Lichfield on Friday night at eleven. Lucy Porter, though she had been well-off since the death of her brother, had never been to London when Johnson introduced Boswell to her in 1776.[6]

Johnson's deep affection for his mother involved no sentimental attribution of virtues she did not have. It has already been shown that he judged almost harshly the mental equipment of both his parents and that he never concealed from himself the fact that they had neither made each other happy nor known how to avoid hurting him with the clumsiness of their affection. There was, nevertheless, more than merely a sense of duty in his devotion to his mother, and more than mere animal affection. He did, to be sure, love her because she *was* his mother and because he had ideas about what was due to parents no more or no less strict than those which he held concerning the limits of parental authority. But in addition he clung to her, to the mere knowledge that she was alive, as he clung to all old acquaintances whose continued existence afforded some protection against that sense of being alone in the world which the superficial intimacy with the great never seemed able to give him. As her end approached, some sense of guilt arising out of the fact that he had not seen her for years intruded, and it reminded him, as so many other things did, that time rolls past; and, as in one of those dreams in which we struggle desperately to do some necessary thing without making any progress toward getting it done, he was again and again overwhelmed with the sense that all his duties had been neglected. He who could not bear to have a visitor depart and leave him alone with himself was terrified whenever an acquaintance bade him an eternal farewell.

Johnson had always been thinking that he would see his mother soon. Now he knew he was either about to see her for the last time or never to see her again. Ten years before she died he had written to Lucy Porter in reply to some bad news about his mother's health that her death "is one of the few calamities on which I think with terror," and it is the noun "terror" that makes the phrase significant.

On January 13, 1759 (she was nearly ninety), he wrote the first of a series of surviving letters in connection with her last illness and death. This first letter was obviously in reply to a communication from her which convinced him that the end was near. Three days later he writes to Lucy Porter that he has sent twelve guineas, and on the same day wrote also to his mother: "I do not think you unfit to face death, but I know not how to bear the thought of losing you. . . . I pray often for you; do you pray for me?" On January 20th he thanked her for her indulgence to him and begged forgiveness "of all that I have done ill, and all that I have omitted to do well." On the other side of the same paper he promised Lucy to come to Lichfield "if it be possible." "God grant," he added, "I may yet [find] my dear mother breathing and sensible."

His wish was not granted, for she died in his absence and was buried on January 23rd while Johnson was in London. On that day, he wrote Lucy promising to send twenty pounds "in a few days" and wrote again on January 25th: "You will forgive me if I am not yet so composed as to give any directions about anything. But you are wiser and better than I, and I shall be pleased with all that you shall do. It is not of any use for me now to come down; nor can I bear the place." On January 27th the forty-first number of *The Idler* was given over to "a letter [which] relates to an affliction perhaps not necessary to be imparted to the public," but which is printed because "I feel no disposition to provide for this day any other entertainment." The author, who is, of course, Johnson himself, remarks:

"Nothing is more evident than that the decays of age must terminate in death; yet there is no man, says Tully, who does not believe that he may yet live another year; and there is none who does not, upon the same principle, hope another year for his parent or his friend: but the fallacy will be in time detected; the last year, the last day, must come. It has come, and is past. The life which made my own life pleasant is at an end, and the gates are shut upon my prospects."

Though there can be no doubt of the depth or the sincerity of Johnson's sorrow, it is legitimate to remark that the reference to "the life which made my own life pleasant" is strongly reminiscent of things he said when Tetty died. Every person lost seemed to Johnson a final one and it may even be that, like many who suffer from apprehension and melancholy, he tended to identify its nameless cause with any event which might seem to furnish rational justification. In the Preface to the *Dictionary* he had written, no doubt with the recent death of his wife in mind: "I have protracted my work till most of those, whom I wished to please, have sunk into the grave, and success and miscarriage are empty sounds." Now his mother seemed, as Tetty seemed then, the last person to whom he had any important tie.[7]

As has already been indicated, Sarah Johnson's death was to be the occasion of a composition much longer and much more important than an *Idler* paper. On January 20th, just three days before the funeral, Johnson wrote to William Strahan, one of those concerned in the publication of the *Dictionary:*

To William Strahan

SIR,

When I was with you last night I told you of a story which I was preparing for the press. The title will be

"The Choice of Life

or

The History of . . . Prince of Abissinia"

It will make about two volumes like little Pompadour [a recently published book], this is about one middling volume. The bargain which I made with Mr. Johnson was seventy five pounds (or guineas) a volume, and twenty five pounds for the second edition. I will sell this either at that price or for sixty, the first edition of which he shall himself fix the number, and the property then to revert to me, or for forty pounds, I share the profit, that is retain half the copy. I shall have occasion for thirty pounds on Monday night when I shall deliver the book which I must entreat you upon such delivery to procure me. I would have it offered to Mr. Johnson, but have no doubt of selling it, on some of the terms mentioned.

I will not print my name, but expect it to be known.

I am, dear Sir,

Your most humble servant,

SAM: JOHNSON

Jan. 20, 1759

Get me the money if you can.

"Preparing for the press" is a vague phrase which does not indicate just how much Johnson had actually written at the time, but he told Reynolds that *Rasselas* was composed "in the evenings of one week," that it was sent to the press in portions as it was written, and that he had never since read it over. The book was not actually published until April 19th, but it must have been within a few days of his mother's death that Johnson wrote the sonorous first sentence: "Ye, who listen, with credulity, to the whispers of fancy, and pursue, with eagerness, the phantoms of hope; who expect, that age will perform the promises of youth, and that the deficiencies of the present day will be supplied by the morrow; attend to the history of Rasselas, prince of Abissinia."

The form which he adopted, that of the pseudo-Oriental tale, was of course perfectly familiar to his contemporaries as a vehicle for moral instruction and Johnson had, indeed, previously used it himself in *The Rambler*. "Abissinia" was no doubt suggested by his youthful translation of Father Lobo's travels in which, indeed, occurs the title and name of one "Rassela Christos, Lieutenant General to Sultan Segued." If any specific source is needed for the thought of the opening sentence, Johnson may have found it in one of the most famous passages of one of his favorite poets, John Dryden, who puts into the mouth of Aureng-Zebe a similar reflection concerning those who "hope tomorrow will repay." The passage was, we know, one of his favorites.[8]

Many who have never read *Rasselas* are, nevertheless, aware of the fact that it tells the story of a prince who escaped from a happy valley in order to find out for himself what men were like and how they fared. In accordance with the peculiar custom of his country (which took this means of preserving highborn persons from the temptations of political intrigue) he had been imprisoned in a sort of earthly paradise provided with every luxury and inhabited by a cultivated group of his fellow countrymen who had voluntarily agreed to commit themselves for life to this luxurious confinement.

Unlike most of his fellow prisoners, Rasselas was not content. He had some need which survived the satisfaction of every definable want and he plotted with his philosopher-guide, Imlac, to escape. Joined by his sister and her maid, they finally practised a tunnel through one of the surrounding mountains, went forth into the world, saw the unhappiness of every human condition and, in the end, decided to return to their prison because they had learned what Imlac knew from the beginning—that "Human life is everywhere a state, in which much is to be endured, and little to be enjoyed."

To Johnson's contemporaries the book was a dazzling specimen of that "true wit" which consists in achieving the perfect statement of something which "oft was thought but ne'er so well expressed." For that reason they admired it with an enthusiasm which the nineteenth century, brought up to admire novelty, paradox, perversity and eccentricity, found it difficult to understand; and in so far as we inherit the taste of that century, we too are likely to approach *Rasselas* with prejudice. But it is actually more original, or at least more tinged with the color of Johnson's own personality, than seems to have been generally remarked—possibly because in the days when it was promptly accepted as a classic there was so much less tendency than there is now to assume that individual personality, the difference between one temperament and another, is the most interesting thing which writing can reveal. Actually, Johnson did something more than merely rephrase the commonplaces which have long served to demonstrate that all is vanity. He was not content merely to indicate how men's plans go astray and men's ambitions are frustrated. His pessimism, in other words, was not merely of that vulgar sort which is no more than a lament over the failure of worldly prosperity. It was, instead, the pessimism which is more properly called the tragic sense of life, and he would undoubtedly have approved the lines of that modern poet who proclaims:

> The troubles of our proud and angry dust
> Are from eternity, and shall not fail.[9]

Since the two things, ordinary pessimism and the tragic sense of life, are easily confused, since, indeed, they are at least mingled if not confused in *Rasselas* itself, it might be worth while in analyzing the tale to build the analysis around some attempt to separate them. Let us, then, begin on the lowest level.

Told in outline as it was told above, the story would seem to be no more than a device for introducing a survey of some of the various conditions of life, and its hero no more than a naïvely neutral observer. Some portion of it is, indeed, precisely that. A series of very short chapters disposes of various ways of life with almost perfunctory brevity, though often with wit. Shepherds, the travelers find, are too rude and too stupid to tell them whether or not the pastoral life is as peaceful as poets have maintained; a hermit they discover just as he is about to return to public life, a philosopher just at the moment when a personal calamity has robbed him of all his philosophy. A professional sage whose society they cultivate soon exhibits Johnson's own weakness by demonstrating that he prefers their foolish conversation to the solitary pleasure of his own wise thoughts, and when they ask him point-blank to advise them what way of life they should choose, he can only reply that he is not able to do so, since he himself has chosen wrongly. Indeed, the only person who will consent to advise them is an optimist who accepts the universe and who believes in living in accordance with nature, but who defines that process thus: "To live according to nature, is to act always with due regard to the fitness arising from the relations and qualities of causes and effects; to concur with the great and unchangeable scheme of universal felicity; to co-operate with the general disposition and tendency of the present system of things." But "The Prince soon found that this was one of the sages whom he should understand less, as he heard him longer. He, therefore, bowed, and was silent, and the philosopher, supposing him satisfied and the rest vanquished, rose up and departed, with the air of a man that had cooperated with the present system."

But by far the best chapter in the latter half of the book is one which deals with a visit to the Pyramids and includes, indeed, what is probably the finest single paragraph in the whole work. Moreover, this chapter is interesting, and one paragraph in it unforgettable, because it treats so powerfully a theme which the earlier sections had introduced but had allowed, for the most part, to remain suggested rather than systematically developed—the theme, that is to say, which has already been called the tragic rather than the merely pessimistic theme.

Rasselas, we here perceive, did not leave the valley merely in order to find out whether, in any vulgar sense, men prospered more outside it than he did within its confines. He knew that he had in the fullest measure that security and plenty and ease for which men commonly say they perform their labors and he was prepared not to be surprised that others led lives more troubled than his. Nor was it merely that he was consumed with vague curiosity. Actually he was seeking the answer to a tremendous question. "That I want nothing," said the prince, "or that I know not what I want, is the cause of my complaint," and it is the "know not what I want" that is really important. Sometimes Rasselas supposes that this sense of wanting something unspecifiable is merely the result of having had all possible desires satisfied. "I have already," he says, "enjoyed too much; give me something to desire." But Johnson is both too little an ascetic and too profoundly concerned with the ultimate nature of man to allow his hero to rest content with so simple an explanation of his infelicity. The difficulty is not merely that all desires are satisfied, but rather that man has some desire which nothing in his experience is capable of satisfying.

" 'What,' said he, 'makes the difference between man and all the rest of the animal creation? Every beast, that strays beside me, has the same corporal necessities with myself: he is hungry, and crops the grass, he is thirsty and drinks the stream, his thirst and hunger are appeased, he is satisfied and sleeps: he rises again and is hungry, he is again fed, and is at rest. I am hungry and thirsty, like him, but when thirst and hunger cease, I am not at rest; I am, like him, pained with want, but am not, like him, satisfied with fulness. The intermediate hours are tedious and gloomy; I long again to be hungry, that I may again quicken my attention. The birds peck the berries, or the corn, and fly away to the groves, where they sit, in seeming happiness, on the branches, and waste their lives in tuning one unvaried series of sounds. I, likewise, can call the lutanist and the singer, but the sounds, that pleased me yesterday, weary me to-day, and will grow yet more wearisome to-morrow. I can discover within me no power of perception, which is not glutted with its proper pleasure, yet I do not feel myself delighted. Man surely has some latent sense, for which this place affords no gratification; or he has some desires, distinct from sense, which must be satisfied, before he can be happy.'

"After this, he lifted up his head, and seeing the moon rising, walked towards the palace. As he passed through the fields, and saw the animals around him, 'Ye,' said he, 'are happy, and need not envy me, that walk thus among you, burdened with myself; nor do I, ye gentle beings, envy your felicity; for it is not the felicity of man. I have many distresses, from which ye are free; I fear pain, when I do not feel it; I sometimes shrink at evils recollected, and sometimes start at evils anticipated: surely the equity of providence has balanced peculiar sufferings with peculiar enjoyments.' " [10]

Perhaps the fact that Rasselas, when he indulges in these reflections, is dwelling in an earthly paradise tends to suggest that such thoughts are likely to occur only to a man so situated, but Johnson's own life was certainly not passed in any happy valley and yet a boredom of tragically grandiose implications was the evil always ready to assert itself even when other evils had been temporarily banished. Indeed, and as we shall see, both his theory of aesthetics and his general theory of human nature rest ultimately upon the desperate assumption that, since man never finds any really self-justifying activity, he must, if life is to be tolerable at all, fill it up with those temporary satisfactions which are gained by the gratification of the easily wearied senses and the parallel gratification of that less easily wearied but still far from limitless appetite for knowledge to which he generally gives no more exalted name than "curiosity."

But though almost the entire substance of another *Rasselas* could easily be compiled out of Johnson's recorded sayings and the identification between himself and his hero could be completely established, he nowhere else takes so definitely as he does in this tale the step which carries him from a rationalistic despair to the point where he asks the question which the Greeks had asked: "What activity is appropriate to man? In doing what does he fulfill his function and thus satisfy himself?"

Sometimes, as for instance when writing to Baretti, Johnson speaks of life as everywhere "supported with impatience and quitted with reluctance." Here his attitude seems almost Schopenhauerian, and suggests the conviction that life is endured only because the irrational will is stronger than the rational judgment. But though the passage from *Rasselas* just quoted seems at least to hint the possibility that the existence of a need must imply the existence somewhere of an answer to it, that hint has disappeared again in the later passage, which is not only the most eloquent Johnson ever wrote on this theme but perhaps, in all literature, the most magnificent tribute ever paid to the power of Boredom.

Rasselas and his companions have, in the course of their travels, just visited the Pyramids.

" 'We have now,' said Imlac, 'gratified our minds with an exact view of the greatest work of man, except the wall of China.

" 'Of the wall it is very easy to assign the motive. It secured a wealthy and timorous nation from the incursions of barbarians, whose unskilfulness in arts made it easier for them to supply their wants by rapine than by industry, and who, from time to time, poured in upon the habitations of peaceful commerce, as vultures descend upon domestick fowl. Their celerity and fierceness, made the wall necessary, and their ignorance made it efficacious.

" 'But, for the pyramids, no reason has ever been given adequate to the cost and labour of the work. The narrowness of the chambers proves that it could afford no retreat from enemies, and treasures might have been reposited, at far less expense, with equal security. It seems to have been erected only in compliance with that hunger of imagination, which preys incessantly upon life, and must be always appeased by some employment. Those who have already all that they can enjoy, must enlarge their desires. He that has built for use, till use is supplied, must begin to build for vanity, and extend his plan to the utmost power of human performance, that he may not be soon reduced to form another wish.

" 'I consider this mighty structure, as a monument of the insufficiency of human enjoyments. A king, whose power is unlimited, and whose treasures surmount all real and imaginary wants, is compelled to solace, by the erection of a pyramid, the satiety of dominion and tastelessness of pleasures, and to amuse the tediousness of declining life, by seeing thousands labouring without end, and one stone, for no purpose, laid upon another. Whoever thou art, that, not content with a moderate condition, imaginest happiness in royal magnificence, and dreamest that command or riches can feed the appetite of novelty, with perpetual gratifications, survey the pyramids, and confess thy folly!' " [11]

According to Boswell, Mr. Strahan and Mr. Johnston bought the copyright of *Rasselas* for a hundred pounds, but afterwards paid the author twenty-five more when it came to a second edition. This seems less than what Johnson had asked in the letter published above, but Baretti told Malone that Johnson was "perfectly contented" with Dodsley's offer of one hundred pounds. In any event, the book was a great success, not only in England but abroad. Six English editions are listed in Johnson's lifetime and translations into Italian, French and German promptly appeared. A review in *The Gentleman's Magazine* for April, 1759, filled nearly five columns. Though composed mostly of excerpt and summary, the last sentence declares that Johnson's tale is full of "the most elegant and striking pictures of life and nature, the most acute disquisitions, and the happiest illustrations of the most important truths." [12]

Voltaire's *Candide* was published the same year as *Rasselas* (probably some two months earlier). Johnson himself, says Boswell, remarked "that if they had not been published so closely one after the other that there was not time for imitation, it would have been in vain to deny that the scheme of that which came latest was taken from the other," and comparison became an inevitable topic for commentators. Johnson thought that "Candide . . . had more power in it than any thing that *Voltaire* had written"; Voltaire, acknowledging a copy of the first French translation sent him by its maker, wrote less ambiguously: "Il m'a paru d'une philosophie aimable, et très-bien écrit." Boswell, who of course was always ready with the correct moral sentiments, remarks:

"Voltaire, I am afraid, meant only by wanton profaneness to obtain a sportive victory over religion, and to discredit the belief of a superintending Providence: Johnson meant, by shewing the unsatisfactory nature of things temporal, to direct the hopes of man to things eternal. Rasselas, as was observed to me by a very accomplished lady, may be considered as a more enlarged and more deeply philosophical discourse in prose, upon the interesting truth, which in his 'Vanity of Human Wishes' he had so successfully enforced in verse." [13]

Such was the line usually taken—as, for example, by one of Johnson's early nineteenth-century editors who did not hesitate to run the risk of exaggerating the effect of the printed word in order to make the contrast more vivid and who roundly announced that, while "the one demoralized a continent, and gave birth to lust, and rapine, and bloodshed; the other has blessed many a heart, and gladdened the vale of sorrow, with many a rill of pure and living water."

But such easy contrasts seem hardly worth drawing. That Voltaire is ribald and ferocious, Johnson melancholy and pietistic, is obvious enough. Yet the very fact that comparisons are drawn seems to suggest that those who make them may have some uneasy sense that, despite the obvious contrasts, there are apparent similarities which ought to be explained away. Indeed, the two lines of argument advanced by the two moralists coincide precisely at the point where Johnson, in a passage quoted above, pays ironical respect to the special system of optimism which is the principal object of Voltaire's attack. However antithetical the temperaments of the two men may have been, they find equally absurd the proposition that this is the best of all possible worlds in the simple sense that Pope had proclaimed when he wrote:

> All discord harmony not understood;
> All partial evil universal good.

Neither is prepared to accept either Spinoza or Leibnitz, or the popular vulgarization of the two.

But the contrast between them is not the simple contrast between the cynic and the Christian, each refusing for a different reason to agree that the world is good. To afford so simple an antithesis, Voltaire would have had to be more of a cynic, and Johnson, if not more of a Christian, at least a Christian of either a more mystical or a more sentimental sort, and hence readier than he was to find a really effective consolation in the reflection that this life is merely the prelude to another. Actually, Johnson was, in one respect, more of a cynic than Voltaire, because Voltaire believed in the possibility of reform while Johnson did not. And if it is not cynicism that prevents him from insisting upon the adequacy of the pietistic solution which he makes a show of offering, it is two things which would have driven a different temperament to cynicism—namely, what he himself called his "obstinate rationality" coupled with an appetite for living which he was too contemptuous of cant to pretend to deny.

Rasselas does not so much end as break off. His contemporaries supposed that Johnson intended to write a continuation, but it seems equally likely that once he had written enough to fill the two small volumes he had agreed to deliver, he stopped because he did not like to write and because, in this particular case, he did not know what more to say. "It was now the time of the inundation of the Nile . . . They deliberated awhile what was to be done, and resolved, when the inundation should cease, to return to Abissinia." Thus the tale concludes, and on the basis of the final sentence one would seem justified in saying that the moral is not that no career leads to happiness and that therefore happiness should not be sought for, but rather the almost Epicurean conclusion that since the ultimate source of human unhappiness "is from eternity," the most fortunate men are those who, like the inhabitants of the Valley, are at least relieved from all the secondary causes of distress and possess in the largest measure the palliatives of security and pleasure. Rasselas and Imlac do return to physical comfort and security.

Shortly before, the sister of Rasselas has been made to say: "To me the choice of life is become less important; I hope, hereafter, to think only on the choice of eternity," and thus Johnson pays to orthodoxy, as he always does, the tribute of formal profession. But these formal professions cannot mean to him what they would have meant had they been as simply and vividly believed in as some have believed them, and here they constitute only the formal rather than the effective moral. Interpreted in the light of his own life as he lived it, the conclusion of *Candide* ("Let us cultivate our garden") would be almost as appropriate to *Rasselas* and therein, perhaps, lies one of the resemblances between the two books which made champions of English respectability so anxious to labor the obvious differences between them.

Boswell, who passed much more easily and more completely than Johnson through the series of steps which lead from the acceptance of orthodoxy to the determination to cultivate pleasantly the garden of this temporary state, could write with enviable ease:

"But if we walk with hope in 'the mid-day sun' of revelation, our temper and disposition will be such, that the comforts and enjoyments in our way will be relished, while we patiently support the inconveniences and pains. After much speculation and various reasonings. I acknowledge myself convinced of the truth of Voltaire's conclusion, *'Après tout c'est un monde passable.'*"

Johnson himself once wrote Mrs. Thrale: "*Vivite laeti* is one of the great rules of health"; and though he might well have suspected of lightness anyone who found it so easy to supply *Rasselas* with Boswell's gloss, he had no theoretical disagreement with it and in his own more troubled way attempted to put its recommendations into practice. Again and again when he is faced with the necessity either of consoling others or of facing some sorrow of his own, the steps are the same. First, the consolations of religion. Then, to others or to himself, the advice: Seek the palliatives for those ills which are susceptible of no radical remedy. That the man as well as the child can be pleased with a rattle and tickled with a straw is indeed one of nature's most kindly laws.[14]

OA'RY. *adj.* [from *oar.*] Having the form or uſe of oars.

His hair transforms to down, his fingers meet
In ſkinny films, and ſhape his *oary* feet. *Addiſon.*
The ſwan with arched neck,
Between her white wings mantling, proudly rows
Her ſtate with *oary* feet. *Milton.*

OAST. *n. ſ.* A kiln. Not in uſe.

Empty the binn into a hog-bag, and carry them immediately to the *oaſt* or kiln, to be dried. *Mortimer.*

OATCA'KE. *n. ſ.* [*oat* and *cake.*] Cake made of the meal of oats.

Take a blue ſtone they make haver or *oatcakes* upon, and lay it upon the croſs bars of iron. *Peacham.*

OA'TEN. *adj.* [from *oat.*] Made of oats; bearing oats.

When ſhepherds pipe on *oaten* ſtraws,
And merry larks are ploughmens clocks. *Shakeſpeare.*

OATH. *n. ſ.* [*aith*, Gothick; að, Saxon. The diſtance between the noun *oath*, and the verb *ſwear*, is very obſervable, as it may ſhew that our oldeſt dialect is formed from different languages.] An affirmation, negation, or promiſe, corroborated by the atteſtation of the Divine Being.

Read over Julia's heart, thy firſt beſt love,
For whoſe dear ſake thou then did'ſt rend thy faith
Into a thouſand *oaths*; and all thoſe *oaths*
Deſcended into perjury to love me. *Shakeſpeare.*

He that ſtrikes the firſt ſtroke, I'll run him up to the hilts as I am a ſoldier
—An *oath* of mickle might; and fury ſhall abate. *Shakeſpeare.*

We have conſultations, which inventions ſhall be publiſhed, which not: and take an *oath* of ſecrecy for the concealing of thoſe which we think fit to keep ſecret. *Bacon.*

Thoſe called to any office of truſt, are bound by an *oath* to the faithful diſcharge of it: but an *oath* is an appeal to God, and therefore can have no influence, except upon thoſe who believe that he is. *Swift.*

OA'THABLE. *adj.* [from *oath.* A word not uſed.] Capable of having an oath adminiſtered.

You're not *oathable*,
Altho' I know you'll ſwear
Into ſtrong ſhudders th' immortal gods. *Shakeſpeare.*

OATHBREA'KING. *n. ſ.* [*oath* and *break.*] Perjury; the vio-

If when you make your pray'rs,
God ſhould be ſo *obdurate* as yourſelves,
How would it fare with your departed ſouls? *Shakeſp.*
Women are ſoft, mild, pitiful, and flexible;
Thou ſtern, *obdurate*, flinty, rough, remorſeleſs. *Shakeſp.*
To convince the proud what ſigns avail,
Or wonders move th' *obdurate* to relent;
They harden'd more, by what might more reclaim. *Milt.*
Obdurate as you are, oh! hear at leaſt
My dying prayers, and grant my laſt requeſt. *Dryden.*

2. Hardned; firm; ſtubborn.

Sometimes the very cuſtom of evil makes the heart *obdurate* againſt whatſoever inſtructions to the contrary. *Hooker.*

A pleaſing ſorcery could charm
Pain for a while, or anguiſh, and excite
Fallacious hope, or arm th' *obdurate* breaſt
With ſtubborn patience, as with triple ſteel. *Milton.*

No ſuch thought ever ſtrikes his marble, *obdurate* heart, but it preſently flies off and rebounds from it. It is impoſſible for a man to be thorough-paced in ingratitude, till he has ſhook off all fetters of pity and compaſſion. *South.*

3. Harſh; rugged.

They joined the moſt *obdurate* conſonants without one intervening vowel. *Swift.*

OBDU'RATELY. *adv.* [from *obdurate.*] Stubbornly; inflexibly; impenitently.

OBDU'RATENESS. *n. ſ.* [from *obdurate.*] Stubbornneſs; inflexibility; impenitence.

OBDURA'TION. *n. ſ.* [from *obdurate.*] Hardneſs of heart; ſtubbornneſs.

What occaſion it had given them to think, to their greater *obduration* in evil, that through a froward and wanton deſire of innovation, we did conſtrainedly thoſe things, for which conſcience was pretended? *Hooker.*

OBDU'RED. *adj.* [*obduratus*, Latin.] Hardned; inflexible; impenitent.

This ſaw his hapleſs foes, but ſtood *obdur'd*,
And to rebellious fight rallied their pow'rs
Inſenſate. *Milton.*

OBE'DIENCE. *n. ſ.* [*obedience*, Fr. *obedientia*, Latin.] Obſequiouſneſs; ſubmiſſion to authority; compliance with command or prohibition.

By now forswearing that he is forsworn. *Shakesp.*

OA'TMALT. *n. s.* [*oat* and *malt.*] Malt made of oats.

In Kent they brew with one half *oatmalt*, and the other half barleymalt. *Mortimer.*

OA'TMEAL. *n. s.* [*oat* and *meal.*] Flower made by grinding oats.

Oatmeal and butter, outwardly applied, dry the scab on the head. *Arbuthnot.*

Our neighbours tell me oft, in joking talk,
Of ashes, leather, *oatmeal*, bran, and chalk. *Gay.*

OA'TMEAL. *n. s.* An herb. *Ainsworth.*

OATS. *n. s.* [aten, Saxon.] A grain, which in England is generally given to horses, but in Scotland supports the people.

It is of the grass leaved tribe; the flowers have no petals, and are disposed in a loose panicle: the grain is eatable. The meal makes tolerable good bread. *Miller.*

The *oats* have eaten the horses. *Shakespeare.*

It is bare mechanism, no otherwise produced than the turning of a wild *oat* beard, by the insinuation of the particles of moisture. *Locke.*

For your lean cattle, fodder them with barley straw first, and the *oat* straw last. *Mortimer.*

His horse's allowance of *oats* and beans, was greater than the journey required. *Swift.*

OA'TTHISTLE. *n. s.* [*oat* and *thistle.*] An herb. *Ains.*

OBAMBULA'TION. *n. s.* [*obambulatio*, from *obambulo*, Latin.] The act of walking about. *Dict.*

To OBDU'CE. *v. a.* [*obduco*, Latin.] To draw over as a covering.

No animal exibits its face in the native colour of its skin but man; all others are covered with feathers, hair, or a cortex that is *obduced* over the cutis. *Hale.*

OBDUC'TION. *n. s.* [from *obductio*, *obduco*, Latin.] The act of covering, or laying a cover.

OBDU'RACY. *n. s.* [from *obdurate.*] Inflexible wickedness; impenitence; hardness of heart.

Thou think'st me as far in the Devil's book, as thou and Falstaff, for *obduracy* and persistency. *Shakespeare.*

God may, by a mighty grace, hinder the absolute completion of sin in final *obduracy*. *South.*

OBDURATE. *adj.* [*obduratus*, Latin.]

1. Hard of heart; inflexibly obstinate in ill; hardned; impenitent.

Oh! let me teach thee for thy father's sake,
That gave thee life, when well he might have slain thee;
Be not *obdurate*, open thy deaf ears. *Shakespeare.*

N° XCIX.

Craves no other tribute at thy hands,
But love, fair looks, and true *obedience*. *Shakesp.*

His servants ye are, to whom ye obey, whether of sin unto death, or of *obedience* unto righteousness. *Rom.*

It was both a strange commission, and a strange *obedience* to a commission, for men so furiously assailed, to hold their hands. *Bacon.*

Nor can this be,
But by fulfilling that which thou didst want,
Obedience to the law of God, impos'd
On penalty of death. *Milton.*

OBEDIENT. *adj.* [*obediens*, Latin.] Submissive to authority; compliant with command or prohibition; obsequious.

To this end did I write, that I might know the proof of you, whether ye be *obedient* in all things. 2 *Cor.*

To this her mother's plot
She, seemingly *obedient*, likewise hath
Made promise. *Shakespeare.*

He humbled himself, and became *obedient* unto death. *Phil.* ii. 8.

Religion hath a good influence upon the people, to make them *obedient* to government, and peaceable one towards another. *Tillotson.*

The chief his orders gives; th' *obedient* band,
With due observance, wait the chief's command. *Pope.*

OBE'DIENTIAL. *adj.* [*obedientiel*, Fr. from *obedient.*] According to the rule of obedience.

Faith is such as God will accept of, when it affords fiducial reliance on the promises, and *obediential* submission to the command. *Hammond.*

Faith is then perfect, when it produces in us a fiduciary assent to whatever the gospel has revealed, and an *obediential* submission to the commands. *Wake.*

OBE'DIENTLY. *adv.* [from *obedient.*] With obedience.

We should behave ourselves reverently and *obediently* towards the Divine Majesty, and justly and charitably towards men. *Tillotson.*

OBE'ISANCE. *n. s.* [*obeïsance*, Fr. This word is formed by corruption from *abaïsance*, an act of reverence.] A bow; a courtesy; an act of reverence made by inclination of the body or knee.

Bartholomew my page,
See drest in all suits like a lady;
Then call him Madam, do him all *obeisance*. *Shakespeare.*

Bathsheba bowed and did *obeisance* unto the king. 1 *Kings.*

18 K The

A page from the first edition of Johnson's *Dictionary*, including the definition of "oats" (Courtesy Columbia University Library) before that time is based either upon cold document or upon the information Johnson himself chose to impart.

All this has, no doubt, something to do with the fact that the Johnson everyone knows seems to have come into being at just about this time, and we shall probably never be able to decide to what extent Johnson really did emerge after the most laborious part of his life was passed. That the impression we have is in part an illusion produced by the sudden flood of light thrown upon him may have been intimated by those portions of this book which have gone before and in which some attempt was made to illuminate certain of Johnson's sayings and doings by relating them to what he said and did in the later period. But that the impression is not *wholly* an illusion there is good reason for believing.

Improved circumstances were now about to make it for the first time possible for Johnson to expand at leisure his social tendencies and to become a great talker rather than merely an industrious hack painfully establishing his fame by doing hack work like a man of genius. It was no mere accident that Boswell met Johnson when he did or that Johnson readily accepted a satellite. He was enlarging the circle of his friends and moving into a social group unlike any of which he had been a member before. He was, in other words, now becoming for the first time a man whom one could advantageously Boswellize. Hitherto he had spent too large a part of his time in the process of writing—an activity that provides little material for the biographers whom the results of it may attract. Moreover, it is by no means certain that Boswell, who was after all very much of an eighteenth-century gentleman, could have brought himself to spend a great deal of time with anyone as shabby and as hard pressed as Johnson had previously been. What Johnson called the "anecdotes of beggary" added picturesqueness to that background of the past against which Boswell sometimes liked to see his hero. But it is doubtful if he would have found much pleasure in chronicling them before it had become evident that they were indeed background only.

Johnson himself can have had no reason for supposing that his material circumstances were likely to undergo any considerable improvement. Indeed, in the period just before that in which relief came the prospects must have appeared more than usually dark. *The Idler* was concluded, he had no regular employment with any periodical, the first proceeds from the subscription to his proposed edition of Shakespeare had already been spent, and his only source of income appears to have been from a few reviews, prefaces, dedications and the like which he turned out from time to time. *The Idler* was not published in collected form until October, 1761, and the sale seems to have been slow; besides, Johnson had already given Newbery two I.O.U.'s, dated May 19, 1759, and March 20, 1760, for sums totaling just under seventy-three pounds. By this time Johnson's reputation was already so well established and his personality so well known that Tobias Smollett could refer to him jocosely as "that great CHAM of literature." But the great Cham was still living from hand to mouth.[1]

In the interests of economy he gave up, by March 23, 1759, the house in Gough Square where he had lived for ten years. Miss Williams was sent into lodgings, where it became Johnson's custom to drink tea with her every night before he went home and her custom to wait up for him no matter how late it might be. Johnson himself took rooms, first at Staple Inn, then in Gray's Inn, then in Inner Temple Lane; and he had no house of his own again until 1765.

It was to the lodgings in Inner Temple Lane that Arthur Murphy paid a call in 1762 and it was them he was to describe as "the abode of wretchedness"; but if the reference was to the lodgings rather than to their inhabitant, the phrase was an exaggeration. Indeed, this last of Johnson's lodgings was, though cheap, probably a pleasant enough place so far as location was concerned, and Johnson stayed on in them for some time after his circumstances had improved. If Miss Williams was absent, Levett was there to get and to share his breakfasts. It was there also that the inveterately picturesque Murphy describes him as living "in poverty, total idleness, and the pride of literature"; receiving solace in his fits of depression from the Rev. John Douglas, later Bishop of Salisbury, and speaking elegant Latin in reply to the colloquial jargon preceeding from the mouth of a traveling Jesuit. It was there also that Mr. Fitzherbert called one morning in hopes of being able to write a letter but found to his great surprise that "an author by profession" could be without pen, ink or paper. "I was once told by a great master," wrote Johnson in *The Idler,* "that no man ever excelled in painting, who was eminently curious about pencils and colours." Perhaps he was one of those writers who feel that to prepare too elaborately for the coming of Minerva is to issue by implication at least one of those invitations which she is said to take pleasure in refusing.

Murphy's description of Johnson's life "in poverty, total idleness, and the pride of literature" certainly suggests a happy bohemianism. Such to him it doubtless seemed and such at moments it doubtless was. Yet it must have been just about the time referred to, or some eight or nine months after Johnson had moved into the chambers in Inner Temple Lane, that this bohemian was writing in his journal under the date "Easter Eve 1761":

"Since the Communion of last Easter I have led a life so dissipated and useless, and my terrors and perplexities have so much encreased, [*sic*] that I am under great depression and discouragement, yet I purpose to present myself before God tomorrow with humble hope that he will not break the bruised reed . . . I have resolved, I hope not presumptuously, till I am afraid to resolve again. Yet hoping in God I steadfastly purpose to lead a new life. O God, enable me, for Jesus Christ's sake."

Nothing is more characteristic of Johnson than the contrast between the desperate vivacity which was the first thing new acquaintances noticed and the black abyss of melancholy into which old friends knew he was slipping when he dropped out of the conversation to mutter incomprehensibly to himself.[2]

Shortly after he first moved into chambers, Johnson visited Oxford, this being, apparently, the first time he had left London in four years; and no doubt because the university always tended to exhilarate him, he wrote from thence a letter of almost undergraduate exuberance. "[Van] is now making tea for me. I have been in my gown ever since I came here. It was at my first coming quite new and handsome. I have swum thrice, which I had disused for many years. I have proposed to Vansittart, climbing over the wall, but he has refused me. And I have clapped my hands till they are sore, at Dr. King's speech." Mrs. Thrale, who was in her time familiar with Johnson's grotesque insistence upon carrying out sudden impulses to schoolboyish exhibitions of physical exuberance, notes, in the margin, not any surprise at Johnson, but only the wonder that Vansittart, whom she obviously knew, "declined any frolic"; and it was probably during this visit that Johnson drank "three bottles of port without being the worse for it"—an achievement of which he boasted nearly twenty years later. Yet such explosions of high animal spirits were less frequent though perhaps no less characteristic than the moods of depression.[3]

Such, then, was Johnson's state, material and spiritual, during the few years preceding the day when a capricious government suddenly decided, for reasons not too clear, to remove him forever from the shadow of actual want. He was famous, he was poor, and he was subject, as he always had been and always would be, to desperate depressions. But he was also better prepared than he had ever been before to expand somewhat in the mild sunshine of moderate prosperity. His visit to Oxford (which has already been referred to) and a visit to Lichfield (which he made during the winter of 1761-62 when he saw his native town for the first time in approximately a quarter of a century) show that he was beginning to feel that need of movement which new prosperity was to enable him to indulge and he was steadily laying the foundations upon which the ramifying structure of his social life was to be built. We know that he had met Dr. Burney, the eminent music scholar and father of the irrepressible Fanny, in 1758 and that he added Topham Beauclerk, the most frivolous of his friends, on the visit to Oxford the following year. It is not always easy to know when he first made the acquaintance of the individual members of the brilliant circle in the center of which he was soon to shine, but it is clear that he knew Reynolds while still living in poverty and the pride of literature. And though Johnson is known to have paid his first visit to Goldsmith's house in May, 1761, Boswell found Goldsmith already proud of his intimacy with the great man when Boswell was just beginning his association.

Apparently Johnson, who prided himself on plain-spoken contempt for politicians in power, had no reason to suspect or hope that he would ever be made the recipient of any bounty until the intention was announced to him. The Earl of Bute, then prime minister, recommended the matter to the king and told Boswell that it was Mr. Wedderburn, later Lord Loughborough, who had made the suggestion to him. But the question who persuaded Mr. Wedderburn must remain a question, for, according to Boswell, Arthur Murphy and Thomas Sheridan both claimed credit as prime movers while Mr. Wedderburn himself would say only: "All his friends assisted." In any event, Mr. Wedderburn was a person important enough to discuss the matter with Johnson without being too important to be able to do so unofficially. Yet, according to Murphy's account, Wedderburn had heard so much of Johnson's independent spirit and of the downfall of Osborne the bookseller whom Johnson was supposed, according to a story which had grown to legendary proportions, to have knocked down with a folio for impertinence, that he asked Murphy to feel his way for him.

Accordingly Murphy went immediately to Inner Temple Lane and "by slow and studied approaches the message was disclosed." Johnson fell into a profound meditation, and asked if the suggestion was seriously intended. He remembered his own definition, which stood in what was the standard dictionary of the English language: "Pension. An allowance made to anyone without an equivalent. In England it is generally understood to mean pay given to a state hireling for treason to his country." And though Murphy does not say so, Johnson was no doubt also balancing the fact that he would undoubtedly be taunted many times if he accepted against the fact that he was being offered the opportunity to change his state from that of a man to whom the third dinner ahead seemed a long prospect to that of one who could be reasonably sure that no dinner would be lacking as long as he lived—for, though the pension was nominally only "at the king's pleasure" rather than for life, it was not likely that he would ever be deprived of it, and of course he was not.

Murphy assured him that "he, at least, did not come within the definition"—i.e., Johnson's own definition of "pensioner." Johnson asked for time and suggested that they meet for dinner next day at the Mitre Tavern. According to Boswell, who has none of the picturesque details just recounted, Johnson sought the advice of Reynolds and Reynolds assured him there could be no objection to his receiving from the king a reward for literary merit. According to Murphy again, Johnson had given up all his scruples when the two next met, and on the following day he was conducted by Mr. Wedderburn to Lord Bute, who assured him that the pension was not offered "for having dipped your pen in faction, nor with a *design* that you ever should." In Boswell's version the words are: "It is not given you for any thing you are to do, but for what you have done," and they were repeated twice so "that he might be sure Johnson heard them." Thus was the great business accomplished.[4]

The sum offered was three hundred pounds per annum, and that was considerable. Many years before, it may be remembered, Johnson had fixed thirty pounds as the annual sum upon which a man might live in London preserved from want, and in the life of his friend Savage he had called two hundred pounds "affluence." The allowance of one thousand pounds which Henry Thrale had as a young man Johnson called "splendid," but he meant that it was such even for a young buck born to the purple of a great brewery, and "splendour" was also the word he chose when, late in life, there was an unrealized hope that his own pension might be doubled and he remarked that with such a sum "a man would have the consciousness that he should pass the remainder of his life in splendour."

Three hundred a year was, then, to Johnson something more than affluence though quite a little less than splendor. It was not, as Boswell once reminded him while administering a characteristic prod, enough to justify keeping a coach; nor was it, so Johnson thought, enough to enable him in his last days to make a long journey in search of health. But the latter of these facts means chiefly that Johnson had always been free with money when he had it, and his own opinion is probably best represented in his reply to the prod above referred to: "Sir, I have never complained of the world; nor do I think that I have reason to complain. It is rather to be wondered at that I have so much. My pension is more out of the usual course of things than any instance that I have known. Here, Sir, was a man avowedly no friend to Government at the time, who got a pension without asking for it. I never courted the great; they sent for me; but I think they now give me up." When Topham Beauclerk heard the news he remarked to Johnson (with Falstaff in mind): "I hope you'll now purge and live cleanly like a gentleman"; if Johnson never quite did that, it was not because three hundred pounds was not sufficient. It was because, as he confessed when answering the charge that Christopher Smart did not love clean linen: "I have no passion for it." [5]

Boswell, who could be ardent friend of liberty or correct High-Church Tory as the occasion seemed to demand, introduces his account of the business with a flourish about the recent accession of George the Third, which "opened new and brighter prospects to men of literary merit, who had been honoured with no mark of royal favor in the preceeding reign," and reports that Johnson expressed himself as overwhelmed "with his Majesties goodness." But of course neither Boswell nor Johnson was naïve enough to suppose that his Majesty had thought the thing up for himself. Indeed, Johnson had said to a friend in the previous year: "You know that we have a new King and a new Parliament. . . . We were so weary of our old King, that we are much pleased with his successor; of whom we are so much inclined to hope great things, that most of us begin already to believe them. The young man is hitherto blameless; but it would be unreasonable to expect much from the immaturity of juvenile years, and the ignorance of princely education. He has been long in the hands of the Scots, and has already favored them more than the English will contentedly endure. But, perhaps, he scarcely knows whom he has distinguished, or whom he has disgusted." The humorous common sense, the placid disenchantment of such a passage is far more characteristic of Johnson than his occasional attempts to recapture for himself the romance of such ancient institutions as that of kingship and he knew well enough, whether Boswell did or not, that the "taste and beneficence" which prompted the new monarch "to be the patron of science and the arts" would not have been remarkable in anyone except a king named George. His Majesty might consent in his later years to have *Paradise Lost* read to him by Mrs. Siddons but, as he confessed to Fanny Burney, he thought a great part of Shakespeare sad stuff, and is said to have been so affected by the representation of a play called *The Mysterious Husband* that he turned his back while exclaiming to his queen: "Charlotte, don't look, it's too much to bear." [6]

How, then, did it happen that a government which posterity has not judged either very generous or very farseeing did, nevertheless, reach down to lift out of his poverty one of the least courtly men of letters in all England? The worst possible motives have on occasion been alleged. It has been suggested, for instance, that Lord Bute had pensioned so many Scotchmen and smarted so under Churchill's attack on the Scotch crew in *The Prophecy of Famine* that he thought it advisable to make a show of generosity to someone born south of the border. But to this it has been replied that, since Churchill did not publish his attack until after Johnson's pension had been granted, it must have been only a bad conscience rather than any prodding from the outside which urged this motive on Lord Bute—if indeed the motive was present at all. Others have suggested that Lord Bute, despite his protestation to the contrary, did expect to get something out of Johnson as he certainly expected to get something out of the pension of two hundred a year to the hireling hack Shebbeare. Indeed, he actually did get something in the form of Johnson's later political pamphlets, though they would probably have been written even if he had not been a pensioner.

Perhaps if we remember how freely and capriciously sinecures and pensions were still being distributed in eighteenth-century England it will appear that we do not need to assume that the Government had any definite end in view when it chose Johnson to be the recipient of a bounty. The system of patronage was so taken for granted and spread its ramifications so widely that a statesman bought favor here and there merely on the chance that the good will of the person concerned might come in handy some day. Moreover, favor given to an eminent man from whom no obvious or immediate return was expected had a tendency to suggest that the statesman responsible was a large-minded lover of virtue.

When a man was professionally in politics, the situation was somewhat different. His support was bought in the course of an honorable transaction which everybody understood, and it was disgraceful, not creditable, for the recipient of a favor not to stay bought. The extent to which this was true is amusingly illustrated by a letter from Sir Robert Walpole's political enemy, Sir William Pultney, to one Dr. Zachary Pearce whom Walpole had just made Dean of Winchester. Writes Pultney: "Though you may think that others besides Sir Robert have contributed to get you this dignity, yet you may depend upon it, that he is all in all. . . . It may happen that some who are of our party, may, if there should be any opposition for members of Parliament at Winchester, prevail upon me to desire you to act there in assistance of some friend of ours; and Sir Robert at the same time may ask your assistance in the election for a friend of his own against the one we recommend. I tell you therefore beforehand that if you comply with my request rather than with Sir Robert's, to whom you are so very much obliged, I shall have the worse opinion of you." In other words, if the dean of a cathedral wishes to be regarded as an honorable man by another honorable man, he will by no means use his influence in favor of this honorable man (and of course not in accordance with the direction of his own conscience), but entirely according to the wishes of the person who saw to it that he became an ecclesiastical dignitary. Surely there can be few instances of an equally paradoxical high-mindedness in the whole range of political history.

But if this was the sort of thing demanded of those with definite political influence, much less was expected of private persons who had been bought merely because they were in some way prominent or connected with prominent people. Thus Horace Walpole, though his liberalism was doubtless sincere and though he certainly mingled not at all in politics, speaks of "all my comfortable apartments in the Exchequer and Custom House" as simply as he would have spoken of paternal estates, and most of his contemporaries would take the situation equally as a matter of course. No wonder then that neither the Government nor the public thought any particular reason need be assigned when some modest bounty was dropped into the lap of anyone not obviously unworthy.

Men of modest achievements, position or connections assumed more frankly than similar people would in the twentieth century that society owed them a living, and the general public, even if it did not always enthusiastically think the same, was not disposed to be resentful if these same not very useful people managed to live at public expense. Pensions had on occasion been given for even less defensible reasons: there is the famous case of John Cleland, whose pension was said to have been given merely in order to make it unnecessary for him to write any more books like *The Memoirs of Fanny Hill!* Today, of course, there would be considerable outcry if a pension were proposed for a notorious provider of obscene literature. Much would be heard about the impudent waste of public funds. But that would be because the average citizen would think his money was being wasted, whereas in the eighteenth century it was less common to think in these terms. It was the king's money that was being spent and "his Majesty's generosity" was more likely to be praised by people who did not stop to realize where his Majesty got the funds with which his Government was being generous.[7]

Johnson's enemies, of course, accused him of venality. His enemies would willingly enough have accused him of worse on slighter pretext. But it is doubtful if anyone who did not think badly of him already thought any worse of him for taking a pension. He himself did not suppose that any return was expected. Once he threatened to resign his bounty when the Government applied to him for a pamphlet, but he reconsidered his threat and it is presumed the pamphlet was not insisted upon. With obvious wisdom he allowed the definition of "pension" to stand in the revised edition of the *Dictionary* which appeared in 1773 after he himself had corrected it. To Boswell he explained what he considered the extent of his obligation: " 'I am the same man in every respect that I have ever been; I retain the same principles. It is true, that I cannot now curse (smiling) the House of Hanover; nor would it be decent for me to drink King James's health in the wine that King George gives me money to pay for. But, Sir, I think that the pleasure of cursing the House of Hanover, and drinking King James's health, are amply overbalanced by three hundred pounds a year.' "

On July 20, 1762, Johnson wrote his formal note of thanks to the Earl of Bute. On the very same day he wrote a long letter to his enigmatic Italian friend, Joseph Baretti, then visiting Milan. Since Johnson, in his early days at least, seldom wrote more than he had to write, his letters are likely to be businesslike at best, scrappy at worst, and likely to begin with some apology for not writing more or oftener. This particular letter is, however, one of the earliest of those extant which reveal him in the humor to express himself with something approaching expansive ease. Somewhat oddly, he makes no mention of the pension, but it is difficult to resist the temptation to believe that the chatty and unhurried tone of this letter reflects the psychological effect of a pressure relieved and that one of the first effects of his new prosperity was to create a sense of what his fellow townswoman, Anna Seward, called "epistolatory leisure."

But the letter also reveals that security did not fundamentally change his tendency to see life through spectacles by no means rose-colored and to suffer from a disenchantment of a rather special sort. It was noted in connection with Johnson's first important piece of writing, the Preface to his translation of Father Lobo's travels, that it was not the drama but the lack of drama in human existence which usually struck him most forcibly. The sense that few things ever come up to our expectation of them was the mild phase of the infirmity which had black ennui as its most virulent manifestation.

After recounting to Baretti some bits of the news of the town Johnson goes on:

"Last winter I went down to my native town, where I found the streets much narrower and shorter than I thought I had left them, inhabited by a new race of people, to whom I was very little known. My play-fellows were grown old, and forced me to suspect that I was no longer young. My only remaining friend has changed his principles, and was become the tool of the predominant faction. My daughter-in-law, from whom I expected most, and whom I met with sincere benevolence, has lost the beauty and gaiety of youth, without having gained much of the wisdom of age. I wandered about for five days, and took the first convenient opportunity of returning to a place, where, if there is not much happiness, there is, at least, such a diversity of good and evil, that slight vexations do not fix upon the heart. Let us trust that a time will come, when the present moment shall be no longer irksome; when we shall not borrow all our happiness from hope, which at last is to end in disappointment." [8]

Inevitably Johnson's biographers have speculated over the question whether or not he would have written more if he had never received a pension, whether it was "a good thing" to relieve of all necessity a great writer who professed that only necessity could make him write. That question is, of course, not likely to be answered and may be dismissed with the reminder that Johnson's two most important literary works (if the *Dictionary* be left out of the count) were published after the pension had been granted. If, however, Johnson the talker, Johnson the rich and powerful personality who sat for Boswell's portrait, is as nearly priceless as many have held him to be, then the world has every reason to be grateful that the well-intentioned stupidity of George the Third blundered into the act which made Johnson a free man.

It has already been said that Johnson was ready for freedom. The time had come for the temperament which had always been his to expand. But the expansion could not have taken place and the record of it could not have been set down except under the conditions now provided, and it is worth noting how rapidly the Johnson of the popular imagination emerged. Within five years after receiving the pension he had not only met Boswell, begun his enormously fruitful association with the Thrales, and taken a house at Johnson's Court; he had also founded with Sir Joshua Reynolds the famous Club and had begun the series of visits and perambulations which were to reach a climax in the tour to the Hebrides.

Some eighteen years earlier Johnson had written in his life of

Savage that the most remarkable thing about that disreputable fellow was his knowledge of men and manners. In speaking of the way in which that knowledge had been obtained, he observed of Savage's behavior with his acquaintances: "He watched their looser moments, and examined their domestic behavior, with that acuteness which nature had given him, and which the uncommon variety of his life had contributed to increase, and that inquisitiveness which must always be produced in a vigorous mind, by an absolute freedom from all pressing and domestic engagements." Despite the fact that Savage was, as Johnson knew well enough, a thoroughgoing rascal, it is obvious that Johnson admired and envied many things about him and that the *Life* owes its vigor to the fact that it is tinged with autobiography in the parts which describe the life of the literary hack as well as enlivened everywhere by Johnson's ability to project himself into experiences which he would, in some sense, have liked to share. He himself had, in other words, the "vigorous mind" and the powerful "inquisitiveness" to begin with. He was now provided with "the absolute freedom from all pressing or domestic engagements" which would allow the inquisitiveness full play.

For this reason he was now about to become a public personage, satirized and caricatured in a way which indicates that he was regarded no longer as merely a writer and man of learning, but as some sort of institution. It is, of course, ridiculous to speak of him as a "dictator" even if Smollett did call him the "great Cham" and even if (as one may guess to be the case) his own contemporaries assumed, as we somehow do, that "the grand panjandrum" of Foote's rigmarole was intended as some sort of reference to him. A dictator cannot remain a dictator if too many people dispute his authority, and once one gets outside the circle of Johnson's intimates one finds a considerable enough number of people ready to pooh-pooh his pronouncements. Yet he did in some sense set up as Sage in Ordinary to the British Public.

Even many of his admirers felt that his political pamphleteering was unfortunate, but it is less to this pamphleteering that allusion is here being made than to various other excursions into fields somewhat outside both his vocation as writer and his avocation as talker. Johnson did not confine himself to the magisterial discussion among friends of the topics which arose or which he brought up. He investigated the Cock Lane ghost, interested himself in the case of the reverend forger Dr. Dodd, pronounced on the authenticity of the poems of Ossian, gave Boswell material for his legal briefs, distributed free advice to various seekers who called on him with their problems; in general, he behaved like a man who thought his position gave him the pleasant duty of setting the public right in any matter which aroused general interest and of distributing free advice to any who felt the need of it.

Such activities did not, to be sure, begin only after he had achieved "freedom from all pressing and domestic engagements." His busy mind and wide-ranging curiosity had led him always to indulge in excursions into fields somewhat outside those of belles-lettres, just as his ready sympathy led him to solicit aid for persons with no immediate claim upon him. As miscellaneous writer—that is to say, as a dealer in words part of whose trade it was to find expression for people unable to find it for themselves—he had, in the decade preceding the granting of the pension, written many pieces on the most varied subjects. For Zachariah Williams he wrote an account of the latter's scheme for determining longitude; he also composed an *Appeal to the People Concerning Admiral Byng;* a preface to a *Dictionary of Trade and Commerce;* and three letters in the *Gazetteer* defending the plan of an architect friend against the attacks of a rival who wanted elliptical arches in the Blackfriars Bridge rather than the semicircular ones proposed by Johnson's protégé. Boswell says that Johnson was "at considerable pains" to study the subject of this last controversy, but it is hardly to be supposed that he learned more than was necessary to present his friend's case or that he felt very differently about it from the way he felt about the writing of the Preface to the trade dictionary. When Boswell asked him concerning the latter, and whether he knew much of the author or of his work, Johnson replied: "Sir, I never saw the man, and never read the book. The booksellers wanted a Preface to a Dictionary of Trade and Commerce. I knew very well what such a Dictionary should be, and I wrote a Preface accordingly."

It is also evident, both from the letters and from Boswell, that even in the years preceding his leisure Johnson found time to solicit charity for unfortunates, to advise individuals on educational problems, and to exert himself in various ways where he had neither any particular obligation to do so nor any hope of material profit. But there also is no lack of evidence that he now found more and more time for such activities, and there is some occasion for the suspicion that he tried to feel that in busying himself in all these ways he was discharging to society an obligation he did not wish to discharge by continuous writing. Once when Boswell was prodding him about his literary work, he replied in effect that he had done as much as he was morally obliged to do, but he was probably not entirely easy in his conscience. On another occasion he remarked more characteristically that it was most mortifying for any man to consider *"what he had done,* compared with what *he might have done."* [9]

One of the occasions upon which Johnson appeared in the role of public arbiter—namely, that on which he took part in the investigation of the Cock Lane ghost—occurred in February, 1762, and therefore a few months before the pension was granted. There are, however, several reasons why the story is worth telling in some detail. For one thing, it drew Johnson still further into the limelight and exposed him somewhat unjustly to much ridicule. For another, it affords an amusing example of a case in which a vulgar and flimsy imposture was approached in a spirit of solemn philosophical inquiry. Finally, the whole affair is typical of one aspect of the London life of the time, when so many men were devoting themselves to the art of getting all there was to be got out of the peculiar privilege of living in a metropolis that a continuous succession of wonders of one kind or another was required to keep the talk of the town going.

In *The Beggar's Opera,* first performed in 1728 but in Johnson's time still the most popular of all theatrical entertainments, Polly and Lucy, the two heroines, sing a duet:

Cock Lane and a Pension

I'm bubbled!
I'm bubbled!
Oh, how I am troubled!
Bambouzled and bit!

Of the three slang words, the only one not still current is said to have originated in reference to the South Sea Bubble, which was the greatest as well as one of the earliest of the eighteenth-century swindles. But a whole series of frauds and cheats was provided for a public which would, apparently, prefer being "bubbled" to not being entertained at all. Just how credulous this public could be was well illustrated by the audience that gathered at the Haymarket Theatre on the evening of January 16, 1749, in response to an advertisement which promised that a performer would enter a quart bottle from which he would discourse sweet music while the bottle was being freely handled by the spectators. Just how much superstition this same public could exhibit was equally well demonstrated by the hundreds of families which left London by coach and the hundreds more who spent the night outdoors in specially made garments, when a crazy soldier predicted that London would be destroyed by earthquake on April 4, 1750. Less than three years later a considerable part of the population divided itself into the pro- and anti-Elizabeth Canning parties over the question whether or not a servant girl of that name really had been kidnaped and persecuted by what we should call "white slavers." And in one respect an earlier sensation is more relevant than any of these in demonstrating how prominent people allowed themselves to become concerned with vulgar impostures: in 1726 the Princess of Wales herself had ordered Sir Richard Manning, one of the leading medical educators of the time, to investigate the case of Mary Tofts, who was alleged to have given birth to a litter of rabbits. Why, in view of such events, should not a great Christian like Johnson make one of an informal committee to inquire into the genuineness of an alleged manifestation of a returned spirit?

In any event, that is precisely what he did do when the whole town lost its head over the mysterious scratchings heard in the bedroom of the eleven-year-old daughter of one Parsons, a man then living in Cock Lane, a slum street of Smithfield. According to Parsons, the sounds emanated from the returned spirit of his sister-in-law, Miss Fanny, who had recently died, supposedly of smallpox. Moreover, the mysterious scratchings could be decoded into the revelation that Miss Fanny had actually been given arsenic by a neighbor named Kent, with whom she and Parsons had formerly lodged and with whom the latter had quarreled. According to Horace Walpole, the Methodists took up the matter; "the whole town of London think of nothing else." Walpole himself, following the example set by many others, went in a coach with the Duke of York, Lady Northumberland, Lady Mary Coke, and Lord Hertford to the house, which they could not manage to get into until the mob of curiosity seekers recognized the duke and made way. When they finally did get into the chamber they found fifty persons crowded into a room lighted by one candle and they "tumbled over the bed of the child to whom the ghosts come, and whom they are murdering by inches in such insufferable heat and stench." Nothing happened; they were told that the ghost would not manifest itself before seven in the morning; and they finally departed with nothing except material for one of Walpole's better-known letters.

The child was later moved to the house of one Stephen Aldrich, rector of St. John's, where the case was investigated by a committee including Sir John Fielding and a renowned exposer of fraud, the Rev. Dr. Douglas, later Bishop of Salisbury. Johnson, as a member of the group, himself wrote a sensible account (published in *The Gentleman's Magazine*) describing how they had required the girl to hold her hands outside the covers and how, after that precaution had been taken, no further scratchings were heard. He reported as the opinion of the committee "that the child has some art of making or counterfeiting a particular noise, and that there is no agency of any higher cause."

It is said to have been discovered later that she had merely taken a piece of wood to bed with her and by that simple means produced the sounds which drew not only Dr. Johnson but Walpole and the Duke of York to her side. At any rate, the outraged Kent, who had been accused of murder, took action. Parsons was condemned to stand in the pillory three times and to go to prison for two years. His wife and one Mary Frazer (who had decoded the messages) got shorter terms and two other persons who had abetted the fraud—a tradesman named James and a clergyman named Moore—paid fines aggregating six hundred pounds. Yet when Parsons stood in the pillory, the mob, which had on a previous occasion made a heroine out of Elizabeth Canning, took his side and not only refrained from exercising the privilege of pelting him with decayed vegetables or more serious missiles, but collected a purse for his benefit—perhaps chiefly because it appreciated the entertainment he had afforded.[10]

Johnson saw no reason why he should be ashamed of his part in the affair. In fact he was still able to talk of it to Boswell "with much satisfaction" more than fifteen years later, and on another occasion he quite properly wished that John Wesley had similarly investigated a trivial ghost story which Wesley accepted without question. But most Londoners were either grossly superstitious or, like Walpole, prepared to scoff without further inquiry. To such sophisticates as the latter, the Cock Lane ghost was merely another entertaining demonstration of the mob's irrationality and the legitimate successor to the rabbit woman, Elizabeth Canning, and the rest—as is shown not only by Walpole's references to both these earlier phenomena in his letter to Edward Montagu but also by a contemporary satiric print in which one observes that the walls of the child's room are ornamented with pictures of Elizabeth Canning and "the bottle conjurer," the latter being just in the act of entering his bottle. Johnson's scientific skepticism, therefore, seemed fair game for the satirist and Charles Churchill seized the opportunity.[11]

The Rosciad had made Churchill famous in the preceding year, but his *Night,* which followed a few months later, was a failure and he knew that Johnson had spoken slightingly of it. He had, therefore, not only what looked like a good topical subject but also an opportunity to pay back an injury. Accordingly he took out of his desk an earlier poem called *The Fortune Teller,* refurbished it somewhat, and added an account of the Cock Lane incident. Books one and two of the resulting mélange were published under the title of *The Ghost* in March, 1762, and Johnson, first referred to as "our letter'd Polypheme," is later drawn at full length. The poem as a whole is certainly not one of Churchill's best and the portrait of Johnson is not especially brilliant; but it is worth quoting not only to indicate that Johnson was already known as a "character" (Boswell would never have sought him out if he had not been), but also that certain of the peculiarities which Boswell makes much of were already well known. Already Johnson was, for example, the man who would knock you down with the butt end of his pistol if the pistol failed to go off.

Pomposo,—insolent and loud,
Vain idol of a scribbling crowd,
Whose very name inspires an awe,
Whose every word is sense and law;
For what his greatness hath decreed,
Like laws of Persia and of Mede,
Sacred through all the realm of Wit,
Must never of repeal admit;
Who, cursing flattery, is the tool
Of every fawning, flattering fool;
Who Wit with jealous eye surveys,
And sickens at another's praise;
Who, proudly seized of learning's throne,
Now damns all learning but his own;
Who scorns those common wares to trade in,
Reasoning, convincing, and persuading,
But makes each sentence current pass
With puppy, coxcomb, scoundrel, ass;
For 'tis with him a certain rule,
The folly's proved when he calls fool;
Who to increase his native strength,
Draws words six syllables in length,
With which, assisted with a frown,
By way of club, he knocks us down;
Who 'bove the vulgar dares to rise,
And sense of decency defies;
For this same decency is made
Only for bunglers in the trade,

> And, like the cobweb laws, is still
> Broke through by great ones when they will—
> Pomposo, with strong sense supplied,
> Supported, and confirm'd by Pride,
> His comrades' terrors to beguile
> "Grinn'd horribly a ghastly smile:"
> Features so horrid, were it light,
> Would put the devil himself to flight.[12]

Churchill's contemporary reputation, not merely as a rough-and-tumble satirist but as a genuine poet, is, of course, rather difficult for us to understand. William Cowper, who certainly had no temperamental affinity with him—although they had, it must be remembered, been schoolfellows—could refer to Churchill, twenty years after the latter's death, as a man who deserved the name poet as it is not deserved more than once in a century. But Johnson was certainly a good prophet and a better critic when he said of Churchill's verse that "it had a temporary currency, only from its audacity of abuse, being filled with living names, and that it would sink into oblivion." When Boswell hinted that Johnson was not an unprejudiced judge, he replied: "Nay. Sir, I am a very fair judge. He did not attack me violently till he found I did not like his poetry; and his attack on me shall not prevent me from continuing to say what I think of him, from an apprehension that it may be ascribed to resentment. No, Sir, I called the fellow a blockhead at first, and I will call him a blockhead still. However, I will acknowledge that I have a better opinion of him now, than I once had; for he has shewn more fertility than I expected. To be sure, he is a tree that cannot produce good fruit; he only bears crabs. But, Sir, a tree that produces a great many crabs is better than a tree which produces only a few."

No doubt it was Churchill's hope that "Dictionary Johnson," as he was still being called, might henceforth be known as "Cock Lane Johnson." Probably, indeed, he did have much to do with the fact that the doings in Cock Lane became a well-known feature of the Johnson legend and that Boswell found it necessary to defend his hero against the notion "which has gained ground" that Johnson was "weakly credulous." That last phrase is certainly no just description of Johnson's attitude, and it happens that we know pretty accurately what the attitude really was. Boswell had a number of conversations with Johnson on the general subject of ghosts, and had them not because Johnson was particularly fond of the topic, but because Boswell himself was, as Edmond Malone took pains to point out. By putting the substance of those conversations together, one may observe that Johnson was genuinely skeptical—which is to say, neither credulous, on the one hand, nor, on the other, unwilling to consider the possibility that anything not disproved might be true.[13]

As a Christian he could not doubt that disembodied spirits could exist. Speaking of apparitions to Boswell he said, very logically: "A total disbelief of them is adverse to the opinion of the existence of the soul between death and the last day; the question simply is, whether departed spirits ever have the power of making themselves perceptible to us." He knew that his old employer, Edward Cave, had once seen a ghost which had so horrified him that he had not liked to talk of the experience; that Goldsmith's brother, a clergyman, had also seen one; and that his early friend "Parson" Ford was reported by a decent person to have been seen in his own cellar shortly after death. He knew also, of course, that religious people like John Wesley —who was not by any means an ignorant man—took the reappearance of departed souls as a matter of course. What is more, he himself had once been "called" by his mother in Oxford just as he was turning the key in his chamber. He had heard her voice saying distinctly "Sam," although he knew she was at that moment in Lichfield.

Despite all this, Johnson had a strong understanding of the nature of evidence. "A man who thinks he has seen an apparition, can only be convinced himself; his authority will not convince another, and his conviction, if rational, must be founded on being told something which cannot be known but by supernatural means." What is more remarkable, he also had something much less common in the eighteenth century than an understanding of evidence—a realization of the importance of psychological factors in influencing belief. Many years before Cock

Lane he had written: "Prodigies are always seen in proportion as they are expected."

Yet he could not consider the question closed because, as he said: "It is wonderful that five thousand years have now elapsed since the creation of the world, and still it is undecided whether or not there has ever been an instance of the spirit of any person appearing after death. All argument is against it; but all belief is for it." He was far from sympathy with those who reject belief in spirits merely out of what Boswell accurately describes as "obstinate contempt"; and when Anna Seward smiled at his wish that John Wesley had investigated a tale he had heard and when Anna asked incredulously: "What, Sir! about a ghost?" he replied with "sudden vehemence": "Yes, Madam: this is a question which, after five thousand years, is yet undecided; a question, whether in theology, or philosophy, one of the most important that can come before the human understanding."

Into the mouth of Imlac, the philosopher in *Rasselas,* he put the argument which must have seemed strong to all who accepted, as most men in the eighteenth century professed to accept, the assumption that what the majority of men have always believed throughout recorded history is probably true:

" 'That the dead are seen no more,' said Imlac, 'I will not undertake to maintain, against the concurrent and unvaried testimony of all ages, and of all nations. There is no people, rude or learned, among whom apparitions of the dead are not related and believed. This opinion, which perhaps, prevails, as far as human nature is diffused, could become universal only by its truth: those that never heard of one another, would not have agreed in a tale which nothing but experience can make credible. That it is doubted by single cavillers, can very little weaken the general evidence; and some, who deny it with their tongues, confess it by their fears.' "

Even deists professed to hold that one might assume as probably true what was common to most religions, and belief in the return of departed spirits would certainly seem to come under this head.

That Johnson himself was actually considerably more skeptical than he allowed Imlac to be seems evident enough from those of his remarks which have already been quoted, and he certainly appears to have approached the Cock Lane ghost with no more predisposition to believe in it than the members of a modern Society for Psychical Research might be expected to show. Since he refused to permit either himself or anybody else to question anything which he regarded as part of the essential minimum of belief required of a Christian, he insisted on assuming without argument that souls exist between the death of the body and the day of resurrection. But since he also refused to believe any more than the essential minimum without what he regarded as either conclusive logic or conclusive evidence, he persisted in regarding the case for apparitions as simply not proved.

During the very last year of his life some reference happened to be made in the course of a conversation with Dr. William Adams to a trivial story then current concerning a ghost which had appeared to warn "the wicked Lord Lyttelton" of his approaching death. Said Johnson: "It is the most extraordinary thing that has happened in my day. I heard it with my own ears, from his uncle, Lord Westcote. I am so glad to have every evidence of the spiritual world, that I am willing to believe it." If that suggests that in his old age Johnson's "stubborn skepticism" had weakened to the point where he was "willing to believe" what he would like to believe, the sequel is significant. Said Adams: "You have evidence enough; good evidence, which needs not such support." There spoke the man who was really, or at least pretended to be, beyond doubt. Replied Johnson: "I like to have more." And there spoke the man to whom the belief he could not imagine himself doing without, nevertheless, never came easy.[14]

CHAPTER VIII

Enter James Boswell

THE FIRST fateful meeting between Samuel Johnson, aged fifty-three, and James Boswell, aged twenty-two, took place by accident in the back parlor of the shop of Tom Davies, actor, author, and bookseller, but now remembered chiefly because he had a pretty wife and because his back parlor was selected by the gods. Topham Beauclerk once declared that "he could not conceive a more humiliating situation than to be clapped on the back by Tom Davies," but it is not likely that anyone experienced that indignity on the afternoon of Monday, May 16, 1763, when the Scotchman and the hater of Scotchmen first laid eyes upon each other.

Boswell, a green but enterprising young man who was desperately anxious to make something out of himself, had come to London some six months before for the purpose of testing his capacities and, above all, meeting interesting people. He had apparently already managed to scrape some sort of acquaintance with Goldsmith; he had certainly got to know three famous and extraordinarily debauched persons: namely, John Wilkes, Robert Lloyd and Charles Churchill. But the Great Moralist, who was definitely on his list, had somehow eluded him.

On this particular afternoon he had just finished drinking tea with Davies and Davies's pretty wife when the former, looking through a glass door, saw Dictionary Johnson approaching. Boswell knew very well how formidable this particular lion—who was really, as Boswell's father was later to call him, a bear—was reputed to be. He had seen the first of the portraits which Reynolds painted, so he was not surprised at the great man's grotesque appearance, but when one considers Boswell's extreme self-consciousness and his frantic eagerness to acquit himself well on all occasions, it is no wonder that Davies's announcement of this "awful approach" seemed to him somewhat in the manner of an actor in the part of Horatio, when he addresses Hamlet on the appearance of his father's ghost, "Look, my Lord, it comes."

Davies introduced Boswell "respectfully" and Johnson, no doubt, responded casually. But Boswell, who could be exasperating when he could not be anything else and always had the art of making people more aware of him than they quite understood why they should be, immediately plunged in, with the result that he almost instantly enjoyed for the first time the painful pleasure of being snubbed by Johnson. "Mr. Johnson," he said in reply to a roguish announcement from Davies, "I do indeed come from Scotland, but I cannot help it"—meaning, Boswell adds apologetically, a "light pleasantry to soothe and conciliate him" and not "an humiliating abasement at the expense of my country." "That, Sir," replied Johnson, "I find, is what a very great many of your countrymen cannot help"—meaning, of course, that swarms of Scotchmen had been "coming from Scotland" to London where not all Englishmen welcomed them.

Johnson, no doubt thinking that he had disposed of the young nobody, turned to Davies and complained that Garrick had just refused him a pass to the theater for Miss Williams because, after the manner of managers from that day to this, he saw no reason why he should give away a ticket to what he knew was going to be a full house. Eager to get back into notice, Boswell then put in with, "O, Sir, I cannot think Mr. Garrick would grudge such a trifle to you." Boswell, of course, did not know that speaking ill of David was a privilege which Johnson reserved exclusively for himself, but he might, had he not been a man who got along in the world as much by saying the wrong thing as by saying the right, have realized that this was impudent, however servilely intended. Johnson, having just knocked the young upstart down once, immediately knocked him down again. "Sir," he replied with a stern look, "I have known David Garrick longer than you have done; and I know no right you have to talk to me on the subject."

According to his own account, Boswell now felt himself "much mortified, and began to think that the hope which I had long indulged of obtaining his acquaintance was blasted." But Boswell was a man who, as the pages of his private papers as well as the pages of his published work abundantly show, was often down but never out. Pride and servility are perhaps incompatible; but vanity and servility certainly are not, as Boswell would demonstrate if any demonstration were needed. Moreover, he was doubtless not sure that to accept such blows as these with gratitude was to be guilty of anything unworthy. He had enough admiration for Johnson's greatness to grant him the right to be rude if he felt like it; he was also enough of a connoisseur of the arts of conversation to consider it a privilege to be snubbed by a man who so obviously knew just how a snub ought to be administered.

In any event, he remained upon the field, and Johnson, evidently confident that the young man had been taught proper behavior in the presence of his betters, began to reward him by scattering pearly pronouncements mixed with delightful personal allusions to persons prominent in the very world Boswell hoped some day to be part of. "People," he remarked, "may be taken in once, who imagine that an author is greater in private life than other men. Uncommon parts require uncommon opportunities for their exertion." The artificial distinctions contributed by fortune, birth and rank are, he went on, "wisely ordered by Providence" because (delightful yet somewhat troubling argument to a young man dreadfully afraid that nothing will ever distinguish him except the fact that he comes of an ancient Scotch family) this preserves "some equality among mankind" by preventing the few people who have any real claim to respect from enjoying a monopoly of it.

In Scotland Boswell had known the philosopher, Lord Kames, a colleague of his father. Lord Kames was certainly a great man. But how much greater must be the man who could pick up a copy of Lord Kames's *The Elements of Criticism* and casually put it in its proper place: 'Sir, this book . . . is a pretty essay, and deserves to be held in some estimation, though much of it is chimerical." Boswell was seeing life. Not, to be sure, the kind he had been seeing in the company of his "classical friend," John Wilkes. But it was a kind that one could boast about in more places, and it was almost—though, as Boswell's subsequent life showed, not quite—as interesting.

He was soon compelled to take his departure because of another engagement at another place. Davies followed him to the door and, when Boswell "complained . . . a little of the hard blows which the great man had given," took it upon himself to be consoling. "Don't be uneasy," he said. "I can see he likes you very well." The fact is surely not evident from the account as Boswell gives it, but Davies was right. Timid, yet persistent, Boswell pursued his advantage by "taking the liberty of waiting upon Mr. Johnson at his Chambers in the Temple"—first, however, inquiring of Davies if he thought such an action permissible. Soon the two were seeing each other quite frequently, and when the time came, a little less than three months later, for Boswell, who was bound for the university at Utrecht, to take ship, Johnson did an extraordinary thing. He made the uncomfortable day-and-a-half-long journey to Harwich and, after an affectionate embrace, saw Boswell safely aboard ship. They were not to meet again for more than two and one-half years.[1]

Anyone who has read Johnson's life as Boswell wrote it is likely to be impressed by the fact that a famous man, already past middle age, should have put himself out to the extent Johnson did when he made the journey to Harwich with a youth whom he had known less than three months. But no such reader will find it difficult to understand why Johnson found the attentions of Boswell to some degree acceptable and pleasant. He had desperate need of company, he was certainly not averse to deferential attention, he liked young men, and Boswell had, besides certain native charms, the attraction of a more than respectable birth. Thus, it is easy to see what he was getting from Boswell. But what, if anything, did Boswell intend? What was he getting from Johnson? What did he hope to get? As it turned out, we know, he got an eternity of fame, and when the time finally came for the *Life* to be written, Boswell himself knew that he was making a bid, certainly his last, for just that. But what conscious motives led him to cultivate Johnson? What kind of man was he and what did he himself think he was about?

Such questions have been asked almost since the *Life* was first published. They were asked by Boswell's own contemporaries, and they were answered after a fashion in Macaulay's famous essay devoted to the paradox that the author of the finest biography in English was a fool, who could write the finest biography in English *because* he was a fool. Since Macaulay's time, this extraordinary judgment has been vigorously challenged on *a priori* grounds as well as on the basis of such evidence as was afforded by the book itself or could be gathered elsewhere. Now, however—thanks to the voluminous, unblushing self-revelations which had lain unsuspected by the world for something like a century and a half in a certain "ebony cabinet" and were finally ferreted out by Colonel Isham—it is possible to give answers which, though by no means simple, are certainly interesting and can be documented about as completely as it is possible to document any pronouncement concerning a thing so mysterious or elusive as human character.

Who, we may now ask with the expectation of getting a fairly satisfactory answer, was this young fellow who appeared in Tom Davies's parlor with a commission from the gods to confer upon a great but difficult and clumsy man a kind of fame he would not otherwise have had; and to be, himself, borne upward into immortality while dangling from the coattails of his master. A contemporary called him "a tom-tit twitt'ring on an eagle's back." But this was not merely an odd and daring flight. It was an apotheosis. The pair never came down again. They entered straight into Elysium together.

James Boswell was the eldest son of one Alexander Boswell, a judge in the Scottish Courts of Session and entitled by virtue of his official position to call himself Lord Auchinleck. James was born in Edinburgh but later he saw enough of the ruined castle of Auchinleck to become imbued with certain romantic notions of the feudal state and of the ancient honors of his family. His mother was a pious lady to whom he was apparently never very close and of whom little is known beyond the fact that, in 1754, her son, then thirteen years old, wrote her a letter about evenly divided between references to "this valley of tears, this world of sin" and a promise not to shoot any more sparrows. The father was a stern, vigorous, domineering man, somewhat uncouth despite considerable learning of the formal, classical sort, and as nearly incapable as any person not absolutely illiterate could be of sympathizing either with his son's early literary ambitions or with his taste for cultivating the acquaintance of bohemians whom his father regarded as riffraff no matter how renowned in their own low circles they might happen to be. To the very end Johnson was to him "a dominie," a "Jacobite fellow," or, more humorously, "Ursa Major." When the two met, they both lost their tempers in argument, and Lord Auchinleck never forgave his son the folly of allowing himself to be seen traveling about his own country "with a *brute*." "Such a Christian as Johnson," he said, "did more hurt to Religion than many Humes."

In due time the young James was sent to the academy of one Mr. Mundell, and afterward to Edinburgh University. He was destined for the law by his father's wishes rather than by his own, and the pressure of parental authority was sufficient to make a lawyer out of him, willy-nilly. But the sternest father can hardly control from a distance the whole twenty-four hours of a son's day, and the young Boswell was soon finding opportunity for indulgence in the three dominant interests of his life—wine, women, and the intimate observation of men acknowledged by the world to possess intellectual distinction. In Edinburgh he formed a strange friendship with a grave, low-spirited, young water drinker and Whig, who was later to become the Rev. William Temple and the recipient of the voluminous letters in which Boswell detailed for his information the most loathsome details of his most sordid debauches. But he also found time left over from study and amusement to scrape an acquaintance with David Hume, doubtless the most distinguished man in Edinburgh but, nevertheless, willing to hobnob with a seventeen-year-old nearly thirty years his junior.

To love wine and women has generally been regarded as an amiable weakness at worst. To admire great men is certainly a positive virtue. But Boswell's love for wine and women was immoderate, to say the least, and his admiration for the great sometimes expressed itself in peculiar ways. It was Oscar Wilde who remarked that the only person for whom all schools of art are equally fine is the auctioneer. One is tempted to add that the only person to whom all great men are equally interesting is the autograph collector. And though Boswell was certainly more than an autograph collector, it was intellectual greatness rather than any one kind of intellectual greatness that interested him primarily. The two first and the five principal objects of his study—Hume, Lord Kames, John Wilkes, Johnson, General Paoli, Rousseau and Voltaire—were very diverse men. Boswell was to some extent interested in poetry and philosophy and morality but he was much more interested in the personality of poets and philosophers and moralists.

It would certainly be the reverse of true to say that he aspired merely to a valet's view of his heroes. He continued to admire his great men and to think them great even though he sometimes badgered and probed and manipulated them in order to note with cool impertinence how they would behave. Johnson, of course, he not only idolized but almost deified. In his relations with none of the others is there the slightest indication of the vulgar impulse to belittle one's betters. He never, in other words, exhibited the methods or the intentions of—to use a word which would have made him stare—the "debunker." But it was, nevertheless, intimacy that he sought, and intimate moments that he valued. It was, to use again the phrase employed in discussing Johnson's own love of biography and prose fiction, the "comedy of manners" that interested him most. He never missed an opportunity to observe a king or queen, but he always noted the little mouse under the chair. Johnson, it will be remembered, warned him in their very first interview that one soon learned not to expect authors to be remarkable in their daily existence. "Uncommon parts require uncommon opportunities for their exertion." But that is precisely what Boswell refused to believe. He wanted to catch the great man off guard, and if "uncommon opportunities" were called for, he would provide uncommon opportunities of a sort by introducing promising subjects, by inventing provocative questions, or by devising provocative confrontations of great man with great man.

Boswell was the first boswellizer the world had ever known. Possibly he felt, without ever putting it just this way, that if the comedy of manners was fascinating when played by ordinary mortals, it ought to be doubly so when the dramatis personae were all remarkable men. Perhaps there was also a more deeply hidden motive. Possibly Boswell, with all his thirst for fame and his determination to experience something of greatness even if only vicariously, realized sufficiently his own limitations to know that he could never distinguish himself as even a critic of literature or philosophy. And possibly, therefore, he determined to see if great men could not be made to exhibit some sort of greatness on some level to a true understanding of which he could reach. In any event, his own renown rests upon the fact that he did succeed in doing just that. "Curiosity," wrote Mrs. Thrale in the margin of her copy of Boswell's *Life,* "carried Boswell further than it ever carried any mortal breathing; he cared not what he provoked so as he saw what *such a one* [i.e., Johnson] would say or do." [2]

Boswell's passion for self-analysis and self-revelation was at least as great as his passion for recording the self-revelation of others. The first published specimen of his many attempts to record some portion of his own life covers exactly two months—from September 14 to November 14, 1762—and fills eighty-three pages of print in the *Private Papers.* It was written, so Boswell says, to be read only by two of his friends; it is concerned with the visits he paid to Scotland between the time he set out from Auchinleck to the time he left Edinburgh for the trip to London which was to result, almost exactly six months later, in the meeting with Johnson; and it reveals the character of the author so vividly that, if we had nothing else, we should know pretty well with what sort of man we have to deal. If we add to it two characteristically fatuous poems which Boswell, already a man who would rather attract attention by his folly than not attract it at all, published in this same year, and also the *Letters Be-*

tween the Honourable Andrew Erskine [a boon companion during his Edinburgh days] *and James Boswell, Esquire,* which he had printed in 1763, we shall know the young Boswell better than we know any but a very few of all the men whose names have survived the attrition of time.

One of the two poems referred to was a song written in memory of the Soaping Club, a convivial association of which he and Erskine were members. It runs:

> Boswell, of Soapers the king,
> On Tuesdays at Tom's does appear,
> And when he does talk or does sing,
> To him ne'er a one can come near;
> For he talks with such ease and such grace,
> That all charm'd to attention we sit,
> And he sings with so comic a face,
> That our sides are just ready to split.
>
> Boswell does women adore,
> And never once means to deceive;
> He's in love with at least half a score;
> If they're serious he smiles in his sleeve.
> He has all the bright fancy of youth
> With the judgment of forty and five.
> In short, to declare the plain truth,
> There is no better fellow alive.

To write even for a convivial group a song so feeble in expression and so oddly ineffectual in its effort to hide vanity under a scant covering of jocularity would be in itself enough to justify some raising of eyebrows. To publish it is certainly to give one's self away. To reprint part of it, as Boswell did, more than twenty-five years later and just four years before his death, is to be really extraordinary.

It has just been said that Boswell had a passion for self-examination (perhaps self-contemplation would be more accurate) and for self-revelation. It needs now to be added that the passion for self-revelation amounted to an exhibitionism hardly this side of the pathological. He loved to get himself up in some sort of fancy dress; he liked to refer to himself as "the friend of Paoli," "the friend of Johnson," or, quite simply, as "Boswell"; his usual method of introducing himself by letter was to draw a romantic picture of his own person; and throughout life he never seemed to tire of sketching self-portraits.

Of these self-portraits the "Soaper" poem may be regarded as the first still extant. The second occurs in the correspondence with Erskine, which he himself printed. It begins with a reference to a very bad poem supposedly anonymous but dedicated to himself and it is worth quoting:

"The author of the *Ode to Tragedy* is a most excellent man: he is of an ancient family in the west of Scotland, upon which he values himself not a little. At his nativity there appeared omens of his future greatness. His parts are bright, and his education has been good. He has travelled in post-chaises miles without number. He is fond of seeing much of the world. He eats of every good dish, especially apple-pie. He drinks old Hock. He has a very fine temper. He is somewhat of an humourist and a little tinctured with pride. He has a good manly countenance, and he owns himself to be amorous. He has infinite vivacity, yet is observed at times to have a melancholy cast. He is rather fat than lean, rather short than tall, rather young than old. His shoes are neatly made, and he never wears spectacles. The length of his walking-stick is not yet ascertained; but we hope soon to favour the Republic of Letters with a solution of this difficulty, as several able mathematicians are employed in its investigation, and for that purpose have posted themselves at different given points in the Canongate. . . ."

If this is what Boswell thought of himself, or wished to think of himself, or hoped others would think that he thought of himself, we may profitably consult the first of the extant journals (previously referred to) in order to fill out the picture and to judge how far it is accurate. Certainly nothing in those pages is inconsistent with the impression produced by the self-portrait even though, as we shall see, certain traits are added more worthy of respect than any which the portrait suggest. The young author was an affected puppy trying to convince himself that a certain adolescent self-consciousness justified any degree of self-indulgence and made him a man of mark. He is complacent about his fits of melancholy, complacent about "the most veering amorous affections that I ever knew anybody have," complacent about his relations with his God. "I adore with humility and gratitude the Lord of the Universe"; and that, coming from James Boswell, is obviously rather more than the Lord of the Universe has any right to expect. He is sure that, for all others may say about being compelled to do this or that, he is master of his own soul, or, as he puts it, "I can and will *soap my own beard.*" As one of the worthy few destined to be owners of the land, he rather regrets that he has "no sort of turn for farming" and even more his "want of taste for planting or gardening, which are really noble and elegant Employments." But "I have lived so much in a town, and have so high a relish of Society and other amusements, that my Attention has had little chance of being employed upon Ploughs and Harrows." In town "Mankind are to be seen more spirited than in the country," and he is soon to settle himself for a while in the greatest of towns. He has obviously already been marked out by fate as a man of bonnes fortunes. The wench who sat next to him at a Punch and Judy show offered to accompany him to London if he so desired—no doubt because "I had my bath great-coat with a gold binding, my gold-lac'd hat smartly set upon my head, and twirled my cane switch with a good deal of gentility." A maid at an inn was seen by one of his companions to enter his room during the night, and if he knew nothing about the matter it was, he assumed, only because "she had not assurance enough to wake me." The shade of another great diarist, long dead but not yet known, must have smiled a sympathetic approval as Boswell noted his reaction to evening prayers: "At night Mrs. Heron read the Evening Service to us, and I beheld with delight so fine a Creature employed in adoring her Creator."

Yet the man has talents far more important than any of the puppyish accomplishments he is priding himself on. One kind of writing—and one kind only—he can already do well. To the end of his life, Boswell's attempts to deal with abstract ideas were usually rather feeble and his verse, which he continued nevertheless to write, very sad stuff. He learned to write a passable familiar essay and he managed to do a considerable amount of literary work of one kind or another but only in portraiture did he ever exhibit anything approaching genius. Thus even this early journal draws some vivid characters, records certain conversations with fine effect, and in the account of the visit to the Punch and Judy show presents a sort of genre picture worthy of any of the great letter or memoir writers of the century.[3]

What is perhaps more important, the outlines of the boswellian method and the boswellian enterprise are already beginning to appear. The young author speaks frankly of the fact that he is attempting certain things by way of practice. When he is not thinking about his own personality, he is thinking about that of others. Lord Kames and David Hume are the two great men whom he has so far met, but he will meet others. He has already begun to boswellize. "I have," he notes, "got into an excellent method of taking down conversations." Of that casually dropped phrase what shall we say? Does it mean that some demon assigned as a guide whispered to him that it was time to prepare for an opportunity he could not know was coming? Or does it mean that a young man, who seemed so proud of his inconstancy, was actually already determined that some great man should be the means of making him also great?

There is no reason for supposing—in fact, there is good reason for not supposing—that Boswell had at this time even tentatively fixed upon Johnson as a subject. But the shadow of Johnson does fall twice across the pages of this first journal, and each time it is evident that the name stirred Boswell's interest.

"I cannot help differing from My Lord Kames, Mr. [Adam] Smith, Dr. Blair and some others whom I have the honor to call my learned friends, with regard to the Author of 'the Rambler.' They will allow him nothing but Heaviness, weakness and affected Pedantry. Whereas in my Opinion Mr. Johnson is a man of much Philosophy, extensive reading, and real knowledge of human life. I can produce numberless papers in the very Work which has led me to examine his character, in proof of what I have asserted. . . . That the people of Britain should have received so grave a work with uncommon Approbation is surprising, considering the Age of effeminate literary taste in which we live. Yet this is a certain fact." Substitute "James Boswell" for "the people of Britain" and the observation increases in interest.

A little more than six weeks later, Boswell, following his "excellent method," was recording in the journal his notes on a conversation with Hume and he records these bits of information:

"Mr. Samuel Johnson has got a pension of £300 a year. Indeed his Dictionary was a kind of national Work so he has a kind of claim to the Patronage of the state. His stile [*sic*] is particular and pedantic. He is a man of enthusiasm and antiquated notions, a keen Jacobite yet hates the Scotch. Holds the Episcopal Hierarchy in supreme veneration and said he would stand before a battery of cannon to have the Convocation restored to its full powers. He holds Mr. Hume in abhorrence and left a company one night upon his coming in. Garrick told Mr. Hume that Johnson passed one Evening behind the Scenes in the Green room. He said he had been well entertained. Mr. Garrick therefore hoped to see him often. 'No, David,' said he, 'I will never come back. For the white bubbies and the silk stockings of your Actresses excite my Genitals.'" No doubt Boswell was greatly intrigued by a man to whom the reason assigned in this last statement seemed a good one for staying away. And here, it should be noted, is the earliest form of the remark which appears in the *Life* translated into more stately and more decorous Johnsonese. The greatest of Boswell's editors was considerably exercised over the story, already current, that Johnson had said something more downright than what was commonly attributed to him, and doubted that he actually had. This passage from the *Journal*, which the editor had never seen, increases the suspision that Birkbeck Hill was wrong.

Boswell is known to have kept a journal of his life in London from the time of his arrival in November until his departure from Harwich on August 6th of the following year. This journal, however, has not been published and though its whereabouts is known it is not available. Hence we are deprived of an opportunity to check the later account of his first reaction to Johnson against a frank record set down at the moment and uninfluenced by any later conception of the meaning of events. But we are not without some significant jottings. It was his habit to scribble down on scraps of paper all sorts of memoranda, resolutions and brief notes—some of them to be used to compile the more orderly journals when he had a moment to spare. Many of these were discovered among his papers and those relating to the period of his first acquaintance with Johnson reveal the author in a light slightly different from that in which he chose to exhibit himself in his published work.

In the *Life* he manages to give the impression that to arrange for a meeting with the author of *The Rambler* was one, at least, of his primary concerns. "I had," he says, "for several years read his works with delight and instruction, and had the highest reverence for their author, which had grown up in my fancy into a kind of mysterious veneration, by figuring to myself a state of solemn elevated abstraction, in which I supposed him to live in the immense metropolis of London." The passages quoted from the first journal hardly suggest feelings on quite this level and the London jottings to be cited presently include hints of a kind of flippancy which few besides Boswell would have thought compatible with them. Moreover, Boswell was more fully occupied with company of a different sort than he cares to admit.

In the *Life* he makes a good deal of the frustration of well-laid plans to secure an introduction—makes a good deal of them, perhaps, in order to explain how it happened that actually the first meeting was accidental. Samuel Derrick, small poet and later master of ceremonies at Bath, whom Boswell called "my first tutor in the ways of London" who "shewed me the town in all its variety of departments, both literary and sportive," promised an introduction but never arranged it. Tom Sheridan, the elocutionist, would have arranged the ceremony but, unfortunately, Tom Sheridan had a falling-out with the Rambler just about this time and was in no mood to introduce anyone. Poor Boswell therefore had to wait on chance.

Now there is no reason for doubting that the facts were as Boswell gives them. But at least until the unpublished journal can be read there seems some excuse for doubting that he was merely moping until he could make contact with the Great Moralist. In London there were gentlemen (and ladies) more easy of access and almost as much to Boswell's taste. In Wilkes he had a companion whose presence was enough to render any debauch "classical." It is significant that Boswell, when he finally did meet Johnson, was compelled soon to leave for another (unspecified) engagement. Moreover, we know that engagements of a sort which Boswell preferred not publicly to specify were often, in the future, to occupy him when he might have been with Johnson. It seems, therefore, reasonable to suspect that he had not been counting every day lost which did not seem to bring him closer to the Great Moralist. In the first journal he had written, with rare lack of self-knowledge: "I have no fondness for riot or extravagant pleasure, and when I am in London I think I may enjoy the bliss of Variety without being debauched." On setting out from Harwich, and with the additional experience of London, he had passed from a calm statement of confidence to the resolution-making stage. "Consider that when you come home with a settled composure you will enjoy life much, without exhausting spirits and setting yourself up as a Buffoon or a jolly dog. . . . Your mind will strengthen by years." But Boswell's mind did not "strengthen by years." He drank more rather than less as time went on and his last years were dismal ones.[4]

The first of the pertinent memoranda is dated May 25th and reads: "Bring up journ. and stop not till 2 so as to have your last rich scenes in good order." The date makes it clear that these "last rich scenes" were provided by Boswell's first call upon Johnson in his chambers, and it is obvious that Boswell had already discovered that the Rambler was a fine source of copy. But he was not drawing on that source as frequently as he himself thought he should. The next memorandum, dated June 14th: "See Johnson oft, and all the Literati and also Places round London, so as to talk of 'em abroad"; the next after that, dated June 17th, reads: "See Johnson on Sat. See him 2 and 3 times a week and have him wt. you next week." These good resolutions were not kept. In the *Life* Boswell states specifically not only that he had seen Johnson only once between the first meeting and June 13th, but also that he was at this time "so occupied, shall I call it? or so dissipated, by the amusements of London" that his next meeting with the man whom he so revered and had been so anxious to meet did not occur until June 25th. Boswell, in other words, despite Johnson's cordiality, saw him for the third time just a little less than a month after their first encounter. Moreover, the phrase "so as to talk of 'em abroad" suggests both that he had some tendency to regard Johnson less as an object of religious veneration than as one of the curiosities of London and also that his motive was quite frankly to make himself interesting rather than to help establish Johnson's fame. A similar motive remained, of course, an important one to the very last though the end sought became larger. In 1763 Boswell hoped that his acquaintance with Johnson might make him listened to in Utrecht. By 1791 he hoped it would make him immortal.

It was just at this time that Boswell's immediate plans underwent a change. He had come to London with the original intention of entering the foot-guards. His father, however, still harping on the law, urged Utrecht; and Boswell, promising himself further European travels, agreed. Possibly the inevitable resolutions about beginning a new and soberer life impelled him to think more seriously of the moral benefits to be derived from Johnson—and strange as it may seem, Boswell did throughout life value these moral benefits and was perhaps justified in his belief that he profited greatly from them.

At any rate, the next memoranda exhibit a new tone. Having listened to Johnson, he now thinks Johnson ought to listen to him—in order to be better equipped to give advice. Some of the notes read: (June 18th) "At 1 call Johnston [*sic*]. Be fine and appoint him to Sup with you next week. Think of telling him your imbecility, your disposition to ridicule, etc. and take his advice"; (July 2nd) "Don't go down, 'twill ruin you . . . You have Johnson and Wilkes and Churchill, etc. to be well with"; (July 9th) "At 2 call Johnson and resolve no more taverns but 1 wt. Johnson and 1 wt. Churchill"; (July 15th) "Bring up Journ. as Johnson desired you should"; (July 21st) "Send your letters [the Erskine Correspondence?] to Johnson, and ask him to say freely whether you have or *may* have powers, or if you had better not try to run"; (July 23rd) "Mem. Johnson's directions; not drunk"; (August 2nd) "Be wt. Johnson at 2 . . . give out linens and pack up and be placid and get into grave humour for Journey." Finally, a special memorandum is added containing resolutions for the conduct of life abroad and including the following: "Go abroad with a manly resolution to improve, and correspond with Johnson. Be grateful to him. Seek to attain a fixed and consistent character, to have dignity. Never despair."

A man who writes a note to remind himself that someone else has advised him not to get drunk is either of a singularly distracted disposition or is singularly addicted to making memoranda for the sake of making memoranda. Boswell was both. He never attained to a "fixed and consistent character," he often despaired, and he never achieved dignity. He was grateful to Johnson, whom he genuinely admired and genuinely revered. But neither admiration nor reverence ever gave him pause when he was probing for Johnson's painful secrets or, what is worse, performing experiments as callous as those of the vivisectionists of animals who were already at work in his century and against whom Johnson, always tenderhearted where physical suffering was concerned, had devoted a bitter number of *The Idler*.

In the popular mind, to boswellize means to record with uncritical enthusiasm the lightest word of some being regarded with extravagant respect. It implies in the boswell an almost masochistic delight in self-extinction, a submergence of one's self in the self of another. But the original Boswell was a much more complicated creature, not merely because he hoped to serve himself quite as much as he hoped to serve Johnson but also because of something that is already revealed in its first crude form by those memoranda where one perceives the beginning of a thought-out scheme for playing a role. "Be fine and appoint him to sup with you next week." He seems resolved to put himself in the light most likely to seem attractive to Johnson while, perhaps, concealing those tastes and habits which would alienate him.

It is not that Boswell did not admire and respect Johnson, but that certain other attitudes which few men would feel to be compatible with admiration and respect were perfectly compatible in the mind of James Boswell. At times his behavior is genuinely that of an admiring disciple. At others it is more like that of the master of a trained bear who shows off the tricks of a shaggy brute for the amusement of sophisticated spectators. When in the course of the *Journal of a Tour to the Hebrides* he calmly and as a matter of course records for public approval his regret that Mrs. Boswell did not seize the opportunity which she had to transcribe Johnson's private diary during his absence, he is revealing not only his own lack of delicacy but the fact that he did not know it was lacking. When, on the same jaunt, he managed to get a Highland girl onto Johnson's lap, and did so in the full knowledge that Johnson was very sensitive on the subject of his own unfitness for the role of gallant, it was in order to entertain himself and others with a spectacle upon which the best comment would be an adaptation of Johnson's own famous remark about women preachers: A bear making love does not make love very well. But we are surprised that he can do it at all.

Perhaps the fact that Boswell had no sense of dignity himself constitutes something of an excuse. A man who could, as Boswell did, imitate a cow in the auditorium of Drury Lane and then be so delighted by public approval as to go on with other and less accomplished animal imitations until his companions were compelled to request him to limit himself to the repetition of his best performance was not likely to be very careful of the dignity of others.

Yet one must take care not to imagine Boswell in too unfavorable a light just because we have self-revelations so frank that they expose him in a way few men have ever been exposed before or since. One recent biographer, reveling in the evidence which Boswell himself supplies, has drawn the picture of a depraved monster in whom it is neither easy nor necessary to believe and that portrait has even more recently been vigorously protested against. Certainly Boswell had no real malice in him. Indeed, and despite what one is sometimes tempted to call the cruelty of his occasional efforts to prod Johnson into an interesting outburst, he had a kind heart. The same letters and journals which record his dissipations furnish evidence to prove that after he had become a Scotch landlord he treated his tenants with solicitous generosity. They reveal also that, toward the miserable end of his life when one is inclined to think of him as suffering through the last stages of degeneracy, he was capable of interesting himself in the hard case of a female convict escaped from Australia and of relieving her distress out of his own pocket. There seems every reason for accepting the judgment of one of the scholars who have studied his life most closely when that scholar describes him as "an idle, unhappy, dissipated man, but a man who in his feckless wandering through life had managed to perform more acts of kindness than the majority of his successful colleagues."

The explanation of most of his discreditable actions lies not in any evil intent but in a willingness to purchase sociability and conviviality at almost any cost. It was good-fellowship, not intrigue or ill feeling, that interested him. He was amiability itself, and nothing would have pleased him better than to see Johnson, Wilkes, Voltaire and Rousseau exchanging expressions of mutual admiration over a bottle. Indeed, he probably saw no reason why they should not get along as well together as they did in his own mind, where his high regard for one existed in perfect harmony with his high regard for the other. But this suggests one of the curious things about Boswell's mind. It means perhaps that he did not so much admire what Wilkes or Johnson or Rousseau or Voltaire actually was, because one cannot really admire all those things at once. He admired each of the men chiefly for being *something,* and if he could not be anything himself he was determined to compensate for the fact by being able to appreciate everybody worth appreciating.

In much of his self-portraiture Boswell exhibits a Rousseauesque determination to stress his own uniqueness. Usually the traits he selects to exhibit it fail lamentably in their purpose. A great many young men are subject to fits of lassitude and melancholy. A great many are astonished at their own "veering amorous affections." But no one else, over the age of twenty, is likely to be astonished by them. Yet Boswell, if not unique, really was unusual in the degree to which he was marked by traits far less common than adolescent melancholy and adolescent susceptibility to female charms. He really was extraordinarily adaptable, sensitive to impressions and experiences of diverse sorts, and capable of a spectator's appreciation of an extraordinary variety of spectacles. Sometimes this capacity for being all this to (and with) all men alarmed or distressed him. Hence his many resolutions and what often seems a genuine hope that by being enough with Johnson he might acquire something of Johnson's fixity of conviction. That he never succeeded has generally been attributed simply to Boswell's "weakness." But this so-called weakness was not simple weakness. It had a positive side. Boswell never succeeded in getting fixed principles because not to have any was, as he himself sometimes realized, the principle most deeply fixed in his nature. His resolution to acquire some was a thing he was trying to force upon himself. When, on the contrary, he boasted that he was equally at home in a church or in "the mansions of gross sensuality" he was following his own nature.[5]

Sensation-seeking as a philosophy of life had not yet been invented, at least in the form in which we are most familiar with it. Eighteenth-century life, as Boswell knew it, was too violent, and vigorous, and coarse to encourage aestheticism. But Boswell's attitude, as he expresses it in later journals and in his letters to Temple, is a philosophy which Huysmans, let us say, would have understood better than most of Boswell's own contemporaries would have understood it. To express his own determination, he would never have used quite Oscar Wilde's words: "To drift with every passion till my soul is as a stringed lute on which all winds can play." There is something finicky and perhaps effeminate about that. Boswell did not want to be anything as subdued as a lute and he did not want to be quite that passive either. But he did see himself and try to picture himself as a man who could and did experience everything from almost insane self-indulgence to pious meditation, and was capable of properly estimating a great whore as well as a great moralist. We may be pretty sure that he never revealed to Johnson what he revealed to Temple, though Johnson probably guessed more than was comfortable. In fact, not revealing it was part of Boswell's pleasure. It made possible the secret enjoyment of a spectacle which it gave him great satisfaction to contemplate—the spectacle provided by James Boswell, the eminent debauchee, becoming the chosen intimate of Samuel Johnson, the Great

Moralist. Describing in the *Life* his first call at Johnson's chambers in the Temple, he writes: "After having been enlivened by the witty sallies of Messieurs Thornton, Wilkes, Churchill and Lloyd, with whom I had passed the morning, I boldly repaired to Johnson." He was far from being unaware of what Johnson would have thought of such company or of the fact that James Boswell was one of the few men who would be welcome both when he joined Wilkes and Churchill at the tavern and when he settled down for a chat with the Rambler.

The old debate over the question whether Boswell was a genius or a fool began more than a hundred years before his *Private Papers* were brought to light. The more one reads in them, the more apparent it becomes that the question was falsely stated. Boswell was not a fool, though he did and said many incredibly foolish things. But he was, as he boasted in a series of periodical essays published between 1777 and 1783, a hypochondriac—which is, of course, one of the eighteenth-century terms for what we call a neurotic, or a man who lives in a world of sick imagination, and creates for himself standards of value which are not only not those of most of his fellows but which tend toward self-destruction. A fool cannot become on occasion a great artist. A normal man who is also an artist cannot on occasion sink to the imbecile level of work like the poem *No Abolition of Slavery, or the Universal Empire of Love,* which Boswell published about a month before the *Life of Johnson* and of which he was very proud. But a neurotic can do both, even though to say that may not carry us far.

Like many neurotics, Boswell sometimes attempted a rational defense of his pathological drinking and his pathological whoring. Wine, he argued, promotes social intercourse and discovers truth. As for whoring, Boswell often thought with comfort of the Old Testament, and wondered, apparently, if he also might not be "like Israel's monarch after God's own heart." But there were other times when he knew that it was no ardor for truth that led him to the bottle. At the very time when he was making his first contacts with Johnson, he could write to Sir David Dalrymple: "I must, however, own to you that I have at bottom a melancholy cast; which dissipation relieves by making me thoughtless, and therefore, an easier, tho' a more contemptible animal." And many years later he could confess: "An hypochondriack is under peculiar temptations to participate freely in wine. For the impatience of his temper under sufferings which are sometimes almost intolerable, urges him to fly to what will give him immediate relief. It has often occurred to me, that one must be obstinate to an extraordinary degree, who feeling himself in torment, can resist taking what he is certain will procure him ease, or at least insensibility." Boswell was certainly not obstinate to that extraordinary degree, and it was obviously forgetfulness of another sort which he sought in the insane pursuit of diseased streetwalkers—an activity which has the same relation to the pleasures of love that lying in the gutter has to the social pleasures of drinking.

No doubt the *Private Papers* will some day be used in an attempt to psychoanalyze their author. Whatever would even remotely suggest such a thing will here be left severely alone; but without even opening the question of what relation, if any, exists between Boswell's neurosis and his genius; without asking whether he was a genius limited and all but destroyed by his neurosis or whether such genius as he exhibited was a product of the neurosis; it is nevertheless evident that this neurotic drunkard and victim of satyriasis could write what is generally regarded as the most remarkable biography in any language because of three characteristics none of which is obviously neurotic: Boswell had a genuine admiration for intellectual greatness; an almost unrivaled sense of what words or gestures or actions reveal personality; and a passionately industrious habit of writing down whatever seemed to him memorable.

All these characteristics might be readily enough deduced from the *Life* itself, and it has just been said that none of them is obviously related to neuroticism. But the *Private Papers* do throw additional light on the last of the three, and do suggest some psychological relationship between it and other aspects of Boswell's personality. In all the nineteen volumes so magnificently presented by Colonel Isham there is no single passage more arresting than this: "I should live no more than I can record, as one should not have more corn growing than one can get in. There is a waste of good if it be not preserved."

For Boswell, then, the making of a record was not an amusement, not a means toward an end, not in any usual sense of the word a scholarly or antiquarian activity. It was the most meaningful portion of life itself. Johnson wrote in order to live and he thought only a fool would write for any other reason. Boswell lived in order to write because only after he had written could he realize that he had lived. We sometimes think of him, properly enough, as one of the innumerable diarists and letter writers who scribbled away so industriously throughout his century. Many of them may have been half aware of what he here so overwhelmingly felt. But were any others conscious of recording their lives and the lives of others for just the reason which Boswell gave himself? It puts Boswell at the opposite pole from, let us say, Horace Walpole, who at least believed that he was writing not so that he or his friends would know that they had lived, but for the benefit of posterity. For a precedent, one must go back to Samuel Pepys, whose devouring curiosity is not wholly unlike Boswell's and whose farewell to his secret record suggests a sense of deprivation somewhat suggestive of what Boswell anticipated when he thought of the possibility that he might no longer be able to put down what he had seen, and said, and thought. But for a full analytical statement and justification of Boswell's feeling one must go, not back but even further forward, to Marcel Proust. Boswell would certainly have read with fascination Proust's attempt to prove that there is nothing significant in anything that has happened until it has been remembered.

Such, then, was the young and unknown man to whom a distinguished and more than middle-aged one was unknowingly entrusting so much of his future reputation. If Johnson had known one-tenth of what we know, he might well have hesitated. But he did not hesitate. Indeed, from the pages of the *Life* which recount the beginnings of the friendship, it would almost appear that he did more than his part toward developing it, and certainly, as things turned out, few would be inclined to say that

Boswell was false to the trust. That he did not, immediately after the first meetings, consider them of overwhelming importance is indicated by the fact that they were not mentioned in either of two letters to Dalrymple, written, respectively, five days after the encounter in Tom Davies's parlor and one month after his first call at the Temple. But this first call had produced the first of Johnson's own many expressions of cordiality.[6]

Boswell entered the first floor of No. 1 Inner Temple Lane with, he tells us, much the same impression which had led the Rev. Dr. Blair to speak of having "found the Giant in his den." The apartment, the furniture, and Johnson's costume were all sufficiently uncouth. "His brown suit of clothes looked very rusty; he had on a little old shrivelled unpowdered wig, which was too small for his head; his shirt-neck and knees of his breeches were loose; his black worsted stockings ill drawn up; and he had a pair of unbuckled shoes by way of slippers." But all these slovenly particulars were forgotten the moment he began to talk. Presently some other callers, whose names Boswell could not remember, went away, and Boswell then also rose. "Nay, don't go"—"Sir, (said I,) I am afraid that I intrude upon you. It is benevolent to allow me to sit and hear you." Johnson seemed pleased and replied: "Sir, I am obliged to any man who visits me"—which of course was pretty close to the literal truth.

And this perhaps is as good a time as any to note that one of the good things which helped Boswell to forget the unpowdered wig and the sagging stockings was a sally apropos the fear that poor Kit Smart might suffer from lack of exercise now that his madness had reached the point where confinement was thought necessary—a sally which exhibits that boisterous sense of fun and that love of the sheerly ludicrous which, though just as characteristic of Johnson as either his moralizing or his wit, is for some reason less often commented upon. "No, Sir," said Johnson, "he has partly as much exercise as he used to have. . . . Indeed, before his confinement, he used for exercise to walk to the alehouse; but he was *carried* back again." And then, as though to make amends for the rough joke, he went on: "I did not think he ought to be shut up. His infirmities were not noxious to society. He insisted on people praying with him; and I'd as lief

DAVID GARRICK IN *HAMLET* (ACT I, SCENE IV)
The start which Johnson thought likely to frighten the ghost
From an engraving by McArdell after a painting by B. Wilson
(Courtesy The Theater Collection, New York Public Library)

pray with Kit Smart as anyone else. Another charge was, that he did not love clean linen; and I have no passion for it."

At the very beginning of his acquaintance with Johnson, Boswell may, as has been suggested, have felt that seeing life with Churchill, Wilkes and the rest was almost as important as any cultivation of the Rambler could possibly be. But, if so, his opinion changed pretty rapidly. He saw Johnson more and more often, and the intimacy proceeded through a series of stages which he carefully noted. A second visit to the Temple on June 13th led Johnson to say: "Come to me as often as you can. I shall be glad to see you." A few days later they met by chance on the street; a few days after that, again by chance, they met at Clifton's eating house and at Boswell's suggestion they agreed to pass the evening of June 25th together at the Mitre, which was then Johnson's favorite tavern. Johnson, not at the moment a teetotaler though he had been one before and was soon to become one again, ordered a bottle of port and Boswell, after his fashion, prepared to relish the full implications of the occasion. "The orthodox high-church sound of the MITRE,—the figure and manner of the celebrated SAMUEL JOHNSON,—the extraordinary power and precision of his conversation, and the pride arising from finding myself admitted as his companion, produced a variety of sensations, and a pleasing elevation of mind beyond what I had ever before experienced." This elevation was certainly not diminished by the fact that the moment was now propitious for something which Boswell never failed to get around to pretty quickly, no matter what great man he had just managed to scrape an acquaintance with. "I opened my mind to him ingeniously, and gave him a little sketch of my life, to which he was pleased to listen with great attention."

Having met at nine, they sat until between one and two in the morning. Exclaimed Boswell as they parted: "Had it been foretold to me some years ago that I should pass an evening with the author of the RAMBLER, how should I have exulted!" Replied Johnson: "Sir, I am glad we have met. I hope we shall pass many evenings and mornings too, together." Plainly Johnson was beginning to see how pleasantly the years of pensioned security might be illuminated, not necessarily perhaps by Boswell, but by lively company of some kind. "Sir," he was to say a few weeks later, "I love the acquaintance of young people; because, in the first place, I don't like to think myself growing old. In the next place, young acquaintances must last longest, if they do last; and then, Sir, young men have more virtue than old men; they have more generous sentiments in every respect. I love the young dogs of this age; they have more wit and humour and knowledge of life than we had; but then the dogs are not so good scholars. Sir, in my early years I read very hard."

July 1st saw Boswell supping again at the Mitre, this time with Goldsmith making a third, but the occasion was somewhat marred by a humiliating reminder that, cordially as he had been received, Boswell was not yet accepted into the last degrees of intimacy. He was not invited to finish the evening by taking tea with the blind Miss Williams, to whose lodgings in Bolt Court Johnson always, it may be remembered, paid a visit before going to bed, and one of whose habits in connection with the pouring of tea, it may also be remembered, was a subject of dispute. "Dr. Goldsmith, being a privileged man, went with him this night, strutting away, and calling to me with an air of superiority, like that of an esoterick over an exoterick disciple of a sage of antiquity, 'I go to Miss Williams.' I confess, I then envied him this mighty privilege, of which he seemed so proud; but it was not long before I obtained the same mark of distinction."

In all, Boswell met with Johnson twelve times during the month of July and there were, indeed, comparatively few periods during the twenty years of their acquaintance when they saw as much of each other within so short a time. On the 6th, Boswell advanced another step by playing host to Johnson, Goldsmith, Tom Davies and another gentleman at the Mitre; on the 9th, he called and found Johnson surrounded by a numerous levee; on the 19th, he got Levett, the medical practitioner who had found refuge with Johnson, to show him his hero's library "which was contained in two garrets over his chambers, where Lintot, son of the celebrated bookseller of that name, had formerly his warehouse." There he found "a number of good books, but very dusty and in great confusion."

"The floor was strewed with manuscript leaves, in Johnson's

own hand-writing, which I beheld with a degree of veneration, supposing they perhaps might contain portions of the Rambler, or of Rasselas. I observed an apparatus for chymical experiments, of which Johnson was all his life very fond. The place seemed to be very favourable for retirement and meditation. Johnson told me, that he went up thither without mentioning it to his servant when he wanted to study, secure from interruption; for he would not allow his servant to say he was not at home when he really was. 'A servant's strict regard for truth, (said he) must be weakened by such a practice. A philosopher may know that it is merely a form of denial; but few servants are such nice distinguishers. If I accustom a servant to tell a lie for *me,* have I not reason to apprehend that he will tell many lies for *himself.'* I am, however, satisfied that every servant, of any degree of intelligence, understands saying his master is not at home, not at all as the affirmation of a fact, but as the customary words, intimating that his master wishes not to be seen; so that there can be no bad effect from it." [7]

On another evening they walked arm in arm along the Strand; on July 30th, they took a sculler at the Temple stairs and made a day of it at Greenwich whence Johnson had suggested they might repair in order to discuss at leisure Boswell's plan of study at Utrecht. It was in Greenwich Park that Johnson asked him: "Is not this very fine?" and that Boswell, sensing what Johnson hoped for, won his heart by replying: "Yes, Sir; but not equal to Fleet-street." Shortly thereafter Boswell "made good my title to be a privileged man" by being taken in the evening to have tea with Miss Williams, and Johnson was in various ways establishing intimate links between himself and his new disciple. He advised Boswell to keep a journal (which Boswell did) and to arrange to have it burned after his death (which Boswell did not do); he glowed with him over the privilege of being a Scotch landlord, advised him to "perambulate Spain," confessed of himself that "he always felt an inclination to do nothing," and most remarkable of all, discussed the desire to make an expedition to "the Western Islands of Scotland" with Boswell when the latter should have returned from the Continent. "There are," he said, "few people to whom I take so much to as you. . . . I should be very unhappy at parting, did I think we were not to meet again." And when the time came to bid good-by on the beach at Harwich, Johnson replied to Boswell's hope that he would not be forgotten by saying: "Nay, Sir, it is more likely you should forget me, than that I should forget you." Boswell adds: "As the vessel put out to sea, I kept my eyes upon him for a considerable time, while he remained rolling his majestic frame in his usual manner: and at last I perceived him walk back into the town, and he disappeared." [8]

So far as sheer brilliance of reporting and arrangement is concerned, Boswell's account of the conversations which he had with Johnson during this period is not so fine as some of his later efforts. Boswell himself was aware of the fact and he offers an apology which, to do him justice, only the supreme excellence of certain pages to come makes appropriate. "I was so wrapt in admiration of his extraordinary colloquial talents, and so little accustomed to his peculiar mode of expression, that I found it extremely difficult to recollect and record his conversation with its genuine vigour and vivacity. In progress of time, when my mind was, as it were, *strongly impregnated with the Johnsonian aether,* I could, with much more facility and exactness, carry in my memory and commit to paper the exuberant variety of his wisdom and wit."

But if the conversations of this period are not quite so completely worked up as some of those of a later date, the material is, nevertheless, rich indeed. Several of Johnson's most often quoted sayings are there, including the one about a dog walking on its hind legs, and the one made in reply to Mr. Ogilvie, a parson-poet, whom Johnson had consented to meet on the secret understanding that he should be spared any of his poetry but who insisted upon singing the praises of his native land. In Scotland, he said, there are "many noble wild prospects," and Johnson, who had little use for wild prospects even if they were not also Scotch, replied: "I believe, Sir, you have a great many. Norway, too, has noble wild prospects; and Lapland is remarkable for prodigious noble wild prospects. But, Sir, let me tell you, the noblest prospect which a Scotchman ever sees, is the high road that leads him to England!"

Apparently Johnson was already talking as well as he ever talked at any time during the twenty years of practice which still lay ahead of him. It is, moreover, remarkable how many of the familiar themes of his discourse he managed to introduce in the course of relatively few sessions, and how skillfully Boswell seized upon them. Between May 16 and August 6, 1763, Johnson ran pretty well through the gamut of his tastes, his prejudices and his deep convictions, from his insistence upon the importance of eating to his sober estimate of the value of Christian evidence.

"Some people (said he) have a foolish way of not minding, or pretending not to mind, what they eat. For my part, I mind my belly very studiously, and very carefully; for I look upon it, that he who does not mind his belly will hardly mind any thing else," and that, of course, prepares one for the later remarks about a "synod of cooks" and about the dinner which was "good enough, to be sure" but "not a dinner to *ask* a man to." All this, as Boswell remarks, is not consistent with what he said on other occasions when he talked with contempt of those who were overly anxious to gratify their palates or with "the 206th number of his Rambler" which "is a masterly essay against gulosity." "His practice," continues Boswell, "I must acknowledge, may be considered as casting the balance of his different opinions upon this subject; for I never knew any man who relished good eating more than he did. When at table, he was totally absorbed in the business of the moment; his looks seemed rivetted to the plate; nor would he, unless when in very high company, say one word, or even pay the least attention to what was said by others, till he had satisfied his appetite, which was so fierce, and indulged with such intenseness, that while in the act of eating, the veins of his forehead swelled, and generally a strong perspiration was visible." Johnson thought himself a gourmet rather than a glutton. "I, Madam, who live at a variety of good tables, am a much better judge of cookery, than any person who has a very tolerable cook, but lives much at home; for his palate is gradually adapted to the taste of his cook; whereas, Madam, in trying a wider range, I can more exquisitely judge." But we have various witnesses besides Boswell (including Mrs. Thrale) to the fact that, whatever might be the undemonstrable niceness of Johnson's perceptions in the realm of eating, his appetites were also, to put it as gently as possible, decidedly hearty. As Boswell acutely remarked: "Johnson, though he could be rigidly *abstemious,* was not a *temperate* man in eating or drinking"; and the fact explains much of his conduct.[9]

To some it may now seem, as it doubtless seemed to some of his contemporaries, that Johnson passed with remarkable ease from magisterial pronouncements concerning the importance of the belly to pronouncements neither more nor less magisterial concerning the importance of religion. He did, indeed, do just that, but those who had heard him often knew that all the area between had also been subject to his survey; that he could easily, if called upon, establish all the links in the chain of considerations which led gradually upward from one to the other, and that he could discourse with the always delightful, if sometimes also absurd, explicitness and clarity which is, after all, perhaps the most remarkable of his gifts. Perhaps we should here examine some of the convictions he was soon expounding to Boswell.

It was, he knew, the business of the wise man to be as nearly happy as he could by employing against the evils of life all those available palliatives (including good food in plentiful quantities) which neither a rational calculus of pleasures nor divine command forbids. It was, furthermore, the business of society to maintain all those institutions which promote the greatest good of the greatest number—even though this formula had not yet been made a formula, and even though Johnson would have disagreed violently enough with those who first made it one. And to Boswell—who was torn between certain feudal notions appropriate to a Highland landowner and a vague aspiration for that liberty which he had never taken the trouble to define—Johnson explained in their early conversations why Toryism actually did tend to produce that greatest good for the greatest number.

One of the subjects upon which he discoursed most gladly was that of "the great scheme of subordination" and the benefits which society as a whole derived from maintaining it by universal agreement. He certainly did not believe that noble birth, exalted position, or great wealth was any more an indication of mental or spiritual superiority than he believed that any one of them guaranteed happiness. He did, however, believe them desirable things in themselves, for, as he remarked with great acuteness to Boswell in the course of one of their earliest meetings: "When I was running about this town a very poor fellow, I was a great arguer for the advantages of poverty; but I was, at the same time, very sorry to be poor. Sir, all the arguments which are brought to represent poverty as no evil, shew it to be evidently a great evil. You never find people labouring to convince you that you may live very happily upon a plentiful fortune.—So you hear people talking how miserable a King must be; and yet they all wish to be in his place." Moreover, though he knew that a lord might be a scoundrel or a sot, he continued to believe that the existence of lords, even if some of them *were* scoundrels or sots, did contribute to the greatest happiness of the greatest number.

The arguments which seemed to him valid were in their essence familiar enough to his century, but today have been largely forgot even by the defenders of the aristocracy, and perhaps they can best be summed up in the language of our own time by saying that Johnson thought a competitive society an unhappy one and thought, in addition, that hereditary rights and hereditary possessions tended to reduce the amount of destructive competition in the society of England.

Pascal and Bernard Shaw have defended certain arbitrary laws in much the same way—Bernard Shaw by comparing them to the rules of the road, despite which no sensible man complains that he has a natural right to drive either to the right or to the left as the mood strikes him; Pascal, by remarking that it is much better to have it understood that a nobleman goes through the door before a valet than it would be to have the question fought out a dozen times every day. Johnson was using the same argument in one of his early meetings with Boswell, when he discussed the possibility that a shoemaker might easily maintain that he was more than the equal of a lord because he did more for society. "Thus, Sir," he concluded, "there would be a perpetual struggle for precedence, were there no fixed invariable rules for the distinctions of rank, which creates no jealousy, as it is allowed to be accidental."

Johnson was not actually overlooking one fact which seems so obvious to the present day—the fact, namely, that the privileges of rank and, more particularly, the privileges of wealth are by no means all as insubstantial as those connected with merely social precedents. But he had convinced himself that even an inequitable distribution of the substantial goods of life was preferable to a perpetual competition for them. Speaking of corporal punishment in education he once said, as the reader may remember: "A child is afraid of being whipped, and gets his task, and there's an end on't; whereas, by exciting emulation and comparisons of superiority, you lay the foundation of lasting mischief; you make brothers and sisters hate each other." Apparently his social opinions are essentially a rational deduction from the same premises. A man who is born rich or privileged may be to some extent envied by his fellows, but they will neither attempt to compete with him nor feel the same self-accusing guilt they are likely to feel in a society where, theoretically at least, everyone has an equal chance to be a president or a plutocrat and where, therefore, not to be either implies an inferiority of merit or ability. It might, moreover, be argued that, in certain respects, Johnson's position is closer to that of nineteenth and twentieth century social pholosophers of the left than it is to that nineteenth century liberalism which was being born in his own day. The Marxian hopes to abolish inequality; Johnson assumed that inequalities could not be abolished. But that difference is possibly less fundamental than the agreement between them. Both find horribly destructive that limitless competition which the philosophy of laissez faire holds out as an ideal.

"What I like about the Garter is that there is no damned nonsense about merit in connection with it." This alleged opinion of a nineteenth-century nobleman has often been quoted as a perfect example of triumphant unreason, but Johnson would probably have nodded his head in approval. "The distinction of rank" is "allowed to be accidental" and that is why such a distinction is harmless. "Sir," he said, "I would no more deprive a nobleman of his respect, than of his money. I consider myself as acting a part in the great system of society, and I do to others as I would have them to do to me. I would behave to a nobleman as I should expect he would behave to me, were I a nobleman and he Sam. Johnson." Yet no man was less of a snob, and the best proof of that fact lies in something other than what is generally alleged. It is true that, as Johnson himself pointed out, a man both poor and humbly born can hardly be accused of being prejudiced for mean ends in favor of either the privileges of birth or the privileges of wealth. It is also true that he stood up for the dignity of literature quite as inflexibly as he did for the dignity of rank. But neither of these facts is as conclusive as another which ought to be mentioned.

Essentially, a snob is a man who assumes that one kind of distinction implies another; that rank is not merely an accident but that a lord is necessarily also a wit, a gentleman, and a scholar. No one was ever further than Johnson from any such conclusion. He granted to rank the rights and the forms of deference which he thought rank might justly claim, but he granted it not one iota of anything more. Once Goldsmith made the company laugh by complaining in his artless way that he had met Lord Camden "in a mixed company" and that Camden took no more notice of him than if he had been an ordinary man. "Nay, Gentlemen," said Johnson, "Dr. Goldsmith is in the right. A nobleman ought to have made up to such a man as Goldsmith; and I think it is much against Lord Camden that he neglected him." [10]

In her *Anecdotes,* Mrs. Thrale watered down another revealing story by making Johnson say, when he troubled her husband by turning his back on the second Lord Bolingbroke, "I am not obliged, Sir, to find reasons for respecting the rank of him who will not condescend to declare it by his dress or some other visible mark: what are stars and other signs of superiority made for?" But Lord Bolingbroke was the divorced husband of the adulterous Diana, now married to Johnson's friend, Topham Beauclerk, and what Johnson actually said (as Mrs. Thrale's manuscript annotation informs us) was something a good deal more pointed and a good deal less respectful. "Why, Sir, I did not know the man. If he will put on no other mark of distinction, let us make him wear his horns." No one, Mrs. Thrale remarked on another occasion, "was so careful to maintain the ceremonies of life," but it is obvious that a due acceptance of the great scheme of subordination did not interfere with a proper estimate of any of his own rights, including those of the tongue.

Neither, it should be added, did his somewhat feudal conception of the social structure make him indifferent to social abuses, for he was as well ahead of his time in a good many of his opinions as he is commonly assumed to have been behind it in others. In the Highlands, Boswell professed to believe that mankind was happier in the "ancient feudal state of subordination," but Johnson had the candor to reply: "To be sure the *Chief* was. But we must think of the number of individuals. That *they* were less happy seems plain; for that state from which all escape as soon as they can, and to which none return after they have left it, must be less happy; and this is the case with the state of dependence on a chief or great man." "I am," he said in a sentence already quoted from the reply to Soame Jenyns, "always afraid of determining on the side of envy or cruelty." And it was that fear which so regularly saved him from most of the brutality often associated with Tory principles by forbidding him to use conservatism as an excuse for inhumanity. He was in favor of popular education at a time when the pious Hannah More was alarmed lest the members of the lower classes should be educated beyond their station. In *The Idler* he protested vehemently against the debtors' prisons, almost a century before any general public indignation was aroused, and in the same series of essays he wrote in flaming indignation concerning those experiments on living animals which his age, under cover of the astonishing Cartesian theory that animals could feel no pain, practiced with almost unparalleled coldness and wanton triviality.

In still another number of the same series of essays, he speaks of "Charity, or tenderness for the poor, which is now justly considered as inseparable from piety," and far from thinking all these things incompatible with Toryism, he quite correctly assumed that they were more readily compatible with Tory doctrine than with that of the Whigs of his day. "They make," he said on another occasion, "a rout about *universal* liberty, without considering that all that is to be valued, or indeed can be enjoyed by individuals, is *private* liberty." "In Dr. Johnson," wrote Hannah More, "some contrarieties very harmoniously meet; if he has too little charity for the opinions of others, and too little patience with their faults, he has the greatest tenderness for their persons. He told me the other day, he hated to hear people whine about metaphysical distresses, when there was so much want and hunger in the world. I told him that I supposed then he never wept at any tragedy but Jane Shore, who had died for want of a loaf. He called me a saucy girl, but did not deny the inference." Indeed, though Johnson quite evidently distrusted "the people" as a source of power, the triumph of the Whigs did not mean to him so much an increase in the power of the people as it did in the power of money used for corruption.

But perhaps the best proof that when Johnson derided the idea of liberty he was thinking only of that sort of which the deprivation produces merely "metaphysical distresses" is to be found in his attitude toward Negro slavery. Boswell was the "friend of Paoli" and hence a champion of liberty—but chiefly, it appears, of the sort whose effects are exclusively "metaphysical." To *him* Negro slavery was an institution so marvelously humane and just that it should be contemplated with delighted wonder. To the Tory Johnson, on the other hand, it was an abomination concerning which he could not speak without rage. Near the very beginning of his career and at a time when the Quakers were still slave dealers, he spoke of "the natural right of the negroes to liberty and independence." A little later he described Jamaica as "a place of great wealth and dreadful wickedness, a den of tyrants and a dungeon of slaves"; and still later he could write: "I do not much wish well to discoveries, for I am always afraid they will end in conquest and robbery." [11]

In 1777 he dictated for Boswell a brief in favor of a Negro suing in Scotland to regain his freedom, and at Oxford, once, this defender of "subordination" and scorner of liberty gave as his toast: "Here's to the next insurrection of the negroes in the West Indies." "An individual," he wrote, "may, indeed, forfeit his liberty by a crime; but he cannot by that crime forfeit the liberty of his children," and it has been argued with at least partial justice that Johnson's scorn for the American rebels (which is so much better known than his hatred of slavery) was the result of the fact that the same Americans who claimed political liberty for themselves imposed personal bondage on others. "How is it," he certainly did ask, "that we hear the loudest *yelps* for liberty among the drivers of Negroes?"; and for once he was in agreement with Horace Walpole, who remarked: "I should think the souls of the Africans would sit heavy on the swords of the Americans."

But Boswell, who seems seldom to have been either consistent or persistent in any opinion or line of conduct except when it was either foolish in itself or could be supported by some foolish argument, remained unconvinced. He thought Johnson discovered in this matter "a zeal without knowledge" and in the *Life* begs "leave to enter my most solemn protest against his general doctrine with respect to the *Slave Trade*. . . . To abolish a *status,* which in all ages GOD has sanctioned, and man has continued, would not only be *robbery* to an innumerable class of our fellow-subjects; but it would be an extreme cruelty to the African Savages, a portion of whom it saves from massacre, or intolerable bondage in their own country, and introduces into a much happier state of life. . . . To abolish that trade would be to shut the gates of mercy on mankind."

Obviously Boswell had not caught Johnson's fear "of determining on the side of envy or cruelty," and after Johnson was dead he ventured to publish an extraordinary poem, *No Abolition of Slavery, or the Universal Empire of Love,* in which he clinches the argument by calling attention to the fact that liberty would not be achieved by the freeing of Negroes since all men must always continue to be Slaves to Love; or, as he puts it—with an infelicity which few other men could achieve:

> Pernicious as th' effect would be,
> T' abolish negro slavery,
> Such partial freedom would be vain,
> Since Love's strong empire must remain.[12]

Johnson's political convictions, like those of most men, were part of an emotional as well as of an intellectual complex in which so many factors were involved that it becomes on occasion quite impossible to judge surely the relative importance of each, or even to be sure which are genuinely causative factors and which are mere rationalizations. If his political opinions are to be understood, it is, accordingly, necessary to remember that they were certainly influenced by tastes and prejudices as important in their own way as the rational theory we have just been examining. It must, first of all, be admitted that his defense of established institutions and hereditary privileges—whether they were those of king, or church, or nobility—had more than a strong tinge of merely romantic prejudice in favor of what was consecrated by age. It must be further admitted that they were also more than a little influenced by that enormous respect for the rights of property which, though usual enough in the eighteenth century, seems to us so excessive that few of even the most conservative today would openly defend it. "Influence," he could say when speaking of the influence of peers upon the election of members to the House of Commons, "must ever be in proportion to property, and it is right it should." He could also, more startlingly, base his estimate of the importance of female chastity on property rights. "Consider of what importance the chastity of women is. Upon that, all the property in the world depends. We hang a thief for stealing a sheep. But the unchastity of a woman transfers sheep and farm and all from the right owner." Small wonder, then, if there are times when he speaks of the claims of the Stuart kings as though he considered the English nation their property and as though the essential thing involved were simply a man's right to his own.

It is also worth noting that, when talking for effect, as he confessedly often did, Johnson took the side of paradox and was well aware of the fact that, in an age when liberalism was everywhere spreading, the arguments of a conservative became paradoxical. In recent years we have heard a good deal about "parlor pinks"—men who love to frighten conservatives with big talk. At times Johnson was a parlor white, similarly delighting to outrage comfortable and self-satisfied people, who regarded their own views as advanced. Finally, he genuinely believed that the current was running so strongly in one direction that someone ought to say what could be said against the prevailing tendency—as was amusingly revealed years later when, on the Scotch tour, Boswell asked him if he did not think that all his enthusiasm for the rights of the crown led him to be insensible of the danger that the rights of the people and their representatives might suffer extinction. Johnson replied that there might have been such a danger once but that there was certainly not one now. And, quoting Samuel Butler, he added that Boswell was like a man who would go right on "crying 'Fire! Fire!' in Noah's flood."

Nevertheless, Johnson's respect for authority was not without limits. During their first meetings, Boswell made an obvious effort to get a clear understanding of his position, and he records with great emphasis the latter's remark apropos of the danger that authority might be abused: "And then, Sir, there is this consideration, that *if the abuse be enormous, Nature will rise up, and claiming her original rights, overturn a corrupt political system.*" The italics are Boswell's, and the latter was, so he tells us, so affected by this generous sentiment that his blood was stirred to "that pitch of fancied resistance, the possibility of which I am glad to keep in mind, but to which I trust I never shall be forced." Boswell might have been stirred still more if he had known that a few years later Johnson was to write in connection with corn riots: "Those who want the supports of life will seize them wherever they can be found."

Johnson's reservation is truly Hobbesian and certainly inconsistent with any literal interpretation of the doctrine of Divine Right, though Mrs. Thrale (in this case obviously in error) calls him "strongly attached" to that "notion." In characteristic eighteenth-century fashion, the remarks to Boswell put original Natural Rights first, and that Johnson thought some contemporary abuses intolerable is clear enough from his remarks about Ireland:

"He had great compassion for the miseries and distresses of the Irish nation, particularly the Papists; and severely reprobated the barbarous debilitating policy of the British government, which, he said, was the most detestable mode of persecution. To a gentleman, who hinted such policy might be necessary to support the authority of the English government, he replied by saying, 'Let the authority of the English government perish, rather than be maintained by iniquity. Better would it be to restrain the turbulence of the natives by the authority of the sword, and to make them amenable to law and justice by an effectual and vigorous police, than to grind them to powder by all manner of disabilities and incapacities. Better (said he) to hang or drown people at once, than by an unrelenting persecution to beggar and starve them.' "

Yet it must be admitted that his fear of confusion was such that he was not likely to consider "enormous" any abuse not literally that. Speaking of the "glorious Revolution" which deprived the Stuarts of their kingship he could say, rather curiously: "What we did at the Revolution was necessary: but it broke our constitution." [13]

Like many men to whom political activity is distasteful, Johnson tried to believe that the private citizen was but little affected by the issues over which politicians, professional and amateur, exercised themselves. "The notion of liberty," he had said at the very first meeting in Tom Davies's parlor, "amuses the people of England, and helps keep off the *taedium vitae*. When a butcher tells you that *his heart bleeds for his country,* he has, in fact, no uneasy feeling." This is indeed one of his favorite themes. Historians, he declared, may say that at the news of the battle of Fontenoy every heart beat and every eye was in tears, but "we know that no man eat his dinner the worse." "I will not trouble you with speculations about peace and war. The good and ill success of battles and embassies extends itself to a very small part of domestic life; we all have good and evil, which we feel more sensibly than our petty part of public miscarriage or prosperity." And to Goldsmith's poem *The Traveller* he contributed the lines:

> How small of all that human hearts endure,
> That part which kings or laws can cause or cure.
> Still to ourselves in every place consign'd,
> Our own felicity we make or find.

In those four lines two of Johnson's profoundest convictions join to reach the conclusion that neither kings nor laws are commonly of great importance to the private citizen. The minor pleasures and the minor pains of existence have, for the most part, their origin in domestic life. The great sufferings, as *Rasselas* had argued, are from eternity and shall not fail.

An age which has seen what ours has seen can hardly be expected to contemplate Johnson's views on this subject with anything less than impatience. We know that kings and laws can and have put whole nations into a state where the influence of domestic affairs is all but obliterated. Yet, in fairness, it ought at least to be remembered that Johnson's experience had been limited to a continent and a century which, while familiar enough with poverty and disease, had had little experience with the extremes of political freedom and political slavery as they exist today. Even Pope would probably have hesitated to designate as fools all those who think one form of government better than another if Pope had had forced upon his attention some of the forms which government has assumed in our time. Mid-eighteenth-century England was in certain respects more like England or America before the First World War than it is like either today. There was a similar prevailing assumption that mankind had definitely left certain kinds of savagery behind it, that "progress" of certain kinds was inevitably continuous, and that mankind would never again be called upon to endure what it had once endured.

Of the many, but relatively humane, wars of his age Chesterfield could write in mock protest: "Even war is pusillanimously carried on in this degenerate age; quarter is given; towns are taken, and the people spared; even in a storm, a woman can hardly hope for the benefit of a rape."

Johnson, who probably supposed that the happy condition he was about to describe would never be changed, could say: "Mutual cowardice keeps us in peace. Were one half of mankind brave, and one half cowards, the brave would always be beating the cowards. Were all brave, they would lead a very uneasy life; all would be continually fighting: but being all cowards, we go on very well." He was, moreover, insular enough to think chiefly not only of his own century, but also of his own nation. And when he argued that government made little difference to the individual, what he really meant was that it made little difference whether the prime minister was a Whig or a Tory; at most, whether the king was a Stuart or a Hanover.

Whether understandably or not, Johnson consistently maintained his attitude. Indeed, and perhaps because he perceived some of its weakness, it was one of those which he tended to defend more and more violently if an objection were so much as hinted. Thus, many years later, Boswell, having expressed the opinion that he might be unhappy in Parliament because he might be vexed when things went wrong, Johnson replied: "That's cant, Sir. . . . Public affairs vex no man." And when Boswell, taking the dangerous liberty of citing Johnson against himself, asked if he had not been vexed by a vote against the influence of the crown, Johnson burst out: "Sir, I have never slept an hour less, nor eat an ounce less meat. I would have knocked the factious dogs on the head to be sure; but I was not *vexed.*" The question whether or not an impulse to knock the members of the House of Commons on the head is prima-facie evidence of vexation was not discussed.

In all his relations with Johnson, though perhaps most notably during the days of their first acquaintance, Boswell appears in two roles which merge one into the other. Sometimes he is an earnest seeker after enlightenment, who wants not only to be advised on his conduct but also to be told what he ought to believe. At other moments he is obviously merely the amateur of character and opinions, bent only on eliciting whatever will enable him to add a trait to the portrait he is already drawing, and more interested that two men can be so different as, say, Johnson and Churchill than he is in deciding how far one or the other is right. Perhaps he did not always himself distinguish between the two roles, and they may have been quite inextricably mingled when he brought up the subject of religion—although his private journals do make it clear enough that he was often quite seriously concerned. In any event, introduce it he did, and in a skillful manner. The topic had been touched upon earlier, and on the occasion of the first visit to the Mitre, when Boswell launched into autobiography, he "acknowledged, that though educated very strictly in the principles of religion, I had for some time been misled into a certain degree of infidelity; but that I was come now to a better way of thinking, and was fully satisfied of the truth of the Christian revelation, though I was not clear as to every point considered to be orthodox." This display of the frankness that was not quite so thoroughgoing as it sounded produced what was no doubt the intended result. Johnson exclaimed: "Give me your hand; I have taken a liking to you" and "then began to descant upon the force of testimony, and the little we could know of final causes; so that the objections of, why was it so? or why was it not so? ought not to disturb us: adding, that he himself had at one period been guilty of a temporary neglect of religion, but that it was not the result of argument, but mere absence of thought." During the ensuing weeks Johnson recurred several times to the topic and at least two things emerge clearly.

One of them is that, for all his religiosity and for all his intolerance of religious skepticism, he remained always in religion as in everything else a rationalist and a rationalizer. He did not believe in the "inner light" because nothing had ever been revealed to him by it. He no more believed that the ordinary mortal could obtain transcendental knowledge of God than (as we shall see later) he believed that imagination in the poet could transcend the senses. And in this, as in so many other respects, he was metaphysically in accord with those philosophers of the English school whom, in general, he professed to despise. Of a certain skeptic it was once said that he could believe anything provided it was not in the Bible. Of Johnson the exact opposite was once remarked by Hogarth, who declared of him: "That man is not contented with believing the Bible, but he fairly resolves, I think, to believe nothing *but* the Bible"; and Mrs. Thrale, who reports the saying, adds: "Mr. Johnson's incredulity amounted almost to disease." He accepted the Bible as revelation, but only because he had, or thought he had, good rational reasons for believing that it *was* revelation. In other words, his arguments in favor of the Christian religion were founded almost exclusively upon an acceptance of those "Christian evidences" which seemed so much more solid than they have seemed, even to most churchmen, in any century since his own. "The Christian religion has very strong evidences. It, indeed, appears in some degree strange to reason; but in History we have undoubted facts, against which, in reasoning *a priori,* we have more arguments than we have for them; but then, testimony has great weight, and casts the balance. I would recommend to every man whose faith is yet unsettled, Grotius,—Dr. Pearson,—and Dr. Clark." A month later he was harping again on the same theme: "As to the Christian religion, Sir, besides the strong evidence which we have for it, there is a balance in its favour from the number of great men who have been convinced of its truth, after a serious consideration of the question. Grotius was an acute man, a lawyer, a man accustomed to examine evidence, and he was convinced. Grotius was not a recluse, but a man of the world, who certainly had no bias to the side of religion. Sir Isaac Newton set out an infidel, and came to be a very firm believer." This, surely, is the language of a man who had the will to believe but no great talent for believing. It is the same language as that of the dialogue quoted previously, in which, discussing the evidence of life after death, Johnson said: "I like to have more." It is also perhaps the language of a man who has forgot for the moment that "prodigies are always seen in proportion as they are expected." [14]

The other important thing which Johnson's talks with his new friend made clear beyond any question is the fact that his orthodoxy (of which much is commonly made) was not the result of any bigoted conviction concerning the unique rightness of the Anglican Church but quite simply a part of his general tendency to favor social unity and social conformity. It is true that when Boswell made the mistake (quite possibly intentional) of mentioning, as one of the absurd things he had heard about Johnson, an alleged statement to the effect that he would stand before a battery of cannon to restore the Convocation to its full powers, Johnson's eyes blazed as he retorted with the anger which always seized upon him when he felt it necessary to defend a proposition he knew to be absurd: "And would I not, Sir?

Shall the Presbyterian *Kirk* of Scotland have its General Assembly, and the Church of England be denied its Convocation?" But when he had not been provoked his High-Church principles qualified themselves away as completely as his Jacobitism did. For all the occasional vehemence of the latter, he could, in the course of these same first conversations with Boswell, explain that the phrase "The King can do no wrong" means only that, since it is desirable to have an ideal of infallible authority, we conventionally attribute the wrongs of a government to the king's ministers, not to the king himself, and thus see to it that the wrong "may not be above our reach." He admitted to Bennet Langton that, so far as James the Second was concerned, "It was become impossible for him to reign any longer in this country," and actually he was no more bigoted as a churchman than he was as a Jacobite.

At the Mitre, for all the "High Church sound" of that name which was so pleasing to Boswell, Johnson declared: "For my part, Sir, I think all Christians, whether Papists or Protestants, agree in the essential articles, and that their differences are trivial, and rather political than religious." That surely is latitudinarian enough; in fact, hardly more than one step away from the deism prevalent in his century. If Johnson expressed, as he often did, extreme irritation against ostentatious dissenters of one kind or another, it was not because he thought doctrinal differences so important but because he thought them so unimportant—far less important than practical unity. When Boswell asked him, on a subsequent occasion, whether it was necessary to believe all the Thirty-nine Articles, Johnson, by refusing to commit himself, made his own opinion clear enough. "That is a question which has been much agitated. Some have thought it necessary that they should all be believed; others have considered them to be only articles of peace, that is to say, you are not to preach against them." [15]

From all this it ought to be clear enough that when Boswell sailed away he carried with him something more than the visual image of an awkward, untidy figure disappearing into the now receding town, and something more than such bits of useful advice as the injunction to recommend himself "to the protection of your CREATOR and REDEEMER" and to get out of the habit of using "words of disproportionate magnitude" to express his thoughts or feelings. He carried also a pretty adequate conspectus of the opinions of a remarkable character which always fascinated him as a specimen and sometimes inspired him with a desire to imitate what it was by no means within the scope of his character to achieve.

Some two months later he drew up a document which he labeled an *Inviolable Plan* and which begins characteristically enough: "You have got an excellent heart and bright parts. . . . The rambler showed you that vacuity, gloom and fretfulness were the causes of your woe." It continues: "You can live quite independent and go to London every year; and you can pass some months at Auchinleck, doing good to your tenants and living hospitably with your neighbours, beautifying your estate, rearing a family, and piously preparing for immortal felicity. . . . Remember Religion and Morality. Remember the dignity of human nature." He did not, unfortunately, always remember these three things. But in later years his misery was perhaps the worse for the fact that he could not for long entirely forget them either. He was now armed with an Inviolable Plan as he set out to visit the German courts in the character of a Scotch gentleman, to fall more or less in love, to meet Rousseau, to meet Voltaire, and finally to become that which, in his own opinion, remained to the end his second-best claim to eminence—"the friend of Paoli."

Boswell's adventures, fascinating as they are when described by himself, hardly come within the scope of this book. They may be followed in the pages of the *Private Papers* or in the volumes which have been devoted to his life. It is, however, not irrelevant to cite several incidents and several expressions which illuminate the character of the man through whose eyes we must so often look at Johnson. It certainly throws some light upon the curious contradictions of his nature and the difficulty he had in reconciling Johnsonian imitations with the native rakishness of his own temperament to know that the charming Dutch girl, with whom he carried on an extraordinarily pompous flirtation and who came pretty close to falling in love with him, could write in a moment of wholly justifiable exasperation that he had exhibited "the puerile vanity of a fatuous fool, coupled with the arrogant rigidity of an old Cato." It is even more enlightening to observe how he stalked his lions and what he thought of his exploit after he had bagged them.

In the case of both Rousseau and Voltaire, the plan of campaign was at least as carefully laid and as persistently prosecuted as it had been and was to be in the case of Johnson. Though he had a letter of introduction to Rousseau from a valued friend, he "determined to put my real merit to the severest test, by presenting myself without any recommendation." Accordingly, he wrote in his own name a letter of which he was very proud and in which "I told him all my worth, and claimed his regard as what I had a title to." And when he had got a far from cordial invitation to present himself, he took all care to get into the mood to appreciate what he knew ought to be memorable.

The same method, with suitable adaptations, was employed to make contact with Voltaire. This time a letter of introduction was presented first but there was a similar hour of meditation to get into the proper mood. "I surveyed wild nature with a noble eye. I called up all the grand ideas which I have ever entertained of Voltaire." And when it became evident that the formal introduction was to gain nothing except a formal interview, Boswell had recourse again to a letter calculated to demonstrate that he was no ordinary pleasure seeker.

It is obvious that neither Rousseau nor Voltaire knew quite what to make of this mad and persistent young foreigner. To begin with, Rousseau treated him with surly impatience, Voltaire with cool irony. Yet it is equally obvious that both soon realized that you could not treat James Boswell as though he were somebody else, even if you had no idea who James Boswell might be. And as his many English acquaintances also found out, he possessed a mysterious capacity for getting himself accepted in a society which would certainly have had little patience with another man whom no easily analyzable reason rendered more acceptable. Within a few minutes of his first meeting with Rousseau, Boswell "thumped him on the shoulder" in his enthusiasm. At the end of the second interview, Rousseau exclaimed: "You are irksome to me . . . Go away." But there were three more meetings, and before the last was over Rousseau was to proclaim: "There are points where our souls are linked." [16]

Nothing in all the *Life of Johnson* is superior to the accounts which Boswell wrote in his journals and in a letter to Temple of the meetings with the two great Frenchmen. In fact, few scenes in the *Life* are actually their equal, and the high point in each of the series of interviews came at the moment when Boswell, perhaps with the Rambler in mind, relentlessly cross-examined his victim on the subject of Christianity.

Perhaps it is only fair to mention here a bit of evidence tending to show that Boswell was genuinely anxious to confirm his own often reiterated but obviously not too secure faith in the Christian religion. When he knew that David Hume's days were numbered, he sought out his old acquaintance, questioned him closely to discover whether the approach of death was shaking his skepticism, and then wrote *An Account of My Last Interview with David Hume, Esq.*, in which he clearly reveals how much Hume's calm persistence in infidelity troubled him. He later mentioned in print the existence of this account "which I may sometime or other communicate to the world," but he never did so; it was presumed lost until it turned up among the papers brought to light by Colonel Isham.

Throughout the whole series of interviews with Rousseau and Voltaire, Boswell's manner was the same ambiguous one which characterizes him in his relations with Johnson. He was at once arrogantly pushing and genuinely humble; reverently worshipful and at the same time as impudently calculating as the most unconscionable of modern reporters. To Temple he boasts of the cleverness of his letters and exults in the fact that he meets the great men on their own level. "Upon that occasion He was one Individual and I another. For a certain portion of time there was a fair opposition between Voltaire and Boswell." And yet it is obvious that a persistent sense of inferiority is expressing itself in this amazement when he realizes that he has spoken up boldly, that Rousseau and Voltaire have deigned to talk to him. Hence to Temple he writes deliriously:

"Think not that I insult you, when you read the full tale of my Felicity. . . . Call me Bombast. Call me what you please. Thus will I talk. No other style can give the most distant expression of the feelings of Boswell. If I appear ridiculous it is because our Language is deficient. I sent my letter on Tuesday by an Express. It was shewn to M. de Voltaire who with his own hand wrote this answer in the Character of Madam Denis. . . . Temple, I am your most Obedient. How do you find yourself? Have you got such a thing as an old friend in this world? Is he to be valued or is he not?"

After he had left Voltaire, Boswell spent more than nine months in Italy, where, incidentally, he renewed his friendship with Wilkes, then in exile, and, with that fine sense of incongruity which may sometimes be rather a fine unawareness of it, urged him to "let *Johnson* teach thee the road to rational virtue and noble felicity." Finally he sailed from Leghorn to Corsica and the last of the lions to be bagged on this expedition. In many respects this rather daring visit to a seldom-visited island and to the leader of its rebel forces was the most important event of the entire foreign residence. Boswell was to publish his *Tour to Corsica* in 1768, it was to sell ten thousand copies in England, to be translated into various European languages, to give him (he hoped) the right to be known as "Corsica Boswell," and to be indeed the only one of his published works to appear before Johnson's death which won any considerable public esteem. And yet his relations with General Paoli were not essentially different, in their beginnings, at least, from those with Rousseau and Voltaire.[17]

On his way to the first meeting with the general, he summoned appropriate reflections concerning the "brave rude men" who were his guides, and was an appreciative spectator of himself when confronted with the sight of Boswell drinking from a brook or making a primitive meal of chestnuts knocked down from a tree overhead. He had a letter of recommendation from Rousseau, who had paid a tribute to Corsica in *The Social Contract,* and once he had reached the general's remote headquarters he was soon exhibiting the melancholy features of his own interesting soul, exchanging with Paoli the inevitable reflections concerning "the being and attributes of God"; repeating to him certain of Johnson's sayings, and, in general, finding that all his usual poses took on a new interest when he was surrounded by the rude champions of liberty. Yet there is the best of evidence that Paoli, like so many others, ended by taking a genuine liking to the odd creature, of whom (according to Fanny Burney's doubtless somewhat burlesqued account) he was later to say: "I was of the belief he might be an impostor, and I supposed . . . he was an espy; for I look away from him, and in a moment I look to him again, and I behold his tablets. Oh! he was to the work of writing down all I say! Indeed I was angry. But soon I discover he was no impostor and no espy; and I only find I was myself the monster he had come to discern. Oh, is a very good man; I love him indeed; so cheerful! so gay! so pleasant!" When Boswell finally took his departure they were on the best of terms, and after Paoli's flight to England they resumed their friendship.

Boswell returned to London in February, 1766, after an absence of about two and a half years, and immediately busied himself with his new-found importance. He hunted up Jean Jacques Rousseau, who was now in his English exile. He sent to the London *Chronicle* various mystifying paragraphs about himself, including one in which it is reported of Mr. Boswell that "he had a good many papers about which he seemed very anxious, and he avoided talking freely of what he had seen in his singular tours." And of course he resumed his acquaintance with Johnson, with whom he had exchanged letters while abroad.

Johnson called, they had another supper at the Mitre, and supper again at the same place a few nights later. Johnson, apparently scenting "enthusiasm," had already written Boswell advising him to "mind your own affairs, and leave the Corsicans to theirs," and he was later, to Boswell's indignation, again to urge him to empty his head of Corsica. But despite this fact Johnson appears to have begun talking where he had left off and Boswell to have resumed his notemaking. Johnson growled a bit over Boswell's taste in friends—"It seems, Sir, you have kept very good company abroad, Rousseau and Wilkes!"—and when Boswell asked him if he thought Rousseau as bad a man as Voltaire he got for reply: "Why, Sir, it is difficult to settle the proportion of iniquity between them."

But Boswell was making only a pause in London. Soon he was back in Scotland, where he was duly admitted to the bar and before the end of the year had begun to practice. He did not see Johnson again until after the publication of his *Account of Corsica;* in the spring of 1768 he was on his way to London to enjoy his glory, and met the Rambler in Oxford.[18]

Boswell's own idea of what the European jaunt had done for him is expressed in the long letter to Temple from which quotations have already been made:

"Before I left Britain, I was idle, dissipated, ridiculous and regardless of Reputation. Often was I unworthy to be the friend of Mr. Temple. [Boswell was perpetually reminding himself that something was or was not worthy of the friend of somebody or other, usually Johnson or Paoli, and the fact indicates how much of his own claim to importance seemed to him to rest in the people who would consent to accept him.] Now I am a very different Man. I have got a character which I am proud of. Speak thou who hast known me from my earliest years, coulds't thou have imagined eight years ago that thy Companion in the Studies of Antiquity, who was debased by an unhappy education in the smoak of Edinburgh, coulds't thou have imagined him to turn out the Man that he now is? We are now, my friend, united in the strictest manner. Let us do nothing of any consequence without the consent of each other."

Actually, Temple was pretty soon to be receiving letters which make it plain that the new man was a good deal worse, or at least a good deal weaker, than the former one. But Boswell's bottles, mistresses and casual whores need concern us little. Johnson knew enough of his friend's drinking, and there is evidence that he knew something of the rest. Indeed, Boswell's failure to give even in his private papers the occasion of a deep offense which he gave Johnson in April, 1776, during a period when, by his own confession, his "moral principle as to chastity was absolutely eclipsed" may mean, it has been suggested, that he had been led into the experiment of confessing more than usual to Johnson. But one may safely assume that Boswell did not usually treat him to such choice bits as that which he communicated to the Rev. Mr. Temple, when he wrote to tell how he had got outrageously drunk at a dinner to some Scotch friends and spent the night with a prostitute—the said dinner having been in payment of a lost bet that "he would not catch the venereal disorder for three years." [19]

During Boswell's absence on the Continent, certain developments had occurred in Johnson's own life, and most of them contributed something to bring about the emergence of his figure in the form most vividly present to our imagination. For one thing, he was granted the degree of Doctor of Laws by Trinity College, Dublin, in 1765 (Oxford did not follow suit until 1775), and thus for the first time actually became the *Dr.* Johnson we so inevitably imagine him always to have been. For another, he moved (at least as early as September, 1765) from his chambers in the Temple to Johnson's Court, Fleet Street, where he was to remain until 1776 and where Boswell, on his return from the Continent, found him established once more in a house, and once more with his household gathered about him—Miss Williams in an apartment on the ground floor, Mr. Levett in the garret, and the faithful Negro, Francis Barber, in attendance.

Boswell gives us no detailed account of Johnson's Court, but Sir John Hawkins speaks of an "upper room, which had the advantages of a good light, and free air," fitted up as a study; also of "some furniture which would not have disgraced a better dwelling" and which "banished those appearances of squalid indigence, which, in his less happy days, disgusted those who came to see him." Arthur Murphy describes how Johnson lived in this same house. "His friend Levett, his physician in ordinary, paid his daily visits with assiduity; attended at all hours, made tea all the morning, talked what he had to say, and did not expect an answer; or if occasion required it, was mute, officious, and ever complying . . . There Johnson sat every morning, receiving visits, hearing the topics of the day, and indolently trifling away the time. Chemistry afforded some amusement." But none of these things makes quite so clear the important fact that Johnson was once again in possession of a home and of a domestic circle, both of which meant so much to him, as does Boswell's surprise, when dining there some years later, to find a decent dinner decently served. Johnson's ultimate aspiration toward domesticity—his dream that he might have a jack in the chimney, and his solemn rejection of the suggestion that in that case he should have a spit also—did not, however, occur until the house in Johnson's Court had been left in 1776 for another.

More important to the new Johnson than even these domestic arrangements was the fact that he was now both adding still more new friends to his circle and cultivating still more assiduously those he already had. Early in 1765, he made the acquaintance of the eminent and haughty brewer Henry Thrale as well as of his sprightly wife, Hester, and the acquaintance ripened so rapidly that as early as 1766 Johnson was to spend more than three months as their guest at their country home at Streatham. Early in 1764, THE CLUB, first proposed by Reynolds and then agreed to by Johnson, came into existence, and for some years thereafter Johnson was assured the opportunity for at least one evening of talk a week in the best imaginable company. The founders included, besides Reynolds and Johnson, Edmund Burke (who was not to make his first speech in Commons until 1766), Oliver Goldsmith, Topham Beauclerk, Bennet Langton, Sir John Hawkins, and two others of less note—the physician, Dr. Nugent, and Anthony Chamier, whom Hawkins described as a retired stockbroker turned gentleman. They met at the Turk's Head Tavern, Gerrard Street, Soho, at seven, dined or supped, and generally remained talking until a late hour. Dozens of such informal groups existed in London and this one was remarkable only because of the character of its members. As time passed some dropped out and a larger number of newcomers was admitted, but it was during the first years that it meant most to Johnson and he to it. Boswell was not elected until 1773, when the insistence of Johnson seems to have brought him in despite the doubts of some of the other members. And to the fact that he *was* admitted is no doubt due in part the further fact that when we think of Johnson we are very likely to think also of THE CLUB—which, by the way, did not become THE LITERARY CLUB until after Garrick's death in 1779.

But perhaps none of the events so far mentioned is more important for what it contributed to the process by which the relatively dim figure of Dictionary Johnson, the scholarly but impoverished hack, is transformed into that of the imposing Dr. Johnson, who would fold his legs and have his talk out, than another which also occurred while Boswell was abroad. It was during that period that Johnson definitely abandoned the use of alcohol (though he had had a previous period of abstinence and though he never became an invariable teetotaler) and became the outstanding exponent in theory and practice of the art of consuming tea on a grand scale and in the grand manner.

Lemonade he also drank gladly as well as freely. Perhaps that beverage ought to figure as prominently in his legend as tea itself. Certainly it ought to be noted that he included it with strict impartiality when he explained to Boswell how impossible it was to consider a certain house in town to which several of his friends had access as the scene of a proposed series of evening conversations. "It will never do, Sir. There is nothing served about there, neither tea, nor coffee, nor lemonade, nor anything whatever, and depend upon it, Sir, a man does not love to go to a place from whence he comes out exactly as he went in." But it would be a hardy biographer who would so disregard established convention as to present Dr. Johnson as pre-eminently a drinker of anything except tea.

It is true that Johnson does not appear ever to have been a real devotee of Bacchus or, except on rare occasion, to have drunk even wine in anything but what was moderation by the standard of his century. It is also true that he had always drunk tea frequently, as indeed had most of his contemporaries, except those who either could not afford it or drank stronger liquids too continuously to find time or room for milder beverages. As early as 1756 he had, in *The Literary Magazine,* reviewed with some indignation the work of an author who attributed to tea drinking a formidable list of evils, ranging from bad digestion and bad teeth to a loss of comeliness among chambermaids, and in response to the author's furious reply he had further inquired and affirmed: "Of tea, what have I said? That I have drank it twenty years without hurt, and, therefore, believe it not to be poison; that, if it dries the fibres, it cannot soften them; that, if it constringes, it cannot relax. I have modestly doubted, whether it has diminished the strength of our men, or the beauty of our women; and whether it much hinders the progress of our woolen or iron manufactures; but I allowed it to be a barren superfluity, neither medicinal nor nutritious, that neither supplied strength nor cheerfulness, neither relieved weariness, nor exhilarated sorrow." This halfhearted championship was, however, undertaken at a time when port was still possible for Johnson and when he might even occasionally have been thinking of himself when he exclaimed with his Lichfield accent: "Who's for *poonsh?*" [20]

He had never made total abstinence a moral principle even for himself. As late as 1781 he had apparently returned to some use of at least fermented liquors, for he told Boswell: "I drink it now sometimes, but not socially." Yet nothing of this need change the general picture of Johnson as a man who, from about 1765 on, sustained his inveterate sociability on tea and lemonade, and who found them sufficient to keep him up as late as any port or punch drinkers cared to stay. About this time he suffered from an illness including an attack of melancholy so severe that he avoided all society and was found by his friend, Dr. Adams, "in a deplorable state, sighing, groaning, talking to himself, and restlessly walking from room to room" in such desperation indeed that he exclaimed: "I would consent to have a limb amputated to recover my spirits." It was apparently as a result of this attack that Boswell found him a water drinker and that, for all practical social purposes, a water-lemonade-tea drinker he remained.

Johnson never smoked, though he did not wholly disapprove of the habit, which he thought had "gone out." Obviously, then, a man who did not like to come out of a house in the same state in which he had gone into it was driven to the consumption of something ante- or postprandial which was not alcoholic, and it appears that legend has been unable to improve much upon fact in describing his addiction to what he left a younger contemporary to call "the cups that cheer but not inebriate." Says

Boswell: "I suppose no person ever enjoyed with more relish the infusion of that fragrant leaf than Johnson," and there is plenty of other evidence to corroborate him, including that of Johnson himself, who wrote that he was one "whose kettle has scarcely time to cool; who with tea amuses the evening, with tea solaces the midnight, and with tea, welcomes the morning." When he was visiting, the kettles of his hosts were allowed no more time for cooling than he was accustomed to grant his own —as Mrs. Boswell was later to discover to her sorrow. It was definitely recorded of him that on one occasion he drank fifteen cups; on another, sixteen. But the best account (which may just possibly mean the most exaggerated) is given by Richard Cumberland, the dramatist, in the course of his memoirs: "At the tea table he had considerable demands upon his favourite beverage, and I remember when Sir Joshua Reynolds at my house reminded him that he had drank eleven cups, he replied—'Sir, I did not count your glasses of wine, why should you number my cups of tea?' And then laughing in perfect good humour he added—'Sir, I should have released the lady from any further trouble, if it had not been for your remark; but you have reminded me that I want one of the dozen, and I must request Mrs. Cumberland to round up my number.' When he saw the readiness and complacency with which my wife obeyed his call, he turned a kind and cheerful look upon her and said—'Madam, I must tell you for your comfort you have escaped much better than a certain lady did awhile ago, upon whose patience I intruded greatly more than I have done on yours; but the lady asked me for no other purpose but to make a Zany of me, and set me gabbling to a parcel of people I knew nothing of; so, Madam, I had my revenge of her; for I swallowed five and twenty cups of her tea, and did not treat her with as many words.' I can only say my wife would have made tea for him as long as New River could have supplied her with water."

Few sayings of Johnson's have been more quoted than one he made late in life when he was persuaded to refresh his memory of the taste of claret and thereupon gave his opinion: "Poor stuff! No, Sir, claret is the liquor for boys; port, for men; but he who aspires to be a hero (smiling) must drink brandy." Perhaps the implied supplement is that tea is the drink of philosophers and wise cowards. In any event, those who are surprised that Johnson, who seldom had anything good to say of intoxication, said what is recorded above, should remember that he added: "Brandy will do soonest for a man what drinking *can* do for him." And when Boswell, always anxious to set one of his own besetting sins in a favorable light, began to tell how, in the days of his first acquaintance with Johnson, he used to suffer a headache from the port drunk while sitting up with him, Johnson cut his friend short with: "Nay, Sir, it was not the *wine* that made your head ache, but the *sense* that I put into it." "What, Sir!" exclaimed Boswell, "will sense make the head ache?" and Johnson promptly laid him flat: "Yes, Sir, when it is not used to it." Johnson assured Boswell that from all his tea drinking "he never felt the least inconvenience" and this, Boswell gravely adds, is "a proof that the fault of his constitution was rather too great tension of fibres, than the contrary." But whatever the state of his fibers, there is nothing to prevent present-day enemies of tea from assuming that there may have been some connection between a dozen or so cups of it and Johnson's difficulty in getting to sleep at night.[21]

From all that has been said above, it must not be assumed that Johnson so far took advantage of his sure three hundred a year to abandon literary work or that, during Boswell's absence, he had devoted himself exclusively to tea, talk and lemonade. In fact, the case was far otherwise. He had written a few dedications, reviews, etc., of comparatively little significance but he had also published one of his most important works. A few months before Boswell's return to England, the long-promised, long-awaited and all but despaired-of edition of the plays of William Shakespeare at last reached his subscribers.

"DR. JOHNSON IN HIS TRAVELLING DRESS
as Described in Boswell's Tour"

From an engraving titled as above, dated 1786, and further described as "Drawn from the Life and Engraved by T. Trotter"

CHAPTER IX

Shakespeare

During Johnson's own lifetime, the reputation of Shakespeare passed through a definite stage in its evolution. Johnson was never to see it reach the point to which romantic critics were to carry it, for his contemporaries still regarded Shakespeare as a human being—even, indeed, as a fallible human being. Shakespeare was, accordingly, treated as a writer and therefore not exempt from criticism; he had not yet become a "force of nature" which must be assumed to be exemplifying some ineffable excellence even when he seemed least worthy of himself. Yet Shakespeare was, nevertheless, already being recognized as the greatest of English writers and hence properly the subject of critical and scholarly attention of a sort hitherto reserved exclusively for the classics of Greece and Rome.

Moreover, and though those concerned were perhaps only partially aware of the fact, he was being contended for by two parties—the representatives of scholarship and criticism, on the one hand, and the representatives of the great public, on the other. Since the beginning of the century, scholars had provided several "editions," that is to say, reprints of his work in which more or less serious attempts had been made to establish an authoritative text and more or less elaborate notes were supplied. But at the same time, the popular theater had not merely maintained him as a living dramatist; it had actually increased his relative popularity until he had outdistanced all the other contributors to the standard repertory and was more firmly established than he had ever been before as a playwright without rival in the estimation of the playgoer.

This did not mean that scholars and theatrical managers were co-operating. Their attitudes were, as a matter of fact, almost diametrically opposed. While the one group was making Shakespeare a sacred classic, the other was treating him with the utmost casualness as a useful theatrical property to be cut, adapted and mangled as freely as though his works had been produced by some anonymous hack. Certain profanations committed by Restoration and early eighteenth-century adapters had, indeed, become standard. Nahum Tate's happy ending for *King Lear* and certain hardly less bold "improvements" invented by Thomas Otway when he rewrote *Romeo and Juliet* as *Caius Marius* were assumed by the average playgoer to be authentic Shakespeare, while one of Colley Cibber's contributions to *Richard III* ("Off with his head. So much for Buckingham") became one of the best-known "Shakespearian" quotations. So far was the actor from concerning himself with nice questions relating to the purity of the text that Mrs. Prichard, most famous Lady Macbeth of the Garrick era, is said never to have read the complete play in any text. Nor was Garrick, for all his love of posing as "the restorer of Shakespeare," by any means guiltless, for at the same time that he expressed reverence for "the bard" he on occasion mangled him recklessly. He used operatic versions of *A Midsummer Night's Dream* and *The Tempest;* in 1756 he reduced *The Winter's Tale* to the length of an afterpiece while retaining a sufficient quantity of cheek after he had finished the job to provide the mangled work with a prologue in which he proclaimed:

> T'is my chief wish, my joy, my only plan,
> To lose no drop of that immortal man.

Worst of all, and late in his career, he modernized *Hamlet* by omitting Osric and the gravediggers entirely, giving Laertes moralizing speeches, managing to drive Gertrude mad with remorse, and setting Hamlet to dueling with the king after Laertes had been killed.[1]

It is hardly necessary to repeat that Johnson was not "a literary dictator." England has never known a man to whom that title could justly be applied, for not even Dryden, whose authority was probably more widely respected in the literary world than Johnson's ever was, never exercised anything like undisputed sway. But Johnson did take all literature for his province, and did, before he had finished his career, manage to have his say concerning most of the English writers whom he thought of as first-rate. It was, therefore, almost inevitable that he should sometime have his say about Shakespeare. It was also almost equally inevitable that it should be not the tradition of the playhouse, but the relatively rather new tradition of scholarship and sober criticism, which he would find congenial. Johnson had the instincts of the scholar as well as the gifts of the critic. He was not an enthusiastic playgoer.

It is true that, more or less in spite of himself, he had had various contacts with the theater. He had once been the teacher and he remained the lifelong acquaintance of the greatest actor of his day. He had come up to London with the manuscript of a tragedy in his pocket, and the actor, out of friendship, had brought the piece to the stage in 1749 when it ran for nine nights before disappearing forever from the boards. Two years before that, he had obliged Garrick with the famous prologue to the opening of Drury Lane under Garrick's management—the prologue which contains two of the far from numerous verses of Johnson still often quoted:

> The drama's laws the drama's patrons give,
> For we that live to please, must please to live.

He wrote three other prologues and, much later in life, again purely for reasons of friendship, concerned himself in Goldsmith's negotiations with the theatrical managers. We know, too, that at one period he even consented to visit Garrick's greenroom.

None of these facts, however, is to be taken as indicating any real interest in the theater. *Irene* was written merely because a tragedy was the first thing likely to occur to an ambitious writer with little knowledge of the world, and Johnson never professed any high regard for its merits. It is true that when Garrick proposed certain alterations, he bridled because he resented any sort of interference, but when asked how he felt about the play's actual failure (which all Garrick's efforts could not hide), "Like the Monument," he replied. Once when someone insisted on reading passages from *Irene* to a social group, Johnson left the room; when asked the reason for this behavior, he replied: "Sir, I thought it had been better." Once when told that a certain gentleman named Pot, to whom he had just been introduced, professed to regard the play as the finest tragedy of modern times, Johnson is said to have retorted merely: "If Pot says so, Pot lies." [2]

Despite, or because of, his connection with Garrick, Johnson's prejudice against actors was one of the strongest and most notorious of the three or four irrational dislikes which have become so large a part of his legend and which were the occasion of those relatively few outbursts of blind unreason and sheer rudeness which are, to a considerable degree, responsible for the opinion held by many of his contemporaries as well as by many people today that he was a surly brute. There is no doubt that he did have a set of apparently unrelated prejudices, that he nursed them to keep them warm, and that the prejudice against actors was one of the most conspicuous. After the manner of men who grow more violent as they become aware of their own unreason, he could become really savage when he realized that what he had said was going to be correctly set down by his hearers as the result of mere prejudice.

After an outbreak of rudeness Johnson sometimes—but unfortunately not always—apologized in manly fashion, from which it is permissible to guess that one who habitually appealed to reason was ashamed of his own lapses into blind dogmatism and that his rage was often really against himself.

Not every harsh judgment which he passed upon individual actors or upon the profession as a whole was either wholly contrary to much respectable opinion of his time or unreasonable in itself. If he never missed an opportunity to sneer at the laureate-player, Colley Cibber, most people sneered at Cibber and had good excuses for doing so. When he complained that the actors of his day had adopted a singsong delivery without regard to the emphasis that would illuminate meaning, he was probably stating a simple fact, since the astonishment caused by Garrick was no doubt due in part at least to the monotonous method of the ruling favorites; for Johnson himself could say of Garrick, toward whom his attitude was notoriously variable: "A true conception of character, and natural expression of it, were his distinguishing excellences."

But Johnson went far beyond reasoned criticism. He seemed to delight in seizing an occasion either to vent what looks like mere vulgar social prejudice or to imagine ingeniously degrading analogies to minimize the whole art of acting. The actor, he declared, was less than a ballad singer; "a fellow who exhibits himself for a shilling"; "a poor player, who frets and struts his hour upon the stage"; "a fellow who claps a hump on his back, and a lump on his leg, and cries *'I am Richard the Third'*"; "no better than creatures set upon tables and joint-stools to make faces and produce laughter, like dancing dogs"; one actor is superior to another only "as some dogs dance better than others." The poet Whitehead "is but a little man to inscribe verses to players"; Lord Camden *"was a little lawyer* to be associating so familiarly with a player"—namely Garrick, who, to be sure, had just been rather too complacently letting the company know that he was just come from a long walk with Camden.

Sometimes, of course, when Johnson made these or similar statements in the happy warmth of exuberant conversation, he was merely arguing for effect or for victory, as he was frank to confess he often did; merely taking the good talker's delight in seeing how successful he could be in an effort to make the worse appear the better reason. Sometimes the context makes it clear enough that this was true, and one passage is worth citing both to make the point and to illustrate the kind of vigorous playfulness to which an incomparable group could abandon itself:

"SIR JOSHUA REYNOLDS. 'I do not perceive why the profession of a player should be despised; for the great and ultimate end of all the employments of mankind is to produce amusement. Garrick produces more amusement than any body.' BOSWELL. 'You say, Dr. Johnson, that Garrick exhibits himself for a shilling. In this respect he is only on a footing with a lawyer who exhibits himself for his fee, and even will maintain any nonsense or absurdity, if the case require it. Garrick refuses a play or a part which he does not like: a lawyer never refuses.' JOHNSON. 'Why, Sir, what does this prove? only that a lawyer is worse. Boswell is now like Jack in "The Tale of a Tub," who, when he is puzzled by an argument, hangs himself. He thinks I shall cut him down, but I'll let him hang,' (laughing vociferously.)" [3]

But despite such fooling, hardly half serious at best, Johnson's prejudice against actors was solidly founded in something and could on occasion express itself with genuine brutality. Mrs. Thrale declared that in a burst of irritation at Garrick's alleged assumption that he could be admitted to The Club merely by expressing his desire to join it, Johnson exclaimed: "I'll black-ball him.—I love my little David dearly, better than all or any of his flatterers do, but surely one ought to sit in a society like ours,

> Unelbow'd by gamester, pimp, or player."

On the authority of Reynolds, Boswell denied that Johnson had said any such thing, but Mrs. Thrale came back in a marginal note to insist "He did say so, and Mr. Thrale stood astonished. They were his very words." There the matter must rest with nothing further except the observation that, at least unless Johnson smiled when he quoted Pope, he was choosing a very odd way of demonstrating his affection for "little David." [4]

It was notorious among members of The Club that Johnson permitted no one except himself to depreciate Garrick—so notorious that Sir Joshua Reynolds made the actor the subject of two imaginary conversations which, though brief, are much the best of all the imitations, pastiches and parodies of Johnson. As Reynolds remarked, Johnson seemed to consider Garrick his property, something which no one could either praise or blame in his presence without being contradicted. While Garrick was still alive, he could say of him on one occasion: "Here is a man who has advanced the dignity of his profession" and, of his undeserved reputation for stinginess, "He has given away more money than any man in England." After Garrick's death, he could write of Garrick's passing that it had "eclipsed the gaiety of nations," and to Mrs. Siddons he could say in tribute to the social charm of this mere player: "After all, Madam, I thought him less to be envied on the stage than at the head of a table." Moreover, he would by no means permit others to criticize in Garrick that sense of his own achievement which Johnson himself was ready to rebuke even when he merely suspected its presence.

Once Boswell, who of course delighted as much in getting Johnson to show his worst side as he did in drawing out his best, "slily [*sic*] introduced Mr. Garrick's fame, and his assuming the airs of a great man." But Johnson replied: "Sir, it is wonderful how *little* Garrick assumes. . . . Consider, Sir: celebrated men, such as you have mentioned, have had their applause at a distance; but Garrick had it dashed in his face, sounded in his ears, and went home every night with the plaudits of a thousand in his *cranium*. Then, Sir, Garrick did not *find* but *made* his way to the tables, the levees, and almost the bed-chambers of the great." One of the company remarked that Garrick was a very sprightly writer too, and Johnson, having once started, was not prevented even by agreement from going on with increased enthusiasm: "Yes, Sir; and all this supported by great wealth of his own acquisition. If all this had happened to me, I should have had a couple of fellows with long poles walking before me, to knock down every body that stood in the way. Consider, if all this had happened to Cibber or Quin, they'd have jumped over the moon.—Yet Garrick speaks to *us*, (smiling)." [5]

Nevertheless, Johnson refused to admit that there was anything very exalted about the nature of an actor's art and scorned to believe that "a mere player" could be trusted to discover the meaning of the words he was declaiming. It is said that when Quin as Falstaff had to carry Garrick as the dead Hotspur off the stage, he used to whisper to the corpse: "Where shall we sup?" and it is evident that this, which illustrates the actor's usual and possibly correct frame of mind, evidently seemed to Johnson more befitting "a mere player" than any high talk about "living a part." "Are you, Sir," he asked Kemble, "one of those enthusiasts who believe yourself transformed into the very character you represent?" And when Kemble admitted that he was not, Johnson went on: "To be sure not, Sir . . . And if Garrick really believed himself to be that monster, Richard the Third, he deserved to be hanged every time he performed it."

One might suppose that if the actor preserved his emotional balance he might be expected at least to be intellectually aware of the meaning of what he was saying, but Johnson, with the not unusual writer's contempt for a man who does not write words of his own but is proud to speak the words of others, would not allow that he actually did speak them intelligently. Shortly after Garrick's first triumphs, Johnson insisted in his presence that "the players, Sir, have got a kind of rant, with which they run on, without any regard either to accent or emphasis," and when Garrick was offended, took great pleasure in challenging him to repeat the ninth commandment. According to Dr. Taylor, who told Boswell the anecdote, both Garrick and a companion tried it and both mistook the emphasis, which should be upon *not* and *false witness.* Boswell doubts that Taylor himself got the story right and believes that Johnson would have insisted upon putting the emphasis on *shalt not.* But it really doesn't matter. The important thing is that "Johnson put them right, and enjoyed his victory with great glee."

Late in his life Johnson was visited by Mrs. Siddons, who, as the reigning queen of Shakespearean tragedy, no doubt felt it her duty to call upon the great literary interpreter of "the bard." Johnson had been irritated by a proposed introduction but he received her politely, discussed Garrick and other actors, and wrote Mrs. Thrale afterwards: "Mrs. Siddons, in her visit to me, behaved with great modesty and propriety, and left nothing behind her to be censured or despised." Just what behavior he expected from this stuffily respectable great lady who, according to Sydney Smith, remained so constantly in buskins that she used, at dinner, to "stab the potatoes," is not explained; but Johnson sounds as though he had been prepared for some untoward incident. That his prejudice never left him is further indicated by the fact that contemptuous references to actors manage somehow to get even into Boswell's account of the tour of the Hebrides.[6]

It has already been suggested that some small part of Johnson's irritable contempt for the player was the contempt of the writer for the mere speaker. Another small part may have been due to the fact that he clung to old-fashioned ways of feeling even more than he did to old-fashioned ways of thinking, and therefore felt toward actors as everyone had felt a few generations back. The members of the players' profession had made their way upward slowly from the status of rogues and vagabonds. Garrick was certainly the first among them to be received by ladies and gentlemen on a footing of absolute equality, for Cibber, despite all the fine company he kept and despite the fact that he had been made poet laureate, was a licensed buffoon rather than an equal, and long after Garrick had supposedly made acting respectable, the prejudice was still so strong that Arthur Murphy was made to feel that, having once appeared briefly on the stage, he could not expect to be regarded as truly a gentleman. Moreover, Johnson, who certainly cannot be called a puritan except in a sense of the term so loose as to be almost meaningless, did come close to being what is popularly called "puritanical" in his attitude toward anything which suggested sexual looseness. The so-called reform of the drama had not signally reformed the lives of theatrical people. Johnson knew that many of them were notoriously loose livers, and being strongly sexed himself he actually feared their example. He also feared, for the same reason, that display of physical charms which members of the theatrical profession take for granted—as is clear enough from the oft-quoted remark which Boswell records as: "I'll come no more behind your scenes, David; for the silk stockings and white bosoms of your actresses excite my amorous propensities" but which he reported elsewhere in much plainer terms.[7]

Boswell assigns several reasons for the vehement unreasonableness of Johnson's attitude. He mentions "first, the imperfection of his organs, which were so defective that he was not susceptible of the fine impressions which theatrical excellence produces upon the generality of mankind," and Johnson certainly did not hear or see very well. Indeed, toward the end of his life he was so nearly blind and so nearly deaf that when he was urged to *see* Mrs. Siddons, he replied: "Well, madam, if you desire it, I will go. See her I shall not, nor hear her; but I'll go, and that will do." Boswell might have added that these same limitations, plus the not unusual tendency of the literary man to be insensitive to all arts but his own, were responsible for the fact that Johnson cared so little, in fact cared not at all, for either music or painting. Boswell does add "the cold rejection of his tragedy" as an additional reason, though it is hardly probable that this was a very powerful one.

"Lastly," he continues, "the brilliant success of Garrick, who had been his pupil, who had come to London at the same time with him, not in a much more prosperous state than himself, and whose talents he undoubtedly rated low, compared with his own." This, most subsequent commentators have agreed, is the factor which accounts for most of at least that part of Johnson's attitude which is sheer violent unreason. Boswell was born too soon to have to decide whether the jealousy was subconscious and therefore constituted a "complex" or whether it was conscious resentment, and it hardly matters much. Johnson was jealous and understandably so. Here was a case where, under peculiarly exasperating circumstances, "the last set out the soonest did arrive."

Few men have achieved fame more slowly, more laboriously or more painfully than Johnson. Few men, on the other hand, ever achieved it with, in appearance at least, such effortless ease as Garrick did. Johnson found writing so distasteful that he could hardly drive himself to the fulfillment of contracted obligations. Acting was, as Garrick wrote his family when he was announcing the dreadful news that he had entered upon a disgraceful profession, "what I dote upon." Moreover, he had prepared himself by no known course of study; luck seemed always to be with him; and he can hardly be said even to have served an apprenticeship. Not long after he arrived in the metropolis, a legacy of one thousand pounds removed all immediate financial difficulties. Only one short summer season in the provinces lay between the evening when he appeared as a substitute in a harlequinade and his triumphant appearance as Richard III in October, 1741. Within a few days, the streets about the unfashionable little theater in Goodman's Fields were clogged with the carriages of the beau monde come to see the new phenomenon. Almost instantaneously he was hailed as an actor who had probably never been equaled, and the rest of his long, brilliant career seemed to follow merely as inevitable step after inevitable step. He was gay, insouciant, instantaneously charming, immediately at home in any society.

No wonder if Johnson—sick, melancholy, clumsy—was envious. It is certainly not to his credit, but it is also certainly not surprising. If he can defend Garrick's self-satisfaction by asking how another would have behaved if similarly seduced, we may ask of Johnson what effect similar provocation would have had on most people. It is doubtless not easy to see a pupil, whom one knows to be in most respects very superficial, have all the luck and get all the attention. Within about a year after his first triumph, while Johnson was just keeping alive by composing parliamentary debates, Garrick was earning something like a thousand pounds a year, or more than three times what Johnson was to get as a pension twenty years later; while Johnson was living on that three hundred a year, Garrick was said to have "got a hundred thousand" by his acting. It is hardly to be wondered at that when Boswell advanced the latter fact as proof of "the merit of great acting, and the value which mankind set upon it" Johnson should have risen to the provocation, as Boswell doubtless hoped he would, and replied: "Is getting a hundred thousand pounds a proof of excellence? That has been done by a scoundrel commissary." Even if Garrick had never existed, Johnson would probably have had no great love for either the theater or theatrical people. But that his resentment against what seemed to him the absurdly resplendent success of his erstwhile pupil helped turn indifference into something like rancor is suggested by the fact that into the life of Savage, written in the early days of Garrick's greatness, he manages to bring contemptuous reference to players and by the fact that he began to bait Garrick in conversation at about the same time.

Number 200 of *The Rambler,* published in February, 1752, includes a portrait of one Prospero, a man raised to sudden wealth who ostentatiously calls attention to his new possessions when a friend of humbler days is calling upon him, and it was generally taken by members of Johnson's intimate circle as a satire on Garrick. Probably it was; for, though Garrick was remarkably free from arrogance, he was quite capable of a childish vanity. But one may certainly suspect the result of an expectation of affront in Johnson's description of his reception: "The best apartments were ostentatiously set open, that I might have a distant view of the magnificence which I was not permitted to approach; and my old friend receiving me with all the insolence of condescension at the top of the stairs, conducted me to a back room, where he told me he always breakfasted when he had no great company." It is, in other words, evident that Johnson accused Garrick of ostentation when he was given his best, of insolence when he was received in relatively humble surroundings; and one can only say that Johnson was fairer when he refused to permit others to accuse little David of faults he himself was all too ready to see. Nor is it particularly remarkable that Garrick, who in general bore all the provocations with long-suffering good humor, did nevertheless permit himself to make an imitation of Johnson's gallant behavior to Tetty one of his drawing-room stunts.

When Boswell, probing a sore spot, ventured to wish that Garrick had been mentioned in the *Preface* to Shakespeare, Johnson replied: "My dear Sir, had I mentioned him, I must have mentioned many more: Mrs. Prichard, Mrs. Cibber,—nay, and Mr. Cibber too; he too altered Shakespeare." But this is obviously an excuse rather than a reason. In the first place, Boswell was not suggesting that Garrick be mentioned as an alterer of Shakespeare. In the second place, Johnson knew as well as Boswell did that none of the other performers was popularly credited as Garrick was with having revealed in a new way the greatness of the dramatist. To be sure, there was no necessity for introducing Garrick's name. Johnson was discussing Shakespeare as a poet rather than as a writer for the stage. But there was, on the other hand, no reason why he might not, had he so desired, pay a graceful compliment to an old friend and introduce a reference which most of his contemporaries would certainly not have thought out of place, and the absence of which Garrick must have taken as a deliberate slight. Indeed, Johnson is said to have remarked: "Garrick, I hear, complains that I am the only popular author who has exhibited no praise of him in print." But Johnson had no desire to pay such a compliment. He maintained that "Many of Shakespeare's plays are the worse for being acted: Macbeth, for instance." And when Boswell insisted on asking if Garrick had not "brought Shakespeare into notice," Johnson replied: "Sir, to allow that, would be to lampoon the age." He was not, in other words, willing to grant that Shakespeare was incapable of attracting notice to himself. He was determined to uphold the dignity of literature by refusing to grant that "a mere player" could contribute a new luster to it.[8]

None of this is, of course, meant to suggest that Johnson undertook to edit Shakespeare in order to provide a counterblast to Garrick's fame and influence. But he did seize the occasion to administer a snub which Garrick's friends were not slow to notice. He was obviously offended by the air of proprietorship which Garrick was exhibiting: by his tendency to act as though he and Shakespeare were necessary complements to each other; by a certain chummy familiarity with "the bard" which finds its perfect expression in the full-length portrait of himself which Gainsborough painted and in which he is represented leaning casually against a bust of Shakespeare with his legs crossed and one arm thrown familiarly about the poet's shoulder. It is, by the way, obviously from this picture that Max Beerbohm got the hint for his sketch of Bernard Shaw in a similar attitude.

Johnson failed to attend the "Shakespeare Jubilee" which Garrick arranged at Stratford in 1769—much to the regret of Boswell, who was so conspicuous on that occasion and who felt that "Johnson's connection both with Shakespeare and Garrick founded a double claim to his presence." This, of course, was several years after the *Shakespeare* had been published, and it is true that a good many other eminent persons stayed away; but it does show that Johnson was still not unwilling pointedly to dissociate himself from the Garrick cult. Garrick might serve Shakespeare (or be served by him) in his way; Johnson would serve Shakespeare in his own. And he had no desire to conceal the fact that he saw little connection between the two ways. Indeed, when he came to prepare the notes to his edition he even seized the opportunity provided by Bottom the Weaver to make one more jibe at a despised profession. Apropos of Bottom's eager offer to undertake a part and to "discharge it in either your straw-colour'd beard, your orange-tawny beard, your purple-in-grain beard, or your French crown-colour'd beard; your perfect yellow," Johnson remarks: "Here *Bottom* again discovers a true genius for the Stage by his solicitude for propriety of dress, and his deliberation which beard to choose among many beards, all unnatural."

It ought, however, to be made clear that, whatever inconsistency may have been involved, Johnson was, despite his contempt for theatrical methods, distinctly on the side of popular judgment when it came to estimating both the kind and the degree of Shakespeare's greatness. He held consistently that enduring popularity was the final test of greatness, and that "the natural feelings of untaught hearers ought never to be slighted." "A man who writes a book," he said on another occasion, "thinks himself wiser or wittier than the rest of mankind; he supposes that he can instruct or amuse them, and the public to whom he appeals, must, after all, be the judges of his pretensions." He did not think Shakespeare above this rule and he was content to make the public the final arbiter. Indeed, in one single instance he went so far as to assume that the popular preference, exhibited over a long period, for the happy ending to *King Lear* established the superiority of that ending.[9]

None of Johnson's other literary projects was so long in maturing as this project to edit Shakespeare. It was the first of the large enterprises which he had definitely announced to the public, for he made the announcement early in 1745, and did not publish the prospectus for the *Dictionary* until 1747, though he had certainly been thinking of the latter for some time previously. Yet the Shakespeare did not actually appear until twenty years later.

Reference has already been made in an appropriate place to the *Miscellaneous Observations on* Macbeth which he published in 1745. Some surviving copies include a single folio leaf of *Proposals for a New Edition of Shakespeare* in the form of an advertisement with specimens of the type to be used. Apparently Boswell did not know why nothing came of the scheme at this time, for he speculates vaguely that "the little encouragement which was given by the public to his anonymous proposals for the execution of a task which Warburton was known to have undertaken, damped his ardour." But it is now known that the publisher, Jacob Tonson, wrote a letter to Edmund Cave in which he claimed to hold the copyright on Shakespeare's works, and it was doubtless this letter which put an effective end to Johnson's plan.

At least we hear no more of it until Johnson, by this time a famous man, not an unknown journalist, published in 1756 "Proposals for Printing by Subscription, the Dramatic Works of William Shakespeare, corrected and illustrated by Samuel Johnson. Subscriptions are taken by J. and R. Tonson, in the Strand; J. Knapton, in Ludgate Street; C. Hitch and L. Hawes, and M. and T. Longman, in Paternoster-Row." These proposals were formerly known only by reprints in the London *Chronicle* during the following year, but an original has now been reproduced in facsimile. Johnson's rights under the contract are also now known by an agreement dated June 2, 1756, in which it is stipulated that "in consideration of Mr. Johnson's care and trouble in preparing the said Work for the Press," he is to receive from Tonson two hundred and fifty sets free in sheets. These, of course, he was to use in supplying subscribers, and it was further agreed that if the number of such subscribers should exceed two hundred and fifty, he was to be supplied with additional sets at one guinea each.[10]

One may suppose that if Johnson ever wrote anything con amore it was the *Preface* of some seventeen thousand words which, despite the acuteness and good sense of some of his notes, is his chief contribution to the understanding and evaluation of Shakespeare. But it is not to be taken for granted that he ever overcame his disinclination to labor so completely as to enable him to write anything con amore. When he made the agreement he was still struggling against poverty; he spent the money received for subscriptions as he got it; and there is no reason for supposing that he was merely maintaining a consistent pose when, according to an anecdote recorded by Horace Walpole, Sir John Hawkins said to Johnson in reference to the Shakespeare: "Now you have finished your *Dictionary,* I suppose you will labour your present work *con amore,"* and Johnson replied: "No, Sir, nothing excites a man to write but necessity." In any event, Johnson appears to have been in no hurry to get along with the work.

The proposals announced that it would be published "On or before Christmas 1757," though it was not actually to appear until nearly eight years later. Letters dated 1757 and 1758 show him writing friends in connection with the effort to get subscriptions. But the receipt of money merely encouraged idleness, as it is evident Johnson's friends were well aware, since Dr. Percy, writing to Dr. Grainger, a poet acquaintance of Johnson's, in 1758 says: "I have several times called on Johnson to pay him part of your subscriptions: I say part, because he never thinks of working if he has a couple of guineas in his pocket," and writing again some weeks later: "As to his Shakespeare, movet sed non promovet. I shall feed him occasionally with guineas." Various other letters reveal the successive postponements which Johnson permitted himself. "I shall publish about March" (of 1758); "It will be published before summer" (of 1758); and "I intend that you shall soon receive Shakespeare" (July, 1762). In entry after entry Boswell expresses his willingness to assume that during this particular year or that Johnson was busy on Shakespeare, but since Johnson usually worked rapidly when he worked at all, the chances are that he was idle with Shakespeare rather than busy with him, or, as Sir Walter Raleigh has put it in interpreting the phrase, "busily engaged with the edition": "That is to say, he worked at it intermittently, and satisfied his conscience, after the manner of authors, by working at nothing else." [11]

A man who accepts subscriptions for a promised work is obviously in honor bound either to produce it or to refund the subscriptions. As the years rolled on, Johnson's delay was in danger of becoming a scandal and Churchill made it one. When the latter had published the first two books of *The Ghost* he had made no strong case against Johnson, whom he charged chiefly with superstitious credulity. When he came, six months later, in September, 1762, to publish Book Three he had two new charges: First, Johnson's acceptance of a pension, since the first books had been published, proved that he was venal as well as credulous. Probably few persons not already disposed to think ill of Johnson took that charge seriously either. But on the second charge he was obviously wide open to the attack embodied in a brief passage of six stinging lines:

> He for subscribers baits his hook
> And takes their cash—but where's the book?
> No matter where—wise fear we know,
> Forbids the robbing of a foe;
> But what, to serve our private ends,
> Forbids the cheating of our friends? [12]

Just what reply, if any, Johnson had to make to this particular passage is not recorded. Boswell says merely: "His throes in bringing [Shakespeare] forth had been severe and remittent; and at last we may almost conclude that the Caesarian operation was performed by the knife of Churchill, whose upbraiding satire, I dare say, made Johnson's friends urge him to dispatch." Hawkins has a vague story that Reynolds and some of Johnson's other friends, "who were more concerned for his reputation than himself seemed to be, contrived to entangle him by a wager, or some other pecuniary engagement, to perform his task by a certain time." But even these methods, if ever actually practiced, cannot have worked rapidly, since slightly more than three years were to elapse between the appearance of Churchill's lines and the only reply which could be effective—namely, the work itself. On October 2, 1765, Johnson wrote his friend, the Rev. Dr. Taylor: "My Shakespeare is now out of my hands." It was entitled *The Plays of William Shakespeare, in Eight Volumes, with the Corrections and Illustrations of Various Commentators; To which are added Notes by Sam. Johnson.* In this title no special mention is made of the *Preface* which was, to Johnson's contemporaries as well as to us, the most interesting feature.

Inevitably the edition was praised and blamed. Boswell tells us that it was virulently attacked by one William Kendrick, an industrious hack who had been honored with an LL.D. from St. Andrew's and whom Johnson was to describe as "One of the many who have made themselves public, without making themselves known." A young student of Oxford wrote an answer to this attack without especially pleasing Johnson who, in the first place, pretty consistently took the position that attacks did an author more good than harm if he refused to dignify them by making an answer, and, in the second place, did not like the assumption that he needed the defense of an unknown youth. But despite the inevitable unfavorable notices, there seems never to have been any real question that the *Shakespeare* was a success. It went through several printings and then, in 1773, was reissued by George Steevens with the latter's revisions and additional notes. Johnson had included selected notes from previous editors; it now became a matter of course to include certain of his observations in popular editions of the plays. What is even more important, the *Preface* came to be pretty generally accepted as the best statement yet made concerning the nature and the extent of Shakespeare's achievement. Nothing since the *Dictionary* had done so much to strengthen with the general literary public Johnson's position as the most imposing man of letters produced by his age.

Just what that reputation finally came to be can perhaps best be illustrated by a paragraph from an account in *The Monthly Review* of a second edition of the Johnson-Steevens *Shakespeare. The Monthly* was one of the two leading critical organs, and the fact that it was Whiggish in politics as well as latitudinarian in religion makes all the more impressive this tribute to an arch-Tory and arch-churchman. Says the reviewer, writing in the number for January, 1780:

"Among the names that have rescued the editorial office from contempt, we may, with strict impartiality, place Dr. Johnson's in the first rank. In spite of the envy of some malignant critics, and their ignorant abettors, who were content to echo their detractions—in spite even of all that a Churchill himself could write to depreciate Dr. Johnson's claim to fame, yet he still commands the admiration of his country, and 'bears his blushing honors thick about him,' even in the very winter of his days.

Nor will posterity censure the present age for having been too prodigal in its applause of this great man. His moral and critical writings will remain a perpetual monument of genius, industry, and learning." [13]

It was, of course, the eighteenth century which saw the birth of Shakespearean criticism, of—one may almost say—the whole art of dealing scientifically with the history of modern literature. Development was so rapid that Johnson's scholarship, strictly so called, was soon outdated, but something must be said of the place of his edition in the series which his century produced before turning to the more interesting question of his attitude toward Shakespeare and the qualities of mind which he exhibited in his approach to that poet who has come to be accepted as a test of any man's intelligence and imagination.

The first "edition" of Shakespeare's works had appeared in 1709, the year of Johnson's birth. Up to that time readers had been compelled to be content with the four successive folios which differed from one another only through the efforts of the printing house to correct printers' errors; and so far was the age from any conception of the problems involved in getting or keeping an accurate text that when the Bodleian Library acquired a clean copy of the third folio, it casually disposed of its copy of the first. The last of the folios had been issued in 1685 and was becoming quite scarce when Nicholas Rowe, later poet laureate and the leading tragic dramatist of his time, issued in 1709 the six octavo volumes in his "edition."

In this edition Rowe did many things which had never been done before. He supplied notes and comments. He also listed the dramatis personae, and saw to it that the plays were divided into acts and scenes—which last two things had not been done for all the plays in any of the folios. Rowe also made some effort to correct obviously corrupt passages and he wrote a preface in which, for the first time, the known facts and current traditions about Shakespeare's career were briefly set forth. For all these reasons, it has been said that no subsequent editor left so deep a mark on the external appearance of the plays.

But Rowe was not a scholar and his principal purpose was

not scholarly. His chief aim was to present his author in conveniently readable form. He boasted that he had endeavored to get a true reading of the text "by comparing the several editions," and he was, indeed, the first person to make any serious pretense of doing this obvious thing. He did not do it very thoroughly, however, and it can easily be demonstrated that sometimes when a word in the text he had at hand was clearly wrong, he made a conjectural substitution when the right word could have been found in an earlier printing of the folio. Nevertheless, Rowe made the first start, and the rapidity with which, once that start had been made, edition followed edition shows how rapidly the eighteenth century caught and developed the conception of the necessity for establishing an authoritative text.

His immediate successor was Alexander Pope, whose six-volume edition appeared in 1725. Pope also made some study of earlier editions but, being a man of letters rather than a scholar, he went much further than Rowe had gone in the direction of frequently printing what he thought Shakespeare ought to have written rather than what there is any sound reason for believing he did write. He provoked Lewis Theobald's *Shakespeare restored: or, a Specimine of the Many Errors, as well Committed, as Unamended, by Mr. Pope,* and this led in turn to Theobald's own edition in 1734. "Piddling Theobald," Pope called him in revenge, and might, with perhaps greater justice, have accused him of following Pope himself more frequently than he should have done.

Like most of his predecessors, Theobald was better in his theory than in his practice, but he was the first clearly to state the new attitude toward Shakespeare's text by calling him "a classic," declaring that the text is "corrupt enough to pass for one of the oldest stamp," and setting forth the general principle that the textual critic who wishes to emend such a text must know the language of the time and support corrections or conjectures by parallel passages. He was the first editor to find all of the forty-one quartos and he has been called the first of our real Shakespearean scholars, though he did not by any means do all his work as carefully as he did some of it. His edition was followed in 1744 by that of Sir Thomas Hanmer, which marks no advance so far as the scientific treatment of the text is concerned.

Such then were the available editions when Johnson issued in 1745 his first *Proposals*. Shortly thereafter, in 1747, appeared an edition by the truculent William Warburton which is also of little importance so far as scholarship is concerned, and there were no more until the long-delayed publication of Johnson's own effort. It was both his good and his bad fortune to come in the middle of the period during which Shakespearean scholarship was evolved. Those who had gone before had not only laid foundations but also clarified, by their mistakes as well as by their achievements, both the nature of the problem and some of the various attitudes which might be assumed in approaching it. On the other hand, it was nearly inevitable that both his own indolence and the rapid advance in scientific method should result in the quick obsolescence of his edition so far as the text is concerned. Speaking only of that text and not at all of aesthetic as opposed to textual criticism, it would perhaps be fair to say two things: First, that no one had ever shown a clearer understanding of what an editor ought to do. Second, that up to date no one, combining his own original work with that of his predecessors, had done a better job. But it must also be added that a better job was soon to be done.

"Sir," Johnson once said to Reynolds, "there are two things which I am confident I can do very well: one is an introduction to any literary work, stating what it is to contain, and how it should be executed in the most perfect manner; the other is a conclusion, shewing from various causes why the execution has not been equal to what the author promised to himself and to the public." Humor aside—and there may have been some in this apparent boast that no one knew better than he did what ought to be done and what excuses to make for not having done it—Johnson was right. Moreover, he never demonstrated better just how right he was in the first part of the boast than in the *Proposals* for his Shakespeare. Here, obviously, was a man who had carefully considered the duties of the editor of a text. He knew very well indeed what ought to be done.[14]

To begin with, and unlike any of the previous editors except

Theobald, Johnson clearly stated the position that the duty of an editor was to establish as far as possible what an author had written rather than what, in the opinion of the editor or his contemporaries, he ought to have written. "The business of him that republishes an ancient book is, to correct what is corrupt, and to explain what is obscure." But it is emphatically not to correct or to explain by conjecture except where all other methods fail, and even then only if the guess is plainly marked for what it is. Neither is it to modernize, or improve, or make more regular. All the modern editions which he consulted printed as "In private to inter him" the line from *Hamlet* which read "In hugger mugger to interr him." Johnson restored what the previous editors had evidently regarded as archaic and inelegant with the remark: "That the words now replaced are better, I do not undertake to prove; it is sufficient that they are *Shakespeare's:* If phraseology is to be changed as words grow uncouth by disuse, or gross by vulgarity, the history of every language will be lost; we shall no longer have the words of any author; and, as these alterations will be often unskillfully made, we shall in time have very little of his meaning."

Before an editor can correct or explain intelligently he must know how corruptions or difficulties arise, and Johnson lists quite exhaustively the sources of such corruptions and difficulties as are met with in Shakespeare's text. That text is corrupt because it was carelessly printed; but difficulties which may appear to be corruptions, though actually they are not, abound for three reasons. First, Shakespeare has so outlived his contemporaries that many references and allusions self-explanatory in his own time are obscure to later readers. Second, he wrote at a time when the language was unfixed and hence made use of words and phrases which are now obsolete. Third—and Johnson seems to have been the first adequately to realize the importance of this fact—because of a characteristic of Shakespeare himself, namely, "the fulness of idea, which might sometimes load his words with more sentiment than they could conveniently convey, and that rapidity of imagination which might hurry him to a second thought before he had fully explained the first."

The good editor, Johnson goes on, will not assume that all

difficulties are the result of corruption, and he will not depend upon "critical sagacity" until all other methods have failed. He will collate all the texts available and he will bring to bear his knowledge of Elizabethan language, customs and beliefs to illuminate any passage which is obscure in all the texts to which he has access. Only when all these methods prove fruitless will conjectures be indulged in. "It has been long found, that very specious emendations do not equally strike all minds with conviction, nor even the same mind, at different times; and, therefore, though, perhaps, many alterations may be proposed as eligible, very few will be obtruded as certain. . . . There is danger lest peculiarities should be mistaken for corruptions, and passages rejected as unintelligible, which a narrow mind happens not to understand." In the proposed edition "nothing shall be imposed, as in the Oxford [i.e., Hanmer's] edition, without notice of alteration; nor shall conjecture be wantonly or unnecessarily indulged." Moreover, and this is, of course, of the greatest practical importance: "The edition now proposed will, at least, have this advantage over others. It will exhibit all the observable varieties of all the copies that can be found; that, if the reader is not satisfied with the editor's determination, he may have the means of choosing better for himself." In other words, Johnson's edition was to be and to a degree did become the first "variorum."

That the work, when it finally appeared some nine years after the *Proposals* were written, is not actually the nearly perfect edition of Shakespeare which the *Proposals* seemed to promise is due, in part, to the conditions and traditions of the time, in part to certain personal characteristics of Johnson which made him something less than an ideal editor even in his own day. His knowledge of Elizabethan language and literature was far more extensive than that of any but a very few of his contemporaries —incomparably better than that of most of his editorial predecessors. It was of a sort which, to take a single but typical example, had enabled him even in the days when he was making his *Miscellaneous Observations* to cite a parallel passage to show that "Aroint thee, witch" was not a printer's error for "Anoint thee." But his knowledge was casual, unsystematic, fragmentary and almost dilettante, not only by present-day standards but by those which were to be introduced by his immediate successors. What is perhaps even more important, his indolence often prevented him from doing what he knew perfectly well ought to be done.

In the *Proposals* "a careful collation of the oldest copies" is mentioned as one of the first and most important duties of an editor. A good deal of such collation he actually carried out—more carefully, it appears, than any previous editor, even Theobald, had taken time for. But there is a telltale sentence in the *Preface* which runs: "I collated such copies as I could procure, and wished for more, but have not found the collectors of these rareties very communicative." Moreover, there is good reason to suspect that if Johnson did not have access to all existing texts, the fault was as much his as that of their owners. He had a clear sense of what scholarship should undertake but very little disposition to do anything that was inconvenient at the same time that it was not indispensable to the fulfillment of his contractual obligations. He was later to take a very cavalier attitude toward the collection of material for the *Lives of the Poets,* and he took on occasion at least an equally cavalier attitude now. Referring to the complaint about "collectors," Boswell writes: "I told him that Garrick had complained to me of it, and had vindicated himself by assuring me, that Johnson was made welcome to the full use of his collection, and that he left the key of it with a servant, with orders to have a fire and every convenience for him. I found Johnson's notion was that Garrick wanted to be courted for them, and that, on the contrary, Garrick should have courted him and sent him the plays of his own accord. But indeed, considering the slovenly and careless manner in which books were treated by Johnson, it could not be expected that scarce and valuable editions should have been lent to him." Evidently Johnson would not, even for the sake of rescuing some of Shakespeare's meaning, run the risk of being thought capable of "courting" little David.[15]

Perhaps nothing demonstrates more clearly the strength and the weakness of Johnson's text as a text than its fate during the next sixty years while Shakespearean scholarship was having its most rapid development. In 1768, or three years after he had published, the supremacy of his edition was unsuccessfully challenged by that of Edward Capell, who collated the editions far more thoroughly than Johnson had done but who largely lost the fruits of his labors because his judgment was as inferior as his industry was admirable and because, accordingly, he made an erratic choice of readings without even following Johnson's practice of printing the alternatives. Five years after that, or in 1773, appeared a new version of Johnson's own edition, the preparation of which he entrusted to the young scholar, George Steevens, and that edition was itself superseded by another revision published by Edmond Malone in 1790. Both of these men were more exact scholars than Johnson could make any pretense of being, and Malone is generally recognized as the first scientific student of English literature in its textual and antiquarian aspects; indeed, he has been called "the greatest of all our Shakespearean scholars." Yet both men took Johnson's work as the basis for their own and both paid high tribute to their predecessor. Of Johnson's edition Steevens said that without it "I . . . could not have kept my legs," and in 1790 Malone wrote: "His admirable preface, (perhaps the finest composition in our language,) his happy, and in general just, characters of these plays, his refutation of the false glosses of Theobald and Warburton, and his numerous explications of involved and difficult passages, are too well known, to be here enlarged upon; and therefore I shall only add, that his vigorous and comprehensive understanding threw more light on his author than all his predecessors had done." If it be further remembered that Malone's last (and posthumous) edition of 1821 furnished the basis for most nineteenth-century editing, it is evident that whatever Johnson's defects may have been he was at least, when everything had been taken into consideration, so much the best yet to appear that no subsequent editor for a very long time to come ever thought either of making a clean sweep of his work or of going back to any of his predecessors for a starting point. Yet to this it certainly must be added that, as an editor, he is the last and best of one school rather more than the first of another. His method was to supplement good sense with knowledge and research. His successors have tended to supplement knowledge and research with good sense—when they could muster it. Perhaps this means that Johnson carried the method of good sense as far as it can be carried.

The whole question of the Shakespearean text is both so technical and so highly controversial that only a specialist has any right to make a pronouncement concerning the absolute merits of the text or the explanatory notes which Johnson provided, and even the specialist who has a right to make such a pronouncement is likely to find himself challenged by another specialist with an equal right. It may, however, be worth while to cite a few judgments which have been passed by qualified persons. Johnson "has the merit of restoring some readings which had escaped Theobald. . . . [His] preface and notes are distinguished by clearness of thought and diction and by masterly common sense." "His text is easily the best that had yet appeared. We have better texts now. But the value of his notes is permanent. . . . In the kind of notes which alone could be written if all the libraries in the world were burned, and we had nothing to guide us but our common sense and what we know of our fellow creatures and of the workings of the head and heart, Johnson is supreme. In all those passages where scholarship and historical knowledge fail to give us their aid there is still no more helpful guide than he. Once we know him we may be trusted to ask, when baffled by a difficult passage, 'What does Johnson say?' "[16]

This last quotation, with its stress on Johnson's explanatory notes, furnishes the necessary link between the discussions of Johnson as scholar and those of Johnson as critic of aesthetic values. The work of the textual critic, like every sort of scientific work, is completely superseded every time it is successfully modified. Johnson's merits or defects as the preparer of a text can be of little importance today to any except a very few specialists. But aesthetic criticism that was good once is never completely outmoded. No successor can build upon it so successfully as to supersede it in the way that scientific work can be superseded. What Johnson had to say about Shakespeare ought to be interesting to anyone capable of being interested in the inexhaustible subject of Shakespeare's greatness. It is also as significant as anything one can possibly know for the understanding and estimating of Johnson's own mind and character. To tell what one thinks—rather, say, what one is capable of thinking—about Shakespeare is to tell what one is.

It has already been said that most of Johnson's contemporaries seem to have received his notes with enthusiasm and to have accepted his *Preface* as the most satisfactory statement ever made of the extent and the character of England's greatest literary genius. It has also been to some extent suggested that many of the most competent of those who have recently written about Shakespeare speak of Johnson with great respect both as editor and as critic—indeed, his literary reputation as a whole has found more and stronger champions in the last quarter of a century than at any other time since his own. But there is also no doubt that the most widely current stereotypes, the most usual textbook commonplaces, tend to dismiss his criticism as pedantic and unimaginative. The great romantics of the early nineteenth century had, of course, no use for him. They cultivated mystical insights and rose to rhapsody. The twentieth century has often accepted the romantics' estimate of Johnson, while moving away from the attitude which led them to formulate it. In many respects he is actually closer to us than the romantics are. Speaking of Johnson's criticism in general, Lytton Strachey declared that it was often ingenious, provocative and interesting; that there is indeed only one virtue which it never has—the virtue of being right. With less wit but with at least some shadow of justification, it has also been said that, though Johnson could appreciate Shakespeare, he could not explain him. But who, one may ask in reply to this objection, has actually done that? And if Johnson indicated—not exhaustively to be sure, but as satisfactorily as any one man ever has—the most important of the kinds of excellence which Shakespeare exhibits, does not that entitle him to a position as high as any among the critics, so many of whom have tried to do more without succeeding in doing it? Perhaps, since Johnson has been so often accused of pedantry, of faultfinding, of lack of feeling, and of lack of imagination, it will be worth while to examine rather closely, not only what he said about Shakespeare in the *Preface* which his contemporaries found so admirable, but also what his attitude was in his private reading and in his familiar conversation.

However little he may have cared for the theater, Johnson had read Shakespeare since early childhood. He remembered how, when he was not more than nine years old, he had somehow got hold of a copy of *Hamlet* and how he read it quietly in his father's kitchen until the ghost scene sent him suddenly scurrying upstairs to the street door "that he might see people about him." Moreover, this simple, direct susceptibility to the sheer power of Shakespeare over the emotions was so far from abating that he could confess nearly half a century later to a sensitivity which few scholars long immersed in "problems" would be likely to exhibit. "I was many years ago so shocked by Cordelia's death, that I know not whether I ever endured to read again the last scenes of the play till I undertook to revise them as an editor." "He that peruses Shakespeare," he wrote in another place, "looks round alarmed, and starts to find himself alone."

A few scattered remarks recorded by Boswell and others have been quoted hundreds of times out of their context just because they seem paradoxical and startling; but in every case the context explains the paradox for what it is. Johnson did once actually say that the description of the temple in Congreve's *The Mourning Bride* "was the finest poetical passage he had ever read" and that "he recollected none in Shakespeare equal to it." But the fact that he said this in Garrick's presence, with the obvious and successful intention of provoking him, is probably even more important than the fact that Johnson, like all his contemporaries, had an admiration which we do not share for formal and rhetorical "descriptive poetry" of the sort which his own century was given to writing. Once Garrick had been successfully provoked and once Johnson had enjoyed the pleasure of smiling at his "enthusiastic jealousy" and his "tragic eagerness," Johnson went on: "Sir, this is not comparing Congreve on the whole, with Shakespeare on the whole . . . What I mean is, that you can shew me no passage where there is simply a description of material objects, without any intermixture of moral notions, which produces such an effect." Congreve, in other words, wrote better than Shakespeare when he wrote about nothing that is capable of calling forth poetical powers or producing a poetical effect.

It is also true that Johnson once remarked, when he was again praising Congreve: "Shakespeare never has six lines together without a fault." But he was merely saying what every critic without exception, from the days of Ben Jonson on, had said and what was perfectly obvious to anyone familiar with what the seventeenth and eighteenth centuries had come to mean by faultless or "correct" rhythm or diction, and by "propriety." Yet Johnson was as far as Dryden from supposing that this put Shakespeare below the "correct" poets. On the one hand, he could say of *The Mourning Bride* that it contained "the finest poetical passage he had ever read"; on the other, he could also say of it, "there is more bustle than sentiment; the plot is busy and intricate, and the events take hold on the attention; but, except a very few passages, we are rather amused with noise, and perplexed with stratagem, than entertained with any delineation of natural characters." Moreover, he could quote with approval Dryden's magnificent and decisive tribute to Shakespeare: "the man, who, of all modern and, perhaps, ancient poets, had the largest and most comprehensive soul." Out of this same sense that Shakespeare's greatness is his *greatness,* he could turn humorously upon Mrs. Thrale, who tried to force him to agree that Edward Young's description of night was better than Shakespeare or Dryden's because it was more "general" and therefore, according to the poetic theory, which Johnson ostensibly accepted, more poetical. "Young froths, and foams, and bubbles," he retorted, "sometimes very vigorously; but we must not compare the noise made by your tea-kettle here with the roaring of the ocean." [17]

If, as may certainly be maintained, the final test of a critic is willingness and ability to recognize excellence even when he cannot account for it; to be able to put loyalty to greatness before loyalty to his own theories, then Johnson passes that test with flying colors. Like all critics of his century—perhaps even like all critics of our own—he did not always know why the good was good or the bad bad; but in the case of Shakespeare, at least, he not only seldom failed to acknowledge what was good but also seldom failed to realize just how good it was. No doubt it was because he thus recognized that a poet can be understood only if we open our minds to receive his impact that he gave in the *Preface* that excellent advice which ought to be surprising to those to whom "Johnson" and "pedant" seem equivalent terms. "Notes are often necessary, but they are necessary evils. Let him, that is yet unacquainted with the powers of *Shakespeare,* and who desires to feel the highest pleasure that drama can give, read every play from the first scene to the last, with utter negligence of all his commentators. When his fancy is once on the wing, let it not stoop at correction or explanation. When his attention is strongly engaged, let it disdain alike to turn aside to the name of Theobald and of Pope. Let him read on through brightness and obscurity, through integrity and corruption; let him preserve his comprehension of the dialogue and his interest in the fable. And when the pleasures of novelty have ceased, let him attempt exactness, and read the commentators." [18]

Others might follow the great Voltaire as well as certain famous native critics in insisting that Shakespeare was at best "a barbarian genius," that Addison's *Cato* could be shown by logic absolutely to be beyond all question the finest tragedy in the English language. Johnson refused to accept logic in the face of experience. To put his foot in contact with a stone may not have been to refute Berkeley, but to put the heads of the critics in contact with the solid fact of Shakespeare's genius was an adequate refutation of them. Moreover, Johnson understood as few of his contemporaries did just what is the nature of the difference between that excellence which consists in the correct expression of laudable sentiments and that sort which involves the ability to capture the imagination and to stir the passions.

The point is so important and Johnson's position is so far in advance of that of most of his contemporaries that it is perhaps worth setting forth. "Correctness" was soon to be vehemently disdained by the romantic poets and their admirers. Indeed, as early as 1759, Edward Young had to some extent anticipated the romantics with his confused and rhapsodical championship of "genius" in the once famous *Conjectures on Original Composition.* But Young, with all his enthusiasm, can hardly be said to have clarified anything and it would be difficult to find in any of Johnson's predecessors, contemporaries or successors a clearer indication of the actual nature of the difference between "correctness" and excellence of the higher kind than one finds in Johnson himself. Let us see what his position was.

To understand it one must first understand that for quite comprehensible reasons he, his immediate predecessors, and his contemporaries did admire also, more than we do, a kind of writing quite different from Shakespeare's—namely, the smooth, consistent and rational style which they practiced. It was new; it was their own invention; and it did exhibit remarkable virtues. Only a very insensitive reader could fail to perceive that, to take one good example, the famous passage from *Aurengzebe* which Johnson quoted and which begins:

> When I consider life 'tis all a cheat
> Yet, fooled with hope, men favor the deceit;
> Trust on, and think to-morrow will repay;
> To-morrow's falser than the former day . . .

is a different kind of writing from the even more famous soliloquy of Macbeth:

> To-morrow and to-morrow and to-morrow.

Moreover, only a very insensitive person could fail to perceive that in certain respects Dryden is better, just as Johnson said the one passage in Congreve was better than any similar passage in Shakespeare. What the one soliloquy communicates by psychological suggestion, the other states as a proposition and develops through a series of completed metaphors. If no post-Elizabethan could possibly have written *Macbeth,* no one before the age of Dryden could possibly have written *Aurengzebe,* because no one before that time had learned so well how to exploit the possibilities of language as an instrument for logical statement as opposed to powerful suggestion.

To use words with a concern for their precise meaning rather than for their emotional association is, if you like, to write prose rather than poetry; but prose is important, and good prose in the sense in which the term has just been used had so rarely been written before the middle of the seventeenth century that one is almost justified in saying that England did not know how to write it. Dryden and Pope provided writing in which the virtues of good prose were exhibited to so high a degree that those to whom the word "poetry" means only a superlatively effective way of writing call this writing by that name, while those to whom the word means exclusively a special kind of good writing, call Dryden and Pope "classics of our prose."

Contemporaries of the latter, even contemporaries of Johnson, could hardly be expected to know, as we do, that the new method, once it had been developed, could be taught and learned while the method of Shakespeare and the other great Elizabethans could not—with the result that reasonably good prose has been written ever since the seventeenth century and that poetry has continued to be written only rarely. Yet that is the chief reason why we regard the achievement of the poets of Shakespeare's age as so much greater than the achievement of Dryden's. It is not because prose—the use of language for logical communication—is less important than poetry. It is merely because we can write passable prose with ease and can rarely manage to write even passable poetry.

If, then, we have any cause to speak condescendingly of the critics of the eighteenth century, it is not because they admired their own kind of writing. When they are guilty of fatuousness and bad taste, it is only when they fail to perceive the excellence of the earlier sort or when they fail to distinguish what the two kinds are. Certainly Johnson cannot be charged with either of these failures. He never for one minute doubted that Shakespeare was the greatest of English poets and the greatest of English dramatists. What is more significant, he realized that Shakespeare was the one *because* he was the other, and he showed clearly what the difference was between statement (wherein the great strength of the eighteenth century lay) and that kind of drama which is also one (and perhaps the chief) kind of poetry.

Dryden had been the first to wrestle seriously with the problem which many of his contemporaries must have sensed dimly and which he saw clearly: How can Shakespeare remain, as he indubitably does, a better poet than any of us, despite the fact

"WALKING UP HIGH STREET"

From The Picturesque Beauties of Boswell, *designed by Samuel Collings and etched by Thomas Rowlandson*

that our many superiorities can so easily be pointed out? Dryden began by denying the fact. He ended by becoming the first important critic definitely to proclaim Shakespeare's unchallengeable position. But in between he could only take refuge in paradox. Of the Elizabethans he could say only: "Theirs was the giant race before the flood." Faced with Shakespeare's "God-like Romans":

> He, in a just despair, would quit the Stage;
> And to an age less polished more unskilled,
> Does, with disdain, the foremost Honours yield.[19]

Yet neither of these statements, despite the memorable quality of the first, can be said to solve the problem. The Elizabethans were gigantic, but like all giants they were uncouth. Shakespeare wrote better than Dryden *because* his age was more uncouth and less skilled. Johnson, on the other hand, sees clearly that skill in statement is not the same thing as skill in drama and illustrates the fact with such simple clarity that one wonders at the gropings of Dryden.

Shakespeare, Johnson says, was concerned with *representing* men and phantoms, not with formulating correct sentiments or avoiding "the petty cavils of petty minds." And with one sweep of the pen he disposes of the whole argument concerning the relative importance of "judgment" and "imagination" to the poet even though he may have on other occasions seemed himself to lean in the direction of the argument here so magisterially dismissed.

"Voltaire expresses his wonder, that our author's extravagancies are endured by a nation, which has seen the tragedy of Cato. Let him be answered, that Addison speaks the language of poets, and Shakespeare of men. We find in Cato innumerable beauties, which enamour us of its author, but we see nothing that acquaints us with human sentiments or human actions; we place it with the fairest and the noblest progeny which judgment propagates by conjunction with learning; but Othello is the vigorous and vivacious offspring of observation impregnated by genius. Cato affords a splendid exhibition of artificial and fictitious manners, and delivers just and noble sentiments, in diction easy, elevated, and harmonious, but its hopes and fears communicate no vibration to the heart; the composition refers us only to the writer; we pronounce the name of Cato, but we think on Addison." [20]

"Corneille," he once said, "is to Shakespeare as a clipped hedge is to a forest," and he never forgot the distinction which ought to be made between either clipped hedges and forests or teakettles and the ocean.

Johnson did not believe that Shakespeare exhibited in perfection every virtue a writer can have. His praise falls short of affirming quite that, but it can hardly be said to fall short of anything that can reasonably be expected. In his judgment, Shakespeare is unquestionably the greatest of English poets as Milton is unquestionably the second. Moreover, if one puts together the items in the long list of supremely important virtues with which Shakespeare is credited, and if one takes note of the fact that not one defect capable of detracting seriously from the supreme greatness of the whole work is admitted, it seems evident that nothing which stops short of sheer Swinburnesque rhapsody could go further. How, then, does it happen that Johnson has frequently been charged with a failure to appreciate Shakespeare's genius?

The answer, stated in the broadest possible terms, comes down to this: Johnson was writing for an audience whose background of expectation and whose background of knowledge and prejudice were different from ours. There are certain other factors involved, but this is the chief one, and the facts to be borne in mind may thus be listed in the order of decreasing importance: (1) Shakespeare's position as a classic rather than as a merely popular writer was not yet fully established. (2) For at least three-quarters of a century it had been obligatory to discuss him in connection with certain critical dogmas now unfamiliar to any except students of literary history. (3) The first function of criticism was generally assumed to be judicial rather than "appreciative" or even expository. (4) Despite the extent of Johnson's admiration and the breadth of his understanding, there did remain aspects of Shakespeare's genius which he could not grasp as completely as certain subsequent critics have grasped them. Let us approach the whole question of Johnson's limitations, real and supposed, in connection with these facts and let us consider them in the order given.

1. *Shakespeare's position as a classic was not fully established.* When Johnson sat down to write a preface in the course of which he would define the nature and extent of his author's importance, his task was in certain respects very different from the task of a critic who should undertake the same thing today, and consequently both his method of approach and the nature of his emphasis were such as to strike us with some surprise. Today, a critic would know, and expect his readers to know, that literary, critical, scholarly and academic—perhaps we had best say frankly "high-brow"—opinion was solidly and dogmatically agreed on the supreme greatness of the author of a certain considerable number of plays which have been read and annotated and argued over almost as earnestly as the sacred texts of the Talmud and the Testaments. He would assume that if there was anyone who needed to be argued with and convinced, anyone whose tastes and prejudices needed to be considered and disposed of, that person was the average reader, who was willing enough to assume (under the crushing weight of opinion) that Shakespeare is great, but who may be disposed to doubt that Shakespeare is for him.

When, on the other hand, Johnson wrote his *Preface,* the existing situation was almost precisely contrary. For some one hundred and fifty years, or ever since the plays were first written, they had been and they continued to be, in the widest sense of the word, popular. "By horny hands," as Dryden says of an even more holy book, "the sacred text was mauled." The plays had been and were being acted with a frequency hard for us to believe possible, and they were also being revised, adapted and generally treated with a casual familiarity that makes us shudder. Shakespeare belonged to the mob. He was adored by the groundlings. But the high-brows were by no means sure that they wanted to claim him.

There was certainly more disposition to do so than there had been even a generation before, but the opinion that Shakespeare was a merely popular playwright rather than a writer whom the refined and instructed could take seriously was older than its opposite, and had behind it not only important names but the weight of much critical analysis. Even those who were prepared, as most Englishmen by now no doubt were, to accept him as, all things considered, their greatest poet, nevertheless granted glaring defects as present beyond the possibility of any argument. They expected them to be assumed, they expected that no one in his right senses would for a moment suppose (as the romantics were soon to suppose) that these defects were subtle virtues; and they expected that any champion of Shakespeare would meet seriously the arguments of those who declared that his imperfections rendered it impossible to consider him a serious writer.

All these expectations Johnson was bound to meet. To realize how far his argument in favor of Shakespeare's supreme greatness was from being won and how much dross even professed admirers like Garrick were still ready to admit was included in Shakespeare's works, one need merely recall that the great name of Voltaire, spokesman for the nation which led in politeness and refinement, had now been added to the list of champions fighting against Shakespeare, just at the time when the English classicists were losing their ground. It was more than ten years after the publication of Johnson's *Preface* that Voltaire was lamenting: "I was the first who showed to the French a few pearls which I had found in his [Shakespeare's] enormous dunghill. I did not expect that what I had done would one day be used in assisting to trample under foot the crowns of Corneille and of Racine, and to place them on the brow of a barbarous mountebank." It was just at this same time that Garrick, spurred on no doubt by his French visit, accomplished his rewriting of *Hamlet* and boasted: "I had sworn I would not leave the stage till I had rescued that noble play from all the rubbish of the fifth act. I have brought it forth without the grave-diggers' trick and the fencing-match. The alteration was received with general approbation." What is more, Garrick had also added speeches composed by himself to make up for some of the Shakespearean rubbish cut away. What is still more, Steevens, the very same who was to revise Johnson's edition, was so pleased that he wrote

Garrick a letter joyously suggesting: "You had better throw what remains of the piece into a farce, to appear immediately afterwards. No foreigner who should happen to be present at the exhibition, would ever believe it was formed out of the loppings and excrescences of the tragedy itself. You may entitle it *The Grave-diggers;* with the pleasant Humours of Osrick, the Danish Macaroni."

Is it, then, any wonder that Johnson should, for instance, have found it advisable to make passing allusion to the fact that "Shakespeare's plays are not in the rigorous critical sense either tragedies or comedies"? But once he has said that, and granted the fact that the ancient poets "according to the laws which custom had prescribed" tended to write about either the momentous vicissitudes of life or the lighter occurrences but not to mingle the two—what could be more modern than his absolute dismissal of the idea that such custom is a law of nature? And what could be more obviously intended to turn the supposed defect of Shakespeare into a virtue than the remarks which follow the simple statement that the plays are not formally either tragedies or comedies? They are, he says: "compositions of a distinct kind; exhibiting the real state of sublunary nature, which partakes of good and evil, joy and sorrow, mingled with endless variety of proportion and innumerable modes of combination; and expressing the course of the world, in which the loss of one is the gain of another; in which, at the same time, the reveller is hastening to his wine, and the mourner burying his friend; in which the malignity of one is sometimes defeated by the frolic of another; and many mischiefs and many benefits are done and hindered without design." Present-day readers may sometimes be bored by Johnson's brief consideration of some of the charges against Shakespeare. They may even, unconsciously, tend to feel that he is giving undue weight to them when he considers them at all. But his contemporaries were more likely to think just the opposite, and in the case just cited it is evident (as it generally is in such cases) that Johnson himself considers the cavils of the pseudoclassicists hardly more weighty than they were considered by later critics no longer under the necessity of even pretending to deal with them.

2. *For three-quarters of a century it had been obligatory to discuss Shakespeare in connection with certain critical dogmas.* Only about seventy-five years before Johnson brushed aside all consideration of "the rules," Thomas Rymer, in a famous and widely read book, had analyzed *Othello* (which seemed to him to break them all) as an outstanding example of bad playwriting, and pronounced it "none other than a bloody farce, without salt or savor." Nearly a generation later Pope was, nevertheless, still calling Rymer one of the best critics and, without agreeing with his strictures, plainly preferring not to argue the points with him. Yet Rymer, it must be remembered, went far beyond a mere insistence that tragedy must rigidly preserve the unities of time and place as well as maintain a decorum unbroken not only by any suggestion of comedy but also free from any allusions to the familiar. Beyond all that, he also insisted that strict Poetic Justice should be administered, and characters so invariably delineated in accordance with what the classicists had declared to be most typical of the profession or social position of the person represented that he could accuse Shakespeare of a mere vulgar attempt to be clever when he made Iago a sly practitioner of the arts of treachery despite the well-known fact that the "character" of a soldier is straightforward and blunt.

When Pope wrote his oft-quoted advice:

> Learn hence for ancient rules a just esteem
> To copy Nature is to copy them [21]

he was merely presenting in brief and much attenuated form a doctrine which Rymer had stated in terms so absolute as to include the conviction that nothing which violated the rules of Aristotle could possibly be pleasing even to the vulgar. Aristotle had discovered once and for all "what pleases." Those who think that they are pleased by something else deceive themselves. It is merely that something not contrary to the rules of Aristotle is pleasing them so much that they fail to notice their inevitable displeasure at the moments when the violations are being committed.

It is true that no subsequent English critic of importance ever reached Rymer's height of absurdity; true that to trace the stream of Shakespearean criticism from him to Johnson is gradually to approach Johnson's own position. But for a long time the tendency of many critics was not to renounce "the rules"; it was, at most, to soften somewhat the rigor of their application and, when that could be softened no further, to apologize for Shakespeare's ignorance and to praise his beauties, which were admitted to be beautiful despite what Voltaire called "the dunghill" in which they were all but lost.

Those critics who have best stood the test of time and are today best remembered are, naturally, those most favorable to Shakespeare. Dryden, in his sketch of a projected reply to Rymer, put himself on the modern side of what is, after all, the crucial question—the question, that is to say, whether "the rules" are "nature methodized" and therefore Aristotle's laws only in the sense that the laws of gravity are Newton's, or whether they are merely generalizations from the practice of a school of writers. " 'Tis not enough," he wrote, "that Aristotle has said so, for Aristotle drew his models of tragedy from Sophocles and Euripides; and if he had seen ours, might have changed his mind." Addison in *The Spectator* is just a bit more cautious, for he insists upon a distinction between those geniuses who have and those who have not "submitted their Greatness to the Corrections and Restraints of Art." But he goes on to say that at least "there is more Beauty in the Works of a great Genius who is ignorant of the Rules of Art, than in those of a little Genius who knows and observes them." And he adds: "Our inimitable Shakespeare is a Stumbling-block to the whole Tribe of these Rigid Critics."

The first two editors of Shakespeare, Rowe and Pope, tended to take a somewhat similar position since they naturally had to defend their assumption that Shakespeare was worth editing. But Pope hedges a bit with his insistence that, after all, the laws of literature and the laws of the stage are not the same. But the usual opinion probably was that Shakespeare was great despite his ignorance and his willfulness; and it is certain that critics whose opinions commanded some respect continued at times to judge much more harshly than that. Charles Gildon, who published *An Essay on the Art, Rise, and Progress of the Stage* in

1710, admits that Rymer "has carried the matter too far," since no one with the least tact can question Shakespeare's genius; but Gildon can account for him only as a "miracle for the age he lived in." Like Rymer he is convinced that "the rules" are "built on an equally solid and infallible reason" and confesses his inability to understand how it is that Shakespeare can please even when he defies them. He is sure, moreover, that he would have pleased even more had he submitted himself to their discipline and in this respect he agrees with John Dennis, whose three letters *On the Genius and Writings of Shakespeare* are supposed to demonstrate that Shakespeare "was a great genius" and to prove their point by arguing that only a great genius could have succeeded at all while disregarding both the Unities and the law of Poetic Justice. Shakespeare, he concludes, "often perform'd wonders" without art and learning; had he possessed both he would have no doubt surpassed the Greeks.[22]

If such arguments as these were coming to have less and less force throughout Johnson's lifetime, they were by no means yet dead, and Voltaire could revive them with an effect sufficiently powerful to make Garrick and Steevens to some extent Voltairians rather than Johnsonians. Voltaire goes back to what is essentially Rymer's position and assumes without argument that it is manifestly absurd that in a tragedy one should see a Roman senator acting clownishly or a king drunk—the unstated reason being, no doubt, not only that a tragedy must be always elevated but also that it is not, in Rymer's sense, part of the "character" of a Roman senator to be undignified or of a king to be drunken. In replying to Voltaire, Johnson—just as he had done in the case of the charge that Shakespeare's plays were neither comedies nor tragedies—makes his appeal to "nature" in the sense of things as they are known to experience as opposed to "nature" in the pseudo-Aristotlian sense of things as they typically are or ought to be. Johnson writes:

"Dennis and Rymer think his Romans not sufficiently Roman; and Voltaire censures his kings as not completely royal. Dennis is offended, that Menenius, a senator of Rome, should play the buffoon; and Voltaire, perhaps, thinks decency violated when the Danish usurper is represented as a drunkard. But Shakespeare always makes nature predominate over accident; and, if he preserves the essential character, is not very careful of distinctions superinduced and adventitious. His story requires Romans or kings, but he thinks only on men. He knew that Rome, like every other city, had men of all dispositions; and, wanting a buffoon, he went into the senate-house for that which the senate-house would certainly have afforded him. He was inclined to show an usurper and a murderer, not only odious, but despicable; he, therefore, added drunkenness to his other qualities, knowing that kings love wine like other men, and that wine exerts its natural power upon kings. These are the petty cavils of petty minds; a poet overlooks the casual distinction of country and condition, as a painter, satisfied with the figure, neglects the drapery."

From all this it is evident that of Johnson's paragraphs on "the unities" one must say just what was said of the briefer discussion of tragedy and comedy as fixed forms—namely, that his concern with the question is no greater than the minimum which every reader would regard as demanded. So far as the position he actually takes is concerned, that position is completely unequivocal. Shakespeare maintains the only unity which is actually important—the unity of action. "His plan has commonly what Aristotle requires, a beginning, a middle, and an end; one event is concatenated with another, and the conclusion follows by easy consequence." The so-called unities of time and place are, he assumes, purely artificial and arbitrary. Authority is not even mentioned as an argument in their favor and the contention that they are based on reason is disposed of by rational analysis. He then concludes: "Whether Shakespeare knew the unities, and rejected them by design, or deviated from them by happy ignorance, it is, I think, impossible to decide, and useless to enquire. . . . Nor, if such another poet could arise, should I very vehemently reproach him, that his first act passed at *Venice*, and his next at *Cyprus*."

Present-day readers who have never met anyone to whom the question of the unities was alive may feel that Johnson devotes several unnecessarily serious paragraphs to disposing of it, but

Johnson was quite aware how differently many of his own contemporaries would feel, and is compelled, after his arguments have been advanced, to admit: "I am almost frightened at my own temerity; and when I estimate the fame and the strength of those that maintain the contrary opinion, am ready to sink down in reverential silence." Moreover, this admission is so far from being merely pretended that he thereupon proceeds to attempt to satisfy those who cannot accept his argument by asking them, as various of his predecessors had done, to "consider the condition of his life" and to "make some allowance for his ignorance." But so far as Johnson's own opinion is concerned, one need only remember that he had just spoken of this ignorance as "happy ignorance."

Nearly fifteen years before the *Preface* was written, Johnson had considered the whole question of "the rules" in *The Rambler,* and as early as that he had come to the conclusion that most of them are merely arbitrary. Those who suppose that he was a blind follower of custom or that he aspired to dictate should ponder the paragraph which concludes this particular essay:

"It ought to be the first endeavour of a writer to distinguish nature from custom; or that which is established because it is right, from that which is right only because it is established; that he may neither violate essential principles by a desire of novelty, nor debar himself from the attainment of beauties within his view, by a needless fear of breaking rules which no literary dictator had authority to enact."

In a subsequent number of *The Rambler,* Johnson had discussed the related and subtler question of "propriety" in connection with poetic diction and the effect of "low" words when found in passages devoted to exalted sentiments. He cites from *Macbeth* the speech:

> Come, thick night!
> And pall thee in the dunnest smoke of hell,
> That my keen knife see not the wound it makes;
> Nor heaven peep through the blanket of the dark,
> To cry, "Hold! Hold!"

and he then proceeds to say of it, among other things: ". . . perhaps scarce any man now peruses it without some disturbance of his attention from the counteraction of the words to the ideas. What can be more dreadful than to implore the presence of night, invested, not in common obscurity, but in the smoke of hell? Yet the efficacy of this invocation is destroyed by the insertion of an epithet now seldom heard but in the stable, and *dun* night may come or go without any other notice than contempt. . . . We cannot surely but sympathise with the horrours of a wretch about to murder his master, his friend, his benefactor, who suspects that the weapon will refuse its office, and start back from the breast which he is preparing to violate. Yet this sentiment is weakened by the name of an instrument used by butchers and cooks in the meanest employments: we do not immediately conceive that any crime of importance is to be committed with a *knife;* or who does not, at last, from the long habit of connecting a knife with sordid offices, feel aversion rather than terrour?"

If such passages as these are quoted out of their context, they seem to accuse Johnson of sharing the rigorous and absurd ideas of some of his contemporaries, but the context puts them in a different light. In the first place, he is primarily concerned, not with convicting Shakespeare of vulgarity but of explaining how he has come to be charged with such a fault by persons who mistake custom for nature. "No word is naturally or intrinsically meaner than another; our opinion therefore of words, as of other things arbitrarily and capriciously established, depends wholly upon accident and custom. . . . Words which convey ideas of dignity in one age, are banished from elegant writing or conversation in another, because they are in time debased by vulgar mouths, and can be no longer heard without the involuntary recollection of unpleasing images." In the second place, Johnson is demonstrating, not that time has served to render Shakespeare ridiculous but that his poetic force triumphs easily over apparent faults which changes of fashion have created. The short passage which is debased not only by the low words "dunnest" and "knife," but also by the vulgar image "peep through the blanket," is, nevertheless, pronounced to be one in which "is exerted all the force of poetry; that force which calls new powers into being, which embodies sentiment, and animates matter." [23]

3. *Like most of his contemporaries, Johnson assumed that the first business of criticism was not enthusiastic eulogy or even interpretation. It was evaluation and discrimination.* He seldom indulged in anything approaching that attempt to recreate in descriptive terms the emotional effect of an author which the nineteenth century came to think of as the chief duty of the critic, but against which the twentieth century has again reacted. For this reason, Johnson's criticism sometimes strikes present-day readers as lacking in enthusiasm. But if one remembers that he regarded judgment as his business, and if one then examines his judgments, it becomes immediately evident not only that Johnson is putting Shakespeare in the very first place, but that he is giving him that place because in Shakespeare's plays he finds the primary virtues of the imaginative writer present in the highest degree and in the greatest possible vigor.

Only time, he begins by reminding us, can definitely establish the greatness of works which are "not raised upon principles demonstrable and scientifick" but which make their appeal "wholly to observation and experience." "The Pythagorean scale of numbers was at once discovered to be perfect; but the poems of Homer we yet know not to transcend the common limits of human intelligence, but by remarking, that nation after nation, and century after century, has been able to do little more than transpose his incidents, new name his characters, and paraphrase his sentiments." Shakespeare also has now endured long enough to pass a similar test. "He has long outlived his century, the term commonly fixed as the test of literary merit. Whatever advantages he might once derive from personal allusions, local customs, or temporary opinions, have for many years been lost; and every topic of merriment, or motive of sorrow, which the modes of artificial life afforded him, now only obscure the scenes which they once illuminated. The effects of favor and competition are at an end; the tradition of his friendships and his enmities has perished; his works support no opinions with arguments, nor supply any faction with invectives; they can neither indulge vanity, nor gratify malignity; but are read without any other reason than the desire of pleasure, and are, therefore, praised only as pleasure is obtained; yet, thus unassisted by interest or passion, they have passed through variations of taste and changes of manners, and, as they devolved from one generation to another, have received new honors at every transmission."

This power to please generation after generation means that the esteem in which Shakespeare is held cannot be based upon any fashion or any prejudice. "What has been longest known has been most considered, and what is most considered is best understood." It means also that Shakespeare is "the poet of nature," not in that vague sense of the word which had come to be intended when pedantic critics talked about "nature versus art" but in a simple sense; he is, that is to say, the poet in whom more often and more continuously than in any other one recognizes truth because what one finds there meets most often the test of one's own experience. He is the poet in whose works one finds most accurately mirrored the world which one knows. "The irregular combinations of fanciful invention may delight awhile, by that novelty of which the common satiety of life sends us all in quest; but the pleasures of sudden wonder are soon exhausted, and the mind can only repose on the stability of truth."

Later critics have preferred to find in Shakespeare (and thereby also to demonstrate in themselves) subtler and more esoteric virtues. Some of these virtues undoubtedly exist though they can hardly bc the most important for Shakespeare's fame since they are, for the most part, beyond the concern or the notice of the great public which has been his firmest support. Johnson prefers to stress the fundamental virtue of fiction: the power to hold the mirror and the power to carry the conviction that it is doing just that.

"The theatre, when it is under any other direction, is peopled by such characters as were never seen, conversing in a language which was never heard, upon topics which never arise in the commerce of mankind. But the dialogue of this author is often so evidently determined by the incident which produces it, and is pursued with so much ease and simplicity, that it seems scarcely to claim the merit of fiction, but to have been gleaned, by diligent selection, out of common conversation and common occurrences. . . .

"To bring a lover, a lady, and a rival into the fable; to entangle them in contradictory obligations, perplex them with oppositions of interest, and harass them with violence of desires inconsistent with each other; to make them meet in rapture, and part in agony; to fill their mouths with hyperbolical joy and outrageous sorrow; to distress them as nothing human ever was distressed; to deliver them as nothing human ever was delivered; is the business of a modern dramatist. For this, probability is violated, life is misrepresented, and language is depraved. . . .

"This, therefore, is the praise of Shakespeare, that his drama is the mirror of life; that he who has mazed his imagination, in following the phantoms which other writers raise up before him, may here be cured of his delirious ecstasies, by reading human sentiments in human language, by scenes from which a hermit may estimate the transactions of the world, and a confessor predict the progress of the passions."

According to Johnson, Shakespeare is, in other words, the greatest of modern poets first and chiefly because he seems most completely to have realized the ideal of knowledge which Imlac had described for the benefit of Rasselas:

" 'Whatever is beautiful, and whatever is dreadful, must be familiar to his imagination; he must be conversant with all that is awfully vast or elegantly little. The plants of the garden, the animals of the wood, the minerals of the earth, and the meteors of the sky, must all concur to store his mind with inexhaustible variety.[24]

" 'But the knowledge of nature is only half the task of a poet; he must be acquainted, likewise, with all the modes of life. His character requires, that he estimate the happiness and misery of every condition; observe the power of all the passions in all their combinations, and trace the changes of the human mind, as they are modified by various institutions, and accidental influences of climate or custom, from the sprightliness of infancy to the despondence of decrepitude. He must divest himself of the prejudices of his age or country; he must consider right and wrong in their abstracted and invariable state; he must disregard present laws and opinions, and rise to general and transcendental truths, which will always be the same; he must, therefore, content himself with the slow progress of his name; contemn the applause of his own time, and commit his claims to the justice of posterity. He must write, as the interpreter of nature, and the legislator of mankind, and consider himself, as presiding over the thoughts and manners of future generations; as a being superiour to time and place.' "[25]

Rasselas, it may be remembered, broke into the harangue with the exclamation: "Enough! thou hast convinced me, that no human being can ever be a poet." But Shakespeare was one.

Some reference, at least, must of course presently be made to the question of how much of Shakespeare's greatness is left—not only unaccounted for but actually unrecognized—when all this has been said of his power to represent what the reader recognizes as a true picture of human nature and human life. For the moment, however, the points to be made are, first, that Johnson insists upon Shakespeare as the supreme modern example of what a poet may accomplish in this respect; and, second, that whatever further excellences he passes over in a silence which may indicate a failure to perceive them, the positive faults which he alleges are both trivial and, except in one instance, recognized as such—at least by comparison with the virtues.

How completely Johnson rejected the whole complex of pedantic objections which learned criticism had built up has already been noted. "There is always an appeal open from criticism to nature," and that appeal he always insists upon taking. But there are certain faults which, Johnson feels, it is not pedantry to notice: Shakespeare's plots are loose and the conclusions, especially, are sometimes hurried. Like others among his contemporaries, he is freely guilty of anachronism. "In narration he affects a disproportionate pomp of diction" and his "declamations or set speeches are commonly cold and weak, for his power was the power of nature." Moreover, and here for once Johnson actually grows bitter: "A quibble is to Shakespeare, what luminous vapours are to the traveller. . . . It has some malignant power over his mind, and its fascinations are irresistible. . . . A quibble is the golden apple for which he will always turn aside from his career, or stoop from his elevation. A quibble, poor and barren as it is, gave him such delight, that he was content to purchase it, by the sacrifice of reason, propriety and truth. A quibble was to him the fatal Cleopatra for which he lost the world, and was content to lose it."

Most of these alleged defects have been, with greater or less success, explained away or turned into virtues by one or another of the subsequent critics. Perhaps the "set speeches" are not always cold; perhaps some of the quibbles are not puerile. But whether Johnson was right or wrong, he did not intend by his censures to detract much from Shakespeare as a dramatist, and the fact that he made them detracts almost as little from his trustworthiness as a critic. Almost at the end of his estimate of Shakespeare, Johnson quotes with approval a judgment of Dryden's which shows clearly enough how relatively unimportant he considers the charges with which we have just been concerned: "But he is always great when some great occasion is presented to him: no man can say, he ever had a fit subject for his wit, and did not then raise himself as high above the rest of poets, Quantum lenta solent inter viburna cupressi."

More serious perhaps is Johnson's more general complaint that Shakespeare enforces no moral. "He sacrifices virtue to convenience, and is so much more careful to please than to instruct, that he seems to write without any moral purpose. . . . He makes no just distribution of good or evil, nor is always careful to show in the virtuous a disapprobation of the wicked; he carries his persons indifferently through right and wrong, and, at the close, dismisses them without further care, and leaves their examples to operate by chance. This is a fault the barbarity of his age cannot extenuate; for it is always a writer's duty to make the world better, and justice is a virtue independent of time or place."

Few present-day critics—Mr. Santayana perhaps excepted—would join Johnson in this particular censure. The dissenters would, however, be about evenly divided between those who praise Shakespeare for refusing to be a moralist and those who insist that a moralist ("in the highest sense," of course) is precisely what he is and precisely why he is great. Perhaps therefore the wisest course to take here will be not to argue the question but to try to understand Johnson's position as clearly as possible.

Some small part of this particular censure of Shakespeare resulted from the fact that Johnson was, in the simplest sense of the words, both a moralist and a moralizer. He enjoyed drawing morals, he enjoyed following the process when others did the same, and in Shakespeare he missed what was to him as obviously a source of pleasure as it has come to seem to most people today an obvious occasion of annoyance. In an even simpler manner he was offended by the incidental bawdiness in Shakespeare's dialogue. Jocose indecency displeased him in ordinary conversation, even though, as we shall see, Boswell occasionally felt impelled to bowdlerize Johnson's own. He boasted that he always repressed it in his company and he saw no reason why he should pass over in silence the offense which a great poet gave him. If he could say that "there is an appeal open from criticism to nature," he could also say no less firmly and in a manner almost evangelical that "there are laws of higher authority than those of criticism." [26]

But Johnson's complaint that Shakespeare gave no moral instruction was founded on something more than taste. It was an inevitable consequence of his theory of literature, and to consider that fact is to come finally to the necessity of considering the charge that the limitations of this theory of literature either disqualify him as a critic of certain highly important aspects of Shakespeare's genius or at the very least make it impossible for him adequately to account for certain supreme virtues which he sensed without being able to specify. One such limitation is connected with the conception of the relation between moralizing and art, which is now under discussion. Considerably more important is his conception of the nature of the imagination. But the two should be discussed one after the other and in each case we may consider, first, what Johnson's assumptions actually were, and then how they affected his understanding of Shakespeare.

Like most of his contemporaries, Johnson found that when he attempted to rationalize and justify the enormous value which he set upon literary excellence, it was difficult to get beyond the contention that literature is important because it helps to make men virtuous, and equally difficult to see how it can help to make men virtuous unless it enforces some morality. Like all the Renaissance critics from whom eighteenth-century classicism derived and whose fundamental concepts even Johnson was liberalizing rather than rejecting, he agreed that poetry should please. But pleasure which runs counter to morality was obviously vicious, and even pleasure which was no more than innocent seemed too trivial an end to justify the feeling that poetry is, next to virtue, the noblest achievement of man. Some form of the statement that poetry is instruction which delights seemed inevitable, and Johnson, again like nearly all of his contemporaries, was unable to do something which many subsequent critics have attempted—namely, seize upon Aristotle's theory of purgation to describe some means by which art may be moral in its effect without being moralizing in its method.

Just how far Johnson was from understanding what, to us at least, it seems clear that Aristotle meant is revealed in a curious passage which records his reply to a leading question addressed to him by Boswell concerning this same "purging of the passions."

"I introduced Aristotle's doctrine in his 'Art of Poetry,' of 'the κάθαρσις τῶν παθημάτων, the purging of the passions,' as the purpose of tragedy. 'But how are the passions to be purged by terrour and pity?' (said I, with an assumed air of ignorance, to incite him to talk, for which it was often necessary to employ some address.) JOHNSON. 'Why, Sir, you are to consider what is the meaning of purging in the original sense. It is to expel impurities from the human body. The mind is subject to the same imperfection. The passions are the great movers of human actions; but they are mixed with such impurities, that it is necessary they should be purged or refined by means of terrour and pity. For instance, ambition is a noble passion; but by seeing upon the stage, that a man who is so excessively ambitious as to raise himself by injustice, is punished, we are terrified at the fatal consequences of such a passion. In the same manner a certain degree of resentment is necessary; but if we see that a man carries it too far, we pity the object of it, and are taught to moderate that passion.' My record upon this occasion does great injustice to Johnson's expression, which was so forcible and brilliant, that Mr. Cradock whispered me, 'O that his words were written in a book!' "

But if we are right in supposing that what Aristotle really meant to say was that evil passions are purged through ritual expression, that by indulging them vicariously through the personages of fiction we render it less likely that we shall indulge them through our own acts, then Johnson completely misses the point and explains away the theory of purgation by making it mean no more than the theory of cautionary example and, at the same time, he misses all opportunity to understand how literature may be moral in effect without resorting to the methods of the nonliterary moralist.[27]

In any event, and in accordance with his habitual assumption, Johnson declares in the *Preface:* "The end of writing is to instruct; the end of poetry is to instruct by pleasing." Neither Rymer himself nor any of his Italian or French predecessors could have spoken more absolutely, and once the absolute principle is thus laid down, one wonders not at Johnson's mild complaint that a failure to enforce moral lessons must be listed among Shakespeare's defects, but that the poet is not therefore summarily dismissed rather than accepted as, all things considered, incomparably the greatest of the moderns. The explanation is twofold. In the first place, Johnson habitually made an important qualification in his demand that poetry should instruct while delighting; in the second place, he found that Shakespeare was after all often moral in effect if not in intention.

One of the most striking features of Johnson as a moralist is his unusual combination of unyielding strictness so far as what he regarded as positively required or positively forbidden to man is concerned, with the greatest indulgence for himself as well as for others in the matter of all activities which he regarded as essentially neutral. He distrusted, as he clearly said, all tendency to multiply scruples, and he shared the contempt of the more worldly men of his century for that kind of "enthusiasm" which led the Puritans in another day and the Evangelicals in his own to assume that every moment not devoted to God was devoted to the devil. He was a hedonist as surely as he was anything else, provided only one admits the provision that pleasure comes second, not first. Moreover, he was a hedonist *because* he was a pessimist; because, in the first place, the evils of life must be palliated and because, in the second place, the mere emptiness of human life, consequent upon its failure to provide man with significant occupations enough to fill his existence, forced him to escape boredom by creating diversions for himself—as the Pharaohs had done when the Pyramids were built, and furnished Imlac with the occasion for one of the most purple of his purple passages. He spoke with contempt of "monastick morality, which holds pleasure itself to be a vice." "Pleasure of itself is not a vice," he declared, and again and again he makes use of phrases like one he wrote to Boswell when he declared it to be "the business of a wise man to be happy."

This attitude he made a part of his theory of literature as it was a part of his theory of life. More than once he calls upon it to soften the neoclassical insistence that poetry which merely pleases has no claim to esteem. Indeed, it is odd that in the *Preface* he finds no occasion to say what he often said elsewhere and what would go far toward removing the apparent inconsistency arising between the contention that Shakespeare is the greatest of modern poets and the statement that he enforces no morality. Twelve years before the *Preface* was issued, he had written in one of his periodical essays two curiously somber sentences which will perhaps stand as the most characteristic expression of his attitude on this point:

"The author is not wholly useless, who provides innocent amusements. . . . There are, in the present state of things, so many more instigations to evil, than incitements to good, that he who keeps me in a neutral state, may be justly considered as a benefactor to life."

For the most part, then, Shakespeare deserves at the very least the praise of the moralist as one of those who keep us "in a neutral state" and "may justly be considered as a benefactor to life"! If this seems but a grudging tribute, it is well to remember with what gusto Johnson the man permitted himself to enjoy those worldly pleasures which, as a moralist, he was compelled to regard as merely permissible palliatives. The *Preface* makes it clear that he abandoned himself to the delights of Shakespeare the poet as completely as he abandoned himself to the joys of the table, or, when he 'folded his legs and had his talk out," to those of conversation. It is hardly to be supposed that in the course of any of these activities he was continuously aware of the fact that, theoretically, nothing more could be said in their favor than that they were morally neutral.

Moreover, Johnson recognized something which seems both so obvious and so highly relevant that it is odd he did not stress it more. In the midst of the very paragraph that contains the strongest censure of Shakespeare's indifference to morality, Johnson drops in the sentence: "From his writings, indeed, a system of social duty may be selected, for he that thinks reasonably must think morally." He that thinks reasonably must think morally! What more could a professed realist like Johnson ask for! What further justification of Shakespeare's method could he demand than that which is implied if one says: He presents life truly and life truly presented must always carry its moral? Perhaps the answer is to be found in the phrase "a system of social duty." Perhaps what Johnson really means is that he finds in Shakespeare no hint of what he himself always demanded as a sort of addendum to the rational and realistic morality which he professed—namely, something specifically Christian.[28]

Perhaps also one may find here another example of the fact that all critics think most of the time in terms of the "problems" set by their predecessors and contemporaries, and that Johnson allows to slip by in one sentence a remark which might have been expanded into one of the most important passages in the whole *Preface* chiefly because it introduces something which critics had not got around to considering fully. Tradition had tended to fix "poetic justice" as the conception in connection with which the poet's regard or disregard of the alleged duty to moralize his plots was discussed, and though Johnson never accepted in any rigid form the doctrine of Poetic Justice, it was undoubtedly present in his mind along with the fact that no poet had ever more obviously disregarded it. Indeed, in the general remarks on *King Lear,* Johnson writes a curious sentence which reveals his own somewhat divided state of mind on the subject:

"A play in which the wicked prosper, and the virtuous miscarry, may doubtless be good, because it is a just representation of the common events of human life; but since all reasonable beings naturally love justice, I cannot easily be persuaded, that the observation of justice makes a play worse; or that, if other excellences are equal, the audience will not always rise better pleased from the final triumph of persecuted virtue." Curious this sentence was because, among other reasons, Johnson has actually shifted his ground from the moral to the aesthetic and defended Poetic Justice, not because it is instructive but because more pleasure is given when one finds a sequence of events ending as one would like them to end rather than as "the common events of human life" frequently do. To the subject he was to return in his *Life of Addison.*

Undoubtedly there are a few, though only a very few, occasions when Johnson's judgment on a particular passage or event is led astray by his concern for formal moralizing. One striking example of such an occasion is a remark in the general comment on *As You Like It* which reads: "By hastening the end of his work, Shakespeare suppressed the dialogue between the usurper and the hermit, and lost an opportunity of exhibiting a moral lesson, in which he might have found matter worthy of his highest powers." Most present-day readers would certainly agree that the opportunity was well lost and, if they are among those who find artistic reason for what the vulgar take to be lapses, would certainly insist that the perfunctory treatment of the usurper's reform is one of Shakespeare's ways of suggesting that no realism is intended in this particular play. In any event, if he had done what Johnson so unwisely wishes, we could only have had a passage more like Addison than like Shakespeare and hence open to the objection which Johnson himself had elsewhere made—that one is reminded of the author rather than of the play.

Such occasional lapses from his own better judgment into the taste of his time might also be illustrated by an occasional emendation which not only weakens the text but violates Johnson's own principle that emendation should never be made simply because one feels that an author ought to have written something different from what he did write. For example, he says of the lines in *Macbeth:*

> I have liv'd long enough; my way of life
> Is fall'n into the sear, the yellow leaf . . .

"As there is no relation between *the way of life,* and *fallen into the sear,* I am inclined to think, that the W is only an M inverted, and that it was originally written, my *May of life.*" Incidentally this emendation was accepted by Steevens but rejected a few years later by Mason and, during the course of the years, Johnson has been overwhelmed by scholars who have cited other Elizabethan uses of the phrase "way of life" and by critics who have felt that, as Richard Grant White finally put it: "Dr. Johnson's emendation is a step proseward, although speciously poetic."

But Johnson did not usually go astray through a preference for eighteenth century "correctness" over Elizabethan spontaneity any more than he usually went astray as the result of a demand that the poet should moralize his tale. Indeed, a fine paragraph in the *Preface* shows clearly how vividly he realized how much better Shakespeare's language was for its purpose than the "more correct" phraseology and diction of his own contemporaries. It should be read with the realization that when Johnson speaks of "common speech" the contrast of which he is thinking is that with "polished" writing.

"If there be, what I believe there is, in every nation, a style which never becomes obsolete, a certain mode of phraseology so consonant and congenial to the analogy and principles of its respective language, as to remain settled and unaltered; this style is probably to be sought in the common intercourse of life, among those who speak only to be understood, without ambition of elegance. The polite are always catching modish innovations, and the learned depart from established forms of speech, in hope of finding or making better; those who wish for distinction forsake the vulgar, when the vulgar is right; but there is a conversation above grossness and below refinement, where propriety resides, and where this poet seems to have gathered his comick dialogue. He is, therefore, more agreeable to the ears of the present age than any other author equally remote, and among his other excellencies deserves to be studied as one of the original masters of our language."

It should also be remembered that in one respect, at least, Johnson's effort to discover the moral as well as the other qualities of Shakespeare carried him a definite step beyond his contemporaries; he saw, as most of them did not, that one must always contemplate the whole of a play rather than its constituent parts. In so far as his predecessors had attempted analytical appreciations, they had tended to discuss "the beauties of Shakespeare"—i.e., isolated poetic passages—or, at most, to analyze individual characters in the plays. If Johnson had really been as much merely a moralist in his attitude toward literature as he is sometimes said to have been, he would have followed in this tradition and added the weight of his influence to those who delight in selecting copybook maxims or proving Shakespeare's greatness by the number of such sayings as "Unto thine own self be true" and "O that men should put an enemy in their mouths" which he has to his credit. But Johnson does nothing of the sort. "Parts," he wrote, "are not to be examined till the whole has been surveyed; there is a kind of intellectual remoteness necessary for the comprehension of any great work in its full design and in its true proportions; a close approach shows the smaller niceties, but the beauty of the whole is discerned no longer." He may have had little conception of what later and more esoteric critics mean by the "unity of Shakespeare," but if so, he at least made a step forward by recognizing that this unity is of the first importance. "His real power is not shown in the splendour of particular passages, but by the progress of the fable, and the tenour of his dialogue; and he that tries to recommend him by select quotations, will succeed like the pedant in Hierocles, who, when he offered his house to sale, carried a brick in his pocket as a specimen." [29] It would, then, seem reasonable to say that Johnson the moralist seldom gets seriously in the way of Johnson the aesthetic critic of Shakespeare and that, at the cost of a certain amount of inconsistency, he treats what he proclaims a major deficiency as though it were, in reality, a very minor one.

4. *There are, perhaps, aspects of Shakespeare's genius which Johnson does not adequately appreciate.* One cannot dispose quite so easily or so completely of this last major objection commonly raised to Johnson's criticism—the objection that he was deficient in the understanding of a certain kind of imagination which is one of Shakespeare's chief glories.

He does not by any means fail to recognize its existence and he does not by any means fail to pay it his tribute. But one must begin by granting that it was not the first thing he saw nor the thing which he considered of the first importance. To him Shakespeare is, first of all, the poet who describes "nature," and by this he meant, as has already been pointed out, the world which is known to human experience and the image of which we recognize because we have known through our senses the thing imitated. He did not mean the world as it might be or the world as it ought to be. Neither did he mean the world in its "essence." He meant, to repeat, the world in which his own common sense believed. To him Shakespeare is great first and chiefly because he "holds the mirror up to nature"; because those wise in the ways of the world recognize the truth of his picture of human behavior, and because those without experience can learn from him the same things experience might have taught them.

Of this emphasis (primary, but not, as we shall see, exclusive) on Shakespeare's truth to fact, one must say precisely what was said of Johnson's concern with moralizing—namely, that it proceeded from both his personal taste and his literary theory. He liked realism—including realism of a much more literal sort than most of Shakespeare. Biography was what he "loved most." The novel found in him an early defender. To know men and manners in intimate detail was one of the principal reasons for reading, as it was one of the principal reasons for talking and for living in London. On the other hand, mythology bored him, and he was comparatively deficient in a sense of wonder—so deficient indeed that an habitual concern with the marvelous seemed to him merely one of the signs of the primitive state of any literature. It is no wonder, then, if he saw first and admired first Shakespeare's knowledge of the world and of human behavior.

There was of course neither in his literary theory nor in that of most of his contemporaries any place for "imagination" as a source of transcendental knowledge. One may no doubt assume that Johnson believed a certain sense of right and wrong innate in man. He certainly makes pronouncements on moral questions which seem to imply as much. But when only the secular is involved, he habitually talked and wrote like a good follower of Hobbes, whose theory of knowledge he seems to accept, not as Hobbesian but merely as self-evident. Again and again and again, both when speaking casually and when writing formally, he assumes that all knowledge (except perhaps that involving moral or religious ideas) comes through the senses. We do not know anything except what we have learned through experience, through vicarious experience, or through logic. Not even poets are "inspired."

"Where nothing has been put in the brain," he said, "nothing can come out of it to any purpose of rational entertainment," and he repeats in the *Preface* the same idea in more philosophical terms: "Nature gives no man knowledge." For him, therefore, no more than for Hobbes can imagination be the actual source of anything. In *The Idler* he had written: "Imagination selects ideas from the treasuries of remembrance, and produces novelty only by varied combinations," and in *Rasselas* he makes Imlac say that he is less unhappy than most in the enforced idleness of the Valley, not because he has a "creative imagination" but because "I have a mind replete with images, which I can vary and combine at pleasure." It is as a result of this same conception of imagination that he says of Shakespeare: "When images are collected by study and experience, [nature] can only assist in combining or applying them."

To romantic critics the most important of all distinctions was that to be made between Fancy and Imagination. At least one aspect of that distinction seems sometimes to have been distinction between merely arbitrary recombinations of the facts of experience and Imagination in the true romantic sense of truth transcendentally acquired without recourse to either experience or logic. But the existence (if it does exist) of this kind of imagination was neither admitted nor even dreamed of by Johnson. To him, as to most seventeenth and eighteenth century critics, the debate was not concerning Imagination versus Fancy but concerning Imagination versus Judgment as the most important endowment of the poet—over, that is to say, the relative importance of Imagination, which recombines the fragments of knowledge retained out of experience by memory, and Judgment, which criticizes the beauty or propriety or usefulness of these recombinations, selecting some and rejecting others.

Johnson implicitly credits Shakespeare with good judgment in general, though many of his small faults evidently show the lack of it. But the processes of his imagination are the processes of all imagination. "Shakespeare, however favored by nature, could impart only what he had learned." And from this it is evident that when Johnson, adopting the familiar distinction between Nature and Art, called Shakespeare (as all previous critics had called him) a poet of Nature, he did not mean as a romantic critic probably would have meant that Shakespeare "looked into his heart and wrote." He meant simply that of the two possible sources of knowledge, experience and learning, Shakespeare got most from the first. Indeed, he says specifically:

"Shakespeare must have looked upon mankind with perspicacity, in the highest degree curious and attentive. Other writers borrow their characters from preceding writers, and diversify them only by the accidental appendages of present manners; the dress is a little varied, but the body is the same. Our authour had both matter and form to provide; for, except the characters of Chaucer, to whom I think he is not much indebted, there were no writers in English, and, perhaps, not many in other modern languages, which showed life in its native colours. . . . Shakespeare, whether life or nature be his subject, shows plainly that he has seen with his own eyes; he gives the image which he receives, not weakened or distorted by the intervention of any other mind; the ignorant feel his representations to be just, and the learned see that they are complete."

It has often been remarked that, though the eighteenth century invented the domestic novel to satisfy a new interest, it never succeeded in finding a satisfactory form for treating the same material on the stage. One may assume that Johnson would have approved a realistic domestic drama, had such a thing existed, and it may sometimes seem that he is praising Shakespeare with especial warmth when he discovers in him a remote approach to the qualities which characterize good domestic drama. "Shakespeare has no heroes; his scenes are occupied only by men, who act and speak as the reader thinks that he should himself have spoken or acted on the same occasion." "The play of Timon," one reads with some astonishment, "is a domestick tragedy, and therefore, strongly fastens on the attention of the reader." Even his answer, already quoted, to Dennis's objection that Shakespeare violates decorum by making a Roman senator play the buffoon, is couched in terms which might well serve a champion of purely realistic drama. "His story requires Romans or kings, but he thinks only on men." And this insistence on the virtue inherent in thinking of men as men rather than as kings or heroes suggests domestic drama rather than high tragedy.[30]

Yet obviously Johnson did not think that Shakespeare's manner was the manner of the eighteenth-century novelist, and he knew that his realism was not the realism of that kind. It will be interesting, therefore, to observe how Johnson defined the difference, to count the steps by which he broadened his conception of what a true representation of Nature might include and, finally, to ask how much of Shakespeare nevertheless continued to remain outside his comprehension.

To begin with, Johnson makes it perfectly clear that to hold a mirror up to nature does not mean to present a perfectly literal reflection of it. Part of Shakespeare's greatness is dependent upon the fact that he does not do that. But the reasons which justify Shakespeare's method have, in Johnson's understanding, nothing to do with "imagination" in any transcendental meaning of the word. They are, on the contrary, simple commonsense reasons. In the paragraph which begins with the phrase about "a faithful mirror" Johnson immediately goes on: "His characters are not modified by the customs of particular places, unpracticed by the rest of the world; by peculiarities of studies or professions, which can operate but upon small numbers; or by the accidents of transient fashions or temporary opinions; they are the genuine progeny of common humanity, such as the world will always supply, and observation will always find. His persons act and speak by the influence of those general passions and principles by which all minds are agitated, and the whole system of life is continued in motion."

Literary "imitations" must, in other words, be modified by the omission of the merely accidental characteristics of the thing imitated, just as the imitator in plastic forms tends to present his personages either nude or in conventionalized garments. But the reason for this practice is not, to Johnson as it might be to certain later critics, esoterically aesthetic. It is simply that to draw attention to what changes from place to place and from time to time tends to distract attention from the permanent and to alienate us from personages who can be interesting only in so far as they are perceived to be identical with ourselves. This is the simplest, as it is also probably the most important, meaning of Johnson's often discussed pronouncements: "Nothing can please many, and please long, but just representations of general nature" and "In the writings of other poets a character is too often an individual; in those of Shakespeare it is commonly a species."

Johnson and his contemporaries may sometimes have been led astray, as critics of all periods sometimes are, by making inadmissible applications of principles sound enough in themselves. Imlac, when he was describing to Rasselas the ideal poet, went so far as to declare: "The business of a poet is to examine, not the individual, but the species; to remark general properties and large appearances; he does not number the streaks of the tulip, or describe the different shades in the verdure of the forest. He is to exhibit, in his portraits of nature, such prominent and striking features, as recall the original to every mind; and must neglect the minuter discriminations, which one may have remarked, and another have neglected, for those characteristics which are alike obvious to vigilance and carelessness."

It is, surely, going rather far to deny the poet the right to note more than carelessness may have observed, and the whole passage is likely to be read with some amusement when one remembers how dead the vast bulk of eighteenth-century descriptive poetry is; how much more alive is that which began to be produced, shortly after Johnson wrote, by poets who felt that "the different shades in the verdure of the forest" were properly the concern of the poet. The very same year that *Rasselas* was published, a child was born who would soon be writing a poem *To a Mountain Daisy;* and before he had written it, another child destined to write another poem, *To the Lesser Celandine,* had also come into the world. Between them they seem to have blown up the theory that poetry can deal only with the general as completely as they seem to have blown up another eighteenth-century theory—the theory, that is to say, that poetry must avoid all that is mean or low. Dr. Grainger (over whom Boswell and Johnson made merry) was said first to have provoked the mirth of his friends by introducing rats into his poem *Sugar Cane,* and then to have saved the dignity of the muse by referring to them in the published version only as "the whisker'd vermin race"; but the poet who did not scruple to write about mountain daisies found it unnecessary to seek out any elegant circumlocution when the occasion arose to speak of a mouse or, even, of a louse.

Johnson himself might go so far astray as to declare once, when Boswell was present: "In the description of night in Macbeth [III, ii,] the beetle and the bat detract from the general idea of darkness,—inspissated gloom." But for all that the question of the general versus the specific in poetry has never really been clearly determined, and for all the successful violations of the rule which Johnson thought established, it still remains true that the individual in art must be something more than merely an individual as surely as the representative of a species must somehow manage to be an individual also. For, as Montaigne once remarked, all men must be different or we could not tell one from the other, and yet all men must be alike or we would not know that they *are* men. In any event, Johnson's theory, besides embodying its element of truth, carried him one step away from any insistence upon literal representation, and hence made him value in Shakespeare some of the very things which a literal insistence upon the "mirror to nature" would render unacceptable.

There still remains in Shakespeare, as in most great poets, much—some would say nearly everything—which makes them great poets; something which even the most generalized image of nature does not obviously include. What of the highest flights of fancy and imagination? what of all the things which seem to be outside anyone's possible experience? what of the world sometimes described as the world of sheer beauty and transcendental truth? That Johnson seems on occasion to recognize its existence has already been stated and will presently be demonstrated. What did he say of it? how important did he consider it? what did he think of its nature? [31]

The most general answer to these last questions no doubt is that Johnson was too little a mystic, too little a romantic, too little interested in the merely marvelous, to value very highly anything of the sort except in so far as it could be shown, or at least felt, to be somehow related to experience. To Boswell he praised Burke's *Essay on the Sublime and Beautiful* and also "Bouhours, who shews all beauty to depend on truth." It was not in his nature to proceed from this to an incantation in the manner of "Beauty is Truth, Truth Beauty." Therefore, anything lacking in truth must be lacking in beauty or, as he wrote in the *Preface:* "The irregular combinations of fanciful invention may delight awhile, by that novelty of which the common satiety of life sends us all in quest; but the pleasures of sudden wonder are soon exhausted, and the mind can only repose on the stability of truth." It is obvious, nevertheless, that Johnson did not think that Shakespeare was always a realistic writer and that he did not admire only the more realistic scenes. Shakespeare's more imaginative flights are not to him always "irregular combinations of fanciful invention." What kind of truth did they seem to him to contain?

The question is not easy to answer because Johnson himself could not answer his part of it. It is plain enough from the *General Observations* which he wrote for each particular play that his most unreserved and enthusiastic admiration was for those—*Othello, Hamlet* and *Lear* especially—where the departures from realism can be accounted for either as generalized representation or as rationally explicable devices for conveying truths by means of symbols as readily interpretable as those of an allegory. It is equally plain from the same series of *Observations* that the fanciful romantic comedy of manners makes relatively little appeal to him. Of *King Lear* he can say: "So powerful is the current of the poet's imagination, that the mind, which once ventures within it, is hurried irresistibly along," and of *Othello* that it contains "such proofs of Shakespeare's skill in human nature, as, I suppose, it is vain to seek in any modern writer." But *The Merchant of Venice* is pronounced improbable; *The Winter's Tale,* full of absurdities; and *Twelfth Night,* though elegant, easy and humorous, is, he tells us, so poorly contrived, in the main plot, that it "wants credibility" and fails to produce the proper instruction required in drama, as it exhibits no just picture of life." Not all present-day critics would find these strictures as shocking as the romantic critics did, or indeed would fail to agree that they are just—at least as far as they go. But this leaves still untouched a more important question: To what extent, if at all, does Johnson meet the test imposed when he is faced with the marvelous rather than the fanciful? What does he make of the tremendous supernaturalism of *Macbeth,* the exquisite delicacy of *A Midsummer Night's Dream,* and the mysteriously exalted harmonies which some, at least, find supremely presented in *The Tempest?* [32]

Johnson's first reaction to all such things was certainly the condescension of the enlightened rationalist. *Macbeth* was the first of the plays upon which he made any extended comment, for it was the subject of those *Miscellaneous Observations* which he published in 1745 when he made the first and abortive proposal for an edition of Shakespeare. Here the point of view adopted is almost exclusively that of the historical scholar bent on accounting for absurdities. The first and last paragraphs of his long introductory note read:

"In order to make a true estimate of the abilities and merit of a writer, it is always necessary to examine the genius of his age, and the opinions of his contemporaries. A poet, who should

TEA AT THE JOURNALISTS HOUSE
IN ST. JAMES COURT

*Designed by Samuel Collings and etched
by Thomas Rowlandson*

"SETTING OUT FROM EDINBURGH"

*Designed by Samuel Collings and etched
by Thomas Rowlandson*

now make the whole action of his tragedy depend upon enchantment, and produce the chief events by the assistance of supernatural agents, would be censured as transgressing the bounds of probability; he would be banished from the theatre to the nursery, and condemned to write fairy tales instead of tragedies; but a survey of the notions, that prevailed at the time when this play was written, will prove, that Shakespeare was in no danger of such censures, since he only turned the system that was then universally admitted to his advantage, and was far from overburdening the credulity of his audience. . . .

"Upon this general infatuation Shakespeare might be easily allowed to found a play, especially since he has followed with great exactness such histories as were then thought true; nor can it be doubted that the scenes of enchantment, however they may now be ridiculed, were both by himself and his audience thought awful and affecting."[33]

The year before the *Miscellaneous Observations* appeared, Johnson wrote *An Essay on the Origin and Importance of Small Tracts and Fugitive Pieces* in connection with the Harleian Miscellany. The two compositions are related by the fact that cach shows how clearly Johnson sensed the importance that was going to be attached to a certain kind of historical study. None of his contemporaries can have had a clearer conception of the kind of light about to be thrown on the older literature by antiquarian research. But it must also be admitted that at the same time Johnson fell into an attitude which still keeps some historical students of literature between the horns of a dilemma. When he explains *Macbeth* by reference to exploded beliefs, he is not merely explaining, he is also explaining away, a work of art which it is worth while to explain only if one assumes that it cannot be explained away. If a modern poet who wrote such a play as *Macbeth* would be banished from the theater to the nursery, then why, since we have so much improved in rationality, should the play not be banished to the nursery now? If it is still worth keeping, it must be either because, at the very least, it is capable of persuading us to some temporary suspension of disbelief or because—and this, of course, would make it more valuable—the use of fictions which we no longer believe in enabled the poet to present something in which we still do believe. Yet in the *Miscellaneous Observations* Johnson can hardly be said to have raised either of these possibilities.

By the time he came finally to compose the notes for his edition of Shakespeare, Johnson seems to have at least retreated somewhat from his original position, and there is certainly no suggestion that he did actually think *Macbeth* fit only for the nursery. The *General Observations* prefixed is much shorter than many of the others and it begins thus: "This play is deservedly celebrated for the propriety of its fictions, and solemnity, grandeur, and variety of its action." To say that is not to illuminate much. But it is to recognize the existence—perhaps fully to recognize the existence—of the qualities which later critics have tried to describe more fully and to analyze minutely.

It can hardly be said that Johnson got much further than this or much further than certain of his predecessors. The question of the meaning of Shakespeare's use of the marvelous and the supernatural was a more or less traditional one, though perhaps more often discussed in connection with the "fairy plays" than in connection with *Macbeth,* and what Johnson does have to say is pretty closely in line with what others had said. Not much less than a hundred years before, Dryden had cited Caliban as a remarkable instance of Shakespeare's power because, though Caliban is a person who was not in "Nature" and was the assumed offspring of an incubus and a witch, nevertheless "the poet has most judiciously furnished him with a language, a person, and a character, which will suit him, both by father's and mother's side." Addison, apparently writing with Dryden in mind, declared: "It shows a greater genius in Shakespeare to have drawn his Caliban, than his Hotspur or Julius Caesar; the one was to be supplied out of his own Imagination, whereas the other might have been formed upon Tradition, History, and Observation." In one of his own contemporaries—namely, Joseph Warton—Johnson might have read an account in which Caliban is described as "the creature of his [Shakespeare's] own imagination, in the formation of which he could derive no assistance from observation or experience," and he may have had any or all of these passages in mind when he himself wrote in the

Preface: "Shakespeare approximates the remote, and familiarizes the wonderful; the event which he represents will not happen, but, if it were possible, its effects would, probably, be such as he has assigned; and it may be said that he has not only shown human nature as it acts in real exigencies, but as it would be found in trials, to which it cannot be exposed." Moreover, Johnson had previously said approximately the same thing, though he had said it more enthusiastically, in the *Prologue* to the opening of Drury Lane:

> Each change of many-colour'd life he drew,
> Exhausted worlds, and then imagin'd new:
> Existence saw him spurn her bounded reign,
> And panting Time toil'd after him in vain.[34]

Faced with the marvelous in Shakespeare, Johnson the realist and rationalist tended, then, to alternate between two explanations and between two attitudes. On the one hand, Shakespeare deals in wonders because his contemporaries had a childish love of such wonders and because they believed in the reality of many things now known to be mere fancies. On the other hand, Shakespeare invented things which might be but are not, thus showing how human nature would behave in circumstances different from those which it will ever encounter. Having exhausted the realm of actuality, Shakespeare imagines new realms in which the possible (if Johnson had been enough a Cartesian, he might have said "the self-consistent") is represented as existent and so linked with portions of the actual that through these links we make imaginative contact and can perceive how we would act if we actually lived within the hypothetical realm.

Whether or not it is possible to understand any more fully the meaning of this aspect of the creative imagination will probably remain a matter on which opinions differ. Romantic critics certainly thought they had said more significant things. Johnson did not; and if what he did say is inadequate, then he is, just to that extent, an inadequate critic of Shakespeare. He certainly did not reject the portions of Shakespeare's work in which this aspect is conspicuous. To introduce his notes on *The Tempest,* he chose a passage from Warburton which begins: "These two first Plays, the *Tempest* and the *Midsummer-night's Dream,* are the noblest Efforts of that sublime and amazing Imagination, peculiar to *Shakespeare,* which soars above the Bounds of Nature without forsaking Sense: or, more properly, carries Nature along with him beyond her established Limits." Perhaps the fact that he quoted this passage is no more significant than the fact that he did *quote* it rather than attempt to say something of the same sort in his own words. If so, then it may be equally significant that when he has almost reached the end of his *Preface* and come to the point where the final tribute has to be paid, he again chooses to quote—this time from Dryden, who had elsewhere expressed greater admiration for "the enthusiastic part of poetry" than Johnson himself habitually felt—and that he chooses for the purpose to begin the quotation on the phrase: "Shakespeare was the man, who, of all modern and, perhaps, ancient poets, had the largest and most comprehensive soul." Whatever truth may be in the charge that Johnson could appreciate Shakespeare but could not as a critic account for him is chiefly to be found in connection with his attitude toward those portions of Shakespeare's work which are the most tenuously connected with the common experience of mankind.

Johnson was following the line of his own interests as well as an established literary tradition when he devoted a considerable portion of his more analytical notes to a discussion of various of Shakespeare's characters.

"But Falstaff, unimitated, unimitable Falstaff, how shall I describe thee! thou compound of sense and vice; of sense which may be admired, but not esteemed; of vice which may be despised, but hardly detested. Falstaff is a character loaded with faults, and with those faults which naturally produce contempt. . . . Yet the man thus corrupt, thus despicable, makes himself necessary to the prince that despises him, by the most pleasing of all qualities, perpetual gaiety, by an unfailing power of exciting laughter, which is the more freely indulged, as his wit is not of the splendid or ambitious kind, but consists in easy scapes and sallies of levity, which make sport, but raise no envy. It must be observed, that he is stained with no enormous or sanguinary crimes, so that his licentiousness is not so offensive but that it may be borne for his mirth.

"The moral to be drawn from this representation is, that no man is more dangerous than he that, with a will to corrupt, hath the power to please; and that neither wit nor honesty ought to think themselves safe with such a companion, when they see Henry seduced by Falstaff."

But Johnson was capable of eloquent and illuminating analyses of poetic excellencies of another kind, though when he can be clearly rational he is usually at his best, as in the well-known passage originally published as part of the *Miscellaneous Observations,* and comparing the speech in *Macbeth* which begins:

> Now o'er half the world
> Nature seems dead, and wicked dreams abuse
> The curtain'd sleep; now witchcraft celebrates
> Pale Hecate's offerings . . .

with that in Dryden's *The Indian Emperor; or The Conquest of Mexico,* which runs:

> All things are hush'd as Nature's self lay dead,
> The mountains seem to nod their drowsy head;
> The little birds in dreams their songs repeat,
> And sleeping flowers beneath the night dews sweat.

Says Johnson: "Night is described by two great poets, but one describes a night of quiet, the other of perturbation. In the night of Dryden, all the disturbers of the world are laid to sleep; in that of Shakespeare, nothing but sorcery, lust, and murder, is awake. He that reads Dryden, finds himself lulled with serenity, and disposed to solitude and contemplation. He that peruses Shakespeare, looks round alarmed, and starts to find himself alone." [35]

Boswell once told Johnson that Adam Smith, lecturing upon composition at the College of Glasgow, had enlarged upon the subject of the superiority in English of rhymed over blank verse. "Sir," replied Johnson, "I was once in company with Smith, and we did not take to each other; but had I known that he loved rhyme as much as you tell me he does, I should have HUGGED him." Smith's rationalism was of a sort so much more inclusive than Johnson's that one may readily assume that he took to Johnson as little as Johnson took to him, but to the distinguished author of *The Wealth of Nations* is attributed one of the finest compliments to Johnson's *Preface*. "The most *manly* piece of criticism," he is said to have called it, "that was ever published in any country."

The phrase is significant because it suggests something more than merely the sturdiness, the vigor and the virility which are always so strikingly present in Johnson's writing. It suggests also something very important in his whole attitude toward Shakespeare and in his approach to the task he had set himself —namely, his manly self-respect even when brought face to face with that poet who had the largest and most comprehensive soul. Readers of Boswell are likely to remember the passages in which he describes Johnson's behavior when he suddenly found himself in the presence of the King in the royal library; and small as George III may seem by comparison with Shakespeare, there is some parallel between the two occasions and the respectful but at the same time self-respecting bearing which Johnson maintained on both. He maintains his right to pass judgment even upon Shakespeare, not because he thinks himself Shakespeare's equal as a poet any more than he thought himself equal in rank to George III. But he did think he had a right to respect his own judgment as well as a duty to grant that it might be wrong; he thought that, as a citizen of the world of letters, he might hold his head high before Shakespeare just as, being a British subject, he might hold it high even in converse with the King.

Coleridge held the typically romantic opinion that a "reverential tone" was the test of Shakespearean criticism. Those who hold with that will certainly think Johnson a bad critic, for his tone is certainly less reverential than it is "manly." But an attitude such as his has one great advantage. It leads a critic to expose freely whatever limitations we need take into consideration when reading him, and it makes it unnecessary for him to obscure his own writing with grandiose tributes to ineffable qualities even when he is discovering them only in order to demonstrate how "reverential" he can be. It is said that after a lecture by a woman critic of the present day, one of her intimates was heard to breathe the comment: "Tonight —— has said things which it will take *even her* months to understand." One is sometimes tempted to say the same of Coleridge. One would never say it of Johnson.

His admiration, like that of an illustrious predecessor whose name is pronounced the same, did stop this side of idolatry, but he paid Shakespeare compliments as high as a human being can deserve. Whether any critic should do more remains, Coleridge notwithstanding, at least an open question. Whatever the uses of incense may be, no one ever maintained that through its enveloping clouds we can see clearly the outlines of the image before which it is burned, and, as has just been suggested, it tends often to obscure the outlines of the worshiper as well. Johnson may not have seen all of the hero (Shakespeare was to him a hero, not a god) whom he was attempting to contemplate. But what he saw he saw clearly, and in describing that much, he at the same time also revealed to us very clearly his own mind.

In concluding, three facts concerning the general tendency of his criticism may be reiterated: (1) Johnson contributed powerfully to the process, already pretty far advanced when he wrote, through which Shakespeare was becoming established as a genuine classic and unquestionably the first of modern poets. (2) Appealing always "from criticism to nature," his discussion of the traditional objections of pseudoclassic criticism is generally for the purpose either of rejecting its premises or of minimizing the importance of the defects which it exposes. (3) His emphasis is always upon the primary virtues of fiction—animation, variety, vividness, and the power to convince—rather than upon refinements and subtleties in any sense esoteric—so far at least as their effect is concerned. On this last point, one final remark may be made.

"Perhaps," Johnson wrote, "it would not be easy to find any author, except Homer, who invented so much as Shakespeare, who so much advanced the studies which he cultivated, or effused so much novelty upon his age or country." Present-day scholars are of course aware that there is less superficial novelty in Shakespeare than Johnson supposed. Present-day critics would no doubt be inclined to deny the great importance attributed to invention in, what would appear to them, its superficial aspects. But the comparison with Homer is important. Johnson was obviously not merely choosing the poet universally admitted to be greatest. He meant something definite, and what he meant was that Shakespeare, like Homer, exhibited the primary virtues.

It was these, rather than any of the more esoteric ones, real or imaginary, which were responsible for keeping Shakespeare alive in the popular mind. To the people he was the teller of incomparable tales, alive with incomparable characters, and Johnson's Shakespeare is, first of all, the people's Shakespeare rather than either the Shakespeare of learned critics or the Shakespeare of the aesthete. And in defense of his attitude, one may recur to a fact often pointed out—the fact, namely, that Shakespeare tended to lose popularity in the widest sense of the term as he became more and more the possession of critics who laid more and more stress upon qualities which the uninstructed could hardly be expected either to perceive or to value.

If Prospero's farewell to his art really is also, as the intriguing fancy makes it, Shakespeare's own farewell to his own art, then it is worth remembering that to rattle thunder, open graves, and call forth the mutinous winds is the "rough magic" of the storyteller—not the work of the philosopher or even of the poet devoted to effects merely exquisite. Something similar may also be said of the praise which makes holding the mirror up to nature an item of first importance. Many would call it aesthetically naïve. Perhaps it is. But it is no more so than Shakespeare himself was, since the phrase is, after all, Shakespeare's own. No doubt it is ordinarily the business of a critic to understand a creative artist better in certain respects than the creative artist understands himself. But what may ordinarily be expected is more than we have any right to expect of the critic of Shakespeare. If Johnson could be said to understand him as well as Shakespeare understood himself, that would indeed be sufficient.[36]

CHAPTER X

Folding His Legs

IN THE spring of 1766, the year following that in which the *Shakespeare* was published, Boswell and Goldsmith engaged Johnson in a particularly revealing conversation. They had called at his home in the hope of taking the Doctor (as we now have a right to call him) for an evening at the Mitre, but they found him indisposed. Accordingly they sent for a bottle of port, which the guests consumed while the host held forth.

Goldsmith, soon to produce his first comedy, complained that Johnson gave himself "no more concern about a new play" than if he had never written one, and from that the conversation proceeded to the question of how the Great Moralist should employ his talents. "Sir," said Goldsmith, "we have a claim upon you." But Johnson—who habitually limited all men's obligations as positively as he insisted upon their fulfillment within the limitations—would by no means admit this claim.

"No, Sir, I am not obliged to do any more. No man is obliged to do as much as he can do. A man is to have part of his life to himself. If a soldier has fought a good many campaigns, he is not to be blamed if he retires to ease and tranquillity. A physician, who has practised long in a great city, may be excused if he retires to a small town, and takes less practice. Now, Sir, the good I can do by my conversation bears the same proportion to the good I can do by my writings, that the practice of a physician, retired to a small town, does to his practice in a great city. Bos-

WELL. But I wonder, Sir, that you have not more pleasure in writing than in not writing. JOHNSON. Sir, you *may* wonder."

Actually, of course, Johnson was to publish two more book-length works—*Journey to the Western Islands* and *The Lives of the Poets*—of which the latter is certainly one of his major achievements and today the most often read of all his works. Indeed, it was less than a year later that George III, having been brought in at his own request to see Johnson, who was reading in the royal library, "expressed a desire to have the literary biography of this country ably executed" and that Johnson "signified his readiness to comply with His Majesty's wishes." But there is no evidence that this was really the beginning of *The Lives of the Poets* or that Johnson's acquiescence at the time was more than politeness. Seven years, consumed chiefly in talk, were to pass between the conversation with Goldsmith on the subject of Johnson's duty and the beginning of the *Journey to the Western Islands;* eleven years, between that conversation and even the engagement to write the *Lives*. Obviously then, Johnson meant what he said about having part of his life to himself and felt that what he had already done relieved him of his moral obligation almost as completely as the pension had relieved him of financial pressure.

Neither the *Journey* nor the few political pamphlets, prefaces and the like that he wrote during the eleven years between finishing *Shakespeare* and contracting for the *Lives* can have occupied more than a very small proportion of his time. As his remarks about the "good he could do by his conversation" make clear, he had by now adopted talk as a vocation as well as an amusement and he tended to reject with increasing vehemence the suggestion that it was his duty to write. "He disliked," as Boswell puts it, "being dunned," and when after Johnson had been at least relatively idle for more than ten years Boswell incautiously expressed the opinion that there was "really a claim upon him" to write something in direct defense of Church and State, he was obviously displeased.

How much and how well Johnson talked we can estimate from Boswell's record and the supplements afforded by the less extensive and less important records of others who heard him. But it ought to be remembered that the record affords, after all, no more than a sampling. In popular speech "a boswell" means someone who is in constant attendance upon his hero—which the original Boswell most certainly was not. His home was Scotland, not London; and his father, as we learn from Boswell's journals, disapproved of jaunts to London. Boswell promised him not to go there without permission, and later "had a palpitation at my heart when I thought of mentioning . . . my wish to go to London this vacation." During the something more than twenty years which elapsed between the first meeting in Tom Davies's parlor and Johnson's death, Boswell was, it has been calculated, within reach of his friend for two years and some weeks even out of what is, roughly, the last quarter of Johnson's life. They did not, of course, meet on anything like every day of the relatively short periods during which they might have met, and Boswell often, as he frankly confesses, failed to make a record of the conversation on the days when they did. What we have, then, is not a remarkably complete record of Johnson's sayings, or even—as we unconsciously tend to assume when reading the *Life*—a selection of the best specimens of his talk. We have only a sampling, and something pretty close to a random sampling at that.

Assiduous as Boswell was when he *was* assiduous, he had, as the journals show, so many other things to write about and so many other amusements to attend to that he does not give us nearly all he might have given if he had actually devoted himself to Johnson, even during his visits to London, as completely as he is popularly supposed to have done. What Mrs. Thrale, Fanny Burney, and less important anecdotists tell us furnishes a valuable supplement which indicates that Johnson talked as well (though in a manner sometimes slightly different) to others as he did to Boswell; yet these reports are far less full than Boswell's and must contain a far less complete account of what the compilers had heard. Perhaps we have as much of Johnson's conversation as we need, even of his, but it should be remembered that he talked many volumes more. And when one considers how large a part chance played in determining what portion of all this talk was recorded, it seems not unreasonable to assume that much of what is lost was quite as good as what has been preserved. Indeed, Boswell, in the preface to the second edition of his work, himself makes precisely this point. "We cannot, indeed, too much or too often admire his wonderful powers of mind, when we consider that the principal store of wit and wisdom which this Work contains, was not a particular selection from his general conversation, but was merely his occasional talk at such times as I had the good fortune to be in his company; and, without doubt, if his discourse at other periods had been collected with the same attention, the whole tenor of what he uttered would have been found equally excellent." [1]

To say that conversation of the sort which Johnson and his friends delighted in no longer exists is to repeat a platitude as familiar as (and perhaps somewhat less easily defensible than) the statement that no one writes letters any more. Talk that is no less talk for its own sake still does go on, sometimes brilliantly; and letters—even long formal letters—still are written. But eighteenth century conversation did have traditions not identical with ours, and Johnson, unique though he was, does undoubtedly maintain a certain relation to them. Good talkers may have been no more appreciated then than they are today, but just as letter writing was more likely then than now to be regarded as one of the recognized forms of literary expression, so, to a somewhat lesser degree, was conversation.

The most obvious and most often repeated explanation of the fact is, of course, that in that day men who had a certain amount of leisure at their disposal moved about less, did not play golf, or tennis, or badminton, had access to fewer commercialized entertainments, and spent far less time in the company of members of the opposite sex—with whom, to be sure, they talked, played cards, and sometimes danced but with whom they did not do most of the fifty things which owe their present-day popularity to the fact that they enable young (and fairly young) people to be together with a minimum of formal communication. Yet even in Johnson's day there were innumerable country gentlemen of Squire Western's type who were as incapable of conversation as any smart sportsman of today, and there were innumerable men about London who spent all their evenings as

Boswell spent many of his—namely, in that "conviviality" which meant little more than getting so completely drunk that no one was more than dimly aware of what anyone else either said or did. It would, in other words, be extremely difficult to demonstrate that in the eighteenth century there were or were not more men in proportion to the total population who talked and enjoyed talk than there are at the present moment. Yet the fact remains that the members of at least certain groups did engage in conversation of a somewhat different kind from that which flourishes today, and the obvious questions to be asked are: "What was this conversation like?" and "Why did that particular sort of talk flourish vigorously at that particular time?"

Certainly Johnson's discourse was not completely typical in either its method or its substance. He would not have been so celebrated or, above all, so often spoken of as some sort of eccentric if it had been. His conversation was certainly more formal, more dogmatic, and more weighty than conversation usually was—even though Boswell's account tends to make it seem less often playful than do the accounts of Mrs. Thrale and Fanny Burney. Not all those who might have been members of his circle cared to be, or found his discourse admirable. But the very fact that a half-dozen men of diverse talents and careers, whom we recognize as among the most intelligent, most talented, and most successful of his day, did regard him with enthusiastic devotion probably indicates something more than merely what is obvious to all who can read—namely, that he was a remarkable man. It probably indicates also that his uniqueness was not absolute, that his particular kind of talk exhibited, to perhaps an unusual degree, certain characteristics in the direction of which the conversation of his age and group tended.

One of the most evident and most general of these characteristics is conscious virtuosity without the triviality which so often accompanies conversation deliberately practiced as an art. Johnson and his companions sat down for a talk as deliberately as another group would sit down to play chamber music or cards. Every member of the group tried to do well, tried within the limits of his capacity to shine. Good things were applauded, the abilities of the players were estimated, and certain sessions were remembered as particularly brilliant. Yet no one was encouraged merely to scintillate. Johnson detested puns, and neither he nor his friends would have tolerated anyone who threw the conversation off the track by irrelevant sallies or any form of exhibitionistic cleverness. Certain traditions were pretty scrupulously observed, and they determined a form of conversation as far removed from the wit combats of the literary men about town whose wisecracks are reported in the gossip columns of today as it is from the earnest debates of those gatherings in which no topic of less than global significance is ever discussed, and talk for talk's sake would be the least admissible of aims.

Johnson and Co. was not composed of men who strove to be "smart" in any of the several meanings of the term; not one of them had what we call "sophistication" as his ideal. But neither was it by any means a little group of serious thinkers. No subject was too slight, none too weighty. The talk might leap from topic to topic and from grave to gay. But it was always *about* something, and though nowhere has the epigram ever been more appreciated, the kind of epigram most admired was the kind which owes its distinction to the fact that it says something more quickly, more adroitly, and more conclusively than it has ever been said before, not the kind which is sheer empty virtuosity or which aims, first of all, at making paradox or perversity appear unanswerable. Indeed, some of the best of Johnson's own witticisms are so completely of the first kind that to certain tastes they do not seem witticisms at all, while even those which are happiest and cleverest seldom fail to have substance. "He who makes a *beast* of himself, gets rid of the pain of being a *man*" is a comment on drunkenness too penetrating to be funny. His reply to the argument "in vino veritas" is ludicrous without ceasing to be at the same time equally powerful: "I would not keep company with a fellow, who lyes as long as he is sober."

Not everyone who heard Johnson's conversation enjoyed it. Anna Seward for one did not, and neither, we may guess, did Gibbon—who was a member of The Club though not, apparently, a very talkative one. But the testimony of various persons in Johnson's intimate circle, as well as that of various others who knew him less well, is overwhelmingly sufficient to prove that many men and many women of many different temperaments rated it almost as highly as Boswell himself did. Richard Cumberland, the playwright, describes him thus:

"I verily think he was unrivalled both in the brilliancy of his wit, the flow of his humour, and the energy of his language. Anecdotes of time past, scenes of his own life, and characters of humourists, enthusiasts, cracked-brained projectors and a variety of strange beings, that he had chanced upon, when detailed by him at length, and garnished with those episodical remarks, sometimes comic, sometimes grave, which he would throw in with infinite fertility of fancy, were a treat, which though not always to be purchased by five and twenty cups of tea I have often had the happiness to enjoy for less than half the number. He was easily led into topics; it was not easy to turn him from them; but who would wish it?"

It was to Edmund Burke that Johnson paid a famous compliment when he said: "That fellow calls forth all my powers. Were I to see Burke now, it would kill me." And yet Burke could himself say of Johnson, when Bennet Langton once wished that Burke had taken a larger part in a certain conversation: "It is enough for me to have rung the bell to him," and it was remarked by Gibbon that even Fox who "could not be afraid of Dr. Johnson" nevertheless "certainly was shy of saying any thing in Dr. Johnson's presence." William Hogarth was not a man who praised readily. It will be remembered that he confessed that when he first laid eyes on Johnson, standing by a window in Samuel Richardson's drawing room, he thought Johnson was an idiot whose relations had put him under the care of the good Mr. Richardson. But Hogarth was later to say of this seeming idiot that his "conversation was to the talk of other men, like Titian's painting compared to Hudson's."

It is somewhat surprising to learn, as from more than one witness we do, that Johnson was sometimes silent in company for considerable periods. Even Boswell sometimes found him unwilling to talk. Mrs. Thrale describes him as "ever musing till he was called out to converse, and conversing till the fatigue of his friends, or the promptitude of his own temper to take offence, consigned him back again to silent meditation"; and in another place she says: "No one was . . . less willing to begin any discourse than himself: his friend Mr. Thomas Tyers said, he was like the ghosts, who never speak till they are spoken to: and he liked the expression so well, that he often repeated it." Fanny Burney records how, at a party in her father's house, Johnson took a book "and began, without further ceremony, to read to himself, all the time standing at a distance from the company." Miss Reynolds adds her testimony thus: "He would rarely, if ever, begin any subject himself, but would sit silent till something was particularly addressed to him." Yet it certainly must be assumed that he usually was spoken to or drawn out and it must not be supposed that it was only to the great or only to his intimates that he talked.

Dr. Maxwell, who was a friend of Johnson's from the time when the *Dictionary* was being compiled to the end of Johnson's life, wrote:

" 'His general mode of life, during my acquaintance, seemed to be pretty uniform. About twelve o'clock I commonly visited him, and frequently found him in bed, or declaiming over his tea, which he drank very plentifully. He generally had a levee of morning visitors, chiefly men of letters; Hawkesworth, Goldsmith, Murphy, Langton, Steevens, Beauclerk, &c. &c. and sometimes learned ladies; particularly I remember a French lady of wit and fashion doing him the honour of a visit. He seemed to me to be considered as a kind of publick oracle, whom every body thought they had a right to visit and consult; and doubtless they were well rewarded. I never could discover how he found time for his compositions. He declaimed all the morning, then went to dinner at a tavern, where he commonly staid late, and then drank his tea at some friend's house, over which he loitered a great while, but seldom took supper. I fancy he must have read and wrote chiefly in the night, for I can scarcely recollect that he ever refused going with me to a tavern, and he often went to Ranelagh, which he deemed a place of innocent recreation.' "[2]

Many of those who consulted him did so on odd questions indeed. Fanny Burney, for instance, records that a clergyman wrote Johnson a letter from the Orkneys, which cost the doctor one and sixpence postage, to say that the writer "labours under a most peculiar misfortune, for which he can give no account; and which is,—that, though he very often writes letters to his friends and others, he never gets any answers; he entreats, therefore, that Dr. Johnson will take this into consideration, and explain to him to what so strange a thing may be attributed." Unfortunately Johnson's reply does not appear to have survived, but we are given by Mrs. Thrale a full account of his dealings with two other strange applicants for advice.

One of them, a clerk to "a very eminent trader," came to beg relief from certain scruples of conscience which were the result of the fact that he had been often tempted to take from his employer paper and packthread enough for his own use and had, indeed, done so so often "that he could recollect no time when ever he had bought any for himself." Johnson suggested the probability that the master would not seriously object and that it was to him that confession should be made. "Oh, Sir!" replied the visitor, "my master bid me have as much as I pleased, and was half angry when I talked to him about it." Johnson, who on more than one occasion expressed his impatience with mere scruples of conscience less fantastic than this, then inquired of his visitor at what hour he left the countinghouse and at what hour he went to bed. When he had learned the answer to these questions he proceeded: "Then I have at least learned thus much by my new acquaintance;—that five hours of the four-and-twenty unemployed are enough for a man to go mad in; so I would advise you, Sir, to study algebra, if you are not an adept already in it: your head would get less *muddy*, and you will leave off tormenting your neighbours about paper and packthread, while we all live together in a world that is bursting with sin and sorrow."

The tale of another strange visitor had best be told entirely in Mrs. Thrale's own words, though it is evident from an earlier record that she improved the tale a bit.

"Another strange thing he told me once which there was no danger of forgetting: how a young gentleman called on him one morning, and told him that his father having, just before his death, dropped suddenly into the enjoyment of an ample fortune, he, the son, was willing to qualify himself for genteel society by adding some literature to his other endowments, and wished to be put in an easy way of obtaining it. Johnson recommended the university: 'for you read Latin, Sir, with *facility.*' I read it a little to be sure, Sir. 'But do you read it *with facility,* I say?' Upon my word, Sir, I do not very well know, but I rather believe not. Mr. Johnson now began to recommend other branches of science, when he found languages at such an immeasurable distance, and advising him to study natural history, there arose some talk about animals, and their divisions into oviparous and viviparous; And the cat here, Sir, said the youth who wished for instruction, pray in which class is she? Our doctor's patience and desire of doing good began now to give way to the natural roughness of his temper. 'You would do well (said he) to look for some person to be always about you, Sir, who is capable of explaining such matters, and not come to us (there were some literary friends present as I recollect) to know whether the cat lays eggs or not: get a discreet man to keep you company, there are so many who would be glad of your table and fifty pounds a year.' The young gentleman retired, and in less than a week informed his friends that he had fixed on a preceptor to whom no objections could be made." [3]

It has already been remarked that some, though apparently not most, of those outside both inner and outer Johnsonian circles were repelled rather than attracted when they happened to come in contact with the great talker. Even within the group of the closest intimates, there were occasional sharp though brief rebellions, and Goldsmith especially, more than once, made ridiculously clear that his ill-concealed vanity was hurt by Johnson's assumption that his right to direct the conversation ought never to be questioned. He complained that Johnson was "for making a monarchy of what should be a republick," and on one occasion he suggested that The Club should have new members since "we have travelled over one another's minds." To that unfortunate observation he got the characteristic Johnsonian reply: "Sir, you have not travelled over *my* mind, I promise you"; and on still another occasion, when the Rev. Mr. Toplady, notorious scourge of the dissenters and author of the hymn *Rock of Ages,* replied ponderously to an unusually long and not very liberal discourse pronounced by Johnson on the subject of toleration by declaring: "Sir, you have untwisted this difficult subject with great dexterity," Goldsmith, who had long been waiting his chance and soon found himself again drowned out, could stand it no longer. In a passion he glared at the Doctor and astonished the company by suddenly throwing down his hat with the senseless exclamation: "Take it." But Goldsmith was notoriously inept in conversation and the occasions were rare indeed when any other member of the inner circle failed to yield the floor to Johnson in accordance with a well-established tradition solidly founded on the group's acceptance of their leader's well-known and humorously accepted foibles.

A certain Dr. John Lettsom, who is mentioned by Boswell as having been present with Johnson at a dinner party given by Mr. Dilly and who is several times mentioned in the *Private Papers,* left *Memorials* in which his impression of Johnson's conversation is briefly noted: "In company I neither found him austere nor dogmatical; he certainly was not polite, but he was not rude; . . . he was sometimes jocular, but you felt as if you were playing with a lion's paw. His body was large, his features strong, his face scarred and furrowed with scrophula; he had a heavy look; but when he spoke it was like lightning out of a dark cloud."

Two phrases in these sentences are remarkably fine, but it is not certain that the stroke of the lion's paw or the flash of lightning out of a dark cloud actually contributed any more to keeping hearers in proper awe than did the sheer resourcefulness and the astonishingly articulate copiousness of the conversation itself even when no threat was implied. How greatly Johnson exulted in the use of his powers is revealed in his remark to Mrs. Thrale when he was twitting her for living in the country and there "feeding the chickens till I starved my own understanding." "There is in this world no real delight (excepting those of sensuality), but exchange of ideas in conversation; and whoever has once experienced the full flow of London talk, when he retires to country friendships and rural sports, must either be contented to turn baby again and play with the rattle, or he will pine away like a great fish in a little pond, and die for want of his usual food." What the deepest source of these powers was is well described by Boswell in his final summing up: "As he was general and unconfined in his studies, he cannot be considered as master of any one particular science; but he had accumulated a vast and various collection of learning and knowledge, which was so arranged in his mind, as to be ever in readiness to be brought forth. But his superiority over other learned men consisted chiefly in what may be called the art of thinking, the art of using the mind; a certain continual power of seizing the useful substance of all that he knew, and exhibiting it in a clear and forceful manner; so that knowledge, which we often see to be no better than lumber in men of dull understanding, was, in him, true, evident, and actual wisdom." But neither Johnson's delight in conversation nor the availability of his knowledge would have been sufficient to make him the great talker he was had both not been united with an astonishingly ready mastery of words, phrases, sentences, paragraphs—of, indeed, the whole technique of expression.

Speaking of the most frivolous of his companions, Johnson is reported once to have said: "Topham Beauclerk has wit, and everything comes from him with ease; but when I say a good thing, I seem to labour." Johnson's hearers seem to have got an opposite impression; he did undoubtedly have what Lord Pembroke called a "bow-wow way," but that way seemed natural to him and his utterance was "laborious" only in the not quite exact sense that it tended to make one assume labor necessary to produce it rather than in the sense that labor was evident. He would, as one acquaintance put it, "take up a topic, and utter upon it a number of the *Rambler*"—which is of course merely the obverse of a fact noted by Mrs. Thrale, namely, that *The Rambler* essays are "expressed—in a style so natural to him, and so much like his common mode of conversing, that I was myself but little astonished when he told me, that he scarcely read over one of those inimitable essays before they went to the press." Another acquaintance, the painter Ozias Humphrey, who was introduced to Johnson in 1764, was so amazed when he heard a man with unbuttoned collar and falling stockings begin to talk with overwhelming precision that he forthwith wrote a letter to his brother declaring "everything he says is as *correct* as a *second edition.*" Indeed, the now vulgar opinion that Johnson was more distinguished as a talker than as a writer began to gain ground shortly after his death, and Reynolds could write: "It has been frequently observed that he was a singular instance of a man who had so much distinguished himself by his writings that his conversation not only supported his character as an author, but, in the opinion of many, was superior. Those who have lived with the wits of the age know how rarely this happens." [4]

Johnson seems, in certain particulars, to have formed a strange idea of himself. "I think myself," he once declared to Boswell, "a very polite man," and he did not even notice the astonishment of his hearers when he declared of himself before a considerable group at Mrs. Thrale's: "No man is so cautious not to interrupt another; no man thinks it so necessary to appear attentive when others are speaking; no man so steadily refuses preference to himself, or so willingly bestows it on another, as I do; no body holds so strongly as I do the necessity of ceremony, and the ill effects which follow the breach of it: yet people think me rude." What this means, no doubt, is that Johnson was strongly impelled to interrupt and to shout down even more often than he did either, but the impression produced upon many was artlessly indicated by simple Lucy Porter, who suddenly cried out when a certain clergyman argued her down in her own house: "Why, Mr. Pearson, you are just like Dr. Johnson, I think: I do not mean that you are a man of the greatest capacity in all the world like Dr. Johnson, but that you contradict one every word one speaks, just like him."

Some part of Johnson's irritability was no doubt physiological, the almost inevitable result of living in a body racked by the complication of diseases which flourished in a system poisoned by scrofulous infection since babyhood. It may also be that his inability to either see or hear well the persons with whom he conversed favored a misunderstanding both of what they said and of the mood in which they said it. But there were also psychological factors in—or at least psychological aspects of—this irritability. Boswell cites, for instance, the presence of an irresistible temptation to employ a gift for saying sharp things and Johnson's tendency to assume that good conversation necessarily implies a contest for superiority. Another clue is supplied by the curious arguments Johnson used in an attempt to defend the rather narrow limits which he tended to place on the rights of free speech.

Milton, in his classic plea for freedom, stressed our duty to truth; Johnson, too much of a skeptic to meet such arguments on their own ground, falls back in rebuttal upon the right of the majority to protect its mental comfort, for when Boswell mentioned his "having heard an eminent physician, who was himself a Christian, argue in favor of universal toleration, and maintain, that no man could be hurt by another man's differing from him in opinion," Johnson replied: "Sir, you are to a certain degree hurt by knowing that even one man does not believe." Only a man unsure of the grounds of his own belief would find himself so hurt and so alarmed by the disbelief of another, and Johnson, who feared mental revolution as much as he did political, responded angrily to anything which suggested the danger of either. After all, it is difficult to cultivate a garden which does not have a fence around it, and fences are rather arbitrary things. Johnson did not like to see them torn down and he vehemently defended his own. One of the comparatively few good things directly relevant to Johnson which Boswell recorded in his notes but did not use in the *Life* is relevant here. Recording, in June, 1784, a conversation with Reynolds, he notes his own observation: "Dr. Johnson's harsh attacks on his friends arise from uneasiness within. There is an insurrection aboard. His loud explosions are guns of distress."

But there is still another explanation, previously alluded to, of Johnson's dictatorial manner, which is, perhaps, the most important of all. Readers may remember both his own explanation of his frolicsome manner at college and his later description of what he called his "defensive pride." Fate had, it must be remembered, added grotesque physique to poverty and mean birth in an effort to keep Johnson down. No matter how completely he might conquer the two latter, the first was always evident and a mighty temptation to those whose natural tendency would have been to find his old-fashioned morality equally grotesque. He would have been the laughingstock of any elegant group which had dared to laugh, and it was up to him to see that it did not dare. Even his brutality—and there were occasions when he was actually brutal—might not unfairly be described as "defensive brutality." [5]

Probably it was because his intimates saw it as such that they tended on the whole to pass it over. Horace Walpole, who lists Johnson among the contemporaries whom he had "no thirst to know" and who judged him by reputation rather than by actual knowledge, said of him in connection with a certain outburst which had become a matter of public discussion: "I have no patience with an unfortunate monster trusting to his helpless deformity for indemnity for any impertinence that his arrogance suggests, and who thinks that what he has read is an excuse for everything he says." But those who knew him intimately judged him less harshly. If they sometimes lost their tempers and, as a result, usually got an apology, they were more likely either to regard the prowess of their friend with admiring awe or to make, even to him, a joke of it, as they did when certain members of The Club, including Reynolds, Gibbon, R. B. Sheridan and others, drew up in the safe form of a round robin their petition that the epitaph for Goldsmith should be written in English.

On an earlier occasion Boswell had called upon Johnson the morning after a session during which the latter had been highly satisfied with his "colloquial prowess" and Johnson said: "Well, we had a good talk," Boswell permitted himself to reply: "Yes, Sir; you tossed and gored several persons." The phrase appears to have become an accepted one, for he used it again when protesting to Johnson over the harsh treatment he thought he had recently received. "JOHNSON. Well, I am sorry for it. I'll make it up to you twenty different ways, as you please. BOSWELL. I said to-day to Sir Joshua, when he observed that you *tossed* me sometimes—I don't care how often, or how high he tosses me, when only friends are present, for then I fall upon soft ground: but I do not like falling on stones, which is the case when enemies are present.—I think this a pretty good image, Sir. JOHNSON. Sir, it is one of the happiest I have ever heard." For once Boswell seems to have failed to sense the full comic implications of a scene he is describing. To do so he would have had to perceive that the image is not, in fact, a very happy one, and that therefore, after Johnson had bestowed praise upon it, he need find only nineteen more ways of making up to Boswell the former rudeness.

A neighbor of Johnson's friend Dr. Taylor, who met the Doctor for the first time at Taylor's house, was so struck, so stunned, by the great man's manner that when asked his opinion of him he could only reply: "He's a tremendous companion." And Mrs. Thrale observed that Johnson's conversation was too strong for those of the great who were accustomed to obsequiousness and flattery—"it was *mustard in a young child's* mouth!" Yet Reynolds as well as Boswell was anxious that Johnson should not be remembered by posterity chiefly as a growler and to insist, as Goldsmith had put it, that Johnson "has nothing of the bear but his skin,"—though it must be admitted that the impulse to compare him to that burly quadruped seems to have irresistibly presented itself to Baretti, to Gibbon, to old Alexander Boswell, and to James's wife, who once made the remark apropos of her husband's tour of Scotland: "I have seen many a bear led by a man; but I never before saw a man led by a bear." "I compared him at this time," writes Boswell, "to a warm West-Indian climate, where you have bright sun, quick vegetation, luxuriant foliage, luscious fruits; but where the same heat sometimes produces thunder, lightning, and earthquakes, in a terrible degree." Reynolds said that if he were to write the life of Johnson he would particularly try to distinguish between what proceeded from his reason and what his passions sometimes drove him into when he was "strenuous for victory." [6]

In Johnson's favor it ought, in any event, to be stated that his tolerance of people was generally (though not quite always) much greater than his tolerance of their ideas; that he numbered among his intimates men of views very different from his own, was frequently surprisingly complaisant when he met by chance persons whom he detested, and often surprisingly generous in granting literary merit to writings which he held in horror. His friend Dr. Taylor was a Whig, and though he and Johnson might shout at one another, they remained friends despite Johnson's declaration: "I do not like much to see a Whig in any dress. But I hate to see a Whig in a parson's gown." Of his old patron, Gilbert Walmsley, he could say: "He was a whig, with all the virulence and malevolence of his party; yet difference of opinion did not keep us apart. I honoured him, and he endured me." And though there was probably no man then alive to whom Johnson ever paid higher compliments than he paid to Edmund Burke, Burke was, or at least became, a "bottomless Whig."

Of the sermons of Dr. Hugh Blair, in favor of which he interceded with a reluctant publisher, and which later became extremely popular, he could say: "I love 'Blair's Sermons.' 'Though the dog is a Scotchman, and a Presbyterian, and every thing he should not be, I was the first to praise them. Such was my candour' (smiling)." Then there was the evening with Dr. Samuel Parr ("the Whig Johnson"), during which the two went to it hammer and tongs over the dangerous subject of the liberty of the press and during which, indeed, Johnson got to the stage of stamping his foot and was stamped back at by Parr who explained when Johnson objected: "I was resolved not to give you the advantage even of a *stamp* in the argument." Yet after even such an evening Johnson said to Bennet Langton, at whose house the dispute had taken place: "Sir, I am obliged to you for having asked me this evening. Parr is a fair man. I do not know when I have had an occasion of such free controversy. It is remarkable how much of a man's life may pass without meeting any instance of this kind of open discussion."

That he was not always so complaisant is evident from the story (told by Mrs. Chapone) of how, when he was introduced in London to the Abbé Raynal, a radical writer, Johnson remarked that he had read the abbé's book and then turned his back upon him. Yet he was polite to John Wilkes, not only on the occasion when Boswell had trapped him, but on at least one other occasion, when he went willingly to meet Wilkes at dinner again. Indeed, Johnson was characteristically willing to knock a friend over the head if it was necessary to win an argument concerning his amiability—as he did when Goldsmith objected to his contention that men who disagreed "on a capital point" could nevertheless live in friendship. "Sir, I am not saying that *you* could live in friendship with a man from whom you differ as to some point: I am only saying that *I* could do it." Even to Rousseau, Johnson could pay the backhanded compliment of saying: "A man who talks nonsense so well, must know that he is talking nonsense," and it is hardly fair to remember, as everyone does, that he described Chesterfield's letters to his son as teaching "the morals of a whore, and the manners of a dancing master" without remembering that he also said: "Lord Chesterfield's Letters to his son, I think, might be made a very pretty book. Take out the immorality, and it should be put into the hands of every young gentleman."

Though Johnson's rudeness cannot always be either excused or explained away, it must be remembered that much of the effect of an anecdote may depend upon how it is told, and what leads up to or follows a remark may all but completely change its character. Mrs. Thrale, who had good reason to remember Johnson's last pain-ridden days when his temper was certainly at its worst and who was, besides, anxious to defend herself before the public from the charges leveled against her after she and Johnson had quarreled, stresses his rudeness more than Boswell does, and against the false impression which the latter accuses her of creating he quotes "an eminent critic" (probably Edmund Malone) who supplied him with the following observations:

" 'Let it be remembered that she has comprised in a small volume all that she could recollect of Dr. Johnson in *twenty years,* during which period, doubtless, some severe things were said by him: and they who read the book in *two hours,* naturally enough suppose that his whole conversation was of this complexion. But the fact is, I have been often in his company, and never *once* heard him say a severe thing to any one; and many others can attest the same. When he did say a severe thing, it was generally extorted by ignorance pretending to knowledge, or by extreme vanity or affectation.' "

The same eminent critic then quotes Mrs. Thrale's *Anecdotes,* where it is told that Johnson "once bade a very celebrated lady [Hannah More], who praised him with too much zeal perhaps, or perhaps too strong an emphasis, (which always offended him), consider what her flattery was worth, before she choked him with it." This certainly sounds shocking enough. But the eminent critic goes on:

"'Now let the genuine anecdote be contrasted with this.— The person thus represented as being harshly treated, though a very celebrated lady, was *then* just come to London from an obscure situation in the country. At Sir Joshua Reynolds's one evening, she met Dr. Johnson. She very soon began to pay her court to him in the most fulsome strain. "Spare me, I beseech you, dear Madam," was his reply. She still *laid it on*. "Pray, Madam, let us have no more of this;" he rejoined. Not paying any attention to these warnings, she continued still her eulogy. At length, provoked by this indelicate and *vain* obtrusion of compliment, he exclaimed, "Dearest lady, consider with yourself what your flattery is worth, before you bestow it so freely."'"

Opinions differ on the question whether or not one account makes Johnson seem significantly less boorish than the other but Miss More (who is clearly identified as the recipient of the reproof by Fanny Burney, who also tells the story) was delighted with the Doctor and was so far from being crushed that she had to be given through Miss Reynolds another hint that Johnson did not like to have flattery laid on too thick.[7]

In reference to that sort of constitutional melancholy and near-madness with which he himself suffered, the following conversation once took place:

"JOHNSON. A man so afflicted, Sir, must divert distressing thoughts, and not combat with them. BOSWELL. May not he think them down, Sir? JOHNSON. No, Sir. To attempt to *think them down* is madness. He should have a lamp constantly burning in his bed-chamber during the night, and if wakefully disturbed, take a book, and read, and compose himself to rest. To have the management of the mind is a great art, and it may be attained in a considerable degree by experience and habitual exercise. BOSWELL. Should not he provide amusements for himself? Would it not, for instance, be right for him to take a course in chymistry? JOHNSON. Let him take a course in chymistry, or a course of rope-dancing, or a course of any thing to which he is inclined at the time. Let him contrive to have as many retreats for his mind as he can, as many things to which it can fly from itself." Boswell's record of this conversation in his journal reveals that it was provoked by a discussion of his own struggles with melancholy.

Now, in so far as the kind of conversation which Johnson cultivated and directed is peculiar to him and came into being as the result of his own particular needs, it may be to some degree understood in the light of what has just been quoted. He, no less than Boswell, desperately needed some activity which would distract him from himself, but his mind was of the sort which must grapple with something substantial and he could not be entertained by rope-dancing either literal or figurative. Hence the talk, in which something is always discussed and yet discussed in a manner which gave full scope to ingenuity, to wit, and to powers of expression which delighted in their own operation. In so far, however, as this conversation was also of a sort which naturally flourished among his contemporaries, it flourished because it provided for the exploitation of interests and attitudes characteristic of intellectual society in his time.

Some considerable part of it was the shoptalk of men professionally concerned with literature and delighting to analyze the strength and weakness both of the accepted masters and of their own contemporaries. It might be gravely judicial, as when Johnson delivered pronouncements concerning Dryden or Pope. At other times it might be tinged with malice: "[Gray] was dull in a new way, and that made many people think him GREAT"; or, more broadly, when Johnson had perversely praised the verses of Samuel Derrick and was trapped by being solemnly asked whether Derrick or Christopher Smart was the better poet, "Sir, there is no settling the point of precedency between a louse and a flea." [8]

Another considerable portion of the conversation was concerned with manners, fashions, and personalities not even nominally connected with literature. Talk of this sort was too rich, too thoughtful, and too responsible to be called merely gossip, but perhaps it would not be unfair to say that it was the thing which gossip is aspiring to be, and that it could rise above the usual level of gossip to achieve some kind of seriousness because of that sense that the comedy of manners is truly important which has already been referred to more than once as characteristic of Johnson and his age. Present-day talkers, if they take themselves seriously, tend to scorn "mere personalities" and confine themselves to "movements" and "forces." Triviality, they feel, can be avoided only by the discussion of "tendencies" and the reduction of persons, when persons cannot be avoided, to "types" either political, psychological or glandular. If Mr. A or Mr. B inevitably comes into the discussion, the only details about him which are really relevant are those which establish him as "fascist," "fellow traveler," "introvert" or "hypoadrenal." But the eighteenth century, having got rid of the doctrine of humors as a short cut to the classification of human beings, had not yet achieved any of the modern simplifications—one of which is so startlingly similar to the doctrine of humors that it really seems to make little difference whether we say "excess of black bile" or "too little thyroid secretion."

To the men of Johnson's century it seemed that that idiosyncrasy was not only fascinating but important just because all classifications were misleading, because only the gossipy details about either a man or a society made any sort of understanding of it possible. It is this conviction which not only dominates much of the conversation of Johnson's circle but also determines Boswell's method in presenting Johnson himself. Boswell was, indeed, uniquely conscious of what the others took for granted without realizing it and a few sentences from his journal make clearer than anything else could what the premise was. Referring, not to Johnson, nor to anyone of whom he intended to make a formal study, but merely to an uncle with whom he drove to Edinburgh in 1775, he wrote:

"The great lines of characters may be put down. But I doubt much if it be possible to preserve in words the peculiar features of mind which distinguish individuals as certainly as the features of different countenances. The art of portrait painting fixes the last; and musical sounds with all their nice gradations can also be fixed. Perhaps language may be improved to such a degree as to picture the varieties of mind as minutely. In the meantime we must be content to enjoy the recollection of characters in our own breast . . . I cannot portray Commissioner Cochrane as he exists in my mind."

Boswell's solution of the difficulty when he came to write the *Life* was to make no serious effort to encompass his subject by any series of generalizations but to supply as many as possible of the details which contributed to the building up of the incommunicable recollection of character in his own breast and to hope that something similar would be built up in the breasts of his readers. Johnson and his friends were following the same method when, for example, they exchanged anecdotes intended to exhibit the paradoxical combination of Garrick's penny-saving habits with his openhanded generosity. Gossip ordinarily excuses itself on the grounds that it is really interest in human character. When the excuse is valid, the thing ceases to be gossip.

No doubt this eighteenth-century faith in the importance of the comedy of manners owed its existence in part at least to a current of skepticism concerning the extent to which it was possible to push our knowledge of human nature beyond the anecdotal stage, and men talked about manners, customs and personalities because they doubted that they could talk profitably about many of the "important" things serious talkers concern themselves with today. Johnson, to be sure, generalized freely enough about morals and about the broad principles of government, but not all of his intellectual contemporaries were as certain as he was that they knew what God intended or what the king had a right to. "Presume not God to scan" and "Let us cultivate our garden" are two injunctions that supplement each other. And both of them tend to emphasize the importance of the comedy of manners. No present-day reader can possibly feel the fascination of either Boswell's *Life* or of Johnson himself unless he is capable of sharing to some extent the conviction that what seems to many mere gossip and chitchat is actually something more.

The skepticism concerning man's ability to know much except the manners and customs of his fellow creatures did not, of course, prevent even those who professed it much more than Johnson did from proceeding sometimes to speculate and to argue concerning all manner of things which they ought, no doubt, to have classified as unknowable and said no more about. Men who adjured others to avoid the presumption implied in any attempt to scan God proceeded forthwith to scan Him in their own way. But the professed skepticism did have other effects beyond that of emphasizing the importance of the social anecdote. Johnson and his friends probably spent almost as much time discussing abstract questions as they did in discussing personalities. But they discussed them in a special manner of their own.

That manner was based on the assumption that, in so far as a subject was discussible at all, it was best discussed in terms of what is generally called (without further definition) "common sense" and that any intelligent and well-educated gentleman, no matter what his special aptitudes might be, was as competent as any other to settle questions philosophical, theological or even scientific. Analysis in the light of "right reason" (which was supposed to be pretty generally attainable) was the final test, and a group composed of an eminent moralist, an eminent actor, and an eminent orator was quite prepared to apply it. That the results are always satisfactory to us one need hardly maintain. But that the assumption made the conversations recorded in Boswell and elsewhere possible is perfectly obvious. That it also makes them, in their own way, interesting is hardly less so. The spectacle offered by the operation of a keen mind trying to see how much it can accomplish with the tools it possesses and with the materials at hand is always a fascinating one. And in all seriousness it may be said that social life in the eighteenth century afforded more abundant opportunity to participate in or to observe such operations than has been afforded in the social life of any age since. It did so, moreover, because the specialist and expert were still in the embryo stage of their development, because most knowledge and most competence was still so highly generalized.

By way of illustration let us take a long report of a single conversation:

"Talking of birds, I mentioned Mr. Daines Barrington's ingenious Essay against the received notion of their migration. JOHNSON. 'I think we have as good evidence for the migration of woodcocks as can be desired. We find they disappear at a certain time of the year, and appear again at a certain time of the year; and some of them, when weary in their flight, have been known to alight on the rigging of ships far out at sea.' One of the company observed, that there had been instances of some of them found in summer in Essex. JOHNSON. 'Sir, that strengthens our argument. *Exceptio probat regulam.* Some being found shews, that, if all remained, many would be found. A few sick or lame ones may be found.' GOLDSMITH. 'There is a partial migration of the swallows; the stronger ones migrate, the others do not.' . . .

"He repeated an argument, which is to be found in his 'Rambler,' against the notion that the brute creation is endowed with the faculty of reason: 'birds build by instinct; they never improve; they build their first nest as well as any one they ever build.' GOLDSMITH. 'Yet we see if you take away a bird's nest with the eggs in it, she will make a slighter nest and lay again.' JOHNSON. 'Sir, that is because at first she has full time and makes her nest deliberately. In the case you mention she is pressed to lay, and must therefore make her nest quickly, and consequently it will be slight.' GOLDSMITH. 'The nidification of birds is what is least known in natural history, though one of the most curious things in it.'

"I introduced the subject of toleration. JOHNSON. 'Every society has a right to preserve publick peace and order, and therefore has a good right to prohibit the propagation of opinions which have a dangerous tendency: To say the *magistrate* has this right, is using an inadequate word: it is the *society* for which the magistrate is agent. He may be morally or theologically wrong in restraining the propagation of opinions which he thinks dangerous, but he is politically right.' MAYO. 'I am of opinion, Sir, that every man is entitled to liberty of conscience in religion; and that the magistrate cannot restrain that right.' JOHNSON.

MRS. THRALE

From an engraving after a painting by Reynolds, said to have been made about 1774

'Sir, I agree with you. Every man has a right to liberty of conscience, and with that the magistrate cannot interfere. People confound liberty of thinking with liberty of talking; nay, with liberty of preaching. Every man has a physical right to think as he pleases; for it cannot be discovered how he thinks. He has not a moral right, for he ought to inform himself, and think justly. But, Sir, no member of a society has a right to *teach* any doctrine contrary to what the society holds to be true. The magistrate, I say, may be wrong in what he thinks; but while he thinks himself right, he may and ought to enforce what he thinks.' MAYO. 'Then, Sir, we are to remain always in errour, and truth never can prevail; and the magistrate was right in persecuting the first Christians.' JOHNSON. 'Sir, the only method by which religious truth can be established is by martyrdom. The magistrate has a right to enforce what he thinks; and he who is conscious of the truth has a right to suffer. I am afraid there is no other way of ascertaining the truth, but by persecution on the one hand and enduring it on the other.' . . . MAYO. 'But, Sir, ought not Christians to have liberty of conscience?' JOHNSON. 'I have already told you so, Sir. You are coming back to where you were.' BOSWELL. 'Dr. Mayo is always taking a return post-chaise, and going the stage over again. He has it at half-price.' JOHNSON. 'Dr. Mayo, like other champions for unlimited toleration, has got a set of words. Sir, it is no matter, politically, whether the magistrate be right or wrong. Suppose a club were to be formed, to drink confusion to King George the Third, and a happy restoration to Charles the Third; this would be very bad with respect to the State; but every member of that club must either conform to its rules, or be turned out of it. Old Baxter, I remember, maintains, that the magistrate should "tolerate all things that are tolerable." This is no good definition of toleration upon any principle; but it shews that he thought some things were not tolerable.' TOPLADY. 'Sir, you have untwisted this difficult subject with great dexterity.' " [9]

Today any casual social group which makes an attempt at conversation that is general but also responsible is constantly impeded by the sense that no member can possibly claim competence in more than one or two very limited fields. We have put our faith in the expert, and however wise we may be in doing so we have made it impossible to take general conversation with the same seriousness that the eighteenth century took it with. When we abandon the merely irresponsible though possibly heated exchange of "opinions," each man speaks on his "subject" and it is immediately granted that only he has a right to speak. Four men educated in four different professions may come together only to discover that their equally good educations overlap so little that they can meet on an equal footing only when they discuss what even the uneducated might discuss with almost equal authority. In Johnson's time there was a body of knowledge which could be assumed in any man designated as "learned" and another body which could equally well be assumed in anyone who had acquired what was called "polite learning." Given one or both of these common bodies of knowledge plus the common faith in the dialectic of common sense, and conversation of the sort which flourished in the Johnson circle, and of which a specimen has just been given, becomes possible.

Boswell himself was submitting to its severest possible test the assumption that any two cultivated men could understand each other when he deliberately tricked Johnson into a meeting with John Wilkes just to see what would happen. But the generalization survived. When the Great Moralist realized that he was about to sit down to dinner with a man whom he regarded as one of the most depraved scoundrels alive, he sat down a moment to compose himself but was presently equal to the occasion. Wilkes helped him to some choice pieces of meat, and one interest which they had in common was established. Presently, that most inevitable of polite subjects—a contested passage in Horace—arose, and there was another subject upon which two men, as antithetical in temperament and experience as two members of the same world could be, could respect each other's knowledge. Presently they were exchanging jokes about the Scotch and Johnson could join with Wilkes in twitting their mutual friend. "JOHNSON (to Mr. Wilkes). 'You must know, Sir, I lately took my friend Boswell and shewed him genuine civilized life in an English provincial town. I turned him loose at Lichfield, my native city, that he might see for once real civility: for you know he lives among savages in Scotland, and among rakes in London.' WILKES. 'Except when he is with grave, sober, decent people like you and me.' JOHNSON. 'And we ashamed of him.'" The fact that Johnson obviously meant Wilkes to take the reference to rakes to include Wilkes himself among those so designated is obvious; but so is the fact that when Wilkes turned the implication aside to link himself with the "sober, decent people" like Johnson, Johnson good-humoredly acquiesced in the joke. As Boswell said, here were "two men, who though widely different, had so many things in common—classical learning, modern literature, wit, and humour, and ready repartee—that it would have been much to be regretted if they had been forever at a distance from each other."

Another way to describe the circumstances which made the age particularly favorable to conversation would be to say that the eighteenth century was the golden age of the amateur, and that conversation is an art of which amateurs are the best practitioners. It flourishes most exuberantly when reasonableness rather than expert knowledge is the thing most trusted, when the assumption is that truth can most often be arrived at not, as the Middle Ages believed, by metaphysical argument and not, as we profess to hold, by scientific method, but by the application of "common sense"; and we may define "common sense" as the acceptance of certain current assumptions, traditions and standards of value which are never called into question because so to question any of them might be to necessitate a revision of government, society and private conduct more thoroughgoing than anyone liked to contemplate.

It would be easy enough to demonstrate that common sense is not so common (i.e., not so self-evident to all sane men) as the eighteenth century liked to assume. Boswell, to take a trivial but extremely revelatory illustration, thought he had demonstrated beyond all possible doubt that Johnson's preference for rhymed English verse over blank verse was founded in "nature" and therefore the result of common sense, when he cited the remark of a rustic who had been discovered by the Earl of Hopeton poring over a copy of *Paradise Lost*. "An't please your Lordship," the rustic is alleged to have observed, "this is a very odd sort of an author; he would fain rhyme, but cannot get at it." Boswell calls this "one of the most natural instances of the effect of blank verse" and it obviously never occurred to him that the rustic expected rhyme, not because it is "in accordance with nature" but simply because most of the verse he had previously met in his doubtless limited previous experience had not been blank. No doubt much that the eighteenth century was ready to accept as "according to nature" was accepted on no better evidence than this. It was one of its most characteristic errors to "assume that the customs of its little island are the laws of the universe."

Faith in common sense certainly implies that "nature" is constant and known, and if we are merely discussing, as we are, what that common sense, upon the acceptance of which conversation of the sort practised by Johnson and his circle depends, really signifies, we must arrive at the conclusion that it signifies an acceptance of a doctrine which we have rejected—namely, the doctrine so well-expressed by Pope when he declared that every normal mind is prepared to recognize truth when it is presented, because his mind is not really a tabula rasa but one on which "the lines though faintly drawn, are drawn right." That Johnson himself ever attempted to think his way through the difficulties presented when his acceptance in some never clearly qualified way of the "tabula rasa" is confronted by his tacit acceptance of the appeal to common sense is nowhere indicated. But he could not have talked as he did had he not made this ever-recurring appeal. He would on many occasions no doubt have been struck dumb if he had said to himself what it not infrequently seems to us that he should have said—something, namely, like this: "The assumption to which I am about to appeal is not really self-evident or universally accepted. Since all knowledge arises out of experience, this also is the product of experience, and since different men have had different experiences, different things seem evident to different people." But Johnson, as we know, was seldom struck dumb.

The reader who follows the discourses and the dialogues reported in Boswell's *Life* or in Mrs. Thrale's *Anecdotes* will no doubt find himself convinced by the analyses only in so far as he agrees that any particular bit of common sense which happens to be appealed to really is common sense; and such will, often enough, not be the case. If he continues, nevertheless, to find the discourse interesting, he will find it so for one or both of two reasons. He will be fascinated by the revelation of an interesting mind and character; or, he will be fascinated by that rational process which consists in reducing opinion to consistency by demonstrating which conclusions are compatible with which others.

And here, perhaps, it should be remarked that it is a capacity to delight in these two things which, more often than anything else, distinguishes that half of literate mankind which finds Johnson one of the most delightful of all companions from that half which finds him only exasperating and wrongheaded. There are, probably, no more High-churchmen or Tories in the one class than in the other. His admirers are rarely, rather than commonly, disciples in the sense of being persons who accept his moral, political and social teaching, or even the majority of his literary judgments. They are, on the contrary, those who, in addition to responding with animal warmth to Johnson's own sturdy goodness and courageous vivacity, are charmed, as men like Burke and Garrick and Reynolds were charmed, by his wit—both in the narrow and in the broad sense of that term; by, that is to say, his ability to make a point with a concision and adroitness which sometimes provokes the smile of delight and sometimes almost paralyzes response by rendering either our agreement or disagreement speechless in the presence of such skill in debate.

Edgar Allan Poe once wrote of Thomas Babington Macaulay that the reader's admiration for that gentleman's writing is the result not of agreement but merely of the fact that we can understand so perfectly *what it is* that he is saying. On occasion much the same thing is true of Johnson. His most dubious propositions and his most farfetched analogies are usually set forth with a stark clarity so striking that even the opponent who feels confident of his ability to find a better argument knows that he is lost because he cannot rival a perspicacity which makes a weak case seem strong. Let us take an example.

Boswell (of all men) was anxious to know if fornication was

to be considered as "a sin of heinous nature" and Johnson (of all men) assured him that it was not. Boswell then countered with the argument presented by an old clergyman, who arose when the question was being debated in connection with an action at law and repeated a text of Scripture denouncing judgment against whoremongers. "JOHNSON. Why, Sir, observe the word *whoremonger.* Every sin, if persisted in, will become heinous. Whoremonger is a dealer in whores, as ironmonger is a dealer in iron. But you don't call a man an ironmonger for buying and selling a pen-knife; so you don't call a man a whoremonger for getting one wench with child."

Boswell, anxious for the reputation of his hero, adds a footnote: "It must not be presumed that Dr. Johnson meant to give any countenance to licentiousness, though in the character of an Advocate he made a just and subtle distinction between occasional and habitual transgression." Johnson of course was frequently talking "in the character of an Advocate" even when law cases were not under consideration. But the point here is neither that fact nor any question as to the justness of his distinction. The point is that Johnson quickly seized upon the word "whoremonger" and, disregarding the fact that, for all he knew, it might be a very loose translation of the original,—disregarding even the fact that he had himself in his Dictionary given as one definition of the word simply "one who converses with a fornicatress"—he produced an analogy so ludicrously appropriate-inappropriate that no other, no matter how much sounder, could possibly seem afterwards other than dull. And if anyone had been so incautious as to challenge him, he would have proceeded to do what Goldsmith called knocking you down with the butt end of his pistol but which is, actually, employing some tactic more subtle. He would have retorted with something like what he said on another occasion to an unnamed disputant who professed not to understand what Johnson had said: "Sir, I have found you an argument; but I am not obliged to find you an understanding." To call that brutal and hectoring is to state only the less important half of the truth. Even those who knew they were going to be knocked down seldom knew well enough just *how* they were going to be knocked down to put up any defense against a blow which usually fell from some unexpected quarter upon some exposed portion of the combatant. Johnson could be rude. But he was seldom rude in any dull, expected or routine way. His rudeness, like all his other activities, was something to which he put his mind and applied his talents.[10]

To say this introduces the subject of a leading characteristic of his discourse even more important than either its perspicacity or its unexpectedness—namely, the extent to which it exhibits a ceaseless intellectual activity of one kind or another. Some allusion has already been made to Lytton Strachey's witty pronouncement upon the *Lives of the Poets:* "Johnson's aesthetic judgments are almost invariably subtle, or solid, or bold; they have always some good quality to recommend them—except one: they are never right." Without stopping to inquire whether the last part of this sentence can possibly mean more than "never in accord with Mr. Strachey's opinion," one must agree that what is here said in favor of Johnson's aesthetic opinions applies with equal force to almost all of his recorded discourse. To find it almost always admirable does not necessarily mean to admire what often seems to most of us perversely wrong. It means only that there is always in it, however wrong it may be, something subtle, or solid, or bold, which is, of course, to say "something good in itself." And that something, in itself good, is nearly always evident because Johnson seems rarely to have ceased, even for an instant, to use the powerful mind that was his.

It has been said by some students of language that a considerable portion of all the words spoken in the course of social interchange is not intended to have any meaning; that the words are ritualistic sounds whose purpose is to demonstrate good will and to cover self-consciousness as well as, sometimes, either to conceal thought or to avoid the necessity of thinking. Few men's discourse can ever have included less than Johnson's did of speaking not intended to have intellectual significance. Certainly, he was not always seeking to find or to communicate Truth; frequently he was endeavoring to win an argument or to exhibit his ingenuity. But he never repeated phrases which had no meaning for him and he seems seldom to have uttered a word to which his intellect had not assigned a purpose. Doubtless no one of his companions failed to recognize the point Garrick once scored when the subject of cards came up and Johnson was about to begin with something like "Why, Sir, as to the good or evil of card-playing—" "Now, (said Garrick,) he is thinking which side he shall take," and it was said of him by another contemporary: "Perhaps no man was ever more happy than Dr. Johnson, in the extempore, and masterly defence of any cause, which, at the given moment, he chose to defend." But once he had decided "which side he would take" he summoned all the resources of his knowledge and of his wit. Thinking, which we may judge to have been good thinking or bad, invariably went on. There were no clichés of thought or of expression. Every idea and every phrase was new-minted for the occasion. Like many men who think that they are lazy but in fact only resent doing what they feel an obligation to do, Johnson expended for the entertainment of his friends a quantity of mental energy which would have sufficed to fill out dozens of the volumes he never wrote.

No doubt it was this more than anything else which his hearers appreciated, which made them seek Johnson out as they would seek out a virtuoso performer upon some instrument which they themselves hoped to master. It is hardly to be supposed that Burke, a political liberal at least at the time of his association with Johnson, or Reynolds and Garrick, worldly men of the world, always found Johnson's conclusions acceptable. But they knew that no one else explored his own mind more thoroughly or communicated it more fully to those privileged to hear him. They were all connoisseurs of wit. Boswell makes in one of his private journals a very accurate distinction between a saying of Chesterfield's which Johnson admired, "Tyrawley and I have been dead this twelvemonth, though we have chosen to keep it secret," and another from the same source about a tall man who was dying by inches. The one, he says, is true wit, the other merely a conceit; and it requires no great connoisseurship to recognize that Johnson's witticisms, like Chesterfield's comment on his own superannuation, condense into a glittering crystal a whole critical and analytical discourse upon some topic. Of music Johnson once said that "it excites in my mind no ideas, and hinders me from contemplating my own," which is comic only because of the contrast between the mental power exhibited by the clarity of statement and the mental limitation implied by the thing stated. But on another occasion, when he had been compelled to suffer distraction from his own ideas while a violinist exhibited his virtuosity and when his companion had informed him that the feat being performed was very difficult, "Difficult," he replied, ". . . I wish it had been impossible." That retort is not merely ludicrous and surprising, for it also implies a whole discourse upon a vulgar error in aesthetics.

Johnson was, of course, perfectly willing to admit that he sometimes talked for victory and sometimes hesitated to decide which side he would take. It is, moreover, evident enough that if he could "untwist a difficult subject with great dexterity" he could also, when he chose, tangle a simple one up for the pleasure of defying his hearers to find the head and tail of it again. The reckless and somewhat malicious Sir John Hawkins goes so far as to say: "I had opportunities of observing what others have taken occasion to remark, viz. not only that in conversation Johnson made it a rule to talk his best, but that on many subjects he was not uniform in his opinions, contending as often for victory as for truth. . . . He would sometimes contradict self-evident propositions, such as, that the luxury of this country has increased with its riches and that the practice of card-playing is more general than heretofore. At this versatility of temper, none, however, took offence."

In one, at least, of his specific examples Hawkins seems rather unlucky since it is difficult to imagine Johnson denying the increase of luxury which he pretty consistently rejoiced in; but the license which he claimed in argument for argument's sake was explicit as well as perfectly understood by his intimates. "When I was a boy," he remarked, "I used always to choose the wrong side of a debate, because most ingenious things, that is to say, most new things, could be said upon it," and on other occasions he admitted with equal freedom that something of the same sort was still true. "I dogmatize and am contradicted, and in this conflict of opinions and sentiments I find delight." Boswell insists upon the clear distinction which he made between the freedom he permitted himself in conversation and the responsibility which he assumed when he wrote. Indeed, it is seldom difficult for the reader to place any of Johnson's recorded utterances in one or the other of the three categories into which they are clearly divided—i.e., what he really believed; what he said only "in the character of an Advocate"; and what he recklessly declared in moments of irritation or anger.[11]

So the talk continued, on every subject and in every place—in Johnson's house, at the Mitre, at the meetings of The Club, at the Thrales' country home, and during the various stays at the various places to which Johnson, increasingly mobile as he grew older, betook himself. Indeed, it continued almost uninterrupted even as, by this time already well past sixty, he plodded on horseback over the Scottish hills or was rowed in an open boat across the rough waters between the Western Islands. "I do not know, Sir, that the fellow [Foote] is an infidel; but if he be an infidel, he is an infidel as a dog is an infidel; that is to say, he has never thought upon the subject."—"A right to a throne is like a right to anything else. Possession is sufficient, where no better right can be shown. This was the case with the Royal Family of England, as it is now with the King of France; for as to the first beginning of the right, we are in the dark."—"Sir, it is so far from being natural for a man and woman to live in a state of marriage, that we find all the motives which they have for remaining in that connection, and the restraints which civilized society imposes to prevent separation, are hardly sufficient to keep them together."—"If a madman were to come into this room with a stick in his hand, no doubt we should pity the state of his mind; but our primary consideration would be to take care of ourselves. We should knock him down first, and pity him afterwards."—"Derrick may do very well, as long as he can outrun his character; but the moment his character gets up with him, it is all over."—"Why, Sir, Sherry is dull, naturally dull; but it must have taken him a good deal of pains to become what we now see him. Such an excess of stupidity, Sir, is not in Nature."—" 'I'd smile with the simple, and feed with the poor'. Nay, my dear lady, this will never do. Poor David! . . . What folly is that! No, no; let me smile with the wise, and feed with the rich."—

"No, Sir; the Irish are a FAIR PEOPLE;—they never speak well of one another."—"A man who exposes himself when he is intoxicated, has not the art of getting drunk."—"Sir, of a thousand shavers, two do not shave so much alike as not to be distinguished."—"If I had no duties, and no reference to futurity, I would spend my life in driving briskly in a post-chaise with a pretty woman; but she should be one who could understand me, and would add something to the conversation."—"My dear friend, clear your *mind* of cant. You may *talk* as other people do: you may say to a man, 'Sir, I am your most humble servant'. You are *not* his most humble servant. You may say, 'These are sad times; it is a melancholy thing to be reserved to such times'. You don't mind the times. You tell a man, 'I am sorry you had such bad weather the last day of your journey, and were so much wet'. You don't care six-pence whether he was wet or dry. You may *talk* in this manner; it is the mode of talking in Society; but don't *think* foolishly."—"Macaulay, who writes the account of St. Kilda, set out with a prejudice against prejudices, and wanted to be a smart modern thinker; and yet he affirms for a truth, that when a ship arrives there all the inhabitants are seized with a cold."—"Swallows certainly sleep all the winter. A number of them conglobulate together, by flying round and round, and then all in a heap throw themselves under water, and lie in the bed of a river."—"I have often thought that if I kept a seraglio, the ladies should all wear linen gowns, or cotton; I mean stuffs made of vegetable substances. I would have no silk; you cannot tell when it is clean. It will be very nasty before it is perceived to be so."—"I will not be baited with *what,* and *why;* what is this? what is that? why is a cow's tail long? why is a fox's tail bushy?"—"Sir, you have but two topics, yourself and me. I am sick of both." [12]

Boswell, as has previously been noted, was by no means always there to catch the good things as they fell. Neither was Fanny Burney, nor Mrs. Thrale, nor any of the others who add their contributions to the record of a stream of discourse which must have begun at least as far back as the days when the young Johnson held forth to his companions before the college gate, must have continued through the time when he was having the best literary talk he ever enjoyed with Jack Ellis, money-changer, and which, therefore, one may suppose, had been going on for nearly thirty years before Boswell's delighted ears heard it for the first time. But once Boswell had entered upon the scene he began to keep some sort of record, and fairly soon the idea of writing Johnson's life must have occurred to him—though just how soon we do not know. In the *Life* he frequently remarks that he did or did not put down notes on a particular conversation soon after it occurred. He tells us also that Johnson "from time to time obligingly satisfied" his inquiries concerning various facts, and that on another occasion, when he expressed desire to be told "all the little circumstances of his life," Johnson did not disapprove of his curiosity but replied: "They'll come out by degrees as we talk together." Yet he never says either when he first decided to make Johnson the subject of his magnum opus or when he first communicated the project to the man whom he proposed to exhibit to the world more completely than any man had ever been exhibited before. He tells us only that Johnson did know of his plan and did approve it.

"As I had," he writes at the beginning of the published *Life*, "the honour and happiness of enjoying his friendship for upwards of twenty years; as I had the scheme of writing his life constantly in view; as he was well appraised of this circumstance; . . . as I acquired a facility in recollecting, and was very assiduous in recording, his conversation, of which the extraordinary vigour and vivacity constituted one of the first features of his character; and as I have spared no pains in obtaining materials concerning him, from every quarter where I could discover that they were to be found, and have been favored with the most liberal communications by his friends; I flatter myself that few biographers have entered upon such a work as this, with more advantages. . . . Had his other friends been as diligent and ardent as I was, he might have been almost entirely preserved. As it is, I will venture to say that he will be seen in this work more completely than any man who has ever yet lived."

Mrs. Thrale records the following conversation which she says took place on July 18, 1773:

"I wonder said he who will be my Biographer? Goldsmith to be sure I replied if you should go first—and he would do it better than anybody.—but then he would do maliciously says Johnson—As for that answered I we should all fasten upon him & make him do Justice in spite of himself. but the worst is the Doctor does not know your Life, nor in Truth can I tell who does, unless it be Taylor of Ashbourne: why Taylor is certainly said he well enough acquainted with my History at Oxford, which I believe he has nearly to himself, but Doctor James can give a better Account of my early Days than most Folks, except Mr. Hector of Birmingham & little Doctor Adams. After my coming to London you will be at a Loss again; though Jack Hawkesworth and Baretti both, with whom I lived quite familiarly, can tell pretty nearly all my Adventures from the Year 1753. however I intend to disappoint the Dogs, and either outlive them all or write my Life myself. But for a Johnsoniana cried I we will defy you at Least; Boswell & Baretti; & myself from Time to Time have a trick of writing down Anecdotes Bons mots &c. & Doctor Percy will be busy at this work I warrant him: He would replied Mr. Johnson, but I have purposely suffered him to be misled, and he has accordingly gleaned up many Things that are not true.

"This Conversation passed on the 18: of July 1773 & I wrote it down that night, as I thought it particularly interesting: I have copied it out this 26: Novr 1777. and am shocked to find three of the People named in it all dead—Goldsmith Hawkesworth & Doctor James." [13]

If we take that alleged conversation at its face value, we will be compelled to assume that as late as 1773 Johnson did not know what Boswell's intentions were. But, according to Boswell's own account, he had, before that, questioned Johnson in a manner which would certainly have given the secret away to even a considerably less acute man than Johnson was, and a little later but still before the date of Mrs. Thrale's conversation, Johnson remarked to him: "I hope you shall know a great deal more of me before you write my Life." Either, then, Mrs. Thrale deliberately suppressed something (which is not likely in the case of a record not intended for publication) or Johnson was for some reason failing to mention a man whom he did not want to suggest to his hostess as a rival. Boswell had certainly determined upon a *Life* before that time and Johnson almost certainly knew that he had. We still, however, do not know either exactly when the resolution was taken or exactly when it was first imparted, for even the publication of Boswell's *Private Papers* does not reveal just when he definitely decided to become Johnson's biographer. His journals record conversations almost from the beginning of the acquaintanceship but they also contain notes on other people with whom Boswell spent his time, and therefore prove nothing beyond the fact that he was an assiduous journalizer.

If these papers throw no light on this question, they do however greatly illuminate a much more important one—namely, the question of Boswell's methods of work and the extent to which his record may be taken as literal. Let us therefore examine them for a moment.

Before the publication of the *Private Papers* it was known from Boswell's own statements that he was accustomed to make notes of a conversation which he considered significant and that he sometimes made them very soon after the conversation had taken place. Moreover, a few pages from one of his note-books containing Johnson material had been seen by Croker while his edition of the *Life* (1831) was in preparation, had later been published somewhat obscurely, and then were edited by R. B. Adam in a tiny volume (*Boswell's Note-Book, 1776-1777*), to which the editor contributed a preface in which is made the categorical statement that the bulk of Boswell's manuscripts had been handed over "to the tender mercies of the Boswell family" and were "at once destroyed."

In the absence of anything more extensive, these few notes and one extant commonplace book known as *Boswelliana* seemed very important; they did enable us to compare certain passages in the *Life* with the notes from which they were constructed. But they are, as we now know, misleading, and the discovery of the great mass of documents which were believed to have been destroyed supplies further evidence in almost unbelievably revealing profusion. In certain cases it is now possible to follow the evolution of important passages of the *Life* through their various stages, to discover what Boswell's aims were, and above all, to judge as we could never judge before just how exact his reports of Johnson's conversations can be assumed to be.

By no means all of Boswell's innumerable manuscripts are even now available. Some may be lost forever. The so-called Fettercairn papers may not be used. Moreover, the nineteen volumes published by Colonel Isham do not include all of even those which did come into his possession. But they do (so we are assured by Geoffrey Scott, who began the preparation of them for the press) contain all the most revealing documents and a sufficiently representative sampling of Boswell's more fragmentary manuscripts to convey an accurate idea of what the whole mass is like. Few men and few books, therefore, have ever been as thoroughly documented as Boswell and his magnum opus, and the first fact that emerges is the fact that the single notebook previously known is quite atypical. That notebook was carried in his pocket to receive bits of information which he wished to jot down immediately, and most of it is devoted to material obtained not from Johnson himself, but from his friends and acquaintances. But Boswell was at the same time keeping the elaborate journals in which the records of his conversations were put down and it was from these rather than from either the notebook or anything like it that most of the substance of the *Life* was drawn.

Thus, though the notebook had seemed to lend some support to the picture which represents Boswell as listening to the conversation of Johnson and his friends with pencil poised over paper, that picture begins to fade when the journals are examined, and Geoffrey Scott's analysis of all the known documents completely disposes of it. Boswell did make his notes in a sort of shorthand, or rather did employ a simple system of abbreviation, achieved by omitting many syllables or words which can readily be supplied. This shorthand was, however, not used to take down words as they fell but merely to save time in making at the first opportunity notes later to be incorporated into his journal.

It is true that Mrs. Thrale is probably referring to Boswell when she disapproves of "a trick I have seen played on common occasions of sitting down steadily at the other end of the room to write at the moment what should be said either by Dr. Johnson, or to him," but she speaks of this as a "trick," not as the habitual practice of Boswell or of anybody else; and the fact that on April 10, 1778, or fifteen years after Johnson and Boswell first met, the former should be told that Boswell used a system of shorthand and should have agreed to test it by reading to him from a book is strong enough proof that Johnson had not been accustomed to seeing his own conversation regularly taken down. Moreover, the existing materials reveal clearly what Boswell's usual method was, and it was not the method of the interviewer. Only on very unusual occasions, at most, did he take down anything on the spot, as is, for that matter, clearly enough indicated by a bit of dialogue which he himself puts into the *Life*. On March 21, 1783, while Johnson went on "talking triumphantly," Boswell, fixed in admiration, exclaimed to Mrs. Thrale: "O, for short-hand to take this down," and she replied: "You'll carry it all in your head; a long head is as good as short-hand." His habitual method was to carry in his long head what he later set down in his shorthand.[14]

Those of the Boswell papers which relate directly to Johnson are of various kinds, but the most important are: first, the rough notes made shortly after the events to which they refer and, second, passages from the stupendous journal which was written up from such notes. As early as October 25, 1764, or while he was on his Continental travels, Boswell wrote: "My method is to make a memorandum every night of what I have seen during the day. By this means I have my materials always secured. Sometimes I am three, four, five days without journalizing. When I have time and spirits, I bring up this my Journal as well as I can in the hasty manner in which I write it." This method he apparently kept up to the end of his life, though the interval allowed to elapse between the notes and the "writing up" tended to lengthen from a few days to a few weeks, as is, for example, illustrated by a sentence in the journal dated October 1, 1776, but carrying as a head the statement "Writing from *notes* (as I always do) 17 October." In few cases have both the rough notes and the completed journal covering the same events survived, for the simple reason that Boswell evidently was accustomed to destroy the former when the latter had been brought up to date, and ordinarily preserved the notes only when he never found time or energy to expand them. But it seems almost certain that nearly all the materials of that part of the *Life* dealing with events of which Boswell was himself a witness went into the journal after having passed through the stage of rough notes.

Just what the relation between the first notes and their expanded form might be can be illustrated by their relationship in one of the rare cases where both survive—namely, that of the notes for June 3, 1784, which were later expanded. From them a brief excerpt will be quoted and followed by a corresponding excerpt from the expanded version.

Note: "Restless but not uneasy night; fond of M.M. [Boswell's wife] Hastened to Dr. J. I met Sr J. Loth introd as Peer, making mouth water. Bid me think how transient. We talked of Langton's inefficiency. He repeated from Dryden, how bold impious get; the conscient wait till prize is gone. Said Lang taught son to save money; wd send him to Parr if for nothing. Talked of Virtue almost never making friendship. Good men and bad never enemies—the thing is not disputed. 'Tis men good different ways. This began by describing the three Langtons. Wore same livery—same colour of virtue."

Journal: "Had past a restless, but not uneasy night. Was full of fondness of M.M. Hastened to Dr. Johnson's as I was to accompany him to Oxford—his first jaunt after his severe illness which confined him so long. I found him calmly philosophical. I told him that Sir James Lowther's introduction into the House of Lords had made my mouth water; and I expatiated warmly on the dignity of a British Peerage. He bid me consider the transient nature of all human honours. I said that would produce indifference. 'But,' said he, 'if you allow your mind to be too much heated with desire for a British Peerage, you will wish to obtain it *per fas aut nefas*.' We talked of Langton's inefficiency. He repeated from Dryden some lines which I shall find; how the bold impious get. The conscientious wait till the prize is gone. He said Langton taught his son himself to save money.

He would send him to Parr if he could do it for nothing. I spoke of Langton's uncle whom I had seen at Rochester. The Dr. said he was a good man. All the three brothers were good men. Virtuous men and virtuous the same way; they wore the same livery, the same colour of virtue. He then made a striking remark: 'Virtue almost never produces friendship. Good men and bad are not enemies. They are not embittered by contest. The thing is not disputed between them. Enmity takes place between men who are good in different ways.'"

From even this brief specimen it is obvious that the journal was more than merely an expansion of what the notes clearly indicated. Obviously the latter were often sufficient to call to mind related circumstances not specifically mentioned, and hence the journal can recount incidents of which the notes themselves contained no hint to anyone except their author.

It so happens that none of the material of the excerpt just quoted—not even Johnson's striking remarks about Virtue as the occasion for friendship—actually found its way into the *Life*, though some of the material in a subsequent portion of the same note did. There is, however, one considerable stretch of Boswell's journal—namely, 119 pages covering 17 days and including his visit with Johnson and Dr. Taylor at Ashbourne in 1777—which has survived with certain corrections which Boswell made in it before it was finally used as the basis for an account of the corresponding period in the published *Life*.[15]

One curious fact which emerges is that though most of the material of the *Life* of Johnson was no doubt drawn from the journals, they were not, primarily, repositories of such material but were instead records of Boswell's own life and experiences in which his intercourse with Johnson inevitably found its proper place. The earliest of the surviving journals—those of the autumn of 1762 and of the Continental tour—are obviously written somewhat self-consciously, with possible readers in mind. All the rest are strictly private, unmistakably intended for no eye but Boswell's, and they owe their existence primarily not to either the determination to gather material about Johnson nor to any preparation for future literary labors but rather to that passion for self-analysis, self-contemplation and self-recording which led Boswell to say in a sentence previously quoted: "I should live no more than I can record."

It is true that he reminds himself from time to time that various books might be quarried out of the journal. No doubt he considered more or less seriously actually undertaking to compose several of such possible books. But they constitute no more than supplementary justifications for a labor that was performed chiefly for the sake of secret and rather unusual pleasures. Even after he had confided to Johnson his intention to write Johnson's life, there is no significant change in the method of the journals and nothing was done toward establishing a plan for the work. Boswell knew, as a surviving entry in one of the journals makes plain, not only that he had announced his intention of becoming Johnson's biographer to Johnson himself but also that his conspicuous position as the great man's intimate would lead the general public to expect at least a memoir from him. Yet when he privately takes stock of himself and his prospects, the *Life* which he will some day write is not generally given an important place in the summing up. As late as 1780 he speaks of it as something which he "is to write" rather than of something which he is actually writing, and it was not until after Johnson's death that he appears to have taken even the preliminary step of revising the journals in order to put them in proper shape for quarrying out the material which had to be separated from all sorts of things relevant to Boswell but irrelevant to Johnson. It almost looks as though his self-absorption, plus his indolence where anything except the passionate making of factual notes was concerned, not only prevented him from actually embarking upon the task to which he had committed himself but also made him doubt that he would ever be able to complete it.

Geoffrey Scott quotes Boswell's second biographer, Fitzgerald, as writing: "he did not scruple to *report* regularly, and it would almost seem that he took so little share in what was going on, or was so privileged, that his proceedings caused as little *gêne* as a professional stenographer would to a practiced speaker." But any such picture as that must be completely dismissed. In Johnson's presence, Boswell may have been a fanatically intent listener and he may have sat as Fanny Burney describes him, as though in terror of missing "the smallest sound from that voice to which he paid such exclusive, though merited homage"— "The attention," Fanny goes on, "which it excited in Mr. Boswell amounted almost to pain. His eyes goggled with eagerness; he leant his ear almost to the shoulder of the Doctor; and his mouth dropped open to catch every syllable that might be uttered; nay, he seemed not only to dread losing a word, but to be anxious not to miss a breathing; as if hoping from it, latently, or mystically, some information." But even if this description is more completely free from exaggeration than one has a right to assume, Boswell was a listener, not a note-taker. He was depending on his "long head" rather than his "short-hand" and it was not, at earliest, until he got home again that he jotted down even the most fragmentary of notes on what he had heard. Some days or some weeks later he reconstructed from these notes a fuller account including circumstances, which the notes recalled without actually recording, and, most frequently at least, this fuller account was not put in any category apart but was embodied in the mountainous journal of his own life. Not until Johnson's death, or not until approximately twenty years after the first Johnsonian items were recorded, did he even go so far as to revise the journals with the idea of using them to write a book about Johnson, and not until this revision had been made did he begin transferring segments of these revised journals into the manuscript of a life of Johnson. Normally, then, what Johnson said was first carried for some hours at least in his head and often passed through two written forms before it went finally into the *Life*. On the other hand many of the long and involved conversations in the *Life* were written up from notes without ever going into the journal.[16]

At first sight this may seem to suggest that the words finally attributed to Johnson are very different from those which he originally uttered, and that Boswell was gradually evolving an idealized version of what he had heard. But his conscious aims as well as his mental limitations are sufficient guarantee that such is not the case. So far as the possibility of any actual invention is concerned, we know that he did not create Dr. Johnson or the Johnsonian manner for the same reasons which convince us that Bacon did not write Shakespeare's plays. Neither Bacon nor Boswell was a simple fool, but the abilities of each were so different from those of Shakespeare, on the one hand, and of Johnson, on the other, that a fool would have been quite as capable as Bacon or Boswell of inventing Hamlet or Dr. Johnson. Moreover—if any moreover is necessary—dozens of others were thoroughly acquainted with Johnson's manner, several of them left accounts of his conversation not too different from Boswell's own, and though the *Life* came in for its share of unfavorable criticism, no one endeavored to maintain that Boswell's hero was the creature of his fancy.

Even more important is the fact, made evident by the surviving documents, that the usual purpose of Boswell's revisions was not to improve on a record but to make it more accurate. The full journal—which, it must be remembered, was written primarily to save the past for Boswell's own delectation—was expanded from the notes merely in order to get down accurately what the notes would enable him to remember after a few days but would not be sufficient to preserve for a longer period, and Boswell would no more have embellished them with fancy than he would have invented imaginary expenditures for his personal account book. To discover what is the relation of the published account to the most literally accurate report Boswell could achieve we need, then, only compare passages in the published *Life* with such of the corresponding passages as survive (often with additional revisions) in the journals.

For this purpose we have the one hundred and eighteen quarto pages of the journal (already referred to) of Boswell's stay with Johnson at Dr. Taylor's. Part of it was enlarged in the usual manner from brief notes and all of it shows what no other surviving portion of the journal does show—namely, that Boswell was using parts of it (with some final revisions) as the actual text of the published *Life*. Most of the material from the journals which finally got into the *Life* appears to have been transcribed from them and probably given its final or next to final revision in the course of the transcript. This was done not only because so much of the irrelevant parts of the journal had to be left out but also because, in addition to the journal itself, Boswell had accumulated all sorts of notes, letters and separate jottings about Johnson which had to be digested and worked in. But in the case of this one section (as was no doubt true in the case of others which do not survive) it was simpler to work on the pages of the journal themselves without making another transcription.

To compare the original text of this section of the journal with the manuscript corrections and with the printed text of the *Life* is to see that, with one somewhat important exception to be mentioned later, the intention is nearly always simply to make the conversation as much like Johnson as possible. Proper names are sometimes suppressed for obvious reasons, but almost nothing recorded of Johnson is omitted, since it was obviously Boswell's theory that the seemingly trivial was of great importance in creating the total effect at which he was aiming. Such stylistic changes as are made are almost always to give greater force or concision to a saying, and what they are like may be illustrated from a single instance, here chosen in part because it does illustrate the exception referred to above—an exception which occurs when, in deference to the growing prudery of the latter part of the century, Boswell softens a coarse expression or omits a plain word. The passage to be quoted concerns the Rev. Mr. Seward, canon of Lichfield. In the journal the passage reads as follows:

"He said [he] was a valetudinarian, one of those who are always mending themselves. He said he did not know a more disagreeable character than a Valetudinarian, who thinks he may do anything that is for his ease, may belch or f—t or desire you to leave the room, and indulges himself in every way. Sir, he brings himself to the state of a Hog in a Stye. Dr. Taylor's nose fell a-bleeding tonight. He said it was because he had omitted four days to have himself blooded after a quarter of a year's interval. Dr. Johnson who is a great Physician disapproved much of periodical bleeding. 'For,' said he, 'you accustom yourself to an evacuation which Nature cannot perform of herself, and therefore she cannot help you, should you, from forgetfulness or any other cause, omit it, and you may be suddenly suffocated. You may accustom yourself to periodical p(urges) or periodical vomiting, because shou(ld) you omit them Nature can pu(rge) you, Nature can vomit you, but (Nature) cannot open a vein to blood (you) and I would advise you some time before the next period of b(lee)ding to purge or vomit.' 'I do not like to vomit,' said Taylor 'for fear of breaking some (small) vessels'. 'Poh', said Dr. Johnson, 'if you have so many things that will break, you had better break your neck, and there's an end on't. You will break no small vessels'. (Blowing with a sort of derision.)"

In revising the journal, Boswell canceled the words "may belch or f—t"; changed "Dr. Johnson who is a great physician" to "who was a great dabler in Physics"; and made several similar but less important changes. In the *Life* the material appeared finally thus:

"Dr. Taylor's nose happening to bleed, he said, it was because he had omitted to have himself blooded four days after a quarter of a year's interval. Dr. Johnson, who was a great dabbler in physick, disapproved much of periodical bleeding. 'For (said he) you accustom yourself to an evacuation which Nature cannot perform of herself, and therefore she cannot help you, should you, from forgetfulness or any other cause, omit it; so you may be suddenly suffocated. You may accustom yourself to other periodical evacuations, because should you omit them, Nature can supply the omission; but Nature cannot open a vein to blood you.'—'I do not like to take an emetick, (said Taylor,) for fear of breaking some small vessels.'—'Poh! (said Johnson,) if you have so many things that will break, you had better break your neck at once, and there's an end on't. You will break no small vessels:' (blowing with high derision.)" *

Evidence exists, it is true, that Boswell occasionally introduced changes somewhat greater than any illustrated here. One instance has long been famous, since it happened to be revealed by a comparison of a passage in *Boswelliana* with the corresponding passage in the *Life,* and was therefore one of the few bits of evidence available before the discovery of the *Private Papers.* In

* The whole question of the extent to which Johnson permitted himself freedom in the use of coarse language is to some extent open. Additional evidence is supplied by the *Private Papers* (X 172 ff.) and by the manuscript diary of Thomas Campbell now being edited by Professor James L. Clifford.

Boswelliana Johnson is reported to have said of old Sheridan and his schemes for the improvement of elocution: "He is like a man attempting to stride the English Channel," and then: "It is like setting up a candle at Whitechapel to give light at Westminster." In the *Life* the two similes are combined and Johnson is made to say: "Sir, it is burning a farthing candle at Dover to shew light at Calais." This appears a definite (and successful) attempt to improve on Johnson by making him say something which Boswell had notes to indicate he did not actually say.

The case just presented is not by any means unique. One might cite, for one other example of a similar freedom, the remarks apropos of "the merit of faith" quoted under the date of June 3, 1781, in a form rather significantly different from the corresponding passage in the *Private Papers*. But the evidence of the *Ashbourne Journal* as well as the evidence of other portions of Boswell's journals is that he did not habitually make changes so great and the parallel passages concerning Seward and Taylor quoted above seem a fair sample of what he actually did do. Moreover, the evidence of the *Ashbourne Journal* is confirmed by that supplied through another series of now published documents second only in importance to the *Ashbourne Journal* itself in establishing the relationship between Boswell's materials and the finished product.

The papers recovered by Colonel Isham include sixteen pages of what appears to be the final ms. of the *Life*. Fortunately, the corresponding pages of Boswell's journal also have survived, and it is therefore possible again to compare what Boswell put into his journal in 1776 with the use which he made of it many years later. The changes are no more drastic than those already illustrated. It is evident that Boswell quite frequently first recorded, as indirect discourse, sayings of Johnson which he presents in the *Life* in direct form, but this seems seldom to have any effect beyond that of increasing vividness. One more brief example of what he did should be sufficient. Under the date of March 16, 1776, he wrote: "But said I, Foote entertains us with stories which are not true. . . . He said Foote was quite impartial; for he lied of everybody." In the ms. of the *Life* (taking account of revisions in the draft itself) this appears as: "observed that Foote entertained us with stories which were not true. . . . JOHNSON. Foote is quite impartial, for he tells lies of everyone." And so it stands in the first edition of the *Life*.

R. B. Adam, editor of the *Note-Book*, having nothing except *Boswelliana* and the *Note-Book* itself to go on, concluded that Boswell "was not afraid to be an artist, and to let his knowledge and genius 'Johnsonize' what was necessarily raw material." Then he adds: "It has hardly been realized how great a license he permitted himself in this, the most important, part of his task." But Geoffrey Scott, with twenty times the evidence at hand, arrives at a different conclusion. "Of *selection* there is but little trace; for the minutest of Johnson's utterances seemed of value; the task was to charge each one with its just intonation. The logic might be rendered more concise, the rhythm more characteristic; the words might be reset to render them more *actual;* this was the full extent of his liberty."

If Boswell had actually taken shorthand notes while Johnson talked and if he had published these notes just as he took them down, then, no doubt, that small portion of Johnson's conversation which could have been preserved in that way would now survive in a form more nearly verbatim than any we now have. But Boswell did not take such shorthand notes; he knew that the earliest notes he did take were not verbatim and he corrected them by reference to what he carried in his long head because he knew that the final result would be nearer to actuality than the first notes themselves. The improvement is an improvement of imperfect notes, not of an actual transcript. We do not, it seems fair to conclude, have precisely the words Johnson spoke. Indirect discourse is often changed to direct. But what (except for the occasional bowdlerization) we do have is for the most part the result of Boswell's best and very competent effort to give us the most accurate possible reconstruction of Johnson's effect. Where what Johnson is made to say is not exactly what he did say, the difference, it seems safe to assume, is more often the result of Boswell's failure to achieve what he wanted to achieve rather than the result of any desire to improve on the original.

All this, moreover, throws light on another old dispute and

shows that the question whether Boswell was a great artist, or a fool whose folly happened to constitute the perfect medium through which an undistorted image was transmitted, is a question wrongly stated. The question really should be: "What kind of artist was Boswell?" or perhaps, even: "Should the method which Boswell employed be called an artistic method or should some other name be found for it?" That he had a method, carefully thought out and laboriously applied, is explicitly revealed through his own statements, and since the publication of the *Private Papers* there is no longer any doubt what the method was.

Consider the passage previously quoted in which Boswell meditates on the impossibility of getting down on paper a portrait of Commissioner Cochrane "as he exists in my mind." That passage indicates not only that Boswell was, in 1775, already pondering seriously and all but despairingly the problems of literary portraiture, but also that he had an almost fanatically earnest conviction concerning what such portraiture should be. Here is no reference to the "interpretation" of character, no hint of any patience with impressionistic theories. Boswell's ideal is not merely realistic, it is "naturalistic" in the nineteenth-century sense of the term. He wants the whole man; and to get that, he thinks he must have everything about him. He must accumulate details, he must reconstruct and recreate. What he needs is not imagination or insight, or even, primarily, the judgment to select. It is documentation and more documentation.

It is evident, moreover, that this conception of the biographer's task underwent no fundamental change and that it dominated the actual writing of the *Life* as well as the accumulation of the materials for it. "No biography," writes Geoffrey Scott of the finished work, "was ever so free from generality; there is no attempt to explain the secret, to forestall the shape that will form itself on the air; scarcely any propounding and summing; all is particular. Boswell weighs out each tested fragment; and the speck of radium inhering in each generates the energy by which the great total, Johnson, strides on among the living." By comparison, Mr. Scott remarks in another place: "How few and insufficient are Plutarch's particulars"; and one might suggest a comparison nearer to Boswell in Johnson's own life of Savage, where an effect somewhat nearer to Boswell's own is achieved through generalization rather than through the endless accumulation of particulars. Yet Boswell stuck for a quarter of a century to an ideal which probably no one before him had ever formulated. "That there is sensitive art in the weighing out," says Mr. Scott, "is plainly evident. But Boswell's conscious effort seems to be fixed far less upon art than upon authenticity. In his letters and diaries we overhear the groans of authorship; but we are witnessing the contrition of an idler or the perplexities of a scholar,—never the doubts, still less the despairs, of an artist. Boswell shrank at times from the sheer material magnitude of his task; he worried over his financial profits; above all he tortured his friends and himself in the effort to gather his harvest of particulars, and he will run over half the city to verify a date. But once at work, never does he question how to give 'effect' to this or that element of humour or poignancy, or whether he can convincingly balance the light and shade in Johnson's character. To collect enough facts, and (since nothing less than all can be enough) to collect more, and to be satisfied of their authenticity: these are his anxieties. Of his power to give life to the vast pile he never hints one doubt." [17]

That no one since has ever used a similar method with equal success, that the *Life* is conspicuously exempt from the dull cumbersomeness of most naturalistic writing, would seem to suggest that Boswell was possessed of some secret to which his literal-minded persistence gives no clue; but the nature of that secret still eludes us, and to know how he wrote his book is important chiefly not because it explains why the book is good but simply because it furnishes a pretty satisfactory answer to the question of how close is Boswell's Dr. Johnson to the actual Dr. Johnson. And that answer seems to be: "As close as Boswell, without the aid of a short hand but with the assistance of a very long head, could make it." He seems to have had as little desire to "interpret" as any biographer who ever lived. Primarily he wants to tell us what Johnson said, not what he might have said or ought to have said. His unconscious motto was the famous one not to be proclaimed until many years later: "I impose nothing, I propose nothing, I expose."

Just how nearly impeccable Boswell's memory was and just how closely his original notes may therefore be supposed to record Johnson's words verbatim is a question still being disputed. Probably the dispute can never be settled, but at the very least it seems safe to say that even if we do not always—even if we almost never—have every one of Johnson's words exactly as he spoke them, we do have, in the vast majority of instances, what Boswell (a man whose extraordinary memory was acknowledged) believed the closest approximation he could give to the fact and the effect of Johnson. Boswell was not an imaginative or a fanciful man. His mind was limited but it did not distort what it was capable of perceiving. He gives us to the best of his extraordinary ability Johnson "as he exists in my mind." To compare a stenographic report of one of the conversations which he reproduces with his own text might be to find many discrepancies. But no one carries away from his intercourse with anyone a stenographic report and it seems reasonable to suppose that the effect produced by what we can remember of a conversation read in Boswell is in no essential particular different from what the effect would be of what we could remember had we actually heard the conversation itself. We are probably, in other words, nearly as close to Johnson as it was ever possible for anyone to get.

At least one thing more remains to be said. Curiously selfless as Boswell's great work turns out to be, the materials for it were gathered in no selfless spirit. They were, as has previously been remarked, not in the first instance recorded as materials for the life of someone else but as part of the records of Boswell's own (to him) matchlessly interesting life. Yet when the *Life of Johnson* finally was written, it proved to be remarkable for the degree to which the author effaces himself and actually writes a life of his subject rather than those "Memoirs of Myself and Johnson" which one would, under the circumstances, expect. Few men have ever been more self-absorbed than Boswell; few men have ever had more acutely the sense that the world does not exist except in connection with themselves. Yet he was ultimately able to write a book based largely on personal observation in which never for a minute is the hero crowded from the stage, and in which the author rarely even shares the spotlight with him. Rare, indeed, are those occasions when Boswell hints the claim that he is of any interest or importance except in so far as interest and importance are conferred upon him by his intimacy with Johnson. Somehow his interest in objective documentation got the best of his interest in self-revelation.

The journals reveal that his methods were rather different from those which had previously been assumed and also that, during most of his life, Johnson played, if not a less important, then at least a less exclusively important, part in his occupations and his plans. But this, in turn, throws new light upon the *Life* itself. It is not a masterpiece accidentally achieved as the result of brainless industry of the sort imagined by Macaulay. It is a work of conscious art. But the conscious art is art of a new scientific, or naturalistic, sort.

CHAPTER XI

Streatham and the Hebrides

THE NAMES of Hester Lynch Thrale and of her husband, Henry, appear quite frequently in the pages of Boswell's *Life.* Some of the references to the lady are decidedly acid, for by the time the *Life* was written she and Boswell had reached a stage of open animosity. But it can hardly be said that Boswell fails formally to acknowledge the extent of her intimacy with the great man over whose memory they were quarreling. Under the date of 1765 he wrote: "Johnson . . . accepted an invitation to dinner at Thrales, and was so much pleased with his reception, both by Mr. and Mrs. Thrale, and they so much pleased with him, that his invitations to their house were more and more frequent, till at last he became one of the family, and an apartment was appropriated to him, both in their house in Southwark, and in their villa at Streatham."

Despite this handsome acknowledgment, the casual reader of Boswell is hardly likely to remember that Johnson saw far more of Mrs. Thrale than he did of Boswell himself or that it is the latter's skill and persistence as a chronicler rather than the actual extent of his association with the hero of his book that is responsible for the impression that they were all but inseparable companions. Mrs. Thrale published her *Anecdotes* five years before Boswell his *Life,* but though she might forestall she could not rival him, and inevitably one tends to judge the opportunities of the competitors by the use which they made of them. Yet it is principally because Boswell wrote more and better that the name of Johnson inevitably suggests to the mind's eye a picture of the Great Moralist laying down the law to his eager disciple rather than the at least equally typical picture of the same great man relaxing into comfortable badinage in Mrs. Thrale's drawing room. Though he and Boswell were so often apart for considerable periods, they did not always maintain any regular or frequent correspondence; though he and Mrs. Thrale saw each other so frequently, she preserved more than four hundred letters which he had written her. Idle compliments may mean little, but it means much to know that in his last dreadful days and in the midst of a bitter quarrel, which only the miseries of a desperate illness can excuse, he thanked her for "that kindness which soothed twenty years of a life radically wretched."

Her *Anecdotes,* though only a small book and not to be compared with Boswell's work, is nevertheless second in importance to nothing except the *Life* itself as a record of Johnson's conversation and a description of his personality. Even so, one would hardly realize from reading it alone just how much his position in the Thrale household meant to him or just how different the life he led there was from anything he had ever known before or from anything he enjoyed elsewhere. One realizes it more vividly perhaps from the brilliant passages of Fanny Burney's diary, which describes social occasions more intimately and warmly gay than any Boswell reports at the Mitre or at The Club; and from the six manuscript volumes of Mrs. Thrale's diary-commonplace book (very recently published in its entirety for the first time and under her own title *Thraliana*) one can form a just estimate of how extremely easy and complete the intimacy became.

It is true that Johnson was already half-domesticated in the Thrale household when Boswell, under the date 1776, reports that "he expatiated on the felicity of England in its taverns and inns" and pronounced quite a discourse on their supreme delights.

" 'There is no private house, (said he,) in which people can enjoy themselves so well, as at a capital tavern. Let there be ever so great plenty of good things, ever so much grandeur, ever so much elegance, ever so much desire that every body should be easy; in the nature of things it cannot be: there must always be some degree of care and anxiety. The master of the house is anxious to entertain his guests; the guests are anxious to be agreeable to him; and no man, but a very impudent dog indeed, can as freely command what is in another man's house, as if it were his own. Whereas, at a tavern, there is a general freedom from anxiety. You are sure you are welcome: and the more noise you make, the more trouble you give, the more good things you call for, the welcomer you are. No servants will attend you with the alacrity which waiters do, who are incited by the prospect of an immediate reward in proportion as they please.' " [1]

Indeed, if Boswell had been less scrupulous (and more capable of happy invention) than we have any reason to believe he was, one might almost suspect him of having invented or at least elaborated this speech. Even as it is, there remains the possibility that he had Mrs. Thrale in mind as a reader when he recorded Johnson's remarks. And there remains also the possibility that Johnson when he made them was reminding himself not to surrender too completely his bohemian freedom in exchange for the ease with which the Thrales provided him. To the end he maintained his own lodgings and his own household to which he periodically returned though he might, no doubt, had he cared to risk it, have made himself a permanent part of the Thrale establishment.

There was surely some lack of candor on his part if he never felt compelled to admit that a chair at the Thrales' well-loaded dinner table or in the Thrales' comfortable drawing room had at least as good a claim as a chair in a tavern to be called "the throne of human felicity"; and he was certainly aware of the fact that there was a qualitative difference between the two felicities. For one thing, the society which he enjoyed in London was pretty largely masculine and he was fond of the company of women. For another, that masculine society never lost a certain formality. Intimate as the members of his inner circle—Boswell, Reynolds, Garrick, Burke and Goldsmith—might be with one another, that intimacy was nevertheless limited by certain unbreachable traditions. They were all gentlemen and they were

108

Of Genius, that power which constitutes a Poet, that quality without which judgement is cold, and knowledge is inert, that energy which collects, combines, amplifies, and animates, the superiority must, with some hesitation, be allowed to Dryden. It is not to be inferred that of this poetical vigour Pope had only a little, because Dryden had more, for every other writer since Milton, must give place to Pope, and even of Dryden it must be said that he has brighter paragraphs, but not better poems. Dryden's performances were always hasty, either excited by some external occasion, or extorted by domestick necessity. he composed without any consideration, and published without any correction. What his mind could supply at call, or gather in one excursion was all that he sought, and all that he gave. The dilatory caution of Pope enabled him to condense his sentiments, to multiply his images, and to accumulate whatever study might produce, or chance might supply. The flights of Dryden therefore are higher, but Pope continues longer on the wing. Of Dryden's fire the blaze is brighter, of Pope's the heat is regular and constant. Dryden often surpasses expectation, and Pope never falls below it. Dryden is read with frequent astonishment, and Pope with perpetual delight

A page from the original manuscript of the *Life of Pope,*
in Johnson's handwriting
(courtesy the Morgan Library)

all jealous of their rights as such. A certain punctiliousness was never neglected. Johnson might be rude, but he apologized or knew that he ought to do so. Gentlemen meeting at a tavern do not and cannot behave to one another like members of a family. They have their reserves and they demand that these reserves be respected. But Johnson was at home with the Thrales as he was not at home anywhere else. Not since Tetty's death had there been any human being with whom he was familiar as he was familiar with Mrs. Thrale; and of course, even while Tetty was alive, he had been too poor to have a comfortable home. Now he came to take an almost comic delight in being consulted on family problems. He discussed budgets and advised on business affairs. There were children to prattle with and to worry over—all the thousand details of an elaborate domestic establishment. And yet he had all this without any real responsibility. He could be, in some respects, more comfortably at home than the real owners of the home could often be. The freedom of his own lodgings was of a sort adequately symbolized by unbuttoned sleeves, uncombed wig and falling stockings. At Streatham, though Mr. Thrale succeeded in achieving some improvement in Johnson's personal appearance, he was, as he had never been elsewhere, truly en pantoufle.

His meeting with the Thrales probably did more to promote his happiness (though less to assure his fame) than his meeting with Boswell, and it took place not long afterwards. The exact date has long been in dispute because it seems impossible to reconcile a statement in the published *Anecdotes* ("The first time I ever saw this extraordinary man was in the year 1764") with another in the manuscript of the earlier but still not contemporary *Thraliana* ("It was on the second Thursday of the month of January 1765 that I first saw Mr. Johnson in a room"). And the confusion seems to be further confounded by the recent discovery of a brief diary kept by Johnson in which the first reference to the "Trails," as he called them then, occurs under the date of January 9, 1765—or one day before the date which Mrs. Thrale had so precisely stated. One is reminded that the fanatical Boswell would never have been so cavalier in fixing the time of a far less significant event and one needs to know scarcely more to rest assured that when he and his rival differ on a question of fact which neither has any reason to misstate, it is Boswell whom one should accept. But the confusion in this particular case seems to resolve itself pretty easily. Johnson's first reference may have been shortly after the first meeting, which must therefore have taken place either early in 1765 or late in 1764, and since many persons still tended to follow their old habit of beginning the new year with March, Mrs. Thrale carelessly wrote "the year 1764" when she meant January, 1765. Johnson was at the time more than fifty-five years old and was about to publish his *Shakespeare*. Mrs. Thrale was twenty-four and her husband, the exact date of whose birth is not known, some eleven or twelve years older.[2]

Arthur Murphy, whom Johnson had known since 1754, was a boon companion of Mr. Thrale and spoke so highly of Johnson's conversation that the Thrales were eager to invite him to their house. Accordingly, Murphy, after taking the precaution (sometimes neglected by others with unfortunate results) of warning his friends not to be surprised by the great man's appearance, brought Johnson to dinner. Boswell was at the moment somewhere in Italy and fresh from his triumphant interviews with Rousseau and Voltaire. When he got back to England he found the intimacy between Johnson and his new friends far advanced. Speaking still of the first meeting, Mrs. Thrale writes: "Mr. Johnson liked his new acquaintance so much however, that from that time he dined with us every Thursday through the winter, and in the autumn of the next year he followed us to Brighthelmstone [Brighton]. . . . From that time his visits grew more frequent, till in the year 1766 his health, which he had always complained of, grew so exceedingly bad, that he could not stir out of his room in the court he inhabited for many *weeks* together, I think months." Taking pity on his lonely and wretched state, Mrs. Thrale (at her husband's suggestion) invited him to come for a stay at her country place and he was there at least from the end of June to the first of October, 1766.

Not even from *Thraliana* (the first entries in which were not made until 1776, though a portion of it refers to a much earlier period) is it possible to reconstruct any accurate calendar of his intercourse with the Thrales, but it obviously became a more and more important part of his existence. When Boswell paid a visit to London in 1769, he found on his arrival that Johnson was again at the Brighton seaside with his friends and he implies that it was for this reason that he was deprived of Johnson's company during his attendance at Garrick's preposterous Shakespeare jubilee in Stratford, to the general absurdity of which Boswell himself added a few characteristic touches fully described in an article published in the *London Magazine* and apparently written by himself: "Of the most remarkable masks upon this occasion was James Boswell, Esq., in the dress of an armed Corsican chief. He entered the amphitheatre about twelve o'clock . . . On the front of his cap was embroidered in gold letters, VIVA LA LIBERTA; and on one side of it was a handsome blue feather and cockade, so that it had an elegant, as well as warlike appearance. . . . He wore no mask; saying that it was not proper for a gallant Corsican. So soon as he came into the room he drew universal attention." [3]

The relationship between Johnson and the Thrales was an extraordinary one and doubly so for the rapidity with which it developed. None of his other admirers had ever cared to make himself responsible for the lonely man to any comparable extent, and responsibility for an aging moralist of uncertain temper, uncouth habits, and failing health was no light one. Yet the Thrales were willing to take him on terms that amounted almost to an adoption, and it has been assumed that Johnson was thinking of his own parallel case when he later described in his *Lives of the Poets* how Watts was for thirty-six years accorded in the house of Sir Thomas Abney "a constancy of friendship and uniformity of conduct not often to be found . . . with all the kindness that friendship could prompt, and all the attention that respect could dictate." "A coalition like this," he goes on, "a state in which the notions of patronage and dependence were overpowered by the perception of reciprocal benefits, deserves a particular memorial." That Johnson came to regard himself not as a guest but as one for whom his friends had assumed a definite responsibility is clearly evident from the reproaches which he permitted himself in his last days when he felt that he was being left adrift.

It is also evident that Henry Thrale fully approved of the arrangement. He was not a man likely to be less than master in his own household or to grant his wife indulgences which in any way discommoded him. Moreover, Johnson always paid him ostentatious deference and was obviously careful, no doubt for reasons connected with his own masculine pride quite as much as because of any desire to flatter his host, to assume that it was the master, not the mistress, whose desires came first, and to whom thanks for benefits received were properly first paid. Indeed, it is chiefly because it was Mrs. Thrale who left notes and published her *Anecdotes* that we tend to think of her as having been the more intimate of the two with Johnson. She bore most of the inconveniences arising out of the arrangement and performed most of the personal services. One looks, therefore, to her character and her earlier life for an explanation of the fact that an uncouth man of genius not only found a refuge in the home of a wealthy brewer but was nursed and coddled there. Mrs. Thrale was, one discovers, a clever and energetic woman whom various circumstances had combined to put in a position where the occupation of hostess had become almost inevitable.

Hester Lynch Salusbury, for so she was born, was the precocious daughter of one John Salusbury, an impecunious, improvident, irascible, and probably not too competent member of a good Welsh family, who had married his kinswoman, Hester Maria Cotton. Hester Lynch came into the world at Bodvel Hall, a farmhouse in a remote part of Caernarvonshire, in January, 1741, and when she was six she had her first instruction in the art of being a dependent, for she was then taken to visit her maternal uncle, Sir Robert Cotton, master of the family estate, Lleweney Hall, Flintshire. The intention was obviously that Sir Robert should find her a sufficient reason for lending a helping hand to his poor relations.

Apparently she made the desired impression, and it is no wonder that she did so if the story dating from this time, which she tells of herself, is typical. "You will see a Mr. & Mrs. Clough at dinner today," said her uncle. "Do you know how to spell

Clough? No, was the reply; I never heard the name; but if it had been spelled like *Buff* you would not have asked me the question. They write it perhaps as we write *Enough*—C,l,o,u,g,h." Though Sir Robert was delighted with the little Hester, he was obviously less pleased with her father. He suggested that the latter might seek a foreign post but he got the reply that, in effect, if he wanted Hester he would have to take her father also.

Presently the child and her mother were staying at Sir Robert's London house and Sir Robert was promising to provide for his niece in his will. When he died, in 1748, it was discovered that he had done nothing of the sort. In desperation her father set forth on an unsuccessful adventure in the New World, while Hester and her mother were passed about among members of the family, usually spending the summers at Lleweney with its new master, Sir Lynch Cotton. By this time Hester's role was pretty clearly outlined. She was to be a pawn in one of those elaborate games habitually played by gentlefolk of the time, in which the prizes were "settlements," "influence," "good marriages" and the like.

While her father was still in the colonies, his younger brother, Thomas Salusbury, had the good luck to fall in love with a stammering epileptic heiress whom he proceeded to marry. Having thus settled himself comfortably, he was ready to do something for the family. Hester was again successfully put through her paces, and when her father gave up the attempt to make his fortune in the New World, brother Thomas, after a good deal of wriggling, finally agreed to put two commitments into writing. He agreed to provide Hester with an allowance of two hundred pounds per year until she should marry *with her mother's consent,* at which time she would receive ten thousand pounds. Having thus done all he could to assure his favorite niece a loveless marriage, he no doubt felt that he had acted with wise generosity.

Meanwhile Hester, the precocious child, was growing up into a clever and amiable show-off, thoroughly accustomed to petted dependency. At sixteen or seventeen, she was translating portions of *Don Quixote* and keeping a diary. Soon she was learning Latin from one Dr. Arthur Collier, who taught Greek to Henry

Fielding's sister Sarah, and who must have made a specialty of developing learned ladies since he became also the mentor of Sophy Streatfeild,* whose calm beauty, swanlike neck, and dog-walking-on-its-hind-legs knowledge of Greek was later to trouble the Streatham waters. Hester herself was piquant, but too short of stature and too prominent of features to be beautiful. One not obviously disqualified suitor did present himself in the person of James Marriott, who was something of a poet and many years later a judge of the Admiralty Court, but the family sent him packing with small ceremony; and when an all but inevitable infatuation with Dr. Collier (already past fifty) showed signs of developing and when he seemed likely to make Hester less amenable to suggestion, he also was banished.

It was evidently everybody's assumption that the phrase "with her mother's consent" covered a good deal of ground and that Hester's own consent to any arrangement which seemed satisfactory to everybody else could be pretty well taken for granted. Sir Thomas, returning one day from the city, announced that he had discovered an all but incomparable young man and informed Hester gravely that she would be expected to like him. Next day the paragon was introduced in the person of Mr. Henry Thrale, the wealthy young heir to one of the noblest names to which the brewing of beer had yet contributed luster and one which was destined to remain such until, after Henry Thrale's death, his establishment was sold to Barclay.

Boswell takes the occasion presented by the first mention of this gentleman to enter upon a long discourse, beginning in the guise of a defense of the respectable position of tradesmen in a commercial nation but ending with the observation that perhaps "the too rapid advances of men of low extraction tends to lessen the value of that distinction by birth and gentility, which has ever been found beneficial to the grand scheme of subordination. . . . The general sense of mankind cries out with irresistible force, 'un gentilhomme est toujours gentilhomme'." Johnson, after he had become domesticated in the Thrale household, was said to have delivered himself of the somewhat unexpected

* Recent research seems to indicate that she spelled it thus.

dictum: "An English Merchant is a new species of Gentleman," and the Salusburys were obviously quite willing to forget their superior birth.

Henry Thrale had, in any event, been given by his father the education of a gentleman—he had, that is to say, attended Oxford (which he left without taking a degree), made a European tour in the company of a future lord, and then, on an allowance of a thousand pounds a year, settled down to the swaggering, practical joking, and whoring which contributed the final polish to a young man of fashion. Heavy drinking seems to have been almost the only accomplishment expected of a gentleman which he never cultivated. An air of *nil admirari* was already becoming the effect aimed at by the superior Englishman, and Henry Thrale seems to have achieved it so early and so completely that one suspects it to have been a part of his original nature. He said little, exhibited no eccentricities, performed his duties adequately but without enthusiasm, and methodically indulged his vices with perfect decorum. Characteristically he paid the proper attentions to the various members of Hester's immediate family, charmed them all, and almost completely neglected Hester herself—partly, no doubt, because he correctly judged that she would not have enough influence to be worth cultivating but partly also, perhaps, because he felt that if he was going to marry the girl, he wanted it understood from the beginning that there was to be no nonsense in connection with the matter.

Not very long thereafter a suitably businesslike marriage contract was drawn up and Hester prepared to enter the marriage state though she made only a halfhearted effort to convince herself that she regarded the prospect with any great satisfaction. Having been for some time in the habit of scribbling verses, she dispatched to the *St. James Chronicle* an effusion entitled *Imagination's Search After Happiness* in which the case for rational submission as opposed to romance and sentiment is set forth. To one of her aunts she wrote in the draft of a letter intended to announce the engagement: "With what Spirits I us'd to sit down to write to my Dear Aunt Sidney and how slowly my Pen moves this Even . . . That the Man my Mother most approves should have luckily fix'd on me for choice seems partly that peculiar

Interposition of Providence . . . Our mutual Preference of each other to all the rest of the World, that Preference not founded on Passion but on Reason, gives us some Right to expect some Happiness." Hester had been too long accustomed to being dependent upon some man whom she managed to please to be especially surprised to find that she was now expected to be similarly dependent upon another. She was, however, later to think it not unworthy of note that she and her husband had never been alone together "for five Minutes till after the nuptial Ceremony was past."

Hester was also, however, too accustomed to being petted condescendingly when she performed her pretty, bright-child tricks not to try the experiment of addressing some coquettish little poetical effusions to her husband after their marriage. But the experiment was not a success. Thrale had married her, certainly not for any mercenary reasons, but chiefly in order that she might bear him children and in order that he might have a mistress at his table of whom he need not be ashamed. Immediately after the ceremony he had taken her some six miles from London to the country place originally built by his father and not yet so pretentious an estate as he was later to make it. There he expected her to perform her duties with a minimum of fuss and, as a sensibly married man, he wanted no verses.

Hester was, as we shall see, apparently much less unhappy than one might suppose. For one thing, she knew that, despite her vivacity and undoubted attractiveness, she was not a beauty and this made her curiously humble so far as certain expectations were concerned. For another, she was at least not being torn from any lover's arms, and she could write some years later: "Though *I* never was troubled with the Tender passion, I will not controvert the Testimony of all Ages and of all Nations: there *is* such a Thing as violent Love I suppose, suddenly excited, and sharply felt; though I should fancy not once for 5000, or even 5,000,000 Times it is imagined by People who wish for the praise of Sensibility." But if she did not have to endure unrequited love, she was, to borrow a phrase used by one of Boswell's recent biographers and applied to quite a different person, destined to suffer "the quiet sorrows of unrequited vivacity."

For years she continued to send squibs of one sort or another to the newspapers and they were frequently published, but her own estimate of her literary powers (despite somewhat more ambitious later efforts) seems just enough: "This is I think the highest Flight of my Genius, to translate a Sonnet or an Epigram—nothing can I write of myself but a Letter." [4]

After more than a decade of matrimony she wrote what has been called "probably the most dispassionate estimate of a husband in the whole range of literary record":

"Mr. Thrale's Person is manly, his Countenance agreeable, his Eyes steady and of the deepest Blue: his Look neither soft nor severe, neither sprightly nor gloomy, but thoughtful and Intelligent: his Address is neither caressive nor repulsive, but unaffectedly civil and decorous; and his Manner more completely free from every kind of Trick or Particularity than I ever saw any person's—he is a Man wholly as I think out of the Power of Mimickry. He loves Money & is diligent to obtain it; but he loves Liberality too, & is willing enough both to give generously & spend fashionably. His Passions either are not strong, or else he keeps them under such Command that they seldom disturb his Tranquillity or his Friends, & it must I think be something more than common which can affect him strongly either with Hope, Fear Anger Love or Joy. His regard for his Father's Memory is remarkably great, and he has been a most exemplary Brother; though when the house of his favourite Sister was on Fire, & we were alarmed with the Account of it in the Night, I well remember that he never rose, but bidding the Servant who called us, go to her Assistance; quietly turned about & slept to his usual hour. I must give another Trait of his Tranquillity on a different Occasion; he had built great Casks holding 1000 Hogsheads each, & was much pleased with their Profit and Appearance—one Day however he came down to Streatham as usual to dinner & after hearing & talking of a hundred trifles—but I forgot says he to tell you how one of my great Casks is burst & all the Beer run out.

"Mr. Thrale's Sobriety, & the Decency of his Conversation being wholly free from all Oaths Ribaldry and Profaneness make him a Man exceedingly comfortable to live with, while the easiness of his Temper and slowness to take Offence add greatly to his Value as a domestic Man: Yet I think his Servants do not much love him, and I am not sure that his Children feel much Affection for him: low People almost all indeed agree to abhorr him, as he has none of that officious & cordial Manner which is universally required by them—nor any Skill to dissemble his dislike of their Coarseness—with Regard to his Wife, tho' little tender of her Person, he is very partial to her Understanding,—but he is obliging to *nobody;* & *confers* a Favour less pleasingly than many a Man *refuses* to confer one. This appears to me to be as just a Character as can be given of the Man with whom I have now lived thirteen Years, and tho' he is extremely reserved and uncommunicative, yet one *must* know something of him after so long Acquaintance. Johnson has a very great Degree of Kindness & Esteem for him, & says if he would talk more, his *Manner* would be very completely that of a perfect Gentleman." [5]

The pair had been married only a year and three months—or since October 11, 1763—when Johnson was for the first time brought to dinner, but they had had ample time to discover that two is not always company. At Streatham, Mrs. Thrale found little to do. On the one hand, she was compelled to give up riding, her favorite outdoor occupation, because her husband thought it too masculine; on the other, she was forbidden the kitchen because Mr. Thrale, later a notorious glutton, considered its management his business, and she was subsequently to confess that she never knew what had been prepared for dinner until she saw it on the table. Loyal to his origins, Mr. Thrale kept a town house in commercial Southwark near the brewery and near the site where the Globe Theatre had once stood, and it was to that house that Johnson was first introduced. But few people came to Southwark and the mistress was not encouraged to launch herself into London society on her own.

Fortunately, however, husband and wife could agree on one thing. Though decidedly no talker, Mr. Thrale discovered that he liked to have talk—even, surprisingly enough, intellectual talk—going on around him. Despite Johnson's almost too determined defense of the mind, character and learning of his host, one cannot help suspecting that Mr. Thrale's satisfaction arose chiefly out of the sense that he was playing an appropriate role as grand seigneur when he gathered the wits about him. But the question is of little importance. For whatever reason, he and his wife agreed on one thing—Dr. Johnson should be cultivated.

Hester, it must be admitted, included in her make-up some of the impulses of the lion hunter and of the social climber. In her old age she seems to have become more and more absorbed in the pursuit of a "brilliant" social life and she was certainly not displeased to discover that, once Johnson had been domesticated, Streatham became an accepted meeting place for a group of distinguished people who would never have found their way there had it not been for him. But in the beginning at least, it was Johnson himself who fascinated her and who satisfied a deep psychological need. There was only one pattern of life to which she was accustomed. It had always been her business to charm someone with her intellectual vivacity and to be petted in return. Had the husband to whom she was handed over been a man like either of her uncles, she would probably have played her accustomed role and been reasonably well-satisfied. But Henry Thrale had no use for an amiably spoiled child. He wanted a submissive and dignified mistress of his house, who would neither show off nor expect to be made over; and hence Hester's occupation was gone. Johnson, on the other hand, was an obvious substitute for Dr. Collier. She knew how to act toward an older man of superior learning and superior intelligence. She did not expect to be taken with entire seriousness. She did not even object to an assumption to which she was entirely accustomed—the assumption, that is to say, that the men of the family were the masters. She asked only that little Hester be praised for her liveliness and her precocity; that she be indulged as a child is indulged. Dr. Johnson was half uncle and half tutor—quite the most distinguished uncle and quite the most learned tutor she had ever had the good fortune to have. Until he put in his appearance she was quite lost. Once he had come upon the scene, the pattern of her life was re-established. Thrale, whose dignity and possessiveness would have tolerated no flirtation, could not even suspect one with Ursa Major, and

Mrs. Thrale was in certain respects too immature to be in any danger of looking for a lover. She wanted to be somebody's child, not somebody's mistress. The fact that she was, by her own statement, only four feet eleven in height must have emphasized the effect of childishness.

As for Johnson, he liked attractive women who were vivacious and intelligent provided they made no attempt to rival him or, for that matter, to rival other members of his sex. He was by no means averse to the avuncular role, and there can have been few things which he ever enjoyed more than he enjoyed the flattering ministrations of a lively woman whom he could, in turn, flatter and tease.

Neither is there any doubt that he enjoyed to the full the new experience of physical luxury. Anna Seward, who made no effort to conceal the bitterness of her dislike for Johnson, who seldom failed to put anything he said or did in the worst possible light, and who tampered with the text of her own letters, gave it as her opinion that "This last and long-enduring passion for Mrs. Thrale was, however, composed equally perhaps of cupboard love, Platonic love, and vanity tickled and gratified from morn to night by incessant homage." And again: "He loved her for her wit, her beauty [which most people certainly did not credit her with], her luxurious table, her coach, and her library; and she loved him for the literary consequence his residence at Streatham threw around her. The rich, the proud, and titled literati, would not have sought Johnson in his dirty garret, nor the wealthy brewer's then uncelebrated wife, without the actual presence, in her saloon *d'Apollon,* of a votary known to be of the number of the inspired."

Johnson certainly did love good eating, for which Streatham was famous, and he did not neglect the table while he was there. It is, moreover, difficult to imagine any contrast greater than that between the uncomfortable disorder of every lodging he had ever known and the perfectly appointed luxury of the Thrale establishment. When he first saw Streatham, it was already a substantial three-story brick house in a park of some hundred acres, within which were included stables, greenhouses, and, besides a kitchen garden, frames for forcing melons, nectarines and peaches—of which last, by the way, Johnson usually ate seven or eight before breakfast and a proportionate number after dinner. In the course of time, Thrale, a lavish spender who had various financial ups and downs but whose brewery in one single year earned fourteen thousand pounds, transformed Streatham into a show place. In 1773 a new library wing was added and many of the rooms, including that regularly occupied by Johnson, were remodeled; four years later, a lake with a small island was added to the grounds; and by 1778, when Fanny Burney first saw the place, it moved her to wondering admiration. Next year Fanny's sister, Susan, described it thus: "As a *place,* it surpassed all my expectations. The avenue to the house, plantations, &c. are beautiful; worthy of the charming inhabitants. It is a little Paradise, I think. Cattle, poultry, dogs, all running freely about, without annoying each other." [6]

Long before these transformations were completed, Johnson had already come to think of Streatham as a second home and his friends had begun to be the most distinguished visitors there. Sir Joshua Reynolds was introduced in 1766, Goldsmith and Burke came, probably, not long before or after. Boswell first encountered Mrs. Thrale outside Johnson's Court sometime in the spring of 1768, just as she was about to drive Johnson out for a visit to Streatham, and on that occasion he only half jokingly admitted that he considered her his rival. But it was nearly a year and a half later before he accepted (and possibly before he received) his first invitation.

Johnson, we know, did not profess to love the country, where he thought the conversation inevitably inferior. Fresh air and exercise he sometimes (but not always) insisted had no influence on health and he once warned Mrs. Thrale that while she was feeding her chickens she was starving her understanding. Yet at Streatham he seemed to be more than passably content and his inconsistency on this point seems to have troubled him no more than certain other inconsistencies did. Thrale's possessions did not seem to have the effect which Garrick's did of making death seem more terrible, and for a man who thought a good inn superior to the best drawing room, he folded his legs very comfortably in the drawing room at Streatham. Indeed, so necessary did the Thrales become to him that during one period at least, and probably at others, he spent only weekends at his own house even when the Thrales were staying in London, since he preferred to pass the rest of the time with them at either Southwark or Streatham.[7]

Whether frequent absence from his own home was cause or effect, it was, at any rate, after he was well established with the Thrales that the company comprising his own household became most numerous and most unruly. In March, 1776, he left the house in Johnson's Court which he had occupied for more than ten years, and moved into No. 8 Bolt Court, where he continued to have his own home during the rest of his life. Sometime before March, 1778, Mrs. Desmoulins—daughter of the Dr. Swinfen who had been Johnson's godfather, and now widow of a writing master—joined Levett, Miss Williams and Francis Barber under his roof. She was, Boswell believed, accompanied by her daughter, and she had been assigned a room which Boswell had previously sometimes occupied. This daughter of Mrs. Desmoulins seems to have left almost no further record of herself, and if she were not mentioned in Johnson's *Prayers and Meditations,* one might almost doubt that she had ever existed. But Boswell had also found in the Johnson household the somewhat shadowy "Poll" Carmichael, who may have been under Johnson's protection for some years before that, since Boswell had previously mentioned an unknown young woman whom he met in Johnson's Court in 1773; and Mrs. Thrale, in her marginal note, identifies this young woman as Poll. To Mrs. Desmoulins, Johnson allowed half a guinea a week (which was, as Boswell points out, more than one-twelfth of his pension); but she was not a happy addition. She and Miss Williams took turns presiding at table, but as Johnson wrote to Mrs. Thrale: "Williams hates everybody. Levett hates Desmoulins and does not love Williams. Desmoulins hates them both. Poll loves none of them." Yet when he was spending the middle of the week at the Thrales', he returned to his own home every Saturday to give his quarrelsome dependents his company and three good dinners before quitting them again Monday afternoon; and it is easy to understand that a weekend at Bolt Court was well calculated to overcome a prejudice against living in another man's house or even against country pleasures.[8]

Boswell, plainly jealous of the Thrales, who saw so much more of Johnson than he did, hints darkly that his hero suffered something of the restraint and humiliations of a dependent. But Johnson was certainly not a man who would play any such role if he felt that he was being compelled to play it, and we may be sure that any deference he paid to Mr. Thrale was paid with pleasure. It is true that he habitually referred to the latter as "my master" and to the latter's wife as "my mistress" but he also referred to both their town house and their country house as "my home" and freely treated these establishments as such. If there is anything in the relationship which remains hard to understand, anything which could remotely suggest the possibility of a sycophancy on Johnson's part, it is the high regard which he felt, or persuaded himself to feel, for Mr. Thrale.

Thrale's character is one which few students of his times have ever succeeded in admiring, but perhaps he was one of those unfortunates whose portraits can do justice only to their less attractive traits. Among his contemporaries, others besides Johnson (though not, as his wife notes, "low people") found him acceptable and, despite both his known infidelity and his venereal infection, the woman who bore him one child after another quite obviously liked him, though she was certainly not "in love"—a fact worth remarking on, since it is much less common to find an unlikable person liked than to find an unlovable one loved. On the other hand, there is some reason for suspecting of Johnson that one of his weaknesses was his ability to shut his eyes almost too completely to the unattractive sides of his friends' characters—as he certainly did, for example, in the case of Topham Beauclerk, who appears so amiable when he is seen through Johnson's eyes but of whom, after his death, Burke could say seriously to Fanny Burney when the subject of Beauclerk's widow came up: "Poor woman! The bowl has long rolled in misery; I rejoice that it has now found its balance. I never, myself, so much enjoyed the sight of happiness in another, as in that woman when I first saw her after the death of her husband." He then, Miss Burney goes on, described Beauclerk's character and "the misery he gave his wife, his singular ill-treatment of her, and the necessary relief the death of such a man must give."

But whether justifiably, mistakenly, or perversely, Johnson spoke of Thrale in the highest terms. For him he had, says Boswell: "a very sincere esteem . . . as a man of excellent principles, was a good scholar, well skilled in trade, of a sound understanding, and of manners such as presented the character of a plain, independent English Squire." Mrs. Thrale glosses this passage with an emphatic dissent: "No, no; Mr. Thrale's manners presented the Character of a Gay Man of the Town; like Millamant in Congreve's Comedy, he abhorred the Country & Every thing in it." But it is significant that she has no comment to make on Boswell's further account of Johnson's remarks. "I know no man (said he) who is more master of his wife and family than Thrale. If he but holds up a finger, he is obeyed. It is a great mistake [which certainly seems to imply that the mistake was sometimes made] to suppose that she is above him in literary attainments. She is more flippant; but he has ten times her learning: he is a regular scholar; but her learning is that of a schoolboy in one of the lower forms."

Certainly Johnson persisted in acting as though this were true, for while he habitually deferred to Thrale he perpetually (if playfully) scolded Thrale's wife for her reckless and restless tongue. "I have been thinking this Morning," he once said to her, "what Creature you most resemble & 'tis the Rattle Snake; I am sure you have its *Attractions,* I think you have its *Venom* too, and all the World knows you have its *Rattle."* As for his support of Thrale's "mastery" of his wife, he carried that to the point where it provoked an amusing teapot tempest described by Mrs. Thrale herself:

"We had a large dinner-party at our house; Johnson sat on one side of me, and Burke on the other; and in the company there was a young female to whom I, in my peevishness, thought Mr. Thrale superfluously attentive, to the neglect of me and others; especially of myself, then near my confinement, and dismally low-spirited; notwithstanding which, Mr. T. very unceremoniously begged of me to change place with Sophy ——, who was threatened with a sore throat, and might be injured by sitting near the door. I had scarcely swallowed a spoonful of soup when this occurred, and was so overset by the coarseness of the proposal, that I burst into tears, said something petulant —that perhaps ere long, the lady might be at the head of Mr. T.'s table, without displacing the mistress of the house, &c., and so left the apartment. I retired to the drawing-room, and for an hour or two contended with my vexation, as I best could, when Johnson and Burke came up. On seeing them, I resolved to give a *jobation* to both, but fixed on Johnson for my charge, and asked him if he had noticed what passed, what I had suffered, and whether allowing for the state of my nerves, I was much to blame? He answered, 'Why, possibly not; your feelings were outraged.' I said, 'Yes, greatly so; and I cannot help remarking with what blandness and composure you *witnessed* the outrage. Had this transaction been told of others, your anger would have known no bounds; but, towards a man who gives good dinners &c., you were meekness itself!' Johnson coloured, and Burke, I thought, looked foolish; but I had not a word of answer from either." [9]

No doubt there are many wives even in the twentieth century who feel that they might say something like what Mrs. Thrale did when she declared: "I never offer to cross my Master's Fancy . . . unless on some truly serious Occasion, nor do I think any Occasion serious enough to excuse Contradiction unless Virtue, Life, or Fortune are concerned. Was I to dye tomorrow I could swear, I never oppos'd his Inclination three Times in the fifteen Years we have been married." But one may wonder if there were many wives even in the eighteenth century who were as nearly justified in saying it.

Even more impressive is the fact that Johnson himself, on occasion, was surprisingly ready to accept a certain amount of mastering from Henry Thrale. He seems to have made no protest when the latter peremptorily put a stop to certain dangerous chemical experiments he was performing at Streatham, or even when he suggested a change in the subject which happened at the moment to be employing Johnson's powers of eloquence with greater satisfaction to himself than to anyone else. According to Fanny Burney, Thrale, "though entirely a man of peace, and a gentleman in his character, . . . had a singular amusement in hearing, instigating, and provoking a war of words, alternating triumph and overthrow, between clever and ambitious colloquial combatants." Nevertheless he was, according to his wife, capable of saying coldly: "There, there, now we have had enough for one lecture, Dr. Johnson: . . . or some such speech," and it is difficult to imagine Johnson accepting that rebuke from anyone else in the whole world. He perpetually read in bed and, since his eyesight was so bad, perpetually singed his wig at the too proximate candle. Mr. Thrale's personal valet had, therefore, orders to keep a presentable one always in his own hands. When Johnson came down to dinner, he was met at the parlor door and handed the company wig. As he went upstairs after dinner, it was taken away from him again. But whether this should be cited as an example of Johnson's meek forbearance or as an example of Thrale's solicitude remains an open question.

Boswell, who had come to hate Mrs. Thrale cordially by the time the *Life* was written, attempts to suggest that she had never done more than tolerate Johnson at her husband's insistence and he gleefully quotes against her a passage from her own *Anecdotes:*

"Veneration for his virtue, reverence for his talents, delight in his conversation, and habitual endurance of a yoke my husband first put upon me, and of which he contentedly bore his share for sixteen or seventeen years, made me go on so long with Mr. Johnson; but the perpetual confinement I will own to have been terrifying in the first years of our friendship, and irksome in the last; nor could I pretend to support it without help, when my coadjutor was no more." And Boswell adds as his own comment: "Alas! how different is this from the declarations I have heard Mrs. Thrale make in his life-time, without a single murmur against any peculiarities, or against any one circumstance which attended their intimacy." [10]

If the passage he had just quoted were the only evidence we possess, it might indeed seem to indicate that Mrs. Thrale, far from loving Johnson, actually resented and even hated him. But there are several things which must be remembered: First, that the passage was written when its author was very much on the defensive against the charge that she had abandoned an old man, who had, as a matter of fact, made quite unreasonable demands upon her. Second, that in the same work from which the passage was extracted there is abundant other evidence of the kindness and affection which she had exhibited toward him over a period of years. Third, that her diary and letters supply independently an impressive testimony to her self-sacrificing solicitude. While he was an inmate of her house she wrote of him in her diary: "Well does he contradict the Maxim of Rochefoucault, that no Man is a Hero to his Valet de Chambre.—Johnson is more a Hero to me than to any one—& I have been more to him for Intimacy, than ever was any Man's Valet de Chambre."

Whatever Mr. Thrale's devotion to Johnson may have been, it was, as has already been suggested, upon his wife that the burden of personal care fell, and the burden was a heavy one. Johnson was first taken into her house when he was suffering from a severe fit of illness and it is evident from a note written on a much later occasion ("My eye is yet so dark that I could not read your note—I wish you could fetch me on Wednesday. I long to be in my own room") that he got into the habit of assuming that he might call upon her when he needed nursing care. As late as 1782, he wrote to Edmond Malone: "I have for many weeks been so much out of order, that I have gone out only in a coach to Mrs. Thrale's, where I can use all the freedom that sickness requires"; and though Mrs. Thrale wrote in the same *Anecdotes* from which Boswell selected the querulous passage, that Johnson required "less attendance, sick or well, than ever I saw any human creature," she would not have thought so had she not loved him.

Even when he was not ill he demanded more constant companionship than most people found it easy to give. In London, Mrs. Thrale, constrained by his lamentations and reproofs whenever she prepared to quit the room, often sat quietly making tea for him until four in the morning. At Streatham, she says, she managed better, "having always some friend who was kind enough to engage him in talk, and favor my retreat." One of those friends—namely, Dr. Burney—told Boswell that he and Johnson had often sat up "as long as the fire and candles lasted, and much longer than the patience of the servants subsisted." But such willing guests were not actually always available, and in her old age Mrs. Thrale could still recall in a letter to her daughter the misery, when she herself was worn out with repeated childbearing, of sitting up with him until her legs began to swell. All in all, her marginal comment on the passage in Boswell where the latter speaks of the "some degree of restraint" which Johnson endured, seems to sum the matter up pretty fairly. "What Restraint," she asks, "can he mean? Johnson kept every body else under Restraint." [11]

While Johnson was thus becoming hardly less than a member of the Thrale family, Boswell was, except for one brief encounter in Oxford, continuing to see him only when Boswell could get to London and when Johnson was either in town or able and willing to have his future biographer invited to the Thrales', to whom he did not pay his first visit until 1769. Between the time when Johnson first met Mrs. Thrale and 1769 he and Boswell were in reach of each other only for a few days in February, 1766, for a short time at Oxford in 1768, and for a few days again in May of the same year. In 1769 they were to meet from time to time between the end of September and early November and not again until March, 1772. It is no wonder, then, if Boswell, who regarded Johnson as to some extent his property, and a valuable property at that, felt that fate was cheating him. In all likelihood, some such feeling was one of the things which led him to arrange that extraordinary "perambulation" around Scotland and into the Western Islands, which was half an adventure in exploration, half a triumphal tour; and in the course of which Dr. Johnson looked at Highlanders and Highlanders looked at Johnson with so much mutual astonishment that one is in some doubt which should be regarded as spectator and which as exhibition. In any event, Boswell and Johnson were, during the tour, continuously in each other's company for a longer time (namely, three months and eight days) than they had ever been before or ever were to be again.

Out of the jaunt, Johnson got his only travel book *A Journey to the Western Islands of Scotland* and Boswell a journal so rich that it served him, just after Johnson's death, as the source of a separate publication preliminary to the *Life*.

Boswell's motives are clear enough, if also multiplex. In addition to the obvious fact that the journey would keep him and Johnson together, it would enable him to prove to Johnson how important the Boswell name was in Scotland and also to show the more learned among the Scotch how much more important that name ought to be if young James could take *The Rambler* in tow. But there was still another motive which may have been stronger than any of the others. Boswell, as we know, was a connoisseur of situations. Here was the prospect of a whole series of situations of hitherto undreamed-of picturesqueness. He knew how Johnson looked and behaved in the surroundings appropriate to him. How would he behave amid surroundings the most unaccustomed and inappropriate that could easily be imagined? Johnson and Boswell made an interestingly odd pair; Johnson and Wilkes, it was later to occur to him, made an even odder one. But Johnson in a Highland inn or Johnson in an open boat between the islands—what a spectacle! and what copy for one's private journal as well, perhaps, as for one's published magnum opus! The learned philosopher would be brought into contact with primitive nature and something not too different from a noble savage.

That Boswell relished the prospect is not difficult to understand; that Johnson ever actually performed the feat is all but incredible. He was, after all, in his sixty-fifth year; he had never been outside of England; he loved comfort; he professed to despise the Scotch; and he had, or pretended to have, as little interest as any man who ever lived in "wild prospects" or primitive men. Coach travel, to be sure, did not displease him and he had shown an increasing tendency to move about; but that he should have agreed to, and then actually made, a really arduous journey, a good deal of it on horseback through the rudest and most difficult country he could have found short of Boswell's own Corsica, is still hard to believe. Yet make it he did, most of the time in pretty good humor and with only occasional complaint. What is more, he evidently regarded the journey as having been well worth his while. To Boswell, of course, the whole thing was, first of all, material for the endless serial story of his own life and he delightedly wrote it up as he went along. Moreover, the original manuscript has very recently been recovered, and it is much richer than the version which he published.

Nearly ten years before they set out on the journey, or shortly after he and Johnson first met, Johnson himself had made the suggestion that the two might someday make a journey to the Hebrides. Probably Boswell did not take the suggestion seriously at the moment, and even after it had been revived nearly a decade later, he was so aware of the inertia which he feared would have to be overcome that he arranged with certain of his dignified countrymen to write letters setting forth their eagerness to have Johnson do their homeland the honor of a visit. But Johnson, no doubt to the surprise of everybody, seemed to need little urging. On August 14, 1773, he joined Boswell in Edinburgh. Four days later they set out from there on a journey of ever-increasing difficulty, which took them up the east coast to Aberdeen and a bit farther north, then west across the country to Inverness, where they took to horseback, or, as Johnson put it, "bid farewell to the luxury of travelling" and entered "a country upon which, perhaps, no wheel has ever rolled." Passing on through Fort Augustus near the end of Loch Ness they reached Glenelg on the west coast. From there they took a boat to the Isle of Skye, made a side trip to Raasay, went by boat again to the islands of Coll and Mull, and regained the mainland at Oban. They then journeyed on to Glasgow, made a visit to Boswell's own Auchinleck, and finally came to Edinburgh again. "My illustrious friend, being now desirous to be again in the great theatre of life and animated exertion, took a place in the coach which was to set out for London."

This circular tour took them just nine days less than three months and was well-calculated to achieve their purpose, which was, in Boswell's words: to "contemplate a system of life almost totally different from what we had been accustomed to see; and to find simplicity and wildness, and all the circumstances of remote time or place, so near to our native great island." Even before they left the mainland for the islands, the country and the people had become primitive enough. Near Loch Ness they entered the earthen hovel of an old woman who fed her eighty-year-old husband and five children upon the milk and curd of sixty goats, and who told them she was as happy as any woman in Scotland, but who feared, when they asked to see where she slept, that they were offering amorous advances. The next night they spent at an inn so dubious that even after Joseph Ritter, Boswell's Bohemian servant and the only attendant of the travelers, had spread their own sheets over the bed, they still hesitated whether or not they should remove their clothes until Boswell exclaimed at last: "I'll plunge in! I shall have less room for vermin to settle about me when I strip!" Often they dined only on such rough fare as the peasants could supply, and when at one village they distributed pennies to the children and gave half a crown to an old woman who furnished them with some milk "the people were very much pleased, gave us many blessings, and said they had not had such a day since the old Laird of MacLeod's time." [12]

The innkeeper at Glenelg "had no bread, no eggs, no wine, no spirits but whisky, no sugar but brown grown black. They prepared some mutton-chops, but we would not have them. They killed two hens. I made Joseph broil me a bit of one till it was black, and I tasted it. Mr. Johnson would take nothing but a bit of bread, which we had luckily remaining, and some lemonade which he made with a lemon which Joseph had for him, and he got some good sugar; for Mr. Murchison, factor to MacLeod in Glenelg, sent us some, with a bottle of excellent rum. . . . I was uneasy and almost fretful. Mr. Johnson was calm. I said he was so from vanity. 'No,' said he, ' 'tis from philosophy.' It was a considerable satisfaction to me to see that the Rambler could practice what he nobly teaches." That night they made beds for themselves by demanding some clean hay upon which they spread their sheets. Johnson further impressed Boswell by so looking on the bright side of things as to observe that they were better off than if they had "been upon the hill."

It is hardly necessary to add, however, that, no matter how philosophical the Rambler could be, nothing in this new experience tended to increase his respect for those who sang the praise of the simple life free from luxury and close to nature. "The philosophers," observed Boswell, "when they placed happiness in a cottage, supposed cleanliness and no smoke." Johnson would not grant them so much foresight. "They did not," he replied, "think about either." Once they had got safely back to civilization, they "heartily laughed at the ravings of those absurd visionaries who have attempted to persuade us of the superior advantages of a *state of nature*."

But it was, of course, chiefly the islands which they had come to see. Here the feudal system of society was to be observed in something like its pristine state. More important, perhaps, was the fact that the idea of an island was something which Johnson contemplated with the fascination of horror. To live on one was almost like inhabiting a ship. It was to feel as isolated as one could possibly feel from all contact with the metropolis and therefore from all civilization. After crossing the narrow body of water separating Skye from the mainland, they were received by Sir Alexander Macdonald, but it was not until six days later, when they set out in a boat for the neighboring island of Raasay, that Boswell felt the real adventure had begun. "We are contending with seas," he called out jubilantly and Johnson repeated an Ode of Horace "Otium divos rogat." The boatman sang; Johnson "observed that naval music was very ancient"; and when they landed, the resident chieftain (called, as was the custom, by the name of his island) welcomed them to his domain. They stayed in comfort at his house, explored the island, ate mutton, and saw a reel danced in the open. Returning to Skye, they visited Kingsburgh, where they reveled in the Jacobite enthusiasm aroused by an introduction to Flora Macdonald and then set out on the much more adventurous journey to the more distant island of Coll.

En route they were caught in a storm, dangerous enough to make Boswell resolve to live ten times better if God should spare him. God did, and Boswell lived worse than before; but they were sheltered by one Captain MacLean who had "a poor temporary house, or rather, hut," and Mrs. MacLean prepared a pleasant rum punch, thus giving Boswell the first lemon he had tasted "for more than a month." From Coll they went to Mull, where Boswell was cheered to discover so much of the fine old feudal spirit remaining that Sir Allan MacLean could angrily remind one of his people: "I can hang you if I please," and where Johnson was highly offended by being asked if he would care for any sheepshead at breakfast. The grand climax was reached by a visit to Icolmkill, the ancient Iona, where St. Columba is supposed to have landed, and when the travelers arrived on the mainland again on October 22nd, they had behind them seven weeks in the Hebrides. They had not visited as many of the islands as they had originally intended, but as Johnson said: "Sir, we have seen enough to give us a pretty good notion of the system of insular life." [13]

The Rambler was not one of those travelers who do as the Romans do. Wrapping the cloak of his philosophy about him, he bore the inconveniences and the actual rigors of the wild journey with somewhat greater equanimity than Boswell could achieve, but he never melted into the landscape or, indeed, made any attempt to appear less incongruous than he was. He dutifully observed what he considered worth observing and made the appropriate philosophical generalizations, but no traveler, not even the traditional Englishman in Italy, ever remained more completely outside the milieu to which he had transferred himself. Spiritually he was never far from Fleet Street and never desired to be. It is this fact, of course, which makes high comedy implicit in the whole "perambulation," and it is Boswell's sense of it that makes the same comedy explicit in his account. But that is not all. Johnson observed the Highlanders, Boswell observed Johnson, and we, observing both, not infrequently find the latter's amusement more amusing than the thing that amused him:

"We rode on well till we came to the high mountain called the Rattachan, by which time both Mr. Johnson and the horses were a good deal fatigued. . . . Going down the hill on the other side was no easy task. . . . Mr. Johnson was prevailed with to mount one of Vass's greys. As he rode upon it down hill, it did not go well, and he grumbled. I walked on a little before, but was excessively entertained with the method taken to keep him in good humour. Hay led the horse's head, talking to Mr. Johnson as much as he could; and just when Mr. Johnson was uttering his displeasure, the fellow says, 'See such pretty goats'. Then *whu!* he whistled, and made them jump. Little did he conceive what Mr. Johnson was. Here was now a common ignorant horse-hirer imagining that he could divert, as one does a child, *Mr. Samuel Johnson!*"

Mr. Samuel Johnson himself found the diversion which sustained him, not by watching the pretty goats, nor even chiefly by observing wild scenery and wild men, but by finding or making opportunities to indulge himself in the same amusement which sustained him wherever he was—namely, general conversation. If the whole tour had consisted of an unbroken series of scenes and incidents like the few which have been alluded to, Johnson would probably have found it, even in Boswell's company, unendurable. But "many green islands there must be." By no means every night was spent in bad inns or every day visiting peasant huts. Considerable time was passed in Edinburgh and at Auchinleck. Even more important was the fact that the houses of gentlemen, wherever they existed, were nearly always open to them, and a good many houses, where comfort and actual provincial elegance was maintained, did exist here and there, despite a degree of isolation now hard to imagine. If, for instance, they fared badly at Glenelg and not too well the next night—their first on Skye—they found Raasay ready to welcome them to his island a week later: "Coffee and tea in genteel order upon the table, . . . diet loaf, marmalade of oranges, currant jelly; some elegantly bound books on a large table, in short, all the marks of improved life." Presently a fiddler appeared. Raasay himself danced. A "kind of wild man" was called in and "made much jovial noise." Boswell found the latter a bit too much for his nerves, but Johnson was delighted and declared: "I know not how we shall get away." That, however, was not exclusively because of the fiddle and the wild man. Says Boswell: "It entertained me to observe him sitting by while we danced, sometimes in deep meditation, sometimes smiling complacently, sometimes looking upon Hooke's *Roman History,* and sometimes talking a little, amidst the noise of the ball, to Mr. Donald Macqueen, who anxiously gathered knowledge from him. He was pleased with Macqueen, and said to me, 'This is a critical man, sir. There must be great vigor of mind to make him cultivate learning so much in the Isle of Skye, where he might do without it.' "

That doors were everywhere thrown open was no doubt due partly to Boswell's respectable name, partly to Johnson's fame which had reached remote places, and partly to the fact that in Scotland what Johnson called "the paucity of human pleasures" was especially pronounced. "Wherever we have come," he declared exuberantly, "we have been received like princes in their progress," and so they had. At Aberdeen they gave him the freedom of the city and, following the custom, he walked about with his patent in his hat. On occasion he was recognized by people where he least expected it, and whatever resident gentlemen, military men, "respectable clergymen" and the like any surrounding country afforded seem always to have been promptly rounded up by the host of the moment. Johnson tried them all out, weighed them in his balance, and if he found them wanting, did not conceal the fact from Boswell or, for that matter, always from the unfortunates themselves. Whenever the occasion presented itself, he acted that "symposiarch" which Hawkins thought him born to be with as much authority as in his own or Mr. Thrale's house and he was little less blunt with strangers than he was accustomed to be with friends. Boswell observed that at neither Aberdeen nor Glasgow did the university professors talk much, since they obviously feared "to expose themselves much to the battery of cannon which they knew might play upon them." [14]

Having come to Scotland convinced that the best of it was merely a lesser England and that "wild prospects" were no adequate compensation for lack of comforts or lack of cultivation, he sometimes seemed to regard the tour chiefly as an opportunity to confirm these prejudices. The scarcity of trees (which ought not to have seemed so important to a Londoner) became the occasion of a positive obsession. Near the beginning of his own account, he gleefully noted that "a tree might be a show in Scotland, as a horse in Venice," and a few pages farther on, "I had now travelled two hundred miles in Scotland, and seen only one tree not younger than myself." Boswell was never allowed to forget this lamentable state of affairs nor allowed to go unreminded of anything—from this absence of trees in the countryside to the overabundance of smells in Edinburgh—which might be calculated to subdue any tendency of his toward national pride. Sometimes Johnson joked. He tasted whisky to see "what it is that makes a Scotchman happy." "I said we had wine before the Union. 'No, sir', said he, 'you had some weak stuff, the refuse of France, which would not make you drunk'. BOSWELL. 'I assure you, sir, there was a great deal of drunkenness'. JOHNSON. 'No, sir; there were people who died of dropsies which they contracted in trying to get drunk'."

Sometimes he worked himself into a state of High-Church indignation over the religious edifices ruined since the Reformation. He told Scotch clergymen to their faces that the Scotch clergy in general were lacking in learning, and he embarrassed Boswell by enlarging too enthusiastically before company on the advantages which Scotland had reaped through the Union. At Auchinleck, when a gentleman of the neighborhood innocently asked him how he liked the Highlands, he exploded: "How, sir, can you ask me what obliges me to speak unfavourably of a country where I have been hospitably entertained? Who *can* like the Highlands? I like the inhabitants very well." Somewhat unnecessarily Boswell adds: "The gentleman asked no more questions."

Of Boswell's wife, he wrote from Auchinleck to Mrs. Thrale: "[she] has the mien and manners of a gentlewoman; and such a person and mind as would not be in any place either admired or contemned. She is in a proper degree inferior to her husband; she cannot rival him; nor can he ever be ashamed of her." But despite this compliment (which he probably regarded as one of which any woman ought to be proud), despite the fact that the lady in question was willing to give up her own bed to him, and had tea ready when he arrived, the two did not hit it off; and when he and old Alexander Boswell (one year his senior) met at Auchinleck, they also could only attempt, quite unsuccessfully, to get along without a quarrel.[15]

Alexander Boswell was "as sanguine a Whig and Presbyterian

as Dr. Johnson was a Tory and Church of England man." He was also, hardly less than Johnson, accustomed to demanding "great attention, in whatever company he was." Moreover, he had read some of Johnson's writing and was not favorably impressed. It is no wonder, then, that Boswell begged his friend to avoid dangerous topics and no wonder that, though for the first day they kept to the safe subject of Anacreon on whom Sir Alexander was something of an authority, the storm could not be indefinitely postponed. No doubt because he was suffering from unnatural restraint, Johnson relieved himself by telling the parish minister, Mr. Dun, who spoke slightingly of the Episcopal clergy, that he knew "no more of our church than a Hottentot," and soon the trouble began. Sir Alexander showed some coins, including one from Cromwell's time. A fatal topic had been introduced, but for once Boswell refuses to tell all and draws the curtain with the most unboswellian of remarks: "It would certainly be very unbecoming in me to exhibit my honoured father and my respected friend as intellectual gladiators, for the entertainment of the public; and therefore I suppress what would, I dare say, make an interesting scene in this dramatic sketch—this account of the transit of Johnson over the Caledonian Hemisphere."

At the distance of today, it seems that Boswell's reputation could hardly have suffered much from one more "unbecoming" revelation, and that he was, if not straining at a gnat, at least straining at a camel no more difficult to swallow than others he had downed with ease. And by way of compensation for the scene that is lost, one is tempted to believe the story which Sir Walter Scott, drawing possibly on nothing but his imagination, told. It ought to be true if it isn't that, when Johnson challenged Sir Alexander to mention one benefit which Cromwell had conferred upon his country, Sir Alexander replied: "God, Doctor! He gart kings ken they had a lith [joint] in their neck."

Yet, in spite of all this, Johnson was more often in a good humor than not and more often complacent than rude. When they dined with the Duke and Duchess of Argyle at Inveraray, Boswell had never seen Johnson "so courtly." With many of his hosts and many of their guests he got on famously, sometimes indeed with the very persons, Lord Monboddo for example, one would have expected him to bridle at. This quite eccentric philosopher not only more than equaled Rousseau in his admiration for the primitive, but also (and in anticipation) went Darwin one better by expressing the conviction that, if proper search were to be made, we would discover some savage tribe whose members bore the tails definitely establishing them as missing links. Boswell knew him of old and knew also that any mention of his name brought snorts of derision from Johnson. But as the pair passed near Monboddo's somewhat dilapidated residence, Johnson agreed to the sending of a note which brought an invitation to call.

Things looked ominous at the beginning when Monboddo, receiving his visitors at the gate, pointed to the Douglas arms, and declared: "In such houses our ancestors lived, who were better men than we." Johnson, determined to let no nonsense pass, replied in fashion equally categorical: "No, no, my lord. We are as strong as they, and a good deal wiser." But Monboddo let the dispute rest there. The two were soon discussing Homer, and soon sitting down to a very satisfactory dinner. In such a mood the recurrent fancy that he was a model of politeness struck Johnson, and after he had stood up to signalize the departure of the ladies, he delivered a little lecture on good breeding and its consequence to society. " 'Tis fictitious benevolence," he said. "It supplies the place of it among those who see each other in public, or little. Depend upon it, the want of it always produces something disagreeable to one or other." He and Monboddo disputed the question whether a savage or a London shopkeeper was the happier, but after they had left, Johnson magnanimously admitted that "he did not know but he might have taken the side of the savage equally, had any one else taken the side of the shop-keeper." He observed that Monboddo had talked no paradoxes that day. "He said he would have pardoned him for a few paradoxes when he found he had so much that was good. But that from his appearance in London he was all paradox, which would not do." [16]

When Johnson came to write his own account of his adventures (published in 1775 as *A Journey to the Western Islands of*

Scotland), he adopted the dignified manner of the philosophical traveler, and one will look in vain for any report of many of the incidents which help to make Boswell's journal so picturesque. But among the things one will find more abundantly than in Boswell is material for judging just what effect was produced upon Johnson by sights so different from any he had seen before or was ever to see again.

"Regions, mountainous and wild, thinly inhabited and little cultivated, make a great part of the earth, and he that has never seen them, must live unacquainted with much of the face of nature, and with one of the great scenes of human existence." In these words he explains to himself why a philosopher should visit some such land as that he had just traversed, but there is no evidence that he was aware of having seen anything worthy of more than curiosity, or anything which a dweller in London might care if he never saw again. To him the question "Who *can* like the Highlands?" was purely rhetorical and meant quite simply that, by comparison with Fleet Street, they were obviously unattractive. Moreover, he was carefully on his guard against any enthusiasm. When Boswell described a mountain as "immense," he bade him call it instead "a considerable protuberance." When Boswell called out: "We are contending with seas," he replied with what must have been to his friend a maddening refusal to be dramatic, "Not much." And so it went. At Leith, Boswell talked "with perhaps too boasting an air" of the beauty of the Firth of Forth. Johnson was patient until Boswell, expanding, compared it with the harbor at Constantinople and the Bay of Naples. "Ay," said Johnson, "that is the state of the world. Water is the same everywhere." He did—though one is here almost ready to doubt Boswell's accuracy—call one prospect "the noblest he had ever seen," but this was certainly not his usual attitude, and his refusal to visit more than one Druid circle is certainly more characteristic. "To go and see one," he said, "is only to see that it is nothing, for there is neither art nor power in it, and seeing one is as much as one would wish." In general, it was no doubt instructive to contemplate a rude civilization once, but once was enough. "Here," he wrote Mrs. Thrale from Skye, "are mountains which I should once have climbed . . . [but] am now content with knowing that by scrambling up a rock, I shall only see other rocks." And in the same letter he laid down the characteristic principle: "The use of travelling is to regulate imagination by reality, and instead of thinking how things may be, to see them as they are." [17]

Well aware that it is the duty of the traveler to note for the benefit of the sedentary whatever is new or strange, he conscientiously observed that in Scottish houses: "Their windows do not move upon hinges, but are pushed up and drawn down in grooves, yet they are seldom accommodated with weights and pulleys," and he added a philosophical reflection: "He that would have his window open must hold it with his hand, unless, what may be sometimes found among good contrivers, there be a nail, which he may stick into a hole, to keep it from falling. What cannot be done without some uncommon trouble or particular expedient, will not often be done at all. . . . The necessity of ventilating human habitations has not yet been found by our northern neighbors; and even in houses well built and elegantly furnished, a stranger may be sometimes forgiven, if he allows himself to wish for fresher air." Torn, as he was later to be when gathering facts for the *Lives of the Poets,* between the desire to give information and a disinclination to put forth the effort necessary to gather it, he observes: "What particular parts of commerce are chiefly exercised by the merchants of Aberdeen, I have not enquired. The manufacture which forces itself upon a stranger's eye is that of knit-stockings, on which the women of the lower class are visibly employed." And of that Scotch invention which was later to become the most popular ever made north of the Tweed, he has this to say: "The word *whisky* signifies water, and is applied by way of eminence to *strong water,* or distilled liquor. The spirit drunk in the north is drawn from barley. I never tasted it, except once for experiment at the inn at Inverary, when I thought it preferable to any English malt brandy. It was strong but not pungent, and was free from the empyreumatick taste or smell. What was the process I had no opportunity of enquiring, nor do I wish to improve the art of making poison pleasant."

Characteristically, Johnson shared the current concern over

SAMUEL JOHNSON

From the painting by Sir Joshua Reynolds (1778) in the Tate Gallery

the wave of emigration that was spreading over the whole country, and it is pleasant to be able to report that, strongly as one would expect his prejudice in favor of maintaining the integrity of the nation, that humanity, which was nearly always dominant when he was confronted with any actual hardship, led him to state the emigrant's case. "From [our host] we first heard of the general dissatisfaction, which is now driving the Highlanders into the other hemisphere; and when I asked him whether they would stay at home, if they were well treated, he answered with indignation, that no man willingly left his native country. Of the farm, which he himself occupied, the rent had, in twenty-five years, been advanced from five to twenty pounds, which he found himself so little able to pay, that he would be glad to try his fortune in some other place."

Scotch breakfasts, Johnson admitted, were probably the best in the world. "If an epicure could remove by a wish, in quest of sensual gratifications, wherever he had supped he would breakfast in Scotland." But it is not recorded that he observed among the habits or the possessions of his northern neighbors any other superiority. The cities, as was to be expected, were merely lesser Londons. Country life, as was also to be expected, was merely less comfortable and less refined than life in the cities. When one comes to the ultimate Thule of the Hebrides, there is only one thing which can possibly be said: "Of these islands it must be confessed, that they have not many allurements, but to the lover of naked nature. The inhabitants are thin, provisions scarce, and desolation and penury give little pleasure." Johnson was not a lover of naked nature and he saw nothing to modify in the slightest degree his conviction that civilization was necessary to comfort, and comfort to that refinement which makes the natural man human.

"The ladies have as much beauty here as in other places, but bloom and softness are not to be expected among the lower classes, whose faces are exposed to the rudeness of the climate, and whose features are sometimes contracted by want, and sometimes hardened by the blasts. Supreme beauty is seldom found in cottages or workshops, even where no real hardships are suffered. To expand the human face to its full perfection, it seems necessary that the mind should cooperate by placidness of content, or consciousness of superiority. . . . It is generally supposed, that life is longer in places where there are few opportunities of luxury; but I found no instance here of extraordinary longevity. A cottager grows old over his oaten cakes, like a citizen at a turtle feast. He is, indeed, seldom incommoded by corpulence. Poverty preserves him from sinking under the burden of himself, but he escapes no other injury of time. Instances of long life are often related, which those who hear them are more willing to credit than examine. To be told that any man has attained a hundred years, gives hope and comfort to him who stands trembling on the brink of his own climacterick."

Even on those few occasions when Johnson opened his mind to romantic impressions, his reactions were tempered not only by his natural tendency in the direction of the undramatic but also by the realization that the country through which he was passing, however wild it might be, was nevertheless only relatively so:

"I sat down on a bank, such as a writer of romance might have delighted to feign. I had, indeed, no trees to whisper over my head, but a clear rivulet streamed at my feet. The day was calm, the air was soft, and all was rudeness, silence, and solitude. Before me, and on either side, were high hills, which, by hindering the eye from ranging, forced the mind to find entertainment for itself. Whether I spent the hour well I know not; for here I first conceived the thought of this narration.

"We were in this place at ease and by choice, and had no evils to suffer or to fear; yet the imaginations excited by the view of an unknown and untravelled wilderness are not such as arise in the artificial solitude of parks and gardens, a flattering notion of self-sufficiency, a placid indulgence of voluntary delusions, a secure expansion of the fancy, or a cool concentration of the mental powers. The phantoms which haunt a desert are want, and misery, and danger; the evils of dereliction rush upon the thoughts; man is made unwillingly acquainted with his own weakness, and meditation shows him only how little he can sustain, and how little he can perform. There were no traces of inhabitants, except, perhaps, a rude pile of clods, called a summer hut, in which a herdsman had rest in the favourable seasons. Whoever had been in the place where I then sat, unprovided with provisions, and ignorant of the country, might, at least before the roads were made, have wandered among the rocks, till he had perished with hardship, before he could have found either food or shelter. Yet what are these hillocks to the ridges of Taurus, or these spots of wildness to the deserts of America?"[18]

He concludes his account thus:

"Such are the things which this journey has given me an opportunity of seeing, and such are the reflections which that sight has raised. Having passed my time almost wholly in cities, I may have been surprised by modes of life and appearances of nature, that are familiar to men of wider survey and much more varied conversation. Novelty and ignorance must always be reciprocal, and I cannot but be conscious that my thoughts on national manners, are the thoughts of one who has seen but little."

It only remains to add that this modesty, as far as it actually goes, is perfectly genuine. But it does not go quite so far as might at first sight be supposed. True, he had "seen but little." On the other hand, he did not suppose that much of that kind of seeing was necessary to make either a cultivated man or a wise one.

The question whether Boswell's *Journal* or Johnson's *Journey* is the better book is inevitably part of the larger controversy concerning the relative importance of the two men. To Boswell's champions, Johnson's account of his experiences is merely another illustration of the fact that its author is lively and interesting only when transmitted to us through the medium of his biographer. To Johnsonians, on the other hand, it is an equally convincing demonstration that a philosopher can hardly owe his reputation to even the most talented of gossipmongers, and one recent critic has tried to dispose of the question by remarking (with perfect truth, of course): "Johnson's unpretentious book is actually on a level of scholarship and literature beyond the reach of Boswell. It is a philosopher's book of travel, in which the traveler is looking less for particular views than for general ideas."

But that hardly proves as much as it seems to prove. Johnson was not especially gifted either as a traveler or as a writer of travel books. Something of his greatness may be sensed in the *Journal,* as something of the greatness of any great man may usually be sensed in anything he does. But to describe journeys was not his metier. Boswell, on the other hand, was practicing upon a very fine subject his one great talent, and to suggest that he did better the one thing which he did well, than Johnson could do something which he was not especially well fitted to do, is not to deny that Boswell was a far lesser man.

Johnson is a more interesting subject than the Hebrides and it is Johnson, rather than the Hebrides, which is Boswell's real subject. Indeed, and thanks partly to the fact that Johnson was so much the same wherever he happened to be, some of the best passages in the *Journal* report incidents or conversations so little affected by the surroundings amidst which they took place that they might easily be transferred to Boswell's later account of events in London. The reader, recalling one of them, may often forget whether it is to be found in the *Journal* or in the *Life.*

If, to be sure, one reads the former, not in the edited version, which Boswell published, but in the much racier original form recently recovered, one will occasionally be surprised at conversations somewhat more raffish than one has come to expect from Johnson. In the published *Journal,* as in the *Life,* Boswell permitted himself to bowdlerize slightly, and had his originals not been recovered we should not imagine that the Great Moralist had called anyone (as he did the Rev. Kenneth Macaulay) "the most ignorant booby and the grossest bastard." So, too, one is a bit surprised to find him discoursing, even though it is with his usual perspicacity, on the luxuries which are, and those which are not, suitable in connection with the convenience known to the eighteenth century as a "little house"; or observing, apropos of his feeling that animal substances are dirty: "I have often thought that if I kept a seraglio, the ladies should all wear linen gowns, or cotton." Boswell, who edited out the rest of the story in order to save his own feelings because of something still to come as well as to preserve Johnson's own reputation, goes on: "To hear Mr. Johnson, while sitting solemn in arm-chair, talk of his keeping a seraglio and saying, too, 'I have *often* thought', was truly curious. Mr. Macqueen asked him if he would admit me. 'Yes', said he, 'if he were properly prepared; and he'd make a very good eunuch. He'd be a fine gay animal. He'd do his part well'. 'I take it', said I, 'better than you would do your part'. . . . He got off from my joke by saying: 'I have not told you what was to be my part'—and then at once he returned to my office as eunuch and expatiated upon it with such fluency that it really hurt me. He made me quite contemptible for the moment."

But most of the time Johnson in Scotland was discoursing upon the same topics and discoursing in the same manner as in England. It was at Leith, but it might just as well have been anywhere else, that Boswell persisted in arguing that suicide might be under some circumstances understandable and supposed the case "that a man is absolutely sure that if he lives a few days longer, he shall be detected in a fraud, the consequence of which will be utter disgrace and expulsion from society." The answer he got was the same he would have received in Fleet Street or Timbuktu: "Then, sir, let him go abroad to a distant country; let him go to some place where he is *not* known. Don't let him go to the devil where he *is* known." Nor does climate or scene have much to do with Johnson's opinion when asked, apropos the alleged naturalness of Garrick's acting: "Would not you, sir, start as Mr. Garrick does if you saw a ghost?" "I hope not," he replied. "If I did, I should frighten the ghost."

The critic who should search through both the *Journal* and the *Journey* to find the one passage which best suggests how Johnson and Boswell reacted to a change of scene might well hesitate amongst several. If romantically inclined, he might choose the passages previously quoted in which Johnson tried to realize how wild the country in which he found himself really was. Or he might, if by inclination one kind of realist, prefer that which describes how the two travelers considered whether to wear their clothes to bed in the hope of keeping vermin at a distance or to take them off in order to give the same vermin fewer places to lodge. But if the critic were neither a romantic nor a realist of the sort referred to, but rather convinced, as Johnson himself was, that men, like water, are much the same wherever you find them and certainly change little when they move about, then he might choose instead the record of a conversation which took place at Ostaig on the Isle of Skye. "I asked him if he had never been accustomed to wear a night-cap. He said, 'No'. I asked if it was best not to do it. He said he had that custom by chance; 'and perhaps no man shall ever know whether 'tis best to sleep with or without a night-cap. . . . Nobody before was ever foolish enough to ask. . . . This comes of being a little wrong-headed'." Perhaps, in other words, the chief thing to be learned from either of the accounts of the great perambulation is simply this: Boswell and Johnson took themselves and one another along for company.[19]

Leaving Boswell in Scotland, Johnson returned alone to London from whence he wrote, on November 27, 1773: "I came home last night, without any incommodity, danger, or weariness, and am ready to begin a new journey." He was not to see Boswell again until March of 1775 but his intimacy with the Thrales was immediately renewed.

He had, indeed, by no means forgotten them while touring Scotland. Mrs. Thrale had been among those who urged him to take the journey, and during his absence he received letters from her husband as well as from herself; moreover, he wrote her a serial account of his adventures, some of the installments of which, though short enough as eighteenth-century letters go, are probably the longest he ever forced himself to write. He also gathered souvenirs for her daughter Queeney; refused to drink her health in whisky; and rather startled Boswell by the vehemence with which he forbade the latter to write in her name a mock epistle to Johnson on his return from Scotland. In the Hebrides he composed for her a Latin ode, which includes the stanza:

> Inter erroris, salebrosa longi,
> Inter ignotae strepitus loquelae
> Quot modis mecum, quid agat requiro,
> Thralia dulcis.[20]

The golden age of the Streatham salon was soon to begin, but at the moment of Johnson's return, his friends were still staggering under a series of misfortunes, which had begun the year before that in which the tour was made.

Mr. Thrale, never a conservative businessman, had allowed himself to be taken in by a schemer named Humphrey Jackson, who claimed to have discovered something of which no doubt all brewers have dreamed—namely, a way of making beer without either malt or hops. Not only did Thrale risk a whole year's output on the new process, but also laid out two thousand pounds to build, for this same Jackson, copper vats, in which, according to Mrs. Thrale, he "was to make Experiments and conjure some curious Stuff, which should preserve Ship's Bottoms from the Worm." To make matters worse, the City was thrown into a panic by the failure of a large banking house in June, 1772, and Thrale, without available capital and without even the year's supply of beer, was faced with ruin which was averted only by his wife's successful efforts to borrow money here and there. Even so, they were left with a debt of one hundred and thirty thousand pounds over and above that of the borrowed money. Meanwhile, Mrs. Thrale continued to bear one child after another; a scandalmongering periodical discovered a good subject in one of Thrale's flamboyant mistresses and, having found that so good a thing, proceeded to invent the story that "An eminent Brewer was very jealous of a certain Author in Folio, and perceived a strong resemblance to him in his eldest son." In June of 1773, Mrs. Thrale's mother, who made her home with the Thrales, died, and in October of the same year, while Johnson was on his tour, her uncle, Sir Thomas Salusbury, from whom, somewhat improbably, she had hoped for some money, proceeded to shuffle off, leaving his wife sole heir. Johnson had been ill in the spring, and despite the fact that he stood the hard journey through Scotland remarkably well, he was soon ill again, and, as usual, asking to be looked after. To Boswell he wrote on February 7, 1774: "I have, indeed, for some weeks past, been very ill of a cold and cough, and have been at Mrs. Thrale's, that I might be taken care of."

Probably Mr. Thrale never completely recovered from these events, and perhaps it is because he is best known from accounts subsequent to this time that he generally appears so silent and morose a man. His wife, on the other hand, was nothing if not resilient, and the sun was soon smiling again. Even during the dark summer of 1773, extensive improvements, including the building of the library wing and much remodeling, were undertaken at Streatham; by the spring of the following year, the brewery was again prosperous, and Mrs. Thrale, who always seemed to think a jaunt or some other form of entertainment the best remedy for sorrow, set off in the summer for a tour of her native Wales with her husband, Johnson, and her eldest daughter, Queeney. Johnson kept a rather dull diary and Mrs. Thrale a not much more interesting one (first published thirty-odd years ago), from both of which it appears that the trip was no great success. Johnson, having just seen one wild country, obviously had no great enthusiasm about seeing another, and not even the company of his favorite child—the bright but rather unpleasant Queeney, aged ten—seems to have enabled him to enjoy it. Nevertheless, the same group made, in the fall of the following year, a journey lasting nearly two months to Paris. It also seems to have meant little to Johnson, and it is a pity that a proposed visit to Italy (which he had long wanted to see) never took place.[21]

On the other hand, the still expanding social life centered at Streatham continued to delight both the hostess and Johnson, who was obviously pleased to be not only part of it but, to some extent, its center. It has earlier been remarked that Reynolds, Goldsmith and Burke had begun to come soon after Johnson himself was established, though the exact date of the first visit of none except Reynolds can be fixed. From a jubilant note written by the hostess, it appears that Mr. and Mrs. Garrick came at least as early as 1777. Garrick never became a real intimate, but a meeting with the famous bluestocking, Mrs. Elizabeth Montagu, two years before had opened up a new field, and she came to dinner at Streatham in the summer of 1777. To celebrate their success as hosts, the Thrales commissioned Reynolds to paint a series of portraits of their distinguished guests to adorn the library. There were ultimately thirteen of them and it was probably Johnson's (given what must have been a position of honor over the fireplace) that he himself is referring to when he writes to Mrs. Thrale on October 30, 1778: "Sir Joshua has finished my picture, and it seems to please everybody, but I shall wait to see how it pleases you." [22]

In 1776, a few weeks before her thirteenth wedding anniversary, Mrs. Thrale received from her husband a set of six handsome quarto blank books bound in undressed calf and each bearing on its cover a red and gold label reading *Thraliana.* Being an inveterate scribbler, she had not waited for this gift to begin keeping notes of one kind or another. Since 1766 she had been keeping a family record known as the *Children's Book.* As early as 1768, Johnson had advised her to "get a little book," and from at least that time on she kept up two more collections —one of anecdotes about Johnson himself and another of miscellaneous anecdotes. Indeed, even after *Thraliana* was begun, she continued to keep separate records of conversations to be copied out later, and thus she worked by a method not wholly different in its mechanical aspects from that of Boswell. But when the new books had been received from her husband, her zeal was redoubled. Imitating the French compilers of ana, she promptly filled the first volume with an extremely heterogeneous collection of anecdotes, character sketches, jeux d'esprit and bons mots—drawn from books and previous notes as well as from memory—and relating indiscriminately to both the living and the dead. Almost exactly one year later, or on September 18, 1777, she began a new volume of which she devoted the first ninety-seven pages exclusively to memorabilia of Johnson before returning then to the previous haphazard method now further complicated by the addition of a detailed record of her own life. After the summer of 1779, by which time she had reached the middle of the third volume, *Thraliana* became more and more exclusively a diary and such it remained until after the death of her husband and then that of Johnson. Something of the old manner, however, was later resumed and continued until, a very old woman living in a new world, she wrote the last entry on March 30, 1809: "Everything most dreaded *has* ensued,—all is over; & my second Husbands Death is the last Thing recorded in my first husband's Present! Cruel Death!"

The existence of *Thraliana* has long been known and certain excerpts made by an early biographer of Mrs. Thrale were used by G. Birkbeck Hill and other great Johnsonians, but the full text was not available to scholars until it was acquired by the Huntington Library, and in 1942 it was published in two volumes totaling more than a thousand pages. Much of the material for her *Anecdotes* was quarried out of *Thraliana,* and it is now obvious that when they were written she had *Thraliana* beside her, and did not write, as was previously supposed, either from memory or with only the earlier notes at hand. Surviving fragments of these early notes show that, at least in the instances they illustrate, the text of the *Anecdotes* is quite close to that of *Thraliana,* much less close to that of the record in its first form. Moreover, the differences between *Thraliana* and the *Anecdotes,* on the one hand, and the earliest record, on the other, indicate quite clearly that Mrs. Thrale allowed herself to modify and improve upon the truth with a freedom which Boswell seldom permitted himself. One must, accordingly, always suspect the precise accuracy of any passage in the *Anecdotes* which cannot be checked at least against *Thraliana* which, one must remember, is itself open to some suspicion, especially if the passage in question is one of those in the compilation which composes the first part of Book II.[23]

But the importance of *Thraliana* is by no means confined exclusively to its usefulness as a check. Scattered here and there are hundreds of references to Johnson and other members of the Streatham circle as well as some highly illuminating character sketches—notably one of the brilliant and dangerous Italian, Joseph Baretti, who had been introduced into the Thrale household in 1773 as a tutor for Queeney; who became an accepted member of the social circle; and who figures frequently in the pages of Boswell. Many of the entries, moreover, are especially valuable from the fact that they represent Mrs. Thrale's contemporary opinions and attitudes rather than what those attitudes and opinions had become when, having begun a new life and being a good deal on the defensive, she composed the *Anecdotes.* At the latter time she would not, for example, have paid Boswell the telling compliment which she wrote down under the date December, 1777: "Mr. Boswell however is the Man for a

Johnsoniana; he really knows ten Times more Anecdotes of his Life than I do who see so much more of him."

It may be remembered that in a passage previously quoted from the *Anecdotes,* Mrs. Thrale blamed her husband for having first imposed the burden of Johnson upon her, and that Boswell protested that she had never complained of his being a burden during his lifetime. Certainly the pages which she devotes to him in *Thraliana* carry no suggestion (until a rupture was approaching) that she found the burden, if burden it was, other than well worth bearing. She began her record of Johnson by a promise "to delight myself by committing to Paper the regard I have for Mr. Johnson" and she speaks of him with almost superstitious veneration.

Yet it is perhaps worth noting that, if the highlights of her portrait are at least as brilliant as Boswell's, the shadows are darker and that—possibly of course in part only because she was a person more given than Boswell to certain kinds of extravagance of statement—she attributes to him faults less excused and less excusable than any Boswell admits. We know, for instance, that Johnson's attitude toward children had something slightly ambiguous in it, but it is startling to find her writing: "He was in his Turn extremely indulgent to Children, not because he lov'd them, for he loved them not, but because he feared extremely to disoblige them: a Child, says he is capable of resentment much earlier than is commonly suppos'd." And this rather farfetched interpretation of Johnson's kindness is not made more persuasive by what follows: "As he was always on the side of the husband against the Wife, so he was always on the side of the Children against the Old ffolks—old People, says he have no Honour, no Delicacy; the World has blunted their Sensibility & Appetite or Avarice governs the last Stage. this was our talk one Morning at Breakfast, when a favorite Spaniel stole our Muffin which stood by the Fire to keep hot;—Fye Bell said I you used to be upon honour, Yes Madam, replied Johnson,—but *Belle grows old.*" It is even more startling to find her committing herself to the opinion: "Of all his intimates and Friends, I think I never could find any who much loved him Boswell & Burney excepted—Mr. Murphy too loved him as he loves People—when he sees them—All the others would rather not have seen him than seen him as far as I have been able to observe; & as to Burney, had they been more together, they would have liked each other less; but I who delighted greatly in them both, used to keep those Parts of their Characters out of Sight wch would have offended the other." Since it was Johnson who first drew to Streatham some of the persons who are here represented as disliking his company, it is difficult to accept Mrs. Thrale's judgment without first assuming that they put up with him for the sake of a good dinner. But at least the judgment ought to be recorded.

Admirers of Johnson may sometimes have wondered if they did not detect in him as he grew older some slight tendency occasionally to identify himself with the prejudices of the privileged class of which he had become an adopted member, but if any such tendency did exist, it was certainly less than Mrs. Thrale would have liked. Her protest in the margin of Boswell's *Life* against Johnson's hankering after the tea and bread of existence has already been noted. A much stronger and more curious example of the same sort of protest occurs in *Thraliana*. To savor it fully, one must remember that Mrs. Thrale was herself a woman active in the good works of charity. One must remember also that, though a sound Tory, a churchwoman and therefore correctly appreciative of the benefits conferred upon society as a whole by the Great Scheme of Subordination, she could call Johnson, by comparison with herself, "warm even to Bigotry" upon that subject. Yet she obviously could not quite forgive him for having "more Tenderness for Poverty than any other Man I ever knew," and once, when he had rebuked her for a contemptuous reference to a "walk through *Porridge Island*" (a Covent Garden Alley famous for cheap cookshops) by saying: "Let us have done laughing at what is serious to so many; Hundreds of your Fellow Creatures dear Lady turn another way that they may not be tempted by the Luxuries of *Porridge Island* to hope for Gratifications they are not able to obtain," she let herself go in the diary: "These Notions—just as they doubtless are; —seem to me the faeculancies of his low Birth, which I believe has never failed to leave its *Stigma* indelible in every human Creature; however exalted by Rank or polished by Learning:—

no Varnish though strong can totally cover primeval meanness, nor can any Situation of Life remove it out of the Sight even of a cursory & casual Observer." In other words, to distribute charity is part of the duty of superior people. But actually to be able to conceive in the imagination "what wretches feel" is Low.[24]

In 1778 Mrs. Thrale records that she had once seen a book in which the author had adopted the device (very modern it seems!) of judging a number of authors by selecting a list of qualities—color, grace, etc.—and then giving each writer a numerical rating under each head. She decided to adopt the same method of grading her acquaintances on their various personal qualities. Following her model, she chose twenty to represent the highest possible degree of any quality and then proceeded to subject thirty-eight men to the test. Her judgment of two of the men certainly deserves to be noted in a biography of Johnson. Here it is:

	RELIGION	MORALITY	SCHOLARSHIP	GEN. KNOWLEDGE	PERSON & VOICE	MANNER
BOSWELL:	5	5	5	10	10	8
JOHNSON:	20	20	19	20	0	0

	WIT	HUMOUR	GOOD HUMOUR
BOSWELL:	7	3	19
JOHNSON:	15	16	0

To give Boswell only 5 on religion is perhaps juster than he would have thought. To give him 19 on good humor seems to be to confirm the opinion of many of his acquaintances. One hardly expects Johnson to stand conspicuously high in respect to the last-named virtue. But an absolute zero is, like some of Mrs. Thrale's other judgments of him, a bit startling. It may, however, mean something that Garrick, Burke, Baretti, Bennet Langton and Beauclerk were also, in her opinion, totally without "good humour."

Whether Johnson at Streatham was good-humored or not, one thing is certain. The whole tone of his conversation and behavior there was lighter than it had ever been anywhere else. A certain tinge of frivolity was seldom absent from anything

Mrs. Thrale did. "Vive la bagatelle" was certainly one of her mottoes and Johnson, who had always been theoretically in favor of gaiety, now managed to put theory into practice. Among the ridiculous parlor games favored by his hostess was one which consisted in imagining what animal or what food each member of the circle would be if he *were* an animal or a dish. Inevitably Johnson was an elephant—also, less obviously, a haunch of venison. But he, like the elephant described by a poet of whom he did not entirely approve, "to make them mirth untwined his lithe proboscis."

This does not mean that he never fell back into what was once described as his "bow-wow way." Reports of the conversation at Streatham indicate that the big guns might be unlimbered at any moment and sometimes when it was least expected. When they were, subjects were disposed of with all the old-time finality. But there was also an abundance of persiflage and many family jokes. When he had first come into the group, Johnson had teased Mrs. Thrale's mother (whose absorption in the news of the world outraged one of his pet prejudices) by inventing imaginary battles supposed to be raging on the Continent. Later, when Mrs. Thrale's distant cousin, the spinster Margaret Owen, spent the winter of 1777 with them, he let it be known that she had refused the offer of his hand in marriage, and that when they all went to Tunbridge together, he warned off other suitors by telling them that if she had turned him down, she obviously would not be easily pleased. He could also turn his hand to charades; choose a motto for a clock; or make, about Belle the spaniel who had developed the habit of snatching, jokes which hardly deserve immortality—e.g., "this Dog would have been a fit member of the Society established by Lycurgus, She condemns one to a State of perpetual Vigilance." And then, of course, there was his favorite, Queeney, whom he rather perversely adored, despite the haughty sullenness of which she gave a splendid example by replying at the age of eleven to a man who asked her at Bath in 1776 if she had ever seen such a sight before: "Yes Sir . . . I think *this* Room very like the South Sea House,—and *this* Company, very like the Clerks." Her birthday and Johnson's (which fell one day later) were once, at least, celebrated together, with a dance for the servants and with the summer house filled with "Food, Fiddles &c." He undertook to teach her Latin (which Mr. Thrale enthusiastically calculated to be better than a thousand pounds added to her fortune) and once, when she put on a fine new dress for a dinner at Mrs. Montagu's, he suddenly came out with an impromptu poem on a classical theme which Queeney did not need to have emphasized:

> "Wear the Gown, & wear the Hat,
> Snatch your pleasures while they last;
> Hadst thou nine Lives like a Cat,
> Soon those nine Lives would be past." [25]

Even when company was present, he would often play his old trick of keeping aloof and busying himself with a book or with scanning the library shelves, "almost touching the backs of them with his eye-lashes, as he read their titles," and then charging into the conversation when something interested or exasperated him. When Dr. Burney had been playing duets with one of his daughters while Johnson had been reading the *Encyclopédie,* he was thrown a question about J. C. Bach's latest concert and promptly exhibited his fine philistine contempt for all the arts except his own by inquiring scornfully: "And pray, Sir, *who is Bach?* Is he a piper?" "Why," said Mrs. Thrale, "you have read his name often in the papers," and then proceeded to give him some account of the concerts. "Pray," said he, gravely, "Madam, what is the expense?" "Oh," answered she, "much trouble and solicitation, to get a Subscriber's Ticket;—or else, half a Guinea." "Trouble and solicitation," said he, "I will have nothing to do with; but would be willing to give eighteen pence."

But despite this effort to put the Burneys and their music in its place, Johnson, thanks to these same Burneys, came, while at Streatham, so far to relax his prejudice as to admit that his failure to appreciate harmony might be due to a defect in him rather than to a defect in music, for when he heard read aloud, from the manuscript of Burney's *History of Music,* the statement that the love of "modulated sounds" must be a passion implanted in human nature, since it is shared by all peoples, he cried out: "Sir! this assertion I believe may be right." And then seesawing a moment in his chair, added: "All animated nature loves music—except myself!"

In the old days he had not been so weakly complaisant. According to Sir John Hawkins, he had once damned the whole art with the declaration: "It excites in my mind no ideas, and hinders me from contemplating my own." And once when Boswell, who ought to have known better than to parade a sensibility which Johnson did not share, told him that he was so affected by music "as often to agitate my nerves painfully, producing in my mind alternate sensations of pathetick dejection, so that I was ready to shed tears; and of daring resolution, so that I was inclined to rush into the thickest part of the battle," Johnson was ready for him. "Sir, (said he,) I should never hear it, if it made me such a fool." But at Streatham he had been known to poke his nose over the keys of the harpsichord while a duet was being played.

When Dr. Burney threatened to make a music lover of him in time, he replied, smiling: "Sir, I shall be very glad to have a new sense put into me." A few months before Johnson's death he went even so far as to request Burney to teach him the scale, and about the same time he told Boswell, on hearing some music accompanying a funeral procession, that this was "the first time that I have ever been affected by musical sounds." It is to be feared, however, that he never got much beyond the point where he was able to direct to one of the Thrale girls, who was playing upon the harpsichord, the discouraging question: "Why don't you dash away like Burney?" The latter's daughter thought Johnson was too deaf to hear what was going on, but it has been objected that other accounts do not suggest that his hearing was as bad as that. Perhaps he merely liked sounds to be strong as he certainly liked flavors to be—a possibility suggested by Boswell's account of how, in the Highlands, he "appeared fond of the bagpipe, and used often to stand for some time with his ear close to the great drone." [26]

By no means the least of the delights of life at Streatham—better even perhaps than the formal parties—was the constant stream of informal sociability supplied by house guests, neighbors and semidependents, who seem to have been always coming or going. It was the custom for everyone to pass the mornings alone, but the rest of the day was spent in highly gregarious fashion. No visitor, moreover, was allowed to go to waste—if he was entertaining, he entertained; if he was not, he at least supplied material for endless discussions and mockeries. The somewhat saturnine Jeremiah Crutchley (believed to be Thrale's natural son), the simple-minded Mr. Rose Fuller, the hypochondriacal William Seward, and the fair Sophy Streatfeild (known as "the S.S.") all furnished some amusement. Even Rose Fuller could at least provoke an epigram: "Is not young Rose Fuller a foolish Fellow—to keep from Church because old Rose is an Infidel?—Is it not foolisher says Johnson in James Harris to be an Infidel, because Lord Shaftsbury wrote the Characteristicks?" Seward could inspire Crutchley with a fine extravagant account of how, on a visit to Crutchley's lodgings, the hypochondriac sought relief from his symptoms by eating cherries, drinking port and madeira, calling for three glasses of peppermint water, a large quantity of ginger, some brandy, and, finally, rhubarb. "I advised him," added Crutchley, "to take a good bumper of gin and gunpowder, for that seemed almost all he had left untried." No wonder that when Streatham was suggested as the possible scene for a play, Johnson cried pompous approval: "Yes! 'Streatham—a Farce!' "

Of all those whom he saw at the Thrales', no one—hardly even the hostess herself—delighted him so much as young Fanny Burney, who had just published *Evelina* when she was first introduced into the household in 1778 and was soon thereafter invited for a stay. Johnson had long known her father but does not seem, until just before this, to have noticed Fanny. Dr. Burney taught music to Queeney, and thus the way was prepared for her entry into the Streatham circle.[27]

Not all the readers of her famous *Diary* have fallen completely under the spell of her charm. Macaulay's defense notwithstanding, some find the assiduity with which she records the compliments paid her a bit tiresome, and Mrs. Thrale herself, after the intimacy had been established, had her reservations. "I fancy She has a real regard for me, if She did not think it beneath the Dignity of a Wit, or what She values more—the Dignity of *Doc-*

tor Burney's Daughter to indulge it"; and again: "She makes me miserable too in many Respects—so restless & apparently anxious lest I should give myself Airs of Patronage, or load her with the Shackles of Dependence—I . . . dare not ask her to buy me a Ribbon, dare not desire her to touch the Bell, lest she should think herself injured." But, on the other hand, the Burneys were far from rich, Mrs. Thrale had a touch of the snob in her make-up, and she may have been quite as much on the lookout for unbecoming airs in a musicmaster's daughter as she thought the latter was on the lookout for the presumptions of a patroness. And Johnson at least had no reservations. It was on both sides something like love at first sight.

Fanny was first aware that she had seen the Doctor when Mrs. Thrale brought him to the Burney house in London in March, 1777. She was prepared for a great experience and somewhat provoked when, instead of talking, Johnson peered at the books on the shelves. Moreover, like most people who saw him for the first time, she was shocked by his appearance. "He is, indeed, very ill-favoured; is tall and stout; but stoops terribly; he is almost bent double. His mouth is almost [continually opening and shutting] as if he was chewing. He has a strange method of frequently twirling his fingers, and twisting his hands. His body is in continual agitation, *see-sawing* up and down; his feet are never a moment quiet; and, in short, his whole person is in *perpetual motion.* His dress, too, considering the times, and that he had meant to put on his *best becomes,* being engaged to dine in a large company, was as much out of the common road as his figure; he had a large wig, snuff-colour coat, and gold buttons, but no ruffles to his [shirt], doughty [perhaps softened from "dirty" in the original version] fists, and black worsted stockings. He is shockingly near-sighted, and did not, till she held out her hand to him, even know Mrs. Thrale." But not much further acquaintance was necessary to banish any unfavorable impressions which had been made. Johnson was presently drawn into the conversation, and Fanny was enraptured.

Writing of her first visit to Streatham the next year, she calls it "the most consequential day I have spent since my birth." Johnson began immediately to devote himself to her and on the subject of the open secret of her authorship of *Evelina* he laid on the flattery as thickly as anyone to whom he ever objected. Mrs. Thrale, before she knew Johnson's opinion, thought *Evelina* amusing enough but "flimzy" compared with Richardson, Fielding and Smollett, but Johnson's admiration was extravagant. He insisted that Fielding never did anything equal to the second volume of *Evelina*. "Richardson would have been really afraid of her; there is merit in *Evelina* which he could not have borne"; "*The Vicar of Wakefield,*" he said, "is very faulty; there is nothing of real life in it, and very little of nature. It is a mere fanciful performance." In so far as Johnson's estimate was serious (and there seems no reason for believing that it was not), the best explanation, aside from that furnished by his liking for the author, is probably suggested by the reference to *The Vicar of Wakefield.* He had, as occasion has previously been taken to observe, a great delight in minutely realistic descriptions of manners, and there was then less prose fiction capable of affording that delight than there is now. *Evelina,* though morally innocent, was marked by a certain knowing worldliness and was a step in a direction he was obviously glad to see the novel taking. Moreover, it is probably not improper to observe that his odd conception of himself as an especially good judge of true polish and gentility was flattered. The false elegance of Mr. Smith, the gentleman manqué, was something which he thought himself capable of savoring more adequately than most.[28]

But Johnson's partiality for *Evelina* was no more marked than that which its author also enjoyed. He was put beside her at table—"we had a noble dinner, and a most elegant dessert"—on her very first evening at Streatham and he was gallant immediately. It was soon understood that he and she should always be partners at table. Boswell, visiting Streatham on a later occasion, was obviously astonished to be waved aside when he prepared "to take a seat that he seemed, by prescription, to consider as his own," and by that time Johnson had taken her completely under his wing, obviously delighting in a kind of half-mocking flirtation at once warmer and more playful than any recorded relationship he had had with any woman since Tetty's death. Once, even, and somewhat to her surprise, he drew her toward him and gave her a kiss—before witnesses, let it be hastily added, lest it be supposed that Johnson was imitating the habits of his future biographer.

Fanny willingly played up to the great man. She had been at first a little astonished by his outspoken ways with others and her remark—"the strength of words he uses would, to most people, be intolerable; but Mrs. Thrale—far from making a point of vindicating herself—generally receives his admonitions with the most respectful silence"—is another rebuttal to Boswell's suggestion that his hero was under restraint. To Fanny herself he was all jokes and smiles. She was amazed that the Great Moralist should take a gay interest in the costumes of the women about him and could even be weighty on the subject: "The truth is, women, take them in general, have no idea of grace. Fashion is all they think of. I don't mean Mrs. Thrale and Miss Burney, when I talk of women!—they are goddesses!—and therefore I except them." He was so anxious to have Fanny make the most of herself that when the Queen of the Blues, Mrs. Montagu (whom he did not too much love), was expected, he tried to lay a plot: "Come, Burney, shall you and I study our parts against Mrs. Montagu comes? . . . Always fly at the eagle! Down with Mrs. Montagu herself!"

Mrs. Thrale might rate Johnson's good humor at zero but Fanny found him positively jovial. "Johnson was in the utmost good humour" and "he was as lively and full of wit and sport as I have ever seen him" are typical sentences in her diary. Indeed, her portrait of her admirer is so much the gayest which survives that the question whether or not it is falsely colored inevitably arises. Fanny was, of course, a novelist. Her diary was revised long after it had been originally written. Moreover, her reports of Johnson's talk represent him as more easily colloquial than he is anywhere else represented. But it must be remembered that his last writing was also the least formal—in certain ways the least "Johnsonian"—he had ever done, and Fanny herself (who had just been reading his *Life of Cowley*) observes: "I could not help remarking how very like Dr. Johnson is to his writing; and how much the same thing it was to hear or to read him; but that nobody could tell that without coming to Streatham, for his language was generally imagined to be laboured and studied, instead of the mere common flow of his thoughts." Doubtless some allowance must be made for the personal equation in Fanny's portrait, but perhaps not so much as one might be inclined to make. Probably she brought out better than anyone else ever had certain things latent in his nature. At least she cannot have invented out of whole cloth things like his joyous account of some of the feminine rascals he had known, from Mrs. Pinkethman (Pilkington?) to Bet Flint, or his imaginary conversation with the dramatist Cumberland apropos of the fact that his daughters had been hissed out of the playhouse because of the extreme height of the feathers they wore.[29]

Sophy Streatfeild, the other recognized charmer prominently a member of the Streatham coterie, was also said to be in Johnson's good graces. But the references to any intercourse between the two are so few both in Fanny Burney's diary and in *Thraliana* that (unless this be set down to jealousy on the part of the two diarists) one is compelled to suspect him to have been less impressed with her rather aloof beauty than anybody else was. Johnson probably preferred pert women like Mrs. Thrale or like Fanny herself, and Sophy was something quite different—soft, insinuating, and yet, with it all, aloof at last; known for her ready but meaningless tears; and suggesting Proust's Odette, who had sorrow on her face but none in her heart, even though she was known to cherish a not too secret passion for one Dr. Vyse, an unhappily married clergyman, who might, so Mrs. Thrale observed, say with Millamant in *The Way of the World:*

> If there's delight in Love; 'tis when I see,
> The Heart *which others bleed for*—bleed for me.

Sophy, said Johnson, "is a sweet creature, and I love her much; but my little Burney writes a better letter," and he refused to be impressed even by the Greek which Dr. Collier had taught her. Mrs. Thrale asserted that "she had a power of captivation that was irresistible; that her beauty, joined to her softness, her caressing manners, her tearful eyes, and alluring looks, would insinuate her into the heart of any man she thought worth attacking," but Johnson insisted that "Taking away her Greek, she was as ignorant as a butterfly." In the Streatham game of comparisons she was a "Pigeon," "pea Green Satten," the "Jessamine" and "White Fricassee." Unfortunately Henry Thrale either needed no encouragement or was one of those whom she thought it worth while to attack, for his open though unsuccessful pursuit of her was a scandal and the subject of a good many ostentatiously high-minded comments in *Thraliana*. But Sophy's greatest gift is most adequately described and celebrated in a long and elaborately worked-up passage of Fanny's diary:

Sir Philip.—Well, I have heard so much of these tears, that I would give the universe to have a sight of them.

Mrs. Thrale.—Well, she shall cry again if you like it.

S.S.—No, pray, Mrs. Thrale.

Sir Philip.—Oh, pray do! pray let me see a little of it.

Mrs. Thrale.—Yes, do cry a little, Sophy (in a wheedling voice), pray do! Consider, now, you are going to-day, and it's very hard if you won't cry a little: indeed, S.S., you ought to cry.

Now for the wonder of wonders. When Mrs. Thrale, in a coaxing voice, suited to a nurse soothing a baby, had run on for some time,—while all the rest of us, in laughter, joined in the request, —two crystal tears came into the soft eyes of the S.S., and rolled gently down her cheeks! Such a sight I never saw before, nor could I have believed. She offered not to conceal or dissipate them: on the contrary, she really contrived to have them seen by everybody. She looked, indeed, uncommonly handsome; for her pretty face was not, like Chloe's, blubbered; it was smooth and elegant, and neither her features nor complexion were at all ruffled; nay, indeed, she was smiling all the time.

'Look, look!' cried Mrs. Thrale; 'see if the tears are not come already.'

Loud and rude bursts of laughter broke from us all at once. How, indeed, could they be restrained? Yet we all stared, and looked and re-looked again and again, twenty times, ere we could believe our eyes. Sir Philip, I thought, would have died in convulsions; for his laughter and his politeness, struggling furiously with one another, made him almost black in the face. Mr.

Seward looked half vexed that her crying for him was now so much lowered in its flattery, yet grinned incessantly; Miss Thrale laughed as much as contempt would allow her; but Dr. Delap seemed petrified with astonishment.

When our mirth abated, Sir Philip, colouring violently with his efforts to speak, said,

'I thank you, ma'am, I'm much obliged to you.'

But I really believe he spoke without knowing what he was saying.

'What a wonderful command,' said Dr. Delap, very gravely, 'that lady must have over herself!'

She now took out a handkerchief, and wiped her eyes.

'Sir Philip,' cried Mr. Seward, 'how can you suffer her to dry her own eyes?—you, who sit next her?'

'I dare not dry them for her,' answered he, 'because I am not the right man.'

'But if I sat next her,' returned he, 'she should not dry them herself.'

'I wish,' cried Dr. Delap, 'I had a bottle to put them in; 'tis a thousand pities they should be wasted.'

'There, now,' said Mrs. Thrale, 'she looks for all the world as if nothing had happened; for, you know, nothing *has* happened!'

'Would you cry, Miss Burney,' said Sir Philip, 'if we asked you?'

'Oh,' cried Mrs. Thrale, 'I would not do thus by Miss Burney for ten worlds! I daresay she would never speak to me again. I should think she'd be more likely to walk out of my house than to cry because I bid her.'

'I don't know how that is,' cried Sir Philip; 'but I'm sure she's gentle enough.'

'She can cry, I doubt not,' said Mr. Seward, 'on any proper occasion.'

'But I must know,' said I, 'what for.'

I did not say this loud enough for the S.S. to hear me; but if I had, she would not have taken it for the reflection it meant. She seemed, the whole time, totally insensible to the numerous strange and, indeed, impertinent speeches which were made, and to be very well satisfied that she was only manifesting a tenderness of disposition that increased her beauty of countenance. At least, I can put no other construction upon her conduct, which was, without exception, the strangest I ever saw. Without any pretence of affliction,—to weep merely because she was bid, though bid in a manner to forbid anyone else,—to be in good spirits all the time,—to see the whole company expiring of laughter at her tears, without being at all offended,—and, at last, to dry them up, and go on with the same sort of conversation she held before they started!

What Sir Philip or Mr. Seward privately thought of this incident I know not yet: but Mr. Delap said,

'Yes, she has pretty blue eyes,—very pretty indeed; she's quite a wonderful miss. If it had not been for that little gush, I don't know what would have become of me. It was very goodnatured of her, really, for she charms and uncharms in a moment; she is a bane and an antidote at the same time.'

Then, after considering it more deeply,

'I declare,' he said, 'I was never so much surprised in my life! I should as soon have expected that the dew would fall from heaven because Mrs. Thrale called for it, as that Miss What-d'ye-call-her would have cried just because she was asked. But the thing is—did she cry? I declare I don't believe it. Yet I think, at this moment, I saw it,—only I know it could not be: something of a mist, I suppose, was before my eyes.'

Sophy is never mentioned by Boswell in the *Life,* she floated out of Fanny Burney's ken, and she disappears from *Thraliana* after 1791. The pages of *Notes and Queries* will, however, reveal both that she has long continued to excite the curiosity of those who lived too late ever to have the opportunity of seeing her cry and that materials to gratify that curiosity have been scant. For this reason it is, perhaps, worth while to note that very recently the editor of *Thraliana* has succeeded in locating the present head of the Streatfeild family and got some new facts. Sophy never got her Dr. Vyse and, as one might have prophesied from one of Mrs. Thrale's remarks about her ("Everybody's Admiration as Mrs. Byron says and nobody's Choice"), she appears to have remained an old maid. She died on November 30, 1835, at the age of eighty-one.[30]

Oddly enough, it was during what one inevitably thinks of as the happiest years of Johnson's life that he composed the most unfortunate of his literary productions—namely, of course, the pamphlet *Taxation No Tyranny* which appeared in 1775 and concerning which his admirers, British as well as American, seem generally to assume the less said the better.

It was not Johnson's first serious attempt at political pamphleteering. As early as 1770 he had composed *The False Alarm,* which was intended to assure the public that it had nothing to fear from the government's attempt to place Colonel Luttrell in Parliament despite the fact that John Wilkes had been duly elected. The next year appeared his *Thoughts on the Late Transactions Respecting the Falkland Islands,* in favor of which it may at least be said that it raises humane objections to the threat of what Johnson thought an unnecessary war. His enemies assumed that these pamphlets were written to repay the Government for his pension, but the truth seems to be that the principal motive was a desire to help Mr. Thrale, who had been elected to Parliament from Southwark at the end of 1765—as a Tory of course. Baretti told Dr. T. Campbell that none of Johnson's political pamphlets would have been written "had it not been for Mrs. Thrale and Baretti, who stirred him up by laying wagers, etc."

At about the same time, Johnson was getting further practice in the art of making the worse appear the better reason by supplying Boswell with writings in support of legal clients, and in this way he produced, among other things, a defense of a schoolmaster accused of brutal treatment of his pupils as well as a defense of a clergyman's "right of immediate, and personal reprehension from the pulpit." Johnson was, therefore, well equipped to prove not only that England had a right to tax her colonists as she saw fit, but also that they should be treated with absolute ruthlessness if they presumed to object. Americans may, nevertheless, regret that Johnson did not remember then a little story which would have been very apt and which he was to tell not long afterwards in his *Life of Waller.* James I, so it seems, once questioned two of his bishops, Drs. Andrewes and Neale, concerning his right to tax. "My lords," he inquired, "cannot I take my subjects' money, when I want it, without all this formality of parliament?" "God forbid, sir, but you should," said Neale. "You are the breath of our nostrils." But when the king turned to Andrewes, the latter, who must surely have been corrupted by Whiggery, gave only a partial answer. "I think," he said, "it is lawful for you to take my brother Neale's money; for he offers it."

We know that Johnson was planning to write "about the Americans" as early as January 21, 1775. Boswell, unlike Dr. Campbell, had "no doubt" that he did so "at the desire of those who were then in power" and adds that Johnson "owned to me, that it had been revised and curtailed by some of them." Boswell, whose liberalism was certainly not anything upon which one could count, admits that he himself had formed "a clear and settled opinion" that the Americans had good right to resist and adds that the extreme violence of Johnson's writing appeared to him "unsuitable to the mildness of a Christian philosopher, and so directly opposite to the principles of peace which he had so beautifully recommended in his pamphlet respecting Falkland's Islands, that I was sorry to see him appear in so unfavorable a light."

Where even Boswell censures unqualifiedly, it is hardly worth while to attempt any defense. Johnson's feeling that a nation which kept slaves had little right to demand liberty has already been mentioned. Benjamin Franklin (who apparently did not meet Johnson in London but who ordered several copies of the *Dictionary*) made reference to this aspect of Johnson's attitude when some time later, about 1786, he wrote a piece called *The Retort Courteous* in which he said: "An order arrives from England, advised by one of their most celebrated *moralists,* Dr. Johnson, in his *Taxation No Tyranny,* to excite these slaves to rise, cut the throats of their purchasers, and resort to the British army, where they should be rewarded with freedom." Johnson no doubt thought of the Americans as a semicivilized mob and they were too far away to call into play that human sympathy which he felt for the Irish and which, as has been so often repeated, tended to temper the harshness of his authoritarian opinions whenever the victims of oppression were presented to his sight or imagination. He was grieved as well as angered to think that British subjects should fail to put any personal or material advantage above the honor of *being* British subjects, and that sorrow is clearly indicated in a remark of his (recorded by Mrs. Thrale) made when a companion congratulated him on the sight of a captured American vessel flying its thirteen stripes, lying in the Thames. " 'Tis a much greater Grief, Sir," replied he, "that any such Ship or any such Colours should *exist,*—than Exultation that they should be *here;* I turn my Eyes from the Sight on't." But anger got the best of grief and one had best rest content with quoting Boswell's remark apropos of *The False Alarm:* "It was wonderful to see how a prejudice in favour of government in general, and an aversion to popular clamor, could blind and contract such an understanding as Johnson's." As one who insisted that "public affairs vex no man" he certainly had no right to be vexed. But vexed he was and possibly, even, like so many other Tories, a little bit frightened.[31]

On June 22, 1779, Mrs. Thrale wrote in her diary: "Publick Concerns now claim every one's Attention: . . . 'tis indeed high Time to be in earnest; France & Spain are leagued against us, & add their Weight to Miseries inflicted on the Mother Country by its revolted Colonies; Bankruptcy & Invasion stare us in the Face, nor can one Ally be found to take our Part. If we have deserved help from Heaven we shall have it; but let us first enquire whether peradventure *ten* righteous may be found—in the two Houses of Parliament . . ."

Next year, stirred by the Gordon riots and the debates concerning the king's sanity but certainly not unmindful also of the American Revolution, she takes up the lament: "How all the World is rushing on to its own Ruin! nations & Individuals & all! the English Constitution is I think at last fairly finished, & my Lady Britannia has cut her own Throat: . . . It was an artificial Form of Government to be sure, and in its Nature difficult to hold together; yet that form of Government which Montesquieu celebrates, & Falkland bled for, demands a Tear or two: Poor Thing! I am sincerely sorry for thy Death." That this lugubrious passage should be immediately followed by "a pleasant Epigram enough" on a frivolous subject may prove that public affairs vex no one. Or perhaps it proves merely that Mrs. Thrale had, as there are other good reasons for believing, a resilient nature.[32]

If the years at Streatham gave Johnson the opportunity to compose his most unfortunate piece of writing, they also gave him the leisure and comfort in which his happiest writing (with the possible exception of *Preface* to Shakespeare) was conceived and executed. To it we may happily turn.

CHAPTER XII

The Lives of the Poets

When Johnson and Boswell were at Ulinish in the Isle of Skye, their activities and their conversations were, as usual, exceedingly various. The Doctor discussed the errors hitherto made by navigators attempting to reach the North Pole, and he also, since he "had never catched any fish in the sea," borrowed from two little girls the lines they were dangling from a rock above the water line. "Mr. Johnson drew one or two cuddies, but he let them go again"—possibly because he was thinking what he is said (on dubious authority) to have on one occasion remarked, namely that "angling—I can only compare to a stick and a string, with a worm at one end and a fool at the other." [1]

Sitting that night before a comfortable peat fire, he forgot that he was at Ulinish, forgot that the fire was peat rather than sea coal, and characteristically began to discourse as though he were somewhere else. "Talking of biography, he said he did not know any literary man's life in England well-written. It should tell us his studies, his manner of life, the means by which he attained to excellence, his opinion of his own works, and such particulars. He said he had sent Derrick to Dryden's relations, and he believed Derrick had got all he should have got, but it was nothing. He said he had a kindness for Derrick, and was sorry he was dead."

Not improbably Johnson was also remembering that in the

course of one of his interviews with George III his Majesty had "expressed a desire to have the literary biography of this country ably executed, and proposed to Dr. Johnson to undertake it." Possibly he was even, by now, considering that he might try his hand at something of the kind. But Boswell refrained from making any comment, no doubt because he had learned how much Johnson resented a hint that he should get to work. Had he been so unwise as to suggest anything of the sort, he would, no doubt, have got some such reply as Johnson later gave to an enthusiastic admirer who insisted that it was now time for the Doctor to do something for England's *prose* writers. The reply was: "Sit down, Sir!"

Johnson was not, of course, a man likely to do even the work he had seriously thought of doing unless subject to the pressure of necessity or, at the very least, the milder pressure of a definite commitment. Though he had apparently long thought of compiling a dictionary, he did not set to work until the contract had been signed, and so it was to be in the case of *The Lives of the Poets,* even though these Lives seem to have been written more nearly con amore than any of his previous works, and even though, for this once, he actually performed more than was nominated in the bond.

Boswell, who was in Scotland when the commission was undertaken, knew nothing of the project until he saw an advertisement (possibly that in the *Publick Advertiser* for April 9, 1777) of a forthcoming edition of the English poets "with a Preface, Biographical and Critical, to each Author, by Samuel Johnson, LL.D." He wrote Johnson a letter of inquiry which he later published in the *Life* along with Johnson's reply wherein the latter speaks of "little Lives and little Prefaces, to a little edition of the English Poets." Boswell also prints a letter to himself from Edward Dilly, who explains how the project came to be conceived.[2]

It seems that an Edinburgh firm had just issued a cheap edition of the poets to be sold also in London. By a recent decision of the House of Lords, it had been decided that the copyright which different booksellers believed they held in works of various of the older poets was not valid, and accordingly these holders of the supposed copyrights decided that their only recourse was to publish on their own account a rival and better edition. "About forty of the most respectable booksellers of London" held a meeting, agreed on "an elegant and uniform edition" and appointed a committee to call upon Johnson with the request that he undertake the prefaces. Johnson seemed pleased with the proposal, and when asked to name his own terms, asked for only two hundred guineas—no doubt because he had no idea at the time how considerable his contribution was to come to be. The terms were immediately accepted.

The oldest of the poets represented was Waller, and the work of all men still living was excluded. In the making of this plan Johnson had no part; he was not in any full sense the editor of the work; and, indeed, he was later to refer in a letter of protest to "your edition, which is very impudently called mine." It is true that at his suggestion the unimportant names of Blackmore, Watts, Pomfret, Yalden (and possibly Thomson) were added to the list of those included, and that (on the authority of Mrs. Thrale alone) Churchill was at his desire omitted. He may also, as one account has it, have seen many of the sheets and been consulted concerning the work of various individual poets, but that he did not always even know what the text was to be is evident enough from his anger at discovering too late that an indecent poem attributed to Rowe was printed. Hence Malone's statement that Johnson was "not the *editor*" is substantially correct. Perhaps most men of his eminence would have refused merely to accept a job of this kind; for a job, defined by others, is precisely what it was. Boswell, who "was somewhat disappointed" in finding that Johnson was to exercise no real direction over the enterprise, asked him if he would be willing to furnish a life and a preface to the works of any dunce whom the booksellers might select. "Yes, Sir," was the reply, "and *say* he was a dunce." [3]

It is equally characteristic of Johnson that though, as it turned out, the payment he received was ridiculously inadequate, he refused to complain. In addition to the two hundred guineas originally promised, he was presented with one hundred more, and then, on the occasion of a revised edition of the *Lives* published separately from that of the poets, given still another hundred; but how niggardly this payment was can be shown from the fact that only a few years later Arthur Murphy received three hundred pounds for *An Essay on the Life and Genius of Samuel Johnson,* shorter than Johnson's own preface to Pope alone. Malone estimated that the booksellers made five thousand guineas from the work in the course of twenty-five years, and believed that if Johnson had asked a thousand or even fifteen hundred he would have got it. Still another indication of what Johnson's name was worth is afforded by the fact that in 1788 Mrs. Thrale got five hundred pounds for the copyright of her *Letters to and from the late Samuel Johnson, LL.D.* Yet apropos of the payment for the *Lives,* Johnson could declare: "Sir, I always said the booksellers were a generous set of men. Nor, in the present instance, have I reason to complain. The fact is, not that they have paid me too little, but that I have written too much." In the "Advertisement" or Preface to the work itself he wrote: "My purpose was only to have allotted to every poet an advertisement, like those which we find in the French Miscellanies, containing a few dates and a general character; but I have been led beyond my intention, I hope by the honest desire of giving useful pleasure." [4]

There were in England other students of literature more industrious than Johnson, and at least one, Edmond Malone, who knew or would quickly have learned more about the lives of the English poets than Johnson knew or had the persistence to discover. But there was no one who could have written critical essays (especially no one who could have written them, as Johnson did, largely out of knowledge in hand) as vigorous and varied and rich as the "little prefaces" turned out to be. Whether his reading had or had not been quite so desultory and fragmentary as he sometimes insisted, he had a prodigious memory which was said, for instance, to have enabled him once to repeat, a year or two later, ten or twelve lines of a Greek hymn he had read at a bookstall. His mind was stored far more richly than the minds of those who might have read more but who certainly retained less. There is a note in his *Prayers and Meditations* which reads: "to treasure in my mind passages for recol-

"SCOTTIFYING THE PALATE"
Designed by Samuel Collings and etched by Thomas Rowlandson

"BOZZY AND PIOZZI"
Designed by Samuel Collings and etched by Gabriel Piozzi

lection," and Mrs. Thrale remarks: "I know nobody but Johnson who has any Store of Poetry in his head if he were struck blind and could read no longer." "If poetry was talked of," she noted on another occasion, "his Quotations were the readiest; & had he not been eminent for more solid & brilliant qualities, Mankind would have united to extol his extraordinary Memory." He had also something which cannot be denied him even by those who find his sympathies narrow, and it was a thing not always possessed by either more industrious scholars or more esoteric critics—namely, a passionate, unwearying enthusiasm for at least that kind of literature, and especially that kind of poetry, which he did like.[5]

It is no wonder, then, that once he had begun to write on a subject so congenial, even Johnson wrote more than he was compelled to write, and that those of the "little prefaces" which had for their subjects the poets whom he found most congenial or most exasperating should have grown under his hand until the entire collection (including the *Life of Savage*, which he republished) fills in a modern edition two fairly substantial volumes. Perhaps, moreover, the attractions of his subjects were hardly less responsible for his tendency to continue on far beyond the limits he had originally set himself than was the fact that he was writing under pleasanter and less lonely circumstances than he had ever written before. The *Dictionary* had been composed "with sluggish resolution" in the midst of poverty and finished, at least, while he was still feeling the first shock of dear Tetty's death. Even the edition of Shakespeare was a labor to which he unwillingly returned after social pleasures and to which he was driven by the growing scandal caused by his delay. But the *Lives* were composed while the comforts of Southwark and Streatham were available to him whenever he chose to take advantage of them.

To Mrs. Thrale, then at Brighton, he wrote on October 6, 1777, mentioning his agreement to do the *Lives*, and in the middle of November he went with her to Streatham for a time. His letters indicate that he preferred, or was compelled, to do much of the actual work in London and in 1779 Mrs. Thrale notes: "tomorrow we set out for Tunbridge & Brightelmstone.—

Fanny Burney goes with us, not Johnson, he stays at home & writes & is diligent." But in May, 1780, he was working at the Thrales' house in Southwark on *Congreve,* and a few of the *Lives* were written at Streatham. Mrs. Thrale sometimes acted as his amanuensis and a portion of the manuscript of the *Pope* is in her handwriting. It is, however, Fanny Burney who gives the coziest picture of Johnson working, no longer "in the gloom of solitude" but surrounded by friends almost as eager as those of Samuel Richardson had been to catch another glimpse of what their great man had been doing. The following account from the *Memoirs* of her father was not published until 1832 and exhibits a pomposity of style for which the readers of the earlier *Diary* are not prepared.

"While this charming work was in progress, when only the Thrale family and its nearly adopted guests, the two Burneys, were assembled, Dr. Johnson, would frequently produce one of its proof-sheets to embellish the breakfast table, which was always in the library; and was, certainly, the most sprightly and agreeable meeting of the day; for then, as no strangers were present to stimulate exertion, or provoke rivalry, argument was not urged on by the mere spirit of victory; it was instigated only by such truisms as could best bring forth that conflict of pros and cons which elucidates opposing opinions. Wit was not flashed with the keen sting of satire; yet it elicited not less gaiety from sparkling with an unwounding brilliancy, which brightened without inflaming, every eye, and charmed without tingling, every ear.

"These proof-sheets Mrs. Thrale was permitted to read aloud; and the discussions to which they led were in the highest degree entertaining. Dr. Burney wistfully desired to possess one of them; but left to his daughter the risk of the petition. A hint, however, proved sufficient, and was understood not alone with compliance, but vivacity. Boswell, Dr. Johnson said, had engaged Frank Barber, his negro servant, to collect and preserve all the proof-sheets; but though it had not been without the knowledge, it was without the order or the interference of their author; to the present solicitor, therefore, willingly and without scruple, he now offered an entire life; adding, with a benignant smile, 'Choose your poet!'

"Without scruple, also, was the acceptance; and, without hesitation, the choice was Pope. And that not merely because, next to Shakespeare himself, Pope draws human characters the most veridically, perhaps, of any poetic delineator; but for yet another reason. Dr. Johnson composed with so ready an accuracy, that he sent his copy to the press unread; reserving all his corrections for the proof-sheets: and, consequently, as not even Dr. Johnson could read twice without ameliorating some passages, his proof-sheets were at times liberally marked with changes; and, as the Museum copy of Pope's Translation of the Iliad, from which Dr. Johnson has given many examples, contains abundant emendations by Pope, the Memorialist secured at once, on the same page, the marginal alterations and second thoughts of that great author, and of his great biographer." [6]

Johnson did—no doubt unwillingly—a certain amount of research. His letters reveal him writing to the printer, Nichols, asking that he be sent certain books; he made, in 1777, a trip to Oxford from whence he wrote Mrs. Thrale to say that he had been searching the library for materials; and in the same year he inquired of Dr. Farmer at Cambridge concerning the manuscripts left by one Baker who had attempted to do for the graduates of that university what Anthony Wood had done for Oxford. More important, perhaps, is the fact that Sir Lucas Pepys borrowed from the Duke of Newcastle the unpublished manuscript of Spence's *Anecdotes*, the value of which Johnson publicly acknowledged. Both Isaac Reed and George Steevens supplied him with a certain amount of information, but Johnson also drew largely from existing editions of the individual poets and even from so familiar a compilation as Langbaine's *Account of the English Dramatic Poets*. None of this is enough to make the *Lives* of great importance as a source of biographical fact, and Johnson was so little concerned to make it such that he distressed Boswell by refusing even to take the trouble to correct two errors which were pointed out to him. "In this minute kind of history the succession of facts is," he is content to say, "not easily discovered"; and when in doubt he takes refuge in the contention that literary scholarship of the sort which Malone was learning to practice is not worth the trouble it costs. Or, as he puts it, "To adjust the minute events of literary history, is tedious and troublesome; it requires, indeed, no great force of understanding, but often depends upon inquiries which there is no opportunity of making, or is to be fetched from books and pamphlets not always at hand."

Once Boswell made the mistake of announcing with too great an air of importance that he had succeeded in persuading Lord Marchmont to invite Johnson to an interview in which Marchmont would "communicate all he knows about Pope." Largely no doubt out of a desire to put Boswell in his place, Johnson replied: "I shall not be in town to-morrow. I don't care to know about Pope," and when Mrs. Thrale, surprised and irritated, put in with "I suppose, Sir, Mr. Boswell thought, that as you are to write Pope's Life, you would wish to know about him," Johnson adopted one of his usual methods of defense which consisted, of course, in being more outrageous than he had been before. "Wish!" he exclaimed. "Why, yes. If it rained knowledge I'd hold out my hand; but I would not give myself the trouble to go in quest of it."

This, of course, is not to be taken as expressing Johnson's real attitude toward his work, but he did actually put so large a part of his dependence on what was already in his mind that he by no means always even reread the works he was about to criticize. According to Nichols, Johnson said, when delivering the *Life of Rowe,* that "the criticism was tolerably well done, considering that he had not read one of Rowe's plays for thirty years!"; and in the *Life of Congreve* ("whom," he writes Mrs. Thrale, "I dispatched at the Borough while I was attending the election"), he remarks concerning the early short tale, *Incognita,* that it has been praised by the biographers, adding with that humor which is more valuable than facts: "I would rather praise than read it." Yet so powerful as well as so full was the mind, on the resources of which Johnson dared so largely to depend, that even the strictly biographical as opposed to the critical portions of his essays often assume a vividness more impressive than any collection of more detailed facts could have achieved. A great deal more is known, for instance, about the life and death of Jonathan Swift than Johnson knew. But has the horror of his last dreadful days ever been presented more simply or more impressively than in the following passage?

"He was always careful of his money, and was, therefore, no liberal entertainer; but was less frugal of his wine than of his meat. When his friends of either sex came to him, in expectation of a dinner, his custom was to give every one a shilling, that they might please themselves with their provision. At last his avarice grew too powerful for his kindness; he would refuse a bottle of wine, and in Ireland no man visits where he cannot drink.

"Having thus excluded conversation, and desisted from study, he had neither business nor amusement; for, having by some ridiculous resolution, or mad vow, determined never to wear spectacles, he could make little use of books in his later years; his ideas, therefore, being neither renovated by discourse, nor increased by reading, wore gradually away, and left his mind vacant to the vexations of the hour, till, at last, his anger was heightened into madness. . . .

"He grew more violent, and his mental powers declined, till, 1741, it was found necessary that legal guardians should be appointed of his person and fortune. He now lost distinction. His madness was compounded of rage and fatuity. The last face that he knew was that of Mrs. Whiteway; and her he ceased to know in a little time. His meat was brought him cut into mouthfuls; but he would never touch it while the servant staid, and, at last, after it had stood perhaps an hour, would eat it walking; for he continued his old habit, and was on his feet ten hours a day.

"Next year, 1742, he had an inflammation in his left eye, which swelled it to the size of an egg, with biles in other parts; he was kept long waking with the pain, and was not easily restrained by five attendants from tearing out his eye.

"The tumour at last subsided; and a short interval of reason ensuing, in which he knew his physician and his family, gave hopes of his recovery; but in a few days he sunk into a lethargick stupidity, motionless, heedless, and speechless. But it is said, that, after a year of total silence, when his housekeeper, on the 30th of November, told him that the usual bonfires and illuminations were preparing to celebrate his birthday, he answered, 'It is all folly; they had better let it alone.'

"It is remembered, that he afterwards spoke now and then, or gave some intimation of a meaning; but at last sunk into perfect silence, which continued till about the end of October, 1745, when, in his seventy-eighth year, he expired without a struggle." [7]

The first four volumes of the *Lives* with the accompanying volumes of the poets' texts appeared in 1779. Despite his interest in the subject and despite the relative comfort in which for the first time he was working, Johnson found as usual that he was reluctant to put forth the effort necessary to complete what he had begun. To Mrs. Thrale he wrote on April 11, 1780: "You are at all places of high resort, and bring home hearts by the dozens; while I am seeking for something to say about men of whom I know nothing but their verses, and sometimes very little of them. Now I have begun, however, I do not despair of making an end." Two months later he was writing to the same lady: "My Lives go on but slowly. I hope to add some to them this week. I wish they were well done." In August, Boswell was informed: "I have sat at home in Bolt-Court, all the summer, thinking to write the Lives, and a great part of the time only thinking. Several of them, however, are done, and I still think to do the rest." Finally, however, he wrote the bookseller, Strahan, in March, 1781, that he had finished at last, and on Good Friday of the same year he entered in his *Prayers and Meditations* the note: "Sometime in March I finished the lives of the Poets, which I wrote in my usual way, dilatorily and hastily, unwilling to work, and working with vigour and haste." [8] Accordingly the six final volumes of the *Lives* were issued with the remaining volumes of the poetical text in 1781 (not 1780, as Boswell in one place mistakenly states). In the same year the *Lives* appeared by themselves as an independent publication, of which a new edition was issued in 1783.

That Johnson allowed his Tory principles to affect his judgment of certain poets, and that the works of certain others (notably those of Gray) were not given the praise which many of his contemporaries thought these works deserved, did not by any means escape the notice of these same contemporaries. A satiric print dated 1782 and entitled *Old Wisdom blinking at the Stars* (its existence is, of course, testimony to Johnson's fame) shows an owl, with Johnson's face and ass's ears, looking sourly ahead and apparently unmindful of the busts of Milton and Pope, which are surrounded with aureoles and placed just above his head. His treatment of Gray, and more especially his condescending remarks on the noble but insignificant poet, Lord Lyttelton, infuriated the bluestockings into whose circle Johnson had recently been introduced, and Mrs. Montagu ceased inviting him to her parties. Nevertheless, *The Monthly Review* devoted a whole series of articles to the two installments of the work and, despite Johnson's Toryism, treated him to the highest praise. Milton's character was, naturally enough, vigorously defended, and exception was taken to the slights visited upon Gray, but the "long-expected edition of the English poets" is declared no disappointment, and Johnson is called: "In the walk of biography and criticism . . . without a rival." "Paradise Lost is a poem which the mind of Milton only could have produced; the criticism before us is such as, perhaps, the pen of Johnson only could have written."

Johnson had said that he expected to be attacked. "However," he added, "I would rather be attacked than unnoticed. For the worst thing you can do to an author is to be silent as to his works. An assault upon a town is a bad thing; but starving it is still worse; an assault may be unsuccessful; you may have more men killed than you kill; but if you starve the town, you are sure of victory." Yet though some attacks were made, at least the "whig-dogs" of *The Monthly* were as generous as anyone had a right to expect. "The world in general," says Boswell, "was filled with admiration." And for all its faults, for all its possibly more serious limitations, the *Lives of the Poets* is still one of the most entertaining and most impressive collections of critical essays in the English language.[9]

In what is still a standard edition of Johnson published in 1825 the editor permits himself to describe the *Lives of the Poets* as "a work that gave to the British nation a new style of biography." Certainly any reader of eighteenth-century literature is likely to agree that he knows no earlier writing quite like these *Lives,* and yet he would probably find it difficult to state in any simple descriptive phrase the exact nature of the novelty. "A new style of biography" ought, one feels, to present some feature immediately identifiable as new. One ought to be able to say, as one can say of Boswell, that no previous writer had ever attempted this method or that of presenting a life and a character. Yet certainly it is not easy to put one's finger on any feature of Johnson's *Lives* which is in any absolute sense novel. Biographical and critical notices prefaced to an author's work had not been uncommon since the seventeenth century, and Johnson was familiar with, among many others, Rowe's preface to his *Shakespeare.* The generalization illuminated by anecdote and including a moral reflection is at least as old as Tacitus and Plutarch. The possibilities of informal and appreciative, rather than formal and pedantic, criticism had been brilliantly illustrated by Dryden a century before the *Lives* were written. Is it possible, then, that the novelty of Johnson is merely excellence; that he seems to be doing something new merely because he is doing something better than it had ever been done in English before?

To that question a qualified affirmative seems a safe enough answer. There is certainly no evidence that Johnson himself aimed at anything which he regarded as original so far as intention or method were concerned. He certainly did not have consciously in mind, as Boswell certainly did, a new theory of biography, and neither, for that matter, was he aware of any theory of criticism of which he intended to present the first exemplification. To be unorthodox in either matter or manner was certainly the last aim he would have been likely to propose to himself, and Young's *Conjectures on Original Composition* or Morgann's *Essay of the Character of Falstaff* are in some senses of the word as much more "original" than Johnson's criticism as Boswell's biography is more original than Johnson's biographical sketches. And yet, when all this has been said, the fact remains that Johnson exploited more fully than any Englishman had ever exploited before the possibilities of a form apparently so casual and, in so far as its origins are merely the "advertisement" like those which we find in the *French Miscel-*

lanies, so trivial that it hardly appears to have any. The fact also remains that it seems foolish to deny the name of originality to exploitation which reveals new potentialities. Moreover, if one now goes on to ask whether Johnson, in addition to the never-resting power of his mind, had any specific convictions or any specific mental habit to which the biographical preface gave congenial opportunity, the answer seems to be that he had not only his passionate interest in character and manners but also a concomitant of that passionate interest—namely, a tendency to look in poetry for the character of the poet.

Of him one is sometimes tempted to say that he is as completely free as any human being can possibly be from any of the beliefs, tendencies or tastes which have a part in the complex called romanticism; that no one of his contemporaries seemed more completely outside the gradually emerging romantic movement, or more insensitive to the novel elements beginning to be evident in the work of Gray or even in that of his friend Goldsmith. Yet the tendency to be as much interested in the poet as in his poetry is certainly a romantic tendency, and Johnson exhibited it, whether or not the fact has any more than an accidental connection with a movement to which he seems to be otherwise completely alien. There is certainly nothing necessarily romantic in saying, as Johnson did, that it was the biographical part of literature which he loved best. And yet when that interest in biography led him, as it sometimes did, to seek in poetry the personality of the poet, the connection, merely accidental or not, becomes apparent.

Perhaps the fact that criticism was first seriously practiced upon ancient classics, concerning whose authors little or nothing is known, is as much responsible as any theory of criticism for the further fact that such criticism tended to be impersonal and to concern itself with the work of art as an isolated fact. The classical theory that poetry is imitation leads naturally to the assumption that if it is to be considered in relation to anything else, that something else is "nature" or "reality" rather than the personality of the poet. But theory or no theory, there could be little tendency to find in Homer, about whom no one knew anything, the meaning of the *Iliad* or, carrying the process still further, to find that the real interest of the *Iliad* is its revelation of Homer's personality. Hence, the methods established in the early English criticism of classical authors would, no less surely than classical theory, incline the critic of the moderns to consider the biography of the writer and his literary works as two separate things.

It is true that the rough criticism of the pamphlet wars is in one sense personal enough. The victim is accused in one sentence of suffering from a shameful disease and in the next of an inability to write scannable verse. But the criticism of the pamphlet wars is something apart from the more serious attempts at dignified literary evaluation; moreover, to abuse a man for his physical and moral defects at the same time that one abuses him for his literary nonentity is not the same thing as to search for the ways in which poetry reveals the poet. And in so far as Johnson's *Lives* are "a new style of biography" they are such largely because of the extent to which the biography of a poet and a criticism of that poet's works are integrated instead of being considered two separate things.

To say this is not to say that Johnson had formulated a theory which he had determined to put into practice. It is possibly worth noting in this connection the obvious fact that biography and criticism tend to retain for him sufficient separateness to lead him usually to begin one of his prefaces with an account of the poet's life and the chronology of his works, and then to proceed to a general exposition and evaluation of those works. Moreover, much of Johnson's criticism confines itself to an analysis of individual poems, and some of it is of the minute sort which seeks for faults of "propriety," and discusses the "correctness" or "incorrectness" of individual lines or phrases. But in so far as there is novelty in his method, the chief element of that novelty is to be found in the extent to which he does unite biography with criticism so as to make the man and his poetry if not one, then at least sometimes related. The reader who comes to Johnson from nineteenth-century biography and criticism will find him conspicuously formal and old-fashioned. But to read him with his predecessors rather than his successors in mind is to understand the way in which he was presenting a new kind of literary biography.

Partly no doubt because he had no formulated theory, Johnson exhibits no tendency either to confine himself exclusively to one method or to carry that method to an extreme. One can no more imagine him sitting down to demonstrate that *the poet is the man* than one can imagine him sitting down, like Taine, to demonstrate that literature is a product of the intellectual *milieu* or, like even more recent critics, that it is the inevitable product of a given system of industrial production. The opposition between the conceptions of "literature as imitation" and "literature as expression" was certainly not present in his mind. Dogmatist though he was in certain departments of his thinking, he was not the sort of literary dogmatist who would suppose that he had to maintain that all literary excellence consists in this one thing or this other thing. So far as literature is concerned, no man was ever more of a pluralist. But for that very reason he was no more likely to be fanatically committed to "pure" criticism than he was to be fanatically committed to a romantic theory of "expression." Hence, Pope and Swift and Dryden and Milton are not merely names attached to certain poems, and information about each of them is relevant to the proper understanding of those poems. Johnson never goes so far as to say that Milton was a bad man and therefore a bad poet. He is so far from saying that Pope was a mean man and therefore a mean poet that he not only gives his poetry supreme praise but singles out as the finest passage in all Pope's writings one which is as little in need as any passage could be of illumination by anecdote. Yet the fact remains that to Johnson a poem is not always merely so many lines on a printed page and as such the sole datum which a critic has to consider. A writer is also a man. His individual experiences and his individual personality have something to do with his writing. And, more successfully than any previous composer of literary biography, Johnson makes that fact significant. "Pope and Swift," he remarks in passing, "had an unnatural delight in ideas physically impure." No statement could be simpler but, simple as it is, it is sufficient to suggest how readily Johnson passed from an analysis of writing to an analysis of the writer. He is not concerned with indecency merely as an aesthetic or a moral problem. He sees it also as a psychological one. The question what these indecent poems are as literature becomes also the question "why did these men write them?"

The limits of Johnson's interests and sensibility remain those revealed in his treatment of Shakespeare. Moreover, that editor of his collected works who was quoted above concerning the novel method of the *Lives* is already sufficiently removed from Johnson's age to accept without reservation the exaggerated romantic estimate of the narrowness of those limitations. "With respect to Johnson's powers as a critic," he writes, "we confess that he had but little natural taste for poetry, as such; for that poetry of emotion which produces in its cultivators and admirers an intensity of excitement, to which language can scarcely afford an utterance, to which art can give no body, and which spreads a dream and a glory around us." But this is a violent—one might almost say a perverse—overstatement of the case. Pope's famous comparison between the progress of the student and the progress of the Alpine traveler, which ends with the line:

> Hills peep o'er hills, and Alps on Alps arise

Johnson calls "perhaps the best that English poetry can show." Yet the passage in which that comparison occurs is certainly one in which the appeal is at least as much emotional as it is intellectual, and the truth is not, as Johnson's critic asserts, that he "wanted that deep feeling which is the only sure and unerring test of poetic excellence" or that he sought in poetry only the didactic and "wished for reasoning in numbers," but merely that the emotions to which, in his case, poetry could make a successful appeal were not the romantic ones. A man who could never, until forced by necessity, bring himself to reread the concluding scene of *King Lear* was certainly not one whose emotions were untouched by poetry. Had Johnson lived to discover how powerfully certain romantic readers were moved by emotions which they could not name, and how frequently they wept for they knew not what sorrow, he would, in all probability, have said of their poetry what he said of Boswell's music—"I should never hear it if it made me such a fool." To admit that may be to admit that he was insensitive to even the genuine beauties of romanticism. But it is not to grant that he was incapable of all poetic feeling.[10]

With the notable exceptions of Milton and Gray, most of the poets whom he treats are poets whose range is well within that of his own comprehension. We do not often, if ever, find him, as it was admitted we sometimes do in his criticism of Shakespeare, so near the limits of that comprehension that he is able to sense the presence of a kind of greatness he is unable to define. Indeed, the present-day reader who comes to the *Lives* without any previous preparation is likely to find that where his sympathy with the critic is imperfect, the difficulty arises as the result of a situation quite different from that which tended to throw him off when reading the *Preface* to Shakespeare. In the latter case, Johnson was dealing with a poet whose greatness the reader grants as readily as Johnson assumes it, perhaps even more readily, and the critic's praise seems (though it really is not) sometimes grudging, because he is defending his author against objections which the present-day reader would never think of raising. In the case of certain of the *Lives,* on the other hand, Johnson (as is quite inevitable so long as he has his contemporary readers in mind), takes for granted the supreme greatness of Dryden and Pope, whom the prejudices and the taste of the present-day reader may make him tend to depreciate. Such a reader finds entirely supererogatory the argument that Shakespeare's greatness is not seriously impaired by his failure to observe the three unities. He is, on the other hand, disappointed not to find any, to him, satisfactory general defense of the kind of poetry which Pope and Dryden wrote.

It is true that Johnson was aware of the attacks which had been begun upon Pope's reputation almost as soon as Pope himself died and that on one occasion he goes so far in the direction of an apology for poetry in Pope's understanding of the word as to write the sentences which Arnold must have had in mind when he wrote his own, now much more often remembered, assertion that Pope and Dryden are "classics of our prose."

"It is, surely," says Johnson, "superfluous to answer the question that has once been asked, whether Pope was a poet? otherwise than by asking in return, if Pope be not a poet, where is poetry to be found? To circumscribe poetry by a definition, will only show the narrowness of the definer, though a definition, which shall exclude Pope, will not easily be made." But that is as close as he will come to arguing a question which on other occasions he refuses even to recognize as askable. Arnold's dictum, "The difference between genuine poetry and the poetry of Dryden, Pope, and all their school, is briefly this: their poetry is conceived and composed in their wits, genuine poetry is conceived and composed in the soul," would have seemed to Johnson arrant nonsense. A soul operating, as Arnold allows himself to seem to suggest a soul ought to operate, as something separate from the wits which inhabit a body along with it is simply, Johnson would certainly have felt, a soul that has lost its wits. And he would have been unwilling to believe that anything or anybody whose wits were absent could possibly compose good poetry or do anything else worth doing.

Shakespeare is to Johnson the greatest of the English poets and his judgment to that effect is freely delivered without any reservation. Milton, he clearly grants, is next in order, but obviously enough the admission is wrung from him despite not only political prejudice but, what is more important, his failure to take much real delight in Milton's work. Nominally, Dryden and Pope come third and fourth, but in his genuine affections they are very nearly tied for second place. The former's *Ode to Mrs. Anne Killegrew* "is undoubtedly, the noblest ode that our language ever has produced"; Pope's translation of the *Iliad,* "the noblest version of poetry which the world has ever seen." [11]

A critic of the present day has recently maintained that a great writer is necessarily a great man writing. Johnson, despite his realization that a poet is a person and that something of his personality is inevitably revealed in his poetry, would have stated the thing more cautiously. A great writer is inevitably a man possessed of certain great qualities; but Johnson certainly did not think that either Dryden or Pope deserved to be called a great man in a sense requiring no qualification. In fact, some of the most penetrating paragraphs in the essays devoted to them, as well as in a number of the others, are paragraphs which analyze with stinging wit the moral and intellectual defects of the men whose life and work are being analyzed. Like most of those who have studied Dryden, Johnson felt for him, despite all the weaknesses of his character, a certain affection, and the sentence in which the significance of Dryden's convenient shift from enthusiasm for Cromwell to enthusiasm for Charles II is palliated became one which almost every commentator since has been constrained to quote: "The reproach of inconstancy was, on this occasion, shared with such numbers, that it produced neither hatred nor disgrace! if he changed, he changed with the nation."

For Pope's less amiable weaknesses Johnson had, on the other hand, even less sympathy than some subsequent critics have managed to cultivate, and he analyzes them with scornful relish. Knowing no metaphysics, Pope was so elated by the confused ideas which he heard from Bolingbroke that he "was in haste to teach what he had not learned," and he was so angry at Cibber that he made him the new hero of the revised *Dunciad* in Theobald's stead without even taking the trouble to fit the old characterization to the new name. The result in the first case is that Pope, "having exalted himself into the chair of wisdom," tells us in the *Essay on Man* "much that everyman knows, and much that he does not know himself." In the second case, it is that he "by showing that what he had said of one he was ready to say of another . . . reduced himself to the insignificance of his own magpie, who, from his cage, calls cuckold at a venture."

"He very frequently professes contempt of the world, and represents himself as looking on mankind, sometimes with gay indifference, as on emmets of a hillock, below his serious attention; and sometimes with gloomy indignation, as on monsters more worthy of hatred than of pity. These were dispositions apparently counterfeited. How could he despise those whom he lived by pleasing, and on whose approbation his esteem of himself was superstructed? Why should he hate those to whose favour he owed his honour and his ease? . . . Pope was far enough from this unreasonable temper: he was sufficiently 'a fool to fame,' and his fault was, that he pretended to neglect it. . . .

"His scorn of the great is too often repeated to be real; no man thinks much of that which he despises; and, as falsehood is always in danger of inconsistency, he makes it his boast, at another time, that he lives among them.

"It is evident that his own importance swells often in his mind. He is afraid of writing, lest the clerks of the post-office should know his secrets; he has many enemies; he considers himself as surrounded by universal jealousy: 'after many deaths, and many dispersions, two or three of us' says he, 'may still be brought together, not to plot, but to divert ourselves, and the world too, if it pleases:' and they can live together, and 'show what friends wits may be, in spite of all the fools in the world.' All this while it was likely that the clerks did not know his hand; he certainly had no more enemies than a publick character like his inevitably excites; and with what degree of friendship the wits might live, very few were so much fools as ever to inquire.

"Some part of this pretended discontent he learned from Swift, and expresses it, I think, most frequently in his correspondence with him. Swift's resentment was unreasonable, but it was sincere; Pope's was the mere mimickry of his friend, a fictitious part which he began to play before it became him. When he was only twenty-five years old, he related that 'a glut of study and retirement had thrown him on the world,' and that there was danger lest 'a glut of the world should throw him back upon study and retirement.' To this Swift answered with great propriety, that Pope had not yet either acted or suffered enough in the world to have become weary of it." [12]

Yet this very imperfect man, whose mental and moral imperfections so communicate themselves to the verses which he wrote as often to mar and sometimes to render them worthless, possessed, nevertheless, talents, as well as moral and intellectual qualities, which enabled him to become third or fourth among English poets, and, indeed, so to exemplify the gifts of The Poet that to read what Johnson says of these gifts is to find as clearly stated as he ever (except perhaps in the *Preface* to Shakespeare) stated his conception of what a poet, and what poetry, is.

That this conception of both the one and the other is different from the romantic one and by no means entirely identical with that held even by most of those of our contemporaries who have revolted against romantic doctrine, hardly needs to be said after the analysis which was made of his tributes to Shakespeare. Johnson did not expect to get from the poetry anything ineffable because (aside perhaps from what revealed Christianity provides) he did not suppose man capable of either discovering or communicating anything ineffable. He did not expect to find anywhere, even in poetry, anything which transcends comprehension or even so nearly transcends it as to be beyond the reach of the same rational judgment which is valid in relation to all other products of the human mind. What he did expect was knowledge of and wisdom concerning the characters and manners of men, and intelligible judgments concerning human life. He expected to find this expressed supremely well, but he certainly supposed that poets would use their wits both in discovering and in formulating what they had to say, and it is unlikely that he supposed any sharp line could be drawn between prose and poetry except that line which distinguishes the metrical from the nonmetrical. However little he would have agreed with Matthew Arnold in many of the latter's pronouncements, he would probably have found his definition of prose as good words in good order and his definition of poetry as the best words in the best order as satisfactory as any likely to be formulated, and he would most certainly have agreed with Mr. T. S. Eliot that the minimal virtues of good poetry are those of good prose. He did not, in other words, believe that there was any clearly definable and absolute qualitative difference between the one and the other or that anything which had no prose meaning could possibly become, by any magic, good poetry.

Imagination is one of the indispensable characteristics of the poet but he is not of imagination all compact. In the *Life of Samuel Butler,* Johnson rephrases the Hobbesian doctrine previously stated in the *Preface:* "Imagination is useless without knowledge: nature gives in vain the power of combination, unless study and observation supply materials to be combined." Thus he reaffirms his acceptance of the theory that imagination, far from being a source of transcendental knowledge, is merely the power of making new combinations of the things learned through the senses or by the operation of reason; and he elsewhere gives recognition to another characteristic pseudoclassic doctrine—the doctrine, namely, which holds that judgment, or the power wisely to choose or to reject any new combination invented by the imagination, is the mental endowment which enables the man of imagination to become a poet. For all these reasons there is nothing lacking to make the following description of Pope and the comparison between him and Dryden very nearly a discussion of the ideal character of The Poet.

"Of his intellectual character, the constituent and fundamental principle was good sense, a prompt and intuitive perception of consonance and propriety. He saw immediately, of his own conceptions, what was to be chosen, and what to be rejected; and, in the works of others, what was to be shunned, and what was to be copied.

"But good sense alone is a sedate and quiescent quality, which manages its possessions well, but does not increase them; it collects few materials for its own operations, and preserves safety, but never gains supremacy. Pope had, likewise, genius; a mind active, ambitious, and adventurous, always investigating, always aspiring; in its widest searches still longing to go forward, in its highest flights still wishing to be higher; always imagining something greater than it knows, always endeavouring more than it can do.

"To assist these powers, he is said to have had great strength and exactness of memory. That which he had heard or read was not easily lost; and he had before him not only what his own meditation suggested, but what he had found in other writers that might be accommodated to his present purpose.

"These benefits of nature he improved by incessant and unwearied diligence; he had recourse to every source of intelligence, and lost no opportunity of information; he consulted the living as well as the dead; he read his compositions to his friends, and was never content with mediocrity, when excellence could be attained. He considered poetry as the business of his life; and, however he might seem to lament his occupation, he followed it with constancy; to make verses was his first labour, and to mend them was his last. . . .

"He professed to have learned his poetry from Dryden, whom, whenever an opportunity was presented, he praised through his whole life with unvaried liberality; and, perhaps, his character may receive some illustration, if he be compared with his master.

"Integrity of understanding, and nicety of discernment, were not allotted in a less proportion to Dryden than to Pope. The rectitude of Dryden's mind was sufficiently shown by the dismission of his poetical prejudices, and the rejection of unnatural thoughts and rugged numbers. But Dryden never desired to apply all the judgment that he had. He wrote, and professed to write, merely for the people; and when he pleased others, he contented himself. He spent no time in struggles to rouse latent powers; he never attempted to make that better which was already good, nor often to mend what he must have known to be faulty. He wrote, as he tells us, with very little consideration; when occasion or necessity called upon him, he poured out what the present moment happened to supply, and, when once it had passed the press, ejected it from his mind; for, when he had no pecuniary interest, he had no further solicitude.

"Pope was not content to satisfy; he desired to excel, and, therefore, always endeavoured to do his best: he did not court the candour, but dared the judgment of his reader, and, expecting no indulgence from others, he showed none to himself. He examined lines and words with minute and punctilious observation, and retouched every part with indefatigable diligence, till he had left nothing to be forgiven. . . .

"His declaration, that his care for his works ceased at their publication, was not strictly true. His parental attention never abandoned them; what he found amiss in the first edition, he silently corrected in those that followed. He appears to have revised the Iliad, and freed it from some of its imperfections; and the Essay on Criticism received many improvements after its first appearance. It will seldom be found that he altered, without adding clearness, elegance, or vigour. Pope had, perhaps, the judgment of Dryden; but Dryden certainly wanted the diligence of Pope. . . .

"Of genius, that power which constitutes a poet; that quality without which judgment is cold and knowledge is inert; that energy which collects, combines, amplifies, and animates; the superiority must, with some hesitation, be allowed to Dryden. It is not to be inferred that of this poetical vigour Pope had only a little, because Dryden had more; for every other writer since Milton must give place to Pope; and even of Dryden it must be said, that if he has brighter paragraphs, he has not better poems. Dryden's performances were always hasty, either excited by some external occasion, or extorted by domestick necessity; he composed without consideration, and published without correction. What his mind could supply at call, or gather in one excursion, was all that he sought, and all that he gave. The dilatory caution of Pope enabled him to condense his sentiments, to multiply his images, and to accumulate all that study might produce, or chance might supply. If the flights of Dryden therefore are higher, Pope continues longer on the wing. If of Dryden's fire the blaze is brighter, of Pope's the heat is more regular and constant. Dryden often surpasses expectation, and Pope never falls below it. Dryden is read with frequent astonishment, and Pope with perpetual delight."

It has already been said more than once that Johnson occasionally perceived, especially in Shakespeare, beauties for which he could not account. It ought now to be added that this fact does not seem ever to have tempted him into any effort to enlarge his own conceptions, and he seems usually to assume that those poets of the seventeenth and eighteenth centuries whose practice confined poetry more and more closely within the limits of what his powers of analysis could deal with wrote the only kind of poetry which would henceforth be written. "What was said of Rome, adorned by Augustus, may be applied by an easy metaphor to English poetry, embellished by Dryden. . . . He found it brick, and he left it marble." [13]

Of the major poets whom the chronological scheme of the *Lives* necessarily included, only two—Cowley and Milton—took Johnson outside the field of his greatest competence, and it is only in connection with them that the present-day reader is likely to find himself out of patience with the critic. Even if such a reader does not share Johnson's admiration for Dryden and Pope, he is, at worst, likely to feel that what Johnson says is excessive rather than that it is wrongheaded; but he may very possibly think him at least blind to the beauties of Donne and certain other poets whom he considers along with Cowley, and deserving, as Cowper thought, to have his breeches dusted for what he said of Milton. Yet the two Lives are among the most interesting of the series and they exhibit certain of Johnson's powers quite as strikingly as they reveal certain of his limitations.

Cowley's reputation was already dying, if it was not already dead. He had certainly long ceased to exercise the influence which is so evident in Dryden's very first verses, though Wilkes names him among the six English poets frequently quoted. But his enormous vogue was still too well remembered not to assure him a place in any collection of the English poets, and Johnson seized the opportunity to discuss, not merely Cowley, but the whole style of poetry which he supposed had been permanently replaced by the purer and more sensible style of Dryden. He would, no doubt, have been astonished to learn that Donne, whom he appears to consider (as indeed all his contemporaries did) merely a minor figure in an unworthy school, would someday become the god of a new idolatry, and that while Cowley continued unread, not only Donne himself but various other, to him, unimportant successors of Donne would be pored over by a new generation of poets who sometimes seem to pay lip service to Dryden less because they genuinely admire him than in order to emphasize the fact that they do not consider themselves romantics.

What led Johnson to expand the *Life of Cowley* was not so much the pleasure of ridiculing a bad kind of poetry as it was the opportunity presented to draw certain distinctions very important in connection with the kind of writing he most admired. He was, no less than Pope himself, concerned with "true wit," by which, of course (and like Pope), he meant something more than we mean by the term as it is most often used, and also something less than had been included in the old general sense which included almost all intellectual as distinguished from volitional activity. What, then, is this "wit" which, so far from being something the poet should disregard in order to write with his soul, is the distinguishing characteristic of the best writing in prose or verse?

Pope's definition:

> True wit is nature to advantage dressed
> What oft was thought but ne'er so well expressed

was already as well-known as any poetic couplet ever could be, but it did not satisfy Johnson. A little later he was to have an almost acrimonious debate with William Pepys on the subject of Pope's definition and in the course of the discussion he said: "That, sir, is a definition both false and foolish. . . . 'What oft was thought' is all the worse for being often thought, because to be wit, it ought to be newly thought." In other words, Johnson evidently realized what, unfortunately, the more conventional poets of his century tended increasingly to forget—namely, that mere truisms, though often not only true but importantly true, grow dull if too often repeated, no matter how well they are expressed, and, indeed, are rarely even well expressed after they have been too often thought or too often said. With Pepys he was "talking for victory" and he allowed himself in the course of the debate to drift into something like mere paradox; but he had already, in the *Life of Pope,* more carefully defined the poet's wit as including the capacity to make the new seem familiar and the familiar seem new. In the *Life of Cowley,* he disposes of Pope's definition by saying more moderately and more accurately that Pope's account of wit "depresses it below its natural dignity, and reduces it from strength of thought to happiness of language."

True wit must, however, be distinguished not only from pompous commonplace but also from something which deviates from it in the opposite direction by becoming a mere display of empty ingenuity; and Cowley, by far the most popular cultivator of this overingenious manner who ever lived, seemed to him to offer an opportunity to analyze the manner which he dubs "the metaphysical." Still referring to Pope's definition, he writes:

"If, by a more noble and more adequate conception, that be considered wit which is, at once, natural and new, that which, though not obvious, is, upon its first production, acknowledged to be just; if it be that, which he that never found it, wonders how he missed; to wit of this kind the metaphysical poets have seldom risen. Their thoughts are often new, but seldom natural; they are not obvious, but neither are they just; and the reader, far from wondering that he missed them, wonders more frequently by what perverseness of industry they were ever found.

"But wit, abstracted from its effects upon the hearer, may be more rigorously and philosophically considered as a kind of 'discordia concors'; a combination of dissimilar images, or discovery of occult resemblances in things apparently unlike. Of wit, thus defined, they [the metaphysical poets] have more than enough. The most heterogeneous ideas are yoked by violence together; nature and art are ransacked for illustrations, comparisons, and allusions; their learning instructs, and their subtlety surprises; but the reader commonly thinks his improvement dearly bought, and, though he sometimes admires, is seldom pleased."

As one of the many examples of "thoughts so far-fetched, as to be not only unexpected, but unnatural," Johnson chose the following lines from Donne:

> Though God be our true glass, through which we see
> All, since the being of all things is he,
> Yet are the trunks, which do to us derive
> Things in proportion fit, by perspective
> Deeds of good men; for by their living here,
> Virtues, indeed remote, seem to be near.

"Who," he asks, "but Donne would have thought that a good man is a telescope?"

"To write on their plan, it was," he grants, "at least, necessary to read and think. No man could be born a metaphysical poet, nor assume the dignity of a writer, by descriptions copied from descriptions, by imitations borrowed from imitations, by traditional imagery, and hereditary similes, by readiness of rhyme, and volubility of syllables." When he wrote that, he was thinking, as too few of his contemporaries seemed to think often enough, of the same disgust with merely "correct poetry," which led him to answer as he did Boswell's question (inspired no doubt by patriotism) concerning the poems of John Ogilvie: "Is there not imagination in them, Sir?" "Why, Sir, there is in them what *was* imagination."

But learning, ingenuity and effort are to him futile as ends in themselves. The metaphysical poets tell him nothing which he recognizes as true or significant about human life. So far as he is concerned, they are merely playing a rather childish game, for he is as far from any conception of "aesthetic experience" as something entirely apart from the ordinary business of daily living as he is from the possibility of imagining that Donne's ingenuities had, for the author, a real emotional meaning. To him all these poets seem to have deliberately avoided the only content which can give value to literature. They neither describe nor comment upon any experience which he recognizes as part of normal human existence. Of Cowley's love poems he says: "that the accusation of lasciviousness is unjust, the perusal of his work will sufficiently evince," but from what follows immediately it is evident that, even if the poet had not been "eminently virtuous," his verses would, nevertheless, have been saved as a eunuch is saved from the sin of lewdness. "Cowley's *Mistress* has no power of seduction. . . . The compositions are such as might have been written for penance by a hermit, or for hire by a philosophical rhymer, who had only heard of another sex; for they turn the mind only on the writer, whom, without thinking on a woman but as the subject for his task, we sometimes esteem as learned, and sometimes despise as trifling, always admire as ingenious, and always condemn as unnatural."

That certain, at least, of the defects which Johnson points out are real and serious, few of even the warmest admirers of the poets whom he discusses would care to deny. That his analysis of the external features of their manner is accurate enough to serve as the basis for classification is sufficiently demonstrated by the fact that his essay fixed upon the school the not too obviously appropriate designation "metaphysical," which has stuck to it through a revolution of taste lifting the school itself from contempt into high esteem. Yet Cowley, "who was almost the last of that race," Johnson calls without qualification "undoubtedly the best," and that fact makes it almost unnecessary to observe that if he saw very clearly what he did see, there were other things to which he was completely blind as well as completely deaf.

For one thing, he was, of course, incapable of catching the subtle rhythms to which present-day ears are again attuned, and which are certainly sometimes (though possibly not as often as modern prejudice likes to assume) achieved by Donne. A man who could refer to the style of versification which he traces from Fairfax through Denham and Waller to its perfection in Dryden as though it represented a self-evident improvement in the course of which nothing worth having was lost and as though no sane person would ever desire to hear any other kind; a man who could say of this "new versification" that, since Dryden's time, "English poetry has had no tendency to relapse to its former savageness," was a man who seems to have had the ability to appreciate to its full one kind of music which many moderns seem to have lost the power of enjoying—namely, the music to be heard in verses exemplifying "the long slow march and energy divine." But words are also capable of making another sort of music of whose existence he was, perhaps, as completely unaware as he was of the sort which his friend, Dr. Burney, professed.

More important, so far as the metaphysical poets are concerned, is the fact that he is obviously forced to deny that any human being ever underwent experiences of certain sorts completely foreign to him. When he sums up the charge against Cowley in one damning word "unnatural" he means to include unnaturalness of thought and feeling as well as unnaturalness in the method chosen to give expression to either. But like so many of his contemporaries who also made "naturalness" their test, Johnson was a little too sure that he knew just how much Nature includes and of just how great a variety she is capable. It may be that the present-day vogue of the metaphysical manner is not due exclusively to the fact that it furnishes contemporary poets with an idiom exactly suited to what they have to say. The vogue may possibly have something to do with the fact that those who suffer from an acute fear of the cliché at the same time that they suffer equally from a paucity of new thoughts find in it a convenient method of escaping the reproach of relying too heavily upon what Johnson called "hereditary similes." Nevertheless, the metaphysical manner is not merely a device by which emptiness may be concealed, and not all metaphysical poetry is unnatural. There are more things in heaven and earth . . .[14]

Few of Johnson's early readers were inclined to protest his judgment upon Cowley or Donne, but his treatment of Milton was greeted by an outcry and is still capable of provoking in certain breasts a lively indignation. Some part of the protest, like some part of the original attack, was political rather than literary in intention—Whig resentment responding to Tory gibes. But the dispute was not wholly political on either side, and when all due allowance has been made for the vehemence of Johnson's dislike of Milton's antiroyalist, antiepiscopal principles, there still remains the fact that some of Milton's poetry merely irritated rather than moved him. It is not easy to see why the republicanism of the one was more "acrimonious and surly" than the Tory prejudices of the other, or how Johnson, who could allow himself to write of a poet's blindness: "This darkness, had his eyes been better employed, had undoubtedly deserved compassion," could say of his antagonist's controversial manner: "Such is his malignity, 'that hell grows darker at his frown'." But had Milton been an Anglican and a royalist, Johnson would still have been constrained to judge his poetry as he does, always taking back with one hand the praise which the other lavishes.

Lavish of praise he certainly is. To no other poet except Shakespeare did he ever pay tributes so high. By a simple process of selection and omission, one might compile from his essay a panegyric that could hardly fail to satisfy even Milton's most idolatrous admirers. "Of the two pieces, L'Allegro and Il

Penseroso, I believe, opinion is uniform; every man that reads them, reads them with pleasure." Of *Comus* it is said that: "A work more truly poetical is rarely found," and *Paradise Lost,* which Johnson regards as completely overshadowing all its author's other work, is assigned a place almost on a level with that of the *Iliad.* "By the general consent of critics, the first praise of genius is due to the writer of an epic poem, as it requires an assemblage of all the powers which are singly sufficient for other compositions." "What other author ever soared so high, or sustained his flight so long? . . . Of all the borrowers from Homer, Milton is, perhaps, the least indebted. He was naturally a thinker for himself, confident of his own abilities, and disdainful of help or hindrance. . . . From his contemporaries he neither courted nor received support. . . . His great works were performed under discountenance, and in blindness; but difficulties vanished at his touch; he was born for whatever is arduous; and his work is not the greatest of heroick poems, only because it is not the first." Moreover, and what may have been more difficult for Johnson, he is even willing to make, in Milton's case, an exception which violates his rooted prejudice against blank verse. "Whatever be the advantages of rhyme, I cannot prevail on myself to wish that Milton had been a rhymer; for I cannot wish his work to be other than it is."

He who, continues Johnson, can put "the faults of that wonderful performance . . . in balance with its beauties must be considered not as nice but as dull," and certain of the faults which Johnson does nevertheless permit himself to specify are merely those which common sense cannot fail to recognize, even if it then dismisses them. An inconvenience of the design is, Johnson remarks, "that it requires the description of what cannot be described, the agency of spirits. . . . His infernal and celestial powers are sometimes pure spirit, and sometimes animated body . . . The confusion of spirit and matter, which pervades the whole narration of the war in heaven fills it with incongruity." Or again: "Some philosophical notions, especially where the philosophy is false, might have been better omitted. The angel, in a comparison, speaks of 'timorous deer,' before deer were yet timorous, and before Adam could understand the comparison."

Johnson himself dismisses such objections as dull rather than nice and they are certainly not adequate to account for a fact which all the panegyric fails to conceal—the fact, that is to say, that the judgments which Johnson pronounces are judgments to which a regular process of reasoned comparisons has led him but in which his taste does not concur and to which his enthusiasm fails to respond. If the epic poem is the greatest of all poems, and if Milton's epic is not the greatest only because it was not the first, then what can we possibly conclude (except perhaps that the greatest poems are dull) from the following sentences in which Johnson the judge steps aside to permit a word from Johnson the reader, who follows his own tastes in contempt of all criticism even when that criticism happens to be his own? "Paradise Lost is one of the books which the reader admires and lays down, and forgets to take up again. None ever wished it longer than it is. Its perusal is a duty rather than a pleasure. We read Milton for instruction, retire harassed and overburdened, and look elsewhere for recreation; we desert our master, and seek for companions." [15]

That last phrase "seek for companions" is no doubt the key to the inconsistency. If no other poet has ever "soared so high or sustained his flight so long," the converse is equally true and, to Johnson, equally important. Neither, that is to say, did any other poet ever transport himself so far beyond or maintain himself so long absent from any contact with man's immediate and daily concerns; say so little of which the truth or falsity may be tested by that appeal to experience which Shakespeare so perpetually invites, and which, so Johnson insists, is one of his chief glories so commonly to survive. Those truths of revealed religion which were the only transcendental truths Johnson was prepared to recognize require no support from poetry. All devotional lyrics are, he declared in the *Life of Watts,* "unsatisfactory" because literary ornament cannot further adorn matter sacred in itself, and he would have refused to suppose that even Milton could add to the glory of God or make the story of man's fall and redemption more awfully impressive. As a poem, therefore, *Paradise Lost* must, like every other piece of fiction, be judged exclusively in terms of its relevance to human life and that relevance seemed to Johnson almost nil.

"The plan of Paradise Lost has this inconvenience, that it comprises neither human actions nor human manners. The man and woman who act and suffer are in a state which no other man or woman can ever know. The reader finds no transaction in which he can be engaged; beholds no condition in which he can, by any effort of imagination, place himself; he has, therefore, little natural curiosity or sympathy.

"We all, indeed, feel the effect of Adam's disobedience; we all sin, like Adam, and, like him, must all bewail our offences; we have restless and insidious enemies in the fallen angels; and in the blessed spirits we have guardians and friends; in the redemption of mankind we hope to be included; and in the description of heaven and hell we are, surely, interested, as we are all to reside, hereafter, either in the regions of horrour or of bliss.

"But these truths are too important to be new; they have been taught to our infancy; they have mingled with our solitary thoughts and familiar conversations, and are habitually interwoven with the whole texture of life. Being, therefore, not new, they raise no unaccustomed emotion in the mind; what we knew before, we cannot learn; what is not unexpected, cannot surprise."

Obviously the pros and cons of Johnson's judgment upon *Paradise Lost* are so difficult to reconcile that he is open to the charge of mere inconsistency: of having said in one paragraph what cannot possibly be true unless what is said in another be false. But his treatment of *Paradise Lost* is not, in the eyes of Milton's admirers, the greatest of his crimes. He grants it supreme greatness at the same time that he declares his inability to take pleasure in excellence of that sort, and having granted so much, he might, by those otherwise constituted, be contemptuously left to do what he predicted any man would do if he persisted in the road Anna Seward had taken when she committed one of Milton's minor poems to heart—namely, "die in a surfeit of bad taste." Far more serious in the opinion of many is the diatribe against *Lycidas,* which is to Johnson a tissue of absurdity, unredeemed by a single positive virtue and hence as reprehensible to his judgment as it is offensive to his taste.

The passage in which this poem is disposed of is one of the most vigorous and amusing which Johnson ever wrote. To anyone who had never read the composition in question, his destructive analysis would probably seem as utterly destructive as Voltaire's ludicrous summary of *Hamlet.* Yet to most people, even to most of those not especially qualified to judge either Milton or poetry, the lines themselves confute the arguments against them and prove Johnson wrong, even though they may not make it clear how one who seems so sensible can be. To understand how he could have gone so completely astray, how in this one instance he was not saved, as he so often was saved, from the worst consequences of his limited theory of poetry by an ability to perceive beauties for which he could not account, one needs to compare what he said of *Lycidas* with what he said of certain other poems which seemed to him in certain respects like it. One needs, in other words, to understand what kind of bad poetry he thought Milton was, in this instance, cultivating.

To do so, one must remember that for what seemed to him *merely poetical* Johnson had complete contempt. This means, for one thing, that, as he wrote in the *Life of Waller:* "Poets, indeed, profess fiction; but the legitimate end of fiction is the conveyance of truth." He would, therefore, have proclaimed readily enough that truth is beauty, but he would never have added "beauty is truth," because to add that would be either merely to repeat the first statement or to be guilty of a dangerous confusion. To him no fiction can be beautiful merely as fiction. It must, if it is to be beautiful, successfully aim at "the conveyance of truth," and it is not only contemptible if it fails but is also at least useless when, as in the case of *Paradise Lost,* the truth it conveys is one which has been adequately conveyed in some other form. Many of the fictions habitually employed in poetry were, he thought, no longer capable of conveying any truth. All that are comprised in what he called "the dark and dismal regions of mythology, where neither hope nor fear, neither joy nor sorrow, can be found" are included in this class.

So too, and *a fortiori,* are those which constitute the whole pastoral tradition. Monsieur Jourdain was never wearier of shepherds than Johnson was, and he never met them in poetry without being impelled to some contemptuous comment. Pope wrote pastorals because "It seems natural for a young poet to initiate himself by pastorals, which, not professing to imitate real life, require no experience." Gay's *The Fan* "is one of those mythological fictions which antiquity delivers ready to hand, but which, like other things that lie open to every one's use, are of little value. The attention naturally retires from a new tale of Venus, Diana, and Minerva." Or again, "There is something in the poetical Arcadia so remote from known reality and speculative possibility, that we can never support its representation through a long work. A pastoral of a hundred lines may be endured; but who will hear of sheep and goats, and myrtle bowers, and purling rivulets, through five acts? Such scenes please barbarians in the dawn of literature, and children in the dawn of life; but will be, for the most part, thrown away, as men grow wise, and nations grow learned." To Johnson, any poet who began to talk of either Amaryllis or Minerva was openly confessing that he had nothing new or useful to say, and not even a novel fancy to propose. He closed his mind when he heard the syllables and refused to listen even to Milton when that strain was taken up.[16]

Moreover, Johnson's contempt for the *merely poetical* included whatever emotions as well as whatever fictions seemed to be generated exclusively for poetical purposes. He would never have used the phrase "poetically true" because he would never have supposed that there was more than one kind of truth. He hated cant (except when it was his own and therefore not recognizable as such) in any form, and poetry which could not meet the test of common sense as he understood it was to him a form of canting, to be exposed as such—not only because it was necessarily bad poetry if it was bad sense, but also for reasons which are moral as much as aesthetic—because, that is to say, any form of insincerity is dangerous and wicked; all the more so if, by being "poetical," it becomes the more seductive. He was not thinking of poetry when he said once to Boswell: "Do not,

Sir, accustom yourself to trust to *impressions*. There is a middle state of mind between conviction and hypocrisy, of which many are conscious." But if he was not thinking of poetry at the moment, he probably felt that those who indulged in merely poetical fancies and merely poetical truths were at best cultivating that dangerous "middle state," to remain long in which is to lose the power of distinguishing between sincerity and pretense. Hence his readiness to apply the test of rational scorn to any poem which seemed likely to be damaged by it—not because he hated poetry but because he loved truth. The injunction "Clear your *mind* of cant" rings repeatedly through his criticism as it does through his conversation.

One hears it, for instance, in the passage devoted to Pope's *Verses to the Memory of an Unfortunate Lady* in which he undertakes to confront the vague sentiments of the poet with what he regards as the facts of the case. The fiction (for it probably was a purely imaginary incident) concerns a young girl, legally a minor, who kills herself when her guardian separates her from her lover. Pope labors to evoke the obvious sentiments suggested by a cruel guardian and a loving girl. He succeeds as well as Pope could be expected to succeed with such a subject, but Johnson calls him back to what in all probability would have been Pope's own prose opinion had he been, for example, one of the relatives of the girl in question rather than her volunteer elegist:

"From this account, given with evident intention to raise the lady's character, it does not appear that she had any claim to praise, nor much to compassion. She seems to have been impatient, violent, and ungovernable. Her uncle's power could not have lasted long; the hour of liberty and choice would have come in time. But her desires were too hot for delay, and she liked self-murder better than suspense.

"Nor is it discovered that the uncle, whoever he was, is with much justice delivered to posterity as 'a false guardian;' he seems to have done only that for which a guardian is appointed: he endeavoured to direct his niece till she should be able to direct herself. Poetry has not often been worse employed than in dignifying the amorous fury of a raving girl."

What, some may ask, is to become of poetry if it is to be regarded with an eye so prone to see things in the light of common sense? What, Johnson would have asked in turn, is to become of common sense if poetry is to be allowed to generate inappropriate emotions because they happen, in a given case, to be more "poetical" than the appropriate ones?

Critics have been known to protest wearily that most tragedies (*Othello,* for a notable example) need never have occurred had either hero or heroine consented for one instant to do what common sense suggests. Such critics obviously wish that such tragedies, at least, had never been written, and Johnson would certainly have agreed, not in the case of *Othello* but at least in the case of most of those tales of woe where the events are obviously invented for the purpose of seeming woeful. When, as a youth, he was composing his own tragic drama, he understood so well what he was doing that when his patron, Gilbert Walmsley, then register of the ecclesiastical court, objected to the part he had read by asking the author how he could manage to plunge his heroine into any deeper distress, Johnson could reply, with a slyness which certainly indicated no deep absorption in the fable he was concocting: "Sir, I can put her into the Spiritual Court!" And when Bennet Langton paused in his reading aloud of the bookseller Dodsley's unusually bloody *Cleone,* Johnson urged him on with the exclamation: "Come, let's have some more, let's go into the slaughter-house again." It is hardly necessary to repeat that such reactions as these are not proof of any insensibility; they are, on the contrary, merely proof that he was tough-minded enough to scoff at pretense even though the pretenders evoked the sacred name of poetry.

Johnson saw no sufficient reason for *willingly* suspending disbelief merely in order to suffer from shadowy distress, and he saw no more reason why the lyric poet should make a fool of himself by supposing personal sorrows he did not really feel. On that subject he expressed himself fully and entertainingly when he came to discuss the love verses which Cowley is said to have addressed to a nonexistent mistress:

"It is surely not difficult, in the solitude of a college, or in the bustle of the world, to find useful studies and serious employment. No man needs to be so burdened with life, as to squander it in voluntary dreams of fictitious occurrences. The man that sits down to suppose himself charged with treason or peculation, and heats his mind to an elaborate purgation of his character from crimes which he was never within the possibility of committing, differs only by the infrequency of his folly from him who praises beauty which he never saw; complains of jealousy which he never felt; supposes himself sometimes invited, and sometimes forsaken; fatigues his fancy, and ransacks his memory, for images which may exhibit the gaiety of hope, or the gloominess of despair; and dresses his imaginary Chloris or Phyllis, sometimes in flowers fading as her beauty, and sometimes in gems lasting as her virtues."

The analysis of *Lycidas* was written in exactly the same spirit and in exactly the same manner as the analyses of Cowley's *Mistress* and Pope's *Unfortunate Lady*. The three passages belong together. They are three illustrations of the same thing—namely, Johnson's reaction to poems which he found offensive because they seemed to him *merely* poetical. Taken by themselves, they are equally good and equally convincing. If the poems with which each is concerned were lost, the three analyses would probably seem equally amusing. Indeed, that concerning *Lycidas* would probably be adequate as a criticism of any translation of the poem into any foreign language. But as one reads the following, one should temporarily suspend one's direct knowledge of the poem in question:

"One of the poems on which much praise has been bestowed is *Lycidas;* of which the diction is harsh, the rhymes uncertain, and the numbers unpleasing. What beauty there is, we must, therefore seek in the sentiments and the images. It is not to be considered as the effusion of real passion; for passion runs not after remote allusions and obscure opinions. Passion plucks no berries from the myrtle and ivy, nor calls upon Arethuse and Mincius, nor tells of rough 'satyrs and fauns with cloven heel'. Where there is leisure for fiction, there is little grief.

"In this poem there is no nature, for there is no truth; there is no art, for there is nothing new. Its form is that of a pastoral: easy, vulgar, and, therefore, disgusting; whatever images it can supply are long ago exhausted; and its inherent improbability always forces dissatisfaction on the mind. When Cowley tells of Hervey, that they studied together, it is easy to suppose how much he must miss the companion of his labours, and the partner of his discoveries; but what image of tenderness can be excited by these lines?

> We drove afield, and both together heard,
> What time the grey fly winds her sultry horn,
> Batt'ning our flocks with the fresh dews of night.

We know that they never drove afield, and that they had no flocks to batten; and, though it be allowed that the representation may be allegorical, the true meaning is so uncertain and remote, that it is never sought, because it cannot be known when it is found.

"Among the flocks, and copses, and flowers, appear the heathen deities; Jove and Phœbus, Neptune and Æolus, with a long train of mythological imagery, such as a college easily supplies. Nothing can less display knowledge, or less exercise invention, than to tell how a shepherd has lost his companion, and must now feed his flocks alone, without any judge of his skill in piping; and how one god asks another god what is become of Lycidas, and how neither god can tell. He who thus grieves will excite no sympathy; he who thus praises will confer no honour.

"This poem has yet a grosser fault. With these trifling fictions are mingled the most awful and sacred truths, such as ought never to be polluted with such irreverend combinations. The shepherd, likewise, is now a feeder of sheep, and afterwards an ecclesiastical pastor, a superintendent of a christian flock. Such equivocations are always unskilful; but here they are indecent, and, at least, approach to impiety, of which, however, I believe the writer not to have been conscious.

"Such is the power of reputation justly acquired, that its blaze drives away the eye from nice examination. Surely no man could have fancied that he read Lycidas with pleasure, had he not known the author." [17]

If Johnson the critic is at his best in dealing with Shakespeare and at his second best with Dryden and Pope, he is, one is tempted to say, obviously at his worst in this treatment of *Lycidas.* Few other literate men have ever found its diction harsh or its numbers unpleasing, and there are certainly many who would read it with pleasure had they never known the author. But Johnson's worst never fails to exhibit some kind of excellence, his darkness is always a darkness visible. If, in this particular instance, his judgment could hardly be worse, his defense of it could hardly be better, and the vigor of his mind animates with an equal vigor the language in which he expresses himself. If he found Milton a poet whom the reader "admires and lays down," there are those who find him a critic one does not want to lay down even when one cannot for the moment admire his judgment.

To most of Johnson's contemporaries, his criticism was eminently readable. "I am not," he remarked in the *Life of Pope,* "writing only to poets and philosophers," and it was by no means in vain that he addressed himself to the general public. That public had never previously been given much critical writing which could be read with easy pleasure. For a long time Dryden's prefaces had stood almost alone as examples of criticism conspicuous for literary charm, and despite Warburton, Mason, Young and Morgann, criticism usually suggested either pedantry, personal abuse, or that curious combination of the two which one found in Rymer, Jeremy Collier or John Dennis. Even the reviews published in the various periodicals were likely to rely so heavily on summary and excerpt as seldom even to approach the form of a critical essay, and Johnson's attempt to popularize criticism—immediately successful enough to create a demand for a separate edition of the *Lives*—gives his essays a certain novelty no more absolute than, but just as important as, the novelty inherent in his tendency to treat biography as relevant to literary interpretation.

Johnson could become a popular critic partly because his premises and his methods were so well adapted to the understanding of the intelligent layman; because, that is to say, literary interpretation and judgment seemed, as Johnson presented them, to be no more than the application to literary questions of that generally applicable common sense in which the eighteenth century placed its faith. His appeal, as he had so explicitly stated in the *Preface to Shakespeare,* was from authority and pedantic rules to "Nature," and Nature was something which his contemporaries, lay as well as literary, were ready to assume that they clearly understood. If, however, one is to define Johnson's literary criticism as common-sense criticism (quotation marks being always understood when the phrase is used), it is even more important to remember that such common-sense criticism is no more clearly distinguished from the pedantic criticism which preceded it than it is from both the romantic criticism which was so shortly to follow, and the sort most frequently practiced by the "serious" critics of today.

Common sense as applied to literature meant, to begin with, the assumption that neither the aims nor the methods of the literary art are peculiar to it. Literature, the assumption is, seeks to give pleasure and to impart instruction; but neither the pleasure it gives nor the instruction it provides constitutes any world apart or requires for its proper appreciation any unique faculties. Johnson, of course, would have been indignantly astonished at anything suggesting the doctrine of art for art's sake. He would have been equally astonished to hear of "significant form" or an "aesthetic experience." To him sound morality and good sense are the same whether in fact or in fiction, in prose or in verse. One of his conscious aims was certainly that of taking literature out of the hands of the pedants. Had he been gifted with the power of foreseeing the future he would undoubtedly have added another: that of keeping it out of the clutches of the romantics and the aesthetes.

Pedantic criticism and romantic criticism are alike in one important respect. Each addresses itself to some sort of specialist. To understand the first, one must be learned. To understand the second, one needs, it is assumed, a special sensibility which is the exclusive possession of a limited class. Both are, therefore, to some extent esoteric; both assume, at the very least, that the reader has either a special equipment or a special endowment without which his judgment is worthless. Johnson, on the other hand, takes it for granted that neither the enjoyment nor the understanding of literature requires any capacities or any knowledge not possessed by every intelligent man. Intelligent talk about books is like intelligent talk about manners or morals or politics because good sense is the key to the intelligent discussion of any subject. There are no unique literary values. No special conceptions, no special sensibilities, no special terms, even, are necessary. Anyone who has the equipment to judge men and manners and morals has the equipment to judge literature, for literature is merely a reflection of men and manners and morals.

To say this is, of course, to say that for Johnson there is no realm of the exclusively aesthetic. As he sees it, aesthetic experience differs from actual experience in being vicarious rather than direct, but in so far as it is an experience at all it is an experience of the same kind as any other. A thing may be valid in poetry though not in accordance with fact only in so far as it can suggest analogy with fact, and if such analogy is not suggested it is poetically false as well as false in every other way. For him there is no world of imagination except the world of memory, and the world of evoked memories is a relatively pale one. As has already been noted, he pooh-poohed the idea that Garrick, or any other actor, was carried away by his role. He was equally contemptuous of the idea that any spectator or any reader lost the distinction between fiction and fact, and he would certainly have been even more contemptuous of anyone who professed to find the world of "dreams" or the world of art either more real or as a whole more satisfactory than the world of reality. In the *Preface to Shakespeare,* he had put into the following few sentences both his theory of imitation and his theory of the effect of such imitation:

"It will be asked, how the drama moves, if it is not credited. It is credited with all the credit due to a drama. It is credited, whenever it moves, as a just picture of a real original; as representing to the auditor what he would himself feel, if he were to do or suffer what is there feigned to be suffered or to be done. The reflection that strikes the heart is not, that the evils before us are real evils, but that they are evils to which we ourselves may be exposed. . . .

"Imitations produce pain or pleasure, not because they are

mistaken for realities, but because they bring realities to mind. When the imagination is recreated by a painted landscape, the trees are not supposed capable to give us shade, or the fountains coolness; but we consider how we should be pleased with such fountains playing beside us, and such woods waving over us. We are agitated in reading the history of Henry the fifth, yet no man takes his book for the field of Agincourt." [18]

Whatever may be the limitations of Johnson's aesthetic theory as it is here revealed, they are also and inevitably the limitations of his criticism. He seldom perceived and never attempted to analyze any aesthetic effect which lies beyond the reach of his "common sense" view of the relation between art and reality. What he has to say in the *Lives of the Poets* is precisely the sort of thing he had to say in his conversation, and he obviously regarded criticism as neither more nor less than good talk about books—which is, in turn, very much like good talk about anything else. He was no less aware than Swinburne or Oscar Wilde that some sort of splendor may surround things wicked or destructive, but he saw no reason why literature should isolate and then acclaim a splendor which experience itself never encounters thus isolated, and the concluding sentence of the following brief passage on Waller's marriage to a lady who was not his "Sacharissa" is, in its own quiet way, an anticipation of Max Beerbohm's *reductio ad absurdum* in his satiric essay on the vulgarity of fire departments. Wrote Johnson of Waller: "He, doubtless, praised some whom he would have been afraid to marry, and, perhaps, married one whom he would have been ashamed to praise. Many qualities contribute to domestic happiness, upon which poetry has no colours to bestow; and many airs and sallies may delight imagination, which he who flatters them never can approve. There are charms made only for distant admiration. No spectacle is nobler than a blaze."

It is obvious that the reader who seeks in Johnson for certain things which he finds or thinks he finds in some later critics will come away disappointed. He will not, to begin with, find Johnson discovering neglected genius or habitually reversing accepted judgments. Johnson happened, it is true, to run counter to general opinion in his estimate of Milton, but on the whole his effort, even there, was to minimize rather than to emphasize the extent of his dissent, and Milton is the only important poet except perhaps Gray upon whom Johnson puts a value conspicuously different from that generally accorded by conservative opinion. In the *Life of Addison* he observed that "About things on which the public thinks long, it commonly attains to think right." It had thought long on Dryden and Pope and the other major poets. Its decision is therefore final for, as he had remarked in connection with some pettishness exhibited by Dryden: "What is good only because it pleases, cannot be pronounced good till it has been found to please."

More important perhaps is the fact that disappointment awaits also the reader who expects from a critic those flashes of half-mystical illumination which were to seem so important in the work of somewhat later exponents of criticism. Johnson would certainly have regarded the claims of "intuition" as skeptically as he did those of the transcendental imagination. He would never have aspired to supply the lightning by which Shakespeare or anybody else could be read and he would have doubted the value of reading done by the aid of any light so dazzling or so fitful. The romantic critic was usually dominated by a sense that the literature upon which he proposed to comment had never been properly understood before. He felt himself surrounded by the mysteries of an undiscovered country and hence perpetually upon the threshold of dazzling discoveries. Johnson, of course, never supposed that he or any other critic could be "creative" and he did not even suppose that unsuspected beauties of major importance remained to be discovered. Pope and Dryden had, like Shakespeare, been appreciated too long and too enthusiastically to permit the supposition that any of their principal excellencies had been unnoticed or insufficiently valued. Had he lived to see the first two dismissed and Shakespeare treated as a poet whom ten generations had admired but never understood, he would certainly have risen to the defense of a public which had thought long and therefore correctly. Literature to him was a country which had been often traversed and often described by competent observers. An intelligent mind might profitably traverse it again, noting details which had previously escaped attention, questioning judgments which had been too hastily made, and retesting in the light of common sense the fictions and the sentiments of the major poets. But discrimination and judgment, not paradox and revelation, were the chief business of the critic, who was usually soundest when he was engaged in nothing more revolutionary than the rationalization and clarification of the general public's perceptions and opinions.

The critic, then, has every right to pass judgment on the poet. No claims to inspiration or membership in a sacred fraternity put the latter above the reach of censure. What is too silly to be said in prose remains no less unacceptable when put into verse. But the critic derives his right from the rights of the general public of which he is a part—not from the fact that he *is* a critic. He will generally agree with the public's considered judgment because literature is to be judged, not in the light of learning (which most readers do not have) or by its effect upon sensibilities undreamed-of except by the few, but in accordance with the same common sense which guides us as we go about the business of life.

Those who read the *Lives of the Poets,* not with disappointment but with delight, get from them something more than merely Johnson's sensible estimate of the merits and the defects of those whom he is discussing. But this something is simply the same thing which they get from the records of his conversation on literary and other topics—namely, the play of a vigorous and entertaining mind over a wide range of subjects. His criticism is not personal in the sense of proposing an account of the adventures of a soul among the masterpieces. Its manner is objective, and its aim is not to present "the truth as I (and probably no one else) see it," but to make statements which the reader will accept as true for himself and for all normal men. This criticism is, however, highly personal in the sense that the manner and the matter alike are so highly characteristic of Johnson that the reader who knew him through his conversation and his other work would have little difficulty in identifying the author even if the *Lives* were unsigned.

Johnson believed in the all but exclusive importance of what has come in our time to be called "public" truths and methods of expression as opposed to "private" ones, but he makes no attempt at "scientific" detachment and no attempt to separate "literary" or "artistic" or "aesthetic" considerations from any others because he did not think such separation possible. In one sense no criticism was ever less "pure." What one gets is, among other things, Johnson on Pope. But one gets the whole Johnson in a sense in which one does not get the whole of the personal critic who self-consciously proclaims his determination to talk about himself in connection with Pope or with Shakespeare. What one gets is, in other words, a personality revealing itself rather than a personality determined to reveal itself. Perhaps, one might add, a personality revealing itself rather than a personality showing itself off.

"The criticism of Dryden is the criticism of a poet; not a dull collection of theorems, nor a rude detection of faults . . . but a gay and vigorous dissertation, where delight is mingled with instruction, and where the author proves his right of judgment by his power of performance." That much, at the very least, must be said of Johnson also. Whatever the admirers of this or that special sort of criticism may feel that he fails to give them, there is rarely a page in which he does not give *something* shrewd, or penetrating, or ingenious, or amusing. Occasionally that something may be a picturesque bit drawn from personal experience or oral tradition, as when he tells us of *Absalom and Achitophel* that the sale was so large "that my father, an old bookseller, told me he had not known it equalled but by Sacheverell's Trial." Sometimes it is a flash of dry wit; sometimes a dissertation on some such subject as the freedom of the press or the place of natural science in education. On still other occasions, it is a defense of one of Johnson's favorite generalizations about literature which happens to be suggested by the poet or the poem at the moment under discussion.

Of the ridiculous furor over Addison's *Cato* he remarks: "Those, who affected to think liberty in danger, affected, likewise, to think that a stage-play might preserve it." Apropos of the same poet's overpraised comparison in the famous compliment to the Duke of Marlborough, he quotes a schoolmaster as having said: "If I had set ten schoolboys to write on the battle of Blenheim, and eight had brought me the angel, I should not have been surprized." But Johnson is equally capable of making fine discriminations which reveal a capacity to appreciate more different kinds of excellence than he is sometimes credited with—as witness, for example, the following comment on Dryden's prose style, which shows how clearly he perceived the difference between Dryden's "naturalness" and the rhetorical methods of his own discourse: "The clauses are never balanced, nor the periods modelled; every word seems to drop by chance, though it falls into its proper place."

Johnson seldom fails to be memorable even when he is wrong, and his criticism is seldom other than interesting even when it is not, by strict definition, criticism at all. The pleasure which we get from reading him is often, at least, as much the pleasure of learning about Johnson as it is that of learning about Dryden, Pope, Milton and the rest; and if to say that is, in the opinion of the austere, to say that he is not really a critic at all, one can only reply that he is, at least, something which it would be a pity to miss. He himself would have considered it the reverse of dispraise had he been accused of mingling moral, social or even merely prudential considerations with aesthetic ones, for he would have maintained that the last are nonsense when isolated from the context which must always be theirs for anyone who is not some sort of literary hermit or monster. He did not think of his literary criticism as something which ought to be essentially different from that general criticism of life which he had made it his business to offer since he first began to write. No praise would have seemed to him higher than that implied in a statement which some might make with derogatory intention: The *Lives of the Poets* was not written by a scholar or by an aesthetician. It was, on the contrary, the work of a man whose wide knowledge of men and manners included, in due proportion, a knowledge of what men had written and what they had found, by the test of time, worth reading.[19]

CHAPTER XIII

Jam Moriturus

When Johnson completed the last of the *Lives* sometime in March, 1781, he was midway between his seventy-first and seventy-second birthdays. Death, which had always seemed very terrible to him, was still some three years and nine months away, but the clouds of misery which were to engulf him were already beginning to gather. The pension preserved him from want and his fame was at its height, but a series of cruel circumstances was to embitter his last days and to deprive him of two solicitous friends upon whom he had come to count very heavily.

The last sad chapter of his checkered existence may be thought of as opening, in the month following that in which the *Lives* had been completed, with the death of Henry Thrale, whose passing was to have consequences even more serious than any which, at the moment, he feared. Nothing in Thrale's life became him less than the leaving of it, but his story and that of his gay widow—as her contemporaries called her—is too clearly an integral part of Johnson's own not to be included in his biography. Had Thrale eaten less he might have lived longer and Johnson might have died less wretchedly.

Not quite two years before his death, Thrale had gone up to London one Monday morning "*to do little things,* as we call it" —which little things were to include listening to a reading of the will of his sister's husband, Arnold Nesbitt. At seven that night he was brought back to Streatham in a state of insensibility which prevented him from recognizing even the members of his family. He had been stricken with apoplexy as he sat at table in his sister's house, and it was not until twelve years later that his wife learned the immediate cause of the stroke. Nesbitt had died insolvent and Thrale was bound to him for a very considerable sum of money. Looking back after the passage of these twelve years, his wife could write: "Mr. Thrale recovering, kept the Secret, tho' he lost his Wits; & kept it I do believe even from Sophy Streatfeild—his health and Happiness forsook him from that Hour however, & tho' he lived near two years . . . he never looked up more." [1]

That he "never looked up more" is perhaps literally true, but it does not mean that Thrale awaited death with quiet dignity. Phlegmatic voluptuary that he was, he sought to rouse himself from melancholy by self-indulgence, and his wife, not made for any tranquil existence, abetted him at least to the extent of trying to provide restless diversion. Though he was soon up and about again, she assumed some of the responsibilities of the brewery, arranged trips to Brighton and elsewhere for the ostensible purpose of driving away the "black dog" of his melancholy, and continued the lavish social life to which they had both become accustomed. Some of the gay gatherings described in the preceding chapter were subsequent to Thrale's first attack, and his wife finally won his consent to a project she had long entertained—the taking of a town house outside unfashionable Southwark, and, as it turned out, in Grosvenor Square. Here, at last, she changed their dinner hour from the citizens' four o'clock to the great world's eight, and set up as one of the spectacular London hostesses. Far from prematurely adopting weeds, she appeared at court in a dress made of a material copied from goods brought from the South Seas and described in the *Morning Herald* as "a striped satin Otaheite pattern, trimmed with crape, gold lace, and foil, and ornamented with a profusion of stones, of a new composition very little inferior in point of lustre to the most brilliant jewels." The trimming alone, according to Mrs. Thrale herself, cost sixty-five pounds.

Thrale, meanwhile, found in all this such solaces as he could

He allowed himself to be conducted from one place of resort to another, and he pursued the presumably always unattainable Sophy Streatfeild with a sort of imbecile earnestness, fawning over her publicly at the dinner table, and visiting her constantly in London while his coach stood discreetly in a neighboring street. In February, 1780, two days before he suffered the third of a series of seizures, there was a large party for tea, cards and supper. "Miss Streatfeild," his wife notes, "was one, & as Mr. Thrale sate by her—he pressed her Hand to his Heart (as she told me herself,) & said Sophy we shall not enjoy this long, & to-night I will not be cheated of my *Only Comfort*— Poor Soul! how shockingly tender! On the first Fryday that he spoke after his Stupor, She came to See him, & as She Sate by the bedside pitying him:—Oh Says he 'who would not suffer even all that I have endured, to be pitied by *you!*' "

But the more lovesick Thrale became the more voraciously he stuffed himself with heavy foods washed down with huge quantities of (presumably) his own beer. It may be remembered that even as early as the first days of his marriage he had considered the kitchen too important to be entrusted to the management of a wife. After the stroke he grew steadily more silent and steadily more gluttonous. His doctors warned him that he was, in Mrs. Thrale's words, "eating himself into an apoplexy." They protested; she protested; Mrs. Montagu protested; Johnson protested; and Fanny Burney protested. But it was to no avail. What, exclaimed his wife in despair, is to be done with a man "whose mouth cannot be sewed up"? A visitor to Streatham described a dinner served there after the master's illness—"two courses of 21 dishes each, besides Removes; and after that a dessert of a piece with the Dinner—Pines and Fruits of all sorts, Ices, Creams, &c, &c, &c, without end."

Thrale, however, did not require the encouragement of these special occasions. At breakfast on Monday, April 2, 1781, he ate so voraciously that Johnson protested firmly: "Sir—after the Denunciation of your Physicians this Morning, such eating is little better than Suicide." But Thrale, they agreed, was only driven to defiantly greater excess. Next day—for restlessness alternated with lethargy—he paid a round of card-leaving visits and came home in fine spirits. "He eat however more than enormously;—six things the Day before, & eight on this Day, with Strong Beer in *such* Quantities! the very Servants were frightened, & when Pepys [the physician] came in the Evening he said this could not last—either there must be *legal* Restraint or certain Death." Mrs. Thrale refused to consider legal action and said: "As he had got the Money he had the best right to throw it away." In the course of the afternoon Thrale retired to bed, where his wife found him, apparently not indisposed. Twenty minutes later Queeney went in to see him. He was lying on the floor because, so he said in reply to the child's frightened question, "I chuse it . . . I lie so o'purpose." Pepys was summoned but Thrale, who had continued to insist that he was quite well and "*chose* to lie so," fell into a violent fit of apoplexy from which he recovered only to sink into another. Early next morning the beloved "master" of the Great Moralist was dead.

To Thrale's widow "the best Consolation is the perfect Amity in which we have lived 17 Years together, the few disputes or Subjects of Complaint either of us have endured from the other, & the Notion I always perswaded myself into, of having been an humble Instrument in the Almighty's hand—to turn the heart of my Husband towards heaven whither he is gone, & whither I hope one day to follow him." The evidence that Thrale's heart had been turning toward heaven seems to have been omitted from *Thraliana.* His funeral cost one hundred and thirty pounds, five shillings, and fourpence.

As for Johnson, he had been summoned during the evening. According to Mrs. Thrale's statement: "Johnson . . . never left him, for while breath remain'd *he* still hoped." According to Johnson's own: "I felt almost the last flutter of his pulse, and looked for the last time upon a face that for fifteen years had never been turned upon me but with respect and benignity." Johnson adds a pious exclamation which seems less inappropriate than Mrs. Thrale's: "Farewel. May God that delighteth in mercy, have mercy on thee." When the will was read, it was found that Johnson, one of the executors, had been left merely the two hundred pounds bequeathed to each of the three others who served with him, and though some thought he should have received an income in addition to this niggardly bequest, he himself made no complaint.[2]

Just how great a change in his own way of life Johnson supposed the death of his "master" would bring about, it is impossible to judge. In his *Prayers and Meditations* he wrote merely, nine days after the event: "The decease of him from whose friendship I had obtained many opportunities of amusement, and to whom I turned my thoughts as to a refuge from misfortunes, has left me heavy." Fortunately, perhaps, he did not suspect that a sort of tenderness had begun to develop even before Thrale's death between Thrale's wife and the man who was before long to be her second husband, and for the moment Johnson was busy with his duties as executor. From the earliest days of his acquaintance with the family he had shown, as scholars frequently do, that it flattered him to be employed in practical affairs. Now he was a businessman as he had never been before.

"If," wrote Mrs. Thrale under the date of May 1, 1781, "an Angel from Heaven had told me 20 Years ago, that the Man I knew by the Name of *Dictionary Johnson* should one Day become Partner with me in a great Trade, & that we should jointly or separately sign Notes Draughts &c. for 3 or 4 Thousand Pounds of a Morning, how unlikely it would have seemed ever to happen! . . . neither of us then being worth a Groat God knows, & both as immeasurably removed from Commerce, as Birth Literature & Inclination could set us. Johnson however; who desires above all other Good the Accumulation of new Ideas, is but too happy with his present Employment; & the influence I have over him added to his own solid Judgment and Regard for Truth, will at last find it *in a small degree* difficult to win him from the dirty Delight of seeing his Name in a new Character flaming away at the bottom of Bonds & Leases." Referring to the same period, Boswell, somewhat maliciously, repeats "a very good story, which, if not precisely exact, is certainly characteristical"—namely, that "when the sale of Thrale's brewery was going forward, Johnson appeared bustling about, with an ink-pen in his button-hole, like an excise-man; and on being asked what he really considered to be the value of the property which was to be disposed of, answered, 'We are not here to sell a parcel of boilers and vats, but the potentiality of growing rich, beyond the dreams of avarice'."

As for the sale, finally made to David Barclay and John Perkins for the sum of 135,000 pounds, Johnson approved of it despite the fact that he may have hesitated to relinquish his new-found employment. He might, however, have been somewhat disturbed had he known that the mistress, about three weeks before the transaction was concluded, was writing in *Thraliana* how, though she had appointed three days a week to attend to the countinghouse, she wished it were possible to "defecate my Mind of Borough Dirt, when I pass the Laystalls at the Stones End." Johnson, a plebeian who hated poverty, had once expressed the somewhat startling opinion that "there are few ways in which a man can be more innocently employed than in getting money." Mrs. Thrale, on the other hand, had the true aristocrat's opinion, which is that, though money is certainly not vulgar, the getting as well as the lack of it most decidedly is. The direction in which her mind was turning she clearly revealed in a letter written three days after the agreement to sell out to Barclay had been signed: "I have lost my Golden Millstone from my Neck, & float once more on the Current of Life like my Neighbours—I long to salute You in my restored Character of a Gentlewoman." That a gentlewoman's money *came* from beer might easily be forgot, but one could hardly claim to be a gentlewoman while it was still *coming* in an amber stream.[3]

Much of the subsequent history of Mrs. Thrale is clearly foreshadowed in the exuberant sentences just quoted. She was, it must be remembered, only forty years old when her husband died, and though that was older then than it is now, it obviously did not seem very old to her. The choice to be made, the choice in which all the subsequent choices were clearly implicit, was the grand choice between the assumption that life was over and the assumption that a very important part of it—quite possibly the happiest part—was still to come. No one of her family or of her friends seems ever to have doubted that the first alternative was the proper one; she herself seems never seriously to have hesitated in her choice of the second. It was this fact rather than the chance appearance in her life, a short time before, of the man she was soon to marry, which made inevitable the general course of her own life and the loneliness of Johnson's last days. The "not impossible she" (or he) rarely fails to appear, once she or he has become "not impossible," and Mrs. Thrale's good luck consisted only in the fact that the "he" presented himself in the person of an honorable man with whom she could live in peace and happiness.

Johnson was old, ailing, and obviously not many years distant from the grave. He could have remained the first concern of his protectress only if she had decided what she did not decide—namely, that she herself had no future other than that of a retiring widow. He was too great a responsibility to constitute a mere incident in her plan of life. She must either build that life about him or neglect him to a degree which he would not quietly tolerate. There was no future toward which they could go together, and she had decided to have a future. There was, therefore, nothing for time to decide except the precise when and the precise why of their parting. In all fairness it must be admitted that she had no choice except that between being cruel to Johnson and being cruel to herself. She was aware of the dilemma and unhappy over it. That she chose to be cruel to Johnson is no cause for surprise and no occasion for easy disapproval on the part of any except those who are quite sure they would have done otherwise.

Disapproval she nevertheless got in full measure from her contemporaries and from posterity; disapproval which found every possible voice, from that of the scandalmongering newspapers to that of the Great Moralist himself, and even today she is so far from being granted peace at last that only a few years ago the Marquis of Lansdowne, in the introduction to *The Queeney Letters,* found it worth while to slay the slain with carefully marshaled arguments intended to re-establish her infamy. No attempt will be made here either to rehabilitate her or to discover a substitute villain, but since the whole course of events may now be followed more closely than was possible before certain documents had come, one after another, to light, it may be worth while to tell the story somewhat fully, with especial attention to the chronology, which Boswell leaves so vague.

Jam Moriturus

Before that story is told, something should, however, be said of Johnson's own life during the period just before he began to be aware that the most intimate of his surviving friends was slipping away. It is possibly no coincidence that his state worsened rapidly as the estrangement grew more and more complete; that he had been, indeed, up to the time when he could no longer shut his eyes to it, surprisingly little changed by increasing age.

Boswell, it may be noted, devotes nearly one-fourth of his long work to the four years 1781-1784. Some part of that fourth is, to be sure, devoted to the last illness and death. There are, moreover, extraneous reasons—including the fact that he was within reach of Johnson during nearly thirty weeks distributed over three of the four years—why the period is treated with unusual fullness. Nevertheless, his pages make it clear that during 1781 and 1782, at least, Johnson was talking as much, as vigorously and, one might guess, with as much delight as ever. Indeed, up to the very end there was astonishingly little flagging so far as the intellect is concerned.

As early as 1778 he was referring to "us old fellows." Even the year before that, he had remarked that "age is a very stubborn disease," but during the same year he was declaring his willingness to sit up all night with Boswell—a sufficient indication that, even though he was afflicted with a very stubborn disease, its ravages were not as evident as they might be expected to be in the case of one who had at the moment already entered upon his sixty-ninth year. Certainly he continued through 1781 and 1782 full of ebullient discourse. His important literary work was done, but he was so far from being finished with his second and best-loved profession that not a few of the best things already quoted from him belong to the period when he was seventy-two or -three—notably, for example, such things as his high-spirited account of Bet Flint, his shrewd warning to Boswell that he should be on the lookout for that "middle state of mind between conviction and hypocrisy," and his ludicrous challenge to the company to find anything funny in his reference to the lady who had "a bottom of good sense." It was also during this same period that he was still young enough to protest: "Sir, it is a very foolish resolution to resolve not to marry a pretty woman.

Beauty is of itself very estimable. No, Sir, I would prefer a pretty woman, unless there were objections to her. A pretty woman may be foolish; a pretty woman may be wicked; a pretty woman may not like me. But there is no such danger in marrying a pretty woman as is apprehended: she will not be persecuted if she does not invite persecution. A pretty woman, if she has a mind to be wicked, can find a readier way than another; and that is all." He was, moreover, still quick enough to retort when Miss Monckton, one of the blues, reproached him for having told her smilingly that she was a dunce for finding Sterne pathetic: "Madam, if I had thought so, I certainly should not have said it." In his seventy-fourth year he was far enough from weariness with literature to find pleasure in the manuscript of Crabbe's *The Village* and still gifted enough to have added to it the well-known line describing the usual pastoral poet as following "where Virgil, not where Fancy, leads the way." It was also about the same time that he delivered to Boswell the memorable discourse on the theme: "Clear your mind of cant."

During most of this period Johnson was, it must be remembered, still ostensibly on good terms with Mrs. Thrale. The fact that his health broke decisively just about the time when he was realizing beyond the possibility of doubt that he could count upon her no longer may or may not be pure coincidence. The fact that a man past seventy takes a definite turn for the worse hardly requires an explanation in outward circumstance. Nevertheless, the coincidence may be mentioned before we return to the affairs of which Johnson was long largely ignorant, but which were to mean so much to him.[4]

Some eight months after her husband's death, Mrs. Thrale took a house in Harley Street. On March 1st she risked public disapproval by inviting her friends to a large assembly before the traditional year of mourning had passed and for this reason had, perhaps, less justification than she supposed for the indignation she professed to feel over the fact that gossip was very busy indeed with sometimes ribald speculations concerning what present-day journalists would call her "love life." On April 17, 1782, she wrote in her diary: "I am returned to Streatham, pretty well in Health & *very* sound of heart, notwi[th]standing the watchers & the Wagerlayers: who think more of the Charms of their Sex by half than I who know them better: Love & Friendship are distinct things; & I would go through Fire to serve many a Man, whom nothing less than Fire would force me to go to Bed to. . . . till I am in Love, I will not marry—*nor perhaps then.*" A month later she notes that she has rejected three proposals—one from a certain Mr. Swale "of good Family & Fortune in Suffolk" whom she scarcely knew, one from Charles Selwin, a retired baker, aged sixty-seven, and one from William Seward, the hypochondriac.

Even before Thrale's death, scandalmongers had, it may be remembered, tried to promote the improbable suspicion that Johnson and the brewer's wife were lovers. Inevitably he was now mentioned as a prospect, though it is difficult to judge just how seriously most people took the suggestion. The *Morning Herald,* we know, included him in a list of possibilities, and Boswell, giving the most striking of various demonstrations of his incredibly bad taste, actually composed a burlesque "Ode by Samuel Johnson to Mrs. Thrale upon their supposed approaching nuptials" which he passed about. Boswell, indeed, makes it clear that he actually considered the union possible, that he hoped it might take place, and that he agreed with a friend concerning "the Doctor's propensity to love The Vain World in various ways." Nothing indicates that Mrs. Thrale ever seriously considered for a moment marrying Johnson, and it is difficult to imagine that Johnson ever had any idea of offering himself. But—or so at least his subsequent attitude strongly suggests —he did consider that she was bound to him by strong ties and that he had something like a moral right to her continued ministrations. His attitude was selfish and the selfishness laid him open to the punishment it was to receive. Had he thought less exclusively of himself he would still have passed his last days in something like desperation, but he would not have been angry, he would not have been bitter, and he would not have been quite so unhappy. "And to be wroth with one we love doth work like madness in the brain." [5]

What he did not know and what, for a long time, Mrs. Thrale

herself probably did not realize, was that her future husband had already been selected by circumstance. We, who are wise after the event, can follow through the pages of her diary the development of an association which has clearly become a love affair long before she is ready to admit the fact. Love at first sight is hardly more favored by novelists and playwrights than is the variation of the theme which adds an element of irony by imagining contempt at first sight, with love at second or third. And it was this pattern which was followed by the romance of Mrs. Thrale. It began a little in the manner of Jane Austen, even though it was soon to involve more disorderly emotions than the author of *Sense and Sensibility* ever approved of in a heroine.

Early in the winter of 1778, Dr. Burney had arranged at his house an evening intended chiefly to bring Johnson forth for the admiration of the aristocratic litterateur, Fulke Greville, his poetess wife, and their daughter, Mrs. Crewe. Miss Burney, Mrs. Thrale and four of her daughters were also of the party, but things did not go well. Johnson, as usual, refused to begin the conversation, and Greville, deciding to play the dignified aristocrat, "planted himself, immovable as a noble statue, upon the hearth, as if a stranger to the whole set." Dr. Burney, who was unable to realize what in fact he knew—namely, that neither Johnson, Mrs. Thrale nor Greville cared anything about music—hoped to save the situation by asking his young protégé, the Italian singer, Gabriel Piozzi, to sing. Piozzi obliged—repeatedly, it would appear—but though he had a fine voice, its only effect on this occasion was to render Greville more aristocratically haughty and to encourage Johnson to pass from waiting silence into frank inattention to all members of the party. Finally, Mrs. Thrale, whose vivacity could not be indefinitely suppressed, stole up on tiptoe to a position just behind the singer who, seated at the piano with his back to his audience, was accompanying himself in an animated *aria parlante*. "She ludicrously began imitating him by squaring her elbows, elevating them with ecstatic shrugs of the shoulders, and casting up her eyes, while languishingly reclining her head; as if she were not less enthusiastically, though somewhat more suddenly, struck with the transports of harmony herself." Fanny Burney, who tells the story not in her diary but in her late memoirs of her father and tells it, therefore, in the style which Professor Tinker has aptly described as one which reminds us "now of Johnson at his worst, and now of Mr. Wilkins Micawber," exclaims: "Strange, indeed, strange and most strange, the event considered, was the opening intercourse between Mrs. Thrale and Signor Piozzi. Little could she imagine that the person whom she was thus . . . holding up to ridicule, would become, but a few years afterwards, the idol of her fancy and the lord of her destiny!"

Johnson did not even observe the little farce, but Dr. Burney made his displeasure clear and the lady sat down. Greville stubbornly kept his place in front of the chimneypiece until finally Johnson, who would soon have burst had he not found some vent for his growing exasperation, rudely exclaimed: "If it were not for depriving the ladies of the fire,—I should like to stand upon the hearth myself!" Greville tried to smile and to hold his place but assurance failed him; he went back to his chair, ringing "with force," as he passed it, the bell for his carriage. The party thereupon broke up and Mrs. Thrale did not consider Piozzi important enough to be mentioned in her diary.

Nearly two and a half years later, or in July, 1780, she saw Piozzi again at the door of a bookseller's shop in Brighton. Perhaps she recognized him, perhaps he had been pointed out by someone else, and perhaps (so the romantic may believe) her demon nudged her elbow. In any event, she spoke to him in Italian and asked if he would be willing to give her daughter music lessons. Piozzi did not remember having met her and did not know who she was. He answered coldly that he had come to Brighton to recover his voice and to finish some musical compositions on which he was engaged. Later in the day, when he had discovered the lady's identity, and hence just how important her patronage might be, he hastened to put himself at her service. In her diary Mrs. Thrale merely noted, under the date July 14th: "I have picked up Piozzi here, the great Italian Singer; he shall teach Hester: she will have some Powers in the Musical way I believe." This is the first mention of him in *Thraliana* and a footnote, which psychologists might find significant, is added: "He is amazingly like my Father."

Piozzi was at the moment just past forty and therefore less than a year older than his new friend. He had been born of middle-class parents at Quinzano in the Venetian State, and after cultivating his musical talents under a wealthy patron, had come to England about 1776. His voice was not strong enough for opera but he acquired considerable reputation as a singer, as a teacher, and as a composer in a small way. Dr. Burney took him up enthusiastically and he was a familiar figure in the Burney household. In later years, at least, he preferred London to Italy, and was described as "as much English as a foreigner can be in manner and way of thinking"; but even this qualified statement may be an exaggeration. He was, it is evident, a good deal of a foreigner, and said to have been embarrassingly ignorant of the kind of familiarity with books and plays which a gentleman in society was supposed to have.

Since he was treated with such venomous contempt by Mrs. Thrale's old intimates, it should be pointed out immediately that there is no evidence whatever to indicate that he was, at the very worst, more than an inoffensive man, and he obviously had considerable charm though it was clearly not of a virile English sort. He was usually described as soft of voice and soft of manner. The romantically impressionable Anna Seward was somewhat later to conclude that so fascinating a musician must inevitably be animated by a refined and delicate spirit. She was "charmed with his perfect expression on his instrument, and with the touching and ever-varying grace with which he sings." "Surely," she continued, "the finest sensibilities must vibrate through his frame, since they breathe so sweetly through his song, though his imperfect knowledge of our language prevents their appearing in conversation." The less gushing Samuel Rogers, who made the acquaintance of the singer in 1789 and became very intimate with him and his wife, says in his own language what is essentially the same thing: "The world was most unjust in blaming Mrs. Thrale for marrying Piozzi; he was a very handsome, gentlemanly, and amiable person, and made her a very good husband. In the evening he used to play to us most beautifully on the piano." [6]

No doubt the very softness which the John Bulls (including

Johnson) found offensive was most appealing to Mrs. Thrale, and it is no wonder that it should have been so to a woman who for nearly twenty years had not only been married to a cold, authoritative husband but also compelled to please a gruff and exacting moralist. Piozzi was "amazingly like my father"—hence easily assimilated into her emotional pattern. But he was also approximately her own age rather than many years older, he was not her "master" but to some extent her dependent; and for once someone anxious to please her, rather than someone whom she had to please. Almost inevitably the relationship developed rapidly.

Thrale, it must be remembered, had suffered the third all-but-fatal stroke some five months before his wife accosted Piozzi at Brighton, and was rapidly approaching his end. In August, 1780: "My Master is got into the most riotous Spirits somehow; he will go here & there, & has a hundred Projects in his Head, so gay, so wild; *I wish no harm may come on't.*" A little more than two weeks later, "Mr. Thrale *would* go to Mitchel Grove the Seat of Sir John Shelley; I did not half like the Expedition, but Pepys bled him first 13 ounces, & gave some rough Medcines too—We just *pulled up in Time* the Dr. says, or here would have been another Stroke." The wonder is only not that Mrs. Thrale found comfort in the tender musician, but that she did not realize (as apparently she did not) the significance of such a passage as the following which went into her diary only a few weeks after the charmer had accepted the invitation which she no doubt genuinely thought was only to teach her daughter rather than herself, and music rather than something else:

"Piozzi is become a prodigious Favourite with me; he is so intelligent a Creature, so discerning, one can't help wishing for his good Opinion: his singing surpasses everybody's for Taste, Tenderness, and true Elegance; his Hand on the Forte Piano too is so soft, so sweet, so delicate, every Tone goes to one's heart I think; and fills the Mind with Emotions one would not be without, though inconvenient enough sometimes—I made him sing yesterday, & tho' he says his Voice is gone, I cannot somehow or other get it out of my Ears,—odd enough!

"These were the Verses he sung to me. . . . I instantly translated them for him, and made him sing them in English thus all'Improviso.

For Love—I can't abide it,
  The treacherous Rogue I know;
Distrust!—I never tried it
  Whether 'twould sting or no:

For Flavia many Sighs are,
  Sent up by sad Despair:
And yet poor Simple I Sir
  Am hasting to the Snare."

In September the Thrales had returned to London in order that Thrale might campaign in the coming election—which, by the way, was to cost him his seat in Parliament. Immediately thereafter, in September, they went to Streatham, and Piozzi soon became a frequent visitor, still teaching Queeney but now also being used as an added attraction for guests. Mrs. Thrale, who had previously been almost as indifferent to music as Johnson himself, became an enthusiastic concert subscriber.

Meanwhile, and largely, it would appear, as the result of mere accident, she had been seeing little of Johnson, though there is no evidence whatever that she was aware of any diminution in her regard. Indeed, under the date of July 14, 1780 (in the same entry as that which first records her having "picked up" Piozzi outside the bookshop), she had written as follows: "Johnson & I have been uncomfortably parted this year, We never lived asunder so long since our first Connection I think, yet our mutual Regard does not decay that's certain—how should it? founded on the truest Principles Religion, Virtue, & Community of Ideas—saucy Soul! Community of Ideas with Doctor Johnson: but why not? he has fastened many of his own Notions so on my Mind before this Time, that I am not sure whether they grew there originally or no: of this I am sure, that they are the best & wisest Notions I possess; & that I love the Author of them with a firm Affection: such is my tenderness for Johnson, when he is out of my Sight I always keep his Books about me, which I never think of reading at any other Time: but they remind me of *him*, & please me more than even his Letters; for in *them* he is often scrupulous of opening his heart & has an Idea that they will be seen sometime, perhaps published."

Apparently neither she nor Johnson saw in the separation anything significant or sought any explanation other than external circumstances. For one thing Johnson had been busy with the *Lives*. For another, the Thrales had been moving restlessly about in search of distraction for the sick husband, and Johnson, though he had become himself much given to visits here and there, never cared for Brighton or any such places of fashionable resort. During the twelve months preceding the date of the passage from *Thraliana* just quoted, he had spent about six weeks partly at Lichfield, partly with his friend Dr. Taylor at Ashbourne, and he had paid a short visit to another friend at Epsom. But he had been at Streatham just before this last going to Epsom, and he was to be with the Thrales at Brighton for a short time just after Mrs. Thrale uttered her lament. That he was in good spirits and unaware that any change in his position was about to take place is clear enough from the fact that he had "in a fit of frolicksome Gaiety" sent her a copy of the satiric verses addressed to a young heir coming of age ("You can hang or drown at last") which are among the best as well as among the best known of his lighter compositions. No shadow, it seems clear, fell between them during Henry Thrale's lifetime.[7]

The latter's death, as we have already seen, brought Johnson to the bedside and plunged him into the affairs of the estate, to which he devoted himself with an enthusiasm which not only reveals how close he still felt to the widow but also suggests an assumption on his part that his fortunes and hers were permanently linked. Throughout the summer there were meetings of the executors, but in October Johnson set out for Oxford and spent there, at Birmingham, Lichfield, and Ashbourne the weeks between October 15th and December 11th. Of the trip he wrote in his *Prayers and Meditations:* "The motives of my journey I hardly know. I omitted it last year, and am not willing to miss it again." But it is just possible that he was beginning to feel that his company was not so welcome as it once was, for on December 8th he wrote Mrs. Thrale a somewhat cryptic letter in which, without explaining himself further, he uttered a plea:

"Do not neglect me, nor relinquish me. Nobody will ever love you better or honour you more."

Johnson's health, always bad, was growing disastrously worse. During the year preceding Thrale's death he had been relatively well—well enough to write: "I am now beginning the seventy-second year of my life, with more strength of body, and greater vigour of mind, than I think is common at that age." He was also, during that time, in high spirits, at least in the presence of Fanny Burney, who describes him at her father's house, where: "He . . . talked all the talk, affronted nobody, and delighted everybody." "I never saw him more sweet," she goes on, "nor better attended to by his audience." All this was in 1780, but by the summer of the next year (that in which Thrale had died) things were very different. During that summer, while on a visit to Sunninghill Park near Streatham, he had soaked his gouty feet in cold water, and it was the opinion of Mrs. Thrale, expressed many years later, that Johnson was "never well" after he had played this "trick" as she calls it, and that he died "of repelled gout." In any event, by September Fanny Burney, who had given so pleasant an account of him the year before, now wrote: "Dr. Johnson has been very unwell indeed. Once I was quite frightened about him; but he continues his strange discipline—starving, mercury, opium; and though for a time half demolished by its severity, he always, in the end, rises superior both to the disease and the remedy,—which commonly is the most alarming of the two." When he returned to London in December from the Oxford-Lichfield-Ashbourne jaunt, Mrs. Thrale, who felt that he had been a vast time away, confided to her diary her fear that he, like her husband, might grow paralytic. She saw "some Symptoms already discoverable I think, about the Mouth particularly" and expressed the conviction of her century when she added "he will drive the Gout away so when it comes, and it must go *somewhere*."

As late as February 27, 1782, Johnson was still assuming that he might enjoy the old privileges, for on that date he wrote Edmond Malone that he has been "for many weeks so much out of order, that I have gone out only in a coach to Mrs. Thrale's, where I can use all the freedom that sickness requires." Mrs.

Thrale herself was at least trying to keep up the pretense (if pretense it was), for only a few weeks earlier she had written in her diary, apropos of his serious condition, "If I lose *him* I am more than undone: Friend, Father, Guardian, Confidant! God give me Health & Patience—what shall I do?" At about the same time she had written to a friend abroad, as though assuming that she accepted responsibility for the old man: "Dr. Johnson has been ill, & is sadly broken; was he either to die or recover a firm state of Health, I think I should try Continental Air for myself." Yet in a letter to Mrs. Strahan, dated February 4th, he had complained that he was "very much deserted" though he had certainly been with Mrs. Thrale the previous week. No doubt he sensed the fact that his patroness, however much she might be trying to feel a responsibility she still acknowledged, was actually spreading her wings. In February she had taken the new house in Harley Street, in March she gave the large assembly already referred to, and by the middle of April they had evidently had some sort of quarrel, and Johnson must have suspected that Piozzi had something to do with it, for late in that month he wrote to her: "I have been very much out of order since you sent me away; but why should I tell you, who do not care or desire to know. . . . Do not let Mr. Piozzi nor anybody else put me quite out of your head, and do not think that any body will love you like—Sam. Johnson." Sometime in May she took him home to Streatham where he remained for more than a month, but jocose rumors of a quarrel began to circulate. He was, until the very last moment, kept in ignorance of the extent to which she was becoming committed to Piozzi, and it seems reasonable to conclude that she was either disingenuous or at least deceiving herself when, in August, she pretended to be injured because Johnson gave his approval to a projected visit to Italy and when, accordingly, she wrote in her diary: "See the Importance of a Person to himself! I fancied Mr. Johnson could not have existed without me forsooth, as we have now lived together above 18 years, & I have so fondled and waited on him in Sickness & in Health—Not a bit on 't! he feels nothing in parting with me, nothing in the least; but thinks it a prudent Scheme,

& goes to his Book as usual. This is Philosophy & Truth; he always said he hated a *Feeler*" [i.e., a sentimentalist].[8]

Those who suppose that Mrs. Thrale would have been more pleased if Johnson had objected to her plans are at liberty to do so. And what a change had taken place in her own estimate of her feelings toward him in the little more than six months since she had confided to her diary the "Friend, Father, Guardian, Confidant" passage! Just six days after she had recorded her conviction that Johnson did not love her appears for the first time an entry which indicates that some sort of vague understanding had been reached between her and Piozzi. Speaking still of the projected foreign journey, she writes: "Piozzi behaves like an Angel . . . he will stipulate nothing, he will set out like Columbus, & see whither he shall be driven—I must be an actual Monster if I *do* treat that Man with Ingratitude."

Did Mrs. Thrale turn to the Italian because she had decided Johnson did not love her, or did she, having turned toward a lover, then arrive at the convenient conviction that to desert Johnson would be to do him no serious injury? To the passage in which Johnson's alleged indifference is described, she added a footnote, which certainly seems to indicate that it was really her feelings rather than his which were changing. "I begin to see (now everything shews it) that Johnson's Connection with me is merely an interested one—he *loved* Mr. Thrale I believe, but only wish'd to find in me a careful Nurse & humble Friend for his sick and his lounging hours: yet I really thought he could not have existed without *my Conversation* forsooth. He cares more for my roast Beef & plum Pudden which he now devours too dirtily for endurance; and since he is glad to get rid of me, I'm sure I have good Cause to desire the getting Rid of *him.*" The last clause of this tirade seems to reveal clearly enough what the author's mental processes were. Johnson had, it is true, always and somewhat oddly put Mr. Thrale first in all formal expressions of his loyalty. He certainly did love beef and pudding, he had always eaten them "dirtily," and no doubt grew grosser as he grew older. But Mrs. Thrale was certainly discovering the importance of all these things at the moment when it became necessary to her peace of mind that she should discover both that

Johnson did not love her and that she was not able to love him.

On October 7th occurred an event of great symbolical importance—Johnson said his last farewell to Streatham. Its owner had let the great house for three years to Lord Shelburne and it has been suggested that she did so in order to get rid of Johnson. But if this is true, she had also other acceptable reasons. Her husband's will had tied up much of the estate in trust for his three daughters, and temporarily Mrs. Thrale was relatively short of funds. Streatham was expensive to keep up and, besides, she was planning to visit abroad. But Johnson must nevertheless have seen that an epoch was ending for him.

In describing the altered relations between the two friends who had once been so close, Boswell, who obviously knew few details of the whole affair, takes refuge in rolling periods. "The death of Mr. Thrale," he writes, "had made a very material alteration with respect to Johnson's reception in that family. The manly authority of the husband no longer curbed the lively exuberance of the lady; and as her vanity had been fully gratified, by having the Colossus of Literature attached to her for many years, she gradually became less assiduous to please him. Whether her attachment to him was already divided by another object, I am unable to ascertain; but it is plain that Johnson's penetration was alive to her neglect or forced attention." Fanny Burney, in *Memoirs of Dr. Burney,* which were composed many years later, and after she had become a bitter critic of Mrs. Thrale, writes of the same period as turgidly as Boswell writes grandiloquently, and her account is obviously open to some suspicion. "Dr. Johnson, while still uninformed of an entanglement it was impossible he should conjecture, attributed her varying humours to the effect of wayward health meeting a sort of sudden wayward power; and imagined that caprices, which he judged to be partly feminine, and partly wealthy, would soberize themselves away in being unnoticed. . . . But at length, as she became more dissatisfied with her own situation, and impatient for its relief, she grew less and less scrupulous with regard to her celebrated guest; she slighted his counsel; did not heed his remonstrances; avoided his society; was ready at a moment's hint to lend him her carriage when he wished to return to Bolt

Court; but awaited a formal request to accord it for bringing him back. The Doctor then began to be stung; his own aspect became altered; and depression, with indignant uneasiness, sat upon his venerable front."

On October 6th, after the farewell to Streatham, Johnson wrote in his *Prayers and Meditations:* "Almighty God, Father of all mercy, help me by thy Grace that I may with humble and sincere thankfulness remember the comforts and conveniences which I have enjoyed at this place, and that I may resign them with holy submission, equally trusting in thy protection when Thou givest and when Thou takest away. Have mercy upon me, O Lord, have mercy upon me." And then he added: "To thy fatherly protection, O Lord, I commend this family." Under the date of the following day he wrote: "I was called early. I packed up my bundles, and used the foregoing prayer, with my morning devotions somewhat, I think, enlarged. Being earlier than the family I read St. Paul's farewell in the Acts, and then read fortuitously in the Gospels, which was my parting use of the library." After that came a paragraph in Latin (for greater solemnity, no doubt) referring to a last visit to Streatham church. "Templo valedixi cum osculo. . . . Streathamiam quando revisam." Curiously the sentences between (still in Latin) describe the dinner of "roast lamb stuffed with raisins, a sirloin of beef, turkey, figs, grapes and peaches—the grapes not very ripe and the peaches hard!" Nearly eight years later, and of course long after Johnson's death, the mistress, still writing in one of the six blank books her first husband had given her, was to describe her triumphant return to Streatham and the celebration there of the seventh anniversary of her second marriage, "with prodigious Splendor and Gayety." "Seventy People ate at our Expense, Thirty-six of which dined at an immensely long Table in the Library—The Plate so fine too, the China so showy, all so magnificent, and at the Time of Dinner Horns Clarinets &c Wch afterwards performed upon the Water in our new Boat that makes such a beautiful, such an elegant Figure." But Johnson was to see Streatham no more.

Boswell, either because he was ignorant or because he wished to make more dramatic Johnson's farewell to the place where he had spent what were, in all probability, the happiest days of his life, seems to imply that this was also his farewell to Mrs. Thrale. But such was by no means the case. He probably left Streatham in her company, and he was certainly with her at Brighton for about six weeks immediately afterward. Fanny Burney was there during part of this time, and he was still gaily gallant though he was certainly in a generally bad humor, and avoided by most of the Brighton society. "Mr. Metcalf," writes Fanny, "is now the only person out of this house that voluntarily communicates with the Doctor. He has been in a terrible severe humour of late, and has really frightened all the people, till they almost ran from him. To me only I think he is now kind, for Mrs. Thrale fares worse than anybody." Her account, which is at considerable length, is indeed one of the severest which survive of Johnson's manners at any time during his life, and the fact that Fanny, though she was at this time still on good terms with Mrs. Thrale, was ultimately to side with Johnson gives it great weight. Yet when Mrs. Thrale returned to London late in November and took a house in Argyle Street, Johnson spent part of his time there and, when he was away, wrote very frequent, if complaining, letters. It was not until April of the next year that they saw each other for the last time.[9]

That Johnson thus prolonged a relationship which had become burdensome to one of the parties concerned is no doubt to be explained not only by the need of companionship and physical comforts, which Mrs. Thrale was ready to find the only reason for his attachment, but also by the further fact that he did not fully comprehend either the cause for her changed attitude or that, its being what it was, it could not be removed. Mrs. Thrale was still not admitting her intentions in regard to Piozzi. No doubt she guessed (and if so, she guessed correctly) that once her intentions were known, a storm would break about her head; and no doubt she desired to put off as long as possible the day when it would do so. But perhaps nothing was so culpable, perhaps nothing was culpable at all, except her refusal to make a clean break, to let Johnson know why everything was over between them. Yet so carefully was the secret kept from him, from most of her acquaintances, and from the general public that as late as October, 1782, while she and Johnson were at Brighton, the *Morning Post* could announce that a treaty of marriage between her and Johnson was said to be "on tap" and jocosely inform its readers that the contract carried among its provisions one to the effect that Johnson was to discard his bush-wig, wear a clean shirt and shave every day. Indeed, other newspapers continued the joke as late as December, when the final breach was close at hand.

Apparently Mrs. Thrale had tried to keep the secret, first from herself, then from all her intimates, and finally from Johnson, who was not to know until the whole world had to be told. We have seen that, even before her husband's death, her diary would have made it clear to any except herself that her infatuation had begun. On the very day upon which Thrale suffered the fatal stroke, and a few hours before it fell, Mrs. Byron, grandmother of the poet of the same name and therefore quite properly one of the "feelers," had seen Piozzi singing to his mistress and had remarked to her: "You know, I suppose, that that Man is in Love with you." But Mrs. Thrale had replied only: "I am too irritated to care who is in Love with me"; and for a time she tried to play her old role of the skeptic where romantic passion was concerned, writing a few weeks after her husband's death: "Miss Owen & Miss Burney asked me if I had never been in Love; with myself, said I, & most passionately. when any Man likes me I never am surprized, for I think how should he help it? when any Man does *not* like me, I think him a Blockhead, & there's an End of the matter."

From July to November of the same year Piozzi was absent on a visit to his parents in Italy. Perhaps as an unconscious gesture indicating the transference of her affections, she had made him a parting gift of a copy of *Rasselas*. She was restless during his absence, and on his return she wrote: "I have got my Piozzi home at last, he looks thin & battered, but always kindly upon me I think." Yet not even in the pages of her private diary would she admit that she was in love. Some five months later, in April, 1782, she was still declaring herself "*very* sound of Heart," though in the same paragraph she added, to an expression of indignation concerning the assumption that she would inevitably marry, an abstract reflection, which certainly must have seemed applicable to her own situation: "a Woman of passable Person, ancient Family, respectable Character, uncommon Talents, and three Thousand a Year: has a Right to think herself any Man's *equal;* & has nothing to seek but return of Affection from whatever Partner She pitches on." Had she, one wonders, been consciously thinking of herself when, somewhat earlier, she had confided to the diary another general reflection: "Concealed Fire burns very fatally—concealed Thoughts lead to Wickedness or Madness . . . 'Tis this *Avarice* of mental Enjoyment, this *Hoarded* Folly; which now & then so blazes out of a sudden under the Name of Love; & I think the Reason of that Furor being more violent among the Female Sex is chiefly because being less tolerated to *declare* their Passion, it preys upon the Mind till it bursts all Reserve, & makes itself amends for the long Concealment." [10]

But concealment she was still to attempt for some time and finally, all but bursting with the secret, she tried merely to whisper enough to give herself relief. By September, 1782, she could no longer keep from *Thraliana* the state of her feelings: "Now! that little dear discerning Creature Fanny Burney says I'm in love with Piozzi—very likely! he is so amiable, so honourable, so much above his Situation by his Abilities." And then, through two printed pages, she debated the objections which might be raised to a marriage—his inferior social position, her greater fortune, his foreign birth, etc., etc. But Johnson, composing the parliamentary debates, never took more care to see to it that the dogs of the opposition did not get the best of the argument. She concludes: "I will however resolve on nothing, I will take a Voyage to the Continent in Spring . . . If he follows me, I may reject or receive at Pleasure the Addresses of a Man who follows with no *explicit Promise,* nor much probability of Success, for I wd really wish to marry no more without the Consent of my Children, (such I mean as are qualified to give their Opinions:) & how should *Miss Thrale* approve of my marrying *Mr. Piozzi?"* By November she had confessed to Queeney and to Fanny Burney "the Strength of my Passion for Piozzi," "the Impracticability of my living without him," and then, nevertheless, declared that she wished she had "two hearts for their Sakes," but that, having only one she would "break it between them." The whole passage and that which follows is almost frenzied in its distress, but Queeney acted as Queeney might have been expected to act. Hoping for nothing better, she temporized and pretended at least to take at its face value her mother's promise to wait. Later in the month Mrs. Thrale had "given my **Piozzi** some hopes.—dear, generous, prudent, noble-minded Creature," but Fanny Burney's shocked disapproval was soon as evident as Queeney's own. By January, 1783, the situation had grown intolerable. Fanny insisted that gossip was spreading and that either the marriage must take place immediately or Piozzi must be renounced forever. Queeney's aversion seemed to be growing daily. Mrs. Thrale threw herself on the bed groaning with anguish while Queeney, looking on with distaste, coldly told her "that if I *would* abandon my Children, I *must;* that their Father had not deserved such treatment from me; that I should be punished by Piozzi's neglect, for that She knew he hated me." Finally, it was decided that Piozzi was to go abroad and that Mrs. Thrale was to live economically till her financial affairs should be in order and she might find herself free to "fly to the Man of my Heart." [11]

The latter kept no diary, or lost it if he did. No one, not even his future wife, seems to have taken the trouble to record except in very general terms what he thought or said. What advances he had made, if any, remain unspecified, and so, for that matter, does everything which would answer the question whether or not Mrs. Thrale, assuming a sort of royal prerogative, did all the proposing. He is, she says, noble, uncomplaining, undemanding, willing to take his chances, etc., etc. But he seems also extremely passive. We do know that he was taken into consultation with Queeney and, according to an account which Mrs. Thrale wrote later, it was he who finally decided to accept Queeney's argument that the marriage would provoke a scandal fatal to the social position of Queeney herself, and, according to this same account, then "went home to Wigmore Street at her [Queeney's] Command; brought all my Letters, Promises of Marriage &c, put them into *her* Hand—& flinging mine from him, cried 'Take your Mama—and make it of her a Countess—It shall kill *me* never mind—but it shall kill her too!' "

If these were his actual words—and they are among the very few belonging to this period which are attributed to him—then his style and that of his mistress must have been much the same. Immediately thereafter, on January 29, 1783, the latter wrote in her diary: "I am parted from my Life, my Soul! my Piozzi." But the latter did not immediately depart for Italy, since it was on April 8th that another final parting took place. At last, however, he did depart, and the result of his absence was only to make one heart at least grow fonder almost to the point of hysteria. On April 5th, Mrs. Thrale had seen Johnson for what was to be—though neither was aware of the fact—the last time. On June 17th he suffered a stroke of apoplexy which was sufficient to deprive him of his powers of speech. Officially at least he still knew nothing of the Piozzi affair, but he was sufficiently aware of the change in Mrs. Thrale's attitude to say in the letter which he wrote her at Bath: "How this will be received by you I know not. I hope you will sympathize with me; but perhaps

> My mistress gracious, mild and good
> Cries: Is he dumb? 'Tis time he shou'd."

That his doubt was reasonable is clear enough from the fact that she not only did not rush to his bedside but wrote in *Thraliana* under the date of June 24th an entry almost in the spirit of the verses which Johnson had quoted from Swift: "A Stroke of Palsy has robbed Johnson of his Speech I hear, dreadful Event! & I at a distance—poor Fellow! a Letter from himself in his usual Style convinces me that none other of his Faculties have fail'd him, & his physicians say that all present Danger is over.

"I sincerely wish the Continuance of a Health so valuable; but have no Desire that he should come to Bath, as my plan is mere retirement & Œconomy which alone can shorten the Absence that destroys my Health, consumes my Soul, and keeps me to mourn *his* Distance to whom only I wish to be near."

The remarkable thing about this passage is the combination of solicitude so detached as to seem almost hypocrisy with the obvious assumption that Johnson is no more to the writer than a somewhat remote acquaintance. The explanation is of course clear enough from the last phrase, which reveals that no one now meant anything to her except Piozzi. That fact continued to become more and more disastrously apparent. Mrs. Thrale, who was by nature so incorrigibly sociable, refused to take part in the life of Bath, her physicians became alarmed at her physical state, and finally they prevailed upon even Queeney to take the necessary step. With her consent a letter was in November dispatched to Piozzi, asking him to return.

Now, however, a new embarrassment—a new scandal, almost—arose. Piozzi seemed in no hurry to come back. A good and sufficient reason was, no doubt, his desire to assure himself that he would not be sent packing again; that the long tragicomedy was at last about over. But to Mrs. Thrale's friends (if they may still be called that) here was another proof that the eagerness was all on her side, that she was shaming herself and them also. But by March, 1784, Piozzi was making preparations to return; in late May or early June he set out; and on July 1st the lovers were reunited at Bath—"The happiest Day of my whole Life, I think—Yes, *quite* the happiest." On July 23rd the pair were married by a Roman Catholic chaplain in London and two days later were married again at St. James Church at Bath. September 4th they set out for the Continent and Mrs. Thrale was not to see England again for more than two years.

On June 30th, just before Piozzi's arrival, she had sent to all the executors of her husband's will a form letter, ostensibly to inform them that Queeney and two of her sisters had departed from Bath for Brighton after having refused to accept their mother's offer to conduct them there, but actually, no doubt, largely for the sake of the last part of the last sentence, which informed the executors that the reason for this conduct was their having "heard that Mr. Piozzi is coming back from Italy, and judging perhaps from our past Friendship & continued Correspondence, that his return would be succeeded by our Marriage." Johnson's copy of this document was enclosed with a letter in which Mrs. Thrale coldly begs pardon "for concealing from you a Connection which you must have heard of by many, but I suppose never believed." "Indeed, my dear Sir, (she adds) it was concealed only to save us both needless pain; I could not have borne to reject that Counsel it would have killed me to take; and I only tell it you now, because all is *irrevocably settled,* & out of your power to prevent."

The unhappy woman was soon compelled to pay the heaviest penalty which it was within the power of her family and acquaintance to inflict. Few persons of either sex, technically independent and merely private citizens, can ever have been so roundly berated, despised and singled out for public scorn merely because they married an unattached man or woman of approximately their own age and of respectable character. Johnson wrote her a letter the brutality and the impudence of which are equally astonishing. If we may believe either Boswell or Fanny Burney (and the existence of the letter removes any *a priori* reason why we should not), he spoke of her with a contemptuous hatred for which there seems no adequate excuse except the assumption that his illness had made him irrational. Yet a number of her other former friends were equally harsh, and that fact makes it impossible to consider Johnson's attitude as one to be explained exclusively on the basis of either his peculiar relationship with her or the desperate state of his health and nerves. Actually that attitude was one shared by many others.[12]

Boswell's venom might be attributed to resentment over her neglect of Johnson or jealousy toward a rival memorialist. That Baretti should have published in 1788 "Strictures" in three numbers of *The European Magazine* and in the course of the articles indulged in sheer vituperation directed toward the "frontless female, who goes now by the mean appellation of Piozzi" is not so surprising as the fact that an editor would print such personal abuse. After all, Baretti was notoriously a violent man, he had long disliked Mrs. Thrale, and in the letters from Johnson, which she had by this time published, were uncomplimentary references to himself, which he professed to believe deliberate interpolations by the recipient. But what of the other former friends? Shortly before the marriage, Mrs. Montagu expressed first the opinion that "the poor woman is mad" and then that "Mrs. Thrale is fallen below pity." Mrs. Vesey seemed to exult in Queeney's declaration that "she can never acknowledge such a father." Mrs. Chapone (and her phrase seems to let out of the bag one of the many cats which must have been confined there) refers sadly to the fact that the "frightful instance of human wretchedness" supplied by the daughters "has given great occasion to the Enemy to blaspheme and to triumph over the Bas Bleu Ladies!"

Neither Johnson nor Boswell can have been much concerned over this aspect of the case, and though Fanny Burney may just possibly have been, her attitude is perhaps the most striking of all. She had, it must be remembered, been extremely intimate with Mrs. Thrale and extravagant in her expressions of admiration. During the earlier stages of the latter's infatuation with Piozzi, she had pretended to be more or less sympathetic though she had at the same time carried on a correspondence with Queeney in which she supported the latter's objections. But when the marriage finally took place, she enthusiastically joined the pack in full cry. In December, 1782, it was "Your dear unhappy mother"; by November, 1783, she is "your poor fallen Mother." Everywhere the assumption seems to have been not that Mrs. Thrale had done a foolish thing (and if her happiness is the test, it turned out to be a very wise one), but that she was disgraced and shamed.

Why? one inevitably asks. What facts are lost to us, or what change has taken place in the social atmosphere which makes the vehemence of the disapproval seem astonishing to most present-day readers, even though some (Lord Lansdowne, for one) seem to share it? And the question must be asked here not only because the whole affair is part of Johnson's story, but also because his own attitude cannot be adequately considered unless one bears in mind the fact that whatever private and perhaps even pathological reasons he may have had, his reaction did not seem unreasonable to most of Mrs. Thrale's circle.[13]

The all but universal opinion of that circle seems to have been, first, that she should not have married anybody; second, that, of all people, she should not have married Piozzi. One reason why she should not have married anybody was simply that a widow who has been left a lot of money should express her gratitude by seeming to be inconsolable even if she isn't. Another and even stronger reason was that her eldest daughter didn't want her to. Everyone seems to have spoken freely of the "abandonment" of her children but, technically at least, it was not she who abandoned her children, but her children who, led by the very determined Queeney, abandoned her.

She should not have married Piozzi of all people for a lengthy list of reasons, any one of which would have been sufficient in itself. He was financially her inferior; he was a foreigner; he was a Roman Catholic; and he was a musician—which latter fact meant, as so many remains from the century make clear, that he was a creature whose claim to respect was approximately that of a tightrope walker, but was nevertheless often more openly despised than any practitioner of the latter or any similar art, because fashion decreed that music should be admired even though musicians should be despised, and under those paradoxical circumstances it was necessary continually to remind foolish persons to keep the distinction clear. Further to justify the objections to Piozzi, the worst characteristics and the worst motives were attributed to him. He was a fortune hunter but he was also, somewhat paradoxically, reluctant to marry the heiress and therefore guilty of forcing her to most unladylike pursuit. The newspapers made merry over his profession; Mrs. Vesey described him as "black ugly" and one who "loves nothing but money." According to Anna Seward, at least, Johnson called him "an ugly dog, without particular skill in his profession." Anna adds that he was, on the contrary, a "handsome man, in middle life, with gentle, pleasing, and unaffected manners, and with very eminent skill in his profession." Surely Johnson had little right to judge of a musician's talent; surely he had even less right to assume that personal beauty (whether Piozzi possessed it or not) was necessary to justify the calling forth of affection. And there seem to be the best reasons for believing that Piozzi was at least pleasing in appearance as well as at least respectable as a performer. It was predicted that he would squander her substance while she would weep her eyes out in recollection of her folly. But if the judgments passed were as far wrong as this prophecy turned out to be, then Piozzi must have been a veritable paragon.

Finally—and this may be more important than it at first seems—everybody appears to have been shocked by the spectacle of a woman no longer young outwardly manifesting an ardor which they thought even younger persons ought to conceal. There seems to have been a general opinion that at her age one might expect the blood more temperately to keep its course—though upon what observations this common expectation was based, then or at any other time, we may properly wonder. "Had the *cause* been a better one," wrote Fanny Burney to Queeney, with unctuous superiority, "the struggles she has voluntarily sustained, would surely have sainted her." "Being such as it [is]," she goes on, "surely, too, they palliate her misconduct,—for she has not yielded weakly or lightly to her inclinations,—she has tried to conquer them, till she has scarce life left for further contest."

Lord Lansdowne, in the course of his statement of the case against Mrs. Thrale, remarks that she was "suffering from what we should now call a 'sex complex,' " and cites the opinion of her physician, Sir Lucas Pepys. There seems little reason to doubt any of this. Mrs. Thrale had, it must be remembered, borne twelve children to a man she did not love and who did not love her. She had also long been a skeptic, if not an atheist, so far as the god of love was concerned. As the ever-sententious Fanny put it to Queeney in urging her not to make the mistake her mother had first made when she married for convenience: "Had she consulted her inclinations when young & not *then* have *scorned & derided* all personal preference, she would now look *forward* with prudence, & *back* with affection." Here one may readily grant was "Vénus toute entière à sa proie attachée," and that is seldom, to spectators, a very pretty sight. As the difficulties in the way of satisfying her passion multiplied, it began to amount almost to nympholepsia. But what was the poor victim to do? It was not a question of illicit indulgence. It was not a question of throwing herself away upon a man whom she would hate as soon as she had possessed him. It was merely a question of a legal and church-blessed union with an honorable man, who would make her happy. Surely one does not need to be a Freudian, surely one does not even need any exaggerated fear of the danger of "suppression," to feel that she took the obviously sensible course. One needs, as a matter of fact, merely to believe a book for which Johnson, as well as she herself, professed the greatest reverence, and in which we are assured that "it is better to marry than to burn."

As to the charge that she "abandoned her children," it has already been suggested that at least there are two sides to any argument based upon it. Four daughters had survived of the twelve children to whom she had given birth. Besides the redoubtable Queeney, they were: Susanna, aged fourteen at the time of her mother's second marriage, Sophia, aged thirteen, and Cecilia, aged seven. Against their mother it must be admitted at once that, in so far as one may judge from her diary, she was a fussy parent, and one more ready to make copy of her children than to find satisfaction in caring for them—quite possibly, indeed, she was too much of a bluestocking really to love them deeply. It should also be admitted that at the time of her second marriage these children were certainly still young enough to need guidance and that it might well have been better for them if she had been able to make them the chief interest in her life. But to do that was beyond her then, as it had always been beyond her before, and it may well be doubted whether they would have profited greatly from the ministrations of an hysterical woman, who had unwillingly sacrificed herself to what she supposed their welfare. "Her actions," writes Lord Lansdowne, "were scarcely those of a devoted mother when she proposed, in 1782, to drag the whole of her little family off abroad in order that she might enjoy her lover's company; or when, having married him in 1784, she departed with him to Italy and left them all at home to shift for themselves."

Putting aside the question whether a visit to Italy in 1782 would have been any great hardship for a group of active children, we must consider whether Mrs. Thrale left them behind after her marriage because she desired to abandon them or because it was made impossible for her to take them with her.

By the terms of Thrale's will, she was made guardian of the children, but they were also to be made wards of chancery. For some reason or other the executors never actually made them the latter, and there seems to have been some disagreement as to whether these executors shared with the mother the guardianship of the children. Contemporary gossip, being very venomous against Mrs. Thrale, insisted triumphantly that the children had been taken away from her, forgetting, possibly, that in so doing this gossip tended to dispose of the charge that it was she who had abandoned them. Sarah Scott, Mrs. Montagu's sister, wrote the latter that the friends of the family, as soon as they "learnt her fix'd purpose . . . informed her the children must not remain with her," and the *Morning Herald* was even more explicit: "Mrs. Thrale, in consequence of her marriage with Piozzi, has the children taken away from her. This the guardians insisted on." Actually, no surviving evidence appears to reveal precisely what did take place, but one may guess that no actual showdown became necessary for the simple reason that Queeney, the executors, and Mrs. Thrale herself were all well enough agreed that the separation should take place. Queeney, if we may believe the statement made in the formal notice sent by Mrs. Thrale and previously quoted, took the initiative by refusing to stay with her mother. The executors would no doubt have objected to subjecting the children to the influence of a Roman Catholic father, and if there had been any insistence on the mother's part, could have taken the matter to chancery, where doubtless their objections would have been sustained. Mrs. Thrale, on her part, knowing that insistence would be vain, and quite possibly having no strong desire to keep, with her, children who did not wish to stay, put up no fight. In one respect everybody was dissatisfied; in another, everybody was satisfied.[14]

If, of course, either Queeney or the executors had approved of the marriage or if Mrs. Thrale had been willing to bow to their disapproval, there would have been no difficulty. The latter's present-day detractors seem to assume that, if she married a man whom her children refused to live with, she was "abandoning" them—which is, after all, a rather odd argument. She had been compelled, by the terms of a previous will, to have her mother's consent for her first marriage. Many seemed to think that she should have waited for her daughter's consent before making a second. But she herself may have felt that she had a right to assume that, if the wishes of parents were decisive when she was young, she ought at least not to be compelled to assume that those of children were decisive when she reached middle age. To Queeney, Johnson wrote on July 1, 1784: "You have not left your Mother, but your Mother has left you." That he put it that way seems to indicate well enough that what he means to imply is: "Though technically you have left your mother, the fact that her outrageous conduct permitted you no alternative makes it possible to say that in reality she left you."

Something, no doubt, turns on the question of Queeney's character and the reasonableness of her attitude. In her favor is the fact that Johnson liked her and that Fanny Burney took her part against her mother. For her part, Queeney had a perfectly practical reason for objecting to the marriage, namely, that the scandal would undoubtedly prove disadvantageous to her in her search for a "good" marriage. Her own letters to Fanny Burney and to her mother certainly confirm the impression that she was cold, haughty and extremely snobbish, and there is abundant testimony to her prudence in the fact that she did not marry until 1808 when she was forty-four—at which time she was united with Admiral Lord Keith, who was by that time sixty, and who had known his bride for twelve years.

During much of her life as Mrs. Piozzi, Hester kept up a correspondence and some pretense of politely amiable relations with Queeney and the other children. In 1787, after her return to England, Queeney and two of her sisters paid a call; shortly thereafter, Mrs. Piozzi took Cecilia away from Queeney (who had assumed a sort of guardianship over the other children) and brought her to live for a time in the Piozzi establishment in London. The ultimate fate of the children who had been "abandoned" is perhaps not irrelevant to the question of their mother's alleged guilt and therefore to the related question of the justification for Johnson's judgment upon her when he wrote in a letter dated July 3, 1784: "What I think of your Mother's conduct I cannot express, but by words which I cannot prevail upon myself to use."

Susanna, said to have been a great beauty, was so successfully launched into society that she moved in the Prince Regent's circle, and though she never married, lived to be eighty-eight. In 1857 she was described as "a stout easy comfortable old lady full of good works and alms, and one who as she has no love for books, or very little, does not care to talk about Dr. Johnson and still less about her mother." Sophia was married in 1807 and died in 1824. Cecilia eloped at eighteen with a Welsh neighbor, who treated her badly, spent her money and died young, but she, like Queeney (who lacked just six months of ninety-three when she died), like Susanna, and like her mother, was vigorous enough to live to a ripe old age—in her case, eighty. On the whole, the four children did neither better nor worse for themselves than many another quartet with a mother to guide them.

Obviously, Mrs. Thrale was no saint, but a desire to put Johnson in the best possible light is hardly reason for trying to make her out a monster. She was obviously a somewhat frivolous woman and no doubt a somewhat selfish one also. Vivacity was her principal charm, and vivacity does not always meet stern tests. The eleven hundred printed pages of her diary tend strongly to support other evidence leading to the conclusion that she had no great emotional depth, that her affections were quick and eager rather than profound. All these things tend to disqualify her as a heroine. She was not fitted to play a tragic role. But she was hardly more shallow or more selfish than thousands who are accepted in society however little acceptable they might be as leading characters in heroic fiction. And to say this is certainly not necessarily to make a villain of Johnson, either. He was, in his relation to Mrs. Thrale during the last days of their association and the last days of his life, irritable, petty and quite unreasonably demanding. But he was not any of these things more than many, perhaps most, people would be under similarly desperate circumstances. In the story of the two, no villain need be. Had not Piozzi appeared on the scene, Mrs. Thrale might well have nursed Johnson to the end; might have postponed her definite entry upon a new life a little while longer. We may wish that, even after she realized the inevitability of her marriage, she had held it off until Johnson was in the grave. But there were so many difficulties to be settled that she refused to make Johnson's feelings into another one. We may be sorry, but we hardly need be either surprised or indignant. "When love comes, many lovely things must go." Mrs. Thrale's devotion to Johnson was one of them.

When she left England on her honeymoon, she passed out of the story with which this book is concerned. It is not improper, however, to add that after her return she did build herself another life in England again, that she apparently never had any reason to regret her marriage, and that she did not die until 1821, when she was past eighty—by which time she had survived her second husband by twelve years. Her *Anecdotes of the Late Samuel Johnson, LL.D., During the Last Twenty Years of His Life* was published in 1786, considerably in advance of the appearance of the first edition of Boswell's *Life,* which came out in 1791. Despite the fact that she was by no means capable of Boswell's scrupulous accuracy, her work is, next to his, the most revealing picture we have of the subject and, despite a few slurs which are really, to use Johnson's word, "defensive," it is a highly favorable picture drawn by a warm admirer.[15]

It will be remembered that when Mrs. Thrale's marriage finally took place, Johnson had not seen her for more than fifteen months. Some correspondence was still maintained even though as early as June, 1783, he had spoken of her "diminution of regard." Not only did he write her the long letter (already quoted) which described his stroke, but shortly thereafter dispatched a whole series of notes informing her of his improved condition, and on November 13th of the same year he says: "Since you have written to me with the attention and tenderness of ancient time, your letters give me a great part of the pleasure which a life of solitude admits." Fanny Burney, who had advised against his being told of the approaching marriage, assured Queeney in a letter written November 15th that Johnson *"knows* of this horrible affair," but that, even considerably later, he still thought the catastrophe might be averted seems to be suggested by the fact that as late as June 26, 1784, just four days before he was sent the formal notification, he had concluded a letter with the adjuration: "Write me if you can some words of comfort."

Broken though he was in health, he had been turning inevitably toward the old solaces. In December, 1783, though he was past seventy-four years old and had already suffered a stroke of apoplexy, he founded a new club, to meet three days a week at the Essex Head Tavern. Illness kept him from many, at least, of its proposed meetings and he wrote to Dr. Taylor on April 12th: "Though it has pleased GOD wonderfully to deliver me from the dropsy, I am yet very weak, and have not passed the door since the 13th of December." In the same letter he says: "I want every comfort. My life is very solitary and very cheerless." Yet nine days later he was at St. Clement's Church, giving thanks for his recovery after 129 days of confinement, and by May 13th he was sending Mrs. Thrale a schedule of his social engagements, which might have frightened a well man half his age: "On Monday I dined with Paradise; Tuesday, Hoole; Wednesday, Dr. Taylor; to-day, with Jodrel; Friday, Mrs. Garrick; Saturday, Dr. Brocklesby; next Monday, Dilly."

Boswell, whom he had not seen for nearly a year, arrived in London on May 5th, and though Boswell himself was going downhill, something like their old association was resumed. Once, they set out together in a coach for a visit to Oxford, and Johnson was enough of his old self, first, to astonish a female passenger into the exclamation: "How he does talk! Every sentence is an essay"; second, to astonish the same lady almost as much by the vehemence with which he resented the bad mutton at an inn, of which he declared in what has by now become a familiar quotation: "It is as bad as can be: it is ill-fed, ill-killed, ill-kept, and ill-drest." Yet he "seemed to feel himself elevated" as he approached Oxford. As usual he dined with one, took tea with another, and laid down the law to all and sundry including a lady who had endeavored to defend her sex against the charge that its members "set no value on the moral character of men who pay their addresses to them."

"'No, no, a lady will take Jonathan Wild as readily as St. Austin, if he has threepence more; and, what is worse, her parents will give her to him. Women have a perpetual envy of our vices; they are less vicious than we, not from choice, but because we restrict them; they are the slaves of order and fashion; their virtue is of more consequence to us than our own, so far as concerns this world.'

"Miss Adams mentioned a gentleman of licentious character, and said, 'Suppose I had a mind to marry that gentleman, would my parents consent?' JOHNSON. 'Yes, they'd consent, and you'd go. You'd go, though they did not consent.' MISS ADAMS. 'Perhaps their opposing might make me go.' JOHNSON. 'O, very well; you'd take one whom you think a bad man, to have the pleasure of vexing your parents. You put me in mind of Dr. Barrowby, the physician, who was very fond of swine's flesh. One day, when he was eating it, he said, "I wish I was a Jew."—"Why so? (said somebody,) the Jews are not allowed to eat your favourite meat." —"Because (said he,) I should then have the gust of eating it, with the pleasure of sinning." ' " [16]

Returning to London on June 19th, he wrote Mrs. Thrale: "I returned last night from Oxford, after a fortnight's abode with Dr. Adams, who treated me as well as I could expect or wish; and he that contents a sick man, a man whom it is impossible to please, has surely done his part well." On June 22nd he went with Boswell to what was to be his last meeting of The Literary Club (earlier The Club), and he was, about the same time, conferring with his friend concerning the possibility that the government might advance him sufficient money for a trip to Italy in search of health. The scheme came to nothing, but on June 30th he and Boswell dined with Sir Joshua Reynolds and without other company. It was the very same day as that on which Mrs. Thrale dated her formal notification of her approaching marriage and curiously it was also the last time that Johnson was to see Boswell. The latter recorded two last dicta uttered by the man whose fame was to owe him so much. Both are characteristic enough: the first is upon the theme of a favorite prejudice; the second, in its simple courageous manliness, at least equally typical:

" 'Sir, (said I), there are many people who are content to live in the country'. JOHNSON. 'Sir, it is in the intellectual world as in the physical world; we are told by natural philosophers that a body is at rest in the place that is fit for it; they who are content to live in the country, are *fit* for the country.'

"Talking of various enjoyments, I argued that a refinement of taste was a disadvantage, as they who have attained to it must be seldomer pleased than those who have no nice discrimination, and are therefore satisfied with every thing that comes in their way. JOHNSON. 'Nay, Sir; that is a paltry notion. Endeavour to be as perfect as you can in every respect.' "

In that last interchange much of the two men was summed up. The dispute is, of course, an ancient one, but there is something "modern" in the neurotic Boswell's perverse championship of the paradox that all gain in sensibility is really loss. Johnson does not answer him with argument. For once at least he does not even rationalize. He falls back, if you like, on pure prejudice. But here is revealed the good, the healthy side of his dogmatic stubbornness. He will put himself, blindly if necessary, on the side of aspiration and health. He was never able to convince himself that life was not more painful than pleasant. But he was never, even to avoid pain, willing to make it less lively.

When Johnson was having this last talk with Boswell (who left London next day), the formal notification from Mrs. Thrale was perhaps already in the post. He certainly received it soon enough to enable him to put the date July 2nd on the first of two letters which have become as famous, almost, as that which he had written so many years before to Lord Chesterfield. Moreover, the second of the two, at least, is almost as forceful as that in which Chesterfield's tardy recognition was rejected. But it does the author considerably less credit.

One way to attempt some explanation and excuse for Johnson's rough impertinence is that which attempts to represent Mrs. Thrale's conduct as morally so reprehensible that it justifies any tone which any friend might choose to take in addressing her. But we have already considered the affair from her point of view and it has already been argued that, though no doubt rather shallow and at the moment quite possibly nearly hysterical, she was no monster. The palliation of Johnson's conduct is to be found less in the provocation than in his own wretched state. If it may be said that Mrs. Thrale was not quite herself, it must in all fairness be said that Johnson was not himself, either; and one justification for the length of the account which has been given of his life during the preceding months must lie in the fact that they remind us of what seems sometimes forgotten—namely, that he was not behaving as he would have behaved had he been really himself.

That he was at the moment dying of gout, dropsy and asthma —all superimposed upon the scrofulous infection from which he had suffered since childhood—is hardly more important than the fact that other old friends—and no friend could he lose without feeling a sort of terror—had been disappearing even from his very household. Levett, whom he had known for some thirty-eight years and who had been a member of his domestic circle during most of that time, died on January 17, 1782. Miss Williams succumbed to a long illness in September, 1783. Though Francis Barber and Mrs. Desmoulins were left, neither was by any stretch of imagination a friend. "I am," Johnson wrote, when Miss Williams was dying, "now broken with disease, without the alleviation of familiar friendship or domestic society; I have no middle state between clamour and silence, between general conversation and self-tormenting solitude. Levet is dead, and poor Williams is making haste to die." Goldsmith, and Garrick, and Beauclerk had disappeared from the scene even earlier, but it is doubtful if their deaths meant so much to Johnson as did those of Levett and Williams. Social companions might to some degree be replaced by other social companions. But the bread and tea of life, the domestic companionship which relieves loneliness without requiring exertion, cannot be casually supplied. Mrs. Thrale had once given him some of that, as well as once provided for him much of more formal sort of sociability. Now, when he was all but alone, she chose to desert him because, forsooth, she was young, hopeful and in love. Filled with pain and indignation, he sat down to write:

July 2, 1784.

MADAM,

If I interpret your letter right, you are ignominiously married: if it is yet undone, let us once [more] talk together. If you have abandoned your children and your religion, God forgive your wickedness; if you have forfeited your fame and your country, may your folly do no further mischief. If the last act is yet to do, I who have loved you, esteemed you, reverenced you, and served you, I who long thought you the first of Human kind entreat that, before your fate is irrevocable, I may once more see you. I was, I once was,

Madam, most truly yours,

SAM. JOHNSON.

I will come down, if you will permit it.

It has been argued that Johnson's indignation was chiefly at a mother who had deserted her children rather than at a friend who had deserted him. Lord Lansdowne states flatly that this was the case and cites in evidence the two letters to Queeney in which Johnson expresses indignation at her mother's conduct in this respect. No doubt Johnson did disapprove, and disapprove all the more strongly since Queeney had been his protégée for many years. But Johnson, though a moralist, had always been conspicuously easygoing when it came to overlooking, in his male friends at least, actions which he would have by no means forgiven either in the abstract or in himself. He had written a biography of Richard Savage. He did not cast off Thrale, or Beauclerk, or Boswell for conduct of which he strongly disapproved. Why would he suddenly become censorious?

Or consider the case of his old school friend, Dr. Taylor, to whose fine estate at Ashbourne he paid frequent and sometimes lengthy visits—for whom, in addition, he wrote sermons. This gentleman was conspicuously unclerical even for an eighteenth-century clergyman. He had inherited wealth and bought ecclesiastical sinecures to make himself wealthier until his income was estimated at seven thousand pounds. Said Johnson himself: "Livings and preferments, as if he were in want with twenty children, run in his head." Indeed, they ran in his head to such good effect that to his living at Market Bosworth he added as other sources of income the following: Prebendary of Westminster; preacher of Broadway Chapel, Westminster; rector of Lawford; perpetual curate of St. Botolph's, Aldersgate; and rector of St. Margaret's, Westminster. Moreover, the general magnificence of Ashbourne pleased Boswell so much that he cited it as an example of a showplace which was actually all that it tried to be. The equipage which Taylor sent to Johnson was "a roomy post-chaise, drawn by four stout, plump horses, and driven by two steady, jolly postillions." Of none of this (especially not of Taylor's concern with fine dogs and fine cattle, or his apparently complete unconcern with spiritual matters) did Johnson approve. "His habits," Johnson complained, "are by no means sufficiently clerical:—As it is said in the Apocrypha, 'his talk is of bullocks'." Indeed, Johnson fancied that his disapproval was so evident as to be disagreeably obvious to the object of it. "No man likes to live under the eye of perpetual disapprobation." Yet, disapprobation was not carried to the point where it would cause any break in the relations. Indeed, Johnson's last known stay outside of London was made partly at Ashbourne, only some three months before his death, and after the final break with Mrs. Thrale. He genuinely disapproved of Taylor. He could not have lived so, himself. "No, Sir," he had once said, "I do not envy a clergyman's life as an easy life, nor do I envy the clergyman who makes it an easy life." But, as has been remarked on previous occasions, he demanded more of himself than of his friends. He did not scruple to associate with publicans and sinners. "How many friendships have you known formed upon principles of virtue?" he once asked, and the very month preceding that in which he is supposed to have rejected Mrs. Thrale because he disapproved her treatment of her children, Boswell records him declaring: "Virtue almost never produces friendship. Good men and bad are not enemies." Surely it is safer to assume that Johnson was human enough to resent being neglected in another's favor. Love had made Mrs. Thrale incapable of seeing any side but her own. Age and ill-health and loneliness had done the same for Johnson.[17]

Two days after he had written his impertinent note, the recipient of it wrote him in reply:

July 4, 1784.

SIR,

I have this morning received from you so rough a letter in reply to one which was both tenderly and respectfully written, that I am forced to desire the conclusion of a correspondence which I can bear to continue no longer. The birth of my second husband is not meaner than that of my first; his sentiments are not meaner; his profession is not meaner, and his superiority in what he professes acknowledged by all mankind. It is want of fortune then that is ignominious; the character of the man I have chosen has no other claim to such an epithet. The religion to which he has been always a zealous adherent will, I hope, teach him to forgive insults he has not deserved; mine will, I hope, enable me to bear them at once with dignity and patience. To hear that I have forfeited my fame is indeed the greatest insult I ever yet received. My fame is as unsullied as snow, or I should think it unworthy of him who must henceforth protect it.

I write by the coach the more speedily and effectually to prevent your coming hither. Perhaps by my fame (and I hope it is so) you mean only that celebrity which is a consideration of a much lower kind. I care for that only as it may give pleasure to my husband and his friends.

Farewell, dear Sir, and accept my best wishes. You have always commanded my esteem, and long enjoyed the fruits of a friendship never infringed by one harsh expression on my part during twenty years of familiar talk. Never did I oppose your will, or control your wish; nor can your unmerited severity itself lessen my regard; but till you have changed your opinion of Mr. Piozzi let us converse no more. God bless you.

That letter seems reasonable, calm and, one is tempted to say, "manly." Johnson replied as follows:

London, July 8, 1784.

DEAR MADAM,

What you have done, however I may lament it, I have no pretence to resent, as it has not been injurious to me; I therefore breathe out one sigh more of tenderness, perhaps useless, but at least sincere.

I wish that God may grant you every blessing, that you may be happy in this world for its short continuance, and eternally happy in a better state; and whatever I can contribute to your happiness I am very ready to repay, for that kindness which soothed twenty years of a life radically wretched.

Do not think slightly of the advice which I now presume to offer. Prevail upon Mr. Piozzi to settle in England: you may live here with more dignity than in Italy, and with more security: your rank will be higher, and your fortune more under your own eye. I desire not to detail all my reasons, but every argument of prudence and interest is for England, and only some phantoms of imagination seduce you to Italy.

I am afraid however that my counsel is vain, yet I have eased my heart by giving it.

When Queen Mary took the resolution of sheltering herself in England, the Archbishop of St. Andrew's, attempting to dissuade her, attended on her journey; and when they came to the irremeable stream that separated the two kingdoms, walked by her side into the water, in the middle of which he seized her bridle, and with earnestness proportioned to her danger and his own affection pressed her to return. The Queen went forward. . . . If the parallel reaches thus far, may it go no further. . . . The tears stand in my eyes.

I am going into Derbyshire, and hope to be followed by your good wishes, for I am, with great affection,

Your, &c.,

SAM: JOHNSON.

Any letters that come for me hither will be sent me.

One might easily suppose, from this and the letter to which it replied, that some sort of reconciliation (good for the future fame of both parties) was still possible, and Mrs. Thrale responded:

Bath, July 15, 1784.

Not only my good Wishes but my most fervent Prayers for your Health and Consolation shall for ever attend and follow my dear Mr. Johnson. Your last Letter is sweetly kind, and I thank you for it most sincerely. Have no Fears for me however; no *real* Fears. My Piozzi will need few Perswasions to settle in a Country where he has succeeded so well; but he longs to shew me to his Italian Friends, and he wishes to restore my Health by treating me with a Journey to many Places I have long wish'd to see: his disinterested Conduct towards me in pecuniary Matters, his Delicacy in giving me up all past Promises when we were separated last year by great Violence in Argylle Street, are Pledges of his Affection and Honour. He is a religious Man, a sober Man, and a Thinking Man—he will not injure me, I am sure he will not; let nobody injure him in your good Opinion, which he is most solicitous to obtain and preserve, and the harsh Letter you wrote me at first grieved him to the very heart. Accept his Esteem my dear Sir, do; and his Promise to treat with long continued Respect & Tenderness the Friend whom you once honoured with your Regard and who will never cease to be my dear Sir

Your truly affectionate and faithful serv

[The signature has been vigorously erased. A postscript adds:]

The Lawyers delay of finishing our Settlements, & the necessity of twenty-six days Residence has kept us from being married till now. I hope your Health is mending.

But Mrs. Thrale was not quite ingenuous. That letter was dated Bath, July 15th, but it was postmarked London, July 16th. Mrs. Thrale was apparently already in London by even the first of the dates, and the suspicion arises that she deliberately avoided letting Johnson know that she was in reach of him. That he knew of the deception seems unlikely, but he never, so far as we know, answered this last communication. All his subsequent references to Mrs. Thrale were couched in terms bitter to the last degree and thus quite oddly inconsistent with the tone of his last communication. "Poor Thrale!" he said, according to Sir John Hawkins, "I thought that either her virtue or her vice would have restrained her from such a marriage. She is now become a subject for her enemies to exult over; and for her friends, if she has any left, to forget, or pity." Less than three weeks before his death, Fanny Burney, calling upon him, asked inadvertently if he ever heard from Mrs. Thrale. And, according, at least, to Fanny's account, he broke out: "No, nor write to her. I drive her quite from my mind. If I meet with one of her letters, I burn it instantly. I have burnt all I can find. I never speak of her, and I desire never to hear of her more. I drive her, as I said, wholly from my mind." No doubt he would have been more accurate if he had said "try to drive her from my mind." We may remember, if he did not, something he once said of Pope and Pope's reiterated contempt for the great. "No man thinks much of that which he despises." [18]

Johnson, it will be remembered, was convinced that men and dogs grew worse as they grew older. Boswell, possibly with this generalization in mind, thought that Johnson himself "by being much more in company, and enjoying more luxurious living . . . had acquired a keener relish of pleasure, and was consequently less rigorous in his religious rites." Once, indeed, Boswell had the courage to raise an eyebrow over the fact that during one particular Passion Week, Johnson dined twice abroad—once with a bishop and despite his own admission that "a Bishop's calling company together in this week, is, to use the vulgar phrase, not *the thing*." But for his pains Boswell got only a specimen of Johnson's sophistry at its most outrageous: "You must consider laxity is a bad thing; but preciseness is also a bad thing; and your general character may be more hurt by preciseness than by dining with a Bishop in Passion-week. . . . You are to consider whether you might not do more harm by lessening the influence of a Bishop's character by your disapprobation in refusing him, than by going to him."

His own opinion was that he was growing more tolerant as he grew older. The charge that he was rude, violent and bitter had always distressed him and, as he considered his own life, he was anxious that he should not be (as he thought) misunderstood. To a certain Mr. Bowles he remarked, some two years before his death: "I look upon myself to be a man very much misunderstood. I am not uncandid, nor am I a severe man. I sometimes say more than I mean in jest; and people are apt to believe me serious; however, I am more candid than I was when I was younger." And then he added: "As I know more of mankind I expect less of them, and am ready now to call a man *a good man*, upon easier terms than I was formerly."

If one may distinguish intellectual tolerance from the sort of testiness which always characterized Johnson and which is certainly not likely to diminish with age, perhaps there was some justification for this opinion that he "expected less" of mankind and therefore judged it less harshly. At least, he was past seventy when Boswell, anxious for a statement that would look well to posterity, got him to dictate a paragraph on the subject of Whigs and Tories which seems almost mealy-mouthed in the light of previous expressions, and begins with the, for him, extraordinary statement: "A wise Tory and a wise Whig, I believe, will agree."

Apparently, it was during the long illness of the spring of 1784 that an amusing little scene involving the question of good humor was played out between him and Bennet Langton. Langton had come to pay a call, and Johnson, in a fit of self-examination, asked his friend to tell him sincerely "in what he thought my life was faulty." Langton, probably not unaware that such questions are dangerous, slyly produced a sheet of paper upon which he had written down several Scriptural texts recommending Christian charity. Johnson glanced at it and soon roared out in high dudgeon: "What is your drift, Sir?" "When," said Johnson indignantly in telling the story, "I questioned him what occasion I had given for such an animadversion, all that he could say amounted to this,—that I sometimes contradicted people in conversation. Now what harm does it do to any man to be contradicted?" "BOSWELL. 'I suppose he meant the *manner* of doing it; roughly,—and harshly'. JOHNSON. And who is the worse for that?' BOSWELL. 'It hurts people of weak nerves'. JOHNSON. 'I know no such weak-nerved people'." It was, as Reynolds "pleasantly observed," "a scene for a comedy, to see a penitent get into a violent passion and belabour his confessor"—especially, it is hardly necessary to add, by way of proving that no mildness was lacking.[19]

Whether "to grow old gracefully" is ever more than a phrase may be questioned. But if any human beings ever achieve in their own last days anything of the sort, it is probably those who approach death if not willingly, then at least with resignation. Johnson's last desperate months were not graceful, whatever else they may have been, and one reason was certainly that he was neither willing nor resigned; that he clutched at and clung to the state "in which there is much to be endured and little to be enjoyed" almost as frantically as Faustus does in the play after the clock has begun to strike. And he did so because he experienced with great urgency both of the motives which lead men to cling to even a few last hours of sickness: He loved life and he feared death.

A large part of all that has gone before in this book was intended as evidence, direct or indirect, in support of the first half of this proposition. Johnson resisted death partly because those delights which he insisted upon calling mere palliatives of a radical ill were to him not in themselves pale but so fiercely vivid as to give fresh meaning to the phrase "a lust for life." He wanted another year, another week even, in which to match his mind against the minds of others; in which to enjoy the sense of his own power as that mind struggled with and triumphed over its friendly antagonists. Moreover, the desperateness of this desire for more time was increased by something which one hardly knows whether to call an additional reason for loving life or one of the reasons for fearing death: the sense that the years which had been granted him and were now past had not been fully or wisely employed.

From as far back as we can follow them, Johnson's conversation and, more especially, the private records of his *Prayers and Meditations* are studded with references to resolutions no more often made than broken. He was always going to be industrious, always going to accomplish more of what he felt himself capable of accomplishing. But he never was able to do it. As the end approached, as it became too late even to resolve, he grew desperate. Self-examination became agony and he could not endure from his friends anything which remotely suggested the things he thought he ought to have done. When, in 1783, Boswell brought up in his presence the fact that Johnson had never complained of the neglect of a world which had rewarded him with neither wealth nor great place, Johnson "flew into a violent passion"—obviously because he reproached himself for a kind of failure, the blame for which he would not shift to "the world." The watch he had long carried bore on its dial (in Greek) the beginning of the New Testament phrase: "The night cometh, when no man can work." The next to the last entry in *Prayers and Meditations* (written apparently only a few days before his death) is merely a prayer that he may remember those same warning words.

But fear of death can be much more than merely a reluctance to quit life, and in Johnson's case it was. He was a courageous man who had borne poverty, ill-health, and long years of insecurity without confessing, at least, any anxiety, and reasonably content if he could see his "third dinner ahead." He had, however, never concealed—in fact, he insisted upon—something very near to panic at the thought of death and he denied that any man could contemplate his own approaching end with equanimity. Boswell once remarked that his visit to Hume just before the latter's death had convinced him that "the thought of annihilation gave Hume no pain." But Johnson was adamant. He himself "never had a moment in which death was not terrible to him." As for Hume: "He had a vanity to be thought easy. It is more probable that he should assume an appearance of ease, than that so very improbable a thing should be, as a man not afraid of going . . . into an unknown state . . . And you are to consider, that upon his own principle of annihilation he had no motive to speak the truth." For the "philosophical" attitude he had indeed nothing but a contempt which he had carefully rationalized—as Boswell had good reason to learn from a little sermon preached to him while the two were in a small boat off the Isle of Skye. Boswell had mentioned "Hawthornden's *Cypress Grove,* where it is said that the world is just a show; and how unreasonable it is for a man to wish to continue in the show-room after he has seen it. Let him go cheerfully out and give place to other spectators. 'Yes', said Mr. Johnson, 'if he's sure he's to be well after he goes out of it. But if he is to go blind after he goes out of the show-room, and never see anything again; or if he does not know whither he is to go next, a man will not go cheerfully out of a show-room. No wise man will be contented to die if he thinks he is to go into a state of punishment. Nay, no wise man will be contented to die if he thinks he is to fall into annihilation. For however bad any man's existence may be, every man would rather have it than not exist at all. No, there is no rational principle by which a man can be contented, but a trust in the mercy of GOD, through the merits of Jesus Christ.' "

There, indeed, is the rub; and unfortunately for Johnson's peace of mind he had no trust "in the mercy of GOD" sufficient to inspire confidence. It may be, as has previously been suggested, that belief in the supernatural was so nearly incompatible with the general tenor of his mind that the exception to skepticism which he professed to make where the doctrines of Christianity are concerned was half in vain and that he therefore did not, at the very bottom of his mind, believe at all. Or, as Colonel Isham has suggested: "Johnson feared death because he was orthodox enough to fear Hell, yet . . . skeptic enough to doubt whether he had been good enough or whether he had faith enough to be saved." Indeed, the most revealing thing which Johnson ever said on the subject of religious faith may just possibly be his answer to a question which Boswell recorded in his journal but which, for some reason, he failed to incorporate into the corresponding section of the *Life*. "I said, 'Has any man the same conviction of the truth of Religion that he has in the common affairs of Life?' He said, 'No, Sir.' "

In any event, Johnson was, by his own admission, too little sure of God's intentions to regard the future with serenity, to consider it as more than unknowable. It is evident that he knew little of the *comforts* of religion. To a sentence in one of Blair's sermons (which in general he so much admired) he took exception so strong that he declared his intention to "have him correct it." The thing, he declared, "was rashly said"; "it may discourage." And the offending statement was this: "He who does not feel joy in religion is far from the kingdom of heaven"! "There are many good men," said Johnson, "whose fear of GOD predominates over their love." It is hardly rash to suggest that he was thinking of himself as one such.

Several times during the last year of his life Johnson discussed in theological terms the justification which he felt for his fear. That God was infinitely good he was willing to admit, but he added (and how his old antagonist, Soames Jenyns would have rejoiced!): "But it is necessary for good, upon the whole, that individuals should be punished. As to an *individual,* therefore, he is not infinitely good." A few weeks before, speaking then also upon the fear of death, he had said: "Some people are not afraid, because they look upon salvation as the effect of an absolute decree, and think they feel in themselves the marks of sanctification. Others, and those the most rational in my opinion, look upon salvation as conditional; and as they never can be sure that they have complied with the conditions, they are afraid."

He himself was far from sure. "I never thought confidence with respect to futurity any part of the character of a brave, a wise, or a good man. Bravery has no place where it can avail nothing. . . . What must be the condition of him whose heart will not suffer him to rank himself among the best, or among the good? . . . The serenity that is not felt, it can be no virtue to feign." But these expressions of opinion are perhaps too well and too elaborately expressed to suggest fully the sheer terror which he felt, and which revealed itself baldly in a brief interchange with his old friend, Dr. Adams, some six months only before Johnson was to come face to face with dissolution: "'As I cannot be *sure* that I have fulfilled the conditions on which salvation is granted, I am afraid I may be one of those who shall be damned'. DR. ADAMS. 'What do you mean by damned?' JOHNSON (passionately and loudly). 'Sent to Hell, Sir, and punished everlastingly'." Shortly before, he had written to Mrs. Thrale: "Write me no more about *dying with grace;* when you feel what I have felt in approaching eternity—in fear of soon hearing the sentence of which there is no revocation, you will know the folly." [20]

On July 6, 1784, a little more than a week before Johnson received the last unanswered letter from Mrs. Thrale, he was writing Reynolds apropos of the scheme to seek health in Italy: "If I grow much worse, I shall be afraid to leave my physicians . . . if I grow much better, of which there is indeed now little appearance, I shall not wish to leave my friends and my domestic comforts. . . . In my present state, I am desirous to make a struggle for a little longer life, and hope to obtain some help from a softer climate." And though the Italian journey was never to be made, he did set out a week later upon what had become an almost annual pilgrimage to Lichfield, and again included, as it so frequently had, a visit to Ashbourne. From the last place, he was writing in September of the restoration of "a great measure of health," and by October he could give this account to a friend: "My diseases are an asthma and a dropsy, and, what is less curable, seventy-five. Of the dropsy, in the beginning of the summer, or in the spring, I recovered to a degree which struck with wonder both me and my physicians: the asthma now is likewise, for a time, very much relieved." While in Lichfield, Anna Seward told him about a "learned pig" which she had seen perform the tricks usually taught to dogs and horses. A gentleman in the company observed that "great torture must have been employed, ere the indocility of the animal could have been subdued." "'Certainly (said the doctor;) but (turning to me,) how old is your pig?' I told him three years old. 'Then, (said he,) the pig has no cause to complain; he would have been killed the first year if he had not been *educated,* and protracted existence is a good recompense for very considerable degrees of torture.' "

At Lichfield he customarily stayed in the very comfortable house of his well-to-do stepdaughter, Lucy Porter. Boswell expresses some surprise that Johnson did not choose to finish his days there rather than return to London where the absence of Mrs. Thrale would leave him without any friend willing to devote himself to his care. Boswell attributes the choice to love of London and he is no doubt right, though Johnson himself repeatedly makes clear his opinion that Lucy had no great affection for him. Indeed, the only known letter from Lucy, one recently discovered and published for the first time, suggests that in 1780 she was not only semi-illiterate but also almost pathologically stingy. In any event, Johnson was in London again on November 16th, after visits to an old friend at Birmingham and to Dr. Adams at Oxford. So eager was he for society that the very next day after his return he dispatched a note to Dr. Burney announcing his arrival.

Levett and Miss Williams, upon whom he had chiefly depended for domestic society, were both gone from Bolt Court. Mrs. Thrale had been "driven from his mind" and Boswell he was not to see again. The devoted Negro servant, Francis Barber, was, however, in attendance and Mrs. Desmoulins was again living in the house. The general tone of Johnson's references to that lady make it doubtful whether he took much pleasure in her society but he was not, fortunately, deprived of whatever solace his remaining friends could give him. There was a constant succession of visitors, so that on occasion his sickroom was crowded.[21]

The apparent improvement in his health during the summer had been a delusion. "I have," he had written Boswell on November 3rd, "this summer sometimes amended, and sometimes relapsed, but, upon the whole, have lost ground very much. My legs are extremely weak, and my breath is very short, and the water is now encreasing upon me." Four days later he wrote to Sir John Hawkins: "I am relapsing into the dropsy very fast"; and by the time he got back to Bolt Court he was already dying though still mentally very active.

On November 25th, Fanny Burney called upon him and found him "very ill." He told her then, apropos of some idea that he might "try what sleeping out-of-town" would do for him, the grim story of the landlord who explained to poor Tetty the battered state of the staircase of the house where she had gone in her last illness, by remarking: "That's nothing but the knocks against it of the coffins of the poor souls that have died in the lodgings!" But he was also quite capable of a discourse on Shakespeare and the nature of genius which is worth quoting both as proof of the continued vigor of his mind and as a further expression of that conception of Imagination which was so important in his critical theory.

"Genius is nothing more than knowing the use of tools; but there must be tools for it to use: a man who has spent all his life in this room will give a very poor account of what is contained in the next.

"Certainly, Sir; yet there is such a thing as invention? Shakespeare could never have seen Caliban.

"No; but he had seen a man, and knew, therefore, how to vary him to a monster. A man who would draw a monstrous cow, must first know what a cow commonly is; or how can he tell that to give her an ass's head or an elephant's tusk will make her monstrous."

Yet when Fanny, seeing him tired, offered to go, he, for the first time in her experience, did not urge her to stay.

Johnson spent a part of his time making translations from the Greek Anthology. Four physicians and a surgeon attended him, all (as Boswell is careful to inform us) without fee. Langton, Burke and the Right Honorable William Windham were among those who sat with him. But as Johnson (preserving to the end the Johnsonian phraseology) himself said: "Sir; you cannot conceive with what acceleration I advance towards death." He had made a will dated December 8th, leaving mementos for Langton, Reynolds and others, as well as small sums of money to various poor people, the largest single bequest being an annuity of seventy pounds a year to Francis Barber. Shortly before, he had asked one of his physicians what would be a proper reward for a faithful servant and was told "that it must depend on the circumstances of the master;—that in the case of a nobleman, fifty pounds a year was considered as an adequate reward for many years' faithful service." "Then," said Johnson, "shall I be *nobilissimus,* for I mean to leave Frank seventy pounds a year."

A few days before that, Sir John Hawkins had seen him destroying papers and Boswell, who was of course not present, cannot keep out of his account of Johnson's last days his own agony at the thought that these papers probably included the autobiographical manuscript in two quarto volumes, a part of which Boswell had read on the sly and one volume of which his wife had missed a chance to copy while its owner and her husband were off on their tour of the Hebrides. It was of this manuscript that Boswell wrote: "I owned to him, that having accidentally seen them, I had read a great deal in them; and apologizing for the liberty I had taken, asked him if I could help it. He placidly answered, 'Why, Sir, I do not think you could have helped it'." Possibly Johnson put the emphasis on "you." That he would have been justified in doing so is clear enough from what follows. "It had come into my mind to carry off those two volumes, and never see him more. Upon my inquiring how this would have affected him, 'Sir, (said he,) I believe I should have gone mad'." This last remark is Johnsonian enough; but the confession which provoked it was even more completely boswellian. Few other men would have made, still fewer would have confessed to having made, his calculation. Would he gain more knowledge of his friend by stealing this friend's papers than he would lose by the forfeiture of all possible future friendship? [22]

By December 10th Johnson had, so Fanny Burney heard, become "perfectly resigned to his approaching fate, and no longer in terror of death." One may hope that this was true, though it is probably an exaggeration. He asked one of his physicians to tell him plainly if he had any chance to recover and the physician, after asking him if he could bear the truth, replied that he could not "without a miracle." " 'Then, (said Johnson) I will take no more physic, not even my opiates; for I have prayed that I may render up my soul to GOD unclouded'." On the morning of the 13th he demanded that Francis Barber should give him a lancet and, conveying it under the covers, he made an incision, immediately afterwards plunging deep into the calves of both legs a pair of scissors, which he took from the drawer of a table beside him—evidently in an effort to relieve the symptoms of his dropsy. About seven that same evening he died, muttering, according to one account, "Jam moriturus." According to another, he succumbed without a word. On December 20th he was buried in Westminster Abbey, and over his grave was placed merely his name, his age, and the date of his death. Perhaps as suitable an epitaph as any would have been achieved by the removal of one word from an exclamation made by Reynolds and recorded by Fanny Burney: "His work is almost done; and well has he done it!"

The next year, when Boswell, sending up a trial balloon before attempting to launch his *Life,* published *A Journal of a Tour to the Hebrides,* he wrote near the beginning of his book:

"Dr. Samuel Johnson's character, religious, moral, political, and literary, nay his figure and manner, are, I believe, more generally known than those of almost any man." [23]

REFERENCES

Passages quoted or cited as authority are listed by chapters below. The superior numbers at the margin refer to those scattered through the corresponding chapter of the text.

When relevant material in a somewhat inaccessible work has been reprinted in either *Johnsonian Miscellanies* or the footnotes to the Hill-Powell edition of Boswell's *Life,* the reference is commonly to one or the other of the latter. References to the writings of Madame d'Arblay are, on the contrary, made by way of editions of her works. Most of the relevant material may, however, be found collected in Professor Tinker's *Dr. Johnson and Fanny Burney* (Moffat, Yard and Company, New York, 1911).

Sincere thanks are due and are hereby extended to the proprietors of the various works quoted, sometimes at considerable length. Permission to quote a number of passages from the private papers of James Boswell in the collection of Ralph H. Isham, privately printed, has very generously been given to me, with the approval of Professor Frederick A. Pottle, the editor, by The Viking Press, Inc., holders of the publication rights, who intend to issue a public edition later. The Clarendon Press, publishers of several of the most extensively quoted works, have graciously granted permission to use their copyrighted material. Miss Balderston, editor of *Thraliana* (also published by the Clarendon Press), was equally generous.

Works infrequently cited are named as they occur in this list of references. Those very frequently cited can be identified by the key words indicated below.

Boswell (Hill-Powell ed.)—*Boswell's Life of Johnson, together with Boswell's Journal of a Tour to the Hebrides, and Johnson's Diary of a Journey into North Wales;* edited by George Birkbeck Hill, D.C.L.; revised and enlarged edition by L. F. Powell. 6 vols. Oxford, Clarendon Press, 1934. (Only the first four volumes, consisting of the *Life* itself, have been published to date in this revised edition.)

Boswell (Piozzi ed.)—*The Life of Samuel Johnson, LL.D.,* by James Boswell, Esq.; with marginal comments and markings from two copies annotated by Hester Lynch Thrale Piozzi; prepared for publication with an introduction by Edward G. Fletcher. 3 vols. Printed for the members of the Limited Editions Club, 1938.

CLIFFORD—*Hester Lynch Piozzi (Mrs. Thrale)*, by James Lowry Clifford. Oxford, Clarendon Press, 1941.

D'ARBLAY—*Diary and Letters of Madame d'Arblay, 1778-1840;* edited by her niece Charlotte Barrett, with preface and notes by Austin Dobson. 6 vols. The Macmillan Company, 1904.

HEBRIDES TOUR—*Boswell's Journal of a Tour to the Hebrides with Samuel Johnson, LL.D.;* now first published from the original manuscript; prepared for the press with preface and notes by Frederick A. Pottle and Charles H. Bennett. The Viking Press, 1936.

LETTERS—*Letters of Samuel Johnson, LL.D.;* edited by George Birkbeck Hill. 2 vols. Harper and Brothers, 1892.

MALAHIDE PAPERS—*Private Papers of James Boswell from Malahide Castle;* edited by Geoffrey Scott and Frederick Pottle. 18 vols. Privately printed, New York, 1928-1934.

MISCELLANIES—*Johnsonian Miscellanies;* arranged and edited by George Birkbeck Hill, D.C.L., LL.D. 2 vols. Oxford, Clarendon Press, 1897.

QUEENEY LETTERS—*The Queeney Letters; being letters addressed to Hester Maria Thrale by Doctor Johnson, Fanny Burney, and Mrs. Thrale-Piozzi;* edited by the Marquis of Lansdowne. London, A. P. Watt & Son; New York, Farrar and Rinehart, 1934.

READE—*Johnsonian Gleanings,* by Aleyn Lyell Reade. 8 parts. Privately printed, London, 1909-1937.

THRALE—*Thraliana; the Diary of Mrs. Hester Lynch Thrale (later Mrs. Piozzi), 1776-1809;* edited by Katherine C. Balderston. 2 vols. Oxford, Clarendon Press, 1942.

TURBERVILLE—*Johnson's England; an Account of the Life and Manners of His Age;* edited by A. S. Turberville. 2 vols. Oxford, Clarendon Press, 1933.

WORKS—*The Works of Samuel Johnson, LL.D.* 9 vols. in 11. Oxford, Oxford Press, 1825.

References

CHAPTER I

[1] *Works,* v. I, p. 226; Boswell (Hill-Powell ed.), v. IV, pp. 112, 405; *Letters,* v. I, p. 392; *Miscellanies,* v. I, p. 128.

[2] Reade, v. IV, pp. 63, 69; *Miscellanies,* v. I, p. 162; v. II, p. 426; v. I, p. 163; *Works,* v. I, p. 255; Reade, v. III, pp. 3 ff., 151, note; Turberville, v. I, pp. 197, 203; Reade, v. III, pp. 81-2.

[3] *Miscellanies,* v. I, p. 133; Boswell (Hill-Powell ed.), v. I, p. 441; Reade, v. III, pp. 51-4; *Miscellanies,* v. I, pp. 129-33; Reade, v. III, p. 61.

[4] Reade, v. III, p. 61 ff.; *Miscellanies,* v. I, pp. 135, 148-9; Boswell (Hill-Powell ed.), v. I, p. 43; Reade, v. III, pp. 78-9, 89, 153-5.

[5] *Miscellanies,* v. II, pp. 32-3, 148; Reade, v. III, pp. 79, 155; *Letters,* v. II, p. 237; Reade, v. III, pp. 72-3; Boswell (Hill-Powell ed.), v. II, p. 238, note 5; *Miscellanies,* v. I, pp. 154, 153; Boswell (Hill-Powell ed.), v. I, p. 46, note 1; v. II, p. 146; v. I, pp. 44-5, 451.

[6] Boswell (Hill-Powell ed.), v. I, p. 47; v. III, pp. 88, 97, 168; v. I, pp. 445, 57, 70; *Miscellanies,* v. I, pp. 319, 181-2; Boswell (Hill-Powell ed.), v. II, pp. 121, 226, 361; v. IV, p. 409; v. I, pp. 71, 182.

[7] Reade, v. III, p. 149; *Miscellanies,* v. II, p. 208; Boswell (Hill-Powell ed.), v. III, p. 162; v. I, pp. 56-7, 81; Pearson, Hesketh: *The Swan of Lichfield,* pp. 36-8; Clifford, James L.: "The Authenticity of Anna Seward's Published Correspondence," in *Modern Philology,* Nov. 1941.

[8] Boswell (Hill-Powell ed.), v. I, p. 58; [illegible]eade, v. III, p. 180; v. V, p. 153 f[illegible] Boswell (Hill-Powell ed.), v. II, [illegible] 52; v. I, p. 347, note 2; Reade, [illegible] V, p. 8; Boswell (Hill-Powell [illegible]), [illegible] p. 59 and note 3; pp. 73-4 [illegible]d note[illegible] pp. [illegible]67, 76, 68.

[9] Reade, v. [illegible] 26; Boswell (Hill-Powell ed.), [illegible] IV, p. 147; v. I, pp. 63, 35; [illegible]eade, v. V, chaps. 3-4.

[10] Reade, v. V, pp. 75 ff., 68; Boswell (Hill-Powell ed.), v. I, p. 80; Reade, v. V, p. 116; Boswell (Hill-Powell ed.), v. I, pp. 324, 94-5; v. I, pp. 81, 71; v. III, p. 7; *Works,* v. V, p. 255; Kingsmill, Hugh: *Samuel Johnson,* pp. 23-4; *Works,* v. I, p. 226.

CHAPTER II

[1] Reade, v. VI, pp. 22, 99, 34; Boswell (Hill-Powell ed.), v. I, p. 96.

[2] Boswell (Hill-Powell ed.), v. I, pp. 93-4, 164; Pottle, Frederick A.: *The Dark Hints of Sir John Hawkins and Boswell.* In *Modern Language Notes,* v. LVI, 1941, pp. 325-9; Boswell (Hill-Powell ed.), v. II, p. 101; v. IV, pp. 551-2; *Miscellanies,* v. I, p. 248; Boswell (Hill-Powell ed.), v. I, pp. 99, 241, note 2; v. II, p. 407.

[3] Boswell (Hill-Powell ed.), v. I, pp. 95, 210, 96; *Miscellanies,* v. I, p. 249.

[4] Reade, v. VI, p. 24.

[5] Seward, Anna: *Letters,* v. I, p. 45; *Miscellanies,* v. I, p. 249.

[6] Reade, v. VI, p. 19; *Miscellanies,* v. II, pp. 173-4.

[7] Reade, v. VI, pp. 29-30; Boswell (Hill-Powell ed.), v. I, p. 97; Reade, v. VI, p. 43; Boswell (Hill-Powell ed.), v. I, p. 98.

[8] Boswell (Hill-Powell ed.), v. I, p.

100; Reade, v. VI, pp. 55, 58; Boswell (Hill-Powell ed.), v. I, p. 101, note 1; p. 59; p. 102, note 2.

9 Boswell (Hill-Powell ed.), v. II, p. 337; Turberville, v. I, p. 166; Lewis, W. S.: *Three Tours Through London,* etc.; Boswell (Hill-Powell ed.), v. II, p. 337; Turberville, v. I, p. 166; *Works,* v. X, p. 240; Turberville, v. I, p. 168.

10 Boswell (Hill-Powell ed.), v. II, pp. 374-5; Turberville, v. I, p. 312; v. II, p. 304; *Rambler,* no. 114; Boswell (Hill-Powell ed.), v. IV, pp. 188-9; Turberville, v. I, p. 162; Boswell (Hill-Powell ed.), v. II, p. 238.

11 *Miscellanies,* v. I, p. 253; Boswell (Hill-Powell ed.), v. IV, p. 204.

12 Carlson, C. Lennart: *The First Magazine.*

13 Boswell (Hill-Powell ed.), v. I, pp. 91, 113, 112, 159, 122-3; v. IV, p. 275, note 1; v. I, p. 122, note 4; p. 113, note 1; Carlson: op. cit., p. 17; Boswell (Hill-Powell ed.), v. IV, p. 409.

14 Boswell (Hill-Powell ed.), v. I, p. 113; Carlson: op. cit., pp. 86, 11, 92, 95, 98-99; Walpole, Horace: *Memoirs of George III.*

15 Boswell (Hill-Powell ed.), v. I, pp. 117, 503, 118; v. IV, p. 409; v. I, pp. 150, 512, 505; *Miscellanies,* v. I, pp. 378-9; Boswell (Hill-Powell ed.), v. I, p. 152; *Miscellanies,* v. II, p. 412.

16 Boswell (Hill-Powell ed.), v. I, pp. 115, 163, 105, 103.

17 *Miscellanies,* pp. 2, 101; Boswell (Hill-Powell ed.), v. I, p. 397; *Miscellanies,* v. I, pp. 247, 248, 246.

18 *Miscellanies,* v. I, p. 135; Boswell (Hill-Powell ed.), v. I, pp. 163, 137; Reade, v. VI, p. 122; Boswell (Hill-Powell ed.), v. I, pp. 133, 469; p. 303, note 1; v. III, p. 195; v. I, p. 135 [compare chap. 6].

19 Reade, v. VI, p. 67; Boswell (Hill-Powell ed.), v. III, p. 21; *Miscellanies,* p. 253; Boswell (Hill-Powell ed.), v. IV, p. 103; *Miscellanies,* v. II, p. 107.

20 *Miscellanies,* v. I, p. 181; Boswell (Hill-Powell ed.), v. I, p. 215; v. III, p. 21, note 3; v. II, p. 452; v. I, p. 106.

21 Boswell (Hill-Powell ed.), v. I, pp. 421-2; v. II, p. 178.

CHAPTER III

1 Boswell (Hill-Powell ed.), v. I, p. 176, note 2.

2 Boswell (Hill-Powell ed.), v. I, pp. 129, 124.

3 *Works,* v. VIII, p. 295; Shakespeare: *Henry V.*

4 *Works,* v. I, p. 4; Boswell (Hill-Powell ed.), v. I, p. 131; *Works,* v. I, p. 3; Boswell (Hill-Powell ed.), v. IV, p. 221.

5 Reade, v. VI, p. 94; *Works,* v. VIII, p. 332; v. I, pp. 16, 20-1; Reade, v. VI, chap. 9; Boswell (Hill-Powell ed.), v. I, p. 134; *Letters,* v. II, p. 126.

6 Shadwell, Thomas: *The Sullen Lovers;* Boswell (Hill-Powell ed.), v. II, p. 184; v. IV, p. 183; v. II, p. 231; v. III, p. 242; *Miscellanies,* v. I, p. 288; *Works,* v. VII, pp. 1-2; *Hebrides Tour,* p. 20; Boswell (Hill-Powell ed.), v. II, p. 231; *Miscellanies,* v. II, p. 404.

7 Boswell (Hill-Powell ed.), v. I, p. 134; Reade, v. VI, p. 120; *Letters,* v. I, p. 5; Reade, v. VI, p. 121; *Letters,* v. I, pp. 3-6; Boswell (Hill-Powell ed.), v. I, p. 234, note 3; Reade, v. VI, p. 122.

8 Reade, v. II, p. 121; Boswell (Hill-Powell ed.), v. I, p. 175 [compare *Works,* v. VII, p. 82, and Boswell (Hill-Powell ed.), v. II, pp. 249-50].

References

[9] *Works,* v. V, p. 191; Boswell (Hill-Powell ed.), v. II, p. 60; *Works,* v. VIII, p. 127.

[10] McAdam, E. L.: "Johnson's Lives of Sarpi, Blake, and Drake," *Publications of the Modern Language Association, 1943,* pp. 466-76.

[11] Boswell (Hill-Powell ed.), v. I, p. 70; *Miscellanies,* v. I, pp. 452, 202-3; Piozzi, Mrs.: *Letters to and from the Late Samuel Johnson,* v. I, p. 187; Boswell (Hill-Powell ed.), v. I, p. 311; *Hebrides Tour,* p. 55.

[12] *Works,* v. VIII, p. 159; Boswell (Hill-Powell ed.), v. II, p. 166.

[13] Saintsbury, George: *Chamfort and Rivarol.*

[14] *Works,* v. VIII, p. 115; Boswell (Hill-Powell ed.), v. I, p. 66, note 4; *Works,* v. VIII, pp. 187-8; Reade, v. VI, p. 80; Boswell (Hill-Powell ed.), v. I, pp. 155, 166, 165.

[15] *Works,* v. VIII, pp. 165, 187, 189, 191, 153, 147, 170.

CHAPTER IV

[1] Boswell (Hill-Powell ed.), v. IV, p. 288; v. I, p. 430.

[2] *Miscellanies,* v. I, p. 382, note 2; Boswell (Hill-Powell ed.), v. II, pp. 83, 189; *Miscellanies,* v. I, pp. 14, 406; Boswell (Hill-Powell ed.), v. I, p. 304.

[3] Boswell (Hill-Powell ed.), v. I, p. 286; v. III, p. 405; v. I, p. 182; *Works,* v. V, p. 1.

[4] Murray, Sir James A. H.: *The Evolution of English Lexicography.*

[5] *Works,* v. V, pp. 5, 3, 27, 11.

[6] *Works,* v. V, p. 20; Segar, Mary: "Dictionary Making in the Early Eighteenth Century," in *Review of English Studies,* v. VII, pp. 210-3.

[7] *Works,* v. V, pp. 19, 7, 13, 39-40.

[8] Boswell (Hill-Powell ed.), v. I, p. 186; p. 82, note 3; pp. 187-8; *Miscellanies,* v. II, pp. 214, 95, 394.

[9] *Hebrides Tour,* p. 29; *Letters,* v. I, p. 189; Boswell (Hill-Powell ed.), v. III, p. 405.

[10] Boswell (Hill-Powell ed.), v. II, pp. 389-90; v. I, p. 191 and note 5; p. 480, note 1; p. 190, note 2; *Miscellanies,* v. II, pp. 96-8; pp. 99-100, 102.

[11] *The Maid of Bath;* Boswell (Hill-Powell ed.), v. IV, p. 75; Vanbrugh, George: *The Relapse,* act 2, scene 1; Turberville, v. I, p. 345; Paston, George: *English Social Caricature in the Eighteenth Century,* p. 20; Boswell (Hill-Powell ed.), v. IV, p. 377, note 1; v. I, pp. 238, 241; *Miscellanies,* v. I, p. 11.

[12] Boswell (Hill-Powell ed.), v. I, p. 277; v. III, p. 305; *Miscellanies,* v. II, p. 317; Boswell (Hill-Powell ed.), v. III, p. 419; *Miscellanies,* v. I, pp. 258, 51; Boswell (Hill-Powell ed.), v. II, p. 393.

[13] Boswell (Hill-Powell ed.), v. I, p. 210, note 1; v. IV, p. 5; v. I, p. 208, note 3; pp. 212, 255; Bradford, C. B.: "Johnson's Revision of the Rambler," in *Review of English Studies,* v. XV, pp. 302-14.

[14] Boswell (Hill-Powell ed.), v. IV, p. 183; *Works,* v. III, p. 201; Wimsatt, W. K.: *The Prose Style of Samuel Johnson; Works,* v. II, p. 242; v. III, pp. 442-3.

[15] Boswell (Hill-Powell ed.), v. I, p. 256 and note 1; p. 252; Powell, L. F.: "Johnson's Part in the Adventurer," in *Review of English Studies,* v. III, pp. 420-9.

[16] Boswell (Hill-Powell ed.), v. I, pp. 261-3; p. 260 and note 3; p. 183; v. IV, p. 332; v. I, p. 261, note 3; p. 265; *The Letters of Chesterfield;* edited by Bonamy Dobree,

v. I, p. 182 ff.; Boswell (Hill-Powell ed.), v. I, p. 332; p. 263, note 3; p. 264, note 4; p. 265.

[17] *Miscellanies,* v. I, p. 404, note 1; MacDonald, Angus: "Johnson as Lexicographer," in *University of Edinburgh Journal,* v. VIII, pp. 17-23; *Works,* v. V, p. 51; Boswell (Hill-Powell ed.), v. I, p. 293; Gove, P. B.: *Notes on Serialization and Competitive Publishing* (Johnson's and Bailey's Dictionaries, 1755); Boswell (Hill-Powell ed.), v. I, pp. 288, 305; v. II, p. 155; v. I, p. 398.

[18] Rypens, Stanley: "Johnson's Dictionary Reviewed by His Contemporaries," in *Philological Quarterly,* v. IV, pp. 281-6; Boswell (Hill-Powell ed.), v. I, p. 296; p. 294, note 7, note 8; *Miscellanies,* v. II, pp. 278, 390, 404; Boswell (Hill-Powell ed.), v. I, p. 287 and note 3.

CHAPTER V

[1] Boswell (Hill-Powell ed.), v. II, p. 405, note 6; *Miscellanies,* v. II, p. 259; Boswell (Hill-Powell ed.), v. I, p. 537; Turberville, v. II, pp. 134-5.

[2] Boswell (Hill-Powell ed.), v. IV, p. 448; v. II, p. 273, note 1; v. I, pp. 247, 244, 147.

[3] Boswell (Hill-Powell ed.), v. I, p. 242 and note 6; pp. 249, 250; p. 249, note 1; p. 248, note 2; p. 251.

[4] *Hebrides Tour,* pp. 177, 226; Boswell (Hill-Powell ed.), v. II, p. 247; v. IV, p. 239; v. II, p. 45; v. III, p. 314; v. I, p. 149; p. 209, note 3; p. 203; v. II, p. 174; v. IV, p. 28, note 7.

[5] *Miscellanies,* v. I, p. 274 and note 1; *Miscellanies,* v. II, pp. 260-2; Boswell (Hill-Powell ed.), v. I, p. 385; p. 245, note 3; v. IV, p. 99.

[6] Boswell (Hill-Powell ed.), v. III, p. 273 and note 1; p. 274 and note 1; pp. 384-5; Thrale, v. I, pp. 167-8.

[7] Thrale, v. I, pp. 167-8; Boswell (Piozzi ed.), v. III, p. 343; Boswell (Hill-Powell ed.), v. II, p. 452 and note 1; pp. 215-6.

[8] *Miscellaneous,* v. I, p. 205; Boswell (Hill-Powell ed.), v. I, p. 463; v. II, p. 99 and note 2; *Miscellanies,* v. I, p. 401; Boswell (Hill-Powell ed.), v. I, p. 301; *Miscellanies,* v. I, p. 401; Boswell (Hill-Powell ed.), v. II, p. 99; v. III, p. 26; v. I, p. 232, note 1; *Letters,* v. II, p. 334; *Miscellanies,* v. II, p. 173, and note 1, note 4; Boswell (Hill-Powell ed.), v. I, p. 232, note 1.

[9] *Miscellanies,* v. I, p. 102; Boswell (Hill-Powell ed.), v. I, p. 243; *Miscellanies,* v. II, pp. 112-3; d'Arblay, v. I, p. 112; Boswell (Hill-Powell ed.), v. I, p. 243, note 2; *Miscellanies,* v. II, p. 110.

[10] Boswell (Hill-Powell ed.), v. IV, p. 137, note 1; *Miscellanies,* v. II, p. 108 ff.; Boswell (Hill-Powell ed.), v. I, pp. 370, 382, 370.

[11] Turberville, chap. 29; Boswell (Hill-Powell ed.), v. IV, p. 293; v. III, p. 22; *Letters,* v. I, pp. 49, 75; *Miscellanies,* v. II, p. 112; Boswell (Hill-Powell ed.), v. I, p. 243; *Miscellanies,* v. II, pp. 111-2; *Works,* v. I, pp. 130-2.

[12] Boswell (Hill-Powell ed.), v. I, p. 239 and note 1; v. IV, p. 401; *Miscellanies,* v. I, pp. 292, 71, 90, 107; Boswell (Hill-Powell ed.), v. IV, p. 402, note 2.

[13] *Letters,* v. I, p. 61; Boswell (Hill-Powell ed.), v. IV, p. 3; v. III, p. 56; v. II, p. 119; *Miscellanies,* v. I, p. 204.

[14] Turberville, v. I, p. 292; Boswell (Hill-Powell ed.), v. IV, p. 137, note 2; *Miscellanies,* v. II, p.

114; v. I, pp. 293, 292; Boswell (Piozzi ed.), v. II, p. 411; *Miscellanies,* v. I, p. 189 [compare Boswell (Hill-Powell ed.), v. IV, p. 347]; *Miscellanies,* v. I, p. 206; v. II, p. 394.

CHAPTER VI

1 Boswell (Hill-Powell ed.), v. III, p. 535; *Letters,* v. I, pp. 61-2, 57; Boswell (Hill-Powell ed.), v. I, p. 307 and note 2.

2 Boswell (Hill-Powell ed.), v. I, p. 471; *Works,* v. VI, pp. 54-5, 64-5.

3 Boswell (Hill-Powell ed.), v. I, p. 330; *Works,* v. IV, p. 449.

4 Boswell (Hill-Powell ed.), v. II, p. 344; v. I, p. 331; v. III, p. 19; v. IV, p. 219; v. I, p. 341.

5 Boswell (Hill-Powell ed.), v. I, p. 175; *Letters,* v. I, p. 32; Boswell (Hill-Powell ed.), v. I, p. 110; Reade, v. IV, p. 8; *Letters,* v. I, pp. 3-6; Boswell (Hill-Powell ed.), v. I, p. 160; *Letters,* v. I, pp. 128, 28; Reade, v. IV, p. 9; *Letters,* v. I, pp. 72-3.

6 Boswell (Hill-Powell ed.), v. I, p. 288; *Letters,* v. I, p. 3; Boswell (Hill-Powell ed.), v. III, p. 451.

7 *Letters,* v. I, pp. 20, 78, 75-82; Boswell (Hill-Powell ed.), v. IV, p. 393; *Works,* v. IV, p. 271; v. V, p. 51.

8 *Letters,* v. I, p. 79; Boswell (Hill-Powell ed.), v. I, pp. 341, 340; v. II, p. 125.

9 *Works,* v. I, p. 226; Housman, A. E.: *Last Poems.*

10 *Works,* v. I, pp. 205, 249, 203.

11 Boswell (Hill-Powell ed.), v. I, p. 365; *Works,* v. I, pp. 268-9.

12 Boswell (Hill-Powell ed.), v. I, p. 341; *Gentleman's Magazine,* April, 1759.

13 Boswell (Hill-Powell ed.), v. I, p. 342; v. III, p. 356; v. II, p. 500; v. I, p. 342.

14 *Works,* v. I, p. 197; Pope, Alexander: *Essay on Man;* Boswell (Hill-Powell ed.), v. IV, p. 289; *Works,* v. I, pp. 309-10; Boswell (Hill-Powell ed.), v. I, p. 344.

CHAPTER VII

1 *Miscellanies,* v. I, p. 407; Boswell (Hill-Powell ed.), v. II, p. 364, note 3; v. I, p. 335, note 1; p. 350, note 3; p. 348.

2 *Letters,* v. I, p. 86; Boswell (Hill-Powell ed.), v. I, p. 421; *Miscellanies,* v. I, p. 418; Boswell (Hill-Powell ed.), v. I, pp. 343, 435; *Miscellanies,* v. I, pp. 26, 416.

3 Boswell (Hill-Powell ed.), v. I, p. 348; Boswell (Piozzi ed.), v. I, p. 245; Boswell (Hill-Powell ed.), v. III, p. 245.

4 Boswell (Hill-Powell ed.), v. I, p. 328; Northcote, James, *Life of Goldsmith,* v. I, p. 75; Boswell (Hill-Powell ed.), v. I, p. 366. *Miscellanies,* v. I, pp. 417-8; Boswell (Hill-Powell ed.), v. I, p. 372 ff.

5 Boswell (Hill-Powell ed.), v. I, p. 491; v. IV, p. 337; p. 116; v. I, pp. 250, 397.

6 Boswell (Hill-Powell ed.), v. I, p. 363; d'Arblay, v. II, p. 344; Parsons, Mrs. Clement: *Garrick and His Circle,* p. 357.

7 Boswell (Hill-Powell ed.), v. I, p. 373, note 1; Turberville, v. I, p. 19; Walpole, Horace: Letter to Montagu, Sept. 17, 1775.

8 Boswell (Hill-Powell ed.), v. I, pp. 429, 376, 370-1.

9 *Works,* v. VIII, p. 136; Boswell (Hill-Powell ed.), v. I, pp. 351, 359; v. II, p. 129.

[10] Boswell (Hill-Powell ed.), v. I, p. 407, note 3; Paston, George: *Social Caricature in the Eighteenth Century,* p. 96 ff.; Turberville, v. II, p. 273; Sidney, William C.: *England and the English in the Eighteenth Century,* v. I, p. 297; Walpole, Horace: Letter to Montagu, Feb. 2, 1762; Boswell (Hill-Powell ed.), v. I, pp. 407-8 and note 3.

[11] Boswell (Hill-Powell ed.), v. III, pp. 268, 297; Paston, George: op. cit., p. 101.

[12] Laver, James: *Poems of Charles Churchill,* v. I, pp. xiv-xxv; Churchill, Charles: *The Ghost,* book 2, lines 1230 ff.; Boswell (Hill-Powell ed.), v. II, p. 10; Churchill, Charles: op. cit., book 2, lines 653 ff.

[13] Laver, James: op. cit., v. I, p. xlix; Boswell (Hill-Powell ed.), v. I, pp. 418-9, 385, 406; v. IV, p. 94, note 2.

[14] Boswell (Hill-Powell ed.), v. IV, p. 94; v. II, pp. 178, 182; v. III, p. 349; v. IV, p. 94; *Works,* v. V, p. 58; Boswell (Hill-Powell ed.), v. III, p. 230; v. IV, p. 95; v. III, pp. 297-8; *Works,* v. I, p. 267; Boswell (Hill-Powell ed.), v. IV, pp. 298-9.

CHAPTER VIII

[1] Boswell (Hill-Powell ed.), v. II, p. 344; v. I, pp. 385, 391-5, 464-72.

[2] *Malahide Papers,* v. I, pp. 47-8; Vulliamy, C. E.: *James Boswell,* p. 116; *Malahide Papers,* v. XVI, p. 149; Boswell (Piozzi ed.), v. II, p. 260.

[3] Pottle, F. A.: *The Literary Career of James Boswell,* p. 14; Vulliamy, C. E.: op. cit., pp. 7-8; *Malahide Papers,* v. I, pp. 133, 105, 79; Abbott, Claude Colleer: *A Catalogue of Papers Relating to Boswell, Johnson and Sir William Forbes found at Fettercairn House,* etc.; *Malahide Papers,* pp. 96-8, 99, 68; Pottle, F. A.: op. cit., pp. 146, xliv.

[4] *Malahide Papers,* v. I, pp. 115, 70, 128; Boswell (Hill-Powell ed.), v. I, pp. 201, 538-9, 383-4, 456, 384-90; *Malahide Papers,* v. I, pp. 112, 152.

[5] *Malahide Papers,* v. I, pp. 149-50; Boswell (Hill-Powell ed.), v. I, p. 400; *Malahide Papers,* v. I, pp. 150-1; *Hebrides Tour,* p. 34; p. 387, note; Pottle, F. A.: *Boswell and the Girl from Botany Bay;* Bronson, Bertrand H.: *Johnson and Boswell,* in University of California Publications in English, v. III, no. 9.

[6] Boswell (Hill-Powell ed.), v. I, p. 395; Pottle, F. A.: *The Literary Career of James Boswell,* pp. 225-7; Tinker, Chauncey Brewster: *Young Boswell,* p. 17; *The Hypochondriack,* no. 30; *Malahide Papers,* v. IV, p. 65; Vulliamy, C. E.: op. cit., p. 17.

[7] Boswell (Hill-Powell ed.), v. I, pp. 395-7, 399, 400-1, 404, 445, 407, 417, 421, 436.

[8] Boswell (Hill-Powell ed.), v. I, pp. 457, 461, 463, 433, 409-10, 450-1, 472.

[9] Boswell (Hill-Powell ed.), v. I, pp. 421, 463, 425, 467, 470, 467-70.

[10] Boswell (Hill-Powell ed.), v. I, p. 441; v. II, p. 219; v. I, pp. 448, 46, 447; v. III, p. 311.

[11] *Miscellanies,* v. I, p. 222 and note 2; v. I, p. 318; *Hebrides Tour,* p. 77; *Works,* v. VI, p. 57; *The Idler,* nos. 10, 17, 24, 28, 38, 4; *Miscellanies,* v. I, p. 204 and note 3; Boswell (Hill-Powell ed.), v. II, p. 60; *Miscellanies,* v. II, pp. 196-7; Boswell (Hill-Powell ed.), v. II, p. 476.

References

12 Boswell (Hill-Powell ed.), v. III, pp. 201-2; v. II, pp. 476-7; v. III, pp. 202-3, 200, 203-4; Pottle, F. A.: op. cit., p. 147.

13 *Hebrides Tour,* pp. 37, 168; Boswell (Hill-Powell ed.), v. III, p. 56; *Hebrides Tour,* p. 37; Boswell (Hill-Powell ed.), v. I, pp. 424, 519; Thrale, v. I, p. 192; Boswell (Hill-Powell ed.), v. II, p. 121; v. IV, pp. 170-1.

14 Boswell (Hill-Powell ed.), v. I, pp. 394, 355; v. II, p. 6; Chesterfield, Lord: Letter to his son, Jan. 12, 1757; Boswell (Hill-Powell ed.), v. III, p. 326; v. IV, pp. 220-1; v. I, pp. 404-5; *Miscellanies,* v. I, p. 241; Boswell (Hill-Powell ed.), v. I, pp. 398, 454-5; *Works,* v. V, p. 58.

15 Boswell (Hill-Powell ed.), v. I, pp. 464, 424, 430, 405; v. II, p. 104.

16 Boswell (Hill-Powell ed.), v. I, p. 471; *Malahide Papers,* v. II, pp. 185, 187, 186, 100-1; v. IV, pp. 12-3, 55, 129, 57, 71, 115, 130, 17.

17 *Malahide Papers,* v. IV, pp. 75, 18, 19; v. XII, p. 227 ff.; *Hebrides Tour,* p. 17; *Malahide Papers,* v. IV, pp. 11, 17; Vulliamy: op. cit., pp. 42-3.

18 Vulliamy: op. cit., pp. 49-55; d'Arblay, v. II, pp. 100-1; Boswell (Hill-Powell ed.), v. II, pp. 3, 22, 59, 11-2, 46.

19 *Malahide Papers,* v. IV, pp. 20-1; Boswell (Hill-Powell ed.), v. III, pp. 86, 474; *Malahide Papers,* v. XI, p. 214; Vulliamy: op. cit., p. 61.

20 Boswell (Hill-Powell ed.), v. II, p. 331; v. I, p. 488; v. III, pp. 535-6; *Miscellanies,* v. II, p. 116; Boswell (Hill-Powell ed.), v. II, p. 50, note 1; [illegible] pp. 490, 520; v. II, pp. 25, 16; *Works,* [illegible] 33; Boswell (Hill-Powell ed.), v. II, [illegible] 464.

21 Boswell (Hill-Powell ed.), v. IV, p. 72; v. I, pp. 483, 521; v. II, p. 8; v. I, p. 317; *Hebrides Tour,* p. 39; Boswell (Hill-Powell ed.), v. I, p. 313; *Works,* v. VI, p. 21; Boswell (Hill-Powell ed.), v. II, p. 269; *Miscellanies,* v. II, pp. 75-6; Boswell (Hill-Powell ed.), v. III, p. 381; v. I, pp. 313-4.

CHAPTER IX

1 Boswell (Hill-Powell ed.), v. II, pp. 348-9; Turberville, v. II, pp. 163-4.

2 Boswell (Hill-Powell ed.), v. I, p. 197 and note 5; *Works,* v. I, p. 24; Boswell (Hill-Powell ed.), v. I, pp. 196, 199; v. IV, p. 5 and note 1.

3 Boswell (Hill-Powell ed.), v. IV, p. 243; v. II, p. 92; v. III, p. 184; v. II, p. 404; v. I, p. 402; v. III, p. 311; v. II, pp. 234-5.

4 Pope, Alexander: *Moral Essays,* no. 3; Boswell (Hill-Powell ed.), v. I, p. 481; v. II, p. 342.

5 *Miscellanies,* v. II, p. 232; Boswell (Hill-Powell ed.), v. III, pp. 312, 263-4; *Works,* v. VII, p. 380; Boswell (Hill-Powell ed.), v. IV, p. 243; v. III, p. 264.

6 Parsons, Florence: *Garrick and His Circle,* p. 131; Boswell (Hill-Powell ed.), v. IV, p. 244; v. I, pp. 168-9; v. IV, p. 242; *Hebrides Tour,* pp. 21-2, 28-9, 93-4.

7 Boswell (Hill-Powell ed.), v. I, p. 201; *Malahide Papers,* v. I, pp. 128-9.

8 d'Arblay, v. II, p. 143; Boswell (Hill-Powell ed.), v. I, p. 167; v. III, p. 184; v. I, p. 99; *Miscellanies,* v. I, p. 248; Boswell (Hill-Powell ed.), v. II, p. 92.

9 Boswell (Hill-Powell ed.), v. II, pp. 68-9; Raleigh, Walter: *Johnson on Shakespeare,* p. 68; *Works,* v. II, p. 14; *The Private Correspondence of David Garrick,* v. I, p. 45; v. II, p. 126; Boswell (Hill-Powell ed.), v. I, pp. 538, 200.

[10] Boswell (Hill-Powell ed.), v. I, p. 175; Courtney, William P., and Smith, D. N.: *A Bibliography of Samuel Johnson,* pp. 17-8; Boswell (Hill-Powell ed.), v. I, p. 545; Raleigh, Walter: op. cit., p. 207; Boswell (Hill-Powell ed.). v. I, p. 545.

[11] Walpole, Horace: Letter to Mason, Feb. 7, 1782; Boswell (Hill-Powell ed.), v. I, pp. 545, 323, 326; v. II, pp. 114-5; v. I, p. 319, note 3; p. 496, note 3; Raleigh, Walter: op. cit., p. 10.

[12] Churchill, Charles: *The Ghost,* book 3, lines 801 ff.

[13] Boswell (Hill-Powell ed.), v. I, p. 319 and note 4; *Letters,* v. I, p. 122; Boswell (Hill-Powell ed.), v. I, pp. 497-8; v. II, p. 204; Spittal, John Ker: *Contemporary Criticism of Dr. Samuel Johnson,* pp. 301-2.

[14] Smith, D. N.: *Shakespeare in the Eighteenth Century,* pp. 31-2, 42; Robinson, H. S.: *English Shakespearean Criticism in the Eighteenth Century,* pp. 64-5; Boswell (Hill-Powell ed.), v. I, p. 292.

[15] *Works,* v. V, pp. 95, 135; Raleigh, Walter: op. cit., p. 193; *Works,* v. V, pp. 96-8, 99, 146; Boswell (Hill-Powell ed.), v. II, p. 192.

[16] Smith, D. N.: op. cit., p. 53; Boswell (Hill-Powell ed.), v. IV, p. 499; Smith, D. N.: op. cit., pp. 48-9.

[17] *Miscellanies,* v. I, p. 158; Boswell (Hill-Powell ed.), v. I, p. 70; *Works,* v. V, pp. 175, 71; Boswell (Hill-Powell ed.), v. II, pp. 85-7, 96; *Works,* v. VIII, p. 26; Dryden, John: *Essay of Dramatic Poesie; Miscellanies,* v. I, p. 187 [compare Thrale, v. I, p. 174, where only Dryden and Young are mentioned].

[18] *Works,* v. V, p. 153.

[19] Dryden, John: *Prologue to Aureng-Zebe.*

[20] *Works,* v. V, pp. 126-7.

[21] Robinson, H. S.: op. cit., p. 244; *The Private Correspondence of David Garrick,* v. I, p. 451; Pope, Alexander: *Essay on Criticism.*

[22] Smith, D. N.: op. cit., pp. 14-5; Robinson, H. S.: op. cit., pp. 24-5, 50-6.

[23] *Works,* v. V, pp. 109, 122-3, 124; v. III, pp. 292-4.

[24] *Works,* v. V, pp. 104, 105-8.

[25] *Works,* v. I, p. 222.

[26] *Works,* v. V, pp. 110, 117-8, 153, 115; Raleigh, Walter: op. cit., p. 95.

[27] Boswell (Hill-Powell ed.), v. IV, p. 295; v. III, p. 39.

[28] *Works,* v. V, pp. 110-1; Boswell (Hill-Powell ed.), v. III, pp. 292, 135; *Works,* v. IV, p. 142; v. V, p. 115.

[29] *Works,* v. V, p. 174; v. VII, pp. 458, 160, 89, 114, 153, 106.

[30] *Works,* v. V, p. 108; Boswell (Hill-Powell ed.), v. I, p. 425; v. IV, p. 17; Seward, Anna: Letters, v. III, pp. 330-1; *Works,* v. V, p. 130; Havens, Raymond: "Johnson's Distrust of the Imagination," in *Journal of English Literary History,* v. X, no. 3; *Works,* v. I, p. 228; v. V, pp. 130-2, 108, 170, 109.

[31] *Works,* v. V, pp. 105-6; v. I, p. 222; Boswell (Hill-Powell ed.), v. II, p. 454; Alleman, G. S.: Letter to London *Times* Literary Supplement, Aug. 13, 1938; Boswell (Hill-Powell ed.), v. II, p. 90.

[32] Boswell (Hill-Powell ed.), v. II, p. 90; *Works,* v. V, pp. 105, 173, 178, 161.

[33] *Works,* v. V, pp. 55, 59.

[34] *Works,* v. V, p. 161; Dryden, John: Preface to *Troilus and Cressida;* Addison, Joseph: *The Spectator,* no. 279; Robinson, H. S.: op. cit., p. 85; *Works,* v. V, p. 108; v. I, pp. 21, 23.

[35] Raleigh, Walter: op. cit., p. 64; *Works,* v. V, pp. 153, 164, 71.

[36] Boswell (Hill-Powell ed.), v. I, pp. 427-8, 496, note 4; *Works,* v. V, p. 132.

References

CHAPTER X

1 Boswell (Hill-Powell ed.), v. II, pp. 15, 34, 40, 441; *Malahide Papers,* v. XII, p. 155; Boswell (Hill-Powell ed.), v. I, p. 11, note 2; p. 11.

2 Boswell (Hill-Powell ed.), v. II, p. 188; *Miscellanies,* v. II, p. 76, note 7; Boswell (Hill-Powell ed.), v. IV, p. 275; v. II, p. 45; v. IV, p. 27; v. III, p. 267; v. I, pp. 146-7; *Miscellanies,* v. I, p. 240; Boswell (Hill-Powell ed.), v. II, p. 213; *Miscellanies,* v. I, p. 290; p. 160 and note 1; v. II, p. 255; Boswell (Hill-Powell ed.), v. II, pp. 118-9.

3 d'Arblay, v. II, p. 41; Boswell (Hill-Powell ed.), v. II, p. 119, note 1; *Miscellanies,* v. I, pp. 300-1, 302-3 [for earlier version see Thrale, v. I, p. 100].

4 Boswell (Hill-Powell ed.), v. II, p. 257; v. IV, p. 183; v. II, p. 253; v. III, p. 68; *Miscellanies,* v. II, p. 402; v. I, p. 324; Boswell (Hill-Powell ed.), v. IV, pp. 427-8; *Miscellanies,* v. I, p. 469; Boswell (Hill-Powell ed.), v. II, p. 326, note 5; *Miscellanies,* v. I, p. 348; v. II, pp. 401, 220.

5 Boswell (Hill-Powell ed.), v. III, p. 337; *Miscellanies,* v. I, pp. 169, 298-9; Boswell (Hill-Powell ed.), v. II, p. 444; v. III, p. 380; *Malahide Papers,* v. VI, p. 62; Boswell (Hill-Powell ed.), v. I, pp. 73-4, 265.

6 Walpole, Horace: Letter to William Cole, April 27, 1773; Boswell (Hill-Powell ed.), v. IV, p. 433; v. III, p. 815; v. II, p. 66; v. III, pp. 338, 139; v. IV, p. 117; v. III, p. 81, note 1; v. II, pp. 66, 348; p. 269, note 1; *Hebrides Tour,* p. 376; Boswell (Hill-Powell ed.), v. III, p. 300; p. 81, note 1.

7 *Hebrides Tour,* p. 219; Boswell (Hill-Powell ed.), v. I, p. 81; v. IV, p. 223; v. III, p. 97; v. IV, pp. 98, 15, 435, 101; v. II, pp. 181, 74; v. I, p. 266; v. III, p. 53; v. IV, p. 341 and note 6.

8 Boswell (Hill-Powell ed.), v. II, p. 440; *Malahide Papers,* v. XI, pp. 166-7; Boswell (Hill-Powell ed.), v. II, p. 327; v. IV, pp. 192-3.

9 *Malahide Papers,* v. IV, p. 17; Boswell (Hill-Powell ed.), v. II, p. 247.

10 Boswell (Hill-Powell ed.), v. III, pp. 64-79; v. IV, p. 43, note 1; v. II, pp. 172, 100; v. IV, p. 313.

11 Strachey, Lytton, quoted in Kronenberger, Louis: *Kings and Desperate Men,* p. 311; Boswell (Hill-Powell ed.), v. III, pp. 23-4 and note 1; *Malahide Papers,* v. VI, p. 87; Boswell (Hill-Powell ed.), v. II, p. 409, note 1; *Miscellanies,* v. II, pp. 308, 97; Boswell (Hill-Powell ed.), v. I, p. 441; *Miscellanies,* v. II, p. 92.

12 Boswell (Hill-Powell ed.), v. II, p. 95; v. III, p. 157; v. II, p. 165; v. III, p. 11; v. I, p. 453; v. II, pp. 79, 307; v. III, pp. 389, 163, 162; v. IV, p. 221; v. II, pp. 51, 55; *Hebrides Tour,* p. 176; Boswell (Hill-Powell ed.), v. III, pp. 268, 57.

13 Boswell (Hill-Powell ed.), v. III, p. 21; v. I, p. 26; v. II, pp. 166, 25-30; Thrale, v. I, p. 173.

14 Boswell (Hill-Powell ed.), v. II, pp. 166, 217; Adam, R. B.: *Boswell's Note-Book,* 1776-1777, pp. xviii-xix; Pottle, F. A.: *The Literary Career of James Boswell,* pp. 274, 277; Abbott, Claude Colleer: *A Catalogue of Papers Relating to Boswell, Johnson and Sir William Forbes Found at Fettercairn House,* etc.; *Malahide Papers,* v. VI, pp. 156-7, 19-24.

15 *Malahide Papers,* v. VI, p. 33; v. V, p. 134; v. VI, pp. 35, 53-5, 189-90.

16 *Malahide Papers,* v. XI, p. 150; v. VI, pp. 66, 161-2, 20; d'Arblay,

Madame: *Memoirs of Dr. Burney,* v. II, p. 194; *Malahide Papers,* v. VI, p. 22.

17 *Malahide Papers,* v. VI, pp. 186-7, 202-3; Boswell (Hill-Powell ed.), v. III, pp. 152-3; Adam, R. P.: op. cit., pp. xvii-xviii, xvi-xvii; *Malahide Papers,* v. VI, pp. 186, 15-6.

CHAPTER XI

1 Boswell (Hill-Powell ed.), v. I, p. 493; *Queeney Letters,* p. 152; Boswell (Hill-Powell ed.), v. II, p. 451.

2 *Miscellanies,* v. I, p. 232; Clifford, p. 545 and note 1; p. 34.

3 Boswell (Hill-Powell ed.), v. I, p. 356 and note 1; *Miscellanies,* v. I, pp. 233-4; Boswell (Hill-Powell ed.), v. IV, p. 340; Clifford, p. 64; Boswell (Hill-Powell ed.), v. II, p. 66, note 2.

4 *Works,* v. VIII, pp. 381-2; Boswell (Hill-Powell ed.), v. IV, p. 340; Clifford, chaps. 1 and 2; Thrale, v. I, p. 17; Boswell (Hill-Powell ed.), v. I, p. 491, note 3; Thrale, v. I, pp. 55, 110; Vulliamy, C. E.: op. cit., p. 33; Thrale, v. I, p. 402.

5 Thrale, v. I, pp. 52-3.

6 Clifford, pp. 46, 51; Thrale, v. I, p. 321; "The Authenticity of Anna Seward's Published Correspondence," in *Modern Philology,* Nov. 1941; Seward, Anna, v. II, p. 103; Clifford, p. 49; *Miscellanies,* v. I, p. 217; Clifford, pp. 104, 165; d'Arblay, v. I, p. 53; Burney, Fanny: *Early Diary,* v. II, p. 265.

7 Clifford, p. 66 and note 2; pp. 77-8; *Miscellanies,* v. I, p. 324; p. 288 and note 3; Clifford, p. 66, note 1.

8 Boswell (Hill-Powell ed.), v. III, p. 222; *Miscellanies,* v. I, p. 188; Boswell (Hill-Powell ed.), v. II, p. 215; Boswell (Piozzi ed.), v. II, p. 54; Boswell (Hill-Powell ed.), v. III, p. 368; *Letters,* v. I, p. 177; *Miscellanies,* v. I, p. 205.

9 Thrale, v. I, p. 53; Clifford, p. 98, note 1; d'Arblay, v. II, pp. 91-2; Boswell (Hill-Powell ed.), v. II, p. 246; Boswell (Piozzi ed.), v. I, p 352; Boswell (Hill-Powell ed.), v. I, p. 496; *Malahide Papers,* v. IV, p. 186; Thrale, v. I, p. 70; Hayward, Abraham: *Autobiography, Letters and Literary Remains of Mrs. Piozzi,* v. I, pp. 89-90.

10 Thrale, v. I, p. 369; *Miscellanies,* v. I, p. 307; d'Arblay, Madame: *Memoirs of Dr. Burney;* Boswell (Hill-Powell ed.), v. I, p. 191, note 2; *Miscellanies,* v. I, pp. 338-9, 307-8, 341; Boswell (Hill-Powell ed.), v. IV, p. 340.

11 Thrale, v. I, p. 385; Clifford, p. 101; Boswell (Hill-Powell ed.), v. IV, p. 141; *Miscellanies,* v. I, pp. 329, 231-2; Boswell (Hill-Powell ed.), v. II, p. 407; Clifford, p. 149; Boswell (Piozzi ed.), v. II, p. 264.

12 Boswell (Hill-Powell ed.), v. I, p. 11, note 2; p. 450; *Hebrides Tour,* pp. 4-6; *Works,* v. IX, p. 24; *Hebrides Tour,* pp. 391, 3, 99-101, 105, 109.

13 *Hebrides Tour,* pp. 111-2, 268, 362, 127-8, 131, 249, 253-4, 337, 345, 303.

14 *Hebrides Tour,* pp. 109-10, 132-3; *Miscellanies,* v. I, p. 288; *Hebrides Tour,* pp. 307, 65; *Letters,* v. I, p. 246; *Hebrides Tour,* p. 365.

15 *Works,* v. IX, pp. 7, 17; *Hebrides Tour,* pp. 348, 210-1, 215, 371; *Letters,* v. I, p. 287; *Hebrides Tour,* pp. 12-3.

16 *Hebrides Tour,* p. 370; p. 375 and note 2; pp. 356, 51, 53, 57-8.

17 *Works,* v. IX, p. 36; *Hebrides Tour,* pp. 107, 127, 34, 99; *Letters,* v. I, p. 254.

18 *Works,* v. IX, pp. 18, 11, 51-2, 33, 52, 153, 80-1, 36-7.

19 *Works,* v. IX, p. 161; Vulliamy, C.

E.: op. cit., p. 108; *Hebrides Tour,* pp. 215, 291, 176-7, 35, 22, 233-4.

20 Boswell (Hill-Powell ed.), v. II, pp. 268, 311; Clifford, p. 103; *Hebrides Tour,* pp. 59, 79, 95, 136; *Letters,* v. I, pp. 223-94, 287; *Hebrides Tour,* pp. 349, 105; Thrale, v. I, p. 215.

21 Clifford, pp. 92-107; Boswell (Hill-Powell ed.), v. II, p. 272; Clifford, p. 104; Broadley, A. M.: *Dr. Johnson and Mrs. Thrale,* pp. 155-252.

22 Clifford, p. 153; Thrale, v. I, p. 364; Clifford, pp. 122, 145; *Letters,* v. I, p. 174; Boswell (Hill-Powell ed.), v. IV, pp. 450-1; Clifford, p. 157.

23 Thrale, v. I, pp. x, xii-xv; v. II, p. 1099; Hayward, Abraham: op. cit., passim.; Thrale, v. I, pp. xix-xx.

24 Clifford, p. 109; Thrale, v. I, pp. 195, 158, 181-2; Boswell (Piozzi ed.), v. III, p. 343; Thrale, v. I, pp. 207, 184, 186.

25 Thrale, v. I, pp. 329-30, 347, 414; Boswell (Hill-Powell ed.), v. II, p. 326, note 5; *Miscellanies,* v. I, p. 231; Clifford, pp. 141, 149; Thrale, v. I, pp. 175-6; p. 182 and note 2; pp. 49, 455, 393, 416.

26 d'Arblay, Madame: *Memoirs of Dr. Burney,* v. II, p. 79; Boswell (Hill-Powell ed.), v. II, p. 409, note 1; v. III, p. 197; *Early Diary of Fanny Burney,* v. II, p. 154; d'Arblay, Madame: *Memoirs of Dr. Burney,* v. II, p. 78; Boswell (Hill-Powell ed.), v. II, p. 409, note 1.

27 d'Arblay, v. I, p. 76; Thrale, v. I, p. 35; d'Arblay, v. II, p. 17; v. I, p. 102.

28 *Edinburgh Review,* Jan. 1843; Thrale, v. I, pp. 443, 400; *Early Diary of Fanny Burney,* v. II, pp. 153-4; d'Arblay, v. I, p. 53; Thrale, v. I, p. 329; d'Arblay, v. I, pp. 90, 77.

29 d'Arblay, v. I, p. 56; d'Arblay, Madame: *Memoirs of Dr. Burney,* v. II, p. 94; d'Arblay, v. I, pp. 67-8; v. I, pp. 117, 66, 85, 118, 84, 69-70.

30 d'Arblay, v. I, p. 102; Thrale, v. I, p. 378; d'Arblay, v. I, pp. 102, 231; Thrale, v. I, pp. 414, 367, 348; d'Arblay, v. I, pp. 237-41; Thrale, v. I, p. 493; v. II, p. 803, note 5.

31 Boswell (Hill-Powell ed.), v. II, p. 3; Clifford, p. 60; p. 74, note 2; *Works,* v. VII, pp. 178-9; Boswell (Hill-Powell ed.), v. II, pp. 292, 313, 312; Thrale, v. II, p. 945; Boswell (Hill-Powell ed.), v. II, p. 112; v. IV, p. 220.

32 Thrale, v. I, pp. 391, 440-1.

CHAPTER XII

1 *Hebrides Tour,* pp. 198, 201; *Notes and Queries,* Dec. 11, 1915.

2 *Hebrides Tour,* p. 204; Boswell (Hill-Powell ed.), v. II, p. 40; *Miscellanies,* v. I, p. 342; Boswell (Hill-Powell ed.), v. III, pp. 108, 488-9, 100-1.

3 Boswell (Hill-Powell ed.), v. I, p. 437, note 2; v. II, p. 272, note 2; *Letters,* v. II, p. 158; Boswell (Hill-Powell ed.), v. III, pp. 109, 370; Thrale, v. I, p. 203; Boswell (Hill-Powell ed.), v. III, p. 490, note 1; *Letters,* v. II, p. 158; Boswell (Hill-Powell ed.), v. III, p. 117, note 8; p. 137.

4 Boswell (Hill-Powell ed.), v. IV, p. 35, note 3; *Miscellanies,* v. II, p. 357, note 3; Nichols, John: *Literary Anecdotes,* v. IX, p. 159; Boswell (Hill-Powell ed.), v. III, p. 111, note 1; *Queeney Letters,* p. 4; Boswell (Hill-Powell ed.), v. IV, p. 35, note 3; *Works,* v. VIII, p. vii.

5 Boswell (Hill-Powell ed.), v. II, p. 318, note 1; *Miscellanies,* v. I, p. 132; Thrale, v. I, pp. 362, 207.

6 Clifford, p. 156; *Letters,* v. II, p.

45; Thrale, v. I, p. 409; Clifford, pp. 196-7; d'Arblay, Madame: *Memoirs of Dr. Burney,* v. II, p. 178 ff.

7 *Letters,* v. II, pp. 13, 15, 196; Thrale, v. I, p. 424; Boswell (Hill-Powell ed.), v. IV, p. 63; *Works,* v. VIII, p. vii; Boswell (Hill-Powell ed.), v. III, p. 359, note 2; v. IV, p. 51, note 2; *Works,* v. VIII, p. vii; v. VII, p. 272; Boswell (Hill-Powell ed.), v. III, p. 344; *Works,* v. VII, p. 417; *Letters,* v. II, p. 160; *Works,* v. VIII, pp. 24, 218-9.

8 *Letters,* v. I, p. 657; v. II, p. 175; Boswell (Hill-Powell ed.), v. III, p. 435; *Miscellanies,* v. I, p. 96.

9 Paston, George: *English Social Caricature in the Eighteenth Century;* Boswell (Hill-Powell ed.), v. IV, p. 73; Thrale, v. I, p. 495; v. II, p. 622; Spittal, John Ker: *Contemporary Criticisms of Dr. Samuel Johnson,* p. 201 ff.; Boswell (Hill-Powell ed.), v. III, p. 375; v. IV, p. 63.

10 *Works,* v. VIII, pp. 339, x, 329; Boswell (Hill-Powell ed.), v. III, p. 147.

11 Arnold, Matthew: *Essays in Criticism;* Second Series (Gray); *Works,* v. VII, p. 325; v. VIII, p. 256.

12 Brooks, Van Wyck: *The Opinions of Oliver Allston; Works,* v. VII, p. 325; v. VIII, p. 256.

13 *Works,* v. VII, p. 151; v. VIII, p. 320 ff.; v. VI, p. 348.

14 Boswell (Hill-Powell ed.), v. IV, p. 102; *Works,* v. VII, p. 31; d'Arblay, v. II, p. 108; *Works,* v. VIII, p. 332; v. VII, pp. 15-6, 20, 17; Boswell (Hill-Powell ed.), v. I, p. 421; *Works,* v. VII, pp. 36, 309.

15 *Works,* v. VII, pp. 116, 105, 79, 121, 123, 125, 138, 142, 139, 136, 138, 135.

16 *Works,* v. VIII, p. 387; v. VII, pp. 134-5; Seward, Anna; *Letters,* v. I, p. 66; *Works,* v. VII, p. 196; v. VIII, pp. 328, 325, 70, 71.

17 Boswell (Hill-Powell ed.), v. IV, pp. 122, 221; *Works,* v. VIII, pp. 244-5; Boswell (Hill-Powell ed.), v. I, p. 101; v. IV, p. 20; *Works,* v. VII, pp. 5, 120-1.

18 *Works,* v. VIII, p. 263; v. V, pp. 121-2.

19 *Works,* v. VII, pp. 182, 456, 252; Boswell (Hill-Powell ed.), v. I, p. 200; *Works,* v. VII, pp. 302, 276, 308, 16, 433, 455, 307.

CHAPTER XIII

1 *Miscellanies,* v. I, p. 96; Thrale, v. I, p. 389; Clifford, pp. 175-6; Thrale, v. II, pp. 803-4.

2 Clifford, pp. 178, 194-5; Thrale, v. I, pp. 432, 441; Clifford, pp. 184, 192; Thrale, v. I, pp. 488-9; p. 489, note 4; pp. 489-90 and note 4; Boswell (Hill-Powell ed.), v. IV, p. 84; *Miscellanies,* v. I, p. 96; Clifford, p. 200.

3 *Miscellanies,* v. I, p. 97; Thrale, v. I, p. 492; *Letters,* v. II, p. 126; Boswell (Hill-Powell ed.), v. IV, pp. 86-7; Thrale, v. I, p. 492; Boswell (Hill-Powell ed.), v. II, p. 325; Clifford, p. 202.

4 Boswell (Hill-Powell ed.), v. I, p. 11, note 2; v. III, p. 303; *Letters,* v. II, p. 33; Boswell (Hill-Powell ed.), v. III, p. 205; v. IV, pp. 103, 122, 99, 109, 175, 221.

5 Clifford, p. 208; Thrale, v. I, pp. 531, 535; p. 530, note 5; Clifford, p. 199; *Malahide Papers,* v. XIV, p. 196; Coleridge, S. T.: *Christabel,* part 2.

6 Thrale, v. I, p. 448, note 7; d'Arblay, Madame: *Memoirs of Dr. Burney,* v. II, p. 101 ff.; Clifford, v. I, p. 87; Thrale, v. I, pp. 448-9; Clifford, pp. 188, 282, 376, 307, 349.

References

[7] Thrale, v. I, pp. 453, 452; Clifford, pp. 189, 193; Thrale, v. I, pp. 445-6; Boswell (Hill-Powell ed.), v. III, p. 454; *Miscellanies,* v. I, p. 92; Boswell (Hill-Powell ed.), v. II, p. 454; *Works,* v. I, pp. 149-50.

[8] Clifford, p. 201; Boswell (Hill-Powell ed.), v. III, p. 454; *Miscellanies,* v. I, p. 101; Clifford, p. 206; Boswell (Hill-Powell ed.), v. III, p. 440; d'Arblay, v. I, p. 435; v. II, p. 22; *Queeney Letters,* p. 254; d'Arblay, v. II, p. 52; Thrale, v. I, p. 521; Boswell (Hill-Powell ed.), v. IV, p. 141; Thrale, v. I, p. 528; Clifford, p. 207; Boswell (Hill-Powell ed.), v. IV, p. 140; Thrale, v. I, p. 528, note 3; Clifford, pp. 209-10; Thrale, v. I, pp. 540-1 and note 2.

[9] Thrale, v. I, p. 541 and note 1; Boswell (Hill-Powell ed.), v. IV, p. 158; d'Arblay, Madame: *Memoirs of Dr. Burney,* passim.; *Miscellanies,* v. I, pp. 108-10; Thrale, v. II, p. 775; Boswell (Hill-Powell ed.), v. IV, p. 158; v. III, p. 454; d'Arblay, v. II, p. 122; Clifford, p. 215.

[10] Clifford, pp. 212-3; Thrale, v. I, p. 541, note 2; Clifford, p. 198; Thrale, v. I, pp. 519, 531, 517.

[11] Thrale, v. I, pp. 544, 546, 549, 551; *Queeney Letters,* p. 66 ff.; Thrale, v. I, pp. 557-9, 562.

[12] Clifford, p. 218; Boswell (Hill-Powell ed.), v. IV, p. 228; *Letters,* v. II, p. 301; Thrale, v. I, p. 568; Clifford, pp. 224-6; Thrale, v. 1, p. 599; v. II, p. 678; *Queeney Letters,* pp. 148-9.

[13] Clifford, pp. 143, 322-3, 229-31; *Queeney Letters,* pp. 66, 80.

[14] Clifford, pp. 230, 307; *Queeney Letters,* pp. 80, 57, 70, xxvi; Clifford, p. 200, note 2; *Queeney Letters,* p. 250; Clifford, p. 230.

[15] *Queeney Letters,* p. 48; Clifford, p. 419; *Queeney Letters,* pp. xvii-xviii, 49, xx-xxi; Masefield, John: *The Widow in the Bye Street.*

[16] *Letters,* v. II, p. 300; v. II, pp. 304-8, 350; *Queeney Letters,* p. 75; Boswell (Hill-Powell ed.), v. IV, p. 253 and note 4; p. 270; *Letters,* v. II, p. 396; Boswell (Hill-Powell ed.), v. I, p. 11, note 2; v. IV, pp. 284, 291-2.

[17] Boswell (Hill-Powell ed.), v. IV, pp. 311, 338, 137, 235; *Letters,* v. II, p. 324; *Queeney Letters,* p. 150; Boswell (Hill-Powell ed.), v. III, p. 181; *Letters,* v. I, p. 396; Boswell (Hill-Powell ed.), v. II, pp. 542, 473; v. III, pp. 181, 455, 304.

[18] *Queeney Letters,* pp. 151-3; Clifford, pp. 228-9; Boswell (Hill-Powell ed.), v. IV, p. 339; d'Arblay, v. II, p. 271; *Works,* v. VIII, p. 316.

[19] Boswell (Hill-Powell ed.), v. IV, pp. 89, 239, 117-8, 281-2.

[20] Boswell (Hill-Powell ed.), v. IV, p. 171; v. II, p. 57; *Miscellanies,* v. I, p. 123; Boswell (Hill-Powell ed.), v. III, p. 153; *Hebrides Tour,* p. 155; Isham, Ralph: *New Invitation to Learning,* p. 295; *Malahide Papers,* v. XIV, p. 245; Boswell (Hill-Powell ed.), v. III, p. 339; v. IV, pp. 299, 278, 395, 299; *Letters,* v. II, pp. 384-5.

[21] Boswell (Hill-Powell ed.), v. IV, pp. 349, 363, 374-5; v. II, p. 463, note 1; Clifford, J. L., in London *Times* Literary Supplement, Aug. 28, 1937; Boswell (Hill-Powell ed.), v. IV, p. 377; *Miscellanies,* v. II, p. 158.

[22] Boswell (Hill-Powell ed.), v. IV, p. 380; *Letters,* v. II, p. 429; d'Arblay, v. II, pp. 270-2; Boswell (Hill-Powell ed.), pp. 384, 399, 411, 401; p. 402, note 2; *Miscellanies,* v. II, p. 127; Boswell (Hill-Powell ed.), v. IV, pp. 405-6.

[23] d'Arblay, v. II, p. 279; Boswell (Hill-Powell ed.), v. IV, p. 415; *Miscellanies,* v. II, p. 134; Boswell (Hill-Powell ed.), v. IV, p. 418; d'Arblay, v. II, p. 277; *Hebrides Tour,* p. 6.

Indexes

INDEX I

GENERAL INDEX

General Index

General Index

General Index

General Index

General Index

General Index

General Index

General Index

General Index

INDEX II

EVENTS OF JOHNSON'S LIFE

INDEX III

JOHNSON'S WORKS

Johnson's Works

INDEX IV

CHARACTER TRAITS AND HABITS, OPINIONS AND SAYINGS

CHARACTER

TEMPERAMENT

SOCIAL CHARACTER

INTELLECTUAL CHARACTER

PHYSICAL CHARACTER

HABITS AND WAY OF LIFE

FINANCIAL CONDITION

Traits, Habits, Opinions, and Sayings

MISCELLANEOUS

WHAT HE LIKED, OR LOVED, OR ADMIRED

WHAT HE DISLIKED, OR HATED, OR HAD NO RESPECT FOR

JOHNSON'S IDEA OF HIMSELF

OTHERS' OPINIONS OF JOHNSON

Traits, Habits, Opinions, and Sayings

EPITHETS AND SIMILES APPLIED TO HIM

MISCELLANEOUS ANECDOTES

SAYINGS OF DR. JOHNSON

NOTE—*Of the sayings quoted in this book not all are listed here. The more extended ones, having defied condensation, are entered under their subjects elsewhere in Index IV.*

Traits, Habits, Opinions, and Sayings

Traits, Habits, Opinions, and Sayings